Introduction to Python Network Automation Volume I - Laying the Groundwork

The Essential Skills for Growth

Second Edition

Brendan Choi

Apress®

Introduction to Python Network Automation Volume I - Laying the Groundwork: The Essential Skills for Growth, Second Edition

Brendan Choi
Sydney, NSW, Australia

ISBN-13 (pbk): 979-8-8688-0145-7   ISBN-13 (electronic): 979-8-8688-0146-4
https://doi.org/10.1007/979-8-8688-0146-4

Managing Director, Apress Media LLC: Welmoed Spahr
Acquisitions Editor: Celestin Suresh John
Development Editor: James Markham
Editorial Assistant: Gryffin Winkler
Copy Editor: Kezia Endsley

Cover designed by eStudioCalamar

Cover image by Freepik (www.freepik.com)

Distributed to the book trade worldwide by Springer Science+Business Media New York, 1 New York Plaza, Suite 4600, New York, NY 10004-1562, USA. Phone 1-800-SPRINGER, fax (201) 348-4505, e-mail orders-ny@springer-sbm.com, or visit www.springeronline.com. Apress Media, LLC is a California LLC and the sole member (owner) is Springer Science + Business Media Finance Inc (SSBM Finance Inc). SSBM Finance Inc is a **Delaware** corporation.

For information on translations, please e-mail booktranslations@springernature.com; for reprint, paperback, or audio rights, please e-mail bookpermissions@springernature.com.

Apress titles may be purchased in bulk for academic, corporate, or promotional use. eBook versions and licenses are also available for most titles. For more information, reference our Print and eBook Bulk Sales web page at http://www.apress.com/bulk-sales.

Any source code or other supplementary material referenced by the author in this book is available to readers on GitHub. For more detailed information, please visit https://www.apress.com/gp/services/source-code.

Paper in this product is recyclable

To Mom and in remembrance of Dad,

Your boundless love and unwavering patience have been the true guiding lights, illuminating every step of this profound journey. Within these pages, this book stands as a testament to the steadfast faith and unwavering encouragement you both have selflessly offered. I am deeply thankful for the profound impact you've had on this endeavor.

Table of Contents

About the Author

Brendan (Byong Chol) Choi, serving as a highly accomplished tech lead at Secure Agility, brings over two decades of hands-on experience in the dynamic world of the ICT industry. He holds certifications in Cisco, VMware, Fortinet, and ITIL. Brendan has lent his expertise to prominent enterprises such as Cisco Systems, Dimension Data (NTT), Fujitsu, and more recently, leading Australian IT integrators like Telstra and NTT. His focus on optimizing enterprise IT infrastructure management and refining business processes sees him utilizing a diverse range of both open-source and proprietary tools. Beginning his journey in the trenches of Cisco TAC Frontline, Brendan transitioned to pivotal IT engineering roles, navigating a spectrum of emerging and legacy technologies. Stemming from a traditional infrastructure background, he ardently explores emerging IT domains like the Cloud, IoT, DevOps, and the transformative technologies linked to the fourth industrial revolution. Brendan's literary contributions include *Python Network Automation: Building an Integrated Virtual Lab, Introduction to Python Network Automation: The First Journey,* and his primary work, *Introduction to Ansible Network Automation: The Practical Primer*. These works are crafted to resonate with and address the current enterprise IT landscape, sharing invaluable industry insights with the wider IT community. His legacy of training over 200 network and systems engineers in Python and Ansible Network Automation is complemented by his passion for disseminating industry-acquired knowledge through social media, blogging, and his YouTube channel. His curiosity spans across diverse domains such as private and public cloud, enterprise networking, security, virtualization, Linux, automation, and the transformative technologies driving the fourth industrial revolution. Amid a cacophony of disingenuous voices in the IT industry, "live by your words" remains Brendan's guiding principle. His unwavering dedication to enterprise infrastructure management echoes through his unwavering commitment to continuous learning, extensive knowledge sharing, and his profound contributions to the rich ICT world.

About the Technical Reviewers

Boyd A Tweed has been in networking for 15 years, working in all types of industries with many different network devices, from a single site to multinational sites spanning the globe.

His passion for automation started when he was building a new data center around Cisco ACI. Trying to learn the new technology was very difficult, because it was unlike any other network device he had touched—everything was GUI based and there was no CLI in sight. He started learning Python to inject the configurations and quickly realized how much easier and faster it was to use programming. He learned everything he could, reading books, taking seminars, and going to classes. Automation really started to take hold of him when he was learning Netmiko to do simple, ad hoc commands. He saw the value in the ability to configure multiple devices from a single script. He hopes, by reading this book, you will gain a better understanding of automation and wishes you the best of luck on your automation journey.

Radhika Shitlani is a network professional with over eight years of experience in network design, implementation, and automation. She has been using Python and contributing to it since its inception in the network domain. She has extensive experience in automating network feature testing and building tools to automate daily tasks in network operations. Currently, she designs and automates networks in data centers of global cloud leaders.

An enthusiast, she is always striving to learn and upgrade her skills. Apart from automating things in Python, she enjoys adventure sports and has completed the first (beginner) level of flying training. She is currently undergoing scuba diving training and dreams of becoming a professional sea diver.

Acknowledgments

I am deeply grateful to my IT industry mentors—Lesek Geba and Truyen Nguyen—and my former managers—Kai Schweisfurth and Ty Starr. Their extensive industry expertise and wisdom, amassed over 40 years in IT, have been invaluable in shaping the first and second editions of this book. My sincerest thanks to Justin (Cheol Yoon) Cheong for his invaluable guidance in the realm of authorship. I extend my deepest appreciation to all of them. My heartfelt thanks also goes to my wife, Sue, and our children, Hugh, Leah, and Caitlin. Their unwavering support has been my bedrock throughout the creation of this book. Their love and understanding have been my unwavering pillars. I also extend sincere gratitude to my extended family, friends, and colleagues for their steadfast support. Lastly, I want to express my gratitude to my readers for embarking on this incredible network automation journey with me.

—Brendan Choi, 2024

Introduction

Python's integration into enterprise network administration has surged in popularity among leading IT organizations. It is increasingly recognized as a pivotal skillset for network engineers in a growing number of organizations, gradually revolutionizing the landscape of network administration and ICT (Information and Communications Technology) infrastructure management.

Written by an ICT expert for real ICT professionals, this book aims to distill core practical knowledge devoid of false assumptions. It's founded on the belief that the book's target audience enjoys hands-on learning approaches over pure theory. This book is not for talkers, idealists, or theorists who merely preach, but for those ready to act. The commitment here is to provide an authentic experience, guiding readers through the actual journey of acquiring network automation skills using Python and its encompassing technologies from scratch. Understanding that individuals in IT come from diverse backgrounds and varying skill levels, this book operates under the notion that its targeted readers are beginners of Python Network Automation. It encourages readers to build everything themselves for a firsthand, immersive experience, emphasizing the importance of holistic comprehension rather than a specialized approach in the enterprise IT and network automation ecosystem. In essence, this book operates on the principle that "seeing is believing!"

In its inaugural edition, *Introduction to Python Network Automation: The First Journey,* this book offered readers a structured path to establish a robust foundation in Python Network Automation. This second edition revisits the original, bolstering the structured learning path with additional new content. The original version was an invaluable resource for IT professionals and students aiming to enhance their automation skills. This revised edition represents a refined iteration, amalgamating five foundational books—Python, Linux, basic networking, essential virtualization, and enterprise networking lab-building techniques—across two comprehensive guides. Tailored specifically for networking students and IT engineers, it provides hands-on experience in constructing a Python Network Automation lab from scratch. With practical examples derived from actual enterprise infrastructure, this edition offers valuable insights into leveraging Python effectively within real enterprise network management scenarios. This book has been divided into two parts—*Part I: Laying the Groundwork: The Essential Skills for Growth* and *Part II—Stepping Up: Beyond the Essentials for Success.* This is Part 1 of the second edition.

While many resources delve into Python-based network automation, few adequately equip students and engineers for Python Network Automation within a comprehensive IT infrastructure management framework. The success of the first edition among genuine ICT professionals stemmed from this book's direct, relatable, and holistic approach to learning network automation using Python and related technologies. Unlike resources that promise a zero-to-hero journey but falter due to their narrow focus, this book stresses the interconnectedness of technologies within the enterprise IT ecosystem. Solely comprehending Python Network Applications focused on software programmability offers limited mileage; a broader perspective becomes essential.

Numerous network automation books tantalize with the allure of Python Network Automation without emphasizing the "no pain, no gain" reality. Conversely, this book adopts a genuine approach, immersing readers in an authentic experience that exposes them to the challenges of acquiring network automation skills using Python. Readers engage in installing and configuring nearly everything themselves, learning from mistakes, overcoming obstacles, and ultimately mastering essential IT skills. This journey empowers readers to overcome initial hurdles in Python Network Automation, fostering the resilience and proficiency necessary to develop functional Python network applications.

By engaging with this book, readers will gain valuable knowledge and well-rounded skills. The book offers a structured learning path, gradually building proficiency in Python and its encompassing technologies. It begins with essential Linux administration skills, progresses through Python basics pertinent to enterprise network automation, explores foundational enterprise network labs, delves into basic networking concepts, and culminates in integrating various technologies. Readers will develop real Python networking applications and optimize code in a production-safe environment—all achievable from a single laptop. Readers can learn, write, and test their Python applications without causing major outages to network services. This journey provides insights into streamlining enterprise network management processes, transitioning from manual tasks to semi- or full automation, thus enhancing efficiency and productivity. Throughout, I share my industry insights gained over the last two decades in the ICT industry, equipping readers with real working knowledge and essential skills to apply Python in network automation. This will empower readers to navigate the ever-evolving landscape of enterprise networking administration confidently.

Designed for diligent readers seeking to enhance their network automation skills with Python, this book caters to IT students, network engineers, and developers managing IP services, networking devices, servers, cloud, and data centers. Technical leaders implementing network automation, mentors training team members, instructors teaching network automation, and Cisco Network Academy students pursuing network administration certifications will also find value in its pages. It's tailored to those interested in integrating network automation into their development process, offering practical knowledge across their enterprise network. Leveraging Python, it effectively teaches network automation techniques and encompassing technologies.

Come along on this expedition with me to enhance your network automation skills and discover new horizons in managing enterprise networks.

CHAPTER 1

Introduction to Python Network Automation

This chapter introduces the book by starting with a casual discussion of the experience of working as an IT professional in today's IT landscape. It then roughly defines the major IT domain groups to which Enterprise IT engineers belong, discusses their responsibilities and required skillsets, and compares their strengths and weaknesses. The chapter also outlines a study plan that serves as the backbone of the book. From the perspective of a working ICT engineer, the chapter considers the importance of learning a programming language and understanding software development, specifically Python within DevOps. Python within DevOps is the primary interest of the readers and core topic of this book, as it kickstarts the reader's journey into network automation. Lastly, the chapter provides information about the minimum system requirements needed to build a fully working Python/Linux/network automation ready-to-use lab on a single laptop/PC, along with the recommended software set for installing virtual devices, such as Linux servers, routers, and switches.

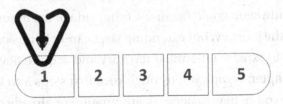

Aiding your journey: The highlighted number indicates the chapter's difficulty, for guidance only.

© Brendan Choi 2024
B. Choi, *Introduction to Python Network Automation Volume I - Laying the Groundwork*,
https://doi.org/10.1007/979-8-8688-0146-4_1

Laying the Foundation

In recent years, network programmability has been revolutionizing the enterprise networking industry, with network automation at the forefront for the past decade. Companies and organizations that once spent millions of dollars on traditional IT lifecycle management are now seeking new frameworks that provide faster, more cost-effective, yet more reliable and predictable network operations. However, many engineers working in the field are still encountering difficulties when trying to embrace network programmability and automation concepts. Reflecting on my journey, I understand that embracing and adopting automation concepts can seem daunting at first—it's like trying to board a moving train or trying to climb Everest. However, with the right resources and guidance, engineers can effectively overcome initial difficulties and master the basic skills needed to excel in network automation.

Jumping on the network programmability bandwagon can be intimidating, especially if you have no prior programming experience or are new to network automation or software-defined networks. It can feel like climbing a mountain—even after reaching the first peak, you realize that an even taller mountain awaits. As a network engineer, you may be comfortable with traditional network administration methods, but now your bosses expect you to upskill and automate your manual tasks with code. If you refuse, someone else will write the code, and you risk losing credibility.

To succeed in network programmability, you must step out of your comfort zone and embrace the learning curve to get up to speed. While it may seem like uncharted territory, with the right resources and determination, you can master the skills needed to excel in network automation. Don't let fear hold you back; Willy Wonka's golden ticket to the automation bandwagon could be on the other side of the mountain. No one can force you to embrace the journey, but extending your career in this cutting-edge industry requires a willingness to explore unfamiliar territory and acquire new skills.

In this opening chapter, I guide you through your first steps into Python Network Automation. Whether you're new to network automation or already on your journey but feel like you're not making progress, this book is for you. I start by identifying the three primary information technology (IT) domain groups that exist in today's IT landscape. Defining the skillsets possessed by each group will give you a clue about where to begin your journey. Through a comparison of these skillsets, I conduct an unbiased gap analysis to determine the strengths and weaknesses of each group. This book is written from the perspective of the enterprise network industry by an experienced network engineer. Additionally, it has been technically reviewed by two Cisco Network Academy

Instructors to ensure the topics remain relevant to real network engineers' work. The goal is to help you develop a realistic learning strategy that enables you to close any identified skill gaps and grow into a cross-functional engineer. As a cross-functional engineer, you will possess strong networking skills, the ability to manage Linux operating systems, and the capability to write code to automate Python applications. This shift will allow you to move away from mundane and repetitive tasks.

Moreover, I introduce you to the concept of a *hybrid engineer*—a cross-functional engineer who is in high demand in the current and future IT job markets. I discuss how the career knowledge growth for such hybrid engineers takes the shape of a "T." The shape of an engineer's career growth mindset can dictate their career path and be the deciding factor for the initial IT domain selection, with the top of the shape representing the potential of an engineer's skillsets and career growth. I have observed network and system engineers who have supported a single technology for over 30 years, content with their comfortable lives and stable jobs. However, technology is evolving rapidly, and manual-driven tasks are gradually being replaced by automated scripts and API-driven applications. Therefore, the new breed of IT engineers may not have the luxury of riding a job into their retirement based on what they learned 5 or 10 years ago.

Figure 1-1 depicts the technologies that are supported by "I-shaped"-minded engineers versus "T-shaped"-minded engineers. Look at the top of the letter—a picture is worth a thousand words. The question is, are you an I or a T? This is a genuine question that all IT engineers and students must ask themselves regularly to develop the best possible career paths. Of course, there is no right or wrong answer to this question, as everyone has different career aspirations and personal circumstances.

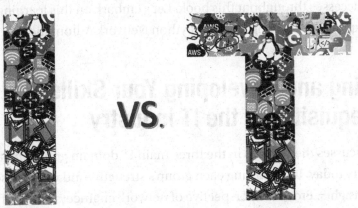

Figure 1-1. I-shape-minded engineer vs. T-shape-minded engineer

Throughout this book, you have the opportunity to install, configure, practice, and write Python code on your laptop (or PC) without needing any other expensive and power-hungry enterprise networking equipment. This aspect is crucial for your success in learning Python Network Automation because you can no longer use the lack of equipment as an excuse for not delving into network automation. You only need your laptop and Internet service to get your network automation journey started. If you are following this book and plan to set up your learning environment on a single laptop, doing so will add mobility and flexibility, allowing you to learn anywhere and anytime at your own pace and convenience. To ensure that you have everything you need to get started, I begin by reviewing the minimum system requirements for your setup and introduce you to the full list of software used to complete the tasks outlined in this book. Additionally, I provide guidance on an Integrated Development Environment (IDE) for Python Network Automation development, enhancing your coding experience. You also have access to the download links for all the necessary software, source code, and files used throughout this book, making it easy for you to access the required resources.

By the end of this chapter—whether you're a network engineer or a student—you will have a better understanding of the current strengths and weaknesses of network engineers compared to software and systems engineers. You will identify any gaps in your knowledge and I will guide you to other areas to expand your horizons, writing Python code, and developing working network automation applications. **Remember, your network automation journey is not a sprint, but rather a series of marathons**. Therefore, it's essential to build the right foundation to endure the race and remain resilient during setbacks. Keep the long-term goal in mind, and with dedication, you'll achieve mini successes throughout this book. Let's embark on this learning journey together and explore the exciting world of Python Network Automation!

Discovering and Developing Your Skills and Prerequisites in the IT industry

This section discusses the skillsets in the three main IT domain groups that are common in the IT industry today. By exploring each group's strengths and weaknesses, you will gain valuable insights. From the perspective of network engineers, I identify areas where your skills may be lacking and work on developing strategies to strengthen them. While understanding Python syntax and concepts is essential for achieving your network automation goals, based on my own experience, it may only account for 25 percent of the equation. To write effective Python Network Automation code, you need to develop stronger foundational skills in various areas. In this chapter, I delve into these areas to help you excel. Additionally, I cover Python basics from a networking perspective, and together, we develop a study plan to address the common weaknesses of network engineers. This plan guides you through acquiring the required foundational skills to meet your initial Python Network Automation goals. The aim is to equip you with a well-rounded skillset, enabling you to approach network automation tasks with confidence and expertise.

Python, networks, and automation are each extensive IT topics on their own, and numerous books have been published on each topic. Every year, countless new books about Python, networks, and automation are released, covering a wide spectrum of knowledge. Some books delve into the basics of a topic, while others combine two or more of these areas into a single book. For instance, you can find books that cover purely Python, solely network, exclusively Linux, specifically Python Automation or uniquely Python Network Automation. However, this book takes a unique approach by combining Python, network, and automation into a single comprehensive guide, with a strong focus on understanding practical Linux skills. Linux serves as the foundation of enterprise network automation, making it a crucial component of this book's content.

While many books have attempted to teach readers how to automate enterprise networks using Python, this book takes a unique approach by following the real-world journey of a network engineer learning Python Network Automation from ground zero. As you progress through each chapter, you'll travel along the author's proven path to success while acquiring essential IT skills and gaining insights into writing effective Python code for network automation. This book incorporates the author's working knowledge, study notes, blog content, tips, and tricks used in networking and virtualization solutions to make the learning experience more pleasant and practical at the same time. By drawing from the author's hands-on experience, this book offers a valuable resource that connects theoretical concepts with real-world applications, giving you a deeper understanding of Python Network Automation in a practical context.

Whether you're a student looking to embark on your first Python Network Automation journey or an IT professional working on enterprise-level routing, switching, and security solutions, this book has something to offer. Even if you're a seasoned IT pro with years of experience in enterprise network administration but have yet to explore Python or network automation studies, the contents of this book introduces you to various topics and technologies you may not have encountered before. Furthermore, this book recognizes that the process of learning and acquiring new skills is just as crucial as achieving study goals and results. The book aims to engage readers whose interests go beyond networking technologies, and who wish to extend their knowledge into Python and Linux. It's not uncommon for IT engineers to feel pressure to be technical experts and know everything, but this book acknowledges the importance of identifying knowledge gaps and helps readers close these gaps for their personal growth and improvement.

Figure 1-2. *A laughable IT engineer logo*

Figure 1-2 may seem laughable, but it sheds light on the behavior of some IT engineers at work. It serves as a reminder for IT professionals to reflect on their past actions and how they support their customers and enterprise infrastructures. Since the invention of personal computers in 1971, the IT industry has undergone significant changes, resulting in the creation and disappearance of various IT jobs. The constantly evolving enterprise IT ecosystem demands that IT engineers keep up with emerging technologies; those who refuse to do so risk being left behind and possibly losing their jobs. The advent of Artificial Intelligence (AI), the emergence of API-based applications, and newer IT automation tools arrived in the enterprise networking industry a few years back. Those who fail to update their skillset and realign their toolsets may find themselves in an uncertain future in terms of job security. IT professionals need to adapt and embrace these advancements to remain relevant and competitive in the job market. Staying current with the latest technologies and continuously improving one's skills will not only ensure job stability but will also open doors to exciting new career opportunities. In essence, as long as you're working in the IT field, it's beneficial to stay engaged in self-education activities to remain relevant.

Reflecting on the Past and Observing the Current Trend for a Better Future

For many years, the IT industry has been primarily focused on reducing operational costs by outsourcing less-skilled jobs to developing countries, where IT operational expenses remain comparatively lower than those in advanced countries. In recent times, numerous organizations have made it a priority to cut down on overhead expenses spent on human resources to drive operational costs to a minimum. Unfortunately, in today's business model, human resources are often perceived as overhead costs, while IT customers demand high-quality services while paying less. This situation can lead to financial pressures, forcing drastic IT cost-cutting measures that may compromise the delivery of quality services. Over the last two decades, outsourcing and offshoring efforts have yielded some success, but they have also fueled a relentless drive to further reduce operational costs. This trend has accelerated the adoption of IT automation solutions, such as Software Defined Networking (SDN) and Infrastructure-as-Code (IaC), which have played a pivotal role in lowering costs and enhancing operational efficiency.

Reflecting on the past 23 years and my own experience, the traditional IT operations model saw the vast majority of organizations bearing the cost of running on-premises IT infrastructure and hosting servers in data centers (DCs). However, since the early 2000s, some organizations perceived internal IT operations and support as being overly expensive, leading them to outsource these functions to external IT Managed Services Providers (MSPs). Others, with a presence overseas, chose to relocate their IT operations to countries like India, the Philippines, and Malaysia. While outsourcing IT functions may not always yield perfect results, it undeniably reduces the cost of running IT operations and improves the organization's profit margin. In the field of enterprise networking, new concepts began emerging around 2012, such as network programmability or programmable networks. As early as 2014, network engineers were grappling with the question, "Do I need to become a programmer to stay relevant in networking?" This is my observation, but initially, automation tools like Puppet (2005) and Chef (2009) were introduced primarily for the automation of system devices, such as Windows or Linux OS, and did not have a significant impact on the uptake of network automation. Python, which had its first version released on February 20, 1991, existed for more than a decade before Ansible emerged in 2012. Ansible, primarily written in Python, became a game-changer as an agentless configuration management tool for automation. Ansible supports both agent and agentless operating systems for automation. Interestingly, since the introduction of Ansible, network engineers have started taking network automation more seriously, and many of them have eagerly embraced this trend, utilizing both Python and Ansible to drive their network automation initiatives.

With the recent migration and widespread adoption of public, private, and hybrid clouds, only a handful of enterprise networking and system devices remain on-premises or within company-owned data centers. In other words, companies have relinquished full control of their platforms in favor of the Infrastructure-as-a-Service (IaaS), Platform-as-a-Service (PaaS), and Software-as-a-Service (SaaS) models. While we cannot predict the exact future, based on the current trends in the ICT industry, this migration trend is likely to continue, unless a major security breach incident occurs to halt the current trajectory. As we progress further, more and more systems will be driven by software and communicate through Application Programming Interface (API) applications. Consequently, it is not difficult to foresee that engineers will increasingly be expected to deliver services and operational support using APIs or other programming languages, surpassing the traditional Graphical User Interface (GUI) or Command Line Interface (CLI) methods.

Staying Relevant as an IT Professional in a Rapidly Evolving Industry

Do you consider yourself an IT professional? If so, you're likely familiar with the self-reflective question, "What sort of IT professional am I?" As an IT engineer, have you ever asked yourself this question? Or perhaps, "What does my future hold in the ever-evolving IT industry?" If you've chosen IT as your lifelong occupation, chances are you've asked these questions many times throughout your career. Staying competitive in the IT industry is crucial; otherwise, you risk being left behind and forced to move on to the next phase of your career and life. Continually studying and developing your skills in current and relevant IT technologies is no easy task. As someone who was once an upcoming IT engineer, I now find myself becoming an "experienced professional" like many others around me. However, even at my age, I continue to pursue my dream of acquiring new technical skills every day and bettering myself in my current career. Though there may be gaps between one's dream and reality, we must strive to live the dream to give meaning to our lives.

In an ideal world, all IT engineers would gain new IT skills every day and work in their dream jobs. However, the reality is that the vast majority of IT engineers are pressured to deliver more in their given hours and contribute toward maximizing their organization's profitability. Consequently, many struggle to keep up with the ever-changing, emerging, and disruptive new technologies. Over the last ten years, a tsunami of new and disruptive IT technologies has flooded the market. To extend their careers, IT engineers must continuously strive to close the gap between demand and their real capabilities. Those who are willing to put in the effort will be able to extend their careers into this decade and beyond. To build a successful IT career, they must love and enjoy their work. To a certain extent, they must be highly dedicated and passionate, in other words, "go crazy with their work". While the word "crazy" typically has a negative connotation, in this context, it is used to emphasize the passion, dedication, and love some IT professionals have for their work. Not all IT professionals are the same; some excel at communications and people management, while others thrive in troubleshooting technical issues. However, in my experience, I've realized that to stay in this field for the whole duration of my professional career, continuous learning habits are essential to staying relevant in this game.

As an IT professional, it's important to have a real passion for your work and always strive to better understand the technologies you support. Because the field of ICT is so broad and ever-evolving, there is no guarantee that what you know today will remain relevant tomorrow. While it's essential to enjoy what you do, it's also crucial to recognize the gaps in knowledge and skillsets. Avoid trying to cover up such gaps, as such actions can lead to more significant problems throughout your IT career. It is important that as an IT professional, you stay honest with yourself and others around you. In this industry, the majority of engineers are honest, yet there are rotten tomatoes who falsely claim knowledge across all IT domains despite their lack of understanding. I usually label these individuals as *posers*.

So, on which side of the spectrum do you fall, and where do you want to take your career? In my experience, many IT engineers tend to be introverts rather than extroverts. Throughout their careers, IT engineers spend an inordinate amount of time communicating with devices as if they were human beings. System engineers work with multiple operating systems in the data center, whereas network engineers communicate with IP devices like routers, switches, and load balancers operating out of dispersed data centers. Security engineers communicate with firewalls operating out of branch offices and data centers, UC engineers work with voice gateways, UC systems, and IP Phones, and programmers use various programming languages and data structures to communicate with various applications. Cloud engineers communicate with applications running from public/private/hybrid clouds hosted in dispersed data centers.

A fascinating observation is how learning a new programming language is similar to learning a new language. While computers and programming languages were created to make our lives easier, it's worth noting that they are designed to communicate with humans. A programmer communicating with a computer uses a programming language that the computer can understand as if they were communicating with another human. In English, an "extrovert" is an outgoing, outspoken person who is not afraid to show their emotions, while a reserved person is called an "introvert." Most often, the vast majority of engineers who continually strive to improve their technical abilities are more likely to have introverted than extroverted personality traits. On the other hand, extroverted engineers often transition into management roles, where they can lead and manage teams and transition into leadership or customer-interfacing roles.

As for the question of who is the more successful engineer, that is ultimately up to individual interpretation. From a technical standpoint, however, I argue that introverted engineers have a better chance of excelling in their roles as long as they continue to learn and keep their technical skills sharp. It's interesting to note that in countries with more mature ICT industries, there are still many senior engineers who continue to enjoy successful careers well into their 50s and 60s (and I am now one of them). These engineers owe their longevity in the industry to staying updated through continuous learning and remaining open to acquiring new skills. In contrast, in countries with less mature IT industries, engineers typically start their careers in their 20s and conclude their technical careers in their late 30s to early 40s.

If you enjoy learning new technologies and are willing to continue living the life of an IT professional until your retirement, being a part of this industry is not a bad personal choice.

Types of IT Automation at the Enterprise Level

In the world of IT automation, the possibilities are vast, catering to various critical functions within an organization. From simplifying application and operating system (OS) installation and upgrades to resource provisioning in both on-premises and cloud environments, IT automation encompasses the power of DevOps and even addresses the crucial task of patching security issues based on common vulnerabilities and exposures (CVEs). Moreover, it extends its reach to configuring OS, network, and security systems, ensuring a comprehensive approach to safeguarding digital assets. At its core, enterprise automation serves straightforward yet profound objectives that resonate with any organization aiming for efficiency and growth. It significantly reduces the reliance on manual processes, empowering businesses to operate seamlessly and efficiently. By providing timely and reliable system maintenance and updates, IT automation mitigates security risks, eliminating the potential for costly human errors.

The transformative impact of automation isn't just confined to the internal workings of an organization. It opens the door to enhanced productivity, unleashing the full potential of available resources. Employees can focus on creative problem-solving and strategic initiatives rather than getting bogged down in repetitive tasks. This newfound freedom from boring work also leads to reduced staff burnout and turnover, fostering a healthier and more engaged workforce. Strangely, this statement does not make sense, as automation will look after the staff's well-being while trying to cut costs and do more with less. So, **in many ways, enterprise IT automation is full of contradictions, as it shows little concern for those who cannot keep up with the pace of changes, while simultaneously claiming to prioritize the well-being of the workforce.**

Ultimately, the true value of IT automation lies in the outcomes and the monetary benefits it brings to organizations. Customer experience is elevated, as the organization can deliver faster and more reliable services. The agility of the business reaches new heights, enabling swift adaptation to keep up with the changing market dynamics. In turn, this enhanced efficiency and customer satisfaction translate into increased revenue, making IT automation an indispensable asset for any enterprise aiming to thrive in today's dynamic ICT landscape.

Key Competencies for IT Professionals in Three Major Domains

According to a report by the National Association of Software and Services Companies (NASSCOM), Bangalore, India, is commonly known as the "Silicon Valley of India" or "IT capital of India," with over 1.5 million people (as of 2020) working in the IT sector. There is a common saying in India, "There are two types of people in the IT profession; one, IT professionals, and two, professionals who manage these people." In this book, to help the readers' understanding, we are dividing IT domain groups into three different groups based on each group's competencies and characteristics. The book then compares the general technical competencies and analyzes them to forecast what the near future IT industry may look like for one group of engineers, that is the network engineering (connectivity) group. Who will be at the forefront of the networking field in the next five years and beyond? Let's review the gaps and requirements to look ahead and develop a plan to study Python, Linux, network automation, and any other basic skillsets.

At the enterprise level, most organizations have **three main domain groups** responsible for managing their IT infrastructure. The first group, known as the **network group**, also known as the connectivity group in some organizations, is responsible for managing all infrastructure and end-user connectivity. The second group, known as the **systems group**, manages servers and applications that provide various services to other infrastructures or end-users. This includes critical business applications such as corporate email, shared storage, and various applications that are essential to the success of the company. The third and last group is the **DevOps group**, which consists of software developers and programmers who specialize in developing software and applications using various programming languages and software development tools.

For the convenience of this book, I refer to these three main domain groups as the network group, the systems group, and the DevOps group for simplicity. The network group is responsible for all IP connectivity and services, including technology sub-domains such as routing and switching, SDWAN, security, data center, cloud, and unified collaboration technologies. Stable and reliable network connectivity forms the foundation of any enterprise business operation, and the network group considers both systems and DevOps-generated IP traffic as the tenants of connectivity services.

Any major network outage on the corporate network or service provider network can bring the entire business to a halt. Therefore, the network connectivity service is one of the most crucial services that can have a significant impact on all business and end-user IP services.

The systems group is responsible for managing critical business applications and operating systems running on both Windows and Linux OS. The DevOps group, on the other hand, is responsible for testing, developing, and implementing various business applications to cater to the company's business requirements. In recent times, both the systems and DevOps groups have extended support for Cloud services or cloud computing. By comparing and analyzing the current capabilities of each group, you will better understand their strengths and weaknesses and identify several weaknesses in the network group so that if you fall under network group, you can improve on any weaknesses.

Although the networking vendor technology used in this book is mainly Cisco, it's important to note that the network automation concepts presented here apply to any vendor networking and security technologies using vendor-compatible Python modules, including Cisco, Arista, Juniper, Fortinet, Check Point, Palo Alto, and HP. First, I compare the technical capability differences among these three domain groups using a spider-web graph to plot and illustrate different technical competencies. Then, I determine and recommend how to embark upon network automation using Python as the preferred programming language.

To facilitate a clear and comprehensive comparison of the three IT domain groups' capabilities, I begin by plotting their competencies on a spider web graph, as depicted in Figure 1-3. This graph uses a ten-point scoring system to rate each competency, where a score of eight out of ten indicates a high level of proficiency, and a score of two out of ten signifies a lower level of proficiency. Between the release of the first edition of this book in May 2021 and the time of authoring this new edition in August 2023, there have been only minor developments in the ICT industry. Therefore, Figure 1-3 still applies to the current ICT industry and the overall IT landscape.

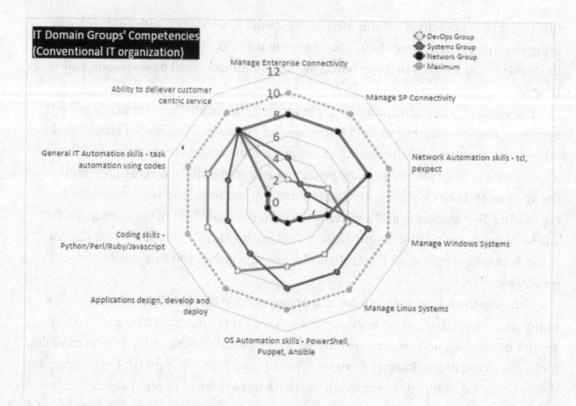

Figure 1-3. *Comparison of general competencies Among IT domain groups in a conventional IT organization*

Figure 1-3 illustrates the standard competencies required by each engineering group over the last decade, providing a bird's-eye overview of each group's strengths and weaknesses. Conventionally, network engineers did not have a strict requirement to learn software engineering or coding, as the traditional network operated at a much slower pace compared to modern networks. As discussed earlier, most network connectivity work was accomplished by conventional network engineers using the good old CLI. On the other hand, the systems group had more exposure to system automation tools and languages due to the nature of their work, which involves completing tasks in bulk with shorter completion times. Until about ten years ago, enterprise network automation wasn't considered a priority for conventional network engineers, and tools like Ansible and Terraform were yet to emerge. Consequently, network engineers didn't feel a real urgency to broaden their skillset to include systems or DevOps competencies. Writing code using high-level interpreted programming languages like Python, JavaScript, and PowerShell typically requires an in-depth understanding of server operating systems, as these languages run on servers, and at times run on network devices.

Achieving enterprise network automation necessitates a combination of competencies from all three groups, as indicated in Figure 1-3. None of the three groups possess all the required competencies, and individuals from conventional network engineering backgrounds are unlikely to have much exposure to managing enterprise systems or participating in enterprise automation tools (application) development projects. In recent times, businesses expect individuals to deliver more with less, a trend particularly evident in smaller companies that prioritize providing more value to customers and businesses. Even in larger companies, increasing the IT budget is often a very low priority. This situation often leads to companies trying to maximize their IT infrastructure investment, which was invested more than ten years ago.

If you study Figure 1-3 once again, it becomes evident that many companies now recognize that no single group possesses all the competencies required to deliver an enterprise network automation solution. Consequently, companies are focusing on upskilling their existing engineers to achieve IT automation, thereby eliminating the overhead costs associated with maintaining all three separate IT domain groups in the future. In fact, industry insiders have been proclaiming that "The walls of different IT domains are crumbling." As a result of this shift, network engineers must learn to administer a Linux Operating System, install a programming language, and develop specific applications to automate the enterprise network they manage. Similarly, engineers from systems or DevOps groups can learn network protocols and networking technologies to automate the network group's repetitive tasks and "low-hanging fruit" work. While the graph represents the general capabilities of each IT domain group, it tells a lot about each group. It is also worth noting that the competencies of individual engineers within a group will vary from one company to the next. Nevertheless, this graph provides valuable insights into how each group of engineers can approach Python Network Automation from different angles.

Comparing the Responsibilities of IT Engineers Across Different Domains

Figure 1-3 reviewed the competencies of the three IT domain groups. This section examines the typical responsibilities of engineers from each group to identify the areas where the network group members can improve to implement enterprise network automation using Python and other automation tools. Take about five minutes to study the responsibilities of each engineer in Figure 1-4. The general responsibilities of IT engineers show that the section labeled "Network Automation Application and System Development Using the Software" highlights the gap that a traditional network engineer needs to address to acquire the necessary skills to create a scripted application that automates their work. As indicated by the shaded area, the first step is to master operating systems such as Linux, in addition to possessing strong networking skills.

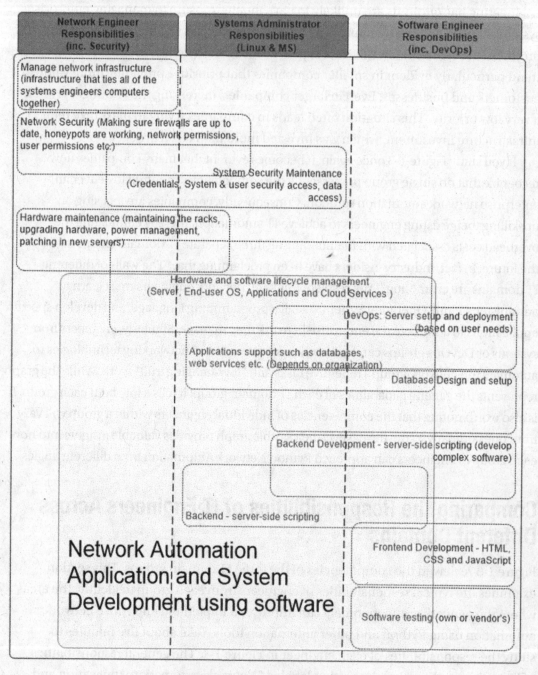

Figure 1-4. *General responsibilities of IT engineers*

To embark on enterprise network automation using Python, mastering the Linux Operating System is fundamental. Once you have gained basic to intermediate Linux administration skills, you can move on to learning basic Python syntax and gradually delve into DevOps concepts. It is also important to gain exposure to Linux grep or general Regular Expressions, as effective data processing is a cornerstone of any programming language. With these foundational skills in place, you can gradually expand your knowledge to other areas of interest, such as network configuration management and system orchestration.

As mentioned in the Introduction, the assumed target audiences of this book are readers who possess working knowledge of Internetworking or are actively pursuing the Cisco Certified Network Associate (CCNA) certification. If you have already taken and passed the CCNA or even the professional-level certification exams, you will undoubtedly derive significant benefits from this book. While this book does not delve into general networking concepts from Cisco Systems, a substantial portion of this book's content is hands-on, and the labs in later chapters are based on Cisco's IOS or IOS XE routers and switches. Thus, if you have prior experience with CCNA, you will find reading this book to be an enjoyable experience. However, even if you are not a certified CCNA, you can still follow along with the exercises and labs, as the book was designed with comprehensive vocational training in mind. If you can comprehend this paragraph and read along, you are capable of understanding and completing all exercises, tasks, and labs presented in this book. Drawing upon the discussions presented in Figures 1-3 and 1-4, this book touches on a broad range of topics, covering various technology domains that may challenge readers from various angles and at the same time, encourage you to upskill your general IT administration skills. It is rare to find a book that encompasses Python, Linux, network automation, and virtualization topics all within a single volume. To aid readers' comprehension, I have tried to include explanations and embedded notes throughout the book.

From Figure 1-4, it becomes evident that network engineers often lack certain essential skillsets. While some individuals may fall outside of this generalization, I concur that the vast majority of engineers I have encountered in my career tend to be lopsided, or what we call "I-shaped" engineers. To transition from being an average network engineer to becoming proficient in network automation, one must enhance their expertise in systems and software development skills. These skillsets are typically associated with the responsibilities of systems and DevOps engineers, which are not traditionally part of a network engineer's core duties.

Here are some of the required skillsets:

- System security maintenance
- Hardware and software lifecycle management
- DevOps, server setup, and deployment
- Application support, such as databases and web services
- Database design and setup
- Backend development: Server-side scripting
- Frontend development: HTML, CSS, and JavaScript
- Software testing (in-house or vendors)
- Cloud services and data center knowledge

By acquiring proficiency in these areas, a network engineer can bridge the gap and successfully venture into the realm of network automation. This diversification of skills is essential for staying competitive and effective in the ever-evolving field of networking.

These responsibilities are quite broad and encompassing; however, there are many sub-domain technologies not covered in the list. Nevertheless, from a network engineer's perspective, it is crucial to establish a solid foundation in network fundamentals before shifting focus toward the responsibilities of systems and DevOps groups.

To facilitate your learning process, I created a study guide for you, which is presented in Table 1-1. This book is a compilation of multiple books into one, carefully curated with topics that will prepare you for your Python Network Automation journey. The skills you will acquire from this book will serve as a primer, helping you build a strong foundation before delving into more advanced topics. Each chapter introduces you to new and fascinating IT skills that may lie outside your comfort zone, progressively layering essential skillsets on top of each other, so you can confidently tackle the challenges of the next network automation mountain. By following the study guide and engaging with the content, you will be well-prepared to embark on your Python Network Automation journey and expand your expertise in the ever-evolving world of network engineering.

The technical approach outlined in Table 1-1 is practical, extensive, and involves several steps, such as installing virtual machines and network services, learning Linux and Python basics, and installing Python. By mastering these skills, you can control networking devices by writing Python code. As a network engineer, most of our time is not typically spent writing code, building programs, or testing codes. Nevertheless, we must start somewhere and begin writing code to transition from relying solely on the CLI and GUI to working with lines of code and APIs. The following approach is one way to embark on your first journey into Python Network Automation, building on the discussions mentioned previously.

Table 1-1. *A Study Plan for Network Engineers Venturing into Python Network Automation*

#	Required Skills	Recommended Topics to Study
①	**Python basics**	✓ Install Python on your computer ✓ Familiarize yourself with the basics of Python syntax ✓ Learn how to apply basic Python syntax to the context of network automation
②	**VMware and virtualization basics**	✓ Install the latest VMware Workstation Pro ✓ Learn virtualization basics ✓ Learn to build virtual machines
③	**Operating system management, patching, upgrading, troubleshooting, and configuration skills**	✓ Install two different flavors of the latest Linux distros: Ubuntu 22.04 LTS and Fedora 37 (at the time of writing this book) ✓ Use a VMware template to install a pre-staged server and import the GNS3 VM Server ✓ Follow a Python installation guide and troubleshoot any installation problems that may arise
④	**Learn Linux basics**	✓ Use the vi and nano text editors without a GUI desktop ✓ Get introduced to the Linux directory structure ✓ Learn file management in Linux with practical exercises ✓ Understand remote connection concepts in Linux, such as SSH, Telnet, and basic APIs ✓ Install FTP, SFTP, TFTP, and NTP servers ✓ Try to install NetBox as IPAM/DCIM as an IP address management tool

(continued)

Table 1-1. (*continued*)

#	Required Skills	Recommended Topics to Study
⑤	**Regular Expressions**	✓ Gain a basic understanding of Regular Expressions ✓ Understand how Regular Expressions are used in Python ✓ Apply Regular Expressions to networking concepts and use cases
⑥	**Network emulator (GNS3) skills**	✓ Learn how to install and set up GNS3 for network emulation ✓ Practice configuring basic and advanced network topologies using GNS3 ✓ Integrate GNS3 with a VMware Workstation to create a more powerful network simulation environment
⑦	**Cisco IOS and IOS XE command lines**	✓ Integrate Cisco IOS, IOS-XE, and CML-Personal L2 and L3 images into GNS3 ✓ Learn basic router and switch commands for network automation lab setup ✓ Write Python codes to control emulated Cisco network devices via SSH, telnet, FTP, and SNMP ✓ Practice Python scripting in a virtual lab environment ✓ Install and configure virtual routers and switches using Python scripts
⑧	**Application development and establishment**	✓ Install Python 3 ✓ Install Python Telnet and SSH modules ✓ Develop applications for network automation with Python codes ✓ Understand basic DevOps development concepts
⑨	**Specific engineer's task automation**	✓ Gain a comprehension of the step-by-step process necessary to automate specific tasks ✓ Embrace self-teaching by adopting a holistic approach, akin to the analogy of "teaching a man to fish," and subsequently narrowing your focus for more effective learning

The chapters in this book essentially follow the order of the study plan mentioned previously. The recommended topics listed serve as the foundation for this book. As you can see, there is a lot of ground to cover, but don't worry too much, as getting started is often the most challenging part. Throughout this book, you will come across various technologies and exercise-based tasks that require you to follow along with the content on your computer. Practically, the entire book requires hands-on work to acquire the targeted skills. This chapter is the only exception where you can read along without typing on your keyboard, and every other chapter requires one. To get the most out of this book, it's recommended you finish all exercises in each chapter to gain enough practice and develop the necessary skills for network automation using Python. My goal in this book is for you to learn the basics right in one place and become a proficient T-shaped mindset engineer. You can do it!

Getting Started with Python and Network Automation: A Guide for Beginners

If you're new to Python and interested in using it for network automation, you might wonder where to begin. A quick Google search for "How to learn Python?" or "How to study network automation with Python?" will yield numerous results on forums and social media platforms like StackOverflow, Quora, and Pinterest. You can also find useful video tutorials on YouTube, some of which are based on AI algorithms. Since November 2021, you can also seek assistance from our new friend, ChatGPT, which can help you start your Python learning journey. However, these general questions may not provide the specific information you need to achieve your immediate work-related goals. Instead, I suggest reframing the question to "Why do you want to study Python for network automation?" and "What is the best way to learn Python for network automation?". These questions will yield better results, helping you understand your motivation and focus on the necessary learning path to achieve your goals. While everyone's questions may differ, the common goal in studying Python for network automation is often to streamline repetitive tasks into code and free up time for more valuable work. The process of network automation using a programming language like Python, PowerShell, JavaScript, or Perl is distinct from automation driven by fully developed automation configuration management tools such as Ansible or Terraform. However, learning Python offers the flexibility to structure your thought and task processes for effective and custom automation. By streamlining your thought processes, you can perform your work more efficiently and systematically using Python code, without being restricted to a specific automation framework or declarative language like YAML or HashiCorp Configuration Language (HCL).

Does this book suggest that many tasks performed manually by network teams all around the world are perhaps inefficient, slow, and lacking structure? Unfortunately, the answer is yes, which is likely why you're here, reading this book. To get started, try reviewing the current inefficient tasks your team performs and break down each logical thinking process and physical task into a document. While many of the repetitive tasks can be automated, some require physical human interaction, such as connecting cables, flicking the power switch, or moving devices during rack and stack procedures. You must learn and practice writing the sequence of tasks, so you can prioritize and incorporate them into your Python codes. An example of this will be provided at the end of Part 2 during the IOS upgrading lab. Writing and documenting all tasks will come in handy when you're trying to determine which tasks you want to automate using Python code. This step will give you a solid foundation to start your first network automation project and tackle your current automation challenges. Instead of immediately diving into Python studies, take some time to identify the manual-intensive and repetitive tasks at work that you want to automate, and again, always document the current processes. Once you've done that, you can start learning Python syntax and begin writing the tasks into lines of code. By following this process, you'll stay motivated and focused on your first Python project, because you're not studying Python just because it's currently the most popular programming language. You're studying it because you're motivated and eager to learn how to use Python to solve specific real-world problems at work. Count on receiving accolades from your bosses and colleagues; you know you have what it takes to achieve it!

What Motivates People to Learn Python?

Since its first release as a programming language in 1991, Python has become incredibly easy to learn and versatile. It is widely used by some of the world's leading IT service vendors and enterprises, including Google, YouTube, Instagram, Netflix, Dropbox, and NASA. By the time the first edition of this book was published in 2021, Python had already secured the position of the second most popular programming language, according to the TIOBE survey. However, in June 2022, Python surpassed all others and claimed the top spot, relegating C to the second position. Python's broad applicability has made it an indispensable tool for solving real-world problems, earning it the nickname "glue language." Its seamless integration of different components, extensive libraries, interoperability, scripting capabilities, web development frameworks, and data integration are six key reasons behind this nickname. Moreover, Python's low entry barrier makes it accessible to learners and professionals of all ages and experience levels, from primary school children to seasoned programmers. Despite the availability of various programming languages, Python stands out as an excellent choice for automating networking tasks. It strikes a balance between ease of learning, power, and versatility, with one of the fastest development times. Python's popularity continues to grow, with abundant study materials, a supportive community, and rankings consistently placing it at the top. In June 2023, the TIOBE survey reaffirmed Python as the world's most popular language, while RedMonk.com ranked it second globally after JavaScript. Furthermore, a superset of Python called Mojo was developed for high-performance applications in machine learning and artificial intelligence. Mojo shares almost identical syntax with Python but overcomes Python's performance limitations using Multi-Level Intermediate Representation (MILR), making it 35,000 times faster than Python. Released in September 2022, Mojo combines Python's usability with the performance of C. Overall, Python's rise to prominence, its extensive applications, and its continuous development highlight its significance as an entry-level language with a bright and promising future.

If you have decided to learn Python for network automation, you may be wondering where to begin and what to study to be effective. Mastering the basic Python syntax and concepts is essential, but it can be challenging to connect these concepts to network automation concepts. There are many books available on Python basics and concepts, and some of them are outstanding, but they may not explain where to start or provide guidance on drills to reach the intermediate or advanced level. Learning any programming language requires persistence and passion, so be prepared to put in the time and effort necessary to become proficient. While Python is easy to learn, it takes time and dedication to become great at any programming language. Be prepared to sacrifice social nights and weekends to study Python library features that seem frivolous and watch hundreds of hours of online training videos from Python gurus.

Ultimately, the effort you put in will be worth it, as learning Python for network automation will enhance your ability to streamline tasks and make you a more valuable asset to your organization.

It's important to note that while Python has a low entry-barrier, it doesn't necessarily mean that it's the easiest language to learn. The reality is that while anyone can start learning Python, it takes persistence, perseverance, and passion to become skilled at writing Python code. The most challenging aspect of learning Python is often keeping your passion alive and consistently pushing yourself to learn different ways of doing things with the language. To achieve this, it's essential to find practical use cases and work on small projects that are personally meaningful and relevant to your job. Automation is a gradual process, and every task you want to automate requires lines of code to be written. In network automation, there is no AI yet that's capable of replicating the experience and logical thinking of a highly skilled network engineer, which is why engineers must automate their tasks until they can teach AI to replicate their actions.

Python was the most wanted programming language for the past few years, as per the 2020 survey (see Figure 1-5), and it is also the fastest-growing language. This indicates that a significant number of developers who have not yet used Python are eager to learn it for developing applications. As per the survey, approximately 30 percent of the respondents (who were developers) expressed their desire to learn Python as their preferred programming language.

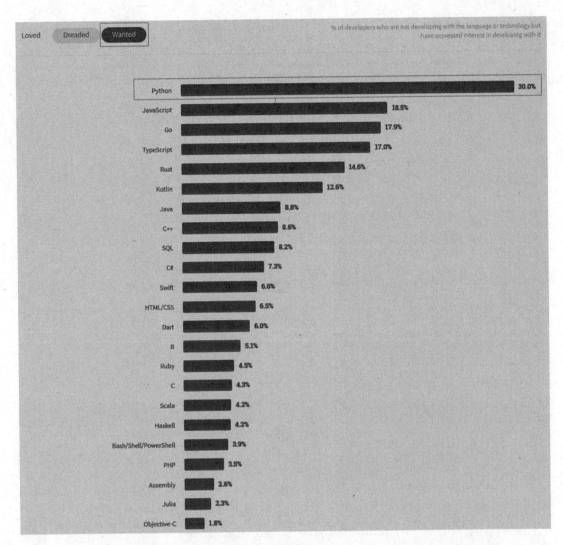

Figure 1-5. *Most wanted programming languages for developers in 2020*
Source: `https://insights.stackoverflow.com/survey/2020#most-loved-dreaded-and-wanted`

Figure 1-6 illustrates the most popular programming languages for 2022 and 2023, with Python leading the pack as the number one programming language of choice since 2022. Despite starting as the third most popular language in the world, following C and Java, Python's popularity has surged over the past decade. As of 2022, Python has overtaken its competitors to become the most widely used language in the programming community.

Feb 2023	Feb 2022	Change		Programming Language	Ratings	Change
1	1			Python	15.49%	+0.16%
2	2			C	15.39%	+1.31%
3	4	^		C++	13.94%	+5.93%
4	3	v		Java	13.21%	+1.07%
5	5			C#	6.38%	+1.01%
6	6			Visual Basic	4.14%	-1.09%
7	7			JavaScript	2.52%	+0.70%
8	10	^		SQL	2.12%	+0.58%
9	9			Assembly language	1.38%	-0.21%
10	8	v		PHP	1.29%	-0.49%
11	11			Go	1.11%	-0.12%
12	13	^		R	1.08%	-0.04%
13	14	^		MATLAB	0.99%	-0.04%
14	15	^		Delphi/Object Pascal	0.95%	+0.05%
15	12	v		Swift	0.93%	-0.25%
16	16			Ruby	0.83%	-0.06%
17	19	^		Perl	0.79%	-0.01%
18	22	^		Scratch	0.76%	+0.13%
19	17	v		Classic Visual Basic	0.74%	-0.09%
20	24	^		Rust	0.70%	+0.16%

Figure 1-6. *The most popular programming languages in 2022*
Source: `https://www.tiobe.com/tiobe-index/`

To begin with, let's analyze these two statements: "I want to learn Python" versus "I want to automate networks using Python." The former statement focuses on mastering the fundamentals of Python syntax and concepts, whereas the latter statement is more specific and encompasses a wider range of objectives. By expressing a desire to learn Python for network automation, you are indicating a practical application of the language. The latter statement demonstrates a specific problem at work that can be resolved through Python. In contrast, the former statement only pertains to learning Python for its own sake. Approaching your Python studies with a clear objective can greatly enhance your learning experience. However, it's important to remember that even with diligent effort, becoming proficient in Python takes time and effort, and cannot be achieved in just a few minutes or hours of watching YouTube videos.

What Are the Necessary Areas of Study to Master Network Automation Using Python?

Most network engineers studying network automation will agree that a flexible integrated development environment (IDE) is essential for learning and developing applications. However, not everyone has access to a network automation development lab environment provided by their organizations or free access to Cisco dCloud or similar online sandboxes. Although timed lab environments are available, they come at significant costs and lack the flexibility and freedom of your lab. Therefore, I recommend using your equipment to build and control every aspect of your lab. **Another advantage of running your lab is the cost-saving perspective, and while you might call me a miser, learning IT should be at a minimal cost to lower the barrier for young and upcoming engineers, who will be the stars of our industry.** This is my perspective, but at the end of the day, automation, especially in large-scale operations like network automation using Python, revolves around cost-driven business activities aiming to reduce operating costs and conserve resources—to achieve more with less. Thus, we need individuals who approach IT with the right mindset, sharing similar thoughts and values. Consequently, it becomes essential to lower the barriers to studying IT automation, encouraging more people to pursue this path and contribute to the field.

There are three ways to configure a lab environment: 100 percent hardware, a hybrid environment that uses both hardware and virtualization, or 100 percent virtualized equipment running on a server or PC. The first method requires a significant initial investment to purchase second-hand equipment and ongoing electricity bills to keep the physical devices operational. A hybrid environment can become cumbersome to manage when some devices run on physical devices and others run on a virtualized environment. The last option, 100 percent virtualized equipment, is the ideal lab environment for studying Python for network automation. This can be achieved by integrating multiple systems and network operating systems running on a virtualization solution. Although it is impossible to experience everything that occurs in a real network environment, building an integrated development lab is the closest you can get to it. **Passive learning through books, Udemy, or YouTube videos is not sufficient.** To master network automation, you need to build your IDE and practice coding actively.

To study Python network automation using this book, all you need is a reasonably powerful desktop or laptop with sufficient CPU power and plenty of RAM. Next, let's discuss the minimum hardware specifications required to follow this book.

Minimum Hardware Specifications for Your Laptop

To successfully install, configure, and engage in all the exercises and Python network automation labs presented in this book, your computer must meet or surpass the minimum specifications listed in Table 1-2. Considering that many network and systems engineers utilize Windows 11 at work, I use this OS as the base operating system for building the IDE Lab environment. However, it might be worth considering upgrading to the latest Windows OS build to leverage the latest features, security, and improvements. If you are using macOS or Linux, you need to find the appropriate software and ensure compatibility on your own. For those with a powerful laptop or PC pre-installed with Windows 11, you are in an ideal position to proceed with the next chapter of this book. If your system is still running Windows 10, 8.1, or 7, it is highly recommended to upgrade to the latest Windows 11. For a seamless experience, a reasonably powerful desktop PC with an optimized CPU and effective system cooling will perform better than a laptop. However, if you own a high-end laptop, utilizing it offers mobility and can lower your utility bill. Because a significant portion of this book concentrates on software installation, creating a practical lab, and running network automation labs on Windows 11 (or newer Windows 12 beyond 2024), your system must meet the minimum hardware and OS requirements specified in Table 1-2. Failure to do so may result in system issues, such as slow response times and delays, while running your lab. Therefore, meeting or exceeding the recommended minimum specifications is imperative.

It's important to note that this book is primarily written for Windows OS users and excludes MacOS/Linux/UNIX desktop users. However, if you choose to follow the book using a non-Windows OS, you should be able to locate compatible versions of different software to complete the exercises. Nonetheless, this falls outside the scope of this book and I recommend using the latest Windows version.

Table 1-2. *Minimum Specifications for Laptops and PCs*

PC Components	Minimum Specification
CPU (Central Processing Unit)	Intel: CPU i7 Gen6 (64-bit) or above CPU benchmark AMD: Ryzen 5 or above CPU benchmark
RAM (Random Access Memory)	16 GB or more for DDR4/DDR5
SSD	240GB or more (with 15% free space for system paging)
Host OS (Operating System)	Microsoft Windows 11/12 (64-bit) or newer

For your reference, the laptop specifications and OS details I used to write this book are shown in Figure 1-7.

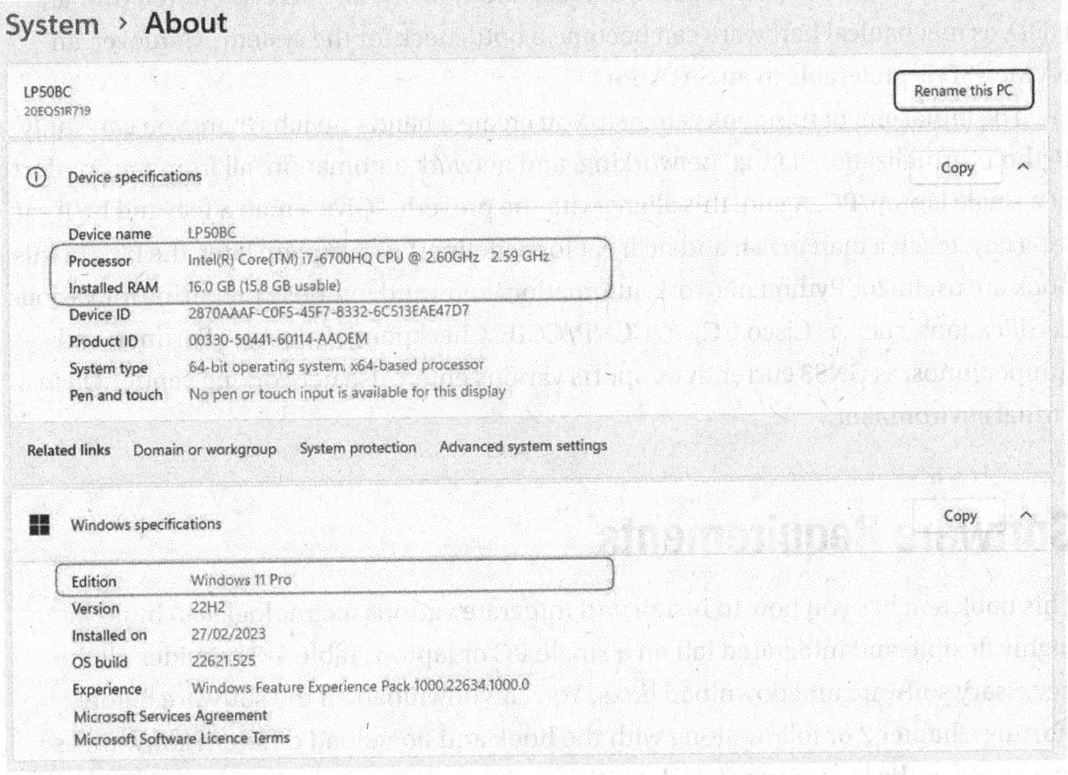

Figure 1-7. *Laptop with Windows 11 and Intel i7 Gen7 system information*

To ensure the smooth running of all labs, your CPU performance benchmark should either be on par with or better than the Intel i7-6700HQ and have at least 16 GB DDR4 memory. At the time of authoring this book in mid-2023, the latest Intel CPU was Generation 13 and the latest AMD CPU was Ryzen 7000 series, so the testing laptop used in this book is an old laptop from the 2015 manufacturing date. Even if your laptop has an older generation of CPU that fails to meet the minimum requirements, most of the labs should still run okay, although performance may not be as optimal when running multiple virtual machines. System delays may arise from the sluggishness of the Windows OS system due to a slower CPU, lack of memory, or several programs running concurrently. These are some of the symptoms from hardware resource contentions if you are using a laptop below the recommended specifications. If you have access to a dedicated ESXi/Proxmox/Cloud environment, I recommend setting up the same lab on external servers for optimal performance. Additionally, an SSD is preferred over an HDD, as mechanical hardware can become a bottleneck for the system. Moreover, an NVMe SSD is preferable to an SATA SSD.

The initial aim of this book is to help you create a hands-on lab where you can study Python, virtualization, Linux, networking, and network automation, all from the comfort of a single laptop/PC. Again, this aligns with the proverb: "Give a man a fish and he'll eat for a day; teach a man to fish and he'll eat for a lifetime." As I explain later, the labs in this book are useful for Python network automation study and for those preparing for various certifications, such as Cisco CCNA/CCNP/CCIE, Checkpoint, Palo Alto, Fortinet, and Juniper Junos, as GNS3 currently supports various enterprise networking vendor OS in a virtual environment.

Software Requirements

This book teaches you how to install and integrate various technologies to build a highly flexible and integrated lab on a single PC or laptop. Table 1-3 provides all the necessary software and download links. You can download all the software before starting Chapter 2 or follow along with the book and download different software as instructed at the beginning of each chapter.

The key technology that ties together and enables multiple types of virtual machines on a single PC is *VMware Workstation*, which is built on its server-based counterpart, the data center solution ESXi (also known as vSphere). While you can use VirtualBox as your desktop virtualization environment, I have opted to use VMware Workstation because it closely resembles the data center (DC) and cloud environments found in the real world. **VMware ESXi is the backbone of many DCs and cloud infrastructure, and many virtual concepts, features, and menus have been passed down and inherited by VMware Workstation. This means that new users of VMware can become familiar with VMware Workstation and already be halfway to understanding vSphere ESXi data center and cloud technologies.** Although the terms VMware ESXi and VMware vSphere are different, they are often used interchangeably to refer to the same vendor's DC technology.

Note that not all software utilized in this book is freeware or open-source, and you may need to use demo software or paid software. For instance, **VMware Workstation 17 Pro** will run in demo mode for the initial 30 days, after which you need to purchase a valid key. However, if you are still using a licensed VMware Workstation 16 or older, you can still use it, as the first edition of this book was written based on versions 16 and 15, and no software compatibility issues were found. If any technical issues arise, you may need to troubleshoot or tweak configurations to make the integration work. Another example is the **Cisco Modeling Labs-Personal Edition** (CML-PE), which requires a yearly subscription of $199 (as of 2023). Nevertheless, for the labs in this book, you only need the three files outlined in Table 1-3. This book continues to use these old files, as you do not need to tap into new IOS-XE features offered by newer IOS-XE software. However, if you have the new CML-PE images, you can use the newer files to integrate Cisco CML-PE images into the VMware Workstation. All other software used in this book is either freeware or open-source.

Table 1-3. *Software and Download Links (At the Time of Writing This Book)*

#	Required Software	Usage	License Type
1	**VMware-workstation-full-17.0.0-20800274.exe** [607.88 MB] or newer URL 1: https://customerconnect.vmware.com/ downloads/info/slug/desktop_end_user_ computing/vmwareworkstation_pro/17_0 URL 2: https://customerconnect.vmware.com/ downloads/info/slug/desktop_end_user_ computing/	Desktop virtualization	Licensed
2	**GNS3-2.2.41-all-in-one.exe** [96.6 MB] or newer URL: https://github.com/GNS3/gns3-gui/ releases	Network device emulator	Open-source
3	**GNS3.VM.VMware.Workstation.2.2.41.zip** [1.08 GB] or newer URL: https://github.com/GNS3/gns3-gui/ releases	VMware Workstation GNS3 VM ova image	Open-source
4	**IOSv-L3-15.6(2)T.qcow2** or newer**IOSv_startup_ config.imgIOSvL215.2.4055.qcow2** or newer URL: https://learningnetworkstore.cisco. com/cisco-modeling-labs-personal/ cisco-cml-personal	Cisco CML L3 imageCML L3 booting fileCisco CML L2 image	Licensed
5	**python-3.12.0a7-amd64.exe** or newer URL: https://www.python.org/ftp/python/	Python for Windows	Open-source
6	**npp.8.5.4.Installer.x64** [4.45 MB] or newer URL: https://notepad-plus-plus.org/ downloads/	Text Editor for Windows	Freeware
7	**putty-64bit-0.78-installer.msi** [3.6 MB] or newer URL: https://www.putty.org/	SSH/Telnet client	Freeware
8	**ubuntu-22.04.2-live-server-amd64.iso** [1.83GB] or newer URL: https://www.ubuntu.com/download/server	Ubuntu Server image: Bootable	Open-source

(continued)

Table 1-3. (*continued*)

#	Required Software	Usage	License Type
9	**Fedora-Server-dvd-x86_64-38-1.6 .iso** [2.27 GB] or newer URL: `https://getfedora.org/en/server/download/`	Fedora Server image: Bootable	Open-source
10	**c3725-adventerprisek9-mz.124-15.T14.bin** (or similar) Option 1: Extract from old used Cisco routers Option 2: Locate an image on Google search result URL: Search Google with the .bin name	Cisco IOS image for GNS3 integration	Licensed
11	**Unpack-0.1_win.exe** [2.5 MB] or newer URL: `http://downloads.sourceforge.net/gns-3/Unpack-0.1_win.zip?download`	Cisco image unpacker 0.1 binary for Windows	Freeware
12	**WinMD5Free.exe** [263 KB] URL: `https://www.winmd5.com/`	Windows MD5 Checker	Freeware
13	**[WinSCP-6.1.1-Setup.exe** [11 MB] or newer URL: `https://winscp.net/eng/download.php`	Secure File Transfer client for Windows-Linux	Freeware
14	**FileZilla_3.65.0_win64-setup.exe** (64bit, For Windows) or newer URL 1: `https://filezilla-project.org/download.php?show_all=1` URL 2: `https://filezilla-project.org/`	Secure File Transfer client for Windows-Linux	Freeware

Building Network Automation Development Environment Using GNS3

A network automation development environment, also known as an Integrated Development Environment (IDE) network lab, is a software platform developed for network application development. In this book, I refer to this environment as "the lab" or "the network lab" for ease of understanding. There are various methods to create a learning lab for Python Network Automation. Around 20 years ago, students studying Cisco routing and switching relied on a combination of hardware-based labs, a Cisco Packet Tracer networking OS simulator, and an open-source emulator called Dynamips, released in 2007 for multiple platforms. GNS3, which is Dynamips with a graphical user interface (GUI) for easy use, was introduced in 2008. While Dynamips was a good networking device emulator for study, it lacked a GUI, making it difficult for beginners to use. GNS3 made managing emulated lab devices more straightforward with its GUI interface.

Initially, GNS3 had numerous bugs and was not always reliable. However, with advancements in CPU architecture, increased RAM capacity, improved software compatibility, and the introduction of Solid State Drives (SSD), emulating vendor network devices from an application on a laptop/desktop has become easier and more accessible. The price drop in PC hardware components and the rise of more open-source network emulators have made studying networking highly accessible. The latest versions of GNS3 are free of many pre-existing bugs and can run a stable lab environment. GNS3 has also evolved to support older Cisco IOSs and to integrate with Cisco IOU and CML's (VIRL) L2 and L3 IOS, enabling emulation of both L2 switches and L3 routers in a virtualized lab environment. While the best way to study any technology is to use real equipment or the same virtual machines in a virtual environment, not everyone has access to such resources. If time and cost are no issue, it is best to study with the real equipment and real virtual devices in a fully blown virtual environment. As the second-best option, an emulator is still preferable to a simulator. For example, GNS3 or EVE-NG is preferred over Cisco Packet Tracer or Boson NetSim Network Simulator. Table 1-4 provides a tabulated list of applications used for network labs, offering insight into the history of network simulators and emulators for networking studies.

Table 1-4. *Network Emulation/Simulation Program for Networking Studies*

Application	Simulator /Emulator and Commercials	Pros and Cons
Cisco Packet Tracer	Simulator & Proprietary	**Pros:** ✓ User-friendly interface ✓ Wide range of network devices ✓ Pre-built network topologies ✓ Simulation and visualization of network activity ✓ Collaboration features ✓ Cost-effective ✓ Built-in tutorials and resources ✓ Integration with other Cisco tools. **Cons:** ■ Limited device support ■ Limited scalability ■ Limited support for advanced networking protocols ■ Limited customization options ■ Limited compatibility with non-Cisco devices ■ Limited real-world application

(continued)

Table 1-4. (*continued*)

Application	Simulator /Emulator and Commercials	Pros and Cons
Boson NetSim Network Simulator & Router Simulator	Simulator & Proprietary	**Pros:** ✓ Realistic network simulation ✓ Comprehensive lab exercises ✓ Supports multiple network devices ✓ Customizable and configurable ✓ User-friendly interface ✓ Instant grading and feedback ✓ Integrated packet tracer **Cons:** ■ Costly ■ Limited platform support ■ Software updates are required ■ No physical hardware interaction ■ Virtualization performance ■ Limited scope of simulations ■ Licensing restrictions

(*continued*)

Table 1-4. (*continued*)

Application	Simulator /Emulator and Commercials	Pros and Cons
GNS3	Emulator & Open-source (Built-on Dynamips)	**Pros:** ✓ Open-source ✓ Emulation of real networks ✓ Cross-platform compatibility ✓ Real-time network simulation ✓ Easy to use ✓ Customizable lab environment ✓ Integration with other tools ✓ Large user community ✓ Cost-effective ✓ Scale and performance **Cons:** ■ Resource-intensive ■ Steep learning curve ■ Limited hardware support ■ Compatibility issues ■ Requires additional software ■ Limited graphical interface ■ Lack of vendor support ■ Security concerns

(*continued*)

Table 1-4. (*continued*)

Application	Simulator /Emulator and Commercials	Pros and Cons
Cisco IOU	Emulator & Proprietary	**Pros:** ✓ Realistic network simulation ✓ Emulation of Cisco hardware ✓ Cost-effective ✓ Open-source ✓ Scalability ✓ Integration with other tools ✓ Large user community ✓ Compatibility **Cons:** ■ Limited device support ■ Limited scalability ■ Limited support for advanced networking protocols ■ Limited customization options ■ Limited compatibility with non-Cisco devices ■ Limited real-world application

(*continued*)

Table 1-4. (*continued*)

Application	Simulator /Emulator and Commercials	Pros and Cons
Cisco CML (VIRL)	Emulator & Proprietary	**Pros:** ✓ High-fidelity network simulation ✓ Wide range of network devices and protocols ✓ Scalability ✓ Integration with other Cisco tools ✓ Robust API for customization and automation ✓ Realistic performance testing ✓ Collaboration features **Cons:** ■ Expensive ■ Resource-intensive ■ Steep learning curve ■ Limited compatibility with non-Cisco devices ■ Limited third-party tool integration ■ Limited community support

(continued)

Table 1-4. (*continued*)

Application	Simulator /Emulator and Commercials	Pros and Cons
UNL Lite (EVE-NG)	Emulator & Proprietary	**Pros:** ✓ High-fidelity network simulation ✓ Support for a wide range of devices and protocols ✓ Scalability ✓ Integration with other tools ✓ Flexible licensing options ✓ Open-source platform with a large user community ✓ Realistic performance testing ✓ Collaboration features **Cons:** ■ Resource-intensive ■ Steep learning curve ■ Limited hardware support for some devices ■ Limited community support for the free version ■ Limited third-party tool integration

(*continued*)

Table 1-4. (*continued*)

Application	Simulator /Emulator and Commercials	Pros and Cons
Vagrant	Emulator & Open-source	**Pros:** ✓ Requires prior knowledge of virtualization and scripting languages ✓ Steep learning curve ✓ Resource-intensive ✓ Limited hardware support for some devices ✓ Limited graphical user interface (GUI) support **Cons:** ■ Requires prior knowledge of virtualization and scripting languages ■ Steep learning curve ■ Resource-intensive ■ Limited hardware support for some devices ■ Limited graphical user interface (GUI) support

In addition to the emulators and simulators discussed in Table 1-4, there are other options available for network simulation. NS-3 is another network simulator that provides a virtual environment for network modeling, testing, and troubleshooting, and it is commonly used for research and education purposes. Dynamips is also a widely used and powerful network simulator that offers a highly realistic simulation of older-style Cisco routers and switches. However, Dynamips is resource-intensive and demands a working knowledge of Cisco IOS, which may make it less accessible to beginners. Users should also be aware of compatibility issues with newer network hardware or software and limited hardware support for some devices. Furthermore, Dynamips lacks vendor support, making it challenging to troubleshoot issues or receive timely updates. Another option for network emulation is Cisco IOU (IOS on UNIX), which is a flexible and popular network emulator that allows users to run virtualized versions of Cisco routers and switches with support for various protocols. However, it was never designed for general public use and requires significant computing power to run it. Similar to

Dynamips, IOU lacks vendor support, making it challenging to troubleshoot issues or receive timely updates. Additionally, it's important to note that Cisco IOU was developed for Cisco internal use and, therefore, does not support other vendor network device OSs.

Over the past two decades, newer emulators such as Unified Networking Lab's UNL Lite (now renamed EVE-NG) and Cisco's CML (Cisco Modeling Lab, old VIRL) have gained popularity due to their versatile features and ease of use. The Cisco Packet Tracer can also be used for studying Cisco certifications through the Network Academy. Many online resources are available to learn how to use these software tools. However, for this book, the recommended option is to use the GNS3 VM running on VMware Workstation Pro, integrated with Cisco IOS and CML images, which provides an emulated network infrastructure for Python network automation labs. Your Python network automation servers will be running as separate and dedicated VMs on the VMware Workstation.

The labs in this book are arranged in a sequence of difficulty from easy to intermediate. As long as you use the same or newer versions of the software as used in this book, most lab setups should work without compatibility issues, making all labs reproducible. If you plan to use the content of this book for group training and solely focus on teaching students in Python labs, one viable option is to create a virtual machine of Windows 11 or 12 on an ESXi 7 or 8 environment or cloud system. From there, you can install all the necessary software, integrate it, and make clones of the original virtual machine to provide designated virtual machines with RDP access. While using a public cloud service provider may be another option, running virtual machines on a public cloud is not cheap and offers less control. **While there are multiple ways to set up your development lab environment, the recommended option in this book is the most cost-effective for learners and provides near-total control over lab management**. After your lab environment has been fully configured, it will run even without an Internet connection. However, it's important to note that cloud-based lab environments can present challenges, because they require a reliable and permanent Internet connection to the cloud resources, and your Internet connection is only as good as your Internet Service Provider (ISP).

Downloading Complementary Guides and Source Codes

For most of the software used in this book, the process of installing the base software is straightforward and can be completed by clicking the Next or Yes buttons a few times, so many readers may not require installation guides. However, if you want to refer to my installation settings in detail, you can download the complementary installation guides from the Author's GitHub page provided in this section. **Before proceeding to Chapter 2, download all pre-installation guides and source code from the following URLs:**

Complementary pre-installation guides are available from:

URL: `https://github.com/pynetauto/apress_pynetauto_ed2.0/tree/main/pre_installation_guides`

Source codes are available from:

URL: `https://github.com/pynetauto/apress_pynetauto_ed2.0/tree/main/source_codes` OR

`https://github.com/orgs/Apress/repositories`

With the general IT automation discussion covered in this chapter, you are now equipped to immerse yourself in the Python exercises presented in Chapters 2 and 3. Let's get started!

Summary

In this chapter, readers were presented with an overview of general IT automation and conducted a comparative analysis of the three primary IT domain groups' skillsets. I identified the specific areas that the network engineer group must focus on and improve on to begin writing Python code for the network automation journey. Additionally, I discussed the minimum hardware and software requirements to build a portable and the most cost-effective network automation lab environment for this book, as well as your CCNA studies. Notably, all network devices used in this book are software-based, including virtual routers and switches.

Storytime 1: Mega Speed Shoe Factory

In 2016, the world was buzzing with excitement about the potential of robotics and automation to revolutionize the manufacturing industry. The shoe manufacturing sector was no exception, as the renowned German brand Adidas announced the launch of its new robotic shoe factory. At that time, predictions were made that up to 90 percent of the nine million workers in southeast Asia could face unemployment due to the introduction of these mega factories.

However, in 2020, Adidas revealed that it would halt production at its two robotic "speed factories" in Germany and the United States. Despite the initial hype and enthusiasm, the reality was that the robots could only produce a limited range of shoes, mainly running shoes with a knit upper. They were unable to manufacture leather shoes with rubber soles, which were in high demand. As a result, the factories could not meet consumer needs, and Adidas was forced to shut down the factories.

This example illustrates the significance of careful planning and the continued need for human involvement in the manufacturing process, countering the fear that machines will completely replace human labor. It also underscores the fact that every industry is learning the potential of automation through trial and error. This failure is reminiscent of the introduction of Automated Teller Machines (ATMs) in the early 1990s, when numerous prominent economists and scholars made inaccurate economic forecasts. The same could be true of predictions regarding the impact of automation and artificial intelligence (AI) on the IT industry. Nevertheless, if we are prepared and embrace change, there should be no fear of automation or AI/ChatGPT. For IT engineers, it is crucial to support their company's IT ecosystem and be honest about their strengths and limitations. It is unrealistic to expect an IT engineer to possess expertise in every aspect of all IT technologies they support. Therefore, being open to learning new skills and acquiring additional knowledge is essential for career advancement and a paved road to a comfortable retirement.

In conclusion, the story of Adidas' failed robotic shoe factory emphasizes the necessity of careful planning and continued human involvement in the manufacturing process. While automation and AI may bring significant changes to the IT industry and beyond, it is vital to approach these changes with an open mind and a willingness to learn. By doing so, we can harness the power of technology to enhance our lives and propel our careers forward.

CHAPTER 2

Learn Python Basics on Windows

Windows is one of the most popular desktop operating systems, especially among new Python learners. This chapter offers hands-on exercises to connect Python syntax with general programming concepts. It guides readers through the process of setting up a simple Python environment on Windows and introduces quintessential Python coding etiquette. The chapter starts with the classic "Hello World!" program and covers basic Python syntax and general programming concepts, laying a strong foundation for learners. By the end of the chapter, readers will have gained the essential Python skills required to write basic scripts. Chapters 2 and 3 serve as primers for the later chapters on Python Network Automation scripting labs. Therefore, you must complete all these exercises to get up to speed.

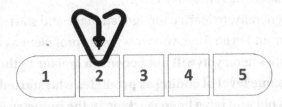

Learn Python Basics on Windows – Part I

Learning a new programming language can present challenges and feelings of uncertainty, which I experienced when embarking on my journey with Python back in 2013. At first, grasping the basic syntax seemed like an arduous and pointless endeavor, leading me to give up after just two months. However, determined to overcome these initial struggles, I decided to give Python another chance in 2015. This time, with persistence and dedication, I managed to grasp the fundamental syntax and concepts

© Brendan Choi 2024
B. Choi, *Introduction to Python Network Automation Volume I - Laying the Groundwork*,
https://doi.org/10.1007/979-8-8688-0146-4_2

within three months. Despite this progress, I faced a new hurdle as I struggled to apply Python to my daily work tasks, leading me once again to abandon my learning journey. It wasn't until 2017 that I discovered the missing pieces of the puzzle: setting clear objectives and creating a roadmap to achieve them. For me, the key was finding ways to utilize Python to automate repetitive tasks in my role as a network engineer. This realization marked a turning point in my learning process. I understood that mastering the language was just one part of the equation. To effectively leverage Python, I also needed to enhance my Linux system admin skills, become proficient in Regular Expressions, and explore various Python modules. In essence, my journey with Python taught me that learning a new programming language is not only about understanding the syntax but also about finding meaningful applications and setting goals that align with one's interests and professional pursuits. It is through such purposeful learning that one can truly unlock the full potential of a programming language like Python.

Starting a new journey to learn a programming language requires strong motivation and personal commitment. However, the learning curve can be steep if this is your first attempt, making it easy to lose focus and give up. To make your Python learning experience more manageable, it's essential to spend some time contemplating your motivations, where you intend to use Python, and what goals you want to achieve. Set realistic expectations and allow yourself ample time to absorb Python syntax and concepts thoroughly. Remember that learning a new language is akin to learning a non-native language and mastering it will take time.

Realistically and generally, to learn a foreign language and start speaking fluently takes about six months, and even then, you won't be as proficient as native speakers. The same analogy applies here; **you will not become a master Python coder in six months or reach the same level of coding as prodigies who started learning Python at the age of ten years old and have been working in the industry for over 20 years. Acknowledge the difference, recognize where you stand and where others stand, and set personal and achievable goals, taking one step at a time. This is extremely important in your journey**. Learning Python is a journey with no finish line, as all learners are at different points in the race. Approach your study strategy with a positive attitude and a willingness to persevere through challenges. The journey of learning never truly ends, and there will always be new aspects to discover and explore.

Now, let's explore the various ways you can interact with your computer. There are three primary methods to instruct the computer to perform a task. The first is to sit in front of the physical computer or use a remote console machine to provide real-time instructions in a one-to-one or one-to-many manner. The second method is to write a piece of code using a text editor or IDE (Integrated Development Environment) and manually execute the code, known as "semi-automation." The third method involves scheduling your code to run automatically at a specific time, referred to as "full automation" or "fully automated." Python is an interactive programming language that doesn't require pre-compiling. As an interactive programming language, it interprets the source code on the spot and provides computer instructions for when the code needs to be executed.

Although this book primarily focuses on Python Network Automation, Python knowledge, and programming skills are essential components and the means to achieve Python Network Automation success. However, you need to know a lot more than Python syntax and programming concepts. As such, this book aims to broaden your perspective on various IT technologies that are crucial for your network automation journey. The book introduces several technologies that will enable you to become a well-rounded technologist capable of coding in Python, administering Linux, developing applications, and building a proof-of-concept (POC) networking lab for work. If your interest lies solely in studying basic Python syntax, it's recommended that you purchase a suitable Python Basics book readily available on Amazon or consume hundreds of free YouTube Python courses. In comparison, this book offers a structured learning strategy that you can follow without taking shortcuts and get over the first mountain.

Your Python knowledge and experience may vary significantly, but in this chapter, I assume that you are a novice Python coder. This chapter covers the essential Python syntax and concepts required to perform selective tasks presented in this book. The book gradually and linearly builds your Python Network Automation skillset. **I encourage you to type the code and complete all exercises in this chapter before proceeding to the next chapters**. This book stands out from others in its presentation of information. Rather than overwhelming you with endless explanations of concepts, it prioritizes required learning to provide practical exercises that you can perform and relate to, followed by explanations of the underlying concepts. I recognize that excessive detail can be counterproductive and I aim to help you become a doer, not just a conceptual thinker. The exercises are accompanied by explanations in the form of embedded comments or follow-up explanations. Additionally, the book includes bullet-point summaries of each concept milestone to help reinforce what you have learned. Unlike other books, I do not burden you with trivial and meaningless before or after quizzes, irrational questions, or absurd challenges that may cause you to feel irritated or lose enthusiasm for the material.

Tip

Install the latest Python for Windows and Notepad++

Before moving on, ensure **that you have installed the latest version of Python for Windows and Notepad++ to follow along with the exercises.** I assume that you have completed the pre-installation tasks before diving into this chapter. When working with Python in a Windows environment, it is recommended to install Python under its folder in the C:\ directory. Doing so allows you to save and modify your Python code without being prompted for Windows folder access permissions, which can improve your coding experience. Additionally, installing Python in its directory helps avoid conflicts with other installed software and ensures that all necessary dependencies are installed correctly. Overall, installing Python in its directory can make it easier to manage and work with Python code on a Windows machine.

For this book, I assume that your Python installation directory is located at C:\python312. It is recommended that you follow this convention while installing Python on Windows (see Figure 2-1).

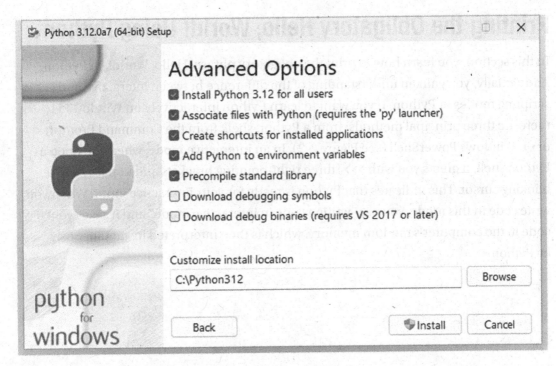

Figure 2-1. *Install Python3 under custom install location C:\Python312*

Warning

Check your Python version

When this book was written, the latest version of Python for Windows was 3.12. If you're using the latest version, your Python version will be newer. While there may be minor version differences, the code in this book is compatible as long as you're using a Python version newer than 3.6.5. To check the Python version, type the python --version or python -V command on your command-line prompt or terminal.

C:\Users\brend>**python --version**

Python 3.12.0a7

Printing the Obligatory Hello, World! Using Python

In this section, you learn how to print the obligatory phrase, Hello, World!, in Python. Additionally, you gain an understanding of the difference between interactive and scripting modes in Python. If you want to learn Python interactively on Windows 11, there are three principal methods: from a Python shell; from the Command Prompt; or on Windows PowerShell (see Figure 2-2). In an interactive mode, when you open a Python shell, it greets you with >>> (three right-pointing brackets and a space) and a blinking cursor. This indicates that Python is ready for your interactive input. When you write code in this mode, you are "writing code in interactive mode" and it saves your code in the computer's random memory, which is then interpreted instantaneously by Python.

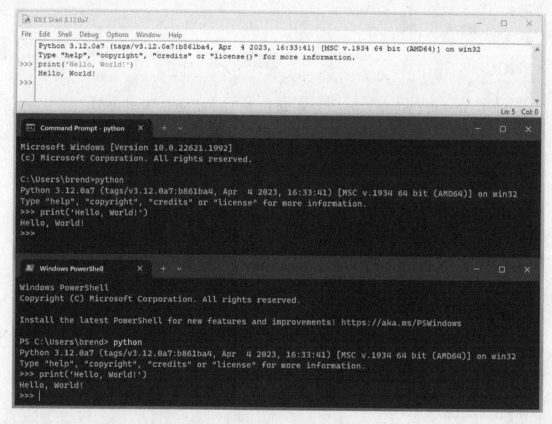

Figure 2-2. *Python interactive coding on Windows*

When starting your journey in Python, you can begin by using a simple `print()` function to display an obligatory "Hello World!" statement on your screen. To accomplish this, you must first write a set of strings enclosed in a set of round brackets, along with single or double quotes surrounding the expression, and then press the Enter key on your keyboard. The Python Interpreter immediately interprets the code and displays the output on your screen. This means that the input is the code you type in, and the output is a result of Python on the terminal screen. The computer program prints out the "Hello World!" statement. The best part is that you do not have to compile the code before running the command, which is the key feature in interpreted languages. Other interpreted programming languages include JavaScript, PHP, Ruby, Perl, and any flavors of shell scripting languages like Bash and PowerShell. On the other side of the spectrum, there are several compiled programming languages in use today, including C and C++, Java, Swift, Kotlin, Rust, and Go.

If you are comfortable with Linux commands and want to learn Python on your Windows PC, the fourth option for practicing Python on a Windows machine is to install WSL (Windows Subsystem for Linux). This option enables you to run a Linux operating system directly on your Windows machine, providing a Linux environment that suits those who prefer it or need to use Linux-specific tools.

To get familiar with the `print()` function, you can open one of the prompt methods discussed earlier and type the mandatory "`print('Hello World!')`" or "`print("Hello, World!")`" statement. **This seemingly simple task will help you learn three things: first, how to use the `print()` function; second, that Python uses either single quotes (' ') or double quotes (" ") to wrap strings; and third, it will introduce you to the mandatory `print('Hello World!')` statement, which serves as a verification tool**. The `print()` function and the use of quotation marks are further explained through various examples in this chapter.

Whether you're new to Python programming or have some experience, it's worth taking the time to learn about the origin and use cases of the Hello, World! program. I've included two URLs that you can visit to learn more about the famous Hello World!. In this book, I use it as a way to verify that Python is functioning properly and can print strings to the console screen when the `print()` function is executed. Before proceeding to the next page, ensure that Python and Notepad++ are correctly installed and configured on your computer.

Expand your knowledge:

The origin of Hello, World!

To expand your understanding, consider reading about the Hello, World! program on Wikipedia:

URL: `https://en.wikipedia.org/wiki/%22Hello,_World!%22_program`

Also, watch the Computerphile video "Hello (World) Abstraction!" on YouTube:

URL: `https://www.youtube.com/watch?v=ycl1VLOq1rs`

These resources delve into the origins and significance of the Hello, World! program in the context of computer programming. While it may seem like a simple program, the use of the Hello, World! statement serves as an important validation tool to ensure that programming languages, compilers, and development environments are functioning correctly. By printing Hello, World! in the examples, you can verify that Python correctly executes your code and displays the output on the console screen.

In Python 3, the `print()` function displays processed data on the user's screen. It takes zero or more arguments separated by commas, which are then printed to the console or standard output stream. In Python 2, `print` was a statement and did not require parentheses. Additionally, Python 2's `print` automatically added a newline character at the end of the output. **The `print()` is a built-in function that requires parentheses around its arguments in Python 3, and you need to add the newline character explicitly**. As Python 2.x has reached its end of life, this book uses Python 3.6.5 or newer. Python 2 is fading out quickly and now, Python 3.x is the de facto version in the ICT industry. The differences between Python 2.x and 3.x are minimal, but if you are a new Python learner, there is no need to learn version 2.x.

Python is commonly referred to as a high-level programming language that is used for a variety of applications, including web development, data analysis, machine learning, and more. One of the main advantages of Python is that it is platform-independent, meaning that code written on one operating system can be run on other operating systems as well. To write Python code, you can use a text editor and save it in the .py file format before running the script. This process is known as "writing a script," "writing code," or "working in scripting mode." Although Python provides a built-in text editor, you can also use a text editor of your choice. While you can use a more feature-rich Integrated Development Environment (IDE), such as PyCharm, Microsoft Visual Studio Code, Atom, or Spyder IDE, mastering how to use Python shell and the built-in text editor is more than adequate while starting your Python study.

In this chapter, you practice each line of code on your keyboard using Python IDLE and the built-in text editor to experience what it feels like to write code in Python. Using a simple Windows text editor such as Notepad, WordPad, or Notepad++ is sufficient to write Python code for now. However, you should take a special note later that other text editors are more feature-rich and provide syntax highlighting, code completion, and debugging capabilities, which can make coding easier and more efficient. In later chapters, I discuss different types of IDE text editors and how they can enhance your coding experience. But for now, focus on learning how to use the Python shell and the built-in text editor to develop a strong foundation in Python programming.

To start writing Python code, you can use Python's built-in text editor by navigating to the File menu in Python IDLE and selecting New. From there, you can begin typing your code. Here's an example line of code to get you started:

welcome.py

```
print("Welcome to the second edition")
```

After writing your Python code, it's important to save it with a name that reflects its purpose. For example, you can save the file as welcome.py. It's also a good practice to keep your Python files organized in a separate folder for better management. To create a new folder for your code, you can navigate to the C:\Python312 directory and create a folder named ch02.

Creating a separate folder for your Python files will help you keep them organized and make it easier to locate them later. Remember to save your code file with a .py extension and run it using the Run command or the F5 key. To execute your code, select Run Module (shortcut key: F5) from the Run menu in the text editor. This will run your Python script and display the output in the console (see Figure 2-3).

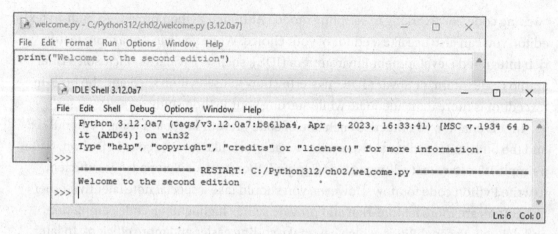

Figure 2-3. *Coding in Python's built-in text editor and IDLE in Windows*

As you progress with learning Python, you will write more complex scripts and modules. However, the process of writing, saving, and running your code will remain the same. Remember to save your code often and test it frequently to catch any errors or bugs. By organizing your code into separate folders and using descriptive file names, you can make it easier to manage and locate your code in the future. Having a well-organized folder (or directory) structure is crucial, especially in Linux systems that operate without graphical interfaces (GUIs). As you venture into Linux in later chapters, you'll understand the vital role and the need for a neatly arranged set of directories.

By completing all the exercises in this chapter, you will become more familiar with the core concepts of Python, which are essential for further learning in the Part 2 of this book. These concepts form the foundation of Python programming and mastering them will enable you to write more complex and sophisticated Python programs. If you are using Linux or macOS, you can open a terminal window and start the interactive mode by typing python or python3. This will allow you to experiment with Python code and test out your ideas in a live environment. Later in this book, I delve deeper into coding in Linux OS and explore more advanced Python programming topics. Overall, mastering the core concepts of Python and becoming proficient with the language will equip you with the necessary skills to tackle real-world programming challenges and build complex applications. Remember to keep practicing and testing your code frequently to catch errors and bugs.

In Part 2 of this book, you learn more advanced concepts such as object-oriented programming, data analysis, and web development using Python. By mastering these topics, you will be able to create powerful and versatile applications for a variety of use cases. So, keep learning and exploring, and always strive to improve your skills.

Preparing for the Python Exercises

According to an article in ZDNet in 2023, Microsoft Windows still dominates the desktop OS market, with a share of 68.15 percent. Therefore, it remains the most popular desktop OS used by end-users. In comparison, macOS accounted for 21.38 percent, Chrome OS for 4.15 percent, and Linux for 3.08 percent. Given these statistics, **starting your Python journey on the Windows environment is an ideal choice for most desktop users**. If you work in an IT profession, transitioning to Linux is recommended as Linux server OS is the true rockstar in the cloud and data center. Many enterprise servers that support Python run on various Linux OS flavors, making it essential for enterprise engineers to become proficient in Linux. Furthermore, the article highlights that more than 96.3 percent of the top websites worldwide run on Linux, and over 90 percent of the cloud operates on Linux. Therefore, if you are involved in coding, application development, cloud, or other cutting-edge technologies, transitioning from Windows to Linux on both the desktop and server side can significantly enhance your efficiency. This chapter, however, focuses on getting you started with Python in the Windows environment. Subsequent chapters cover Linux basics and help you become familiar with working within the Linux OS environment. So, let's begin with Python on Windows and later explore using Python on Linux. If you have been a Windows user all your life, it is strongly recommended to start working on Linux OS to stay ahead of the pack in most IT technician jobs. On the other hand, if you are already familiar with Linux, you will have a smooth journey in business class while taking your Python Network Automation career to new heights.

Throughout this chapter, you go through various exercises and use the explanation and concept summary to review what you have learned from these exercises. To get started with Python coding, you first learn about four essential Python concepts with some examples, and then you try out all the exercises as you follow along with this chapter:

1. Python data types

2. Indentation and code blocks

3. Commenting

4. Basic Python naming conventions

You can practice all exercises presented in this chapter on Linux or macOS with minor modifications to directory locations. To open Python on these operating systems, simply open a terminal window and type python or python3 to start the interactive mode. Python will greet you with a friendly interactive prompt. Pay close attention, and you will notice that the prompt has three greater-than symbols followed by a single whitespace. This is called the Python prompt, and it indicates that Python is ready to receive input from you. From there, you can type in Python code and experiment with the language. In the next few sections of this chapter, you learn about the basics of Python programming, including data types, code indentation, commenting, and naming conventions. These concepts are essential to understanding how to write clean and maintainable Python code and mastering them will enable you to tackle more complex programming challenges later on.

Tip

PEP 8, the official style guide for Python code

When you encounter the three greater-than signs (sometimes referred to as "chevrons") followed by a single whitespace in Python, it indicates that Python is ready for you to type the next line of code. As you continue practicing writing code, you'll become very familiar with this symbol. The combination of the three chevrons and the space represents four objects in total. This serves as a reminder of PEP 8, the official style guide for Python code, which advocates using four spaces for indentation to enhance code readability. Adhering to PEP 8's recommendations and including the use of four spaces for code blocks will help you develop a habit of writing clean, readable code. Remember, following the official style guide is the best approach to achieving a consistent and professional coding style.

>>>□

Note: "□" represents a space.

Visit the following site to read a full PEP 8 style guide for Python code.

URL: https://peps.python.org/pep-0008/

Understanding Data Types

In this section, you gain an understanding of the different data types used in Python. It's essential to grasp these concepts early on to save time and prevent potential errors while writing code. **In Python, a data type is a group of values that share similar characteristics.** There are several data types in Python, including numbers, sequences, mappings, sets, and None. Familiarizing yourself with these data types will help you write more concise, efficient, and effective code.

To learn about each data type, I use Python's built-in function type(). This function allows you to determine the data type of a particular value or variable. By understanding the different data types in Python and how to use them (see Figure 2-4), you'll be on your way to writing more compliant and scalable Python codes.

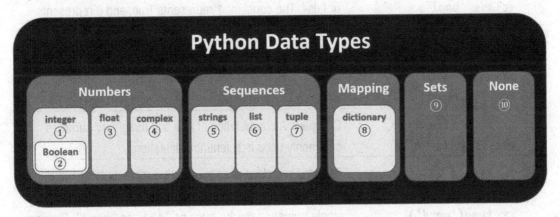

Figure 2-4. *Python data types*

Python is an object-oriented language that treats everything as an object. This means that every element in Python can be classified into different data types based on its characteristics. Understanding the most commonly used data types and how they are used in Python is essential to comprehend basic to intermediate Python coding concepts while developing various applications or scripts. Note that the circled numbers in the following examples correspond to each of the Python data types shown in Figure 2-4. It is important to understand the differences between these data types and how they can be used in various scenarios to write efficient and effective Python code. By mastering these data types as the building blocks or code elements, you will be able to develop more complex programs and applications with ease.

In the following examples, I aim to provide a foundational understanding of the most used Python data types required to comprehend the concepts and applications presented. To validate different data objects, let's use Python's built-in function type(). To do this, open your Python shell and enter the text in bold, next to >>>, and press the Enter key. Let's get started.

#	Examples	Explanation
①	>>> **type (3)** `<class 'int'>`	**Integer**: A subclass of numbers that represents whole numbers with + or − signs, like -3, 0, and 5. Integers are commonly used in numeric data for calculation purposes.

②	>>> **type (True)**
	 `<class 'bool'>`
	 >>> **type (False)**
	 `<class 'bool'>`
		Boolean: A subclass of integer that tests conditions for true or false. The constant 1 represents True, and 0 represents False.

③	>>> **type (1.0)** `<class 'float'>`	**Float**: A subclass of numbers that represents numbers with fractions or decimal points. For example, 1.0 is a float.
④	>>> **type (1 + 2j)** `<class 'complex'>`	**Complex**: A combination of real and imaginary numbers, commonly used in scientific calculations.

⑤	>>> **type ('123')**
	 `<class 'str'>`
	 >>> **type('word')**
	 `<class 'str'>`
		String: A subclass of sequence that represents an ordered sequence of characters. Strings are enclosed in double or single quotation marks, such as `'123'` or `"word"`. They are mutable and indexed by integers from 0 to n.

⑥	>>> **type ([1, 2, 3])** `<class 'list'>`	**List**: A subclass of sequence that represents an ordered collection of items of any data type. Lists use square brackets [ ] to contain items in the order, and they are mutable.
⑦	>>> **type ((3, 2, 1))** `<class 'tuple'>`	**Tuple**: A sequence of values of any data type that is indexed by integers. Tuples are immutable and list their elements in round brackets ( ), separated by commas. The main difference between a list and a tuple is its immutability.

(continued)

#	Examples	Explanation
⑧	`>>> type ({'a': 'apple', 'b': 'banana'})` `<class 'dict'>`	**Dictionary**: An unordered mapping data type that consists of "key: value" pairs separated by commas and enclosed in braces { }. For example, 'a' that precedes 'a':'apple' is a key, and 'apple' that follows a colon is a value. The order of elements is ignored, and the value is accessed by calling a key.

⑨	`>>> type ({1, 2, 3, 3, 2, 1})`
	 `<class 'set'>`
	 `>>> {1, 2, 3, 3, 2, 1}`
	 `{1, 2, 3}`
		Set: An unordered collection of values of any data type that does not allow duplicate entries. Sets are also immutable, and they only allow a single entry of the same value.

⑩	`>>> type (None)` `<class 'NoneType'>`	**None**: In Python, None is a data type that represents the absence of a value and is often used as a placeholder to indicate null or empty variables.

You have looked at different Python data types in these examples, so now you know what they are and what they look like. Next, let's look at the concept of type casting in Python. **Type casting in Python is the process of converting a variable from one data type to another, allowing for operations between different data types**. To perform explicit type casting in Python, you can use built-in functions, also known as constructors:

#	Example	Explanation

⑪	```>>> int(3.45)```
	```3```
	```>>> float(3.00)```
	```3.0```
	```>>> str("365")```
	```'365'```
	```>>> bool(1)```
	```True```
	```>>> bool(0)```
	```False```
		While Python does an excellent job of automatically detecting data types, there are times when **explicit type casting is necessary to ensure accurate data representation and prevent confusion**. In such cases, built-in data type constructors such as int(), float(), str(), and bool() can be used to convert data into a specific type. These constructors are frequently used in Python code to handle various data types and ensure consistency in the data processing.

Expand Your Knowledge:

Read More About Python Built-in Data Types

For more detailed explanations of each data type in Python, the official documentation site of Python.org provides comprehensive information. You must develop a habit of reading and referencing the official Python documentation when you have any questions. You can visit the following URL to access this documentation: https://docs.python.org/3/library/stdtypes.html

Indentation and Code Blocks

While most programming languages like C, C++, and Java use braces { } to structure code, Python uses indentation instead. Indentation is used to define a code block, which is a group of statements in a program consisting of at least one statement and declarations. In Python, a code block starts with indentation and ends with the first unindented line. Examples of code blocks include the body of a function, loop, and class. It is essential to use four spaces to differentiate between code blocks in Python.

The following examples teach you how to use indentation or whitespace as code blocks. To start, navigate to the C:\Python312\ch02 folder and create a new text file using Notepad. Write the IP addresses 10.10.10.1, 20.20.20.2, and 30.30.30.3 on separate lines in the file. Save the file as ip_addresses.txt.

ip_addresses.txt

10.10.10.1
20.20.20.2
30.30.30.3

#	Examples	Output

①	```with open("C:\\Python312\\ch02\\ip_addresses.txt",```
	```"r") as file:```
	```□□□□for line in file:```
	```□□□□□□□□print(line)```
		10.10.10.1
		20.20.20.2
		30.30.30.3

②	```with open("C:\Python312\ch02\ip_addresses.txt", "r")```
	```as f:```
	```□□for l in f:```
	```□□□□print(l, end="")```
		10.10.10.1
		20.20.20.2
		30.30.30.3

Explanation

① Python uses whitespace or indentation to group statements. When the statement ends with a colon (:), the next line needs to be indented to show that it is part of the group. Example 1 opens a file with IP addresses, which reads the IP addresses. The recommended indentation convention in Python is four spaces, as specified in PEP 8. The example shows the second line with four spaces, followed by eight spaces on the third line. You can create a text file named ip_addresses.txt under C:\Python312\ch02 with a few IP addresses and test the code shown in your Python Interpreter. The output shown in the example is for demonstration purposes only. Notice the automatic newline addition and the output of each line are separated by the newline character \n automatically.

② Consistent spacing is essential in Python code blocks, with four spaces being the most widely used indentation convention. However, using any consistent whitespace works, including two spaces used in Google's Python coding standard. In the provided code example, the last line uses the end parameter to manage unwanted spaces in the output. By default, the end parameter is set to \n, which adds a new line after each print statement. However, you can set it to other characters like " " (a space), "/", or ":", and more to manipulate the spaces.

Commenting

Python comments provide context and explanation about code snippets to make the code more readable and provide useful information to other programmers. Comments describe the code's functionality or purpose and start with the # sign, and any text following is ignored by the interpreter. Multiline comments can be created using triple-single or triple-double quotation marks. Comments can explain code snippets, describe the function or variable purposes, or temporarily disable code during development. Good commenting habits save time, as code is read more often than written, and correct grammar and punctuation enhance readability. Good commenting habits make code more accessible to others and improve overall code quality.

#	Examples

① `# This code upgrades Cisco IOS on multiple devices using a TFTP server.`

②
```
# Ask new driver's age.
age = 17
if age > = 18:
print('You are old enough to drive a car.')
# elif age > 80:
# print('You are too old to drive a car!') else:
print('You are too young to drive a car.')
```

③
```
"""
This code can be used to remotely access multiple devices via SSH and upgrade their IOS to the latest version available on a TFTP server. Before uploading the new IOS image to the device's flash, please verify its MD5 value to ensure its integrity.
"""
```

Explanation

① Adding comments to your code is an essential practice for improving its readability and maintainability. In Python, comments start with the # (hash) symbol and continue to the end of the line. Comments can be used to explain the purpose of the code, clarify its meaning, or provide guidance to users. For example, the comment in this snippet concisely describes the code's purpose, making it easier to understand at a glance. To add a comment, simply start the line with the # symbol. By including clear and informative comments, you can make your code more accessible to others and reduce the time it takes to understand and modify it.

② This example shows how comments can be used to make code more readable and provide context. The comments in this code explain the purpose of the code and the decision-making process behind it. The first line asks for the new driver's age, and the next line sets the variable age to 17. The `if` statement checks if the age is greater than or equal to 18, and if so, it prints a message saying the driver is old enough to drive a car. The `elif` statement is commented out, but it would have checked if the age is greater than 80 and printed a message if it is. Finally, the `else` statement prints a message if the age is less than 18. By commenting out the `elif` statement, the programmer can temporarily disable it during development without deleting it entirely.

③ The use of triple quotation marks is recommended for comments that span three or more lines in Python. Triple quotation marks can be used to create multiline strings, which can also be used for commenting purposes. By using triple quotation marks, you can create comments that span multiple lines without having to add a hash symbol (#) at the beginning of each line. This can make the commenting process more efficient, especially for longer comments that require more explanation. Additionally, using triple quotation marks allows for greater flexibility in the formatting and presentation of comments, which can improve the readability and organization of the code. It's worth noting that both single triple quotation marks (`'''`) and double triple quotation marks (`"""`) can be used for multiline comments in Python

Python Naming Convention

Programming languages are governed by naming conventions, and Python is no exception. For consistency and readability, Python developers have established standard naming conventions for objects such as variables, functions, modules, classes, and constants. It is imperative to adhere to these conventions to ensure that your code is easy to understand and maintain. Here is a concise guide to the standard naming conventions:

- **Variables**: Use all lowercase letters and separate words with underscores. Avoid capitalizing any letters in the variable name. Use descriptive and meaningful names.

- **Functions and methods**: Use lowercase words or words with underscore separators.

- **Modules**: Use a short, lowercase word or words with no underscores. When saving a module as a .py file, use a short, lowercase word or words without underscore separator(s).

- **Packages**: Use a short, lowercase word or words with no underscores.

- **Classes**: Use camel casing, starting each word with a capital letter without underscore separator(s).

- **Constants**: Use uppercase letters and separate words with underscores.

By adhering to these conventions, you can create descriptive and meaningful names, enhance the clarity and maintainability of your code, and make it easier for others to read and understand your code. The inclusion of code comments, utilizing the # symbol or triple quotation marks, can also greatly enhance code clarity. Refer to Table 2-1 for a comprehensive overview of recommended naming conventions for new Python programmers.

Table 2-1. *Python Objects, Naming Conventions, and Examples*

Type	Conventions	Examples
Variable	✓ Use all lowercase letters in your variable name. ✓ Separate words in the variable name with underscores instead of capitalizing them. ✓ Avoid capitalizing any letters in the variable name. ✓ You can use a single word or multiple words in the variable name. ✓ If you need to separate words within the variable name, you can use underscores. ✓ By following these conventions, you can create descriptive and meaningful variable names that enhance the clarity and maintainability of your Python code. This convention ensures consistency and readability in your code, making it easier for others to read and understand your code. ✓ Avoid excessively short or abbreviated variable names in Python, but in some cases, using clear and commonly accepted ones like x, y, z, var, tmp, f_n, or s_n may be acceptable. Nonetheless, using descriptive variable names is generally recommended for the sake of code clarity and maintainability.	num_of_items: This variable name uses underscores to separate words and avoids capitalization, making it more readable and consistent with the rest of the codebase. input_file_name: Also consistent with Python variable naming conventions, this name uses underscores and all lowercase letters to separate words. It is also descriptive, making it clear what the variable represents. engineer_kpi: By using underscores to separate words and avoiding capitalization, this variable name is consistent with Python conventions. It is also descriptive, conveying the purpose of the variable within the code.

(continued)

Table 2-1. (*continued*)

Type	Conventions	Examples
Function	✓ Use all lowercase letters in your function name. ✓ Separate words in the function name with underscores instead of capitalizing them. ✓ If your function name requires multiple words, you can use underscores to separate them. ✓ Avoid capitalizing any letters in your function name. ✓ By following these conventions, you can create descriptive and meaningful function names that are easily understood and recognized by others, leading to more effective and user-friendly Python code.	camelCase: First word in lowercase, subsequent words capitalized. For example, getUserName or calculateTotalMemory. snake_case: All words in lowercase, separated by underscores. For example, get_user_name or calculate_total_memory. verb_noun: Start with a verb, followed by a noun. For example, calculate_speed or validate_input.
Method	✓ When naming a method in Python, use the same conventions as for naming functions. ✓ Specifically, use all lowercase letters and separate words with underscores. ✓ Avoid capitalizing any letters in the method name. ✓ If your method name requires multiple words, use underscores to separate them. ✓ By following these conventions, you can create descriptive and meaningful method names that are consistent with the rest of your codebase, leading to more maintainable and readable Python code. Additionally, this convention can help others more easily understand the purpose of your methods, leading to more effective collaboration and teamwork.	calculate_distance(): Uses all lowercase letters and underscores to separate words, making the method name more readable. get_user_input(): Follows the convention of using all lowercase letters and underscores, while also being descriptive and conveying the purpose of the method. create_file_path(): Consistent with Python naming conventions, using underscores to separate words and avoiding capitalization. The method name is also descriptive and helps clarify its purpose.

(*continued*)

Table 2-1. (*continued*)

Type	Conventions	Examples
Module	✓ Use the same convention as for functions (camelCase, snake_case, verb_noun). ✓ When saving a module as a `.py` file, use a short, lowercase word or words with underscores as separators.	`snake_case`: Use all lowercase letters and separate words with underscores. For example, `network_tools.py`, `file_utils.py`, or `comparison_tools.py`. **short words**: Use short, meaningful words to name your module. For example, `module.py`, `math.py`, `sys.py`, or `os.py`.
Package	✓ Use all lowercase letters with no underscores to name your package. ✓ Use short, meaningful words without underscores as separators.	`requests`: This is a popular Python package used for sending HTTP requests. Its name is a short, descriptive word with no underscores. `netmiko`: This is another widely used Python package for scientific computing. Its name is a short, lowercase word with no underscores.

(*continued*)

Table 2-1. (*continued*)

Type	Conventions	Examples
Class	✓ Start the name of your class with a capital letter. ✓ Avoid underscores in your class names. ✓ Use camel case to separate words in your class names, starting each word with a capital letter.	`RouterModel`: This class represents a router model and follows the naming convention by starting with a capital letter, avoiding underscores, and using camel case to separate words. `CaseRecord`: This class represents a student's academic record and also follows the naming convention by starting with a capital letter, avoiding underscores, and using camel case to separate words.
Constant	✓ Use all uppercase letters when naming a constant in Python. ✓ You can use a single letter, a word, or multiple words separated by underscores for the constant name. ✓ The purpose of using uppercase letters for constants is to distinguish them from variables. ✓ Following this naming convention helps ensure consistency and readability in your code. ✓ Using descriptive and meaningful names for your constants can enhance the clarity and maintainability of your Python code.	`AVG_VALUE`: This is a constant representing the mathematical value of pi. It follows the convention of using all uppercase letters and underscores to separate words. `MAX_THROUGHPUT`: This is a constant representing the maximum number of attempts allowed for a particular operation. It also follows the convention of using all uppercase letters and underscores to separate words.

I recommend that you take the time to thoroughly review each type, example, and convention outlined in this section before progressing to the next section. As you continue to write Python code, you may find it helpful to refer to this table for guidance.

Tip

Mu editor: An alternative to Python IDLE

For those seeking a more GUI-driven text editor, consider downloading the Mu text editor. It allows you to perform the same exercises with ease. Mu offers smoother GUI navigation, making it an excellent choice for first-time Python learners to grasp the basics. Additionally, it provides lookahead functionality and syntax explanations, aiding beginner programmers in their coding journeys (see Figure 2-5).

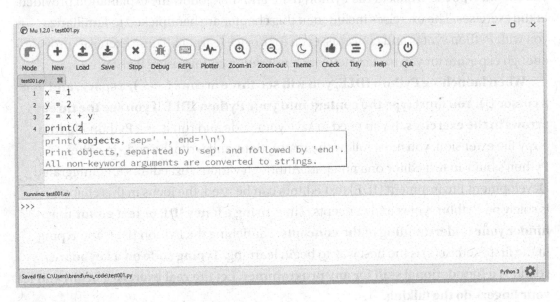

Figure 2-5. *Mu Python text editor*

You can download Mu from this link:

URL: https://codewith.mu/en/download

Python Exercises: Start!

Currently, most technologies and programming languages require coding by typing on a keyboard. However, new technologies like voice recognition and AI-powered tools such as ChatGPT (Chat Generative Pre-Training) could potentially make coding by voice more common in the future. Nonetheless, typing code on a keyboard remains the most effective way to acquire vocational skills in coding. Completing all coding exercises is crucial to mastering the basic Python syntax and concepts required for network automation coding. A solid grasp of Python basics is essential to continue and succeed in your Python Network Automation journey.

For Python learners, it's recommended that you complete all coding exercises in the Python IDLE. These exercises are designed to enhance understanding of Python syntax and concepts needed for network automation coding. To aid comprehension, you should type the syntax in the Python IDLE and then follow the explanation provided in the exercises. The exercises included in this chapter are handpicked to familiarize you with Python syntax and concepts, even for novice learners. These exercises provide enough exposure for you to start network automation coding using Python.

When launching Python IDLE, you will see three arrows (>>>), a space, and a cursor (|). You must type the content into your Python IDLE if you see the three arrows in the exercises. If you need to save your code and run it as a Python file with a `.py` file extension, you must follow the instructions and write the code in either Python's built-in text editor or a notepad. Although various text editors and Integrated Development Environment (IDE) text editors can be used, the focus in this chapter is solely on Python syntax and concepts. Thus, **using a fancy IDE or text editor may hinder your understanding of the concepts**. Launching the Python IDLE and typing in the first exercise(s) is the best way to begin learning. **Typing code on a keyboard remains a foundational skill for any programmer. Let the real exercises begin and let your fingers do the talking.**

Tip

Want to complete all the exercises in one go?

You can download all the exercises used in this chapter from my GitHub site. The file name is `Ch02_end_to_end_exercises.txt`. Use this file to follow along and complete all exercises in one go.

URL: `https://github.com/pynetauto/apress_pynetauto_ed2.0/tree/`
`main/chapter_exercises`

Variables and Strings

Python variables and strings are fundamental concepts in programming. **Variables are used to store values in a program, while strings are used to represent textual data.** To learn these concepts effectively, it is important to practice by typing the information in the exercises provided. **Remember to type everything in bold in the interactive mode to get the most out of your learning experience.**

Exercise 2-1: Create Variables and Assign Various Data Types

#	Exercise	Explanation

①	`>>> x = 1`
	`>>> y = 2`
	`>>> x + y`
	`3`
	`>>> type(x + y)`
	`<class 'int'>`
		Two variables, called x and y, are created with the digits 1 and 2, respectively. The values of x and y are added together using the + operator. The result, which is the sum of x and y, is printed to the console as 3.
		The type() function is used to determine the data type of the result. The data type is an integer (int).

②	`>>> x = '1'`
	`>>> y = '2'`
	`>>> x + y`
	`'12'`
	`>>> type(x + y)`
	`<class 'str'>`
		Two variables x and y are created and assigned strings, '1' and '2', respectively. The + operator is used to concatenate the two string values of x and y, resulting in '12'.
		The type() function is used to confirm that the result of the concatenation is a string, which is denoted as <class 'str'>.

(continued)

#	Exercise	Explanation

③	`>>> x, y, z = 1, 2.0, "3.18"`
	`>>> print(type(x), type(y), type(z))`
	`<class 'int'>`
	`<class 'float'>`
	`<class 'str'>`
		The code assigns the values 1, 2.0, and "3.18" to the variables x, y, and z, respectively using multiple assignments. The `print()` function is used to display the data types of the variables x, y, and z in the console. The output shows that the variable x is of type integer (`int`), y is of type float (`float`), and z is of type string (`str`).

④	`>>> fruit = 'apple'`
	`>>> applause = 'bravo'`
	`>>> dec1 = 1.0`
	`>>> bool_one = True`
	`>>> bool_0 = False`
	`>>> _nada = None`
		The variable `fruit` is assigned the string value of `'apple'`. The variable `applause` is assigned the string value of `'bravo'`. The variable `dec1` is assigned the float value of `1.0`. The variable `bool_one` is assigned the Boolean value of `True`. The variable `bool_0` is assigned the Boolean value of `False`. The variable `_nada` is assigned the value of `None`.

Exercise 2-2: Create Variables and Use the print() Function to Print Output

#	Exercise	Explanation

①	`>>> x = 1`
	`>>> y = 2`
	`>>> z = 3`
	`>>> total = x + y + z`
	`>>> print(total)`
	`6`
	`>>> total`
	`6`
		Here, the variables x, y, and z are assigned the values 1, 2, and 3, respectively. Then, these values are added together and stored in the variable total. Finally, the value of the total is printed to the console using the `print()` function. The output of the code is 6. When working in a Python Interpreter, simply typing a variable name will display its information on the console. However, in a Python script, you need to use the `print()` function to output information to the console.

Exercise 2-3: Abbreviated Variable Assignment

#	Exercise	Explanation

①	```>>> x, y, z = 1, 2, 3```
	```>>> print(x, y, z)```
	```1 2 3```
	```>>> x, y, z```
	```(1, 2, 3)```
		In Python, you can assign multiple variables to multiple values on a single line using a comma (,) as the separator. When you print an individual variable, it is displayed as an integer object. However, when you print multiple variables using commas to separate them, they are returned as a tuple object. Also, note that the print statement returns the values in sequence, but the interpreter returns the values in a tuple, which you learn about later.

②	```>>> a = "apple"```
	```>>> b,c = 'banana',```
	```'coconut'```
	```>>> b,c```
	```('banana', 'coconut')```
	```>>> print(b,c)```
	```banana coconut```
	```>>> print(b,c, sep=',')```
	```banana,coconut```
		When working with strings in Python, you can use either single or double quotes to define them, as long as you are consistent throughout your code. This helps avoid confusion and errors.
		
		Additionally, the print() function in Python separates the values by a space character by default. You can use the sep argument in the print() function to specify a different separator between the values. For example, sep=',' will separate the values with a comma followed by a space.

Exercise 2-4: Enter a String, Escape Character Backslash (\), and type() Function

#	Exercise	Explanation
①	```>>> 'He said, "You are one of a kind."'``` ```'He said, "You are one of a kind."'```	You can express a string of text in a set of single or double quotation marks. Both single and double quotes can be used interchangeably, but it's important to be consistent with your choice of quotation marks within a codebase.

②	```>>> said = "He said, \" You are one of a kind.\""```
	 ```>>> print(said)```
	 ```He said, "You are one of a kind."```
	 ```>>> type(said)```
	 ```<class 'str'>```
		In Python, backslashes (\) can be used to escape special characters within strings. For example, when defining a string with double quotation marks, you can include a double quotation mark within the string by using a backslash character just before it. This removes the special meaning of the inner double quotation mark and treats it as a regular character within the string. It's common practice to use a consistent style of quotation marks within a codebase to improve code readability. For example, you can choose to always use single quotes or double quotes for string literals and use the other type only when necessary. To check the data type of an object in Python, you can use the type() function.

Table 2-2 provides examples of backslash use cases. Review the table before moving onto the next exercise. You can also type in your Python Interpreter to learn the subtle differences between each example.

Table 2-2. *Backslash Examples*

\ Use	Example	Explanation
\\	>>> **print('\\\\represents backslash\\\\')** \represents backslash\	**The backslash character (\) is used to escape special characters in a string, including itself.** This process is called **escaping** or **negating the meaning of the metacharacter** and treating it as a literal character instead.
\'	>>> **print('\\'Single quotes in single quotes\\'')** 'Single quotes in single quotes'	**The backslash character (\) can be used to escape special characters within a string, including single quotes.** This allows you to include a single quote within a string that is defined with single quotes.
\"	>>> **print("\\"double quotation marks inside double quotation marks\\"")** "double quotation marks inside double quotation marks"	**The backslash character (\) can be used to escape special characters within a string, including double quotes.** This allows you to include a double quote within a string that is defined with double quotes
\n	>>> **print('Line 1\\nLine 2\\nLine 3')** Line 1Line 2Line 3	**The newline character \n is used to represent a new line in a string on both Windows and Linux operating systems.** However, **it's important to note that the newline sequence \r\n is commonly used on Windows, while on Linux, \n is typically used alone.** To ensure portability across different operating systems, it's generally recommended to use only \n for new lines in Python strings.

(continued)

Table 2-2. (*continued*)

\ Use	Example	Explanation
\t	```>>> print('No tab\tTab\tTab')``` No tab Tab Tab	**\t is the escape sequence used for a horizontal tab, and it works the same way on both Windows and Linux operating systems.** This is because a horizontal tab is a universal character that is recognized and displayed the same way on all systems. Therefore, you can use \t to insert a horizontal tab in your code regardless of the operating system you are using.
\r	```>>> print('Line 1\rLine 2\rLine 3')``` Line 3	**The carriage return character \r is used to return the cursor to the beginning of the current line in a string on both Windows and Linux operating systems.** It's generally recommended to use \n for new lines and \r for returning the cursor to the beginning of the line, but in practice, the usage may vary depending on the context and the specific requirements of the platform or application.
\r\n	```>>> print('Line 1\r\nLine 2\r\nLine 3')``` Line 1Line 2Line 3	**\r\n is the escape sequence used for a new line on Windows operating systems, while \n is used on Linux operating systems.** Using the correct escape sequence for the respective operating system will ensure that the program behaves as intended.
\rn	```>>> print('Line 1\rnLine 2\rnLine 3')``` nLine 3	**In Python, \rn is not a valid escape sequence.** On Windows, the correct escape sequence for a new line is \r\n, while on Linux it is \n. Using the incorrect escape sequence may result in unexpected behavior or errors in the program.

Exercise 2-5: Is the Variable a Container, a Tag, or a Pointer?

#	Exercise	Explanation

①	```>>> x = "apple"```
	```>>> y = "apple"```
	```>>> id(x)```
	```2590130366512```
	```>>> id(y)```
	```2590130366512```
	```>>> x == y```
	```True```
		The concept of Python variables as containers is a common analogy used in teaching, but it's not entirely accurate. Instead, Python variables are more like tags or pointers pointing to an object (see Figure 2-6). In the example of x and y being assigned to the same string "apple", they are both pointing to the same object, and you can validate this using the id() function to check their object IDs. Comparing x and y with the comparison operator confirms that they are equal, meaning they are both pointing to the same object. Therefore, **the container analogy does not work entirely, and understanding variables as tags or pointers provides a more accurate perspective.**

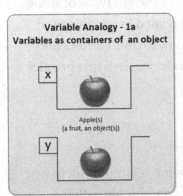
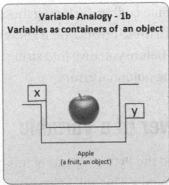
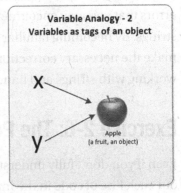

Figure 2-6. *Variables: container vs. tag/pointer analogy*

Tip

Python variable naming conventions recommendations

1. Use a lowercase single letter, word, or words.

2. In case more than two words are used, separate words with an underscore (_) for readability. Use numbers to differentiate the same variables with similar object characteristics, for example, `fruit_1= "apple"` and `fruit_2 = "orange"`.

3. Variable names are case-sensitive. `fruit_1` and `Fruit_1` are two separate variables.

4. Avoid using Python reserved words, which is discussed further in a later exercise.

In the following example, you can practice defining a character or sentence using double or single quotation marks. It's important to learn about different types of string errors that you may encounter while coding, including those related to variables and strings. By becoming familiar with these errors, you'll know how to troubleshoot and make the necessary corrections. Before you dive into string indexing, let's first practice working with strings and handling potential errors.

Exercise 2-6: The Power of a Variable

Even if you don't fully understand the Python syntax at this point, it's important to type out each line of code in the interpreter. This will help you get comfortable with the syntax and build your confidence in writing Python code. In the later exercises, I provide additional examples and explanations of concatenation and string formatting to help solidify your understanding of these concepts.

#	Exercise	Explanation
①	`>>> print("Python is awesome!")` `Python is awesome!`	This is a simple Python code to print a single awesome thing.

②	`>>> word = "awesome"`
	`>>> print("Python is " + word + "!")`
	`Python is awesome!`
		Use a **variable** and **string concatenation method** to put the strings together. Here you use the + sign.

③	`>>> word = "awesome"`
	`>>> print("Python is {}!".`
	`format(word))`
	`Python is awesome!`
		Use a **variable** and **string formatting method** to produce the same output.

④	`>>> word = "awesome"`
	`>>> print(f"Python is {word}!")`
	`Python is awesome!`
		Use a **variable** and **f-string method**, which was introduced in Python 3.6 (PEP498), to print the same output. You may not see the immediate benefit of the variable. Now complete exercises ⑤, ⑥, and ⑦.

⑤	`# awesome_things.py`
	`word = "awesome"`
	`print(f"Python is {word}!")`
	`print(f"Sydney weather is {word}!")`
	`print(f"League of Legends is`
	`{word}!")`
	`print(f"Disneyland is {word}!")`
	`print(f"You're {word}!")`
		Now, open a text editor and create a file called awesome_things.py under C:\Python312\ch02 and enter the lines of code shown here.

⑥	`PS C:\Users\brend> cd /`
	`PS C:\> cd Python312\ch02`
	`PS C:\Python312\ch02> python`
	`awesome_things.py`
	`Python is awesome!`
	`Sydney weather is awesome!`
	`League of Legends is awesome!`
	`Disneyland is awesome!`
	`You're awesome!`
		Open the PowerShell on your Windows and enter the text in bold to run the awesome_things.py Python script.
		You should expect a similar output to what's printed on the left.

(continued)

#	Exercise	Explanation
⑦	PS C:\Python312\ch02> **get-Content** **.\awesome_things.py** word = "**fabulous**" *[...omitted for brevity]* PS C:\Python312\ch02> **python** **.\awesome_things.py** Python is fabulous! Sydney weather is fabulous! League of Legends is fabulous! Disneyland is fabulous! You're fabulous!	Now open the file again and replace the word, "awesome" with "fabulous", then run the code again. It will produce new output. You only updated a single variable and now you have turned your five awesome things into five fabulous things! Imagine there were over 100 of the same things you had to update. This demonstrates the power of a variable.

As demonstrated, by changing the value of a single variable, you can update five sentences in the output. This approach avoids the need to update the same information multiple times and instead only requires updating the variable once. This not only saves time and effort but also reduces the risk of errors that can occur when making repetitive changes.

Exercise 2-7: String Indexing

#	Exercise	Explanation

①	>>> **bread = 'bagel'**
	>>> **bread [0]**
	'b'
	>>> **bread [1]**
	'a'
	>>> **bread [4]**
	'l'
		Python indexing starts at 0. For the word bagel used in the exercise, the alphabet 'b' is the 0 index, and the alphabet 'l' is the index 4.
		String: **b a g e l**
		Index: <u>0</u> 1 2 3 <u>4</u>

When writing Python code, it is common to encounter various error messages. Familiarizing yourself with commonly encountered errors in advance can help you resolve these errors quickly and make the most of your Python coding experience. The following examples intentionally trigger several Python errors to help you better understand them.

Exercise 2-8: Variable Assignment-Related Errors

A SyntaxError is a type of error in Python that occurs when there is a violation of the language's syntax rules.

#	Exercise	Explanation

①	`>>> +lucky7 = 7`
	`SyntaxError: can't assign to operator`
	`>>> 7lucky= 7`
	`SyntaxError: invalid syntax`
	`>>> 7_lucky = 7`
	`SyntaxError: invalid decimal literal`
	`>>> lucky7 = 7`
	`>>> lucky7`
	`7`
		A SyntaxError, called `"can't assign to operator"` is triggered, because a variable name cannot start with an operator like +.
		
		Similarly, a SyntaxError, called `"invalid syntax"`, is triggered, because a variable name cannot start with a number like 7.
		
		A SyntaxError, called `"invalid decimal literal"`, is triggered, because a variable name cannot start with a number followed by an underscore, like 7_.
		
		Finally, `lucky7` is the correct Python syntax for variable assignment. There is no SyntaxError during this variable assignment.

Syntax errors are triggered by incorrect variable naming conventions. If you use an arithmetic operator symbol at the beginning, Python will raise an error. If you place a number at the beginning of the variable name, Python will return an invalid syntax error. If you assign variables correctly, you will not encounter error messages, as shown in the last example. Syntax errors are an essential part of any coding—they are there to help you correct your coding mistakes.

Exercise 2-9: SyntaxError: Unterminated String Literal

We will generate several syntax errors in this exercise to study their differences and similarities.

#	Exercise	Explanation

①	```>>> q1 = Did you have a wonderful day?```
	``` File "<stdin>", line 1```
	``` q1 = Did you have a wonderful day?```
	``` ^^^```
	
	```SyntaxError: invalid syntax```
		The code attempts to assign a string to a variable "q1" with different variations of syntax, resulting in various syntax errors.

②	```>>> q1 = "Did you have a wonderful day?```
	``` File "<stdin>", line 1```
	``` q1 = "Did you have a wonderful day?```
	``` ^```
	
	```SyntaxError: unterminated string literal (detected at line 1)```
		In the first attempt, the code tries to assign a string without enclosing it in quotes, which causes an invalid syntax error.

③	```>>> q1 = "Did you have a wonderful day?'```
	``` File "<stdin>", line 1```
	``` q1 = "Did you have a wonderful day?'```
	``` ^```
	
	```SyntaxError: unterminated string literal (detected at line 1)```
		In the second and third attempts, the string is enclosed in a single quote, but it's not terminated correctly, causing an unterminated string literal error.

④	```>>> q1 = Did you have a wonderful day?'```
	``` File "<stdin>", line 1```
	``` q1 = Did you have a wonderful day?'```
	``` ^^^```
	
	```SyntaxError: invalid syntax```
		In the fourth attempt, the string is not enclosed in quotes, causing another invalid syntax error.

(continued)

#	Exercise	Explanation

⑤	>>> **q1 = 'Did you have a wonderful day?'**
	>>> **q1**
	'Did you have a wonderful day?'
		Finally, in the last attempt, the string is enclosed in single quotes, and it's correctly assigned to the variable "q1" without errors. It's essential to use the correct syntax when assigning values to variables in Python to avoid syntax errors.

When assigning a string in Python, use consistent quotation marks to avoid a scanning string literal error. This error occurs when single and double quotes are mixed in a string literal, causing the interpreter to be unsure where the string ends. The error can occur in both the Python shell and the Windows PowerShell. To fix it, use the same type of quotation marks at the beginning and end of the string. By being mindful of quotation marks, you can avoid errors and write Python code that runs smoothly.

Exercise 2-10: NameError: name 'variable_name' is not defined

#	Exercise	Explanation

①	>>> **print(a1)**
	Traceback (most recent call last):
	  File "<pyshell#1>",
	  line 1, in <module>
	    print(a1)
	NameError: name 'a1' is not defined
		A NameError occurs when the code tries to reference a variable that hasn't been defined yet.

②	>>> **a1 = 'Yes, I had a**
	lovely day.'
	>>> **print(a1)**
	Yes, I had a lovely day.
		To avoid this error, it's important to define your variable first before trying to use it in a function like print(a1).

In Python, it's crucial to define all variables before using them in your code. This ensures that the variable exists and has a value that can be used in the function or statement. By defining your variable first, you can avoid NameErrors and ensure that your code runs correctly.

Exercise 2-11: SyntaxError: Invalid Syntax and Python Reserved Keyword

#	Exercise	Explanation

①	```>>> for = 'I enjoy driving'```
	``` File "<stdin>", line 1```
	``` for = 'I enjoy driving'```
	``` ^```
	```SyntaxError: invalid syntax```
	```>>> fav_hobby = 'I enjoy driving'```
		The issue with the code is that the variable name for is a reserved keyword in Python and cannot be used as a variable name. To fix this, you must choose a different variable name that is not a reserved keyword.
		
		Using a different variable name will solve the syntax error.

②	```>>> import keyword```
	```>>> print(keyword.kwlist)```
	```['False', 'None', 'True', 'and',```
	```'as', 'assert', 'async', 'await',```
	```'break', 'class', 'continue', 'def',```
	```'del', 'elif', 'else', 'except',```
	```'finally', 'for', 'from', 'global',```
	```'if', 'import', 'in', 'is', 'lambda',```
	```'nonlocal', 'not', 'or', 'pass',```
	```'raise', 'return', 'try', 'while',```
	```'with', 'yield']```
		Python reserves certain words, called reserved keywords, which have special meanings and functions in the language. To view the full list of reserved keywords, you can import the keyword module. It's important to avoid using reserved keywords as variable names or identifiers in your Python code. This is because they are already assigned to specific functions in the language and using them as variable names can cause unexpected errors.

To avoid syntax errors and unexpected behavior, it's important to choose descriptive variable names that are not among the list of reserved keywords. In Table 2-3, you can find the Python reserved keywords and Table 2-4 provides a brief explanation of each keyword for further study. There is no need to memorize these, some you will pick them up as you work more with Python and some you can always reference from the import keyword's keyword_kwlist. By understanding the meanings and functions of these keywords, you can write cleaner and more efficient code in Python without encountering errors or unexpected behavior.

Table 2-3 lists Python's reserved keywords.

Table 2-3. *Python 3 Reserved Keywords*

and	del	from	not	while
as	elif	global	or	with
assert	else	if	pass	yield
break	except	import	~~print~~	**False**
class	exec	in	raise	**True**
continue	finally	is	return	**None**
def	for	lambda	try	**nonlocal**

Table 2-4 contains a brief explanation of each Python keyword.

Table 2-4. *Python 3 Keyword Explanation*

Keyword	A brief explanation
and	A logical operator that returns True if both operands are True and False otherwise.
as	Used to create an alias for a module, class, or function.
assert	Used to check if a condition is True and raise an exception if it's not.
async	Used to define an asynchronous function.
await	Used to wait for an asynchronous function to complete.
break	Used to break out of a loop.
class	Used to define a class.
continue	Used to skip the current iteration of a loop and continue with the next.
def	Used to define a function.

(continued)

Table 2-4. (*continued*)

Keyword	A brief explanation
del	Used to delete a variable, list element, or attribute.
elif	Used in an if statement to specify an alternative condition.
else	Used in an if statement to specify what to do if the condition is False.
except	Used to handle exceptions.
finally	Used in a try-except block to specify code that will always be executed.
for	Used to loop over a sequence of values.
from	Used to import a specific part of a module.
global	Used to declare a global variable.
if	Used to specify a condition.
import	Used to import a module.
in	Used to check if a value is present in a sequence.
is	Used to compare if two objects are the same.
lambda	Used to define a small, anonymous function.
not	A logical operator that returns True if the operand is False and False otherwise.
or	A logical operator that returns True if at least one operand is True.
pass	Used as a placeholder for code that will be added later.
raise	Used to raise an exception.
return	Used to return a value from a function.
try	Used to specify code that might raise an exception.
while	Used to loop while a condition is True.
with	Used to specify a context in which an object is used.
yield	Used to return a value from a generator function.
FALSE	A Boolean value representing False.
TRUE	A Boolean value representing True.
None	A value that indicates the absence of a value, similar to null in other languages.
nonlocal	Used to declare a non-local variable.

Exercise 2-12: TypeError: 'str' Object Is Not Callable

#	Exercise	Explanation

①	`>>> help = 'Please help me reach my goal.'`
	`>>> print(help)`
	`Please help me reach my goal.`
	`>>> help (print)`
	`Traceback (most recent call last):`
	`File "<pyshell#77>", line 1, in`
	`<module> help (print)`
	`TypeError: 'str' object is not callable`
		When you use a built-in function name as a variable name, you effectively overwrite the function name, making it unusable. This can cause errors and unexpected behavior in your code. Therefore, it's important to avoid using keywords and built-in function names as variable names.

②	`>>> dir(__builtins__)`
	`['ArithmeticError', 'AssertionError',`
	`'AttributeError', 'BaseException',`
	`'BlockingIOError', 'BrokenPipeError',`
	`'BufferError', 'BytesWarning',`
	`'ChildProcessError', [...omitted for brevity]`
		You can use the dir(__builtins__) command in Python to check all built-in modules available in the Python Interpreter. The dir() function without arguments will return a list of names in the current local scope, which includes all built-in names by default. The __builtins__ attribute is a module containing all built-in names. By calling dir(__builtins__), you can view a list of all built-in modules available in Python.

Avoid using Python built-in module names as variable names, as doing so can lead to issues and unexpected behavior in your code. It's best to choose descriptive variable names that are not among the built-in modules to avoid conflicts and errors. If you're unsure whether a name is a built-in module or not, you can check by using the dir(__builtins__) command.

Tip

Getting help troubleshooting errors

When programming in Python, you will encounter various error codes as you write and run your code. While some error codes are easy to troubleshoot, and solutions may already be available on the official Python documentation site (`https://docs.python.org/3/`), others can be more challenging, stubborn, and require more time and effort to resolve. When faced with such stubborn errors, one useful resource for finding solutions is the Stack Overflow website (`https://stackoverflow.com/questions`). There, you can search for similar errors and find suggestions and solutions from the community. However, it's important to carefully evaluate any solutions you find and make sure they're appropriate and applicable to your specific use case.

Exercise 2-13: Handle Long Strings

In Python, triple quotation marks (either three single quotes or three double quotes) can be used to create multiline strings, which can be used for commenting. By using triple quotes to enclose the string, you can include line breaks and another formatting without having to manually add escape characters. This makes the code easier to read and less error-prone.

#	Exercise

①	```>>> """You're one of a kind. You're my best friend.```
	```... I've never met someone like you before.```
	```... It's been wonderful getting to know you."""```
	```"You're one of a kind. You're my best friend.\nI've never met```
	```someone like you before.\nIt's been wonderful getting to know you."```

(continued)

#	Exercise
	In Python, you can create multiline strings by enclosing a string within triple quotation marks (either three single quotes or three double quotes). This feature allows you to enter multiple lines of text, which is particularly useful when you need to write long descriptions or comments that would be too complex to express in a single line of code. Multiline strings are also helpful when working with text data or when formatting output that requires line breaks. Overall, using multiline strings is a valid and flexible commenting method that can enhance the readability and organization of your code.

②	`>>> macaroni_cheese = "Boil water, cook macaroni for 7-8 mins, drain, add milk, cheese sauce mix, and butter (optional), mix well, and serve for a delicious Macaroni and Cheese! Enjoy!"`
	`>>> macaroni_cheese`
	`'Boil water, cook macaroni for 7-8 mins, drain, add milk, cheese sauce mix, and butter (optional), mix well, and serve for a delicious Macaroni and Cheese! Enjoy!'`
	This example assigned a long alphanumeric sentence string to be assigned to a variable without the line breaking. This reduces the code readability. This example does not follow the PEP 8 style guide.

③	`>>> macaroni_cheese = "Boil water, cook macaroni for 7-8 mins, drain, add milk, \`
	`... cheese sauce mix, and butter (optional), mix well, and \`
	`... serve for a delicious Macaroni and Cheese! Enjoy!"`
	`>>> macaroni_cheese`
	`'Boil water, cook macaroni for 7-8 mins, drain, add milk, cheese sauce mix, and butter (optional), mix well, and serve for a delicious Macaroni and Cheese! Enjoy!'`
	If you use the backslash, you can assign a long macaroni_cheese recipe in a string on multiple lines and improve the code readability. The output is the same as ② with increased readability. This example can be said to be adhering to the PEP 8 style guide.

Expand Your Knowledge:

Why Follow the PEP 8 Style Guide?

The appendix of this book includes a quick guide to Python PEP 8, which is a widely accepted standard for coding style in Python. While the quick guide provides a summary of the main principles, if you want to delve deeper into PEP 8 details, you can visit the official python.org site for more information. The site contains the full PEP 8 documentation, which provides detailed guidelines on coding conventions and best practices for Python developers. By adhering to PEP-8 standards, you can write code that is easier to read and understand, making it more maintainable in the long run. URL: `https://peps.python.org/pep-0008/`

Exercise 2-14: Use \ (Backslash) as an Escape Clause to Remove Special Character Meanings

#	Exercise

①
```
>>> single_quote_string = 'He said, "arn\'t, can\'t shouldn\'t
woundn\'t."'
>>> print(single_quote_string)
He said, "aren't, can't shouldn't wouldn't."
```

The escape character, represented by the backslash symbol (\), is a powerful tool in Python coding. It allows you to use special characters like quotes and newlines in your strings without them being interpreted as their usual meanings. For example, if you need to include a single quote within a string enclosed in single quotes, you can use the backslash to "escape" the special meaning of the quote and treat it as plain text. So, Python will recognize ' as a plain text single quote. This is just one example of how the escape character can be used in Python to enhance the functionality and readability of your code.

(continued)

#	Exercise

② `>>> double_quote_string = "He said, \"aren't can't shouldn't wouldn't.\""`
`>>> print(double_quote_string)`
He said, "aren't can't shouldn't wouldn't."

The escape character can also be used within a string that is enclosed in double quotation marks. Unlike in single-quoted strings, where you would need to use escape characters repeatedly for special characters, you can simply use the regular ' (single quote) character without escaping it. This is because the outer enclosing quotation marks are different (double quotes). An escape character is a useful tool in Python coding that handles special characters within strings. Fewer backslash escapes are used in this example compared to exercise ①.

Exercise 2-15: Enter (Inject) Values/Strings into a String Using %s

#	Exercise

① `>>> exam_result = 95`
`>>> text_message = 'Congratulations! You scored %s on your exam!'`
`>>> print(text_message% exam_result)`
Congratulations! You scored 95 on your exam!

You can insert a variable containing a digit into a string message using the %s placeholder.

② `>>> wish = 'You need %s to make your wish come true.'`
`>>> genie = 'a Genie in the bottle'`
`>>> print(wish% genie)`
You need a Genie in the bottle to make your wish come true.

You can include the value of a string variable in another string using string formatting. One way to do this is by using the placeholder %s, which represents a string value. To use this method, simply place the %s in the desired location within the string, and then follow the string with the % operator and the string variable you want to insert. For example, the 'Hello, %s!' % name would replace %s with the value of the variable 'name'.

(continued)

#	Exercise

③
```
>>> fast_car = 'Faster electric cars have %s & %s to make them go
faster.'
>>> part1 = 'dual motors'
>>> part2 = 'bigger batteries'
>>> print(fast_car%(part1, part2))
Faster electric cars have dual motors & bigger batteries to make them
go faster.
```

You can insert one or more variables into a string using the string formatting operator %. To do this, you can use one or more format specifiers %s inside the string, each of which will be replaced by a corresponding value when the string is formatted. To pass multiple values to the string formatter, you can wrap them in a tuple or list sequence and then pass that sequence as an argument to the % operator. The sequence should contain one value for each %s in the string.

④
```
>>> my_score = 'My exam scores are %s for English, %s for Math, and %s
for Science.'
>>> my_score% (95, 92, 90)
'My exam scores are 95 for English, 92 for Math, and 90 for Science.'
>>> print(my_score% (95, 92, 90))
My exam scores are 95 for English, 92 for Math, and 90 for Science.
```

When using string formatting with the % operator, you can directly pass the expected values (arguments) instead of defining them as variables beforehand. This can be useful when you need to use the values only once and don't want to define extra variables. To pass arguments directly, you can provide them inside a tuple or a list after the % operator. The number of values in the sequence should match the number of format specifiers (%s) in the string. Note that the order of the values in the tuple should match the order of the %s format specifiers in the string, so this example provided three arguments (95, 92, 90).

Printing, Concatenating, and Converting Strings

Printing strings refers to the process of outputting a string to the console or terminal. In Python, you can use the print() function to print strings. The print() function can take one or more arguments (strings or other data types), and it will output each argument separated by a space by default.

Concatenating strings refers to the process of joining two or more strings together to create a new string. In Python, you can concatenate strings using the + operator. When you concatenate strings, you create a new string that includes the characters of all the original strings in the order in which they were joined.

Converting strings refers to the process of changing the data type of a string to another data type. In Python, you can convert strings to other data types using built-in functions such as `int()`, `float()`, and `bool()`. The new data type will have a different representation of the same value. For example, converting the string `"38"` to an integer will produce the integer value 38.

One effective way to learn Python is by typing code directly into the Python Interpreter using your keyboard. While it may seem intimidating at first, practicing and learning by doing it yourself is a great way to build confidence and proficiency. With regular practice using the Python Interpreter, you can quickly become proficient in Python programming and develop a better understanding of Python syntax. So grab your keyboard, launch the Interpreter, and start typing!

Exercise 2-16: Use the print() and len() Functions and Create a Simple Function

#	Exercise	Explanation

①	```>>> print('Paris baguette')```
	```Paris baguette```
	```>>> bread = 'NY bagel'```
	```>>> print(bread)```
	```NY bagel```
		You can use the `print()` function to display output on your screen. To use it, simply pass the item you want to print as an argument within the parentheses. You can print strings, numbers, and expressions using `print()`.

②	```>>> aussie = 'meat pie'```
	```>>> print(len(aussie))```
	```8```
	```>>> print(type(aussie[4]))```
	```<class 'str'>```
		You can use the `len()` function to determine the length of a string. The `len()` function counts all characters in the string, including spaces and special characters. To use `len()`, simply pass the string as an argument within the parentheses, and the function will return the length of the string.

(continued)

#	Exercise	Explanation
③	```\n>>> bread = 'naan'\n>>> def bread_len():\n▯▯▯▯length = len(bread)\n▯▯▯▯print(length)\n>>> bread_len()\n4\n```	To create a simple function in Python that counts the characters in a string, you can define a variable and then write a function that reads the length of the variable and prints the character count. To define a function, use the `def` keyword followed by the function name and arguments in parentheses, and end the header line with a colon. The function body should be indented using four spaces. To call the function, simply type its name followed by parentheses. For example, if you defined a function named `count_characters`, you would call it by typing `count_characters()`. With these steps, you can create your first Python function and use it to perform a specific task.

Exercise 2-17: Use the lower() and upper() String Methods

#	Exercise	Explanation
①	```\n>>> "Bagel Is My Favorite\nBread!".lower()\n'bagel is my favorite bread!'\n>>> bread = 'BAGEL'\n>>> print(bread.lower())\nbagel\n```	`lower()` and `upper()` are built-in string methods used for text manipulation. The `lower()` method converts all uppercase characters in a string to lowercase, while the `upper()` method converts all lowercase characters to uppercase.
②	```\n>>> "baguette is also my\nfavorite bread.".upper()\n'BAGUETTE IS ALSO MY FAVORITE\nBREAD.'\n>>> bread = 'baguette'\n>>> print(bread.upper())\nBAGUETTE\n```	In this example, the `upper()` string method works precisely opposite to `lower()` string method. If there are no uppercase or lowercase characters in the string, `lower()` and `upper()` will simply return the original string. These methods are useful for normalizing text data and preparing it for analysis or display.

Exercise 2-18: String Concatenation and the str() Method

#	Exercise	Explanation

①	```>>> print('Best' + 'friends' + 'last' + 'forever.')```
	```Bestfriendslastforever.```
	```>>> print('Best ' + 'friends ' + 'last ' + 'forever.')```
	```Best friends last forever.```
	```>>> print('Best' + ' ' + 'friends' + ' ' + 'last' + ' ' + 'forever.')```
	```Best friends last forever.```
	```>>> print('Best', 'friends', 'last', 'forever.')```
	```Best friends last forever.```
	```>>> print('~'*79)```
	```>>> love = ('like' * 10)```
	```>>> print(love)```
	```likelikelikelikelikelikelikelikelikelike```
		String concatenation is an essential skill for working with text data. By using operators like +, ,, *, and whitespace, you can manipulate strings to create more complex and useful outputs. By practicing string concatenation, you will gain a deeper understanding of how to manipulate text data in Python, which is a crucial skill for working with data in many different domains.

②	```>>> time = 30```
	```>>> print('You have' + time + 'minutes left.')```
	```Traceback (most recent call last):```
	```File "<stdin>", line 1, in <module>```
	```TypeError: can only concatenate str (not "int") to str```
	```>>> print('You have ' + str (time) + ' minutes left.')```
	```You have 30 minutes left.```
		The str concatenation error occurs when you try to combine a string with an integer or other data types. This error can be fixed by using the str() method to convert the integer into a string, allowing it to concatenate with other strings. **Converting between data types like this is called "casting," and it's an important concept in Python and other programming languages.** By understanding casting and how to manipulate data types in Python, you'll be able to work with a wide range of data more effectively.

Exercise 2-19: Learn to Change Strings Using Curly Brackets and .format()

#	Exercise

①
```
>>> 'She is {} years old.'.format(25)
'She is 25 years old.'
>>> 'She is {{}} years old.'.format(25)
'She is {} years old.'
>>> 'She is {{{}}} years old.'.format(25)
'She is {25} years old.'
```

You can change the contents of a string using curly brackets {} and the .format() method. If you want to include a pair of curly brackets in your string, you can do so by using double curly brackets {{}}. To include a value in curly brackets, use triple curly brackets {{{value}}}. By mastering this technique, you can create dynamic, customizable strings that are perfect for a wide range of programming applications.

②
```
>>> 'Learning Python 101 is {}.'.format('important')
'Learning Python 101 is important.'
>>> '{} {} {} {} {}'.format ('Learning', 'Python', 101, 'is',
'important.')
'Learning Python 101 is important.'
```

You can use the .format() method to construct a string by including one or more curly brackets {}. To include multiple curly brackets, simply double them up, like this: {{}}. Within the curly brackets, you can insert variable names, string literals, and even arithmetic expressions. By mastering this technique, you can create powerful and dynamic strings that are perfect for a wide range of programming applications.

(continued)

#	Exercise

③
```
>>> '{} | {} | {}'.format ('bread', 'quantity', 'date')
bread | quantity | date
>>> '{} | {} | {}'.format ('bagel', '100', '01/12/2020')
'bagel | 100 | 01/12/2020'
```

You can create a table-like format for your output by using curly brackets and the pipe symbol (|). To do this, simply enclose your variables or literals in curly brackets and separate them with pipes to create columns. You can even use the colon symbol to format the output further, such as specifying the field width or the number of decimal places. With this technique, you can create elegant and easy-to-read tables that are perfect for displaying complex data in a clear and concise format.

Exercise 2-20: Adjust Text Position with Curly Brackets and .format()

#	Exercise

①
```
>>> '{}|{}'.format ('bagel', '10')
'bagel|10'
>>> '{} | {}'.format ('bagel', '10')
'bagel | 10'
>>> '{0:1} | {1:1}'.format ('bagel', '10')
'bagel | 10'
```

The first example formats two items without any spacing between them, using the curly brackets {}. The second example formats two items with a space and a pipe symbol between them, using {} | {}. The third example uses indexing in the curly brackets to specify the order of the items and add spacing between them, using {0:1} | {1:1}.

(continued)

#	Exercise

②
```
>>> '{0:1} | {0:1}'.format ('bagel', '10')
bagel | bagel
>>> ('{0:1} | {0:1} | {1:1} | {1:1}'.format ('bagel', '10'))
'bagel | bagel | 10 | 10'
```

The given examples demonstrate how to format a string using curly brackets and the
.format() method. The curly brackets contain the index number of the item in the
.format() method. By default, the indexing starts from 0, and you can change the item's
position using special characters like < (left-align), ^ (center-align), or > (right-align). In the
first example, the string is formatted to have a width of 1, and the items are called out by their
index numbers. In the second example, the string is formatted to have a width of 1, and the
items are called out in a specific order by their index numbers.

③
```
>>> '{0:>1} | {1:1}'.format('bagel', '10')
'bagel | 10'
>>> '{0:>10} | {1:1}'.format('bagel', '10')
'     bagel | 10'
>>> '{0:>20} | {1:1}'.format('bagel', '10')
'               bagel | 10'
```

The first one aligns 'bagel' to the leftmost position and '10' to the rightmost position with
a space in between. The second one aligns 'bagel' to the 10th position from the left and
'10' to the rightmost position with spaces in between. The third one aligns 'bagel' to the
20th position from the left and '10' to the rightmost position with spaces in between.

④
```
>>> '{0:^10} | {1:^10}'.format ('bagel', '10')
'  bagel    |     10    '
>>> '{0:^20} | {1:^20}'.format ('bagel', '10')
'        bagel         |          10          '
>>> '{0:^30} | {1:^30}'.format ('bagel', '10')
'            bagel              |               10             '
```

(continued)

#	Exercise

These examples show how to center-align the items in a formatted string using the ^ (caret) symbol for the text positioning option. Here are some improved explanations:

The ^ (caret) symbol is used to center-align items in a formatted string. You can specify the width of the field to allocate for the items, and the ^ symbol will center the item within that field. In the previous examples, the items 'bagel' and '10' are centered within fields of 10, 20, and 30 characters wide, respectively. The resulting output shows the items centered within their fields with whitespace padding on either side.

Exercise 2-21: Adjust the Number of Decimal Places

#	Exercise

①
```
>>> '{0:^10} | {1:10}'.format('pizza', 27.333333)
' pizza   | 27.333333'
>>> '{0:^10} | {1:10.2f}'.format('pizza', 27.333333)
'  pizza   |      27.33'
```
Using nf, you can format the number of decimal places. Here, n is the number of decimal places, and f represents the format specifier. Hence, 2f means to reduce the float to two decimal places. To better understand the format specifier or any other content in this book, you must enter the lines and learn from your keyboard and screen.

②
```
>>> '{0:^10} | {1:10}'.format('Cisco IOS XE 4351', 16.1203)
'Cisco IOS XE 4351 |    16.1203'
>>> '{0:1} | {1:10.2f}'.format('Cisco IOS XE 4351', 16.1203)
'Cisco IOS XE 4351 |      16.12'
```
Apply the formatting method to an authentic example.

③
```
>>> '{0:1} | {1:1.2f}'.format('Cisco IOS XE 4351', 16.1203)
'Cisco IOS XE 4351 | 16.12'
>>> router = ('Cisco IOS XE 4351', 16.1203)
>>> router[0] + ' | ' + str( round(router[1], 2))
'Cisco IOS XE 4351 | 16.12'
```

(continued)

#	Exercise

Another way to achieve the same result is to use the concatenation and round methods in your code. First, use the indexing method to call out the router name with 'router[0]. Second, index the second item, float (Cisco IOS XE version number), then third, use the round method with decimal reference of 2, then fourth, convert the shortened float as a string. Finally, fifth, use the + method to concatenate the values as a string. You do not have to understand all of what is going on here, as you will get more familiar as you write code.

Exercise 2-22: Ask and Receive User Input with input()

#	Exercise

①
```
>>> fav_bread = input('Name of your favorite bread: ')
Name of your favorite bread: pita
>>> print(fav_bread)
Pita

>>> num_bread = input("How many " + fav_bread + " would you like? ")
How many pita would you like? 5
>>> print(num_bread)
5

>>> 'So, you wanted {} {} bread.'.format(num_bread, fav_bread)
'So, you wanted 5 pita bread.'
```

You can use input() to receive the user's input through the keyboard. This example shows that the input() function takes user input and can store the returned information as variables. You can recall the stored information from your computer's random memory.

Exercise 2-23: Change a Word or Character in a String

#	Exercise	Explanation
| ① | ```python
>>> your_phone = 'iPhone 14 Pro'
>>> your_phone.split()
['iPhone', '14', 'Pro']
>>> your_phone = your_phone.
split()
>>> your_phone
['iPhone', '14', 'Pro']
>>> your_phone[2] = 'ProMax'
>>> your_phone
['iPhone', '14', 'ProMax']
>>> " ".join(your_phone) # " " has
a white space
'iPhone 14 ProMax'
``` | In this first exercise, you learned how to manipulate strings by splitting them and replacing specific words. Your goal was to replace the word 'Pro' with 'ProMax' in the string 'iPhone 14 Pro'. To accomplish this, you used the split() method to break the string into individual words, accessed the third item 'Pro', and replaced it with 'ProMax'. Then, you joined the modified words back together using the " ".join() method with a space separator. As a result, you transformed the original string into 'iPhone 14 ProMax', reflecting the updated model of your phone. Congratulations on completing the exercise! |

(*continued*)
```

#	Exercise	Explanation

②	```python
	>>> my_phone = 'Galaxy S20 +'
	>>> len(my_phone)
	12
	>>> my_phone = list(my_phone)
	>>> my_phone
	['G', 'a', 'l', 'a', 'x', 'y', ' ', 'S', '2', '0', ' ', '+']
	>>> my_phone[9], my_phone[11] = '3', 'Ultra'
	>>> my_phone
	['G', 'a', 'l', 'a', 'x', 'y', ' ', 'S', '2', '3', ' ', 'Ultra']
	>>> "".join(my_phone) # "" has no white space
	'Galaxy S23 Ultra'```
		The goal of this exercise is to transform the string 'Galaxy S20 +' into 'Galaxy S23 Ultra' using Python string-manipulation techniques. However, because strings are immutable in Python, you need to use a workaround to replace characters in the string. Specifically, you must replace the 9th character, which is 'O', with '3', and the 12th character, which is '+', with the word 'Ultra'. Keep in mind that Python string indexing starts at 0, so the 9th character is actually at index 8, and the 12th character is at index 11.
		To achieve this transformation, you can start by using the list() method to split the string into a list of individual characters. Then, use indexing to replace the appropriate characters with '3' and 'Ultra'. Finally, use the .join() method with an empty string as a separator to concatenate all the characters back together into a new string. With these steps, you can convert 'Galaxy S20 +' into 'Galaxy S23 Ultra'.

In the previous exercise, you had to replace specific characters in a string, which may have seemed overly meticulous. However, if you find the exercise enjoyable, you likely possess great attention to detail, which is an essential skill in coding. As you continue to develop your programming skills, attention to detail will prove valuable in producing clean, effective code that runs smoothly. By being meticulous in your code, you can identify and address potential issues before they become problems, resulting in higher quality and more reliable software. So, don't underestimate the power of paying attention to details in coding, and keep honing this skill as you progress in your coding journey.

Recap: Variables and Strings

To recap, this chapter has covered some key concepts related to variables and strings in Python:

- A string is a sequence data type in Python that represents a sequence of characters. Once created, it cannot be changed (immutable).

- Strings can be expressed in either single or double quotation marks.

- Variables are labels for locations in memory that hold values. They allow you to store and manipulate data in your code.

- Python follows basic variable naming conventions to improve the readability and usability of code. Variable names should start with a letter or underscore, followed by letters, digits, or underscores. Spaces and special characters are not allowed, and multiple words in a variable name should be separated by underscores.

- It's best practice to avoid using reserved words or function names as variable names to prevent conflicts and confusion.

- A function is a block of reusable code written to perform a specific task. Python provides built-in functions such as `print()`, `len()`, `str()`, and `list()` to work with strings and other data types.

By understanding these concepts, you can start working with variables and strings in Python effectively. Keep these concepts in mind as you continue to learn and practice Python programming.

Numbers and Arithmetic Operators

In this section, you continue learning about numbers, operators, and functions with simple examples. Arithmetic involves working with numbers, while mathematics is concerned with theory. This section focuses on the practical aspects of working with numbers in Python.

Python arithmetic operators are symbols used to perform mathematical operations such as addition, subtraction, multiplication, division, and more on numerical values in Python. Let's quickly type these on the Interpreter to learn about each one of them.

Exercise 2-24: Arithmetic Operators

#	Exercise	Explanation
①	```>>> 5 + 2``` ```7```	Addition (+): Adds two values together
②	```>>> 5 - 2``` ```3```	Subtraction (-): Subtracts one value from another
③	```>>> 5 * 2``` ```10```	Multiplication (*): Multiplies two values together
④	```>>> 5 / 2``` ```2.5```	Division (/): Divides one value by another, resulting in a float value
⑤	```>>> 5 // 2``` ```2```	Floor Division (//) (returns the quotient without the remainder): Divides one value by another, resulting in an integer value
⑥	```>>> 5 % 2``` ```1```	Modulus (%): Returns the remainder of a division operation
⑦	```>>> 5 ** 2``` ```25```	Exponentiation (**): Raises a value to a power

⑧	```>>> 5 + 2.0```
	```7.0```
	```>>> 5 - 2.0```
	```3.0```
	```>>> 5 * 2.0```
	```10.0```
	```>>> 5 / 2.0```
	```2.5```
		When performing a calculation between an integer and a float in Python, the result will always be a float value. This is because Python automatically converts integer values to float values during calculations involving both types.

⑨	```>>> 5 / 2```
	```2.5```
	```>>> type(5 & 2)```
	```<class 'int'>```
	```>>> type(2.5)```
	```<class 'float'>```
		For example, the expression 5 / 2 would evaluate to 2.5 instead of 2, as one of the operands is a float. It's important to keep this in mind when working with numerical data types in Python to avoid unexpected results in your calculations.

(continued)

#	Exercise	Explanation

⑩	`>>> 5 / 0`
	`Traceback (most`
	`recent call last):`
	`File "<stdin>", line`
	`1, in <module>`
	`ZeroDivisionError:`
	`division by zero`
		Be aware of potential division by zero errors. **Division by zero is not allowed in Python and will result in a ZeroDivisionError**. For example, the expression 5 / 0 will result in a ZeroDivisionError. It's important to check for and handle these errors in your code to prevent your program from crashing or producing unexpected results. One way to handle this error is to use a `try-except` block to catch the ZeroDivisionError and handle it gracefully in your code.

Exercise 2-25: Integer vs. String

#	Exercise	Explanation

①	`>>> int_2 = 2`
	`>>> str_5 = "5"`
	`>>> str_5 + int_2`
	`Traceback (most recent`
	`call last):`
	`File "<stdin>", line 1,`
	`in <module>`
	`TypeError: can only`
	`concatenate str (not`
	`"int") to str`
		If you assign an integer to one variable and a string to another variable in Python and then attempt to add them using the + operator, you will encounter a TypeError. This is because you can only perform additions of the same object types in Python. For example, the expression "5" + 2 will result in a TypeError.

②	`>>> str_5 + str(int_2)`
	`'52'`
	`>>> int(str_5) + int_2`
	`7`
		To add two variables of different types, you need to convert one of them to the other type. For example, you could convert the integer value to a string using the `str()` function before performing the addition, like this: "5" + `str(2)`. This would result in the string "52". Alternatively, you could convert the string to an integer using the `int()` function before performing the addition, like this: 5 + `int("2")`. This would result in the integer 7.

105

Recap: Arithmetic Operators

Python provides a range of arithmetic operators that allow you to perform calculations with integers. When used with strings, the plus sign (+) can concatenate a series of strings, and the multiplication sign (*) can repeat a string n number of times. Table 2-5 shows the available arithmetic operators in Python.

Table 2-5. Arithmetic Operators

Operator	Description
+	Addition
–	Subtraction
*	Multiplication
/	Division (returns a float)
//	Integer division (returns an integer)
%	Modulus (returns the remainder of a division operation)
**	Exponentiation (raises a value to a power)

When entering numerical values, it is important not to enclose them in quotation marks. If a value is enclosed in quotation marks, Python will treat it as a string object. You can convert a string to an integer using the int() function or to a decimal using the float() function. It's also worth noting that when performing arithmetic operations on different types of data, Python will automatically convert the values to a common type. For example, if you add an integer and a float, Python will convert the integer to a float before performing the addition operation. However, if you attempt to perform arithmetic operations on incompatible data types (such as adding a string and an integer), Python will raise a TypeError.

Booleans and Relational Operators

Booleans are a data type that represents one of two values: True or False. Booleans are used in programming to control the flow of code execution by checking whether a condition is true or false. Relational operators are used to compare values and return a Boolean result of either True or False.

Exercise 2-26: Booleans

#	Exercise	Explanation

①	```>>> a = True```
	```>>> b = False```
	```>>> print(a)```
	```True```
	```>>> print(b)```
	```False```
	```>>> type (a)```
	```<class 'bool'>```
	```>>> type (b)```
	```<class 'bool'>```
		Booleans are a data type that can hold one of two possible values, either True or False. They are commonly used in programming to test conditions and evaluate whether they are True or False.

②	```>>> type (True)```
	```<class 'bool'>```
	```>>> print((1).__bool__())```
	```True```
	```>>> type (False)```
	```<class 'bool'>```
	```>>> print((0).__bool__())```
	```False```
		In Boolean operations, the value of True is represented by the constant 1, while the value of False is represented by 0. To test whether a value is True or False in a Boolean context, you can use the bool() method.
		
		Several constants are defined to be False, including None and False. Additionally, any numeric type that evaluates to zero, such as 0, 0.0, 0j, decimal(0), and integer(0.1) are also considered False in a Boolean context. Empty sequences and collections, such as ' ', (), [], {}, set(), and range(0) are also considered False in Boolean operations.

Exercise 2-27: Relational Operators

These are examples of using relational operators in Python to compare the values of 1 and 2.

#	Exercise	Explanation
①	`>>> 1 == 2` `False`	The first comparison, "`1 == 2`", tests for equality. Because 1 is not equal to 2, the result is `False`.
	`>>> 1 > 2` `False`	The second comparison, "`1 > 2`", tests whether 1 is greater than 2. Because this is not true, the result is `False`.
	`>>> 1 >= 2` `False`	The third comparison, "`1 >= 2`", tests whether 1 is greater than or equal to 2. Because this is not true, the result is `False`.
	`>>> 1 < 2` `True`	The fourth comparison, "`1 < 2`", tests whether 1 is less than 2. Because this is true, the result is `True`.
	`>>> 1 <= 2` `True`	The fifth comparison, "`1 <= 2`", tests whether 1 is less than or equal to 2. Because this is true, the result is `True`.
	`>>> 1 != 2` `True`	The sixth comparison, "`1 != 2`", tests for inequality. Because 1 is not equal to 2, the result is `True`.

In summary, these comparisons illustrate how relational operators can be used to compare values in Python and return Boolean results of either `True` or `False`.

Exercise 2-28: Use Boolean Expressions to Test for True or False

These are examples of using Boolean operators in Python.

#	Exercise	Explanation

①	```>>> True and True is True```
	True
	```>>> True and False is False```
	True
	```>>> False and True is False```
	False
	```>>> False and False is False```
	False
	```>>> not True is False```
	True
	```>>> not False is True```
	True
		The first two examples use the and operator. "True and True is True" evaluates to True because both operands are true. "True and False is False" evaluates to True because one operand (False) is false.
		The next two examples also use the and operator. "False and True is False" evaluates to False because one operand (False) is false. "False and False is False" evaluates to False because both operands are false.
		The next example uses the not operator. "not True is False" evaluates to True because the not operator negates the value of True, resulting in True. The final example also uses the not operator. "not False is True" evaluates to True because the not operator negates the value of False, resulting in True.

In summary, these examples illustrate how Boolean operators can be used in Python to combine Boolean values and return new Boolean values. The and operator returns True if both operands are true, and the not operator negates the value of a Boolean expression.

Exercise 2-29: Logical (Membership) Operators

These are examples of using Boolean operators in Python to combine Boolean expressions and return new Boolean values.

#	Exercise	Explanation

①	`>>> True and False or not False`
	`True`
	`>>> True and False or True`
	`True`
	`>>> False or True`
	`True`
	`>>> True or False`
	`True`
		The first example, "True and False or not False", evaluates to True. This is because the and operator has higher precedence than the or operator, so "True and False" is evaluated first. Because this expression is false, the or operator then evaluates the next expression, which is "not False". Because "not False" is True, the overall result is true.
		The second example, "True and False or True", also evaluates to True. This is because the and operator has higher precedence than the or operator, so "True and False" is evaluated first. Because this expression is false, the or operator then evaluates the next expression, which is "True". Because "True" is true, the overall result is True.
		The third example, "False or True", evaluates to True. This is because the or operator returns True if at least one operand is true, and in this case, the second operand ("True") is true.
		The fourth example, "True or False", also evaluates to True. This is because the or operator returns True if at least one operand is true, and in this case, the first operand ("True") is true.

In summary, these examples illustrate how Boolean operators can be used in Python to combine Boolean expressions and return new Boolean values. The and operator returns True if both operands are true; the or operator returns True if at least one operand is true; and the not operator negates the value of a Boolean expression.

Exercise 2-30: Change the Order of Operation with () (Parentheses)

#	Exercise

① >>> **True and False or not False**
True

The expression "True and False or not False" is an example of combining Boolean expressions using the and and or operators in Python. In this case, the and operator has higher precedence than the or operator, so the expression is evaluated from left to right as follows: "True and False" is evaluated first. Because "False" is one of the operands, the overall result of this expression is False.

The or operator then evaluates the next expression, which is "not False". Because "not False" is true, the overall result of this expression is True. Therefore, the final result of the expression "True and False or not False" is True.

② >>> **(True and False) or (not False)**
True

In this case, the parentheses indicate the order of evaluation. The parentheses around "True and False" indicate that this expression is evaluated first, and because one of the operands is False, the overall result of this expression is False. The parentheses around "not False" indicate that this expression is evaluated next, and because "not False" is True, the overall result of this expression is True. Finally, the or operator combines the results of the two expressions inside the parentheses, and because one of the expressions is True, the overall result of the expression is True.

③ >>> **((True and False) or (not False))**
True

The parentheses indicate the order of evaluation. The parentheses around "True and False" indicate that this expression is evaluated first, and because one of the operands is False, the overall result of this expression is False. The parentheses around "not False" indicate that this expression is evaluated next, and because "not False" is True, the overall result of this expression is True. Finally, the or operator combines the results of the two expressions inside the parentheses, and because one of the expressions is True, the overall result of the expression is True.

In summary, this example illustrates how parentheses can be used to control the order of evaluation of Boolean expressions in Python, and how the and, or, and not operators can be used to combine Boolean values and expressions to produce new Boolean values.

Control Statements: if, elif, and else

Python's control statements—if, elif, and else—are used to create conditional branching in programs. They allow programmers to execute different sections of code based on whether certain conditions are met.

Exercise 2-31: Use if and else

Type these if statements in Python and study the output.

#	Exercise
①	```
>>> if 1 < 2:
...   print('One is less than two.')
...
One is less than two.
```
The if keyword is followed by a condition, which in this case is 1 < 2. This condition evaluates to True because 1 is indeed less than 2. If the condition is True, then the code indented under the if statement is executed. In this case, the code is a print statement that outputs the string "One is less than two." to the console. Therefore, when the code is executed in the Python Interpreter, **it checks if 1 is less than 2, which is** True, **and then executes the** print **statement, resulting in the output** "One is less than two." **appearing on the console.** |
| ② | ```
>>> if 1 > 2:
...     print('One is bigger than two.')
...
>>>
``` |

(continued)

#	Exercise
	The if keyword is followed by a condition, which in this case is 1 > 2. This condition evaluates to False because 1 is not bigger than 2. If the condition is False, then the code indented under the if statement is skipped and not executed. In this case, the code indented under the if statement is a print statement that would output the string "One is bigger than two." to the console if the condition were True. Therefore, when the code is executed in the Python Interpreter, **the if statement is skipped because the condition is** False**, and there is no output to the console.**
③	```
>>> if 1 > 2:
...   print('One is bigger than two.')
... else:
...   print('One is NOT bigger than two.')
...
One is NOT bigger than two.
```
The if keyword is followed by a condition, which in this case is 1 > 2. This condition evaluates to False because 1 is not bigger than 2. Because the condition is False, the code indented under the if statement is skipped and the code indented under the else statement is executed. The else statement provides an alternative block of code to be executed if the if condition is False. In this case, the code indented under the else statement is a print statement that outputs the string "One is NOT bigger than two." to the console. Therefore, when the code is executed in the Python Interpreter, the if condition is False, and the code indented under the else statement is executed. This results in the output "One is NOT bigger than two." appearing on the console. |
```

Exercise 2-32: Use if, elif, and else

This exercise involves using different types of conditional statements in Python.

#	Exercise
| ① | ```python
>>> age = 21
>>> if age >= 18:
...    print('You are old enough to get your driver\'s license.')
...
You are old enough to get your driver's license.
``` |
| | In the given code, a variable named age is assigned the value of 21. Then, an if statement is used to check whether the value of age is greater than or equal to 18. Because 21 is greater than 18, the condition is True and the code indented under the if statement is executed. The code indented under the if statement is a print statement that outputs the string "You are old enough to get your driver's license." to the console. Therefore, when the code is executed, the output "You are old enough to get your driver's license." is displayed on the console. |
| ② | ```python
>>> age = 17
>>> if age >= 18:
...    print('You are old enough to drive a car.')
else:
...    print('You are too young to drive a car.')
...
You are too young to drive a car.
``` |
| | In the given code, a variable named age is assigned the value of 17. Then, an if statement is used to check whether the value of age is greater than or equal to 18. Because 17 is less than 18, the condition is False and the code indented under the else statement is executed. The code indented under the else statement is a print statement that outputs the string "You are too young to drive a car." to the console. Therefore, when the code is executed, the output "You are too young to drive a car." is displayed on the console. |

(continued)

#	Exercise

③
```
>>> age = 100
>>> if age <18:
...     print('You are too young to drive a car.') elif age> 99:
...     print('You are too old to drive a car.')
else:
...     print('You are in an eligible age group, so you can drive a
car.')
...
You are too old to drive a car.
```

The given code first assigns the value of 100 to the variable age. Then, the code uses an if-elif-else statement to check the value of age. Because 100 is greater than 99, the code block indented under the elif statement is executed, which prints the message "You are too old to drive a car." to the console. Therefore, when the code is executed, the output "You are too old to drive a car." is displayed on the console.

Exercise 2-33: Write Code with if, elif, and else

To complete this exercise, go to the C:\Python312\ch02 folder, open a text editor, and create a new Python file named driver_age.py under your working folder. Once you have saved the new Python file with the .py extension, you can execute the Python code by typing python driver_age.py in the command line prompt or terminal. Each time you execute the program, you can enter a different age value.

#	Exercise	Explanation
①	```# driver_age.py
q1 = input ('What is your legal age? ')
age = int(q1)
if age < 16:
print('You are too young to take a driving test.')
elif age > 99:
print('You are too old to take a driving test.')
else:
print('You\'re in the right age group to take a driving test.')```	This Python code prompts the user to enter their age as input. The input is then converted from a string to an integer. The code then checks the age and prints a message based on the age input. If the age is less than 16, it prints a message saying that the user is too young to take a driving test. If the age is greater than 99, it prints a message saying that the user is too old to take a driving test. Otherwise, it prints a message stating that the user is in the right age group to take a driving test.
②	```C:\Python312\ch02>python driver_age.py.py
What is your legal age? 15
You are too young to take a driving test.```	Enter 15 for the Python program to return the if statement.
③	```C:\Python312\ch02>python driver_age.py.py
What is your legal age? 100
You are too old to take a driving test.```	Enter 100 for the Python program to return the elif statement.
④	```C:\Python312\ch02>python driver_age.py.py
What is your legal age? 17
You're in the right age group to take a driving test.```	Enter 17 for the Python program to return the else statement.

You have created an interactive program that prints out different messages based on the user's age. Essentially, this is how many computer programs operate when interacting with humans.

Recap: Boolean and Conditionals

- Boolean data types determine if a condition is True or False.

- Relational operators compare values and return Boolean values.

- Round brackets ( ) can be used to change the order of operations in a Boolean expression.

- Complex conditionals can be expressed using Boolean logical operators such as and, or, and not.

- The Boolean logical operators and, or, and not are also known as membership operators.

- and returns True if all conditions are true.

- or returns True if at least one of several conditions is true.

- not returns the inverse of the used operator.

- Boolean operations are executed in the order of not, and, then or.

- Python control statements like if, elif, and else are used with Boolean operators to control program flow.

Tip

Feeling fatigued?

If you're feeling tired, take a break before tackling the rest of the exercises in this chapter. Taking time to recharge can make a significant difference, helping you approach the tasks ahead with renewed energy and focus.

Learn Python Basics on Windows – Part II
Functions

In Python, a *function* is a reusable block of code that performs a specific task. Functions help in modular programming, making code more organized, efficient, and easier to read. They take arguments as input, process them, and return the result. Functions in Python can be defined using the def keyword, followed by the function name, parameter list, and code block. Functions can have optional default parameters and can also return multiple values. Python provides a rich library of built-in functions, and users can also define their custom functions to fit their specific needs.

Exercise 2-34: Define a Function

#	Exercise	Explanation

①	```>>> def say_hello():```
	```... print('Hello')```
	```...```
	```>>> say_hello()```
	```Hello```
		In Python, you define functions using the keyword def and always end the function definition with a colon. You can create a new function in the following format:
		def function_name(): # *Code block*
		When you run the function, it will perform the action defined in the function, in this case, say 'Hello'.

②	```>>> say_goodbye()```
	```Traceback (most recent call```
	```last): File "<stdin>", line 1,```
	```in <module>```
	```NameError: name 'say_goodbye'```
	```is not defined```
		If you use a function without defining it, you will encounter a NameError.

Exercise 2-35: Assign Default Values to a Function

#	Exercise	Explanation

①	```>>> def say_hello(name):```
	```... print(f'Hello {name}')```
	```...```
	```>>> say_hello('Hugh')```
	```Hello Hugh```
		A function that returns a "Hello" when you enter a name. "Hello" and the entered name is concatenated using the f-string method.

②	```>>> say_hello()```
	```Traceback (most recent call last):```
	```File "<stdin>", line 1, in <module>```
	```TypeError: say_hello() missing 1```
	```required positional argument: 'name'```
		If you forget to enter a name, a TypeError will be returned.

③	```>>> def say_hello(name = 'son'):```
	```... print(f'Hello {name}')```
	```...```
	```>>> say_hello()```
	```Hi son```
	```>>> say_hello('John')```
	```Hi John```
		You can assign a default name to make the code run without a TypeError. You can consider it as an error-handling mechanism. You learn about error handling in the later exercises.

Exercise 2-36: Define Hello and Goodbye Functions

#	Exercise	Explanation

①	```>>> def say_hello(f_name, s_name):```
	```... print('Hello! {} {}'. format```
	```(f_name, s_name))```
	```...```
	```>>> say_hello ('Mike', 'Smith')```
	```Hello! Mike Smith```
	```>>> say_hello ('Mike')```
	```Traceback (most recent call last):```
	```File "<stdin>", line 1, in <module>```
	```TypeError: say_hello() missing 1```
	```required positional argument:```
	```'s_name'```
		In this example, you define the say_hello function with two variables using the format string method. This means when the function runs, it would expect two positional arguments. If you give only a single argument, you will encounter a TypeError with a missing argument.

②	```>>> say_hello(f_name='Leah',```
	```s_name='Taylor')```
	```Hello! Lea Taylor```
	```>>> say_hello(s_name = 'Rose',```
	```f_name = 'Kate')```
	```Hello! Kate Rose```
		If variable names are used to call the function, the order of the variables does not matter, as the function uses the named variables.

③	```>>> def say_goodbye(f_name,```
	```s_name = 'Doe'):```
	```... print('Goodbye! {} {}'.```
	```format (f_name, s_name))```
	```...```
	```>>> say_goodbye('John')```
	```Goodbye! John Doe```
	```>>> say_goodbye('John', 'Citizen')```
	```Goodbye! John Citizen```
		You can also assign a default variable value to the function to accept just a single positional argument response. In this example, one or two arguments are accepted and processed without a TypeError. This could be an acceptable error avoidance strategy to continue your code.

Exercise 2-37: Use the odd or even Function

#	Exercise	Explanation

①	```>>> def odd_or_even(number):
	... if number%2 == 0:
	... return 'even'
	... else:
	... return 'odd'
	...
	>>> odd_or_even(3)
	'odd'
	>>> odd_or_even(4)
	'even'```
		This exercise returns whether a number is even or odd. Do not look at the function's simplicity; think about how you can apply it at work.

②	```>>> def even_num(number):
	... if number%2 == 0:
	... return True
	... else:
	... return False
	...
	>>> even_num(1)
	False
	>>> even_num(2)
	True```
		You can tweak Example 1 and make it into a True or False function. Try to learn the basics of Python each day and think about scenarios or applications to use such functions.

Exercise 2-38: Nest a Function Within a Function and a lambda Function

#	Exercise	Explanation

①	```
	>>> def name():
	... n = input('Enter your name: ')
	... return n
	...
	>>> def say_name(n):
	... print('Your name is
	{}.'.format(n))
	...
	>>> def say_the_name():
	... n = name()
	... say_name(n)
	...
	>>> say_the_name()
	Enter your name: Mike Smith
	Your name is Mike Smith.
	``
		You create two functions, and then on the third function, you nest (reused) them. This is a straightforward exercise, but if a function is lengthy and complicated, you can save the code lines as a separate file and import a specific function as a customized module. You learn about modules in later chapters, so in this section, try to focus on the Python syntax.

(*continued*)

#	Exercise	Explanation
②	```python\n>>> say_the_name = lambda: (lambda n:\nprint('Your name is {}.'.format(n)))\n(input('Enter your name: '))\n>>> say_the_name()\nEnter your name: Jane Doe\nYour name is Jane Doe.\n```	To simplify the nested function in ①, you can use the lambda function. A Python lambda is a type of function. A lambda function in Python is a small, anonymous function that can have any number of arguments but can only have one expression. This lambda function combines the name and say_name functions and is executed immediately. When you run the code, it will prompt you to enter your name, and then it will print Your name is [your name].

Recap: Functions

- Define functions before you use them. The basic function syntax begins with def function_name(parameter_name):

- A function can perform any action with small code in the reusable main code and return data.

- Functions can take parameters, or you can set default parameter values to use arbitrary parameters.

- Functions can be used to control the flow of your script.

- You can get more help by using the built-in function help() and then typing def.

- Lambda functions are defined using the lambda keyword and are commonly used when you need a simple, short-lived function for a specific purpose.

Lists

In this section, you practice Python list-related concepts. Let the fingers do the talking.

Exercise 2-39: Create a List and Index Items

#	Exercise	Explanation

①	```>>> vehicles = ['car', 'bus', 'truck']```
	```>>> print(vehicles[0])```
	```car```
	```>>> print(vehicles[1])```
	```bus```
	```>>> print(vehicles[2])```
	```Truck```
		In Python, lists are written with square brackets. In this example, only string items are used, but the list supports all other data types. The indexing starts from 0 and increases by one, so to page 'truck', which is the third item in the list, you use index [2].

②	```>>> vehicles = ['car', 'bus', 'truck']```
	```>>> vehicles[0] = 'motorbike'```
	```>>> vehicles```
	```['motorbike', 'bus', 'truck']```
		A list is a collection that is ordered and mutable. So you can replace an item using the indexing method. In this exercise, car has been replaced with motorbike.

③	```>>> print(vehicles[-1])```
	```truck```
	```>>> print(vehicles[-2])```
	```bus```
	```>>> print(vehicles[-3])```
	```Motorbike```
		You can use minus signs to index items backward. More slicing examples follow soon.

④	```>>> vehicles```
	```['motorbike', 'bus', 'truck']```
	```>>> vehicles[0] = ['sedan', 'wagon', 'convertible', 'SUV']```
	```>>> vehicles```
	```[['sedan', 'wagon', 'convertible', 'SUV'], 'bus', 'truck']```
		The list can also contain most of the other data types. This example shows a list of cars as part of the parent list, vehicle.

(*continued*)

#	Exercise	Explanation

⑤	`>>> cars = ['sedan', 'wagon', 'SUV', 'hatchback']`
	`>>> for car in range(len(cars)):`
	`...   print('{} is at position {}.'.format(cars[car], car))`
	`...`
	`sedan is at position 0. wagon is at position 1. SUV is at position 2. hatchback is at position 3.`
		In Example 1, you saw that the indexing starts at 0. Quickly write a function to check the item positions and see if it starts at 0.

Exercise 2-40: Use append, extend, and insert in a List

#	Exercise	Explanation

①	`>>> cars = ['sedan', 'SUV', 'hatchback']`
	`>>> cars.append('convertible')`
	`>>> cars`
	`['sedan', 'SUV', 'hatchback', 'convertible']`
		Append adds an item to the end of a list.

②	`>>> cars.extend(['crossover', '4WD'])`
	`>>> cars`
	`['sedan', 'SUV', 'hatchback', 'convertible', 'crossover', '4WD']`
		To add multiple items to the end of a list, use the extend() function.

③	`>>> cars.insert(1, 'wagon')`
	`>>> cars`
	`['sedan', 'wagon', 'SUV', 'hatchback', 'convertible', 'crossover', '4WD']`
		To insert an item in a specific location, use an index number to insert the new item. In this example, wagon was inserted in index 1 and it pushed the other items to the right index.

Slicing

Exercise 2-41: Slice a list

#	Exercise	Explanation

①	```>>> bread = ['bagels', 'baguette', 'ciabatta', 'crumpet', 'naan', 'pita', 'tortilla']```
	 ```>>> some_bread = bread[1:3]```
	 ```>>> some_bread```
	 ```['baguette', 'ciabatta']```
	 ```>>> print('Some Bread: {}'.format (some_bread))```
	 ```Some Bread: ['baguette', 'ciabatta']```
		You can use the slicing method to call the items in a list. In this example, you want to index items 1 and 2, so you have to use [1:3]. The first indexed item is included but not the last indexed item. You can also use the print() function to "prettify" your output.

②	```>>> first_two = bread[0:2]```
	 ```>>> first_two```
	 ```['bagels', 'baguette']```
		If you want the first two items, use [0:2] as the slicing index.

③	```>>> first_three_bread = bread[:3]```
	 ```>>> print(first_three_bread)```
	 ```['bagels', 'baguette', 'ciabatta']```
		If you do not specify the start index number, Python will page from index 0.

④	```>>> last_two_bread = bread[-2:]```
	 ```>>> print('Last two bread: {}'.format (last_two_bread))```
	 ```Last two bread: ['pita', 'tortilla']```
		You can also page backward using minus indexing.

⑤	```>>> bread = ['bagels', 'baguette', 'ciabatta']```
	 ```>>> ciabatta_index = bread. index('ciabatta')```
	 ```>>> print(ciabatta_index)```
	 ```2```
		You can also create a variable and check the index number of an item from the list.

Exceptions and Error Handling

Look at the following example and think about how you could handle the error. In this section, you learn how to handle Python exceptions and errors.

#	Example	Explanation

①	```>>> bread = ['bagels', 'baguette', 'ciabatta']```
	```>>> crumpet_index = bread.index('crumpet')```
	```Traceback (most recent call last): File```
	```"<stdin>", line 1, in <module> ValueError:```
	```'crumpet' is not in the list```
		You will encounter ValueError if you page an item that does not exist in a list.

Exercise 2-42: Handle Errors with try and except in a List

You are going to learn the concept of error handling here. When an error occurs, your program will suddenly stop. When Python runs into an error, it detects it as a sign to stop and exit the application. If you know what errors are expected, in most cases, you'll want to be in control of how errors are handled. Do not let Python decide what to do with the errors.

Note: After completing Exercise ①, save the same code in a file under `C:\Python312\ch02\` as `ex2_42.py`.

#	Exercise	Explanation
①	```>>> bread = ['bagels', 'baguette', 'ciabatta'] >>> try: ... crumpet_index = bread.index('crumpet') ... except: ... crumpet_index = 'No crumpet bread found.' ... print(crumpet_index) ... No crumpet bread found.```	When you encounter errors in an application, the program must continue running the rest of the application or it will stop to prevent more significant problems. **Errors are a constructive part of the script, and they help your application stop, so it does not cause more problems. So, as a programmer, you want to know which errors are expected and how to handle them when they occur.** If you know how to handle errors like the ValueError in the previous example in this exercise, you will have cleaner Python code. You can customize and process the error message as you want to express it. In the previous example, the error message tells explicitly that the paged bread type, crumpet, does not exist.
②	```# ex2_42.py bread = ['bagels', 'baguette', 'ciabatta'] try: crumpet_index = bread.index('crumpet') except: crumpet_index = 'No crumpet bread found.' print(crumpet_index)```	It is much easier to use a text editor than coding it directly on the Python IDLE in this example. Use text editors such as Notepad, Wordpad, or Notepad++ (NPP) to save the Python code and save it as ex2_42.py under the C:\Python312\ch02 folder.
③	```C:\Python312\ch02>python ex2_42.py No crumpet bread found.```	Run the Python script to get the expected output. Working in interactive mode is fun, but you have to start thinking about writing your code on a text editor or an IDE.

Exercise 2-43: Find an Index of an Item in a List with the Customized Exception

Note: Save the code with the exercise name given and run it from the Python prompt. All the code is available for download from the GitHub site. The file names are ex2_43_1.py for Exercise 2-43-1 and ex2_43_2.py for Exercise 2-43-2.

#	Exercise	Explanation
①	```# ex2_43_1.py
bread = ['bagels', 'baguette',
'ciabatta', 'crumpet']
try:
crumpet_index = bread.index
('crumpet')
except:
crumpet_index = 'No crumpet bread
was found.'
print(crumpet_index)```	In this example, you are trying to find the index number of crumpet. bread. index('crumpet') will look for the index number of the item. In the output, index 3 is returned.
②	```# ex2_43_2.py
bread = ['bagels', 'baguette',
'ciabatta', 'naan']
try:
crumpet_index = bread.index
('crumpet')
except:
crumpet_index = 'No crumpet bread
was found.'
print(crumpet_index)```	If you replace crumpet with naan bread and run the script, it will return the customized except error, as shown in the output.

Practicing Lists

Practice the list of concepts you have learned so far. **I encourage you to type every single word and character shown.** While you are typing, try to guess what the exercise is trying to teach you. You might be getting tired, but nobody will practice these exercises for you; you have to do everything yourself.

Exercise 2-44: Practice a List

Note that the following exercise should be completed in a single attempt.

#	Exercise

①	```>>> shopping_list1 = 'baseball hat, baseball shoes, sunglasses, baseball bat, sunscreen lotion, baseball meat'```
	 ```>>> print(shopping_list1)```
	 baseball hat, baseball shoes, sunglasses, baseball bat, sunscreen lotion, baseball meat
	 ```>>> type(shopping_list1)```
	 `<class 'str'>`
	 You have just created shopping_list1 as a string.

②	```shopping_list2 = ['baseball hat', 'baseball shoes', 'sunglasses', 'baseball bat', 'sunscreen lotion', 'baseball meat']```
	 ```>>> print(shopping_list2 [2])```
	 sunglasses
	 ```>>> type(shopping_list2)```
	 `<class 'list'>`
	 shopping_list2 is a list as the items are wrapped around [ ] (square brackets), a square bracket set. Use indexing to return sunglasses.

(continued)

#	Exercise

③
```
>>> shopping_list2 = ['baseball hat', 'baseball shoes', 'sunglasses',
'baseball bat', 'sunscreen lotion', 'baseball meat']
>>> shopping_list2.pop(5)
'baseball meat'
>>> shopping_list2
['baseball hat', 'baseball shoes', 'sunglasses', 'baseball bat',
'sunscreen lotion']
```
Indexing does not change the list, but if you use the pop() method, it will take the called item out permanently.

④
```
>>> print(shopping_list2 [2])
sunglasses
>>> print(shopping_list2 [2: 5])
['sunglasses', 'baseball bat', 'sunscreen lotion']
```
Using a single index or a range of indexes, you can call out the items from a list.

⑤
```
>>> shopping_list2 [2] = 'ball'
>>> print(shopping_list2)
['baseball hat', 'baseball shoes', 'ball', 'baseball bat',
'sunscreen lotion']
```
You can insert a new item into the list using indexing as a mutable object.

⑥
```
>>> some_numbers = [1, 3, 5]
>>> some_strings = ['which', 'Olympic', 'sports']
>>> numbers_and_strings = ['which', 1, 'Olympic', 3, 'sports', 5]
```
The list can contain numbers, strings, or a combination of unique items.

⑦
```
>>> numbers = [3, 6, 9, 12]
>>> strings = ['soccer', 'baseball', 'basketball', 'swimming']
>>> new_list = [numbers, strings]
>>> print(new_list)
[[3, 6, 9, 12], ['soccer', 'baseball', 'basketball', 'swimming']]
```
A list can store another list.

(*continued*)

#	Exercise

⑧	>>> **summer_sports = ['swimming', 'diving', 'baseball', 'basketball', 'cricket']**
	 >>> **summer_sports.append ('beach volleyball')**
	 >>> **print(summer_sports)**
	 ['swimming', 'diving', 'baseball', 'basketball', 'cricket', 'beach volleyball']
	
	 You can use the append() method to add two lists and make them into one list.

⑨	>>> **print(summer_sports)**
	 ['swimming', 'diving', 'baseball', 'basketball', 'cricket', 'beach volleyball']
	 >>> **del summer_sports [1]**
	 >>> **print(summer_sports)**
	 ['swimming', 'baseball', 'basketball', 'cricket', 'beach volleyball']
	
	 Use del and indexing to delete items you want to delete from your list.

⑩	>>> **summer_sports = ['swimming', 'baseball', 'basketball', 'cricket']**
	 >>> **winter_sports = ['skiing', 'ice skating', 'ice hockey', 'snowboarding']**
	 >>> **print(summer_sports + winter_sports)**
	 ['swimming', 'baseball', 'basketball', 'cricket', 'skiing', 'ice skating', 'ice hockey', 'snowboarding']
	
	 You can concatenate lists using the + operator.

⑪	>>> **summer_sports = ['swimming', 'baseball', 'basketball', 'cricket']**
	 >>> **winter_sports = ['skiing', 'ice skating', 'ice hockey', 'snowboarding']**
	 >>> **sports_list = list(zip(summer_sports, winter_sports))**
	 >>> **print(sports_list)**
	 [('swimming', 'skiing'), ('baseball', 'ice skating'), ('basketball', 'ice hockey'), ('cricket', 'snowboarding')]
	
	 Here, zip() combines the elements from both lists into pairs of tuples, and then list() converts the result into a list of tuples. Each tuple contains a summer sport and its corresponding winter sport.

The for loop and the while loop (Loops)

Exercise 2-45: Use the for Loop's upper() and capitalize() Methods

#	Exercise	Explanation
①	```>>> bread_type = ['bagels', 'baguette', 'ciabatta'] >>> for bread in bread_type: ... print(bread.upper()) ... BAGELS BAGUETTE CIABATTA```	As the name suggests, for loop loops through a list until the last item is paged from the list. This example calls out the index 0 item first, then goes back to the loop, calls the index 1 item, and then the last item, which has index 2. Also, appending upper() will convert the returned values into uppercase.
②	```>>> bread_type = ['bagels', 'baguette', 'ciabatta'] >>> for bread in bread_type: ... print(bread.capitalize()) ... Bagels Baguette Ciabatta```	You can also use Python's capitalize() method to change each bread's first letter into capital letters.

133

Exercise 2-46: Use the while Loop and the len() Function

#	Exercise
| ① | ```
>>> basket = ['bagels', 'baguette', 'ciabatta', 'crumpet', 'naan',
'pita', 'tortilla']
>>> bread = 0
>>> while bread < len(basket):
...     print(basket[bread], end=" ") # " " contains a white space
...     bread += 1
...
bagels baguette ciabatta crumpet naan pita tortilla >>>
``` |

The while loop and len() functions are used to call out and print each bread. This while loop uses indexing and loops until the list is empty. Although the len() function returns the number of items in an object, in this example, it is used with a for loop to return each item until the list is empty. Notice that end=" " is used to print the output on a single line.

Sorting and Ranges

Exercise 2-47: Use sort() vs. sorted() to Sort a List

#	Exercise	Explanation
| ① | ```
>>> bread = ['naan', 'baguette',
'tortilla', 'ciabatta', 'pita']
>>> bread.sort()
>>> bread
['baguette', 'ciabatta', 'naan',
'pita', 'tortilla']
``` | When you use the sort() function on a list, it sorts the items from A-Z permanently. |

(continued)

#	Exercise	Explanation
| ② | ```python
>>> bread = ['naan', 'baguette',
'tortilla', 'ciabatta', 'pita']
>>> bread_in_order =
sorted(bread)
>>> bread_in_order
['baguette', 'ciabatta', 'naan',
'pita', 'tortilla']
>>> bread
['naan', 'baguette', 'tortilla',
'ciabatta', 'pita']
``` | The sorted() function only sorts A-Z temporarily. It does not change the order of the original data. The different effect of the sort() and sorted() seems to be insignificant and unnoticed to novice Python programmers, but in programming fundamentals, sorted() is the recommended method over the sort() method, as it does not permanently alter the original item. You can reuse the original item as well as the newly created item as objects. |

Exercise 2-48: Link Two Lists

#	Exercise	Explanation
| ① | ```python
>>> bread = ['naan', 'baguette',
'tortilla', 'ciabatta', 'pita']
>>> more_bread = ['bagels', 'crumpet']
>>> all_bread = bread + more_bread
>>> print(all_bread)
['naan', 'baguette', 'tortilla',
'ciabatta', 'pita', 'bagels', 'crumpet']
>>> all_bread.sort()
>>> print(all_bread)
['bagels', 'baguette', 'ciabatta',
'crumpet', 'naan', 'pita', 'tortilla']
>> all_bread.reverse()
>>> all_bread
['tortilla', 'pita', 'naan', 'crumpet',
'ciabatta', 'baguette', 'bagels']
``` | In this example, you create two lists and then merge them into one list. Then the sort() function organizes the items in the list from A-Z. Finally, you use the reverse() method to reverse the list's order to Z-A. |

Exercise 2-49: Find the List Length Using the len() Function

#	Exercise	Explanation
| ① | ```
>>> bread = ['bagels',
'baguette', 'ciabatta']
>>> print(len(bread))
3
>>> bread.append('naan')
>>> print(len(bread))
4
``` | You use the len() function to check how many bread types are in the list. Next, you add another bread type using the append method, and then recheck the number of bread types with the len() function. It has increased by 1. |

Exercise 2-50: Use range() with the for Loop

#	Exercise	Explanation
| ① | ```
>>> for number in range (3):
...    print(number)
...
0
1
2
``` | If you use a for loop with the range() function, you can call out the list items with ease. range(3) means up to but not including 3, so this example loops through 0, 1, and 2. |
| ② | ```
>>> for number in range (2, 5):
...    print(number, end=" ")
...
2 3 4
``` | Using commas, you can specify where to begin and where to finish. In this for loop example, the first argument (digit) represents the first number and the second argument (digit) represents the ceiling number of finishing the loop, so the last number is always going to be n-1, which is number 4 in this example. |

(continued)
```

#	Exercise	Explanation
③	```>>> for number in range (1, 8, 2): ... print(number, end=" ") ... 1 3 5 7 ```	In the last example, you use three arguments to loop through a range of numbers. The first and last numbers carry the same meaning as explained in Example ②, but the last digit 2 represents the interval or frequency. Starting from 1, it will loop through to odd numbers only until it reaches the ceiling number 8. So, as expected, Python only prints the odd numbers 1, 3, 5, and 7. You must master the `for` loop well to make your Python scripts work harder for you.
④	```>>> for bread in ['bagels', 'baguette', 'crumpet', 'naan']: ... print(bread, end=" ") ... bagels baguette crumpet naan ```	**You are applying the** `for` **loop to a list**. Instead of a `range()` function, you use a list with items inside the list.
⑤	```>>> for bread in ('bagels', 'baguette', 'crumpet', 'naan'): ... print(bread, end=" ") ... bagels baguette crumpet naan ```	**You are applying the** `for` **loop to a tuple. Do you wonder what the difference is between this and the previous example in Example ④? You cannot feel it in these examples, but the difference is in the speed.** Because tuples are immutable and have fewer indexing pointers than lists, they can process the data faster while looping through each item in a tuple. If you need to process a million data lines, speed will matter, so use tuples over lists.

Exercise 2-51: Create a string list for loop() and range() with Arguments

#	Exercise

①
```
>>> bread = ['bagels', 'baguette', 'ciabatta', 'crumpet', 'naan', 'pita', 'tortilla']
>>> for number in range (0, len (bread), 2):
...     print(bread [number] , end=" ")
...
bagels ciabatta naan tortilla
```

In this example, you nest the len() function inside a range() function to loop through a bread list with three arguments, similar to Exercise 2-50's ③. Because the last argument is 2, it will step through the bread list and index items 1, 3, 5, and 7.

②
```
>>> bread = ['bagels', 'baguette', 'ciabatta', 'crumpet', 'naan', 'pita', 'tortilla']
>>> for number in range (0, len (bread), 3):
...     print(bread [number] , end=" ")
...
bagels crumpet tortilla
```

This is the same example as the previous example, but with a stepping value of 3—indexed items are bagels, crumpet, and tortilla.

③
```
>>> bread = ['bagels', 'baguette', 'ciabatta', 'crumpet', 'naan', 'pita', 'tortilla']
>>> for number in range (0, len (bread), 5):
...     print(bread [number] , end=" ")
...
bagels pita
```

This is the same example with a stepping value of 5, so this example prints out the first value and sixth value—bagels and pita bread.

Recap: Lists and Loops

- When creating and assigning a variable to a list, enclose the elements in square brackets [ ] and separate each item in the list with a comma. A typical list syntax looks like this:

  List_name = [element_1, element_2, ..., element_n]

- List items can be indexed by the index number starting from 0 to n. To index the first item in a list, use index number 0. To index an item from the last item, use an index number of -1.

- Use slicing to index part of a list. For example, List_Name [3, 6].

- Use for loop() to index a range of numbers in a list.

- A while loop will continue to run as long as the condition is True and only stops when the condition becomes False.

- You can sort a list using the sort() and sorted() list methods.

- If you use built-in functions like range(), you can index sequential numbers.

- Handle Python exception errors using "try and except" code blocks.

Tuples

Exercise 2-52: Tuple Basic Examples

#	Exercise	Explanation

①	>>> **tuple1 = (0, 1, 3, 6, 9)**
	>>> **tuple2 = ('w', 'x', 'y', 'z')**
	>>> **tuple3 = (0, 1, 'x', 2, 'y', 3, 'z')**
		These are examples of tuples. Notice that tuples are almost identical to lists, except the items are wrapped around a set of round brackets ( ). Notice that they are aesthetically different.

(continued)

#	Exercise	Explanation

②	```>>> tuple1 = (0, 1, 3, 6, 9)```
	```>>> tuple [1] = 12```
	```Traceback (most recent call last):```
	```File "<stdin>", line 1, in <module>```
	```TypeError: 'type' object does not support item assignment```
		You have tried to replace 1 with 12, and the tuple will spit the dummy back at you with a TypeError. Therefore tuples are known as immutable sequential objects in Python.

③	```>>> tuple1 = (0, 1, 3, 6, 9)```
	```>>> tuple2 = ('w', 'x', 'y', 'z')```
	```>>> print(tuple1 + tuple2)```
	```(0, 1, 3, 6, 9, 'w', 'x', 'y', 'z')```
		You can still combine two tuples by using the + sign.

Exercise 2-53: Tuple to List Conversion

#	Exercise	Explanation

①	```>>> tuple3 = (0, 1, 'x', 2, 'y', 3, 'z')```
	```>>> list (tuple3)```
	```[0, 1, 'x', 2, 'y', 3, 'z']```
		To change a tuple into a list, use ```list(tuple_name)```.

②	```>>> tuple1 = (0, 1, 3, 6, 9)```
	```>>> tuple2 = ('w', 'x', 'y', 'z')```
	```>>> list (tuple1 + tuple2)```
	```[0, 1, 3, 6, 9, 'w', 'x', 'y', 'z']```
		You can combine two or more tuples and still convert them using the ```list()``` conversion technique.

Exercise 2-54: Handle Tuples (Are Tuples Immutable?)

#	Exercise

①	```>>> days_of_the_week = ('Monday', 'Tuesday', 'Wednesday', 'Thursday', 'Friday', 'Saturday', 'Sunday')>>> for day in days_of_the_week:```
	```... print(day, end=" ")```
	```...```
	```Monday Tuesday Wednesday Thursday Friday Saturday Sunday```
	
	This is a simple tuple example containing the days of the week.

②	```>>> days_of_the_week = ('Monday', 'Tuesday', 'Wednesday', 'Thursday', 'Friday', 'Saturday', 'Sunday')```
	```>>> days_of_the_week [0] = 'Funday'```
	```Traceback (most recent call last):```
	```File "<stdin>", line 1, in <module>```
	```TypeError: 'tuple' object does not support item assignment```
	
	When you try to update an item with another, Python will return a TypeError to remind you that a tuple is an immutable object in Python.

③	```>>> days_of_the_week = ('Monday', 'Tuesday', 'Wednesday', 'Thursday', 'Friday', 'Saturday', 'Sunday')```
	```>>> print(days_of_the_week)```
	```('Monday', 'Tuesday', 'Wednesday', 'Thursday', 'Friday', 'Saturday', 'Sunday')```
	```>>> del days_of_the_week```
	```>>> print(days_of_the_week)```
	```Traceback (most recent call last):```
	```File "<stdin>", line 1, in <module>```
	```NameError: name 'days_of_the_week' is not defined```
	
	Although tuples are immutable, it does not mean you cannot delete the whole tuple. Use del tuple_name to delete a tuple.

Exercise 2-55: Tuple-to-List and List-to-Tuple Conversions

#	Exercise	Explanation

①	```>>> weekend_tuple = ('Saturday', 'Sunday')```
	```>>> weekend_list = list (weekend_tuple)```
	```>>> print('weekend_tuple is {}.'. format (type (weekend_tuple)))```
	weekend_tuple is <class 'tuple'>.
	```>>> print('weekend_list is {}.'. format (type (weekend_list)))```
	weekend_list is <class 'list'>.
		This is a simple example of converting a tuple to a list. You can check the data type using the type() function.

②	```>>> country_list = ['US', 'England', 'Germany', 'France']```
	```>>> country_tuple = tuple (country_list)```
	```>>> type (country_list)```
	<class 'list'>
	```>>> type (country_tuple)```
	<class 'tuple'>
		Similarly, this is an example of converting a list to a tuple.

Exercise 2-56: Use a for Loop in a Tuple

#	Exercise	Explanation

①	```>>> countries = ('US',```
	```'England', 'Germany', 'France')```
	```>>> for country in countries:```
	```... print(country, end=" ")```
	```...```
	```US England Germany France```
		Like a list, you can index items in a tuple by using a for loop. Tuples and lists have a lot of common properties. The differences are that one is immutable (tuple), one is mutable (list), one is faster (tuple), and one is slower (list) during indexing.

Exercise 2-57: Assign Multiple Variables to a Tuple

#	Exercise

①	```>>> weekend = ('Saturday', 'Sunday')```
	```>>> (saturn, sun) = weekend```
	```>>> print(saturn)```
	```Saturday```
	
	```>>> weekdays = ('Monday', 'Tuesday', 'Wednesday', 'Thursday',```
	```'Friday')```
	
	```>>> (moon, tiu, woden, thor, freya) = weekdays```
	```>>> print(thor)```
	```Thursday```
	
	You can assign multiple variables to items in a tuple. This example uses the seven-day week and the meanings of the names of the days. Sunday and Monday were named after the Sun and Moon, and other days were named after mythological gods.

(continued)

#	Exercise

②	```>>> country_info = ['England', '+44']```
	 ```>>> (country, code) = country_info```
	 ```>>> print(country)```
	 England
	 ```>>> print(code)```
	 +44
	
	 You can also use a list as items in a tuple.

Exercise 2-58: Create a Simple Tuple Function

#	Exercise	Explanation

①	```>>> def high_and_low (numbers):```
	 ```... highest = max (numbers)```
	 ```... lowest = min (numbers)```
	 ```... return (highest, lowest)```
	 ```...```
	 ```>>> lotto_numbers = [1, 37, 25,```
	 ```48, 15, 23]```
	 ```>>> (highest, lowest) = high_and_low```
	 ```(lotto_numbers)```
	 ```>>> print(highest)```
	 48
	 ```>>> print(lowest)```
	 1
		You can make a simple function and use a tuple to page the highest number or the lowest number. Spend a few minutes understanding how this function works and then move to the next exercise.

Exercise 2-59: Use Tuples as List Elements

#	Exercise	Explanation

①	```python
	>>> country_code = [('England',
	'+44'), ('France', '+33')]
	>>> for (country, code) in
	country_code:
	... print(country, code)
	...
	England +44
	France +33
	>>> for (country, code) in
	country_code:
	... print(country, end=" ")
	...
	England France
	>>> for (country, code) in
	country_code:
	... print(code, end=" ")
	...
	+44 +33
	``
		You can use tuples as elements in a list. You can choose to call out single items in each tuple. Enter something meaningful to you to get more practice on this.

Recap: Tuples

- Tuples are sometimes called immutable lists, and once created, they cannot be changed in the same tuple form. You need to convert tuples back into a list first, and then elements can be changed. The general tuple syntax is:

  Tuple_name = (element_1, element_2, ..., element_n)

- However, you can delete the entire tuple in Python.

- You can convert a tuple to a list using the built-in function `list()`.

- You can convert a list to a tuple using the built-in function `tuple()`.

- You can find the maximum and minimum values of a tuple using the `max()` and `min()` methods.

Dictionary

Exercise 2-60: Dictionary Basics

#	Exercise

①	`>>> fav_activity = {'hugh': 'computer games', 'leah': 'ballet', 'caitlin': 'ice skating'}`
	`>>> print(fav_activity)`
	`{'hugh': 'computer games', 'leah': 'ballet', 'caitlin': 'ice skating'}`
	Create a dictionary called `fav_activity`. Make your family members' favorite hobbies into a dictionary. A dictionary usually has key and value elements, as in a real dictionary. Python's dictionary key: value elements are wrapped in a curly bracket set { } with comma separators.

②	`>>> fav_activity = {'hugh': 'computer games', 'leah': 'ballet', 'caitlin': 'ice skating'}`
	`>>> print(fav_activity ['caitlin'])`
	`ice skating`
	You can use a key called `caitlin` to call out the value of the key.

③	`>>> fav_activity = {'hugh': 'computer games', 'leah': 'ballet', 'caitlin': 'ice skating'}`
	`>>> del fav_activity ['hugh']`
	`>>> print(fav_activity)`
	`{'leah': 'ballet', 'caitlin': 'ice skating'}`

(continued)

#	Exercise
	Delete the key hugh using the del statement. When you delete a key, its value is also deleted. Now you know that a dictionary in Python is a mutable object.

④
```
>>> print(fav_activity)
{'leah': 'ballet', 'caitlin': 'ice skating'}
>>> fav_activity ['leah'] = 'swimming'
>>> print(fav_activity)
{'leah': 'swimming', 'caitlin': 'ice skating'}
```

Change the value of the key leah in the dictionary to swimming.

Exercise 2-61: Dictionary TypeError and Converting Two Lists as a Single Dictionary

#	Exercise	Explanation
①	```>>> fav_activity = {'leah': 'swimming', 'caitlin': 'ice skating'} >>> fav_subject = {'leah': 'math', 'caitlin': 'english'} >>> print(fav_activity + fav_subject) Traceback (most recent call last): File "<stdin>", line 1, in <module> TypeError: unsupported operand type (s) for +: 'dict' and 'dict'```	In Python, you cannot link two or more dictionaries into a single dictionary. Trying to join two dictionaries into one will return TypeError: unsupported operand.
②	```>>> keys = ['a', 'b', 'c', 'm', 'p'] >>> values = ['apple', 'banana', 'coconut', 'melon', 'pear'] >>> fruits = dict (zip (keys, values)) >>> fruits {'a': 'apple', 'b': 'banana', 'c': 'coconut', 'm': 'melon', 'p': 'pear'}```	However, if one list contains only keys, and the other list contains the same number of corresponding values, the two lists can be joined together to form a dictionary. In this example, you create a dictionary called fruits using one list with alphabets (keys) and another list with corresponding fruit names (values).

Exercise 2-62: Use Keys to Print Values from a Dictionary

#	Exercise
| ① | ```
>>> dialing_code = {'France': '+ 33', 'Italy': '+ 39', 'Spain': '+ 34', 'England': '+ 44'}
>>> France_code = dialing_code ['France']
>>> Italy_code = dialing_code ['Italy']
>>> Spain_code = dialing_code ['Spain']
>>> England_code = dialing_code ['England']
>>> print('Press {} first to call France.'. format (France_code))
Press +33 first to call France.
>>> print('Press {} first to call Italy.'. format (Italy_code))
Press +39 first to call Italy.
>>> print('Press {} first to call Spain.'. format (Spain_code))
Press +34 first to call Spain.
>>> print('Press {} first to call England.'. format (England_code))
Press +44 first to call England.
``` |

In the dictionary example, you used the keys to call corresponding values and printed them on your computer monitor. Try to practice all the examples. Many newbie programmers ask the same question about how to get better at coding; there is no substitute for practice.

Exercise 2-63: Change a Dictionary Value

#	Exercise
| ① | ```
>>> dialing_code = {'France': '+ 33', 'Italy': '+ 39', 'Spain': '+ 34', 'England': '+ 44'}
>>> dialing_code ['England'] = '+ 44-20'
>>> England_London = dialing_code ['England']
>>> print('Dial {} to call London, England.'. format (England_London))
Dial + 44-20 to call London, England.
``` |

As with other mutable objects in Python, you can also change dictionaries. In this exercise, you update the value of the key, England. You included the area code of 20 for London behind the country code +44. Then you print out a simple statement using the format() function.

Exercise 2-64: Add a New Set of Keys and Values to a Dictionary

#	Exercise
| ① | ```
>>> dialing_code = {'France': '+ 33', 'Italy': '+ 39', 'Spain': '+
34', 'England': '+ 44'}
>>> dialing_code ['Greece'] = '+30'
>>> dialing_code
{'England': '+44', 'Greece': '+30', 'Italy': '+39', 'Spain': '+34',
'France': '+33'}
``` |

You can add other keys and value pairs as you like. Dictionaries, like lists, are mutable containers. Notice the unordered manner of the dictionary in this example. There is no need for number indexing in Python dictionaries, as the keys are used to call the values.

Exercise 2-65: Find the Number of Dictionary Elements

#	Exercise
| ① | ```
>>> dialing_code = {'England': '+44', 'Greece': '+30', 'Italy': '+39',
'Spain': '+34', 'France': '+ 33 '}
>>> print(len (dialing_code))
5
``` |

Use len() to find the number of key: value pairs in a dictionary.

Exercise 2-66: Delete Dictionary Keys and Values

#	Exercise

①
```
>>> dialing_code = {'England': '+44', 'Greece': '+30', 'Italy': '+39',
'Spain': '+34', 'France': '+ 33 '}
>>> del dialing_code ['Italy']
>>> print(dialing_code)
{'England': '+44', 'Greece': '+30', 'Spain': '+34', 'France': '+33'}
```

To delete a key: value pair in a dictionary; use del with a key. The value will automatically be removed along with the key.

Exercise 2-67: Write a Python Script with a Dictionary

#	Exercise

①
```
# ex2_67.py
dialing_code = {'England': '+44', 'Greece': '+30', 'Italy': '+39',
'Spain': '+34', 'France': '+33'}
for code in dialing_code:
    print('The country code for {0} is {1}.'. format (code, dialing_
code [code]))
# Output:
The country code for England is +44.
The country code for Greece is +30.
The country code for Italy is +39.
The country code for Spain is +34.
The country code for France is +33.
```

Note: Try to save the ex2_67.py script on Notepad++. Save the file with the same name and run the code using Ctrl+F6 keys.

Now let's get familiar with making simple scripts like this and running them on IDLE or Notepad++. In this example, you used the format function to call both key and value pairs and put them through a for loop to print each country's international dialing codes.

Exercise 2-68: Dictionary for Loop and Formatting

#	Exercise
①	```
>>> countries = {'England': {'code':'+ 44', 'capital_city':'London'},
'France': {'code':'+ 33', 'capital_city':'Paris'}}
>>> for country in countries:
...   print("{} 's country info:" .format (country))
...   print(countries [country] ['code'])
...   print(countries [country] ['capital_city'])
...
England 's country info:
+ 44
London
France 's country info:
+ 33
Paris
```
You can nest dictionaries within a dictionary. Use a `for` loop to print elements of the dictionary, countries. |
| ② | ```
>> countries = {'England': {'code':'+ 44', 'capital_city':'London'},
'France': {'code':'+ 33', 'capital_city':'Paris'}}
>>> for country in countries:
...     print(f"{country}'s country info:")
...     print(countries [country] ['code'])
...     print(countries [country] ['capital_city'])
...
England's country info:
+ 44
London
France's country info:
+ 33
Paris
```
print("{} 's country info:" .format (country)) in Exercise ① is the same as print(f"{country}'s country info:") in Exercise ②. The second version is the simplified version and helps you write shorter code. |

Recap: Dictionary

- A dictionary comprises key: value pair collections, separated by commas, and wrapped around braces { }. The general dictionary syntax is:

  ```
  dictionary_Name = ['Key_1': 'Value_1', 'Key_2': 'Value_2',
  'Key_n': 'Value_n']
  ```

- To call a value stored in a dictionary, you must use a key rather than indexing. The dictionary doesn't use number indexing, so it is an unordered sequence collection.

- You can change the value of a key using the key as an index. Example: `dictionary_name ['key_1'] = 'new_value_1'`.

- Deleting a key using `del` deletes both the key and the value. Example: `del dictionary_name ['key_1']`.

- `value_x` in `dictionary_name.values()` will tell you if a key is part of a dictionary or not.

- `dictionary_name.keys()` returns only the keys of the dictionary.

- `dictionary_name.values()` returns only the value of the dictionary.

- You can use a `for` loop on a dictionary, as in lists and tuples.

- Dictionaries can have any data type as an element as long as they have the correct key: value pairings.

Handling Files

File-handling skills in Python are fundamental, as business-critical data must be processed using various file-handling modules and methods. The simplest form of file handling is reading and writing a text file. As you become familiar with more complex file handling, you can learn more advanced file-handling methods using Python modules such as pandas and NumPy for data processing or xlrd and openpyxl for Excel files. However, even before becoming familiar with such modules, it's important to master basic data processing using indexing or slicing or using regex to process your data. There is a 500-page book written alone on how to use the Python pandas module, so it is an unenviable task to cover all the topics on data processing and file handling.

However, this book aims to expose you to various basic data-processing exercises and file-handling methods. You become familiar with how Python processes data, and then the processed data can be processed through a basic file-handling method.

Exercise 2-69: Read and Display the Hosts File from Your PC

#	Exercise	Explanation

①	Run this from Microsoft Windows Python interactive shell.
	
	`>>> hosts = open('c://windows//system32//drivers//etc//hosts')`
	`>>> hosts_file = hosts.read()`
	`>>> print(hosts_file)`
	`# Copyright (c) 1993-2009 Microsoft Corp. #`
	`# This is a sample HOSTS file used by Microsoft TCP/IP for Windows. #`
	`# This file contains the mappings of IP addresses to host names. Each`
	`# entry should be kept on an individual line. The IP address should`
	`# be placed in the first column followed by the corresponding host`
	`name. # The IP address and the host name should be separated by at`
	`least one # space.`
	`#`
	`# Additionally, comments (such as these) may be inserted on individual`
	`# lines or following the machine name denoted by a '#' symbol.`
	`#`
	`# For example:`
	`#`
	`#     102.54.94.97 rhino.acme.com              # source server #`
	` 38.25.63.10    x.acme.com# x client host`
	
	`# localhost name resolution is handled within DNS itself. #`
	`127.0.0.1    localhost`
	`#     ::1    localhost`	

(continued)

#	Exercise	Explanation
		You have just read the hosts file from your Windows machine and printed it out on your computer screen.
		Reading a file is this easy, and if you do not specify the reading method, it usually opens in r (reading) mode.
		Notice while opening the hosts file, how each \ backslash in the Windows OS file system has been replaced with // slashes. If you insist on running Python on Windows and must handle files, this is a significant point to take away from this example.
②	Optionally, run this from Linux or the macOS Python interactive shell.	

```
>>> hosts = open ('/etc/hosts')
>>> hosts_file = hosts.read()
>>> print(hosts_file)
127.0.0.1 localhost.localdomain localhost
:: 1 localhost6.localdomain6 localhost6

The following lines are desirable for IPv6 capable hosts
:: 1 localhost ip6-localhost ip6-loopback fe00 :: 0 ip6-localnet
ff02 :: 1 ip6-allnodes ff02 :: 2 ip6-allrouters
ff02 :: 3 ip6-allhosts
```

You can use the same code on a Linux or macOS system to read the hosts file (object), but this time the hosts file exists under /etc/hosts instead. **In Python, it only takes three lines of code to open, read, and print a file's contents.**

Exercise 2-70: Open and Close Hosts Files

#	Exercise	Explanation

①	```>>> hosts = open('c://windows//system32//drivers//etc//hosts')```
	```>>> hosts_file = hosts.read()```
	```>>> print(hosts_file)```
	`# Copyright (c) 1993-2009 Microsoft Corp.`
	`.`
	`[... omitted for brevity]`
	`.`
	`# localhost name resolution is handled`
	`within DNS itself.`
	`#       127.0.0.1     localhost`
	`#       ::1     localhost`
	```>>> hosts.close ()```
		After opening a file with the open('file_path') method, you must close the file after use. This process is the same as you when open a text or word file on your computer, and after use, you close the file. You can close the file using the file_variable. close() method. In this example, close the open file using hosts. close().

Exercise 2-71: Create Code to Close a File in Two Ways

#	Exercise

①	```>>> hosts = open ('c://windows//system32//drivers//etc//hosts', 'r')```
	```>>> hosts_file_contents = hosts.read()```
	```>>> print('File closed? {}'.format(hosts.closed))```
	`File closed? False`
	`>>>`
	```>>> if not hosts.closed:```
	```... hosts.close()```
	`...`
	`>>>`
	```>>> print('File closed? {}'.format(hosts.closed))```
	`File closed? `**`True`**

(*continued*)

#	Exercise

Type in simple Python scripts to open the hosts file and then close it. Then check if the file has been properly closed. True means the file has closed correctly. Sometimes this file open option comes in handy.

②
```
>>> with open ('c://windows//system32//drivers//etc//hosts', 'r') as
hosts:
...     print('File closed? {}'.format (hosts.closed))
...     print(hosts.read())
...     print('Finished reading the file.')
...
File closed? False
# Copyright (c) 1993-2009 Microsoft Corp.
.

[... omitted for brevity]

.

# localhost name resolution is handled within DNS itself.
#     127.0.0.1     localhost
#     ::1     localhost

Finished reading the file.
>>>
>>> print('File closed? {}'. format (hosts.closed))
File closed? True
```

When you use the open() option, this removes the need to add a close() line. The with open statement opens the file and closes the file automatically with no close() statement. Try to open files using this option rather than the file.open() method.

③
```
try:
f = open('c://windows//system32//drivers//etc//hosts',
encoding = 'utf-8')
f_read = f.read()
print(f_read)
finally:
f.close()
```

(continued)

#	Exercise

If you insist on using the file open() method, open the file in a try-finally **block**, so if a file operation fails and suddenly closes, it closes the file correctly. Also, notice that the encoding has been specified as UTF-8. On Python 3.4+, this is already the default encoding method, but it is specified for demonstration purposes only in this example.

Exercise 2-72: Create a Text File, Read, Write, and Print

#	Exercise

①
```
>>> f = open('C://Python312//ch02//file1.txt', 'w+')
>>> for i in range(3):
...     f.write('This is line %d.\r' %(i + 1))
...
16
16
16
>>> f.close() # Always close file. Data gets written as the file
closes.

>>> f = open('C://Python312//ch02//file1.txt')
>>> f_read = f.read()
>>> print(f_read)
This is line 1. This is line 2. This is line 3.
 # white space

>>> print(f_read.strip())# Removes undesired whitespaces.
This is line 1. This is line 2. This is line 3.

>>> print(f_read, end='') # Removes undesired whitespaces.
This is line 1. This is line 2. This is line 3.

>>> f.close()# Always close file.
```

(continued)

#	Exercise

This is a basic example of opening (creating) a file in write mode (w+) and writing to the file. The file is closed after the information is written. Then the file is opened again in reading (r) mode, and the contents of the file is printed out on the screen. The file has to be closed after each use. Use strip() or end='' to remove any spaces created during file writing. You can remove the unwanted spaces if you want to.

②
```
>>> with open('C://Python312//ch02//file1.txt', 'w+') as f:
...    for i in range(3):
...      f.write('This is line %d.\n' %(i + 1))
...
16
16
16
>>> with open('C://Python312//ch02//file1.txt', 'r') as f:
...    for line in f:
...      print(line)
...
This is line 1.
□# white space
This is line 2.
□# white space
This is line 3.
□# white space
```

In this second example, you used the open with method to create and read the file, so there is no need to close the file. Also, while you created the file, you used \n (newline) rather than \r (return carriage), and when the content was read, you could see that the new lines had been added. Whitespace includes \t (tab), \n (newline), and \r (return carriage).

(*continued*)

#	Exercise

③
```
>>> with open('C://Python312//ch02//file1.txt', 'r') as f:
...     for line in f:
...     print(line, end=' ')
...
This is line 1. This is line 2. This is line 3.
```
Once again, you used end=' ' to remove the undesired whitespace.

④
```
>>> with open('C://Python312//ch02//file1.txt', 'r') as f:
...     for line in f:
...     print(line.strip())
...
This is line 1. This is line 2. This is line 3.
```
Similarly, use strip() to remove any whitespace.

⑤
```
>>> with open('C://Python312//ch02//file1.txt', 'r') as f:
...     skip_header = next(f) #Removes the header or the first line.
...     for line in f:
...         print(line.strip())
...
This is line 2. This is line 3.
```
skip_header = next(f) can remove the header or the first line of your file to print from the second line.

(*continued*)

#	Exercise

⑥
```
>>> with open('C://Python312//ch02//file1.txt', 'w+') as f:
...    for i in range(3):
...        f.write('This is line %d.\r\n' %(i + 1))
...
17
17
17
>>> with open('C://Python312//ch02//file1.txt', 'r') as f:
...    for line in f:
...        print(line)
...
This is line 1.
☐# white spaces
☐
☐
This is line 2.
☐# white spaces
☐
☐
This is line 3.
☐# white spaces
☐
☐
```

Be careful using \r and \n together, as the end product will behave differently depending on your operating system. If you are handling files in Linux or macOS, the use of \r and \n will differ.

Exercise 2-73: Use rstrip() or lstrip() to Remove Whitespace

#	Exercise

①
```
>>> with open('C://Python312//ch02//file1.txt', 'w+') as f:
...     for i in range(3):
...     f.write('□□□□This line contains white spaces %d.□□□□\n' %(i + 1))
...
42
42
42
>>> with open('C://Python312//ch02//file1.txt', 'r') as f:
...     for line in f:
...     print(line)
...
□□□□This line contains white spaces 1.□□□□ # white spaces
□ # white space
□□□□This line contains white spaces 2.□□□□
□
□□□□This line contains white spaces 3.□□□□
□
```

Create a file with four spaces on the left and four spaces on the right.

②
```
>>> with open('C://Python312//ch02//file1.txt', 'r') as f:
...     for line in f:
...     print(line.lstrip())
...
This line contains white spaces 1.□□□□
□
This line contains white spaces 2.□□□□
□
This line contains white spaces 3.□□□□
□
```

Use lstrip() to remove spaces on the left side.

(continued)

#	Exercise

③
```
>>> with open('C://Python312//ch02//file1.txt', 'r') as f:
...     for line in f:
...         print(line.rstrip())
...
☐☐☐☐This line contains white spaces 1.
☐☐☐☐This line contains white spaces 2.
☐☐☐☐This line contains white spaces 3.
```

Use rstrip() to remove space on the right side, including \n, the newline character.

④
```
>>> with open('C://Python312//ch02//file1.txt', 'r') as f:
...     for line in f:
...         print(line.strip())
...
```
This line contains white spaces 1. This line contains white spaces 2. This line contains white spaces 3.

Use strip() to remove all whitespace.

Exercise 2-74: Python File Mode Exercise in r Mode

When you open a file in reading (r) mode, the file pointer is placed at the beginning of the file, which is the default mode.

#	Exercise	Explanation

①	<pre>>>> with open('C://Python312//ch02//file2.
	txt', 'r') as f:
	... print('Created file2.txt')
	...
	Traceback (most recent call last):
	File "<stdin>", line 1, in <module>
	FileNotFoundError: [Errno 2] No such file or
	directory: 'C://Python312//ch02//file2.txt'</pre>
		You try to create a file in default reading mode, but Python does not allow file creation in only read (r) mode.

(continued)

#	Exercise	Explanation

②	```
	>>> import os
	>>> os.path.isfile('C://Python312//ch02//file2.txt')
	False
	``
		You import the os module and use the os.path.isfile() method to check if a file has been created, but as expected, no file has been created.

③	```
	>>> with open('C://Python312//ch02//file2.txt', 'w') as f:
	... print('Created file2.txt')
	...
	Created file2.txt
	``
		Now open and create file2.txt in write (w) mode.

④	```
	>>> import glob
	>>> print(glob.glob('C://Python312//ch02//*.txt'))
	['C://Python312//ch02\\file1.txt', 'C://Python312//ch02\\file2.txt']
	``
		You import the globe module to confirm that the file exists in your document folder.

⑤	```
	>>> import os
	>>> os.path.isfile('C://Python312//ch02//file2.txt')
	True
	``
		Using the os.path.isfile() method, you double-check that the file was created and exists in the folder (the directory in Linux).

⑥	```
	>>> with open('C://Python312//ch02//file2.txt') as f:
	... print(f.mode)
	...
	r
	``
		You use .mode to validate file mode. If file mode is not specified, the file opens in default reading only.

⑦	```
	>>> with open('C://Python312//ch02//file2.txt') as f:
	... f.write ('Writing to a file is fun.')
	...
	Traceback (most recent call last):
	File "<stdin>", line 2, in <module>
	io.UnsupportedOperation: not writable
	``
		You open file2.txt in reading mode and attempt to write to the file, but Python reminds you that you cannot write to the file in this case.

Exercise 2-75: Python File Mode Exercise in r+ Mode

Open a file for both reading and writing. The file pointer will be at the beginning of the file.

#	Exercise	Explanation

①	```>>> import os```
	```>>> os.remove('C://Python312//ch02//file2.txt')```
	```>>> os.path.isfile('C://Python312//ch02//file2.txt')```
	```False```
		Use the os.remove() method to remove an existing file, called file2.txt. This file was created in Exercise 2-74. You can also check if the file has been deleted successfully using the os.path.isfile() method.

②	```>>> with open('C://Python312//ch02//file2.txt', 'r+') as f:```
	```... f.write('* Test Line 1')```
	```... print('Trying to write the first line.')```
	```...```
	```Traceback (most recent call last):```
	```File "<stdin>", line 1, in <module>```
	```FileNotFoundError: [Errno 2] No such file or directory: 'C://Python312//ch02//file2.txt'```
		Try to open and create a file in r+ mode; just as in r mode, Python will return FileNotFoundError. You cannot create a new file using r+ mode.

③	```>>> with open('C://Python312//ch02//file2.txt', 'w+') as f:```
	```... f.write('* Test Line 1')```
	```... print('Just created file2.txt with line 1')```
	```...```
	```13```
	```Just created file2.txt with line 1```
		This time use w+ mode to recreate the file2.txt file and write the first line for testing. As in Exercise 2-74, w+ allows you to open and create a new file; you will find more on this in the following w and w+ exercises.

(continued)

#	Exercise	Explanation

④	```>>> with open('C://Python312//ch02//file2.txt', 'r+') as f:```
	```... print(f.mode)```
	```...```
	```r+ # Opens a file for both reading and writing.```
		Use the .mode method to check your file-handling mode.

⑤	```>>> with open('C://Python312//ch02//file2.txt', 'r+') as f:```
	```... f_read = f.read()```
	```... print(f_read)```
	```...```
	```* Test Line 1```
		Now reopen text2.txt in r+ mode and write to the file.

⑥	```>>> with open('C://Python312//ch02//file2.txt', 'r+') as f:```
	```... f.write('# This will overwrite Line 1')```
	```...```
	```28```
	```>>> with open('C://Python312//ch02//file2.txt', 'r+') as f:```
	```... f_read = f.read()```
	```... print(f_read)```
	```...```
	```# This will overwrite Line 1```
		When you read the file, you can see that the last action has overwritten the old information.

Exercise 2-76: Python file Mode Exercise in a Mode

Perform the following exercises to learn about 'a' or append mode. In 'a' (append) mode, the file pointer is at the end of the file if the file exists. Also, if the file does not exist, it creates a new file for writing.

#	Exercise	Explanation
| ① | ```python
>>> import os
>>> os.remove('C://Python312//ch02//file2.
txt')
>>> os.path.isfile('C://Python312//ch02//
file2.txt')
False
``` | Remove file2.txt and recreate a file with the same name in an (append) mode. As you may have already noticed, append mode will also allow you to create a new file if it does not exist. |
| ② | ```python
>>> with open('C://Python312//ch02//file2.
txt', 'a') as f:
...    f.write('This is line 1.')
...
15
``` | Open file2.txt in append mode to read the file. Python will tell you that in this mode, you cannot read the file. |
| ③ | ```python
>>> with open('C://Python312//ch02//file2.
txt', 'a') as f:
...    f_read = f.read()
...    print(f_read)
...
Traceback (most recent call last):
File "<stdin>", line 2, in <module>
io.UnsupportedOperation: not readable
``` | Open the file in reading mode and print out the contents on the screen. |
| ④ | ```python
>>> with open('C://Python312//ch02//file2.
txt', 'r') as f:
...    f_read = f.read()
...    print(f_read)
...
This is line 1.
``` | This time, open the file in append mode and add more information. |

(continued)

#	Exercise	Explanation
⑤	```>>> with open('C://Python312//ch02//file2.txt', 'a') as f:... f.write('This is line 2.')...15```	Open file2.txt in append mode and write This is line 2.
⑥	```>>> with open('C://Python312//ch02//file2.txt', 'r') as f:... f_read = f.read()... print(f_read)...This is line 1.This is line 2.```	Open file2.txt in append mode and add a new line. This time, add \r to add the line to the next line.
⑦	```>>> with open('C://Python312//ch02//file2.txt', 'a') as f:... f.write('\rThis is line 3.')...16```	Confirm the entry in reading mode.
⑧	```>>> with open('C://Python312//ch02//file2.txt', 'r') as f:... f_read = f.read()... print(f_read)...This is line 1.This is line 2. This is line 3.```	This time, use \n to add another line.
⑨	```>>> with open('C://Python312//ch02//file2.txt', 'a') as f:... f.write('\nThis is line 4.')...16```	When you use the strip() method, whitespace such as \r and \n is deleted.

(*continued*)

#	Exercise	Explanation
⑩	``` >> with open('C://Python312//ch02//file2.txt', 'r') as f: ... for line in f.readlines(): ... print(line.strip()) ... This is line 1.This is line 2. This is line 3. This is line 4. ```	When you use the read() method, Python reads the entire file and dumps out the information. Sometimes this is not the desired method, as you only want to read a line at a time. Use readline() to read one line at a time.

⑪	```
	>>> with open('C://Python312//ch02//file2.txt', 'r') as f:
	... f.readline()
	...
	'This is line 1.This is line 2.\n'
	``
		If you use the readlines() method, Python will read each line and return them as a string item list.

⑫	```
	>>> with open('C://Python312//ch02//file2.txt', 'r') as f:
	... f.readlines()
	...
	['This is line 1.This is line 2.\n', 'This is line 3.\n', 'This is line 4.']
	>>> with open('C://Python312//ch02//file2.txt', 'r') as f:
	... f.tell()
	...
	0
	>> with open('C://Python312//ch02//file2.txt', 'a') as f:
	... f.tell()
	...
	63
	``
		Python file method tell() returns the file's current position read/write pointer within the file. As you can observe, when a file is opened in r/r+ mode, the pointer starts from index 0. Whereas, if you open the file in a/a+ mode, the pointer will begin at the end of the index.

Exercise 2-77: Python File Mode Exercise in a+ Mode

Opens a file for both appending and reading exercises. The file pointer is at the end of the file if the file exists. The file opens in the append mode. If the file does not exist, it creates a new file for reading and writing.

#	Exercise	Explanation

①	```>>> import os```
	```>>> os.remove('C://Python312//ch02//file2.txt')``` # Removes old file2.txt
	```>>> with open('C://Python312//ch02//file2.txt', 'a+') as f:```
	```... print(f.mode)```
	```... f.write('This is line 1.\rThis is line 2.\rThis is line 3.\r')```
	```...```
	```a+```
	```48```
		Remove file2.txt once again, then open and re-create the file2.txt file in a+ mode with three lines.

②	```>>> with open('C://Python312//ch02//file2.txt', 'a+') as f:```
	```... f_read = f.read()```
	```... print(f_read, end='')```
	```...```
		Open the file in a+ mode, then read and print the file. But because the pointer is at the end of the file in a+ mode, no information is printed.

③	```>>> with open('C://Python312//ch02//file2.txt', 'r') as f:```
	```... f_read = f.read()```
	```... print(f_read, end='')```
	```...```
	```This is line 1. This is line 2. This is line3.```
		When you open the file in the default r mode again, the pointer starts at the beginning of the file and prints out the contents on the screen. Although a+ supports file-reading mode, because of its pointer location when the file is opened, there is no fair use case to open a file in this mode over the normal a mode.

Exercise 2-78: Python File Mode Exercise in w Mode

Open a file for writing only. Overwrites the file if the file exists. If the file does not exist, creates a new file for writing.

#	Exercise	Explanation

①	```>>> with open('C://Python312//ch02//file2.txt', 'w') as f:```
	```... f.tell()```
	```... print(f.mode)```
	```... f.write('This is line 1.')```
	```...```
	```0```
	```w```
	```15```
		No need to remove the old file. Opening a file in w mode will overwrite the old file and create a new file. If there is no file with the same name, Python will create a new file.

②	```>>> with open('C://Python312//ch02//file2.txt', 'r') as f:```
	```... f_read = f.read()```
	```... print(f_read)```
	```...```
	```This is line 1.```
		You open file2.txt in read mode and print the contents in r mode.

③	```>>> with open('C://Python312//ch02//file2.txt', 'w') as f:```
	```... f_read = f.read()```
	```... print(f_read)```
	```...```
	```Traceback (most recent call last): File "<stdin>", line 2, in <module>```
	```io.UnsupportedOperation: not readable```
		If you try to read the contents in w mode, you will encounter an IO-related error, as shown in this example.

Exercise 2-79: Python File Mode Exercise in w+ Mode

Open a file for both writing and reading. This overwrites the existing file if the file exists. If the file does not exist, it creates a new file for reading and writing.

#	Exercise	Explanation
①	```>>> with open('C://Python312//ch02//file2.txt', 'w+') as f:... f.tell()... f.write('This is line 1.')... f.tell()... print(f.read())...0151515```	When you open a file in w+ mode, the pointer begins at index 0 after writing to the file. It moves to the end of the contents. When you try to print information while the pointer is at the end of the line, Python will return a blank.
②	```>>> with open('C://Python312//ch02//file2.txt', 'w+') as f:... print(f.mode)... f.write('This is line 1.')... f.seek(0)... print(f.read())...w+150This is line 1.```	To write in w+ mode and read and print out the file contents, you have to move the pointer to position zero using the seek(0) method. In this example, you reset the pointer position to 0, or the beginning of the file, and Python prints the lines correctly.

171

Exercise 2-80: Python File Mode Exercise in x Mode

x is like w. But for x, if the file exists, it raises FileExistsError.

#	Exercise	Explanation

①	```>>> with open('C://Python312//ch02//file2.txt', 'x') as f:```
	```... print(f.mode)```
	```...```
	```Traceback (most recent call last):```
	```File "<stdin>", line 1, in <module>```
	```FileExistsError: [Errno 17] File exists:```
	```'C://Python312//ch02//file2.txt'```
		file2.txt already exists from the previous exercise. When you try to open file2.txt in x mode, it it will raise FileExistsError. This new file-handling mode can come in handy if you do not want to overwrite the existing file mistakenly using w/w+ mode.

②	```>>> with open('C://Python312//ch02//file4.txt', 'x') as f:```
	```... print(f.mode)```
	```...```
	```X```
		Create a new file in x mode. Python is happy with this operation.

Exercise 2-81: Python File Mode Exercise in x+ Mode

x is writeable only. x+ can write and read.

#	Exercise	Explanation

①	```>>> with open('C://Python312//ch02//file5.txt', 'x+') as f:```
	```... print(f.mode)```
	```...```
	```x+```
		This is the write and read version of the x mode. Almost identical to w+ mode, but it will not overwrite the existing file. It will require exclusivity to create a new file. Look at Table 2-6 for all file modes. You do not have to memorize all these modes now; you will get familiar with each mode as you write more Python code.

Table 2-6. *File Processing Modes*

Mode	Descriptions
r	Opens a file for reading only. This mode places the file pointer at the beginning of the file. This is the default mode.
rb	Opens a file for reading only in binary format. This mode places the file pointer at the beginning of the file.
r+	Opens a file for both reading and writing. The file pointer will be at the beginning of the file.
rb+	Opens a file for both reading and writing in binary format. The file pointer will be at the beginning of the file.
a	Opens a file for appending. The file pointer is at the end of the file if the file exists. The file is in append mode. If the file does not exist, it creates a new file for writing.
ab	Opens a file for appending in binary format. The file pointer is at the end of the file if the file exists. The file is in append mode. If the file does not exist, it creates a new file for writing.
a+	Opens a file for both appending and reading. The file pointer is at the end of the file if the file exists. The file opens in append mode. If the file does not exist, it creates a new file for reading and writing.
ab+	Opens a file for both appending and reading in binary format. The file pointer is at the end of the file if the file exists. The file opens in append mode. If the file does not exist, it creates a new file for reading and writing.
w	Opens a file for writing only. Overwrites the file if the file exists. If the file does not exist, it creates a new file for writing.
wb	Opens a file for writing only in binary format. Overwrites the file if the file exists. If the file does not exist, it creates a new file for writing.
w+	Opens a file for both writing and reading. Overwrites the existing file if the file exists. If the file does not exist, it creates a new file for reading and writing.
wb+	Opens a file for both writing and reading in binary format. Overwrites the existing file if the file exists. If the file does not exist, it creates a new file for reading and writing.
x	x mode is like w mode. But for x, if the file exists, it raises `FileExistsError`.
x+	x is only writable. x+ can write and read.

Exercise 2-82: Open a Byte File in Python

#	Exercise

①
```
>>> with open('C://Python212//ch02 //ex82_horse.jpg', 'rb') as horse_
pic:
...     horse_pic.seek(2)
...     horse_pic.seek(4)
...     print(horse_pic.tell())
...     print(horse_pic.mode)
...
2
4
4
Rb
```

Python can also open and read byte files such as images and other files. This example shows you how to open and use the seek method to read byte files. When you open in byte mode, you add b behind the normal r/r+, a/a+, and w/w+ modes.

Tip

Downloading the horse image

You can download the ex82_horse.jpg file from the pynetauto GitHub site as part of Chapter 2 code. This JPEG file is included in the chapter2_codes.zip file. This is my photo, so there are no copyright issues.

URL: https://github.com/pynetauto/apress_pynetauto_ed2.0/tree/main/source_codes

Exercise 2-83: Handle Errors with try and except

Optionally, you can download the source code files, ex2_83_countries.py and ex2_83_countries.txt, and then run the code from Notepad++.

#	Exercise

①
```
>>> try:
...     countries = open('C://Python312//ch02//ex2_83_countries.txt', 'r')
... except FileNotFoundError as e:
...     print(str(e))
... else:
...     nations = countries.read()
...     print(nations)
...     countries.close()
...
[Errno 2] No such file or directory: 'C://Python312//ch02//ex2_83_
countries.txt'
```

You can use try and except, try, except and else or try and finally to handle errors that occur during file handling. This first exercise shows you an example of an error where there was no file in the directory. Download and drop the ex83_countries.txt file in your documents folder and perform the next task.

②
```
>>> try:
...     countries = open('C://Python312//ch02//ex2_83_countries.txt',
'r')
... except FileNotFoundError as e:
...     print(str(e))
... else:
...     nations = countries.read()
...     print(nations)
...     countries.close()
...
```
United States England Germany France
Japan Italy Spain Australia

If you have the correct file in the directory, the Python code will reach the else statement and print out the names of the countries in the file. Try and except error handling becomes very handy while working with errors, especially while working with files.

Recap: The Python File-Handling Concept

- Use the open() built-in function to open a file. The general syntax is:

  open(file_location, mode)

- If the file mode is not specified, the file opens in default r (read) mode.

- If in read() file mode, the entire contents of the file is read.

- When a file is opened with the open() function, the best practice is to close the file with the close() function.

- If you open a file using open ~, you do not have to use the close() function to close the opened file.

- The for loop reads the file contents line by line.

- Whitespace created during the handling of a file can be deleted using the strip(), rstrip(), lsetrip(), and end=' methods.

- You can write data to a file using the write() function.

- The file opens in text mode unless specified to be opened in byte mode using b mode. Computers prefer to handle data in binary format.

- English alphabets or numbers are recognized as 1 byte in size, but some characters in UTF-8 format, such as Korean, Chinese, and Japanese, can be larger than 1 byte in size.

- Try and except error handling can help you write more robust Python scripts.

Using Python Modules

The two words—modules and packages—could be used interchangeably in Python, but how are they different? They are closely related and novel Python learners often get confused. They both serve the same purpose in organizing code, but there are some subtle differences between the two, as they each provide slightly different ways

of organizing code. Usually, **a module is a single** .py **Python file with some function.**
A package is a directory that contains multiple Python modules. So, **a package is
a collection of modules.** A module can be considered a self-contained package, and
a package is a collection of various modules that are separated across multiple files.
Usually, you start with a module, and as requirements grow, you turn the multiple
modules into a package to serve some purpose in your work.

As you work more with Python, you will use many built-in modules and packages, as
well as adopt and use someone else's modules and packages, or create custom modules
and packages to use them in your Python applications. Let's learn some basics about
using modules.

Time Module

Exercise 2-84: Import a Time Module

#	Exercise	Explanation

①	>>> **import time**
	>>> **print(time.asctime())**
	Sun Apr 12 00:48:07 2020
		Import the time module and print the time from your computer.

②	>> **print(time.timezone)** -36000	Find your time zone using the time.timezone method. -36000 is the time zone value for Sydney, Australia.

③	>>> **from time import asctime**
	>>> **print(asctime())**
	Sun Apr 12 00:49:44 2020
		Use from ~ import ~ to import only the required functions from the time module. You can import multiple functions on the same line.
		For example, from time import gmtime, strftime.

Sleep Method

Exercise 2-85: The time.sleep() Function

#	Exercise	Explanation

①	`#Ex2_85.py (optional)`
	`>>> from time import asctime, sleep`
	`>>> print(asctime())`
	`Sun Apr 12 01:00:01 2020`
	`>>> sleep(10)`
	`>>> print(asctime())`
	`Sun Apr 12 01:00:11 2020`
	`# Output:`
	`Sun Apr 12 01:02:05 2020`
	`Sun Apr 12 01:02:15 2020`
		`time.sleep()` is used to put your script into sleep for a designated period. Whenever you can, **avoid using** `import` * **(import all) when importing modules**; only import the explicit function you are going to use. The * wildcard loads all modules and functions, so it will slow down your code loading all the modules.

For example, try to avoid using:

```
from time import * # Avoid *, as * is too greedy
```

Preferred:

```
from time import asctime, sleep # importing two modules here
```

If you don't remember the name of the function from the module, you can import the module first and use `dir(module_name)` to find the name of all the methods you can choose from.

```
>>> import time
>>> dir(time)
['CLOCK_MONOTONIC', 'CLOCK_MONOTONIC_RAW', 'CLOCK_PROCESS_CPUTIME_ID',
'CLOCK_REALTIME',
'CLOCK_THREAD_CPUTIME_ID', '_STRUCT_TM_ITEMS', ' doc ', ' loader ',
' name ', ' ' asctime ',' clock ',' clock_getres', 'clock_gettime',
'clock_settime', 'ctime', 'daylight', 'get_clock_info', 'gmtime',
'localtime', 'mktime', 'monotonic', 'perf_counter' , 'process_time',
'sleep', 'strftime', 'strptime', 'struct_time', 'time', 'timezone',
'tzname', 'tzset']
```

Exercise 2-86: Browse a Path Using the sys Module

#	Exercise

①	**# For Windows**
	```>>> import sys```
	```>>> sys.path```
	```['', 'C:\\Python39\\python39.zip', 'C:\\Python39\\DLLs', 'C:\\Python39\\lib', 'C:\\Python39', 'C:\\Python39\\lib\\site-packages']```
	
	# For Linux
	```>>> import sys```
	```>>> sys.path```
	```['', '/usr/lib/python36.zip', '/usr/lib/python3.6', '/usr/lib/python3.6/lib-dynload', '/ usr/local/lib/python3.6/dist-packages', '/ usr/lib/python3/dist-packages']```
	
	First, import the target module and then use `sys.path` to find the Python files on your system.

②	**# For Windows**
	```>>> import sys```
	```>>> for path in sys.path:```
	```... print(path)```
	```...```
	```C:\Python39\python39.zip```
	```C:\Python39\DLLs```
	```C:\Python39\lib```
	```C:\Python39```
	```C:\Python39\lib\site-packages```
	
	# For Linux
	```>>> import sys```
	```>>> for path in sys.path:```
	```... print(path)```
	```...```
	```/usr/lib/python36.zip```
	```/usr/lib/python3.6```
	```/usr/lib/python3.6/lib-dynload```
	```/usr/local/lib/python3.6/dist-packages```
	```/usr/lib/python3/dist-packages```
	
	To prettify the output, use the `for` loop method to produce a line-by-line of the system directory path. In this example, you can compare where PYTHONPATH and related packages are installed in Windows vs. Linux. PYTHONPATH is an environment variable that adds directories where Python will look for modules and packages.

Exercise 2-87: Add a New FILEPATH Using the sys Module

#	Exercise
①	

```
# For Windows
>>> import sys
>>> sys.path.append('C:\Python39\
my-packages')
>>> for path in sys.path:
...    print(path)
...
C:\Python39\python39.zip
C:\Python39\DLLs
C:\Python39\lib
C:\Python39
C:\Python39\lib\site-packages
C:\Python38Python39\my-
packages # Newly added FILEPATH
```

```
# For Linux
>>> import sys
>>> sys.path.append('/Users/root/
my-packages')
>>> for path in sys.path:
...     print(path)
...
/usr/lib/python36.zip
/usr/lib/python3.6
/usr/lib/python3.6/lib-dynload
/usr/local/lib/python3.6/dist-
packages
/usr/lib/python3/dist-packages
/Users/root/my-packages # Newly
added FILEPATH
```

If you want to create and add new modules/packages to a FILEPATH, Python will also look at the customized modules/packages under the new directory. You can add the new FILEPATH using the sys module.

Exercise 2-88: Check Builtins and the sys.builin_module

#	Exercise
| ① | ```
>>> dir(__builtins__)
['ArithmeticError', 'AssertionError', 'AttributeError',
[... omitted for brevity]
'staticmethod', 'str', 'sum', 'super', 'tuple', 'type', 'vars', 'zip']
>>> import sys
>>> for name in sys.builtin_module_names:
...     print (name, end=' ')
...
_abc _ast _bisect _blake2 _codecs _codecs_cn _codecs_hk
[... omitted for brevity]
``` |

In the Python Interpreted session, you can use the `dir()` function to view built-in modules. You can also use the `for` loop method to view what's inside built-in modules. There are other ways to view this information, and this is just a way to check builtins and modules.

Exercise 2-89: Create a Simple Import sys Module

#	Exercise	Explanation
| ① | ```
# ex2_89.py
import sys
file = 'C://Python312//ch02//test.txt'
try:
with open (file) as test_file:
for line in test_file:
print(line.strip())
except:
print('Could not open {}'. format(file))
sys.exit(1)
``` | |

First, create a script called ex2_89.py and copy the code. This example script was created and saved under the C://Python312//ch02 folder.

(*continued*)

#	Exercise	Explanation

② `C:\Python312\ch02>` **`python C://Python312//ch02//ex2_89.py`**
`Could not open C://Python312//ch02//test.txt` # *output*

From the Windows command line prompt or Windows PowerShell, run the `ex2_89.py` script. Optionally, if you set up Notepad++ for Python, run the code. Because there is no `text.txt` file in the designated folder, Python will trigger the customized exception error. The script had an `import sys` module statement, and it triggered an exit action after printing the exception error.

③ `>>>` **`with open('C://Python312//ch02//test.txt', 'w') as f:`**
`...`   **`f.write('This is a test file only.')`**
`...`   **`f.write('Study Python, Network, Linux and Automation all from a single book.')`**
`...`
`26`
`67`

Now create a `test.txt` file and add a couple of lines.

④ `>>>` **`with open('C://Python312//ch02//test.txt', 'r') as f:`**
`...`   **`print(f.read())`**
`...`
`This is a test file only.` # *output*
`Study Python, Network, Linux, and Automation all from a single book.` # *output*

To check the contents, open and read the file, and then print the lines.

⑤ `C:\Python312\ch02>` **`python C://Python212//ch02//ex2_89.py`**
`This is a test file only.` # *output*
`Study Python, Network, Linux, and Automation all from a single book.` # *output*

Now run the Python script (`ex2_89.py`) to print the contents. This was a small exercise, but I hope you are taking away something from it. If you didn't, go back and review what you learned here.

Exercise 2-90: Understand Lambda by Making a Calculator

#	Exercise	Explanation

①	```>>> def sum(x, y):```
	```... return x +y```
	```...```
	```>>> sum(3, 2)```
	```5```
		This is a simple function that adds and returns the sum of x and y.

②	```>>> sum = lambda x, y: x + y```
	```>>> sum(3, 2)```
	```5```
		You can use lambda on a single line of code to achieve the same result. This is the re-creation of the function in Example ① but with fewer lines.

③	```>>> lamb_cal = [lambda x,y:x+y, lambda x,y:x-y, lambda x,y:x*y, lambda x,y:x/y]```
	```>>> lamb_cal[0]```
	```<function <lambda> at 0x000001BF34AFC3A0>```
	```>>> lamb_cal[0](3, 2)```
	```5```
	```>>> lamb_cal[1]```
	```<function <lambda> at 0x000001BF34AFC670>```
	```>>> lamb_cal[1](3, 2)```
	```1```
	```>>> lamb_cal[2]```
	```<function <lambda> at 0x000001BF34AFC700>```
	```>>> lamb_cal[2](3, 2)```
	```6```
	```>>> lamb_cal[3]```
	```<function <lambda> at 0x000001BF34AFC790>```
	```>>> lamb_cal[3](3, 2)```
	```1.5```
		You have just created a simple calculator on a single line using lambda. The calculator is self-explanatory; lamb_cal can perform basic arithmetic. As you become more familiar with Python coding, there are certain situations in which you can apply lambda. You do not have to use lambda, but you can see the real value of it in this exercise.

(*continued*)

Recap: Module Concept

- Modules use a set of variables, functions, and classes in the .py file format.

- You can import a module by issuing `import module_name`.

- The default location of a module is set during Python installation.

- The Python built-in library is a set of reusable Python programs that contain a variety of code.

- The `dir()` built-in function allows you to view the modules in a package.

- If you do not have the required module, you can create one, add `FILEPATH`, and add your packages.

I hope you have been busy on your keyboard throughout this chapter and got some real hands-on practice. An interpreted programming language such as Python was designed to mimic the human language. Many years ago, I studied the pragmatics of language as part of my master's course at Macquarie University, Sydney. According to the Cambridge dictionary, "pragmatics" is defined as "the study of how language is affected by the situation in which it is used, of how language is used to get things or perform actions, and of how words can express things that are different from what they appear to mean." As you become more comfortable with Python as a programming language or a tool, you must continue to learn to communicate with computers (machines), become comfortable giving a set of instructions to computers, and learn to interpret Python's feedback and errors. This chapter covered the most basic Python concepts through practical examples and exercises. The best way to learn a programming language is through more exercises that are relatable to real scenarios. Now that you have learned the basics, you get some more practice in linking the concepts to the real scenarios in Chapter 3. The next chapter contains general Python exercises as well as work-related exercises.

Summary

As I draw the curtains in this chapter, you can see how Windows, being one of the most popular desktop operating systems, has become a welcoming gateway for countless Python learners. The hands-on exercises presented here have allowed readers to seamlessly merge Python syntax with fundamental programming concepts, providing them with sturdy groundwork. From the simple yet iconic "Hello World!" program to mastering basic Python syntax, readers have acquired the essential skills necessary to craft basic scripts. As you embark on the next chapters, which will prepare you to jump into the exciting realm of Python Network Automation scripting labs in the latter half of the book, it will become evident that **completing all exercises is of utmost importance, ensuring a swift and confident journey to mastery**. So, march forward with renewed enthusiasm, for there are fascinating challenges ahead awaiting the Python pioneers. Happy coding!

CHAPTER 3

More Python Exercises

In ancient times, the Romans borrowed a valuable concept from the Athenians and transformed it into a timeless proverb: "Repetito master sturdiorum," which can be translated to "Repetition is the mother of all learning." Building upon the basics learned in the previous chapter, this chapter dives into Python exercises that offer practical scenarios to enhance your skills. These exercises are directly related to real-life applications, preparing you for the scripts you'll create later. Engage your mind as you let your fingers type out the code. Consider how each exercise contributes to automating and streamlining your work. Throughout the chapter, you'll strengthen your Python proficiency, visualizing how coding can optimize productivity. Embrace the power of repetition and relatable exercises to become a skilled Python programmer. By the chapter's end, you'll be able to tackle the challenges in the Part 2 of this book confidently.

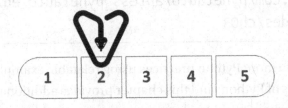

Getting Ready for the Exercises

This book assumes that you are new to network automation using Python. When comparing the day-to-day tasks of typical IT analysts, systems engineers, and network engineers, it becomes evident that they do not have to type as much as DevOps engineers. The nature of the DevOps engineer's job requires constant learning and adopting new ideas, writing code, and creating applications. On the other hand, most non-DevOps IT staff reading this book spend their time planning, implementing, installing, configuring, and troubleshooting various issues in their IT specialties.

© Brendan Choi 2024
B. Choi, *Introduction to Python Network Automation Volume I - Laying the Groundwork*,
https://doi.org/10.1007/979-8-8688-0146-4_3

Finding time during work hours to practice coding and developing automation applications can be challenging, as it is not their primary focus, and they are not paid to do so. Despite these challenges, most enterprise IT teams encourage their engineers to learn a programming language and automate repetitive tasks. Many dedicated IT engineers have used their time outside of work to learn and develop coding skills. However, it is crucial to recognize the inherent disparity between the starting points of the book's audience and professional programmers who began coding in their teens. Catching up may require investing many years and countless hours in front of the computer. Unfortunately, some may find it discouraging and give up, never reaching their intended goals. **Not everyone will grasp programmability concepts or learn Python basics on their first or second attempt. The key is to be consistent and keep trying until you succeed.** Overcoming these challenges is possible through more exercises. Whenever you encounter specific Python challenges, get into the habit of searching for relevant topics on Google, YouTube, ChatGPT, and reading reputable books.

Tip

All Chapter 3's code and files are available from the author's GitHub page.

```
https://github.com/pynetauto/apress_pynetauto_ed2.0/tree/
main/source_codes/ch03
```

Now, let's dive into more Python practices using relatable examples. In Chapter 2, you learned the basics of Python, and this chapter provides additional practice to prepare you for network automation. Remember, the more you practice, the better you will become.

Exercise 3-1: Concatenate a List and a Tuple Into a Single List

#	Exercise	Explanation

①	```>>> fruits = ['apple', 'orange', 'mango']```
	```>>> vegetables = ('broccoli', 'potato', 'spinach')```
	```>>> favorites = fruits + list(vegetables)```
	```>>> print(favorites)```
	```['apple', 'orange', 'mango', 'broccoli', 'potato', 'spinach']```
		Create a variable in the list and another variable in a tuple. Use the list() method to convert the tuple into a list. Finally, concatenate and merge the list and tuple into a single list.

Exercise 3-2: Use Python as a Calculator

#	Exercise

①	```>>> eigrp, ospf, rip = 90, 110, 120 # Real routing protocol distances used```
	```>>> path1, path2, path3 = 3, 6, 9```
	```>>> admin_distance = (eigrp * path1) + (ospf * path2) + (rip * path3)```
	```>>> print(admin_distance)```
	```2010```
	Use Python as a calculator to compute the administrative distance.

Exercise 3-3: Do Some Basic String format() Exercises

#	Exercise

①	```>>> name = 'Hugh'```
	```>>> age = 18```
	```>>> detail = 'His name is %s and he is %d.'```
	```>>> print(detail %(name, age))```
	His name is Hugh and he is 18.
	
	This is a basic string (%s) and digit (%d) formatting example.

②	```>>> Name, age, height = 'Hugh', 18, 174.5```
	```>>> detail = ('His name is {}, he is {} and {} cm tall.'.format(name, age, height))``` #1
	```>>> print(detail)``` #2
	His name is Hugh, he is 18 and 174.5 cm tall. #3
	```>>> detail = ('His name is {0}, he is {1} and {2} cm tall.'.format(name, age, height))``` #4
	```>>> print(detail)```
	His name is Hugh, he is 18 and 174.5 cm tall.
	```>>> detail = ('His name is {name}, he is {age} and {height} cm tall.'.format(name='Joshua', age=20, height=178))```
	```>>> print(detail)```
	His name is Joshua, he is 20 and 178 cm tall.
	```>>> detail = ('His name is {0}, he is {age} and {height} cm tall.'.format('Michael', age=14, height=170))```
	```>>> print(detail)```
	His name is Michael, he is 14 and 170 cm tall.

#1. format() example: Default arguments
#2. format() example: Positional arguments
#3. format() example: Keyword arguments
#4. format() example: Mixed arguments

(continued)

#	Exercise
③	```python
>>> person = {'height':174.5, 'name':'Hugh', 'age':18}
>>> print('{name} is {age} years old and {height} cm tall.'.format(**person))
Hugh is 18 years old and 174.5 cm tall.
```
This is a `str.format(**mapping)` example. This is an example of the argument parsing used in Python, so make a special note of the two asterisks used in the example. |

## Exercise 3-4: Ask for a Username

To prepare for Exercise 3-4, ensure you've installed the most recent version of Microsoft Visual Studio Code (VSC) on your computer. Additionally, download and install a Python plugin for your VSC, as demonstrated in the following TIP.

---

**Tip**

**Installing Microsoft Visual Studio Code and the Python Plugin**

Step 1. Download the Windows version of Visual Studio Code

`https://code.visualstudio.com/download`

Step 2. Install VSCodeUserSetup-x64-1.81.0.exe or later on your computer. Your software version may be different.

Step 3. Install the Python extension for Visual Studio Code, as shown in Figure 3-1.

*Figure 3-1. Find and install the Python plugin*

---
```

Create a new working folder, called "ch03" under C:\Python312\. You will be working under the C:\Python312\ch03 folder in this chapter for any exercises with the file creations.

Open the C:\Python312\ch03 folder and create a new Python code named ex3_4.py with the following content in exercise ①.

#	Exercise	Explanation
①	```# ex3_4.py
print('Please enter your name: ')
name = input()
print('Thank you, ', name)```	Create some Python code that will ask for the user's name. You are going to use this as the basis of the username and password tool development. You will have some fun while asking for someone's name.
②	As shown in Figure 3-2, click the Run icon in the top corner. Then type in your name and press the Enter key. Enter a name to get a thank you.	

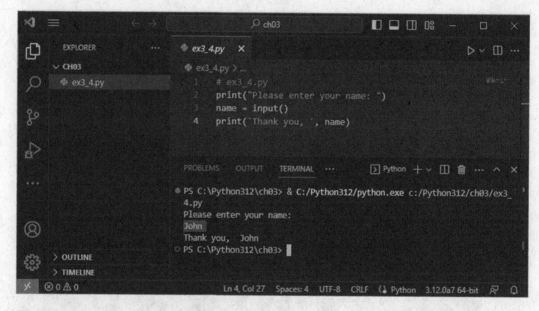

Figure 3-2. *User input, thanking the user*

Exercise 3-5: Get a Username: Version 1

Write the code, save it as ex3_5.py, and run the code in Notepad++ (see Figure 3-3).

#	Exercise
| ① | ```python
name = input('Please enter your name: ')
print(f'Hi, {name}.')
```<br><br>Reiterate ex3_4.py and write simplified code in ex3_5.py. The number of code lines has shrunk. In this exercise, you are learning how to reduce two code lines into a single line of code and use an abbreviated formatting method, the f-string method. |
| ② | Run the modified script on Visual Studio Code. |

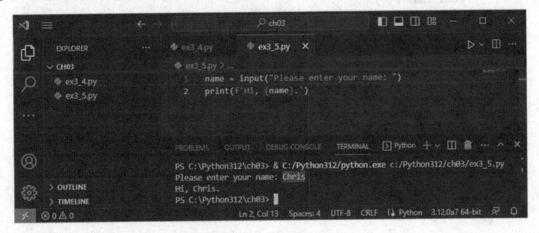

Figure 3-3. *Refactoring Python code*
```

Exercise 3-6: Get a Username: Version 2

#	Exercise	Explanation
| ① | ```python
import re

name = input("Enter your name: ")
while True:
  while not re.match("^[a-zA-Z]+$", name):
    name = input("Enter your name: ")
  else:
    print(name)
exit()
``` | Using ex3_5.py as the basis, create a simple Python application asking for someone's name with some requirements. Name this file ex3_6.py for convenience. You have imported the re (Regular Expression) built-in Python module to force the user to provide a name starting with an alphabetical letter that accepts letters only.

^[a-zA-Z]+$ means any character starting with a letter with one or more characters and ending with a letter. So, you cannot enter a number or a special character as a name. If the user does not adhere to this rule, the script asks until the user provides an expected response. Once the correct response is received, the name is printed and the user exits the application.

You learn more about Regular Expressions in Chapter 9. An entire chapter is dedicated to learning Regular Expressions and how to use the re module. Scripting is all about data handling and processing. You must master Regular Expressions and conquer your fear of Regular Expressions to become confident programming engineers. |

(continued)
```

#	Exercise	Explanation
②	Run and test the improved Python code, as shown in Figure 3-4 . You must enter the correct data type and format to print the name.	

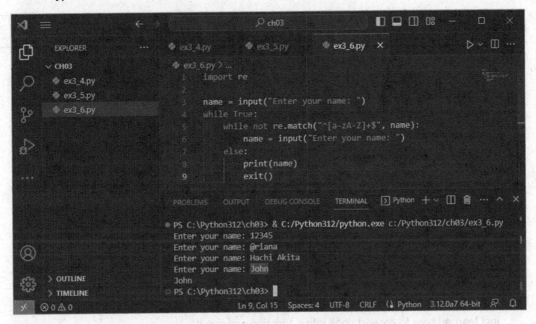

Figure 3-4. User input, getting correctly formatted input

Exercise 3-7: Get a Username: Version 3

Enter the code and save the file as ex3_7.py on Visual Studio Code. Run the code as shown in Figure 3-5.

#	Exercise	Explanation
| ① | ```python
import re

def get_name():
  name = input("Enter your name: ")
  while True:
    while not re.match("^[a-zA-Z]+$", name):
    name = input("Enter your name: ")
    else:
      print(name)
      exit()

get_name()
``` | Create the ex3_7.py script and run it to learn how you can create a function based on ex3_6.py and convert it into a function. The last statement, get_name(), will trigger the script to run. This is the same script as ex3_6.py, but I have converted it into a function so you can understand the reiteration process. |
| ② | Run the script once you have completed writing the code, as shown in Figure 3-5. You have just learned how to convert code into a function and run it. | |

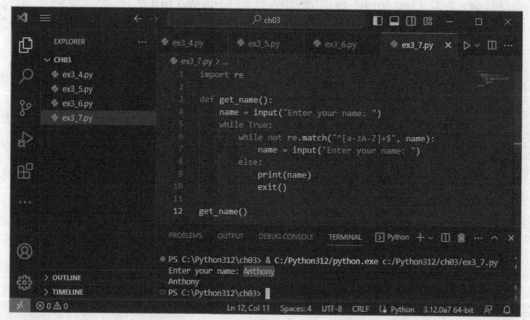

Figure 3-5. *User input, getting the username script into a function*
```

Exercise 3-8: Import and Use a Custom Module

Open your Windows command-line prompt and navigate to the folder containing the
ex3_7.py file. In my case it's called C:\Python312\ch03>. Use the cd C:\Python312\
ch03> command. Run "python" and import ex3_7.py as a module, it will prompt you for
your name.

#	Exercise
| ① | ```
C:\Users\brend>cd C:\Python312\ch03
C:\Python312\ch03>python
Python 3.12.0a7 (tags/v3.12.0a7:b861ba4, Apr  4 2023, 16:33:41) [MSC
v.1934 64 bit (AMD64)] on win32
Type "help", "copyright", "credits" or "license" for more information.
>>> import ex3_7.py
Enter your name: Tim
Tim
``` |

If you selected Add Python 3.12.0a7 to PATH during the Python installation, you should be able
to call the Python script as a module and run it from anywhere on your Windows operating
system. You have just learned how to import Python as a module in your Python Interpreter.

Exercise 3-9: Use Commas to Add Spaces Between Strings and Speed Test the Methods

#	Exercise
| ① | ```
>>> print('Around' + 'the' + 'World' + 'in' + '100' + 'days.')
AoundtheWorldin100days. # By default, no spaces are added when '+' is
used
>>> print('Around ' + 'the ' + 'World ' + 'in ' + '100 ' + 'days.') #
manually enter spaces between words
Around the World in 100 days.
>>> print('Around', 'the', 'World', 'in', '100', 'days.')
Around the World in 100 days. # adds spaces automatically
``` |

(continued)

#	Exercise
	Practice the previous exercises and compare the output. Notice that commas are used in the previous exercise, and the output adds spaces between the strings.

②
```
# Method 1: String Concatenation
>>> print('Around ' + 'the ' + 'World ' + 'in ' + '100 ' + 'days.')
Around the World in 100 days.

# Method 2: String Formatting
>>> Print('{} {} {} {} {} {}'.format('Around', 'the', 'World', 'in',
'100', 'days.'))
Around the World in 100 days.

# Method 3: String Join
>>> print(' '.join(['Around', 'the', 'World', 'in', '100', 'days.']))
Around the World in 100 days.

# Method 4: f-Strings
>>> print(f"{'Around'} {'the'} {'World'} {'in'} {'100'} {'days.'}")
Around the World in 100 days.

# Method 5: String Literal with Spaces
>>> print('Around the World in 100 days.')
Around the World in 100 days.
```

These methods achieve the same output, but they use different approaches to concatenate/
format strings with spaces in Python 3.

(continued)

#	Exercise

③ Are you curious about the execution times of each method? Create a new Python file and name it ex3_9_speed_test.py. Using the timeit built-in module, this code will compare the execution times of the various methods used in the previous task. Tip: The following code is available from the Author's GitHub page. Download the file and use it to save time.

```python
import timeit

# Method 1: String Concatenation
method1_time = timeit.timeit("'Around ' + 'the ' + 'World ' + 'in ' +
'100 ' + 'days.'", number=1000000)

# Method 2: String Formatting
method2_time = timeit.timeit("('{} {} {} {} {} {}'.format('Around',
'the', 'World', 'in', '100', 'days.'))", number=1000000)

# Method 3: String Join
method3_time = timeit.timeit("' '.join(['Around', 'the', 'World',
'in', '100', 'days.'])", number=1000000)

# Method 4: f-Strings
method4_time = timeit.timeit("'Around' + ' the' + ' World' + ' in' +
' 100' + ' days.'", number=1000000)

# Method 5: String Literal with Spaces
method5_time = timeit.timeit("'Around the World in 100 days.'",
number=1000000)

# Print the execution times in microseconds
print("Method 1 Time:", method1_time * 1e6, "microseconds")
print("Method 2 Time:", method2_time * 1e6, "microseconds")
print("Method 3 Time:", method3_time * 1e6, "microseconds")
print("Method 4 Time:", method4_time * 1e6, "microseconds")
print("Method 5 Time:", method5_time * 1e6, "microseconds")
```

(continued)

#	Exercise
	Run the speed test application on your computer, and the output should resemble the following example. While there's no definitive right or wrong way to write your code, certain methods in Python might perform faster or slower than others.

```
C:\Python312\ch03>python ex3_9_speed_test.py
Method 1 Time: 59652.2000269033 microseconds
Method 2 Time: 711086.3999696448 microseconds # over-convoluted,
hence the slowest
Method 3 Time: 200708.79999548197 microseconds
Method 4 Time: 26748.99995326996 microseconds
Method 5 Time: 15409.399988129735 microseconds # simplest, hence the
fastest
```

Exercise 3-10: Practice if; if and else; and if, elif, and else

#	Exercise	Explanation

①	```>>> x = 3```
	```>>> y = 5```
	```>>> if x > y:```
	```... print('x is greater than y.')```
	```...```
	```>>> # No output as if the statement was False```
		You have just practiced if; if and else; and if, elif, and else. These exercises are self-explanatory; Python does not require a lot of explanation and the barrier to entry is lower than other programming languages.

②	```>>> x = 3```
	```>>> y = 5```
	```>>> if x < y:```
	```... print('x is less than y.')```
	```...```
	```x is less than y. # prints output as if the statement was True```	

(continued)

#	Exercise	Explanation
| ③ | ```python
>>> x = 3
>>> y = 5
>>> if x >= y:
...   print('x is greater or equal to y.')
... else:
...   print('x is smaller than y.')
...
x is smaller than y.
``` # *prints output of else statement* | |
| ④ | ```python
>>> x = 3
>>> y = 5
>>> z = 3
>>> if x < y > z:
...   print('y is greater than x and greater than z.')
...
y is greater than x and greater than z.
``` # *all conditions are met* | |
| ⑤ | ```python
>>> x = 5
>>> y = 10
>>> if x < y:
...   print('x is smaller than y.')
... elif x > y:
...   print('x is greater than y.')
... else:
...   print('x is equal to y.')
...
x is smaller than y.
``` # *if the statement was satisfied* | |
```

Exercise 3-11: Practice for ~ in range with end=' '

#	Exercise

①
```
>>> for n in range (1, 11):
...     print(n)
...
1
2
[...omitted for brevity]
9
10
>>> for n in range (1, 11):
...   print(n, end='')
...
12345678910
>>> for n in range (1, 11):
...   print(n, end=' ') # adds spaces and print horizontally
...
1 2 3 4 5 6 7 8 9 10
>>> for n in range (1, 11):
...   print(n, end=',') # adds commas between output
...
1,2,3,4,5,6,7,8,9,10,
>>> for n in range (1, 11):
...   print(n, end='/') # adds forward slashes
...
1/2/3/4/5/6/7/8/9/10/
>>> for n in range (1, 11):
...   print(n, end='|') # adds pipes (vertical bars)
...
1|2|3|4|5|6|7|8|9|10|
```

Practice each for ~ in range statement with end= and compare the variations in the outcome.

Exercise 3-12: Practice for ~ in range

#	Exercise

①
```
>>> for n in range (2, 11):
...     print(("Creating VLAN") + str(n))
...
```

Creating VLAN2 Creating VLAN3 Creating VLAN4 Creating VLAN5 Creating VLAN6 Creating VLAN7 Creating VLAN8 Creating VLAN9 Creating VLAN10

for ~ in range() becomes handy when you have to loop through several lines to add configuration to networking devices. You will apply the previous code in later Python network automation labs. Try to get familiar with this example.

Exercise 3-13: Practice for line in ~

#	Exercise	Explanation

①
```
>>> txt1 = "Seeya later
Alligator"
>>> for line in txt1:
...         print(line)
...
S
e
e
```
[...omitted for brevity]
```
o
r
>>> txt1 = "Seeya later
Alligator"
>>> for line in txt1:
...     print(line,
end='')
...
Seeya later Alligator
```

For strings, you can use the for line in ~ method, and you will get the same effect as the for n in range() method for numbers.

Exercise 3-14: Use the split() Method

#	Exercise	Explanation

①	```>>> txt1 = "Seeya later Alligator"```
	```>>> print(txt1.split())``` # splits at every white spaces
	```['Seeya', 'later', 'Alligator']```
	```>>> print(txt1.split( ))``` # same as above
	```['Seeya', 'later', 'Alligator']```
	```>>> print(txt1.split('e', 1))```
	```['S', 'eya later Alligator']``` #splits at the first instance of 'e'
	```>>> txt2 = (txt1.split('e', 1))```
	```>>> print(txt2[0])``` # You only want to extract the letter 'S'
	```S```
	```>>> txt3 = (txt1.split('a', 3))```
	```>>> print(txt3)``` # splits at every 'a', three times
	```['Seey', ' l', 'ter Allig', 'tor']```
	```>>> print(txt3[1])``` # You only want to extract the first letter 'l'
	```L```
		Getting enough practice with string indexing and splicing becomes a powerful tool when used with Regular Expressions. Unfortunately, to become a good programmer, you must get familiar with general data handling: data gathering, data processing, and data flow control.

Exercise 3-15: Practice with lstrip(), rstrip(), strip(), upper(), lower(), title(), and capitalize()

#	Exercise

①	```>>> australia = ' terra australis incognita '```
	```>>> print(australia.title())``` # title() method capitalizes first letters
	Terra Australis Incognita
	```>>> print(australia.rstrip().upper())``` # upper() for capitalization
	TERRA AUSTRALIS INCOGNITA
	```>>> x = (australia.lstrip().lower())``` # lower() for lower casing
	```>>> print(x.capitalize())``` # capitalize() for capitalization of first letter only
	Terra australis incognita
	```>>> print(australia.strip().upper())``` # strip() remove both left and right white spaces
	TERRA AUSTRALIS INCOGNITA

You have just completed the uppercasing, lowercasing, and strip method practice. Can you think of some interesting and relatable words for you to practice? Add some fun to your exercise by changing the words to have more meaning to you.

Exercise 3-16: Create a File and Read It Four Different Ways

#	Exercise	Explanation

①	```>>> with open('test123.txt', 'w') as f:```
	```... f.write('This is line 1.\nThis is line 2.\nThis is line 3.\n')```
	```...```
	48
		Create test123.txt in w mode and write something.

(*continued*)

#	Exercise	Explanation
| ② | ```python
>>> with open('test123.txt', 'r') as f:
...     lines = f.readlines()
...     print(lines)
...
['This is line 1.\n', 'This is line
2.\n', 'This is line 3.\n']
``` | This is the with open method with a readlines() example. |
| ③ | ```python
>>> with open('test123.txt', 'r') as f:
...     lines = list(f)
...     print(lines)
...
['This is line 1.\n', 'This is line
2.\n', 'This is line 3.\n']
``` | This is the with open method with a list() example. |
| ④ | ```python
>>> f = open('test123.txt', 'r')
>>> lines = f.readlines()
>>> print(lines)
['This is line 1.\n', 'This is line
2.\n', 'This is line 3.\n']
>>> f.close()
``` | This is a simple open() method with a readlines() example. Always close the file after use. |
| ⑤ | ```python
>>> f = open('test123.txt', 'r')
>>> lines = list(f)
>>> print(lines)
['This is line 1.\n', 'This is line
2.\n', 'This is line 3.\n']
>>> f.close()
``` | This is a simple open() method with a list() example. Make sure f.close() is issued to close the file. |

Exercise 3-17: Read and Output Files for a More Detailed Understanding

#	Exercise	Explanation

①	```>>> with open('test123.txt', 'w') as f:```
	```... f.write(' this is a lower casing```
	```line.\n')```
	```...```
	```33```
	```>>> with open('test123.txt', 'r') as f:```
	```... print(f.read())```
	```...```
	```this is a lower casing line.```
		Create a new test123.txt file. Because the file opens in w mode, it will overwrite the file created in Exercise 3-16. Write to the file in the same way as shown in this book.

②	```>>> with open('test123.txt', 'a') as f:```
	```... f.write('THIS IS AN UPPER CASING LINE.```
	```\nThisIsACamelCasingLine.\n')```
	```...```
	```58```
		You can write more content to your file in a mode.

③	```>>> with open('test123.txt', 'r') as f:```
	```... print(f.read())```
	```...```
	```this is a lower casing line. THIS IS AN```
	```UPPER CASING LINE.```
	```ThisIsACamelCasingLine.```
	```>>> with open('test123.txt', 'r') as f:```
	```... print(f.readline())```
	```...```
	```this is a lower casing line.```
	```>>> with open('test123.txt', 'r') as f:```
	```... print(f.readlines())```
	```...```
	```[' this is a lower casing line. \n',```
	```'THIS IS AN UPPER CASING LINE .\n',```
	```'ThisIsACamelCasingLine.\n']```
		Try to read and print in three different modes: read(), readline(), and readlines(). Do you see the difference?

(continued)

#	Exercise	Explanation
| ④ | ```python
>>> with open('test123.txt', 'r') as f:
...     print(f.read().lower().strip())
...
this is a lower casing line. this is an
upper casing line. thisisacamelcasingline.
``` | Practice using other methods to manipulate your strings and whitespace. |
| ⑤ | ```python
>>> with open('test123.txt', 'r') as f:
...     x = (f.read().lower().strip())
...     y = set(x.split())
...     print(y)
...     print(len(y))
...
{'lower', 'casing', 'a', 'this', 'is',
'upper', 'thisisacamelcasingline.', 'an',
'line.'} 9
``` | You are using the set() and split() methods together to count the total number of words and characters in your file. |

Exercise 3-18: Use the getpass() Module and User Input

For this exercise, open the Python IDLE (interpreter) to write the code.

#	Exercise	Explanation
| ① | ```python
>>> import getpass
>>> def get_pwd():
...     username = input('Enter
username : ')
...     password = getpass.getpass()
...     print(username, password)
...
>>> get_pwd()
Enter username : admin
Password: **********
admin mypassword
``` | Use import to load the getpass library. Use def to change your password into a function. Then use the input() function to ask for the user's name; then use the getpass. getpass() module to ask for the user's password. While the password is entered, the getpass() module will hide it. Just for testing, I have printed out the username and password. The getpass() module comes in handy when creating a login request for SSH and Telnet to networking devices. |
```

Exercise 3-19: Understand the Difference Between Encoding and Decoding

#	Exercise	Explanation

①	```>>> text_1 = 'Network Automation'```
	```>>> print(text_1)```
	```Network Automation```
	```>>> byte_1 = text_1.encode()```
	```>>> print(byte_1)```
	```b'Network Automation'```
		Computers communicate in bits (0s and 1s), and the computer handles files in bytes. But we humans want to communicate in plaintext to machines, so encoding and decoding are required. This is a simple exercise to convert a string into bytes. You will see this in action during the Telnet Python lab exercises in Chapter 13. Make a special note of this exercise.

②	```>>> byte_2 = b'Mission completed.'```
	```>>> print(byte_2)```
	```b'Mission completed.'```
	```>>> text_2 = byte_2.decode()```
	```>>> print(text_2)```
	```Mission completed.```
		In Python 3, all strings are recognized as Unicode, and the decode() method must be used to convert bytes, which are binary stream data that computers understand. When executing commands on machines such as routers and switches, be wary of byte-to-string conversion and string-to-byte conversion to avoid code execution errors.

Exercise 3-20: Handle CSV Files in Python with the csv Module

#	Exercise

① # Use the following information to create .py called ex3_20.py and save it to your 'C:\Python312\ch03' folder.

```python
# ex3_20.py
import csv

with open ('C://Python312//ch03//2020_router_purchase.csv', 'w',
newline='') as csvfile:
    filewriter = csv.writer (csvfile, delimiter = ',', quotechar = '|',
    quoting = csv.QUOTE_MINIMAL)
    filewriter.writerow (['Site', 'Router_Type', 'IOS_Image', 'No_of_
    routers', 'Unit_price($)', 'Purchase_Date'])
    filewriter.writerow(['NYNY', 'ISR4351/K9', 'isr4300-
    universalk9.16.09.05.SPA.bin', 4, '$ 9100.00', '1-Mar-20'])
    filewriter.writerow(['LACA', 'ISR4331/K9', 'isr4300-
    universalk9.16.09.05.SPA.bin', 2, '$ 5162.00', '1-Mar- 20'])
    filewriter.writerow(['LDUK', 'ISR4321/K9', 'isr4300-
    universalk9.16.09.05.SPA.bin', 1, '$ 2370.00', '3-Apr- 20'])
    filewriter.writerow(['HKCN', 'ISR4331/K9', 'isr4300-
    universalk9.16.09.05.SPA.bin', 2, '$ 5162.00', '17-Apr-20'])
    filewriter.writerow(['TKJP', 'ISR4351/K9', 'isr4300-
    universalk9.16.09.05.SPA.bin', 1, '$ 9100.00', '15-May-20'])
    filewriter.writerow(['MHGM', 'ISR4331/K9', 'isr4300-
    universalk9.16.09.05.SPA.bin', 2, '$ 5162.00', '30-Jun-20'])
```

Create a new code file called ex3_20.py using the information. The file needs to be saved in the C:\Python312\ch03 folder.

(*continued*)

#	Exercise
②	Open the ex3_20.py file on your Microsoft Visual Studio Code and run the code to create your CSV file (see Figure 3-6).

Figure 3-6. *Running the CSV script to create an Excel file on Windows PowerShell*

When you run ex3_20.py on your Visual Studio Code, it will create a CSV file with the name 2020_router_purchase.csv in the same folder.

(*continued*)

#	Exercise
③	Use Microsoft Excel to open the file and check the newly created file. It should look similar to Figure 3-7.

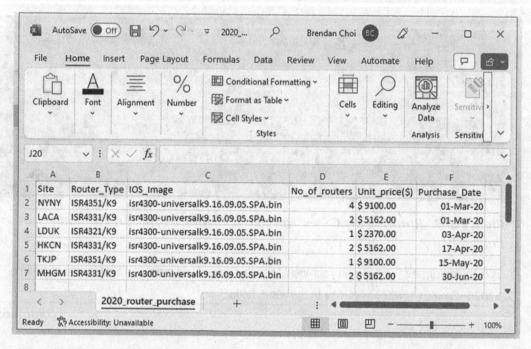

Figure 3-7. Checking 2020_router_purchase.csv in Excel

Open the newly created 2020_router_purchase.csv file in Microsoft Excel to check it.

(*continued*)

#	Exercise

④ # For Windows users, open your Python interpreter from the command-line prompt to run the following.

```
C:\Python312\ch03>python
Python 3.12.0a7 (tags/v3.12.0a7:b861ba4, Apr  4 2023, 16:33:41) [MSC v.1934 64 bit
(AMD64)] on win32
Type "help", "copyright", "credits" or "license" for more information.
>>> f = open('C://Python312//ch03//2020_router_purchase.csv', 'r')
>>> f
<_io.TextIOWrapper name='C://Python312//ch03//2020_router_purchase.
csv' mode='r' encoding='cp1252'>

# For Linux users (optional)
>>> f = open ('2020_router_purchase.csv', 'r')
>>> f
<_io.TextIOWrapper name = ''2020_router_purchase.csv' mode = 'r'
encoding = 'UTF-8'>
```

If you open and read the file, you can see that the Windows-created file will use the encoding of cp1252, whereas on Linux, UTF-8 encoding will be used as the default decoding method.

(*continued*)

#	Exercise

⑤

```
>>> f = open('C://Python312//ch03//2020_router_purchase.csv', 'r')
>>> routers = f.read()
>>> routers
'Site,Router_Type,IOS_Image,No_of_routers,Unit_price($),Purchase_
Date\nNYNY,ISR4351/K9,isr4300-universalk9.16.09.05.SPA.bin,4,
$ 9100.00,1-Mar-20\nLACA,ISR4331/K9,isr4300-universalk9.16.09.05.SPA.
bin,2,$ 5162.00,1-Mar- 20\nLDUK,ISR4321/K9,isr4300-
universalk9.16.09.05.SPA.bin,1,$ 2370.00,3-Apr- 20\nHKCN,ISR4331/
K9,isr4300-universalk9.16.09.05.SPA.bin,2,$ 5162.00,17-Apr-20\
nTKJP,ISR4351/K9,isr4300-universalk9.16.09.05.SPA.bin,1,$ 9100.00,
15-May-20\nMHGM,ISR4331/K9,isr4300-universalk9.16.09.05.SPA.bin,2,
$ 5162.00,30-Jun-20\n'
>>> print(routers)
Site,Router_Type,IOS_Image,No_of_routers,Unit_price($),Purchase_Date
NYNY,ISR4351/K9,isr4300-universalk9.16.09.05.SPA.bin,4,$ 9100.00,
1-Mar-20
LACA,ISR4331/K9,isr4300-universalk9.16.09.05.SPA.bin,2,$ 5162.00,
1-Mar- 20
LDUK,ISR4321/K9,isr4300-universalk9.16.09.05.SPA.bin,1,$ 2370.00,
3-Apr- 20
HKCN,ISR4331/K9,isr4300-universalk9.16.09.05.SPA.bin,2,$ 5162.00,
17-Apr-20
TKJP,ISR4351/K9,isr4300-universalk9.16.09.05.SPA.bin,1,$ 9100.00,
15-May-20
MHGM,ISR4331/K9,isr4300-universalk9.16.09.05.SPA.bin,2,$ 5162.00,
30-Jun-20
>>> f.close ()
```

Use read() to read the file. The content is a long string of data. If you use print(), the new lines will be displayed as individual lines, and it becomes easier to read.

(*continued*)

#	Exercise

⑥
```
>>> with open('C://Python312//ch03//2020_router_purchase.csv', 'r') as
f:
...     routers = f.readlines()
...     for router in routers:
...         print(router, end=(" "))
...
Site,Router_Type,IOS_Image,No_of_routers,Unit_price($),Purchase_Date
NYNY,ISR4351/K9,isr4300-universalk9.16.09.05.SPA.bin,4,$ 9100.00,
1-Mar-20
LACA,ISR4331/K9,isr4300-universalk9.16.09.05.SPA.bin,2,$ 5162.00,
1-Mar- 20
LDUK,ISR4321/K9,isr4300-universalk9.16.09.05.SPA.bin,1,$ 2370.00,
3-Apr- 20
HKCN,ISR4331/K9,isr4300-universalk9.16.09.05.SPA.bin,2,$ 5162.00,
17-Apr-20
TKJP,ISR4351/K9,isr4300-universalk9.16.09.05.SPA.bin,1,$ 9100.00,
15-May-20
MHGM,ISR4331/K9,isr4300-universalk9.16.09.05.SPA.bin,2,$ 5162.00,
30-Jun-20
```

If you do not want to be bothered with the ending `f.close()` statement, you can also use the
`with` open command to open the file and read it. This example uses the `f.readlines()`
method to read each line separately and then uses the `for` loop to call out each line
in the CSV file. Take your time and carefully study the difference between the `read()`,
`readlines()`, and `readline()` methods.

(*continued*)

Exercise 3-21: Output a CSV File

#	Exercise
| ① | ```
>>> f = open('C://Python312//ch03//2020_router_purchase.csv', 'r')
>>> for line in f:
...    print(line.strip())
...
Site,Router_Type,IOS_Image,No_of_routers,Unit_price($),Purchase_Date
NYNY,ISR4351/K9,isr4300-universalk9.16.09.05.SPA.bin,4,$ 9100.00,
1-Mar-20 LACA,ISR4331/K9,isr4300-universalk9.16.09.05.SPA.bin,2,
$ 5162.00,1-Mar-20 LDUK,ISR4321/K9,isr4300-universalk9.16.09.05.
SPA.bin,1,$ 2370.00,3-Apr-20 HKCN,ISR4331/K9,isr4300-
universalk9.16.09.05.SPA.bin,2,$ 5162.00,17 -Apr-20
TKJP,ISR4351/K9,isr4300-universalk9.16.09.05.SPA.bin,1,$ 9100.00,
15 -May-20
MHGM,ISR4331/K9,isr4300-universalk9.16.09.05.SPA.bin,2,$ 5162.00,
30 -Jun-20
>>> f.close()
``` |

As in a normal text file, you can use the `for` loop method to read each line and print one line at a time. Make sure you use the `strip()` method to remove any leading or trailing whitespace, newlines, or tabs.
```

Exercise 3-22: Find the Price of a Cisco ISR 4331 Router from a CSV File

#	Exercise

①
```
>>> f = open('C://Python312//ch03//2020_router_purchase.csv', 'r')
>>> x = f.read().split('\n') #1
>>> x
['Site,Router_Type,IOS_Image,No_of_routers,Unit_price($),Purchase_
Date', 'NYNY,ISR4351/K9,isr4300- universalk9.16.09.05.SPA.bin,4,
$ 9100.00,1-Mar-20', 'LACA,ISR4331/K9,isr4300- universalk9.16.09.05.
SPA.bin,2,$ 5162.00,1-Mar-20', 'LDUK,ISR4321/K9,isr4300-
universalk9.16.09.05.SPA.bin,1,$ 2370.00,3-Apr-20', #2 'HKCN,ISR4331/
K9,isr4300- universalk9.16.09.05.SPA.bin,2,$ 5162.00,17 -Apr-20',
'TKJP,ISR4351/K9,isr4300- universalk9.16.09.05.SPA.bin,1,$ 9100.00,15
-May-20', #3 'MHGM,ISR4331/K9,isr4300- universalk9.16.09.05.SPA.bin,2,
$ 5162.00,30 -Jun-20', '']
>>> y = x[2] #4
>>> y #5
'LACA,ISR4331/K9,isr4300-universalk9.16.09.05.SPA.bin,2,$ 5162.00,
1-Mar-20'
>>> z = y.split(',')
>>> z
['LACA', 'ISR4331/K9', 'isr4300-universalk9.16.09.05.SPA.bin', '2',
'$ 5162.00', '1-Mar-20']
>>> price_4331 = z[4]
>>> print(price_4331)
$ 5162.00
```

In this example, you practiced reading data from a CSV file and extracting specific information.

#1. The read().split() method reads the file, splits the items, and saves the items in a list for each line.

#2. x's index 2 was assigned to variable y.

#3. Once again, split() breaks the string into a list. The list was assigned to a variable z.

#4. z's fifth or index 4 elements were assigned to a variable called price_4331.

#5. The price of a Cisco 4331 was printed on the screen.

Exercise 3-23: Calculate the Total Cost of the Router Purchases: No Module

Create ex3_23.py on your Visual Studio Code.

#	Exercise
①	```# ex3_23.py```

```
# ex3_23.py

total = 0.0
with open ('C://Python312//ch03//2020_router_purchase.csv', 'r') as f:
  headers = next (f)
  for line in f:
    line = line.strip ()
    devices = line.split (',')
    devices[4] = devices[4] .strip ('$')
    devices[4] = float (devices[4])
    devices[3] = int (devices[3])
    total += devices[3] * devices[4]
    print('Total cost: $', total)
```

Using the method learned in Exercise 3-23, create a program that calculates the total cost of routers called ex3_23.py. Set the initial value of the total at 0.0 dollars. Use indexes 3 and 4 in the list to find the sum spent on the router purchase. To avoid errors that can occur during calculations, use header=next(f) to skip the first line's header information. Split, strip, and convert between various data types. Save the script in the Document folder and make sure you change the file path to suit your computer settings.

② C:\Python312\ch03> **python ex3_23.py**
Total cost: $ 78842.0

Run the Python application to find the total cost of the router purchases. You can also run this from the Visual Studio Code optionally. According to the script, the total cost was $78,842. These exercises seem very anal and meaningless, but will become useful while processing meaningful data and developing real work applications.

Exercise 3-24: Calculate the Total Cost of the Router Purchases Using the csv Module

#	Exercise
①	```# ex3_24.py
import csv # using csv module

total = 0.0
with open ('C://Python312//ch03//2020_router_purchase.csv') as f:
  rows = csv.reader (f)
  headers = next (rows)
  for row in rows:
    row [4] = row [4].strip ('$')
    row [4] = float(row [4])
    row [3] = int(row [3])
    total += row[3] * row[4]

print('Total cost: $', total)``` |

I re-created the same application using Python's built-in csv module. First, import the csv module and follow the same process of stripping and converting between data types. There is a famous saying in programming, "There's more than one way to gut a fish."

#	Exercise
②	```C:\Python312\ch03> python ex3_24.py
Total cost: $ 78842.0```

Run the new code, but the total cost will be the same. Optionally, you can run the Python code from the Visual Studio Code.

Exercise 3-25: Convert dd-mmm-yy and Calculate the Difference in Days and Then in Years

While working in networking, you'll notice that different vendors have different date and time formats in their software. One good example is the date format of Cisco routers and switches. While I was manipulating the data collected from actual Cisco IOS software, I had to spend an hour converting and manipulating the release date of Cisco IOS in a particular format and work out how old the IOS image was since its release date. This exercise is from a real production example script. Here's the format of the IOS release date given: 12-Jul-17.

The objective is to manipulate and convert the date to the correct format so Python can work out how old the IOS is since its release date. Note that your date will differ from the result given in this example, as it uses today() as the calculation date. Follow along with example ① first and then follow through with the iteration example ②.

#	Exercise
①	```# Follow this exercise in Python IDLE```
	```>>> from datetime import datetime #1```
	```>>> IOS_rel_date = '12-Jul-17' #2```
	```>>> x = IOS_rel_date.replace('-', ' ') #3```
	```>>> y = datetime.strptime(x, '%d %b %y') #4```
	```>>> y #5```
	```datetime.datetime(2017, 7, 12, 0, 0) #6```
	```>>> y_day = y.date() #7```
	```>>> datetime.today() #8```
	```datetime.datetime(2023, 12, 22, 11, 34, 11, 903372) #9```
	```>>> datetime.today().date() #10```
	```datetime.date(2023, 12, 22) #11```
	```>>> t_day = datetime.today().date() #12```
	```>>> delta = t_day - y_day #13```
	```>>> print(delta.days) #14```
	```2354```
	```>>> years = round(((delta.days)/365), 2) #15```
	```>>> years #16```
	```6.45```

(continued)

#	Exercise

#1. Import the `datetime` module from the `datetime` library. You need this library to complete the challenge.

#2. Enter the IOS release date as a string to begin this exercise.

#3. Replace - with blank spaces.

#4. Use the `datetime` module's `strptime` method to convert x to the correct date format. %d represents days, %b represents abbreviated months such as JAN, Jun, and Jul, and %y represents the abbreviated year without the first two leading digits. Python's `datetime` module expects the date to be in a specific format, and we are trying to normalize the format to achieve this goal.

#5. Now type y to check the current format. It has two 0s separated by a comma, which is the hour and minute. You have to lose these two zeros.

#6. Now use the `date()` method on y to drop the hour and minute information. Check first before applying this. This is the date format required to solve half of this challenge. You are at 50 percent now.

#7. It is time to work with today's date. To find the number of days since the IOS release, you need to work out what today is and then subtract the day of the release date. Use the `datetime()` module again, this time `today()`.

#8. If the result is acceptable, then append `.date()` at the back to drop the time elements. This will return the date in the correct format.

#9. Now assign the object from #9 to a variable, called t_day.

#10. The delta or the difference between the two dates is t_day – y_day.

#11. Print the result, and it will return the delta in the number of days.

#12. Now divide the delta by 365 days to convert the days to years. Use the `round()` function to give the last two decimals. This single exercise will give you some insight into how to massage specific data, in this case, dates.

#13 & 14. Find the delta and print it in days.

#15 & 16. Calculate the days in years and print the value in years.

(continued)

#	Exercise

②
```
# Reiterated and reduced version of example 1:
>>> from datetime import datetime
>>> x = IOS_rel_date.replace('-', ' ')
>>> y_day = (datetime.strptime(x, '%d %b %y')).date()
>>> t_day = datetime.today().date()
>>> delta = t_day - y_day
>>> years = round(((delta.days)/365), 2)
>>> print(years)
6.45
```

This example is a reiterated version of Example 1. I crunched some functions into one line to shorten the conversion processes. This is just one example of data manipulation, and there are many other ways to do the same conversion. Still, the important thing is to understand the thought process so you can adapt it to your situation. Finally, if you have 10 minutes, visit the following site to review which `strftime` code formats are available: `https://strftime.org/`.

Furthering Your Understanding of Python Functions

In Python, there are four types of functions, each serving different purposes. Understanding these different types of functions is crucial when working with Python, as they provide a wide array of tools and capabilities to streamline and enhance programming tasks. Let's explore these:

1. **Built-in functions** are already integrated into Python and can be used directly without any additional setup. Python comes with a rich library of built-in functions that offer various functionalities to perform specific tasks.

2. **Module functions** (a.k.a. module) in Python are files containing Python definitions and statements. They can include functions, variables, classes, and more. Developers and companies create modules to organize and bundle related functionalities, making them readily available for various projects and applications. By importing the module, Python users can access and leverage its

functionalities.

3. **User-defined functions** are defined by users or programmers themselves to meet specific requirements. User-defined functions allow developers to encapsulate a set of operations into a single function, promoting code reusability and maintainability.

4. **Lambda functions** (anonymous functions) are small, temporary functions without a name. They are defined using the `lambda` keyword and are typically used for short tasks when a full function definition is unnecessary.

Exercise 3-26: Structure of a Function

#	Exercise	Explanation

①	```def function_name(argument):```
	``` code_to_run```
	``` return value```
		This is an example showing the basic structure of a function.

②	```>>> def my_func():```
	```... print('Hello Skippy')```
	```...```
	```>>> my_func()```
	```Hello Skippy```
		This is an example of a function, printing a single line.

③	```>>> def add(num1, num2):```
	```... return num1 + num2```
	```...```
	```>>> print(add(2, 3))```
	```5```
		This is another function example, returning the sum of num1 and num2.

④	```>>> def all(num1, num2):```
	```... return num1 + num2, num1 -```
	```num2, num1 * num2, num1 / num2```
	```...```
	```>>> print(all(2, 3))```
	```(5, -1, 6, 0.6666666666666666)```
		Using a function, you can perform multiple tasks at once in this example. The results returned are the addition, subtraction, multiplication, and division of num1 and num2.

Exercise 3-27: Random Module with a List

#	Exercise	Explanation
①	`import module_name`	There are thousands of pre-made modules, which brings down the development time. To use a module, use the `import` command.

②	```>>> import random```
	```>>> animals = ['cat', 'dog', 'horse', 'pig']```
	```>>> print(random.choice(animals))```
	```'pig'```
		Import the `random` module and the code randomly prints one of the animals from the list of domesticated animals.

③	```>>> import random```
	```>>> animals = ['cat', 'dog', 'horse', 'pig']```
	```>>> print(random.sample(animals, 2))```
	```['dog', 'horse']```
		When selecting a specific number of items randomly, use the `sample` method.

Exercise 3-28: Random Module with Numbers

#	Exercise	Explanation

①	```>>> import random```
	```>>> list = random.sample(range(1, 46), 6)```
	```>>> print(list)```
	```[32, 30, 29, 22, 10, 40]```
		The code provided imports the `random` module and generates a list named `list` containing six random and unique integers within the range from 1 to 45 (inclusive). The `random.sample()` function is used to achieve this. It ensures that no number is repeated in the generated list.

(continued)

#	Exercise	Explanation
| ② | ```python
>>> def lotto():
...     list = random.
sample(range(1, 46), 6)
...     print(list)
...
>>> lotto()
[32, 8, 21, 19, 44, 20]
>>> lotto()
[6, 26, 2, 7, 13, 37]
``` | Now use the random.sample to get the six numbers for your weekly lottery entry. |

Exercise 3-29: random.randint Example

#	Exercise	Explanation
| ① | ```python
import random
random.
randint(first_num,
last_num)
``` | The random.randint() function takes two arguments, first_num and last_num, and returns a random integer from the range specified by those arguments, including first_num and last_num. |
| ② | ```python
>>> import random
>>> print(random.
randint(5, 10))
5
>>> print(random.
randint(5, 10))
8
...
``` | If you just want a single number between the first number and the last number, you can use random.randint. |
```

Exercise 3-30: Use the Random Module to Play PowerBall

Working on Visual Studio Code, create the ex3_30.py file under the C:\Python312\ch03 folder with the following code.

#	Exercise	Explanation
①	```#ex3_30.py
import random
def powerball():
    main_numbers = random.sample(range
    (1, 36), 5)
    pb_number = random.randint(1, 20)
    print("Main numbers:", main_numbers)
    print("PowerBall number:", pb_number)

powerball()``` | This code can be used to play the PowerBall lottery. It imports the random module, defines a function called powerball(), and then generates five random and unique main numbers from 1 to 35 using random.sample(). It also generates a random PowerBall number from 1 to 21 using random.randint(). |
| ② | ```C:\Python312\ch03> python ex3_30.py
Main numbers: [3, 14, 35, 20, 7]
PowerBall number: 11
C:\Python312\ch03> python ex3_30.py
Main numbers: [25, 1, 3, 32, 18]
PowerBall number: 7
...``` | Run the code over and over. You will get the random five numbers for the main numbers and a PowerBall number. |

As discussed, this chapter focuses solely on fundamental and selective Python topics, making it far from comprehensive. To enhance your Python skills further, I recommend exploring additional basic Python books and other study materials that delve deeper into the subjects covered here. By completing these basic Python exercises, you are now well-prepared for Python network automation. However, keep in mind that more advanced topics await you in the upcoming chapters. Embrace the journey of continuous learning, as it will undoubtedly lead to greater proficiency and mastery of Python programming.

Exploring the Python IDE Environment

After completing this chapter, you need to start thinking about an integrated development environment (IDE) for Python code development. Working in a text editor is straightforward, but it has its limitations. Working within an IDE is not compulsory, but as you write more complex and longer Python code, your coding efficiency drops when using text editors such as Notepad, EditPlus, or Notepad++ on Windows or vi, Emacs, Gedit, or Nano on Linux. IDEs provide many features not available from standard text editors. When you work in collaboration with team members, suddenly the version control of your documents becomes essential. Many organizations use GitHub or similar cloud-based Git applications with cloud storage as their code version control solution. Still, you do not have to worry about version control at this stage. You must learn to crawl before you can walk. Hence, this topic is not discussed beyond this section in this book. You do not have to start using an IDE application in this book, but you have been introduced to Microsoft Visual Studio Code and I encourage you to explore others and find the perfect match for your coding style. On enterprise Linux systems, you rarely see graphical user interfaces (GUIs), so only Windows-compatible IDEs are discussed here. MacOS has a similar number of IDEs that you can choose from, but that is out of this book's scope. To help you explore various Python IDEs available for Windows, see Table 3-1. Although Jupyter Notebook (Anaconda) is not an IDE, it is included in Table 3-1 to give you another path to studying Python.

Table 3-1. *Python IDEs and Anaconda (Jupyter Notebook)*

Recommended IDE	Pros and Cons, Download URL
PyCharm*	**Pros**: Feature-rich, intuitive user interface, supports cross-platform, made for Python, free Community version, friendly for both beginners and experts **Cons**: Paid Professional version **URL**: `https://www.jetbrains.com/pycharm-edu/` (Education edition link)
Microsoft Visual Studio	**Pros**: Windows-friendly, easy to use (especially if you are a Windows user), feature-rich, Community version free **Cons**: The interface can be slow to start up **URL**: `https://visualstudio.microsoft.com/vs/features/python/`

(continued)

Table 3-1. (*continued*)

Recommended IDE	Pros and Cons, Download URL
Eclipse	**Pros**: Multiple programming language support, familiar user interface, free **Cons**: JRE (JDK) dependency, tricky to set up for beginners, older IDE **URL**: `https://www.eclipse.org/downloads/packages/installer`
Atom	**Pros**: Developed by GitHub's Electron text editor, supports cross-platform and multiple programming languages, feature-rich via extensions and plugins, good documentation on application programming interface (API), free, easy to use, light yet still powerful **Cons**: Not as intuitive as PyCharm; closer to a text editor than PyCharm **URL**: `https://sourceforge.net/projects/atom.mirror/files/latest/download`
Sublime Text 3	**Pros**: Popular code editor with a fast, stable, and mature user interface; many features with modular approach and extendability **Cons**: Not as versatile as other IDEs; still feels more like a text editor than an IDE; must purchase a license for continued use; no debugging option **URL**: `https://www.sublimetext.com/download`
Spyder	**Pros**: Tailored for data science and scientific computing, interactive console for quick code testing, variable explorer for easy data inspection **Cons**: Resource-intensive for large datasets, steeper learning curve compared to some other IDEs, limited support for non-data science projects URL: `https://www.spyder-ide.org/`
Anaconda – Jupyter Notebook	**Pros**: Beginner-friendly, excellent Python learning tool, web-based, used by scientific communities for data analytics **Cons**: Not an IDE, web-based, system resource-heavy **URL**: `https://jupyter.org/install`

Summary

This chapter offered more substance than Python's print() function and syntax. It served as a test drive, giving you a glimpse of what's ahead in the upcoming chapters. You learned additional Python basics by exploring new Python modules, handling files, and processing data with simple Python code. Chapters 2 and 3 form a solid foundation for the Python network automation labs later in this book and Part 2. If you find some exercises challenging, don't worry; feel free to review and repeat them two to three times. It's beneficial to reinforce your understanding through repetition. If time permits, I recommend revisiting the exercises in both chapters several times before reaching Chapter 11. Chapters 4-6 and 10 focus on building virtually integrated Python network automation labs, starting with Linux server VM creations on VMware Workstation Pro. You dive into VMware Workstation Pro basics and general virtualization technology in Chapter 4. VMware Workstation, along with its virtualization technologies, will facilitate building a comprehensive virtual networking lab, acting as the glue that connects virtual machines. I encourage you to read the next chapter in its entirety to continue your learning journey.

Storytime 2: Machine vs. Human, The First Confrontation

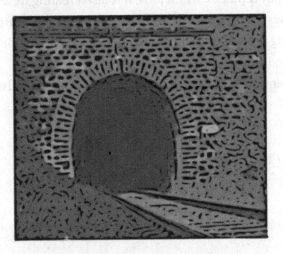

Figure 3-8. An old train tunnel (Representation only)

According to historical records and folklore, a significant human versus machine confrontation occurred in the United States around the 1870s. The legendary story of John Henry, a skilled railway worker, challenging an automatic steam drilling machine to construct a railway tunnel, has been passed down through generations in American folklore. Although the exact details of the story may be subject to debate, it symbolizes the emergence of automation and its impact on the workforce during the Industrial Revolution. In those times, railway workers, including miners, had to use traditional tools like hammers, chisels, and drills, along with dynamite, to manually create tunnels. The introduction of steam-powered drilling machines represented a leap in technology, paving the way for automation in various industries.

Fast forward to today's technology landscape, where automation has become an integral part of the IT industry. While it is true that automation generally enhances efficiency and improves the quality of human life, it also raises concerns about job displacement and the need for upskilling to keep pace with technological advancements. In the rapidly evolving world of IT automation, existing engineers and professionals may find themselves facing similar challenges as John Henry did in the past. However, the key to navigating this changing landscape lies in continuous learning and staying up-to-date with the latest IT technologies. Embracing the opportunities that automation presents and developing expertise in emerging fields can open new doors and lead to fulfilling career paths.

In conclusion, automation continues to play a significant role in shaping the IT industry. While it may replace certain jobs, it is also creating new opportunities for skilled professionals. This IT book aims to explore the fascinating world of IT automation, equipping readers with the knowledge and skills needed to thrive in an increasingly automated world.

Source: `https://en.wikipedia.org/wiki/John_Henry_(folklore)`

CHAPTER 4

Introduction to VMware Workstation

VMware Workstation Pro is one of the most popular end-user desktop virtualization solutions used by enterprise IT personnel. It allows IT engineers to build and test real-world-like virtual machines and network devices from their PC/laptop. Learning to build a fully functioning and integrated virtual lab on a single computer and mastering Python network automation basics on a single PC is this book's underlying goal. This chapter is designed to teach you the basics of the most popular and versatile VMware product, VMware Workstation 17 Pro, and basic virtualization concepts. After reading this chapter, you will gain the following knowledge: you'll understand the difference between Type-1 and Type-2 hypervisors, understand various IT vendors offering different desktop virtualization solutions, learn how to install VMware Workstation, learn how to perform general administration on VMware Workstation, and understand how VMware Workstation's network adapters operate.

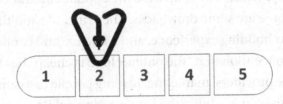

VMware Workstation at a Glance

In this chapter, you learn about VMware Workstation Pro, a Windows Desktop Hypervisor that enables you to build your Python network automation labs. Except for the first three chapters, this book relies on VMware's desktop virtualization technology, specifically VMware Workstation 17 Pro. Keep in mind that this chapter is solely focused

© Brendan Choi 2024
B. Choi, *Introduction to Python Network Automation Volume I - Laying the Groundwork*,
https://doi.org/10.1007/979-8-8688-0146-4_4

on the exploration of VMware Workstation 17 Pro. While it may not offer hands-on practical activities, it provides detailed insights into the functioning of virtual network interfaces, virtual switch types, and the various menus and features. By thoroughly understanding these concepts, you can enhance your proficiency in virtualization technology. Before delving into Python automation, it is crucial to approach your studies with an open mind toward various IT technologies. Learning Python coding alone does not guarantee success in network automation; you must also grasp concepts like Regular Expressions, Linux administration, and cloud services, even if they are outside a network engineer's comfort zone. Becoming proficient in Python may take months or even years, and applying Pythonic concepts to real-world scenarios presents its challenges. You need to integrate your Python knowledge with your existing networking and general IT expertise. Writing Python code is just the initial step; it requires a comprehensive understanding of Linux, networking, basic mathematics, regular expressions, interaction with APIs, emerging cloud infrastructure, and more.

Given limited time and resources, you aim to acquire essential skills to embark on network automation using Python, all on a single Windows PC/laptop. The most convenient way to achieve this is by utilizing VMware's desktop virtualization, specifically VMware Workstation 17 Pro. Throughout this book, I consistently use the term *VMware Workstation* to refer to VMware Workstation 17 Pro. The reason for choosing VMware Workstation is its suitability for novice Python coders like you—it is fairly easy to learn. It provides a practical and flexible platform to build a virtual lab environment for learning multiple technologies in various scenarios, all from the convenience of a laptop. While setting up a lab on a public cloud such as AWS, Azure, or GCP is an option, there are some drawbacks. These include additional costs, a lack of an end-to-end Linux building experience, and a reliable and continuous Internet connection. The misconception that "the public cloud is cheap" has been perpetuated by public cloud service providers' marketing, leading people to assume the cloud is free. Due to these limitations, you will build the lab on a physical PC.

In this chapter, I want you to become comfortable with the basic virtualization concepts and the fundamental functions of the VMware Workstation. Even if you are already experienced with various virtualization solutions, including VMware products, you may still find new insights here. By the end of this chapter, you should be well-prepared to follow the rest of the book's content and create a functional proof-of-concept (PoC) lab. In the previous chapter, you installed Python 3 on your Windows host PC and learned Python basics on Windows 11. However, in this chapter and the upcoming ones, you are guided through installing two flavors of Linux distribution servers on your Windows host using VMware Workstation. This will allow you to comfortably transition to Linux servers, practice building Python applications on Linux, and gradually acquire foundational Linux administration skills.

Virtualization technology—particularly Type-2 hypervisors like VMware Workstation and Oracle VirtualBox—helps run multiple operating systems (OSs) on a single host. As a pre-task for this chapter, you need to download and install VMware Workstation on your PC. VMware Workstation Pro offers a fully functional 30-day trial period, making it an excellent starting point for your learning journey. After installation, you will learn the basics of VMware Workstation and proceed to install the latest Ubuntu and Fedora servers in the next two chapters. By installing two popular Linux distributions—Red Hat Enterprise Linux (RHEL)/Fedora and Debian/Ubuntu—you will gain exposure to more than one Linux environment. Throughout this book, these two servers serve as the training ground for teaching basic Linux and Python coding. Additionally, you will build the Fedora server as an all-in-one IP services server, which will prove useful in the PoC labs in this book.

Note that in the first edition of this book, the CentOS 8 Server was used. However, since the book's release, Red Hat (owned by IBM) has made CentOS the upstream for RHEL. In December 2020, CentOS shifted its focus to CentOS Stream, a rolling-release distribution serving as the upstream for future RHEL releases. Consequently, there are no significant benefits to using CentOS over Fedora. For this study, it does not matter whether you use RHEL, CentOS Stream, or Fedora, as they all serve the same purpose. If you want to follow along with all the content exactly, use Fedora. However, choosing another flavor of RHEL Linux should also work, although it might require some additional repositories and processes.

Tip

Is it OK to use VMware Workstation 15 or 16?

Although VMware Workstation 17 Pro includes some bug fixes, if you have a genuine license for version 15 or 16, you can still create your learning labs on these older versions. With minimal feature changes since version 15, most of the learning in this book will also function on the previous versions, akin to how a Windows application can be installed and operate on both Windows 10 and 11, and soon on Windows 12.

The more you know about VMware Workstation Pro's features and basic virtualization functions, the more effective you will become in building your study lab and testing environment. When designing and constructing a PoC lab for enterprise IT solutions, it is common to use expensive and highly powerful devices to test like-for-like features and performances. In some cases, real equipment is necessary and justified, especially for stress testing hardware-related system performance. However, the procurement process for acquiring the right equipment can be time-consuming, taking weeks or even months. Additionally, finding sufficient rack space with the appropriate power voltage and cooling to maintain a smoothly running lab can be challenging. A physical lab also involves dealing with the right cables and connector types to suit vendor equipment interfaces, which can slow down the process of building a company's PoC lab. Often, thousands of dollars are wasted on a company lab that is only utilized by a few people in the organization. Allocating the budget more effectively could be a solution, but there is still a lack of green IT in this domain. Thanks to advancements in virtualization and cloud technologies over the past decade, more and more equipment is transitioning to virtualization and cloud platforms. This can be observed in the rapid expansion of cloud-based computing, software-as-a-service (SaaS), platform-as-a-service (PaaS), and more recently, serverless technologies with Kubernetes and cloud computing. Virtually anything related to IT-as-a-service leverages the power of virtualization and cloud technologies in one form or another.

VMware Workstation Pro is VMware's most popular cross-platform desktop virtualization program, supporting both Windows and Linux. For macOS, VMware Fusion offers the same functionality. While there is a free version called VMware Workstation Player, it lacks several key features that prevent you from setting up a more robust lab. Hence, you will use VMware Workstation Pro. You will install a series of software applications, one at a time, on the Microsoft Windows host system. According to a recent ZDNet research in July 2023, Microsoft Windows still dominates the desktop operating system (OS) space worldwide, holding a share of over 68 percent. Apple's macOS comes in second place with over 21 percent, followed by Chrome OS with over 4 percent, and Linux desktop at over 3 percent. From my observation, even within the IT industry, similar user percentages are reflected. However, with enterprise-level automation solutions, administrators spend very little time on the desktop (or the GUI). In many production environments, Linux servers are deployed without the GUI, making Linux the default operating system for many enterprise systems. This offers added flexibility, higher performance, a low cost of ownership, and better security.

At the time of authoring this book in July 2023, users were allowed to download the latest version of VMware Workstation Pro evaluation for Windows from VMware's official website without registering an account. It offers a 30-day free trial period for all customers. You can purchase a Pro license within the trial period for permanent activation and support. At the time of writing this book, the latest VMware Workstation for Windows version was 17.0.0, build 20800274, but your downloaded version will likely be newer. As mentioned in the TIP, other versions of the software should work just fine. If you are using VMware 14 or an older version, I recommend upgrading to the next version to follow the content of this book. Figure 4-1 displays the exact VMware Workstation used in this book.

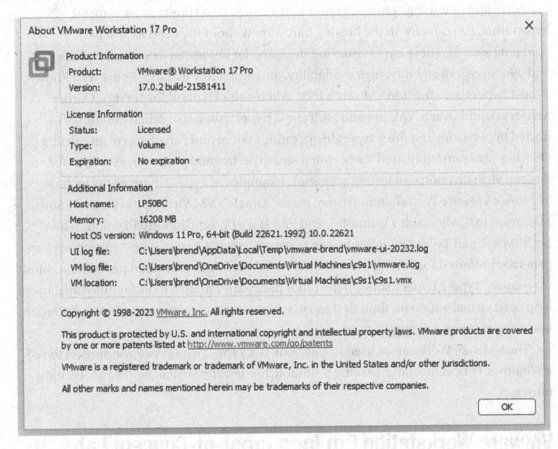

Figure 4-1. *About VMware Workstation 17 Pro*

Even if you are not yet familiar with the concept of virtualization, you will not have any problem following this chapter's content, as this book assumes that you have had no previous experience with this VMware product. Those who are not familiar with a

235

desktop virtualization program such as this can read through the chapter to get familiar with this software and some basic desktop virtualization concepts. For those who have many years of virtualization experience, skim through this chapter and jump to the next two chapters, which cover installing Ubuntu 22.04 LTS and Fedora 38 Linux virtual machines (VMs).

Type-1 vs. Type-2 Hypervisors

Virtualization (hypervisor) software can be classified into two main types: Type-1 and Type-2 hypervisors. The key distinction lies in how they interact with the underlying hardware and operating systems. Type-1 hypervisors, also known as bare-metal hypervisors, run directly on the hosting hardware without the need for a separate operating system. These hypervisors are designed for enterprise-level server platforms and offer excellent stability, high availability, and scalability features. Some well-known Type-1 hypervisors include VMware's ESXi, Microsoft's Hyper-V for Servers, Citrix's XenServer, and Oracle VM. In contrast, Type-2 hypervisors, also called desktop or hosted hypervisors, require a separate operating system and run on top of an existing OS. They are commonly used for personal and experimental purposes, as well as for desktop virtualization and testing scenarios. Examples of Type-2 hypervisors include VMware's VMware Workstation, Fusion, Player, Oracle's VM VirtualBox (formerly Sun Microsystems), Microsoft's VirtualPC, and Red Hat's Enterprise Virtualization. While both Type-1 and Type-2 hypervisors can serve various use cases, Type-1 hypervisors are generally preferred for enterprise environments due to their enhanced performance and robustness. Type-2 hypervisors, on the other hand, are valuable tools for individual users who need virtualization on their desktop machines or want to experiment with different operating systems and applications.

The VMware Workstation used in this book is a Type-2 hypervisor running on top of a Windows 11 host machine, making it suitable for desktop virtualization and learning purposes.

VMware Workstation Pro for a Proof-of-Concept Lab

VMware Workstation 17 Pro is VMware's leading desktop virtualization program, initially released in 1999, with the latest version available during the authoring of this book being version 17. While the book is centered on version 17.x, you can effortlessly create the lab using earlier versions like 16.x or even 15.x without encountering any issues.

Installing and using this desktop virtualization program is intuitive and requires no user training. Such virtualization programs, running on top of the operating system, are sometimes referred to as experimental virtualization programs. The installation process is straightforward, and you can complete the initial software setup with just a few mouse clicks. VMware Workstation Pro is one of the most robust desktop virtualization programs commonly found on IT engineers' laptops or desktops.

When selecting desktop virtualization software for lab use, you may come across other popular options from Microsoft and Oracle, such as Oracle's VirtualBox and Microsoft's Hyper-V. However, due to considerations of software compatibility and system stability, you utilize VMware Workstation 17 Pro in this book. While enterprise-level virtualization programs like VMware's ESXi, Microsoft's Hyper-V, Debian KVM, XCP-ng and Proxmox Virtualization were also considered, it's essential to note that Type-1 hypervisors such as these have higher hardware specification requirements. For example, Type-1 hypervisor software necessitates installation on hypervisor-specific hardware (bare-metal) servers. Additionally, operating Type-1 hypervisor software requires a separate client PC to remotely access the server console. Consequently, Type-1 hypervisors are typically deployed in data centers or company communication rooms and are not intended for mobile use.

Before Using VMware Workstation

When installing Type-1 hypervisor software like ESXi 7.0 or 8.0, there are strict hardware requirements during the installation process. The software has a built-in process to check for minimum and stricter hardware prerequisites. However, for VMware Workstation 17 Pro installation on your host operating system, there are only minimal hardware prerequisites, as the software runs on top of your host OS. If your computer's CPU and motherboard support virtualization technology, you can proceed with the installation. Newer PCs or laptops usually come with the Virtualization Technology option enabled in the BIOS by default. If you are using an older PC or laptop, you may need to enable this setting before installing the software.

Until recently, VMware's virtualization solutions tended to favor Intel's CPU architecture slightly more than AMD's. In my experience, Intel CPUs have demonstrated superior performance, compatibility, and efficiency. However, AMD has made significant advancements in CPU development, and their CPUs are now better suited for individual users who prioritize PC gaming.

237

Before installing the VMware Workstation, ensure that the virtualization support is enabled in the BIOS of your laptop or PC motherboard, as illustrated in Figure 4-2.

```
                 Phoenix TrustedCore(tm) Setup Utility
      Advanced

      Advanced Processor Configuration              Item Specific Help

  CPU Mismatch Detection:            [Enabled]     When enabled, a VMM
  Core Multi-Processing:             [Enabled]     (Virtual Machine
  Processor Power Management:      · [Disabled]    Monitor) can utilize
  Intel(R) Virtualization Technology [Enabled]     the additional hardware
  Execute Disable Bit:               [Enabled]     capabilities provided
                                                   by Vanderpool
  Adjacent Cache Line Prefetch:      [Disabled]    Technology.
  Hardware Prefetch:                 [Disabled]
  Direct Cache Access                [Disabled]    If this option is
                                                   changed, a Power Off-On
                                                   sequence will be
  Set Max Ext CPUID = 3              [Disabled]    applied on the next
                                                   boot.




  F1   Info  ↑↓  Select Item  -/+    Change Values    F9   Setup Defaults
  Esc  Exit   ·  Select Menu  Enter  Select ▶ Sub-Menu F10  Save and Exit
```

Figure 4-2. *Checking the Intel CPU motherboard virtualization support setting*

If the use of Intel VT (or AMD-V) is set to Disabled in the BIOS, change the setting to Enabled, and then press the F10 key to save the changes and log into Windows 11 normally. Tables 4-1 and 4-2 list the BIOS entry keys for major motherboard and laptop manufacturers. The function key or key combination to enter the BIOS varies from one manufacturer to another, and the most common manufacturers' keys are provided for your reference. If you can't find your laptop manufacturer in the table, visit the manufacturer's website and locate the BIOS information to change the BIOS settings.

Table 4-1. *BIOS Setup Entry Key by Laptop Manufacturer*

Manufacturer	BIOS Key Combo
Acer	F2/Del (new)
	F1/Ctrl+Alt+Esc (old)
Asus	F2/F10/Del/Insert/Alt+F10
Compaq	F1/F2/F10/Del
Dell	F1/Del/F12/F3 (new) (press when the Dell logo appears on the screen)
	Ctrl+Alt+Enter/Fn+Esc or Fn+F1/Ctrl+F11 (old)
eMachines	F2/Del
Fujitsu	F2
Gateway	F1/F2
HP	F1/F2/F6/F9/F10/F11/Esc
	Tablet PC: F10/F12
Lenovo	F1/F2/F11 (new)
	Ctrl+Alt+F3/Ctrl+Alt+Ins/Fn+F1 (old)
LG	F10/F11/F12
Samsung	F2/F4
Sony	F1/F2/F3/Assist
Toshiba	F2/F1/ESC/F12
Other	Refer to the respective vendor's website

Table 4-2. *BIOS Setup Entry Key by Motherboard*

Manufacturer	BIOS Key/Key Combo
ASROCK	F11
ASUS	F12/F2/F8/F9
BIOSTAR	F7/F9
Compaq	F10
EMTec	F9
Foxconn	F7/Esc
GIGABYTE	F12
HP	F9
Intel	F10
LG	F12
MSI	F11
Pegatron	F11
Samsung	ESC
Other	Refer to the respective vendor's website

Before moving on, make sure you have finished installing VMware Workstation Pro.

Warning

Download and install VMware Workstation now!

Downloading and installing VMware Workstation 17 (or newer) Pro on your
Windows 11 PC is super easy, but, in case you need some help or a reference
point, the software download link and step-by-step installation guide are
provided here:

Download VMware Workstation 17 Pro from the following URL:

URL: `https://www.vmware.com/au/products/workstation-pro/`
`workstation-pro-evaluation.html`

The `2_Install_VMware_Workstation_v1.0` `(Python).pdf` guide is available here:

URL: `https://github.com/pynetauto/apress_pynetauto_ed2.0/tree/main/pre_installation_guides`

What's Next on VMware Workstation 17 Pro?

As a pre-task for this chapter, ensure that you have installed VMware Workstation 17 Pro on your host PC. I will briefly review the menu options for those who are new to virtualization technology and this program before proceeding to install two Linux virtual servers and importing the GNS3 VM. If you are confident in your knowledge of VMware Workstation features, feel free to skip to Chapter 5.

In simple terms, you can think of a virtual machine (VM) as another independent computer running on the host computer's operating system (Type-2). Users can interact with the VM through VMware Workstation's main user console and utilize various operating system installation media files to create, install, configure, import, export, control, and manage VMs. After the pre-task, you have already seen the main user console of VMware Workstation, and you may have noticed that the user interface is concise and intuitive. However, the operations and behaviors of VMs are much more sophisticated than they might appear at first glance. A VM may resemble an application, but it functions as a complete computer with many native features of a real hardware computer. To become more familiar with VMware Workstation, the best approach is to use it actively. Nevertheless, to ease your learning process, I explain some console-related terminology in the next section, including a look at the user interfaces, menus, and the Virtual Network Editor.

After a quick review, you are guided to download and install a couple of VMs and import a VM using the GNS3 .ova file. It is essential to create all three VMs by the end of chapter 6, as they serve as the foundation for the rest of the book. These VMs will enable you to learn Linux, understand regular expressions, install Python and network-related modules, and develop Python network automation scripts in the virtual labs. Emulating real lab scenarios, you will test various networking concepts and become familiar with commonly used file-sharing services. In the book's final chapters, you encounter lab scenarios involving FTP, SFTP, and TFTP servers based on the Fedora 38 virtual machine (VM). If you want to create new VMs here and export them to a real production environment, you can do so using the VMware Converter software. VMs can be pre-staged on VMware Workstation and later converted into Type-1 VMs, running on VMware's ESXi 7/8. But for now, let's focus on exploring the main user console and its menus of Workstation 17 Pro.

VMware Workstation 17 Pro User Console

The Workstation 17 Pro user console allows you to install, control, and manage various types of VMs. Figure 4-3 displays the main user interface and default buttons found in VMware Workstation 17 Pro. This figure provides information on various components of the interface, menus, and buttons. Take some time to familiarize yourself with the names of each item shown in the figure. No special skills are required to use this program, and you can easily create and use a VM after installation.

The virtual machine depicted in Figure 4-3 is Red Hat Enterprise Linux 9.2 with a user GUI, and it only took 15 minutes to have the server up and running. Now, let's delve into learning about the menus and key features.

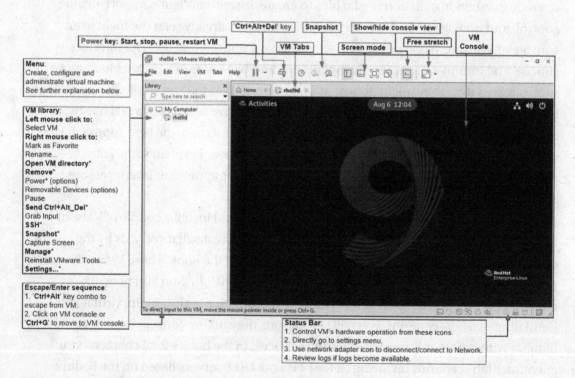

Figure 4-3. *VMware Workstation, user interface*

Basic Operations of VMware Workstation 17 Pro

Figure 4-4 illustrates the main user interface for VMware Workstation 17 Pro, which serves as the primary interface for managing your VMs. When compared to Microsoft Hyper-V on Windows 11 and Oracle VirtualBox, VMware Workstation Pro stands out with its friendly user interface and powerful features readily accessible to the user. The next section familiarizes you with the most basic functions of this program.

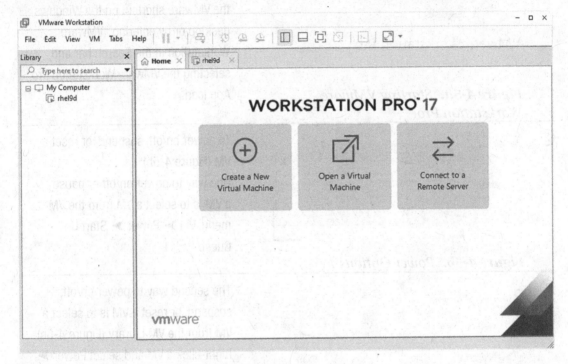

Figure 4-4. *VMware Workstation, main user window*

VMware Workstation Pro: Basic Operations

To start VMware Workstation Pro, and to start and stop VM, follow these instructions:

#	Task	Description
①	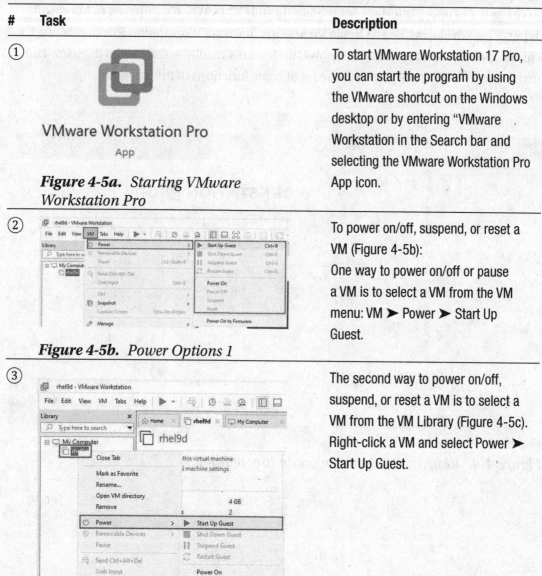 **VMware Workstation Pro** App *Figure 4-5a.* *Starting VMware Workstation Pro*	To start VMware Workstation 17 Pro, you can start the program by using the VMware shortcut on the Windows desktop or by entering "VMware Workstation in the Search bar and selecting the VMware Workstation Pro App icon.
②	*Figure 4-5b.* Power Options 1	To power on/off, suspend, or reset a VM (Figure 4-5b): One way to power on/off or pause a VM is to select a VM from the VM menu: VM ➤ Power ➤ Start Up Guest.
③	*Figure 4-5c.* Power Options 2	The second way to power on/off, suspend, or reset a VM is to select a VM from the VM Library (Figure 4-5c). Right-click a VM and select Power ➤ Start Up Guest.

(*continued*)

#	Task	Description
④	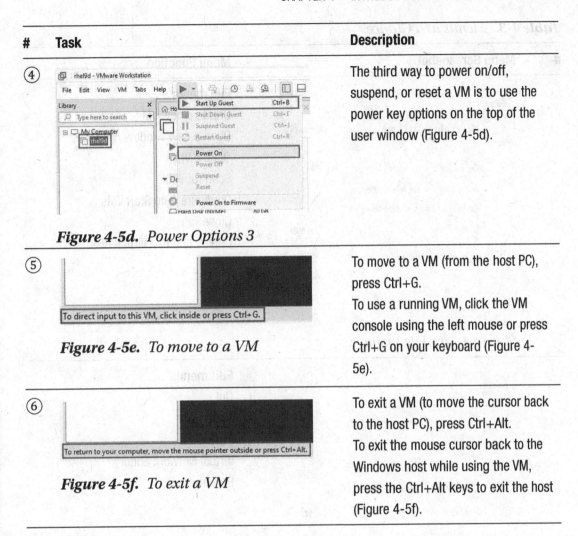	The third way to power on/off, suspend, or reset a VM is to use the power key options on the top of the user window (Figure 4-5d).

Figure 4-5d. Power Options 3

#	Task	Description
⑤	To direct input to this VM, click inside or press Ctrl+G. *Figure 4-5e. To move to a VM*	To move to a VM (from the host PC), press Ctrl+G. To use a running VM, click the VM console using the left mouse or press Ctrl+G on your keyboard (Figure 4-5e).
⑥	To return to your computer, move the mouse pointer outside or press Ctrl+Alt. *Figure 4-5f. To exit a VM*	To exit a VM (to move the cursor back to the host PC), press Ctrl+Alt. To exit the mouse cursor back to the Windows host while using the VM, press the Ctrl+Alt keys to exit the host (Figure 4-5f).

For more detailed user instructions, refer to "Using VMware Workstation Pro" at https://docs.vmware.com/en/VMware-Workstation-Pro/17/workstation-pro-17-user-guide.pdf.

VMware Workstation Menu

Table 4-3 shows all the menus at a glance. The most commonly used features are marked with an asterisk (*). You may find it helpful to check the features and skip to creating virtual machines.

Table 4-3. *Menus at a Glance*

#	Menu Screenshot	Menu Function
①	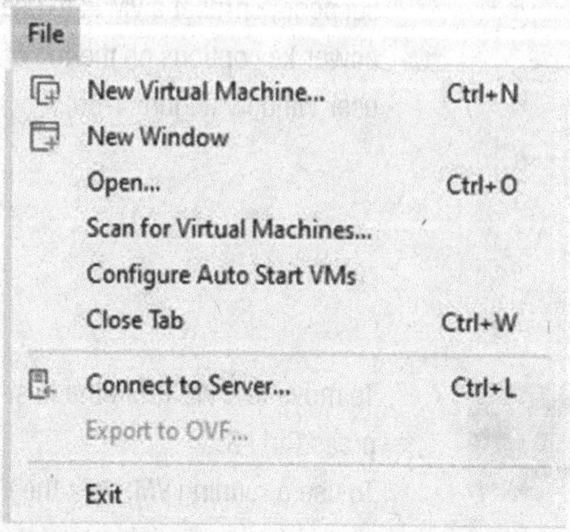	**File menu:** Create a new VM Open a new window Open a VM* Scan for VMs Configure Auto Start VMs Close Tab Connecting to a virtual disk Exit*

Figure 4-6a. *File menu*

#	Menu Screenshot	Menu Function
②	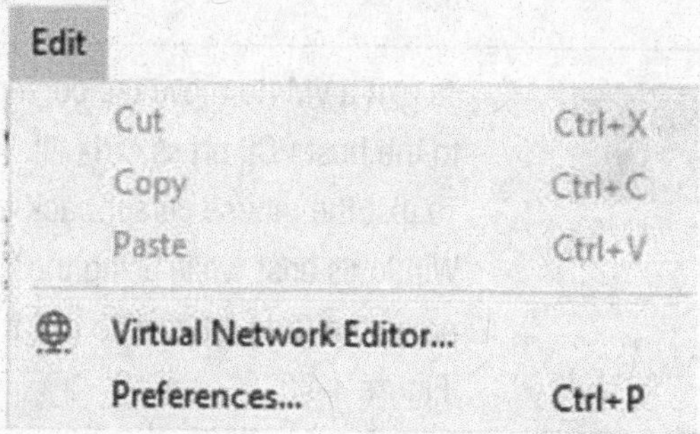	**Edit menu:** Cut Copy Paste Virtual Network Editor* Preferences*

Figure 4-6b. *Edit menu*

(continued)

Table 4-3. (*continued*)

#	Menu Screenshot	Menu Function
③	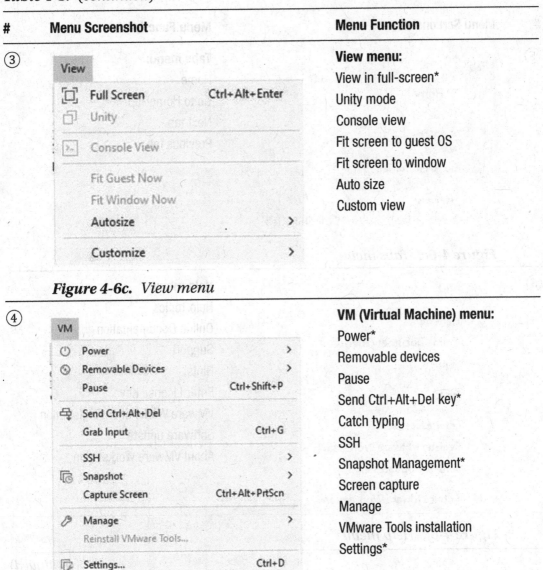	**View menu:** View in full-screen* Unity mode Console view Fit screen to guest OS Fit screen to window Auto size Custom view

Figure 4-6c. *View menu*

#	Menu Screenshot	Menu Function
④		**VM (Virtual Machine) menu:** Power* Removable devices Pause Send Ctrl+Alt+Del key* Catch typing SSH Snapshot Management* Screen capture Manage VMware Tools installation Settings*

Figure 4-6d. *VM menu*

(*continued*)

Table 4-3. (*continued*)

#	Menu Screenshot	Menu Function
⑤	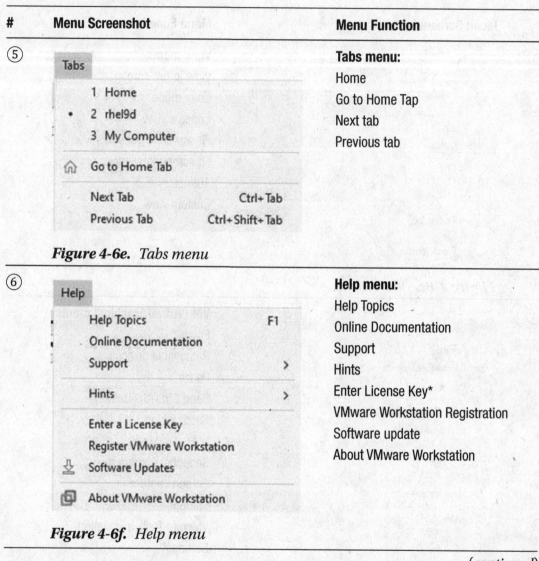	**Tabs menu:** Home Go to Home Tap Next tab Previous tab

Figure 4-6e. *Tabs menu*

#	Menu Screenshot	Menu Function
⑥		**Help menu:** Help Topics Online Documentation Support Hints Enter License Key* VMware Workstation Registration Software update About VMware Workstation

Figure 4-6f. *Help menu*

(*continued*)

Table 4-3. (*continued*)

#	Menu Screenshot	Menu Function
⑦		**VM power icon:**
		Guest On*
	Start Up Guest · · · · · · · · Ctrl+B	Guest Off*
	Shut Down Guest · · · · · · Ctrl+E	Guest Suspend
	Suspend Guest · · · · · · · Ctrl+J	Restart/Resume Guest*
	Restart Guest · · · · · · · · Ctrl+R	Power on
		Power off
	Power On	Pause
	Power Off	Reset
	Suspend	Enters BIOS when powered on *
	Reset	
	Power On to Firmware	

Figure 4-6g. VM power icon

#	Menu Screenshot	Menu Function
⑧		Send Ctrl+Alt+Delete to the VM

Figure 4-6h. Send Ctrl+Alt+Del icon

#	Menu Screenshot	Menu Function
⑨		Take a snapshot of this VM
		Revert this VM to its parent snapshot
		Manage snapshots for this VM

Figure 4-6i. Snapshot icons

#	Menu Screenshot	Menu Function
⑩		Show or hide the library
		Show or hide the thumbnail bar
		Enter full-screen mode
		Enter Unity mode

Figure 4-6j. Screen mode option icons

(*continued*)

Table 4-3. (*continued*)

#	Menu Screenshot	Menu Function
⑪		Show or hide the console view

Figure 4-6k. *Show or hide the Console view icon*

#	Menu Screenshot	Menu Function
⑫		Free stretch

Figure 4-6l. *Free stretch icon*

Virtual Network Adapters

One of the most common questions beginners ask about VMware Workstation 17 Pro is how to use different virtual network adapter settings. Providing a concise answer is challenging, as reading the lengthy documents on the VMware website may not be feasible for most of us, due to time constraints. Here, I cover the basics to help you get started with VM networking. For first-time users, it's essential to understand the differences between each virtual network adapter and how to use them effectively. To explain this, I review the available virtual network adapters and their definitions. Then, you can explore the adapter settings in your programs to see how each adapter is configured on your PC. Let's start by looking at the Virtual Network Editor to review the out-of-the-box virtual network adapter settings. This will provide a solid foundation for understanding and configuring network adapters in your VMware Workstation environment.

Virtual Network Editor Overview

VMware Workstation offers virtual network features through virtual switches, with three specific networks mapped to three virtual switches. Additionally, users can create up to 17 virtual switches as needed. The various networking types are discussed in detail in the next section. This means you can have a total of up to 20 virtual switches, ranging from VMnet0 through VMnet19, each representing a single flat network or subnet. Similar to a real production environment, you can connect multiple VMs to the same network or virtual switch. To get started, open the Virtual Network Editor menu to review the default connection types available for your configuration.

#	Screenshot	Description
①	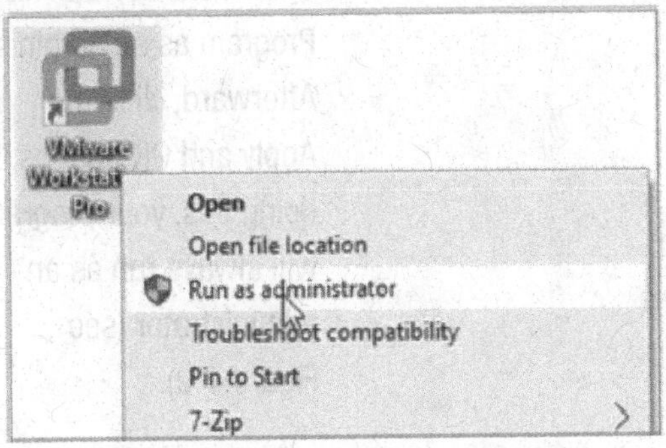 **Figure 4-7.** *VMware Workstation Pro, running as administrator*	When starting VMware Workstation Pro, it is best practice to launch the program by right-clicking the desktop icon and selecting the Run as Administrator option, as illustrated in Figure 4-7. This ensures that you are launching the program with full administrator-level privileges, enabling you to make any necessary changes to program settings.
②	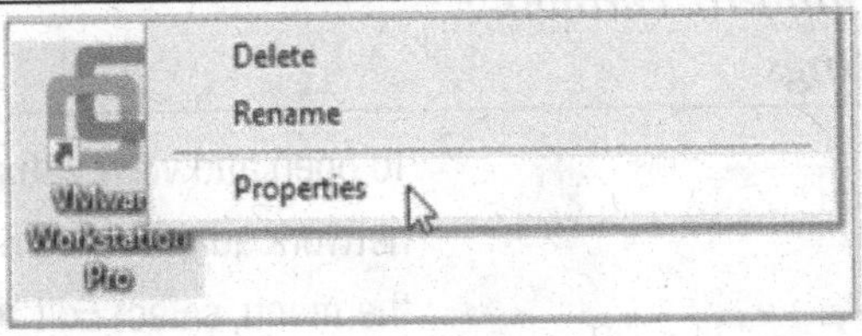 **Figure 4-8.** *VMware Workstation Pro, shortcut icon Properties*	If you don't want to click the Run as Administrator option every time you start the program, you can change the shortcut properties to make the program run in administrator mode. To do this, right-click the VMware Workstation Pro's desktop icon and select Properties, as shown in Figure 4-8.

(continued)

#	Screenshot	Description
③	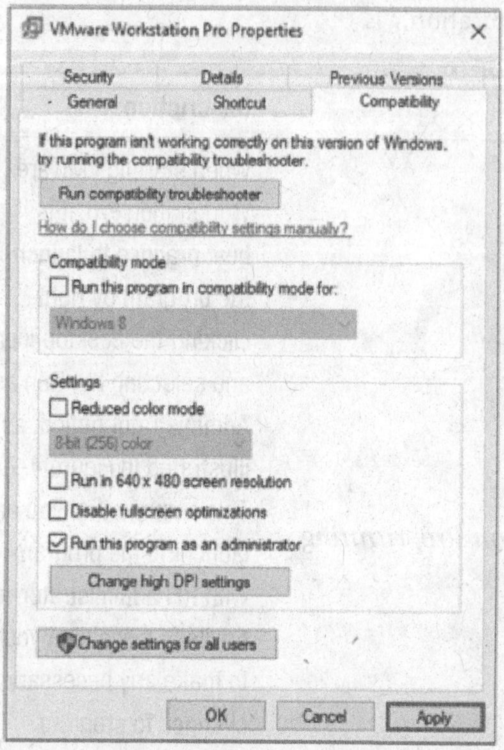 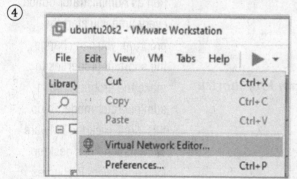	In the shortcut properties menu, click Compatibility, and under the Settings option, check Run This Program as an Administrator. Afterward, click the Apply and OK buttons. By doing this, your program will always run as an administrator (see Figure 4-9).

Figure 4-9.   *VMware Workstation Pro, changing the properties Compatibility settings*

#	Screenshot	Description
④		To open and view virtual network adapters from the menu, select Edit ➤ Virtual Network Editor (see Figure 4-10).

Figure 4-10.   *Selecting Virtual Network Editor*

(continued)

#	Screenshot	Description
⑤	*Figure 4-11.* *Virtual Network Editor, default adapter types*	When you open the Virtual Network Editor the first time, you will find three virtual switches (VMnets), as expected. Similar to a real network adapter, a virtual adapter can be referred to as a virtual NIC or a virtual network interface. The Virtual Network Editor serves as the default control tower to manage various virtual networks, allowing you to perform tasks such as adding or removing networks, enabling or disabling DHCP, and more (see Figure 4-11).

Expand your knowledge:

Read the Virtual Network Editor documentation!

In the Virtual Network Editor window shown in Figure 4-10, click the Help button, which will open the documentation on the official VMware site to "Using the Virtual Network Editor."

Virtual Network Interface Description

This section contains a quick overview of the different network modes and networking jargon discussed so far. If you have studied or are studying Cisco CCNA, you will already be familiar with these networking terminologies used in the network industry. If you are preparing for the CCNP or have completed CCNP studies, you will likely be able to relate these network adapter modes to real production environments. However, even if you are not familiar with networking technologies, you will have no trouble understanding the following explanations.

As mentioned, there are three out-of-the-box network adapters, but you can add or remove more adapters as needed. Additionally, you can specify the subnets according to your preferences as you build your lab. Table 3-4 provides descriptions for the three virtual network modes and one user (custom) mode.

Virtual Network Adapter Modes Explained

Figure 4-12 illustrates a typical bridged network setup on VMware Workstation Pro.

#	Bridged Network Illustration	Explanation
①	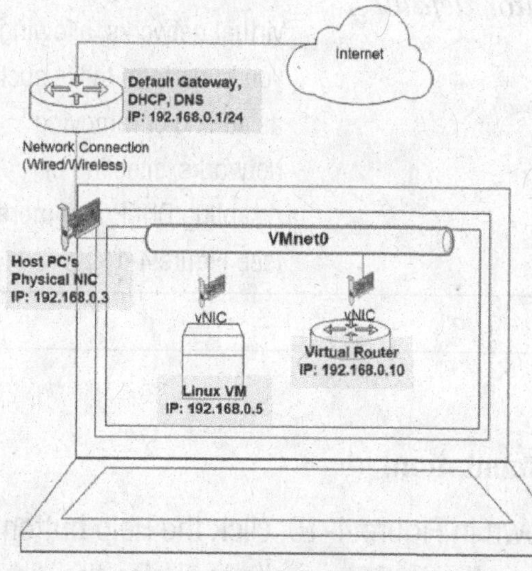	By default, in *bridged network adapter mode,* all virtual machines share the host machine's network connection. VMware Workstation uses VMnet0 as the default bridged network, and all computers, including the host PC and virtual machines, use the same gateway, DHCP, and DNS server. Consequently, both the host PC and the virtual machines acquire IP addresses from the same subnet, with the same default gateway address.

Figure 4-12. VMware network adapters, bridged mode

In Figure 4-13, in host-only mode, the workstation provides the DHCP service.

#	Host-Only Mode Illustration	Explanation
②		*Host-only mode* is perfect for testing two or more VMs in an isolated network within the virtual environment. By default, the host-only mode connects to VMnet1, enabling VMs to be connected in the same subnet for experimentation with no interaction outside of the experimental network. Your host PC and VMs can still communicate via VMnet1.

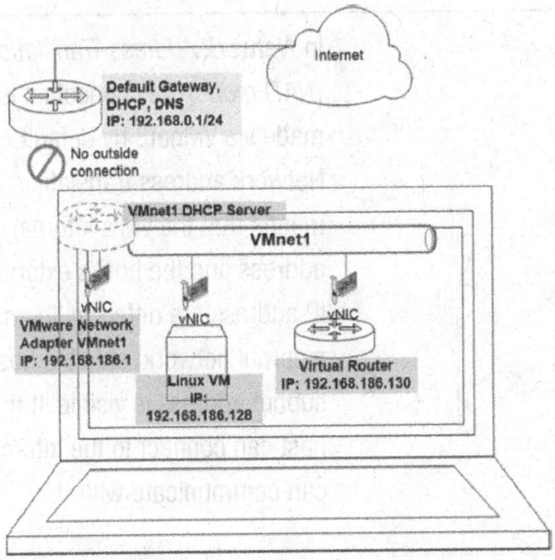

Figure 4-13. *VMware network adapters, host-only mode*

Figure 4-14 illustrates an example of a NAT configuration on VMware Workstation Pro.

#	NAT Mode Illustration	Explanation
③	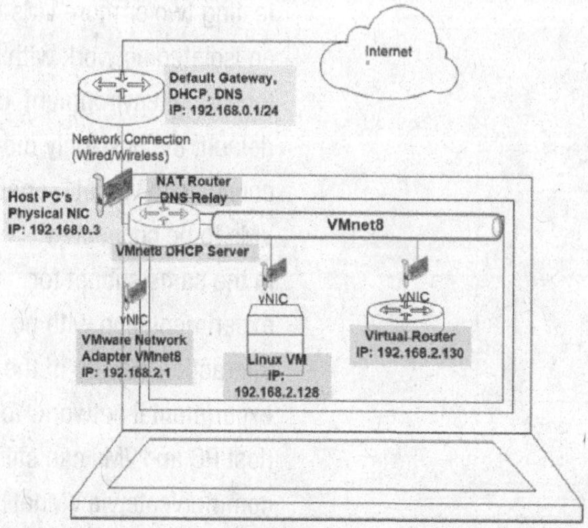	In *Network Address Translation (NAT) mode*, the connection is made via VMnet8 by default. Network address translation means that the VM's internal IP address and the host's external IP address are different. In an external network, only the host's subnet address is visible. If the host can connect to the Internet, it can communicate with it.

Figure 4-14. VMware network adapters, NAT mode

In custom networking, you can select one of the previous modes and customize it to suit your scenarios. It is the same mode as NAT mode, but with some changes in the default settings.

You are encouraged to spend enough time understanding the different virtual network modes and how they differ from the real physical network. Visualize how you can use these different modes in your PoC labs. Getting familiar with how each network mode interacts with your host machine and other networks will help you build a lab that can test more advanced IT theories. Open the Virtual Network Editor from the menu and spend some time exploring the settings, adding or removing new VMnets, and customizing the settings. In the following section, you review VM settings in more detail.

Tip

Why perform a Proof-of-Concept (PoC)?

The information provided in the previous response is accurate and does not contain any factual errors. The idea of "proof-of-concept" (PoC) in the field of IT refers to validating and testing an existing or new IT concept or solution in specific scenarios. PoC labs are used to experiment and demonstrate that a certain theory or technology works as intended and aligns with the intended design.

To gain deeper understanding and expertise in IT, spending significant time in PoC labs is highly beneficial. It allows IT professionals to explore and test various theories, technologies, and solutions, providing a broader knowledge base than what can be gained solely from books or real-life scenarios. By engaging in PoC labs, individuals can learn how different technologies and concepts interact and can better prepare themselves to address complex challenges that may not arise in a standard production environment.

In summary, PoC labs are valuable tools for IT professionals. They enable individuals to enhance their skills, explore new ideas, and gain practical experience beyond what traditional learning methods offer.

Revealing Each Virtual Network Interface Type

To gain a comprehensive understanding of the virtual network interface options available in VMware Workstation, let's examine each type.

Host-Only Networking

In this mode, your VMs share a private network with the host and other virtual devices within the same subnet. This configuration is ideal when your VMs don't require external communications beyond the host. By default, when using host-only networking, all VMs will be connected to VMnet1, which can be visualized as a single virtual network switch. A built-in DHCP server within this network provides IP addresses to hosts for added convenience. Figures 4-15 to 4-19 illustrate the configuration of VMnet1, and you can find related settings on your host's operating system. For more detailed clarification of VMware networking concepts, refer to the following tutorial: `https://rednectar.net/2011/07/20/vmware-interfaces-tutorial/`.

Figure 4-15 shows that the out-of-the-box VMnet1 subnet is assigned as 192.168.65.0/24. However, you can modify the subnet and CIDR as needed. Additionally, there is an option to disable the DHCP service, allowing you to manually assign IP addresses within a VM's OS.

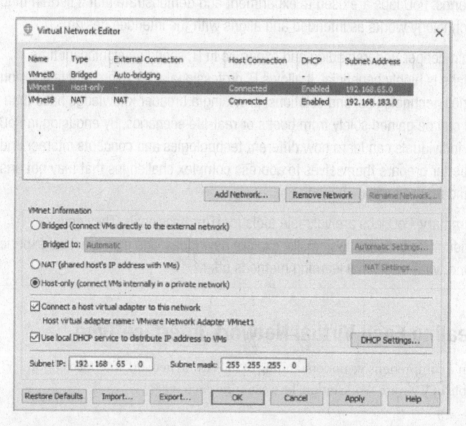

Figure 4-15. *Virtual Network Editor, VMnet1 host-only network*

Figure 4-16 shows you the VM settings where the relevant network connection is configured.

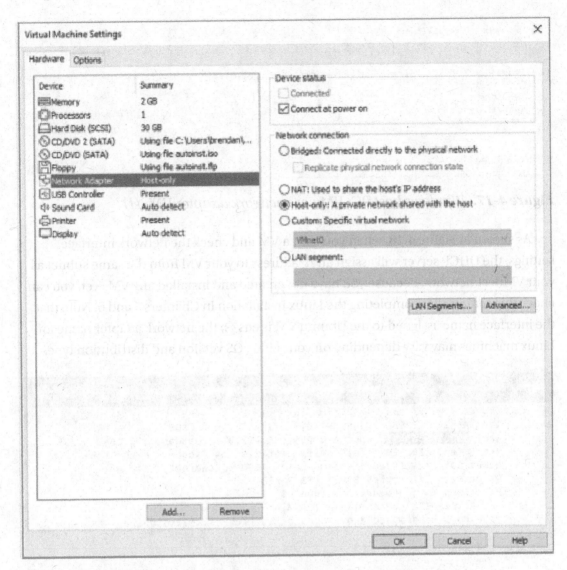

Figure 4-16. *Virtual machine settings, host-only network connection*

Figure 4-17 displays the result from the `netsh interface ip show addresses`
"VMware Network Adapter VMnet1 command, which reveals the configuration settings
for VMnet1 on your host PC. As expected, the IP address assigned to the host's VMnet1
adapter is 192.168.65.1/24, with an interface metric of 35. The interface metric of 35
indicates that the DHCP service configured this IP address.

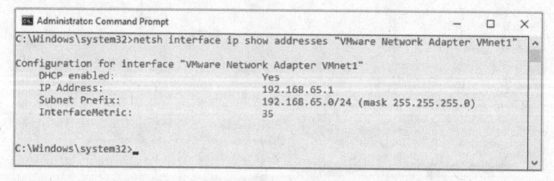

Figure 4-17. Windows host PC, VMware network adapter VMnet1

As shown in Figure 4-18, when you start a VM and check the network interface settings, the DHCP server will assign an IP address to your VM from the same subnet as your VMnet1 network. Because you have not created and installed any VMs yet, you can check this setting after completing the Linux installation in Chapters 5 and 6. Note that the interface name assigned to the Ubuntu VM is ens33; the network adapter name for Linux machines may vary depending on your Linux OS version and distribution type.

Figure 4-18. A virtual machine, ens33 network adapter

To visualize and better understand the host-only network mode, refer to the earlier Figure 4-13. This will help you locate the information on the host-only virtual network for your VMs. Now, let's move on to explore bridged mode.

Bridged Networking

In bridged mode, a VM acts as if it is another computer on the same network as the host computer, and it receives an IP address from the real network. By default, the VMnet0 network is assigned in bridged mode. If you are using your home network to connect to the Internet, your home network router usually provides DHCP services. The IP subnet of ISP-provided Internet modems/routers is typically either 192.168.0.0/24 or 192.168.1.0/24, with the default gateway taking the first IP (.1) or last IP (.254) addresses on the network. In bridged mode, other physical computers can communicate with your VMs, and you can also emulate multiple computers from one computer. By default, your VMs in bridged network mode can communicate with the Internet and other VMs on your network.

Figure 4-19 displays the default bridged network in the Virtual Network Editor. The IP address will be assigned from the real network device on the host's physical adapter network, so the DHCP options are grayed out under the settings.

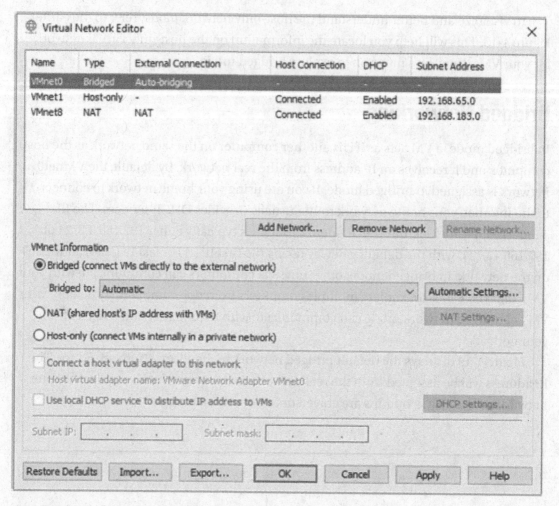

Figure 4-19. *Virtual Network Editor, VMnet0 bridged network*

Figure 4-20 displays the VM settings where the bridged network is configured and used.

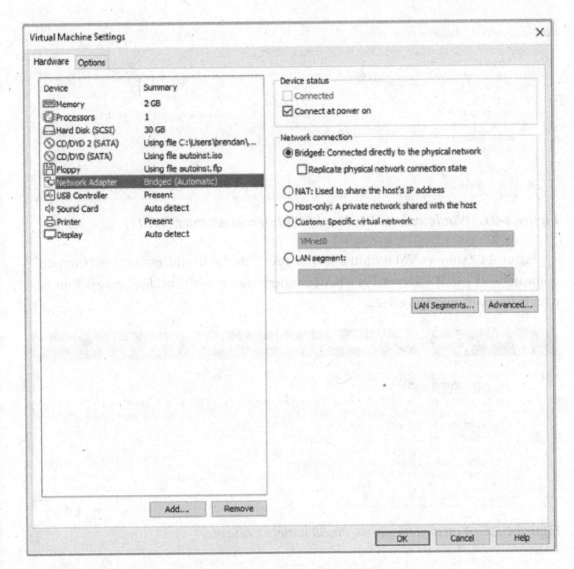

Figure 4-20. *Virtual machine settings, bridged network connection*

Figure 4-21 reveals the host's physical adapter network configuration from the DHCP server at 192.168.0.1; the default gateway doubles as a DHCP server in a typical home network. In my case, the host connects to the Internet via wireless, so a Wi-Fi 3 interface is shown as the adapter name. However, your settings may differ from those shown in Figure 4-21.

Administrator: Command Prompt
C:\Windows\system32>netsh interface ip show addresses "Wi-Fi 3"
Configuration for interface "Wi-Fi 3"
DHCP enabled: Yes
IP Address: 192.168.0.232
Subnet Prefix: 192.168.0.0/24 (mask 255.255.255.0)
Default Gateway: 192.168.0.1
Gateway Metric: 0
InterfaceMetric: 55
C:\Windows\system32>

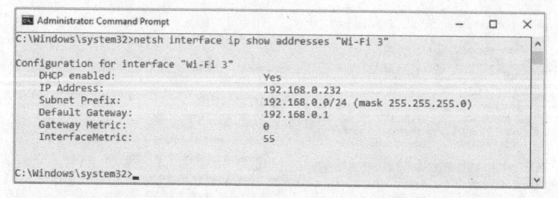

Figure 4-21. *Windows host PC, local PC's Internet adapter (Wi-Fi)*

Figure 4-22 shows a VM terminal session revealing the IP address received from the home network's DHCP server. For a better understanding of the bridged network mode, refer to the previous Figure 4-12.

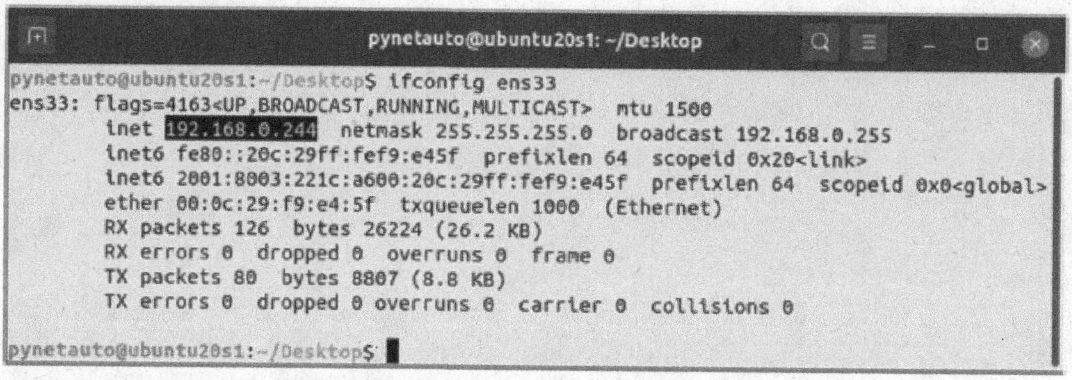

pynetauto@ubuntu20s1: ~/Desktop
pynetauto@ubuntu20s1:~/Desktop$ ifconfig ens33
ens33: flags=4163<UP,BROADCAST,RUNNING,MULTICAST> mtu 1500
inet 192.168.0.244 netmask 255.255.255.0 broadcast 192.168.0.255
inet6 fe80::20c:29ff:fef9:e45f prefixlen 64 scopeid 0x20<link>
inet6 2001:8003:221c:a600:20c:29ff:fef9:e45f prefixlen 64 scopeid 0x0<global>
ether 00:0c:29:f9:e4:5f txqueuelen 1000 (Ethernet)
RX packets 126 bytes 26224 (26.2 KB)
RX errors 0 dropped 0 overruns 0 frame 0
TX packets 80 bytes 8807 (8.8 KB)
TX errors 0 dropped 0 overruns 0 carrier 0 collisions 0
pynetauto@ubuntu20s1:~/Desktop$

Figure 4-22. *A virtual machine, ens33 network adapter*

Network Address Translation Networking

In Network Address Translation (NAT) mode, a VM shares the host's IP and MAC addresses. The outside network (the Internet) sees your network as a single network identity, and the internal network is not visible outside the network. Typically, and in the traditional sense, NAT is used to hide the internal network from outsiders and extend the number of useful IPv4 IP addresses within your network. If you have already undertaken Cisco CCNA routing and switching studies, understanding NAT or PAT is part of the study curriculum, so comprehending this type of networking mode will also make immediate sense. Throughout this book, you will utilize NAT's features for your entire lab configuration to keep the networking configuration to a minimum.

Look at Figure 4-23 and review how NAT is configured under VMware Workstation Pro configuration. In NAT mode, VMware Workstation provides the DHCP service, meaning that another subnet is used inside the network; in this case, the subnet assigned to NAT is in the 192.168.183.0/24 range, and this is the primary method in which your lab will connect to the Internet and the host.

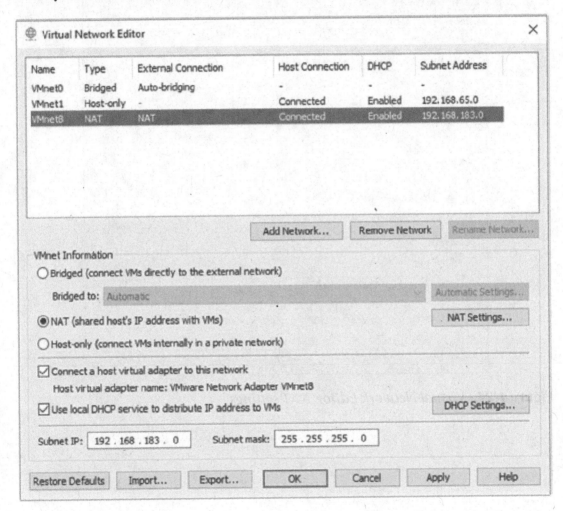

Figure 4-23. *Virtual Network Editor, VMnet8 NAT adapter*

Click the NAT Settings button in Figure 4-23; it reveals NAT or VMnet8 settings. You will notice that the gateway IP address for this subnet is 192.168.183.2, and you can assume that 192.168.183.1 would have been assigned to the VMnet8 adapter on the host PC; this is verified in Figure 4-24.

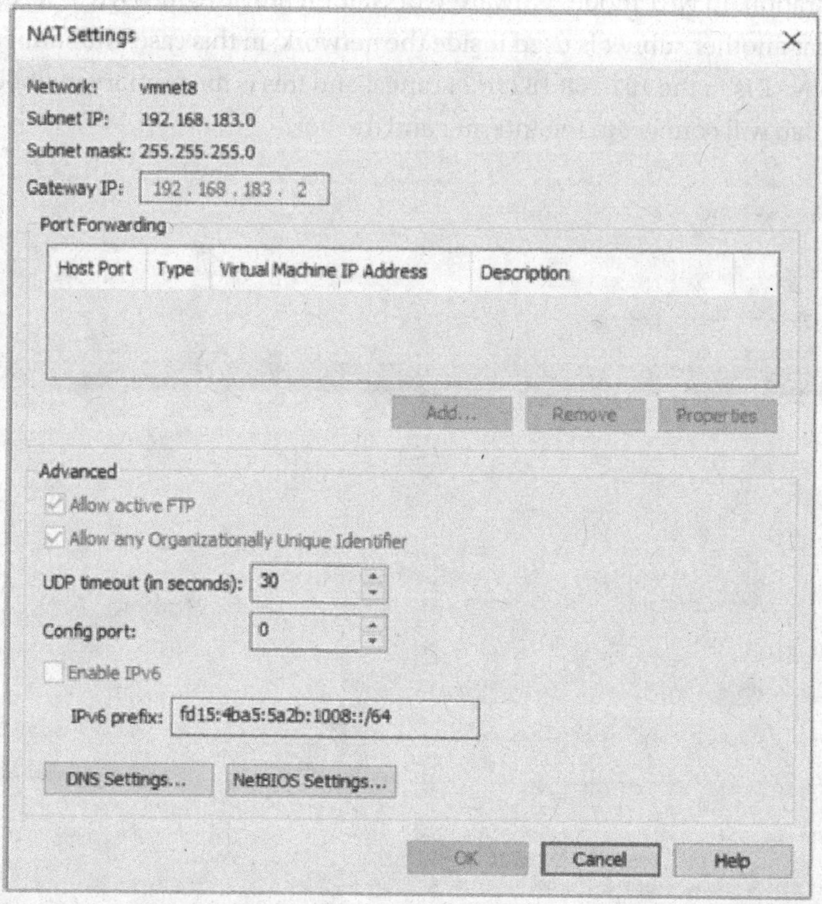

Figure 4-24. *Virtual Network Editor, NAT settings*

Figure 4-25 displays the network connection configuration of a VM.

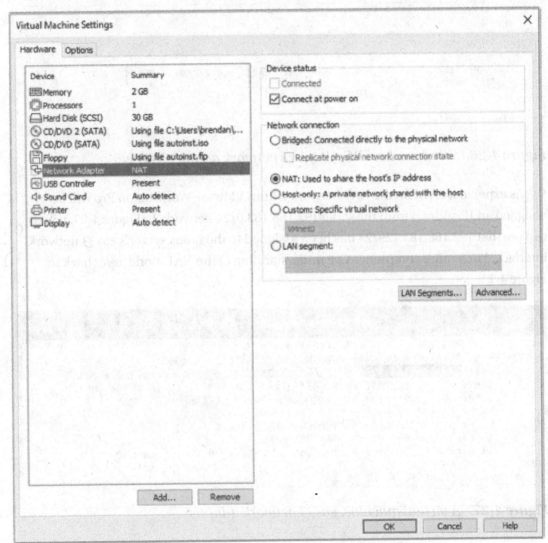

Figure 4-25. *Virtual machine settings, NAT network connection*

In Figure 4-26, the IP address configuration from the DHCP server is shown, and as discussed earlier, 192.168.183.1/24 is assigned to VMnet8 on the host. However, the default gateway for the VMs is set to 192.168.183.2.

```
Administrator: Command Prompt                                        —    □    ×

C:\Windows\system32>netsh interface ip show addresses "VMware Network Adapter VMnet8"

Configuration for interface "VMware Network Adapter VMnet8"
    DHCP enabled:                      Yes
    IP Address:                        192.168.183.1
    Subnet Prefix:                     192.168.183.0/24 (mask 255.255.255.0)
    InterfaceMetric:                   35


C:\Windows\system32>_
```

Figure 4-26. *Windows host PC, VMware network adapter VMnet8*

As expected, a VM on the NAT network within VMware Workstation Pro will be assigned an IP address from the same 192.168.183.0/24 network. In Figure 4-27, you can see that 192.168.183.129/24 has been assigned to the Linux server's ens33 network interface. For a more comprehensive understanding of the NAT mode, refer back to Figure 4-14.

```
                        pynetauto@ubuntu20s1: ~/Desktop          Q   ≡   _   □   ×

pynetauto@ubuntu20s1:~/Desktop$ ifconfig ens33
ens33: flags=4163<UP,BROADCAST,RUNNING,MULTICAST>  mtu 1500
        inet 192.168.183.129  netmask 255.255.255.0  broadcast 192.168.183.255
        inet6 fe80::20c:29ff:fef9:e45f  prefixlen 64  scopeid 0x20<link>
        ether 00:0c:29:f9:e4:5f  txqueuelen 1000  (Ethernet)
        RX packets 298  bytes 56459 (56.4 KB)
        RX errors 0  dropped 0  overruns 0  frame 0
        TX packets 240  bytes 25864 (25.8 KB)
        TX errors 0  dropped 0 overruns 0  carrier 0  collisions 0

pynetauto@ubuntu20s1:~/Desktop$ █
```

Figure 4-27. *A virtual machine, ens33 network adapter*

Summary

In this chapter, you explored virtualization technology, a cornerstone of cloud services and modern IT infrastructure. You learned the distinctions between Type-1 and Type-2 hypervisors, understanding their respective use cases. Opting for VMware Workstation 17 Pro as the virtualization solution, you learned about its user-friendly interface and powerful features. After successfully installing VMware Workstation Pro, you explored various virtual network modes, including bridged, host-only, and NAT modes, each offering unique benefits for your virtual lab environment. Emphasizing the importance of proof-of-concept (PoC) labs, you read about their value in hands-on learning and testing IT theories. Now, equipped with this knowledge, you are ready to dive into practical aspects by creating virtual machines and setting up Ubuntu 22.04 LTS and Fedora 38 servers in the upcoming chapters. Virtualization technology opens up endless possibilities, and I am thrilled to embark on this virtual journey with you.

Creating an Ubuntu Server Virtual Machine (VM)

In this chapter, you download the latest Ubuntu Server 22 bootable image, a critical step in setting up and configuring your virtual machine within the VMware Workstation environment. Ubuntu, a prominent Debian Linux–based distribution, is renowned for delivering a top-tier user experience within the Linux realm. While Ubuntu Desktop traditionally serves as the gateway for many Windows users venturing into the Linux world, the focus in this book shifts to Ubuntu Server 22, albeit with an innovative twist: you'll integrate a Graphical User Interface (GUI), enriching the versatility of your lab setup. By the end of this chapter, you'll have mastered installing an Ubuntu Server virtual machine from the ground up. Not only will you gain expertise in tailoring specific server settings, but you'll also learn how to capture a virtual machine's snapshot and adeptly clone it. This chapter serves as the first attempt to convert you (a Windows user) to a Linux user, empowering you to wield the potential of Linux servers to your advantage and forging a solid foundation for your Python Network Automation endeavors.

© Brendan Choi 2024
B. Choi, *Introduction to Python Network Automation Volume I - Laying the Groundwork*,
https://doi.org/10.1007/979-8-8688-0146-4_5

Aim for Immersive Learning by Creating the Virtual Machine Yourself!

While the appeal of public cloud platforms like Amazon Web Services (AWS), Microsoft Azure, and Google Cloud Platform (GCP) is undeniable, there are compelling reasons why installing a Linux virtual machine on VMware Workstation trumps deploying on a public cloud for IT Engineers and students aiming to truly master the intricacies of Linux. In the realm of public cloud computing, the convenience of swiftly provisioning templated or pre-built virtual machines is indeed remarkable. Amazon EC2, Azure Virtual Machines, and Google Compute Engine all offer quick solutions for those seeking immediate VM deployment. However, this convenience comes at a cost, particularly for those aspiring to become adept Linux users.

Imagine these cloud-based virtual machines as finely tuned automobiles, handed over to you as the driver. While this is perfect for those with specific destinations in mind, it falls short of nurturing true expertise. Aspiring IT engineers and students seeking to delve into the core mechanics of Linux face limitations in such environments. Here's where the distinction lies: Becoming a Linux mechanic requires you to intimately understand the inner workings and troubleshoot, tweak, and optimize the system. Think of yourself not just as a driver, but as someone who aspires to be a mechanic—one who can fine-tune the engine, modify components, and craft unique solutions. Installing and configuring various Linux flavors from scratch, as offered by VMware Workstation, grants you the raw material to truly build and comprehend Linux from the ground up.

By immersing yourself in the process of setting up a Linux virtual machine within VMware Workstation, you cultivate an in-depth understanding of each step: choosing the distribution, partitioning drives, installing packages, configuring services, and more. This hands-on approach enables you to grasp the foundational principles that underpin Linux, transforming you from a casual user to a Linux virtuoso. While public cloud platforms serve their purpose of swift deployments, they present pre-worked environments that hinder the immersive learning experience you seek. VMware Workstation, on the other hand, places you firmly in the driver's seat of building and nurturing Linux environments. As you read this book and embark on your journey to become a Linux mechanic, remember that the depth of knowledge and expertise lies in the process—in building, troubleshooting, and innovating within your Linux VMs.

Tip

What are n-1 and five 9s?

In practical production scenarios, administrators often opt for the *n–1* (n minus one) version of the software, foregoing the very latest release to enhance stability and circumvent potential bugs and compatibility issues. This strategy is aligned with the pursuit of achieving "five 9s," signifying 99.999 percent yearly uptime, equal to approximately 5.26 minutes of allowable downtime annually. The aim for four 9s translates to 99.99 percent uptime, corresponding to around 52.56 minutes of yearly downtime, while three 9s represent 99.9 percent uptime, allowing for about 8.76 hours of downtime per year. The five 9s goals embody an unwavering commitment to maintaining an exceptionally reliable system. While the n–1 approach supports this objective, administrators retain the flexibility to transition to a newer version if performance or desired features warrant such a shift. This balance between stability and adaptability underscores the nuanced decisions made to ensure both steadfast dependability and operational versatility in production environments.

From Image to Server: Mastering VM Installation and Linux Proficiency

You can create virtual machines (VMs) by using bootable image files from various operating systems or by loading preconfigured VM images created by others. However, opting for the latter choice, involving importing or converting pre-built VMs, may deprive you of the opportunity to grasp the process of installing a virtual server from scratch. Nevertheless, thanks to more powerful desktop and laptop hardware components, creating and running a VM from the ground up requires minimal effort and time investment. Thus, this chapter leads you through the complete installation experience—starting with image file downloads and culminating in basic configuration steps. Even though the VM creations in this book offer a desktop version of more intricate enterprise and cloud infrastructure solutions, the fundamental concepts and techniques of VM provisioning hold striking similarities.

In the past decade, the IT realm has been abuzz with the term "cloud computing." At its core, cloud computing encapsulates the consolidation of potent servers within centralized or distributed data centers, delivering on-demand services via the Internet. Everything operates off-premises, with users interfacing through thin client machines or applications hosted on remote nodes. Beneath the surface of cloud computing reside containerization, virtualization, and Linux technologies—understanding them propels you closer to the world of cloud computing.

After installing VMware Workstation 17 Pro on your laptop, the next step involves securing a bootable image file for your host's operating system for VM installation. This image can span a spectrum of Windows or Linux variants. Given the clear intent to pivot away from the Windows OS and become comfortable with Linux, you'll download a couple of bootable Linux images and begin the installation process. Notably, this exploration extends to two prominent Linux distros—Ubuntu and Fedora. Ubuntu is a widely recognized Debian-based distribution, and Fedora is a community development version rooted in Red Hat. To provide you with comprehensive hands-on familiarity with these Linux distributions, you'll install Ubuntu Server in this chapter, followed by the Fedora server installation in Chapter 6. Both servers are versatile platforms to develop and test your Python network applications throughout the book. While the core kernels bear remarkable resemblance between these Linux distributions, nuanced distinctions emerge through side-by-side usage. Hence, immersing yourself in both installations and navigating basic administrative tasks will amplify your learning and career prospects. In essence, all Linux distributions possess similar fundamental characteristics—they run on the Linux kernel and exhibit common functionalities. However, their distinctions arise from the tailored approach each distribution adopts. Different Linux distributions are like diverse vehicles optimized for specific terrains or tasks. One distribution might be designed with server performance in mind, another for desktop usability, and yet another for security-focused applications.

When you are ready, let's create an Ubuntu Server 22.04 LTS virtual machine.

Tip

Ubuntu Server 22.04 LTS: What's in a name?

In the world of Ubuntu Linux, the nomenclature of server versions follows a consistent *YY.MM* format, denoting the release year and month. Therefore, Ubuntu Server 22.04 bears testament to its debut in the market during the fourth month of 2022. The acronym LTS holds a pivotal role, representing "Long Term Support." This signifies that this particular software iteration enjoys an extended support duration of five years, distinct from its beta counterparts. This naming pattern is mirrored in Ubuntu 18.04 LTS, which emerged in the fourth month of 2018. Additionally, note that even-numbered Ubuntu releases, such as 22.04 LTS, prioritize stability and offer long-term support, while odd-numbered versions, such as 23.04 beta, focus on testing new features with a shorter support window and potential instability. Choosing between them involves weighing stability and long-term support versus the desire for cutting-edge features and innovation.

Downloading and Installing an Ubuntu Server 22 Image

To install the latest Ubuntu Server, you must first download a bootable Ubuntu Server image (`.iso`) file from Ubuntu's official download site. Ensure a reliable Internet connection for the download and then follow the directions in the following sections.

#	Task
①	Launch your preferred web browser and navigate to the Ubuntu download page at `https://ubuntu.com/download/server`. Download the latest server version, at the time of writing the latest long-term support version of 22.04 train was 22.04.3 (`ubuntu-22.04.3-live-server-amd64.iso`), so these instructions use this version, but you can use a newer Ubuntu Server version instead (see Figure 5-1).

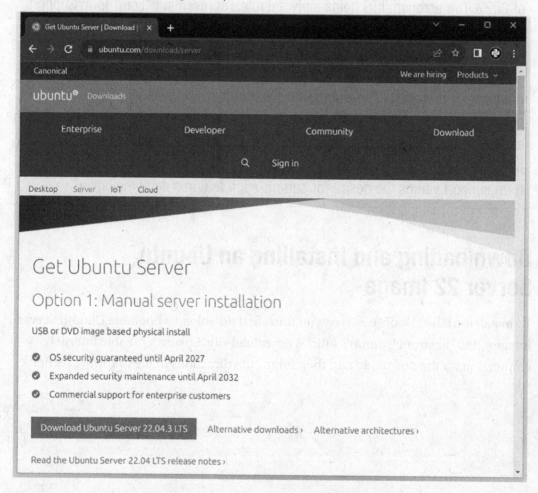

Figure 5-1. *Ubuntu Server 22.04 LTS image download page*

Installing Ubuntu Server 22.04 LTS

Creating a Linux VM on VMware Workstation is a straightforward process. However, honing the skill of creating and installing various VMs using different bootable ISO images can be perfected through practice. For guidance on installing and creating a working Ubuntu Server 22.04 virtual machine, refer to a supplementary guide named Ch05_Create_an_Ubuntu_Server_22_VM.pdf. Follow the guide found on my GitHub page for creating a virtual machine, which walks you through the process of installing an Ubuntu 22.04 server on your Windows PC.

Guide link:

https://github.com/pynetauto/apress_pynetauto_ed2.0/blob/main/pre_
installation_guides/Ch05_Create_an_Ubuntu_Server_22_VM.pdf

At this juncture, the chapter proceeds with the understanding that you have completed an installation of an Ubuntu Server 22.04. Your virtual machine (VM) should now be operational and running as intended.

Warning

Download installation guides and source codes from GitHub

In the first edition of this book, the foundational installation guides were included as an integral part of the content. However, in this updated edition, these essential installation instructions have been classified as supplementary guides, available separately in PDF format. It's important to note that these guides are now provided externally to the book.

To ensure you have easy access to all the guides and code downloads, remember to bookmark my GitHub page at the following URL:

https://github.com/pynetauto/apress_pynetauto_ed2.0/tree/main

---

Logging In to a New Ubuntu Server 22 via SSH

As you'll soon discover, accessing the new VM through VMware Workstation's console screen can be cumbersome. A simpler approach to managing your server involves connecting to it via SSH, using SSH client software on your Windows host PC.

SSH operates over TCP port 22 and is ubiquitous in the network and systems realm for enterprise device management, much like how systems and network administrators oversee their systems within their networks.

Suppose you have already memorized the server's allocated IP address during the Ubuntu Server installation process in the Network Connections section. In that case, your memory is sharp. However, if the assigned IP address has slipped your mind, let's identify the IP address to enable you to SSH into the server.

① The initial and most direct approach to discovering the IP address on an Ubuntu system involves executing the `ip address show` or `ip add` command. An IP address from the VM NAT network should be assigned to your `ens33` network adapter. In this example, u22s1 has been allocated the IP address 192.168.127.129/24. It's worth noting that your server's assigned IP address doesn't necessarily need to match this, but if your Ubuntu Server acquired a valid IP address, it serves as a positive sign that your VM's network functionality is operating correctly.

However, if you've acquired an IP address from a distinct subnet or haven't obtained a valid IP address altogether, then it's imperative to retrace your steps and start the network troubleshooting process from your VM network editor or VM network settings.

```
jdoe@u22s1:~$ ip address show
1: lo: <LOOPBACK,UP,LOWER_UP> mtu 65536 qdisc noqueue state UNKNOWN group
default qlen 1000
   link/loopback 00:00:00:00:00:00 brd 00:00:00:00:00:00
   inet 127.0.0.1/8 scope host lo
    valid_lft forever preferred_lft forever
   inet6 ::1/128 scope host
    valid_lft forever preferred_lft forever
2: ens33: <BROADCAST,MULTICAST,UP,LOWER_UP> mtu 1500 qdisc fq_codel state
UP group default qlen 1000
   link/ether 00:0c:29:cf:71:3d brd ff:ff:ff:ff:ff:ff
   altname enp2s1
   inet 192.168.127.129/24 metric 100 brd 192.168.127.255 scope global
dynamic ens33
    valid_lft 962sec preferred_lft 962sec
   inet6 fe80::20c:29ff:fecf:713d/64 scope link
    valid_lft forever preferred_lft forever
```

② The alternative, more conventional, method of locating the IP address on any Linux server involves executing the `ifconfig` command. For those just beginning to shift from Windows OS to Linux OS, it's evident that this command closely resembles the `ipconfig` command used in the Windows command prompt.

In the context of Ubuntu Server 22.04, it's necessary to install `net-tools` before this command can be used. To do so, execute the `sudo apt install net-tools` command. This step also serves as a convenient test for confirming your virtual Ubuntu Server's Internet connectivity.

```
jdoe@u22s1:~$ ifconfig
-bash: ifconfig: command not found
jdoe@u22s1:~$ sudo apt install net-tools
[sudo] password for jdoe: **********
[...omitted for brevity]
```

Recall that the interface, ens33, serves as the server's virtual NIC connecting to the network. Once the installation is completed, proceed to execute the `ifconfig` command for IP address verification. The ens33 adapter holds the IP address 192.168.127.129/24, accompanied by a broadcast address of 192.168.127.255. If you know the name of the virtual network interface, you can include it in your `ifconfig` command, as shown here:

```
jdoe@u22s1:~$ ifconfig ens33
ens33: flags=4163<UP,BROADCAST,RUNNING,MULTICAST>  mtu 1500
       inet 192.168.127.129  netmask 255.255.255.0  broadcast 192.168.127.255
       inet6 fe80::20c:29ff:fecf:713d  prefixlen 64  scopeid 0x20<link>
       ether 00:0c:29:cf:71:3d  txqueuelen 1000  (Ethernet)
       RX packets 536  bytes 316773 (316.7 KB)
       RX errors 0  dropped 0  overruns 0  frame 0
       TX packets 479  bytes 88511 (88.5 KB)
       TX errors 0  dropped 0 overruns 0  carrier 0  collisions 0
```

③ Pause here for a moment and consider this: The gateway IP for the 192.168.127.0/24 subnet is not 192.168.127.1, but rather 192.168.127.2. Specifically, 192.168.127.2 functions as the NAT gateway IP, while 192.168.127.1 represents the designated IP address of the Windows 10 host's VMnet8 (VMware Network Adapter VMnet8) interface. To verify this information directly from the Ubuntu Server console, utilize the ip route | grep ^default" (or "ip r | grep ^def) command. The purpose of this command is to examine the IP route using a general Regular Expression (grep) and locate a string that starts with ^ and the term default (see Figure 5-2).

```
jdoe@u22s1:~$ ip route | grep ^default
default via 192.168.127.2 dev ens33 proto dhcp src 192.168.127.129 metric 100
```

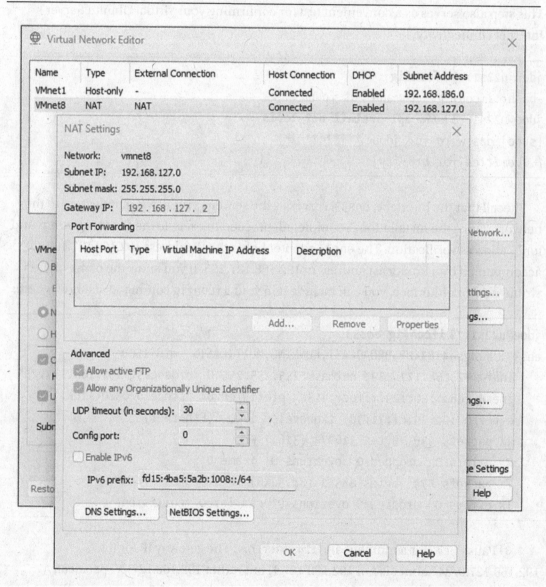

Figure 5-2. *VMware VMnet8, confirming the default gateway on VMware Workstation*

④ Open the Windows Command Prompt using the cmd command and then run the netsh interface ip show addresses "VMware Network Adapter VMnet8" command from your Windows 11 host PC. This confirms your understanding of the VMware NAT network and now you can connect to the u22s1 with the DHCP-assigned IP address of 192.168.127.129.

```
C:\Users\brend>netsh interface ip show addresses "VMware Network Adapter
VMnet8"
Configuration for interface "VMware Network Adapter VMnet8"
  DHCP enabled:                 No
  IP Address:                   192.168.127.1
  Subnet Prefix:                192.168.127.0/24 (mask 255.255.255.0)
  InterfaceMetric:              35
```

---

⑤ If you haven't already downloaded PuTTY from the Internet, visit PuTTY's official website (https://www.putty.org/) to download a copy. Once downloaded, launch PuTTY on your Windows 11 host. Note that there are installable and portable versions— if you want to use it as a stand-alone tool, download the portable version (.exe), but if you plan to use PuTTY with SuperPuTTY later, download the installable version (.msi) and install the software.

Next, enter the IP address of your Ubuntu Server along with port 22 for the SSH connection (see Figure 5-3). Finally, click the Open button located in the bottom-right corner of the PuTTY Configuration window.

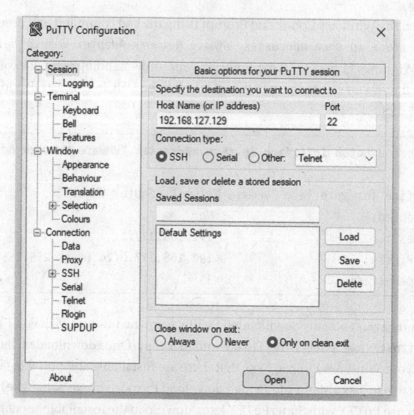

Figure 5-3. *SSH login to u22s1 using PuTTY*

⑥ The server will transmit its `ssh-ed25519` key fingerprint to your PuTTY (SSH) session. To continue to the server's login screen, click Accept (see Figure 5-4).

Figure 5-4. Accepting the PuTTY security alert from the Ubuntu Server

⑦ Enter your username and password and press the Enter key on your keyboard to log in to your Ubuntu Server. Now you are connected to your server via SSH (see Figure 5-5).

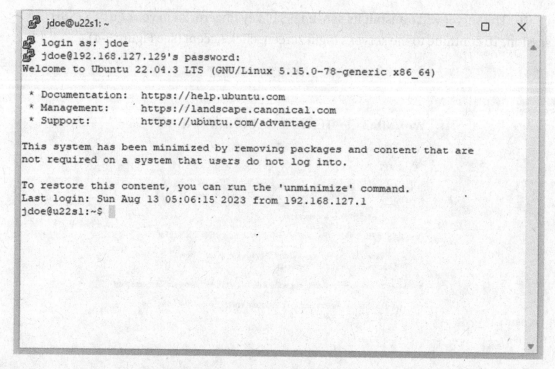

Figure 5-5. *Log in to the Ubuntu Server on PuTTY*

Customize the Ubuntu Server

After creating your Ubuntu Server virtual machine, it works out of the box; however, Ubuntu has a few critical settings disabled by default. You want to get full access to these settings for your testing lab purposes to add more flexibility. You can tweak a few things to make this server more user-friendly to add more value to your learning. If you are running an Ubuntu Server in production, do not enable these settings to reduce the security attacking surface—always follow your organization's security best practices. Because this is your lab VM, you are going to perform some system customizations. First, enable root user SSH login from remote clients; this allows you to connect to this server via SSH as the root user, saving time during system administration. Second, install a desktop GUI; this will allow you to log in to the desktop settings, use the desktop as a standard end-user machine, and use the available applications via the Linux GUI. Third, enable root user GUI access. This feature is disabled by default too, but often the root user GUI access to the server may be required for quick troubleshooting.

Ubuntu VM Customization 1: Enable Root User SSH Login on Ubuntu Server 22.04

As a general rule, most recent Ubuntu Servers prioritize security by disallowing root users from logging into the terminal console or connecting via SSH. While this security measure is essential, it can sometimes impede efficiency during lab scenarios. This situation may necessitate the constant use of sudo before each command, restricting the flexibility you require for your lab activities. For this reason, introducing SSH logins can infuse a bit more flexibility into your lab environment. Additionally, this divergence from the best practice stems from the understanding that learning how to adjust or troubleshoot issues is as important as learning to set things up correctly. Given that these actions are performed within a controlled lab environment on your laptop, you can undertake tasks that might not be permissible in a production setting. However, it's important to emphasize that leaving the root console and SSH login disabled remains a security best practice in real production environments.

To enable direct root user SSH access, start by logging into your server as your regular user. Run the sudo passwd command. Following the password prompt, enter your password, and you will be immediately prompted to create a new Linux password for the root user. Note that while asterisks are used for illustration, your password will remain hidden as you type it.

Let's enable root user SSH login first. Go to u22s1's VMware Console and log in as the user jdoe. You will be working on the console to enable root user SSH login.

#	Task
①	Enable the root user password by performing the following tasks:

```
jdoe@u22s1:~$ sudo passwd
[sudo] password for jdoe: ************** # jdoe's password
New password: ************** # root user's new password
Retype new password: **************
passwd: password updated successfully
```

(*continued*)

#	Task
②	The previous action doesn't automatically grant SSH access to the server. This needs to be manually enabled by updating the SSH server configuration file. To begin, log in as the root user using the `su` - command and enter the password created in the previous step. To enable SSH login for the root user, you must access and modify the `sshd_config` file located under `/etc/ssh`. As you opted for a minimal server installation, most of the desired packages will need to be installed. It's worth noting that there isn't a usable text editor available to open this file initially. Therefore, installing a text editor is necessary. Because I cover the usage of both vi and nano later, install both Linux text editors, as demonstrated here:

```
jdoe@u22s1:~$ su -
Password: ************** # root user's password
root@u22s1:~# vi /etc/ssh/sshd_config # try to open the sshd_config
file
-bash: vi: command not found
root@u22s1:~# apt install vim # install vim text editor
[...ommitted for brevity]
root@u22s1:~# vim --version # check vim version
VIM - Vi IMproved 8.2 (2019 Dec 12, compiled Aug 01 2023 05:37:49)
Included patches: 1-3995, 4563, 4646, 4774, 4895, 4899, 4901, 4919
[...ommitted for brevity]
root@u22s1:~# nano /etc/ssh/sshd_config # try to open the sshd_config
file
-bash: nano: command not found
root@u22s1:~# apt install nano # install nano text editor
[...ommitted for brevity]
root@u22s1:~# nano --version # check nano version
GNU nano, version 6.2
(C) 1999-2011, 2013-2022 Free Software Foundation, Inc.
[...ommitted for brevity]
```

(continued)

#	Task

③ With both text editors installed, you can update the `sshd_config` file to allow root user SSH login and take the next steps. If you are familiar with the vi/vim text editor, use it. Assuming that you are a first-time Linux user, you use the nano text editor here to update the information on the config file.

First, open and locate the line beginning with `#PermitRootLogin prohibit-password` and add a new configuration, `PermitRootLogin yes`, on the next line.

root@u22s1:~# **nano /etc/ssh/sshd_config**

`[...omitted for brevity]`

`#LoginGraceTime 2m`

`#PermitRootLogin prohibit-password # Leave the original value for`
`future reference`

PermitRootLogin yes `# Add this new line to enable root user SSH login.`

`#StrictModes yes`

`[...omitted for brevity]`

If a line of configuration is already disabled by default, I developed a habit of adding a new line below the original settings and enabling the feature, so I know that this setting was something I have modified. Also, you can add a comment above the changed settings using a leading # followed by a change description.

After you have modified the file, save the changes by using Ctrl+S and then exit by using Ctrl+X.

④ To make the previous change take effect, you must restart the SSH server service.

root@u22s1:~# **service ssh restart** `# restart ssh server service`

root@u22s1:~#

If you get no error, the service has been restarted successfully. In Linux, this is called "a silent yes."

(continued)

287

#	Task
⑤	Now, from your Windows 11 host PC, launch PuTTY, enter the IP address of your server, and SSH in with port 22. Log in with the user name `root` and your root user's password. Once you successfully log in to your server via an SSH session, you will see a screenshot like the one in Figure 5-6.

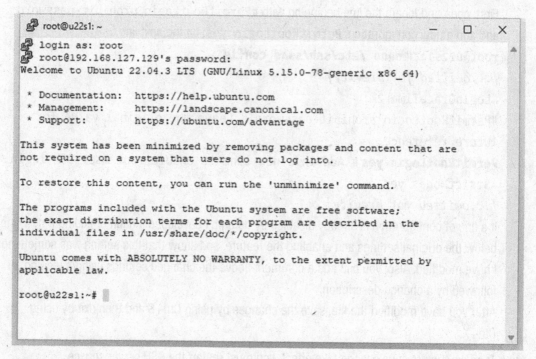

Figure 5-6. *root user SSH login on Ubuntu*

Tip

Enabling root user SSH login with a single command

To quickly grant SSH access to the root user, you can use a concise `sed` command in your terminal session. By executing this single command, you make the necessary modification in the SSH configuration file:

```
$ sudo sed -i 's/#PermitRootLogin prohibit-password/
PermitRootLogin yes/' /etc/ssh/sshd_config
```

$ [sudo] password for jdoe: *******************

Keep in mind that following this config change, it's essential to restart the SSH service for the changes to take effect:

```
$ sudo service ssh restart
```

A noteworthy point to remember is the usage of the $ symbol. When this symbol is present, it signifies that you're logged in as a regular user. To execute root user-privileged commands, you need to prefix them with the `sudo` command. Conversely, the # symbol denotes that you're logged in as the root user. In such cases, there's no requirement to add `sudo` before your commands.

You have now installed two text editor programs—vim and nano—on your Ubuntu Server and successfully enabled SSH login for the root user on your Linux server. You've successfully added some flexibility to your lab server.

Ubuntu VM Customization 2: Install a Desktop GUI and Other Packages

In a production environment, a Linux server is commonly deployed without a Graphical User Interface (GUI) to enhance security and performance. This aligns with the preferred security practice followed by many Linux administrators. However, this choice doesn't mean you cannot utilize a Linux server with a GUI. You have the option to install a desktop GUI on an Ubuntu Server if desired. A GUI can be particularly useful in a testing lab setting, providing additional capabilities needed for testing diverse IT scenarios. For instance, it allows you to test an HTTPS connection via a web browser. In a typical production environment, Linux is frequently configured as a headless server without a GUI. This choice bolsters server performance and security, making a GUI for the Linux server non-essential in such scenarios. Additionally, operating without a GUI is different than operating a system in headless mode. A server is designated as headless when it operates without connected KVM (keyboard, video, and mouse) peripherals, emphasizing its lack of direct keyboard, video, and monitor connections for user interaction.

Nevertheless, understanding how to install/remove a GUI on an Ubuntu Server remains helpful. Let's delve into the process of installing a desktop GUI directly from the VMware Workstation console of Ubuntu Server, u22s1. You'll update the apt packages index first, install the `tasksel` tool, and then install the Ubuntu desktop. Follow the provided instructions:

#	Task

①	First, update the apt package index.
	`jdoe@u22s1:~# `**`sudo apt update`**
	`[sudo] password for jdoe: **********`
	`[...omitted for brevity]`

②	To install Ubuntu Desktop, run the following `sudo apt` command. Be patient, as it may take some time to complete the desktop installation. `jdoe@u22s1:~# `**`sudo apt install ubuntu-desktop -y`** `[...omitted for brevity]` Appending the '-y' flag to your Linux command expedites software installations by automating your responses throughout the command execution.

(continued)

#	Task
③	At the end of Ubuntu Desktop installation, it will prompt you with the restart of services. We can ignore this one by selecting <Cancel> and exiting the application (see Figure 5-7).

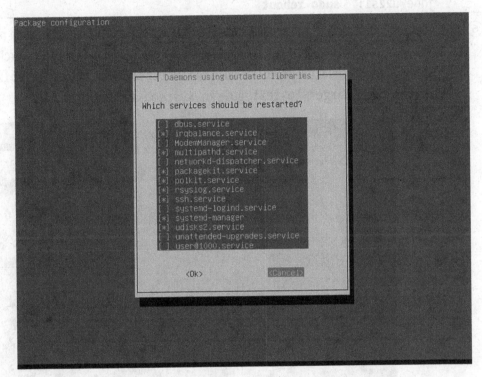

Figure 5-7. *Select <Cancel> to complete the Ubuntu Desktop installation*

④ Once you have exited, to ensure that the system starts with the GUI, you have to run
the following command to create the symlink to the default.target. This command
changes the default systemctl set-default multi-user.target settings to
systemctl set-default graphical.target.

```
jdoe@u22s1:~# sudo systemctl set-default graphical.target
[sudo] password for jdoe: **********
Created symlink /etc/systemd/system/default.target → /lib/systemd/
system/graphical.target.
```

(continued)

#	Task
⑤	Next, execute the sudo reboot command to restart the server and apply the Ubuntu desktop. jdoe@u22s1:~$ **sudo reboot**
⑥	After the reboot, as you can see in Figure 5-8, you will see a welcoming GUI login page with your user's name. If the GUI does not load up properly, you may need to search the Google to troubleshoot the issue. One such site is https://www.cyberciti.biz/faq/ switch-boot-target-to-text-gui-in-systemd-linux/ 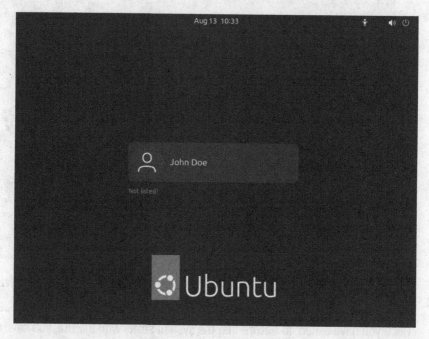 *Figure 5-8.* *Ubuntu login GUI*
⑦	**Optionally**, you can switch the default target back to the multi-user target, which doesn't load the GUI by default. To do this, use the following command: jdoe@u22s1:~# **sudo systemctl set-default multi-user.target** jdoe@u22s1:~# **sudo reboot**

(continued)

#	Task
⑧	**Optionally**, if you want to remove the Ubuntu Desktop environment, it's possible; however, it may not eliminate all related packages or configurations. The purge command eradicates the ubuntu-desktop package and its configuration files, while autoremove eliminates any unnecessary dependencies. It's important to note that removing the desktop environment might not fully restore the server to its initial state. In my tests, these commands solely removed the Ubuntu desktop, leaving the base Gnome desktop untouched. Hence, you also have to remove the base Gnome desktop to remove the GUI. I am going to leave this for you to investigate at your leisure. jdoe@u22s1:~# **sudo apt purge ubuntu-desktop** jdoe@u22s1:~# **sudo apt autoremove**

Congratulations, you've now acquired the knowledge to update your server and install a GUI on your Ubuntu Server 22.04 LTS. The GUI interface will prove invaluable in the upcoming troubleshooting and testing tasks you'll undertake, providing a streamlined way to address specific challenges.

Ubuntu VM Customization 3: Enable Root User GUI Access

If you have keen observation skills, you might have already noticed that the root user GUI login isn't functional. You might be wondering, "How can I enable root user GUI login?" Given that this is a lab server, providing you the freedom to explore and customize, let's proceed to enable the root user GUI login. Note that this is separate from the SSH root user login, which was covered earlier.

Initially, you need to be logged into the server as a regular user (jdoe in the example) to accomplish this task. Alternatively, you can choose to SSH into the server using PuTTY if you prefer.

#	Task

① Open and edit /etc/gdm3/custom.conf, which is the GDM configuration file, using the nano text editor to allow root login. Add AllowRoot=true and save the file.

```
jdoe@u22s1:~$ sudo nano /etc/gdm3/custom.conf
[sudo] password for jdoe: ***************
jdoe@u22s1:~$ cat /etc/gdm3/custom.conf
# GDM configuration storage
#
# See /usr/share/gdm/gdm.schemas for a list of available options.
[daemon]
# Uncomment the line below to force the login screen to use Xorg
#WaylandEnable=false
# Enabling automatic login
#  AutomaticLoginEnable = true
#  AutomaticLogin = user1
# Enabling timed login
#  TimedLoginEnable = true
#  TimedLogin = user1
#  TimedLoginDelay = 10
AllowRoot = true # Add this line here!
[security]
[xdmcp]
[chooser]
[debug]
# Uncomment the line below to turn on debugging
# More verbose logs
# Additionally lets the X server dump core if it crashes
#Enable=true
```

(*continued*)

#	Task

② Next, edit the PAM authentication daemon configuration file at /etc/pam.d/gdm-password and comment on the specific line that denies root access to the graphical user interface. Use the nano or vi editors and open the /etc/pam.d/gdm-password file. Put # at the beginning of the line that starts with auth required pam_succeed_if.so user!= root quiet_success. You are commenting that line out, which means you are disabling the feature.

```
jdoe@u22s1:~$ sudo nano /etc/pam.d/gdm-password
jdoe@u22s1:~$ cat /etc/pam.d/gdm-password
#%PAM-1.0
auth      requisite        pam_nologin.so
#auth     required         pam_succeed_if.so user != root quiet_success # Put the
                                             '#' to hash out the line (disable feature)

@include common-auth
auth      optional         pam_gnome_keyring.so
@include common-account
# SELinux needs to be the first session rule. This ensures that any
# lingering context has been cleared. Without this it is possible
# that a module could execute code in the wrong domain.
session [success=ok ignore=ignore module_unknown=ignore default=bad]
pam_selinux.so close
session required         pam_loginuid.so
# SELinux needs to intervene at login time to ensure that the process
# starts in the proper default security context. Only sessions which are
# intended to run in the user's context should be run after this.
# pam_selinux.so changes the SELinux context of the used TTY and configures
# SELinux in order to transition to the user context with the next execve()
# call.
session [success=ok ignore=ignore module_unknown=ignore default=bad]
pam_selinux.so open
session optional         pam_keyinit.so force revoke
session required         pam_limits.so
session required         pam_env.so readenv=1
session required         pam_env.so readenv=1 user_readenv=1 envfile=/etc/default/
                         locale
@include common-session
session optional         pam_gnome_keyring.so auto_start
@include common-password
```

(continued)

#	Task
③	A mandatory reboot is required here once again. Reboot your Ubuntu Server using the `sudo reboot` command or using the power button on the top-right corner of your Ubuntu desktop. Once the server has been restarted, log in as another user, enter `root` as the username, and enter the root user's password. jdoe@u22s1:~$ **sudo reboot**
④	After the reboot, select the Not `listed` option on the GUI login page and use `root` as the user ID. Then use the root user password to log in to the desktop as a root user. Congratulations! You can now log in to the Ubuntu desktop as a root user (see Figure 5-9).

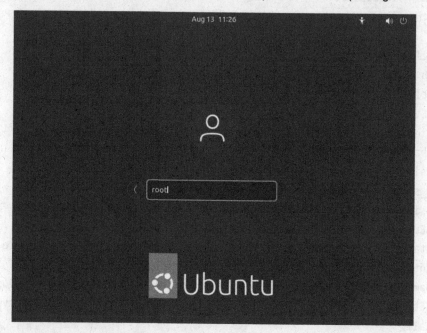

Figure 5-9. *Ubuntu Server customization 3, root user GUI login*

You've now achieved success in implementing three customizations on your initial Ubuntu Server and are primed to delve deeper into the realms of Linux and Python. The next step involves swiftly mastering the process of taking snapshots of the current virtual machine status. This action augments your flexibility, facilitating the execution of an array of tasks within your lab environment.

Taking a Snapshot of a Virtual Machine

One of the most potent advantages of using a virtual machine for your operating system lies in the capability of snapshots. In enterprise settings utilizing ESXi and vCenter-based VMware solutions, snapshots and cloning stand as remarkable methods to avert system failures and facilitate recovery from such events. Within the VMware technology sphere, additional recovery mechanisms include high availability, vMotion, and DRS. However, when using a desktop-friendly solution such as the VMware Workstation 17 Pro, snapshots and clones are two key tools to preserve the current condition of your virtual machines (VMs).

Consider a snapshot akin to capturing an image of your system at a given moment. This permits you to revert any undesired or unsuccessful system alterations to the pristine operational state of the VM. On the other hand, the cloning feature empowers you to create either partial or complete backups of your VMs, thereby safeguarding the system state in scenarios of system failures. A crucial point to consider is that snapshots and cloning, while powerful tools, are not immune to data loss. This is especially true for servers configured as databases, where intricate data structures might not be effectively captured. Additionally, newly implemented configurations could potentially be lost and unrecoverable in some cases.

In the context of Python network automation labs, snapshots or full clones can serve as fail-safe recovery mechanisms. Snapshots enable you to navigate through different moments within your lab, essentially letting you travel back in time. In the upcoming steps, I guide you through the process of creating a snapshot for your Ubuntu Server before proceeding with further software installations on the server.

#	Task
①	To capture the present state of your server, access your VMware Workstation menu and follow this sequence: VM ➤ Snapshot ➤ Take Snapshot. Refer to Figure 5-10 for visual guidance.

Figure 5-10. *VMware snapshot, navigating to the Snapshot menu*

(*continued*)

#	Task
②	Enter a descriptive name detailing the status/stage of the VM, and then click the Take Snapshot button to initiate snapshot creation, as depicted in Figure 5-11. It's important to recognize that generating a snapshot while the VM is powered on takes more time and requires additional storage space compared to creating a snapshot while the VM is powered off.

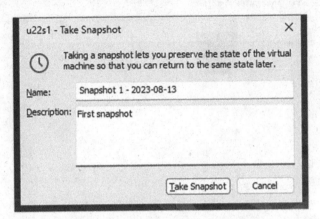

Figure 5-11. *VMware snapshot, creating a VM snapshot*

(*continued*)

#	Task
③	In the bottom-left corner of the window, the percentage of snapshot progress will be displayed. Once it reaches 100 percent, navigate to the Snapshot Manager from the menu and confirm the snapshot (see Figure 5-12).

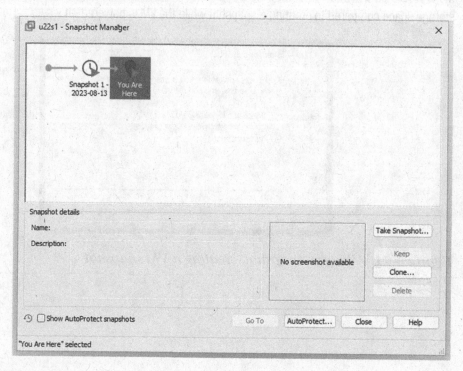

Figure 5-12. *VMware snapshot, confirming snapshot*

Cloning a Virtual Machine

You now have a customized Ubuntu virtual server. Should you desire to create an additional VM, you can achieve this by cloning the existing VM. Cloning enables you to re-create an identical machine at the speed of lightning, a remarkable contrast to the considerable time spent installing a new VM from scratch. Furthermore, cloning offers the advantage of generating a comprehensive backup of the current VM state, thereby preserving the server's configuration. With this understanding, let's delve into the process.

Power off your virtual machine, u22s1, to begin the cloning process. Only cold cloning is supported in VMware Workstation Pro.

#	Task
①	To clone a VM, navigate to VM ➤ Manage ➤ Clone (see Figure 5-13). Alternatively, you can also start the cloning process within the Snapshot Manager.

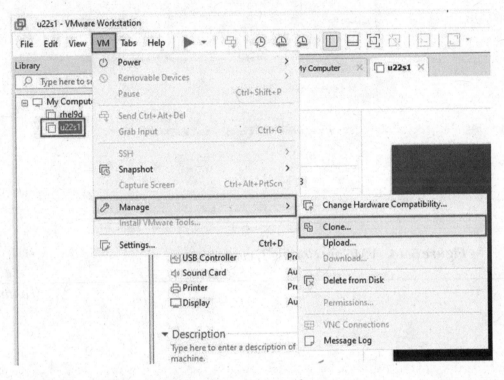

Figure 5-13. *VMware cloning 1, making a clone*

②	From the Welcome message, select Next to quickly move to the next page.

(continued)

#	Task
③	Leave the default settings and click the Next button (see Figure 5-14).

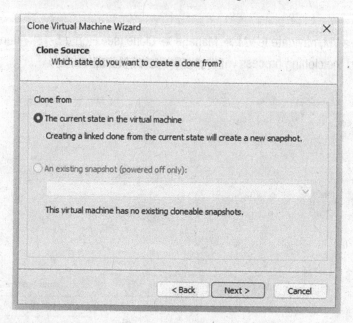

Figure 5-14.   *VMware cloning 1, clone source*

(*continued*)

#	Task
④	Select Create a Full Clone and click the Next button (see Figure 5-15).

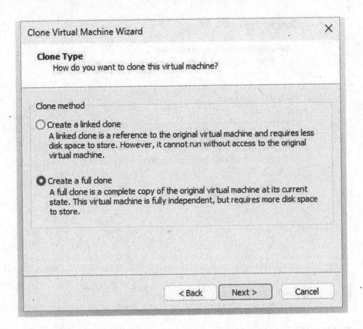

Figure 5-15. *VMware cloning 1, clone type, a full clone*

(*continued*)

#	Task
⑤	Rename the cloned VM and click the Finish button (see Figure 5-16).

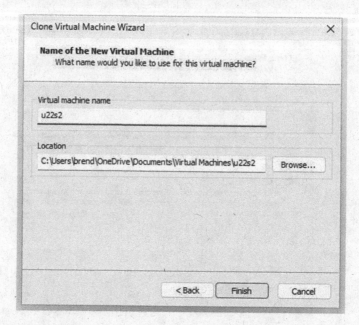

Figure 5-16. *VMware cloning 1, renaming the cloned VM*

(*continued*)

#	Task

⑥ Now click the Close button (see Figure 5-17).

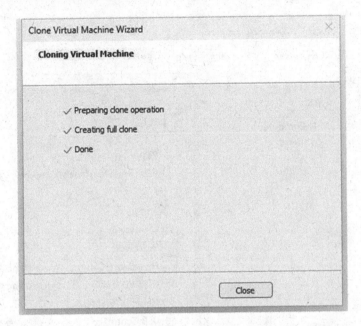

Figure 5-17. *VMware cloning 1, closing the VM cloning wizard*

(*continued*)

#	Task
⑦	You will now see another Ubuntu Server added to your VM library (see Figure 5-18).

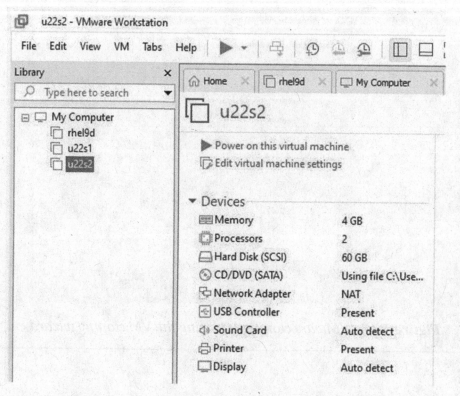

Figure 5-18. *VMware cloning 1, cloned VM added to the library*

(*continued*)

#	Task
⑧	**Optionally**, if you want to copy and duplicate your VM simply, simply copy the folder containing all the VM files to other storage. This method will take up a lot of hard disk space, so if you are using a smaller SSD, a snapshot is a better option than fully cloning a VM (see Figure 5-19).

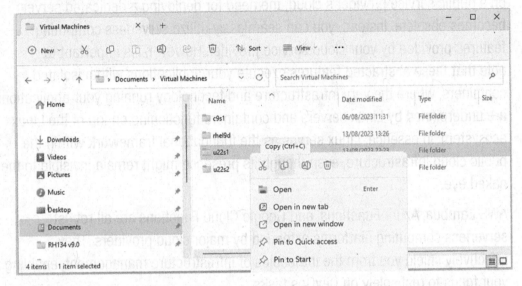

Figure 5-19. *VMware cloning 2, copying the VM folder to an external drive*

Well done! You've successfully created a snapshot and a full clone of a functional Ubuntu 22.04 server. This accomplishment sets the stage for your upcoming learning journey. In the next chapter, you explore the installation of Fedora using a similar method. This will allow you to delve into crafting a Red Hat-flavored VM and exploring its customized configurations.

Now equipped with the skills to install, customize, back up, and clone an Ubuntu Server VM, you're ready for the next phase: creating another Linux server, your third server. This forthcoming chapter guides you through the process of creating a virtual machine for Fedora 38, serving as an all-in-one IP services server. This installation will play a pivotal role in the network automation labs.

Expand Your Knowledge:

What Does It Mean to Go Serverless?

Featuring AWS Lambda, Azure Functions, and Google Cloud Functions

If you're aiming to develop an application and operate it as a serverless service on a public service provider's cloud, the need for deploying a dedicated server becomes obsolete. Instead, you can seamlessly utilize serverless computing features provided by your cloud service provider. However, it's important to note that these abstracted features execute your applications within isolated containers, where the very infrastructure and technology running your applications are underpinned by Linux servers and containers functioning on top of the Linux ecosystem. In essence, Linux serves as the foundational framework within the public cloud infrastructure, even though its presence might remain invisible to the naked eye.

AWS Lambda, Azure Functions, and Google Cloud Functions are all robust serverless computing platforms extended by major cloud providers. They effectively shield you from the intricacies of infrastructure management, enabling your focus to rest solely on DevOps tasks.

AWS Lambda, with its support for multiple languages and seamless integration with AWS services, offers auto-scaling triggered by events.

Azure Functions amplifies language diversity, seamlessly fits within the Microsoft ecosystem, and expands through automated scaling.

Google Cloud Functions, starting with Node.js and now embracing languages like Python and Go, smoothly integrates with Google Cloud services.

All three platforms excel in event-driven execution, auto-scaling, integration with SQL and no-SQL databases, and pay-as-you-go billing. While AWS Lambda boasts extensive community adoption, Azure Functions prospers within Microsoft's domain, and Google Cloud Functions optimizes Google's service integration. Selecting a suitable platform for your use case hinges on factors such as cloud provider preference, language proficiency, integration requisites, and your existing ecosystem, all culminating in effective serverless application development.

Nevertheless, even in the era of serverless computing at your disposal, understanding Linux is as an indispensable asset for all IT engineers, particularly for both upcoming and seasoned network engineers who have yet to explore the Linux realm. The pervasive influence of Linux across the bedrock infrastructure of these technological advancements further accentuates the imperative for a heightened grasp of Linux systems. Such insight is pivotal in enabling adept adaptation to the continuously shifting terrain of contemporary computing.

Summary

You began this chapter by downloading the latest Ubuntu Server 22 bootable image, a pivotal step in configuring your very own virtual machine within the VMware Workstation environment. Ubuntu, a prominent Debian-based Linux distribution, is renowned for delivering an exceptional user experience in the Linux realm. While Ubuntu Desktop traditionally acted as a gateway for Windows users venturing into Linux, the approach in this book took a unique turn. You delved into Ubuntu Server 22 with minimal installation, and then with a surprising twist, you integrated a GUI, enriching the versatility of your lab setup. Installing an Ubuntu Server as a virtual machine proved to be a straightforward process, but it still presents many challenges for novice Linux users. By the end of the chapter, you had adeptly installed the Ubuntu Server virtual machine from the ground up. This newfound mastery extends not only to customizing specific server configurations but also to the art of capturing snapshots and skillfully creating clones of virtual machines.

CHAPTER 6

Creating a Fedora Server Virtual Machine (VM)

You begin this chapter by downloading the latest Fedora Server 38 bootable image and creating a Fedora Linux virtual machine (VM) in the VMware Workstation environment. Fedora, a community-driven development distribution rooted in Red Hat Linux, stands as the upstream of Red Hat Enterprise Linux (RHEL). It's known for its cutting-edge software experience and serves as another popular Linux entry point for new Linux learners. The focus in this chapter is building and tailoring Fedora 38 Server to align with the lab requirements. The aim is to enrich your lab journey by customizing the server for specific needs. You will also acquire the knowledge of recovering a forgotten password for the root user. A forthcoming chapter will introduce various IP services, augmenting the server with time and file storage functionalities. As you traverse this chapter, you'll gather hands-on experience customizing a Fedora Server VM from scratch, modifying the hostname, and assigning a static IP address. You'll also master creating a VM via a .ova file for GNS3 VM. This chapter signifies the second step in your transition from a Windows user to a novice Linux enthusiast.

In the previous chapter, you created an Ubuntu Server machine and learned how to customize its settings to make it more usable for your lab. Although you could simply clone the existing Linux VM to create more virtual machines, this would prevent you from learning the basic operations of other Linux distributions, such as Fedora. Fedora, along with its sister Linux distributions CentOS and RHEL, are among the most popular

© Brendan Choi 2024
B. Choi, *Introduction to Python Network Automation Volume I - Laying the Groundwork*,
https://doi.org/10.1007/979-8-8688-0146-4_6

first-time Linux user operating systems. First-time Linux users are likely to start their journeys with either Ubuntu or Fedora, as they both offer great graphical user interfaces, which lower the entry to Linux. Therefore, you will download and install a second Linux distribution, Fedora. You also learn how to turn this server into a server with multiple IP services for lab testing purposes in Chapter 8. As in the previous chapter, you will search for and download the bootable image, install the image, and then create another virtual machine. After creating the Fedora 38 virtual machine, you will test the server's connection via SSH and learn an easy way to manage the network adapter on a RHEL flavored Linux server. To prepare for GNS3 integration, you also need to download the correct copy of the GNS3 VM file for VMware Workstation. That way, using the downloaded GNS3 VM .ova file, the GNS3 VM will be created ahead of time for smoother integration. But before jumping into VM creation tasks, I quickly clarify some Linux terminologies and the Linux distribution relationship to expand your knowledge.

Understanding the Fedora, CentOS Stream, and RHEL Relationship

Using the example of Fedora, CentOS Stream, and Red Hat Enterprise Linux (RHEL), this section explores their interconnected relationships. First and foremost, **Fedora** serves as the cutting-edge, community-driven Linux distribution that functions as **an upstream project for RHEL**. Known for its constant delivery of cutting-edge features, technologies, and software, Fedora 38—the most recent version of writing this book—empowers users with the latest advancements within the RHEL-based Linux ecosystem. It functions as a testing ground for novel features, ideas, and technologies, potentially adopted by CentOS Stream and eventually integrated into RHEL 9. While Fedora may not offer the same long-term stability as RHEL, it provides an environment for community developers to venture into new realms of possibility within the Linux landscape.

   CentOS Stream occupies an intermediary role, bridging the development stage of Fedora with the steadfastness of RHEL. For instance, CentOS Stream 9 **operates as a rolling-release preview platform, showcasing features that will later be incorporated into the subsequent RHEL 9 release**. This avenue permits users to preview forthcoming changes and contribute feedback before their integration into RHEL 9. Additionally, CentOS Stream serves as a community development platform, enabling the creation of applications and solutions that align seamlessly with RHEL. In essence, it acts as a vital connection between upstream development and enterprise-grade readiness.

Red Hat Enterprise Linux (RHEL) stands out as **a commercially supported and enterprise-grade Linux distribution**, renowned for its unshakable stability, security, and sustained support. RHEL 9 epitomizes this stability, designed to provide a reliable operating system for mission-critical environments. Developed by Red Hat, an IBM-owned software company, RHEL benefits from extensive testing, certifications, and premium support options. Organizations seeking a dependable and well-supported platform for their applications and services often choose RHEL 9. Typically, RHEL releases patch version upgrades every six months and major version changes every three years. As of 2023, RHEL 10 was under development and slated for release in two years.

In other words, the interplay between these three Linux OSs is as follows: **Fedora 38 functions as the upstream source**, introducing fresh innovations and concepts. **CentOS Stream 9 bridges the gap between Fedora and RHEL**, offering a preview platform and inviting contributions to forthcoming RHEL modifications. Lastly, **RHEL 9 serves as the enterprise-ready, commercially supported distribution that draws from developments in both Fedora and CentOS Stream**. It caters to organizations seeking stability, security, and long-term and technical support under a subscription model. Like the relationship between Fedora and RHEL, Ubuntu, developed by Canonical, maintains a similar dynamic with Debian Linux.

Tip

Linux chaos? Community-driven, upstream, downstream, stable, commercial

"Linux chaos" refers to the diverse and dynamic nature of the Linux ecosystem. With thousands of contributors, distributions, and projects, the Linux world can seem chaotic at times. This chaos is also the source of Linux's strength, as it enables rapid innovation, customization, and collaboration.

Community-Driven

Both Debian and RHEL have strong community-driven elements. Debian is developed and maintained by a large community of volunteers and enthusiasts. The Debian Project emphasizes openness, collaboration, and inclusivity, allowing anyone to contribute to its development.

Upstream

In the context of Debian and RHEL, "upstream" refers to the source of software that is incorporated into their distributions. Debian draws software from various upstream projects and integrates it into its repositories. RHEL's upstream source includes projects like Fedora, from which it derives many of its features and innovations.

Downstream

"Downstream" refers to projects or distributions that build on the work of upstream sources. In the case of Debian, Ubuntu is a downstream distribution that takes Debian as its base and adds its features and modifications. For RHEL, CentOS Stream serves as a downstream distribution that previews upcoming RHEL features.

Stable

Both Debian and RHEL offer stable releases. Debian's stable release focuses on reliability, security, and long-term support. RHEL is renowned for its enterprise-grade stability, making it a preferred choice for organizations seeking a dependable platform.

Commercial

While Debian is maintained by a community of volunteers and offers free access to its software, RHEL is a commercial distribution developed by Red Hat. RHEL comes with professional support, certifications, and advanced features tailored for enterprise environments. This commercial model helps fund RHEL's development and support services.

In summary, both Debian and RHEL exemplify the complexity and vibrancy of the Linux ecosystem. They embrace community-driven development, leverage upstream sources, create downstream distributions, offer stable releases, and showcase a commercial model with varying focuses and objectives.

Downloading and Installing Fedora Server Image

The procedure for downloading and installing a Fedora virtual machine (VM) in VMware Workstation mirrors the process for installing the Ubuntu 22 server. Similar to creating an Ubuntu VM, the initial step involves downloading a bootable Fedora installation image file in the .iso (bootable) file format. As of the writing of this book, the latest version was 38. Should you be reading this at a later time, you can download either version 38 or a more recent version for this chapter. While there may be minimal differences between major features in recent Fedora versions, the core mechanics should remain consistent. Additionally, it's worth noting that Fedora 38 can be interchanged with CentOS Stream 9 or RHEL 9, with only minor deviations in packaging support. Nonetheless, considering Fedora's status as the cutting-edge version within the RHEL lineage and its cost-free nature, it's highly recommended, particularly for newcomers.

Before proceeding, verify your Internet connectivity, then follow these steps to create and install your new Fedora 38 VM in VMware Workstation 17 Pro. If you opt to download and install an alternative version of Fedora (or CentOS Stream, or RHEL), rest assured that the installation process will remain nearly identical. Chapter 8 delves into installing various software to transform this server into a versatile lab hub and the Python Automation server. Pay special attention to the software installation guidelines tailored to your specific Fedora version, as compatibility may vary across versions. This Fedora VM can also serve as a versatile lab server for your future IT studies, servicing various IP services to aid in your future IT certification preparations or used as the basis for proof-of-concept labs.

Expand Your Knowledge:

Ding-dong, the Source Code's Closed!

With IBM's acquisition of Red Hat for $34 billion in 2018, changes have surfaced in the realm of CentOS server support and development. Community support for CentOS 8 servers ceased on December 31, 2021, shifting users toward CentOS 8 Stream or newer versions. Positioned between Fedora and Red Hat Enterprise Linux, CentOS Stream functions as an early-release variant of RHEL. Implementing Stream in production can lead to support challenges from Red Hat, detaching their obligation for outdated CentOS server versions. However, Stream versions suit lab environments, meeting most testing needs. July 2023 saw Red Hat's pivotal announcement of exclusively catering RHEL source code to only paying customers, impacting projects relying on RHEL's code, like AlmaLinux, Rocky Linux, and Oracle Unbreakable Linux. The adjustment disrupts free compatibility and carries implications for various projects and their users. Indeed, IBM has decided to lock the gates and keep RHEL's source code behind closed doors, barring non-paying customers from the grand code unveiling.

First, let's download the latest Fedora installation `.iso` file from the official Fedora site.

Downloading the Fedora 38 Server Image

#	Task
①	From your favorite web browser, go to the Fedora Project Official site and click the DVD iso download button for Fedora Server on the web page (see Figure 6-1). URL: `https://fedoraproject.org/server/download/`

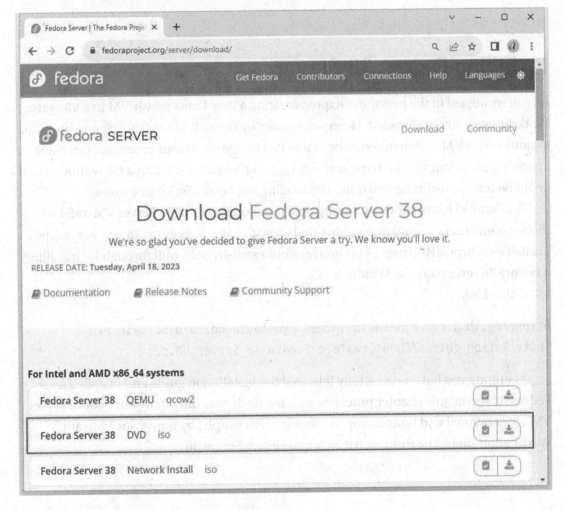

Figure 6-1. *Fedora 38 download page*

(continued)

#	Task
②	Alternatively, you can search for the Fedora Linux release index for any previous version. `https://dl.fedoraproject.org/pub/fedora/linux/releases/`
③	After downloading, your file will be stored in the `Downloads` folder under your username. Once you've obtained the bootable `.iso` file and it's ready for use, make sure to keep track of where you saved it.

Installing Fedora 38 Server

As you witnessed in the previous chapter, creating a new Linux server VM in a VMware Workstation is straightforward. However, mastering the skill of configuring and installing various server VMs using different bootable ISO images demands practice. Moreover, acquiring proficiency in the basic text editing and navigating the Linux OS without a GUI could be time-consuming and quite challenging, especially for novice users.

For detailed instructions on setting up a functional Fedora 38 Server VM, refer to the supplementary installation guide titled `Ch06_Create_a_Fedora_38_Server_VM.pdf` available on my GitHub page. This guide offers a step-by-step walkthrough for installing a Fedora 38 server on your Windows PC.

Guide Link:

`https://github.com/pynetauto/apress_pynetauto_ed2.0/blob/main/pre_`
`installation_guides/Ch06_Create_a_Fedora_38_Server_VM.pdf`

Assuming you have successfully followed the installation guide and installed a Fedora 38 server, this chapter proceeds with the understanding that your Fedora Server VM is operational and functioning as intended. Put simply, by now, your VMware Workstation should be running a functional Fedora Server 38.

Accessing Fedora 38 Server via SSH

In Fedora 38, there's no need to modify any settings to establish a remote connection using SSH. By default, the regular users are permitted but the root user is not permitted to connect to the server using the SSH protocol. To confirm this, don't just take my word for it. You can verify this by launching PuTTY on your Windows 11 host and establishing an SSH connection to the Windows 11 host PC.

#	Task
①	On your VMware Workstation Console, use the Linux command ip address show or ip add show to confirm the DHCP-acquired IP address of your Fedora Server. In my example, the allocated IP address is 192.168.127.130 for the interface ens160. Note that your IP address and IP address subnet may be different from mine; see Figure 6-2.

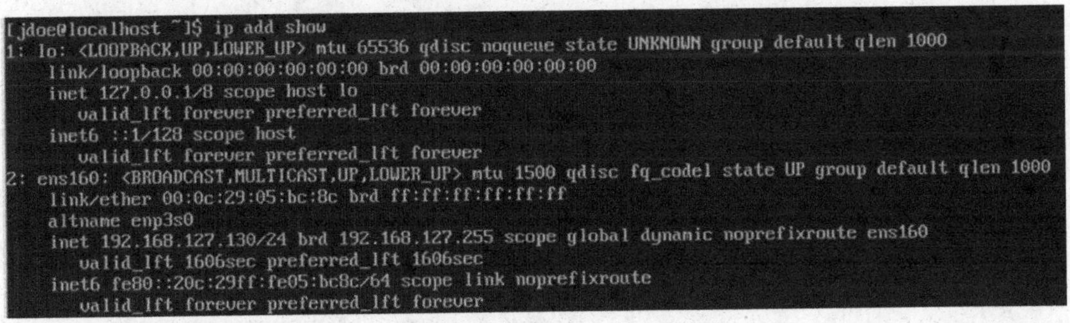

```
[jdoe@localhost ~]$ ip add show
1: lo: <LOOPBACK,UP,LOWER_UP> mtu 65536 qdisc noqueue state UNKNOWN group default qlen 1000
    link/loopback 00:00:00:00:00:00 brd 00:00:00:00:00:00
    inet 127.0.0.1/8 scope host lo
       valid_lft forever preferred_lft forever
    inet6 ::1/128 scope host
       valid_lft forever preferred_lft forever
2: ens160: <BROADCAST,MULTICAST,UP,LOWER_UP> mtu 1500 qdisc fq_codel state UP group default qlen 1000
    link/ether 00:0c:29:05:bc:8c brd ff:ff:ff:ff:ff:ff
    altname enp3s0
    inet 192.168.127.130/24 brd 192.168.127.255 scope global dynamic noprefixroute ens160
       valid_lft 1606sec preferred_lft 1606sec
    inet6 fe80::20c:29ff:fe05:bc8c/64 scope link noprefixroute
       valid_lft forever preferred_lft forever
```

Figure 6-2. *ip add show command output*

(*continued*)

#	Task
②	Next, from your host's Windows 11 desktop, open PuTTY and enter the IP address of your Fedora 38 VM. You already confirmed the IP address and it was 192.168.127.130. Enter the IP address into PuTTY's Host Name (or IP Address) field, as shown in Figure 6-3.

Figure 6-3. *PuTTY login screen*

(*continued*)

#	Task
③	When the PuTTY security alert is prompted, accept the rsa2 key and click the Accept button (see Figure 6-4).

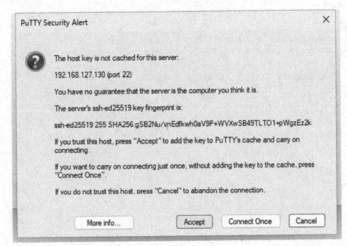

Figure 6-4. *Fedora 38 SSH login, accepting the ssh-ed25519 server key*

(*continued*)

#	Task
④	Now use your user ID and password to confirm that the SSH login works (see Figure 6-5).

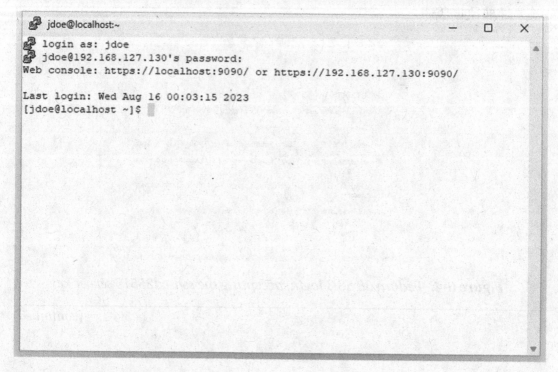

Figure 6-5. *SSH normal user login*

(*continued*)

#	Task
⑤	If you prefer, you can initiate another PuTTY session and log in as the root user this time. You haven't made any system changes at this point and if you attempt to log in as the root user vis SSH, you will get an Access Denied error, as shown in Figure 6-6.

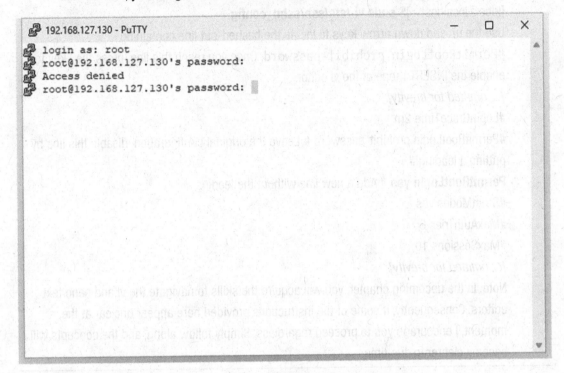

Figure 6-6. SSH root user login first attempt—access denied

(*continued*)

#	Task
⑥	Now go back to your normal user SSH session and use the vi text editor to open the `sshd_config` file under the `/etc/ssh` directory. You have to enter the exact command with the leading `sudo`.

[jdoe@localhost ~]$ **sudo vi /etc/ssh/sshd_config**

Use the up and down arrow keys to locate the hashed-out line containing `#PermitRootLogin prohibit-password`. Once you reach this line, press the I key to enable the INSERT mode of the vi editor.

[…omitted for brevity]

#LoginGraceTime 2m

#PermitRootLogin prohibit-password # Leave the original configuration, disable this line by putting a leading #

PermitRootLogin yes # Add a new line without the leading '#'

#StrictModes yes

#MaxAuthTries 6

#MaxSessions 10

[…omitted for brevity]

Note: In the upcoming chapter, you will acquire the skills to navigate the vi and nano text editors. Consequently, if some of the instructions provided here appear unclear at the moment, I encourage you to proceed regardless. Simply follow along, and the concepts will become clearer in due time.

(*continued*)

#	Task

⑦ Once you have completed the configuration file change, it should look like Figure 6-7. Use the Esc key to move into the Command Mode. You will notice that the colon appears at the bottom of the screen. Type wq next to the colon to write and quit (save, change, and close vi).

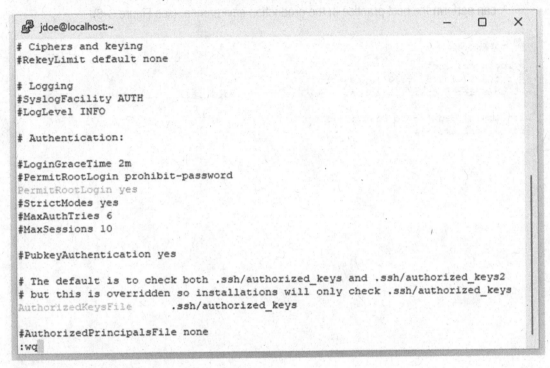

```
jdoe@localhost:~                                    —    □    ×
# Ciphers and keying
#RekeyLimit default none

# Logging
#SyslogFacility AUTH
#LogLevel INFO

# Authentication:

#LoginGraceTime 2m
#PermitRootLogin prohibit-password
PermitRootLogin yes
#StrictModes yes
#MaxAuthTries 6
#MaxSessions 10

#PubkeyAuthentication yes

# The default is to check both .ssh/authorized_keys and .ssh/authorized_keys2
# but this is overridden so installations will only check .ssh/authorized_keys
AuthorizedKeysFile          .ssh/authorized_keys

#AuthorizedPrincipalsFile none
:wq
```

Figure 6-7. *Enabling root user SSH login*

⑧ Run the sshd restart command for this change to take effect.
[jdoe@localhost ~]$ **sudo systemctl restart sshd**
[sudo] password for jdoe: ****************

(continued)

#	Task
⑨	Now restart another PuTTY session to log in as the root user for the second time. This time the system will allow you to log in as the user root. This is against the best practice, but you have to explore different settings to learn more from your lab environment and so that can perform the best practice in the production environment (see Figure 6-8).

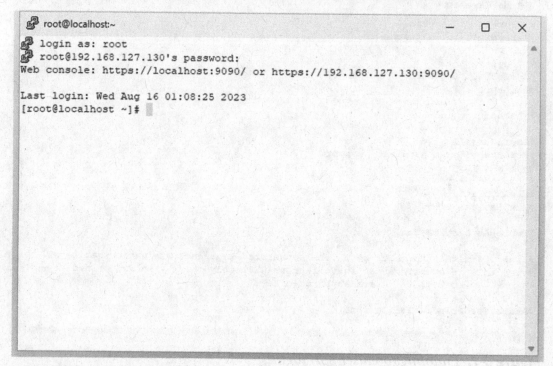

Figure 6-8. SSH root user login second attempt

You have now completed Fedora 38 Server installation and the initial customization. Before delving into the next topic, I'd like to share some of my insights regarding the Linux operating system.

Linux powers today's cloud infrastructure; what meets the eye isn't the reality of **the** operational world. A brief Google search on the Internet reveals that the percentage of PC users favoring Linux as their operating system with a desktop interface is relatively modest compared to the prevalence of Windows OS with a desktop interface. However, when it comes to the domain of enterprise and cloud services, the adoption of Linux OS significantly surpasses that of Microsoft Windows OS. Notably, the Linux system has gained remarkable traction in backend and cloud systems. Sometimes, what you see is merely the tip of the iceberg. Behind the scenes, much of the digital world, abstracted from users, is powered by Linux operating systems rather than Windows. While Linux continues to gain strength, its influence remains largely unseen by the average user. For individuals embarking on a journey within the world of IT, particularly newcomers to the industry, this is a noteworthy fact. The increasing prominence of Linux operating systems at both the enterprise and cloud service provider levels can offer a multitude of opportunities for those who diligently learn and master Linux operating systems.

As someone who has worn the hat of a network engineer for many years, I must admit that I grew quite accustomed to my Windows operating systems. Regrettably, I was guilty of harboring resistance toward expanding my horizons to encompass Linux for many years. This paradigm shifted when I embarked on a journey of self-taught Python programming. The limitations and challenges I encountered while attempting to accomplish more complex tasks using the Windows OS led me to the realization that my journey would be much smoother on the Linux platform. Upon gaining proficiency in Python, I discovered that network automation, a vital skill, was inherently more streamlined on Linux OS than on Windows OS. Despite recognizing the importance of learning Linux, I resisted it for many years. **Like many IT professionals entrenched in the familiarity of Windows and gravitating solely toward its OS, I experienced the typical psychological hurdles toward embracing Linux—denial, emotional resistance, cognitive dissonance, external influences, and attachment to a preferred reality.** However, upon focusing on Python and Network Automation, I finally embraced the reality and began my conversion to Linux, involving acknowledgment, understanding, adaptation, emotional processing, and integration. The takeaway is simple: Learn from my mistake; don't postpone learning Linux.

Forgotten Root User Password Recovery for Fedora 38

To my astonishment, a typographical error occurred while I was inputting the root user's password, rendering me unable to access the system using the designated root user credentials, as outlined in the preceding steps. This unexpected turn of events required an impromptu password recovery procedure on the Fedora 38 platform. It's intriguing to note that the situation of misplacing the root user's password is a fairly common occurrence, often requiring Linux administrators to perform a root user password recovery.

The methodology for regaining access to the root user's account varies between different Linux distributions and even across versions in the same distribution. Nonetheless, the fundamental principle underpinning the password recovery process remains consistent, if not identical. The following comprehensive guide explains how to perform a root user password recovery on the Fedora 38 server, with applicability extending to RHEL 9 and CentOS 9 Stream.

You can recover your root user password by following each step carefully.

#	Task
①	Initially, you need to **edit the Boot Entry within the Grub Menu** during the Power-On Self Test (POST) phase. To initiate the process, start your Fedora 38 server. Once the GRUB screen materializes, press the e key to initiate edits on the currently selected boot entry, as exemplified in Figure 6-9.

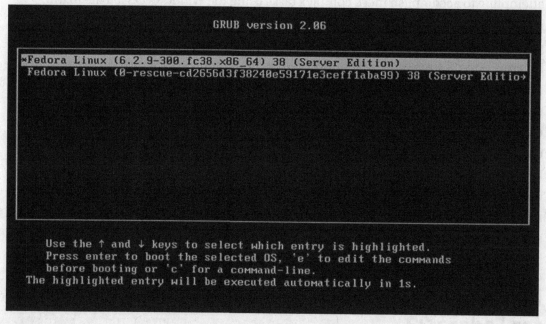

Figure 6-9. *Press e to enter the edit booting parameter*

(*continued*)

#	Task
②	Subsequently, proceed to **boot into Emergency Mode** and make minor adjustments to the booting parameters. On the ensuing screen, an array of boot parameters are presented. Navigate to the line commencing with `linux ($root)/vmlinuz-6.2.9-300...` and utilize either the **END** key or the key combination **CTRL+e** to direct the cursor to the line's termination. Append `rw init=/bin/bash` to the end of the line as pointed by the arrow, mirroring the illustration provided in Figure 6-10.

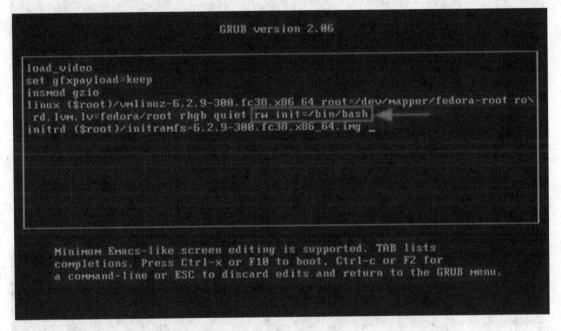

Figure 6-10. *Change the boot parameter*

After appending the extra configuration to the end of the line, **press CTRL+x or F10 to boot into emergency mode**.

(*continued*)

#	Task
③	Once the system reboots, follow the steps to reset the root user's forgotten password. Accomplish this by running the `passwd` command to reset the password for the root user, as shown in Figure 6-11.

```
 Booting a command list
[  OK  ] Stopped systemd-tmpfiles-setup.service - Create Volatile Files and Directories.
[  OK  ] Stopped systemd-udev-trigger.service - Coldplug All udev Devices.
         Stopping systemd-udevd.service - Rule-based Manager for Device Events and Files...
[  OK  ] Finished plymouth-switch-root.service - Plymouth switch root service.
bash-5.2# passwd
Changing password for user root.
New password:
Retype new password:
passwd: all authentication tokens updated successfully.
```

Figure 6-11. *Reset the root user password and update the .autolabel timestamp using the touch command*

④	Upon successfully resetting the root password, proceed to execute the `touch` `/.autolabel` command. This command serves the purpose of updating and activating SELinux relabeling upon the subsequent system reboot, as demonstrated in Figure 6-12.

```
 Booting a command list
[  OK  ] Stopped systemd-tmpfiles-setup.service - Create Volatile Files and Directories.
[  OK  ] Stopped systemd-udev-trigger.service - Coldplug All udev Devices.
         Stopping systemd-udevd.service - Rule-based Manager for Device Events and Files...
[  OK  ] Finished plymouth-switch-root.service - Plymouth switch root service.
bash-5.2# passwd
Changing password for user root.
New password:
Retype new password:
passwd: all authentication tokens updated successfully.
bash-5.2# touch /.autorelabel
bash-5.2#
```

Figure 6-12. *execute touch /.autorelable command*

Note: SELinux stands for "Security-Enhanced Linux." It is a security mechanism implemented in Linux operating systems to provide fine-grained access control and mandatory access controls (MAC) for processes and users.

(continued)

#	Task
⑤	Finally, exit the single-user mode and initialize the rest of the boot process by running the `exec /sbin/init` command, as shown in Figure 6-13.

```
 Booting a command list
[  OK  ] Stopped systemd-tmpfiles-setup.service - Create Volatile Files and Directories.
[  OK  ] Stopped systemd-udev-trigger.service - Coldplug All udev Devices.
         Stopping systemd-udevd.service - Rule-based Manager for Device Events and Files...
[  OK  ] Finished plymouth-switch-root.service - Plymouth switch root service.
bash-5.2# passwd
Changing password for user root.
New password:
Retype new password:
passwd: all authentication tokens updated successfully.
bash-5.2# touch /.autorelabel
bash-5.2# exec /sbin/init
[  195.963406] selinux-autorelabel[649]: *** Warning -- SELinux targeted policy relabel is required.
[  195.964051] selinux-autorelabel[649]: *** Relabeling could take a very long time, depending on file
[  195.964447] selinux-autorelabel[649]: *** system size and speed of hard drives.
[  195.983395] selinux-autorelabel[649]: Running: /sbin/fixfiles -T 0  restore
[  214.209208] selinux-autorelabel[655]: Warning: Skipping the following R/O filesystems:
[  214.209746] selinux-autorelabel[655]: /run/credentials/systemd-resolved.service
[  214.209854] selinux-autorelabel[655]: /run/credentials/systemd-sysctl.service
[  214.210093] selinux-autorelabel[655]: /run/credentials/systemd-tmpfiles-setup-dev.service
[  214.210189] selinux-autorelabel[655]: /run/credentials/systemd-tmpfiles-setup.service
[  214.210453] selinux-autorelabel[655]: /run/credentials/systemd-vconsole-setup.service
[  214.211681] selinux-autorelabel[655]: Relabeling / /boot /dev /dev/hugepages /dev/mqueue /dev/pts /d
l/debug /sys/kernel/tracing /tmp
```

Figure 6-13. *SELinux relabeling*

Wait for the SELinux relabeling process to complete, this will take a few minutes depending on the filesystem's size and speed of your SSD and system clock speed. If you only see the Plymouth boot screen, simply press the ESC key to view the SELinux progress.

(*continued*)

#	Task
⑥	Once the filesystem relabeling process is finalized, the system will undergo a reboot. Subsequently, you will be able to access your Fedora system by logging in with your recovered root password, as depicted in Figure 6-14.

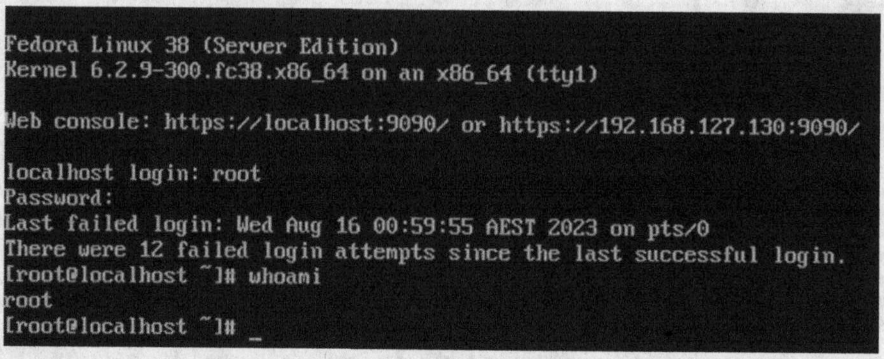

```
Fedora Linux 38 (Server Edition)
Kernel 6.2.9-300.fc38.x86_64 on an x86_64 (tty1)

Web console: https://localhost:9090/ or https://192.168.127.130:9090/

localhost login: root
Password:
Last failed login: Wed Aug 16 00:59:55 AEST 2023 on pts/0
There were 12 failed login attempts since the last successful login.
[root@localhost ~]# whoami
root
[root@localhost ~]#
```

Figure 6-14. *Log in as the root user with the newly recovered password*

You have now successfully reset the root user password in Fedora 38. The process for root user password recovery on Fedoras 37, 36, and 35 are identical. For detailed guidance on root user password recovery for earlier Fedora OS versions, refer to the Fedora documentation specific to each version.

Changing the Hostname on the Fedora Server

You may have already observed that the hostname of the Fedora Server remains as localhost instead of f38s1. Unlike the process for the Ubuntu Server, updating the hostname for the Fedora Server requires manual intervention using a single command, followed by logging out and logging back in. If you haven't previously set the hostname, you can do so using the following steps:

#	Task
①	Run the `sudo hostnamectl set-hostname <server_name>` command to change your Fedora Server's hostname to f38s1. [jdoe@localhost ~]$ **sudo hostnamectl set-hostname f38s1** [sudo] password for jdoe: *****************
②	Use the `logout` or `exit` command to log out of current session. [jdoe@localhost ~]$ **logout**
③	Log back in. Notice that the server name has been updated correctly. login as: **jdoe** jdoe@192.168.127.130's password: *************** Web console: https://localhost:9090/ or https://192.168.127.130:9090/ Last login: Sat Aug 19 13:37:05 2023 from 192.168.127.1 [jdoe@f38s1 ~]$

Managing a Network Adapter on Fedora Linux

If you need to modify the network settings on your Linux server, such as assigning a static IP address to your Fedora Server to prevent IP changes after the DHCP lease expires, it's common in production environments to use static IP addresses. This practice eliminates DHCP dependencies and enhances operational stability. Achieving this can be done through different approaches. There are two primary methods for configuring a static IP address on your Fedora (Red Hat/CentOS) server. The first involves using nmcli commands via the terminal console, while the second method relies on nmtui, a graphical user interface tool. For simplicity, you could use the second approach but then you will only know one half of the method, so I guide you through assigning a static IP address to your Fedora Server using both methods. You can choose either method to set the static IP address, but it's beneficial to familiarize yourself with both techniques. If you're logged in as the root user, you can exclude sudo from your commands.

Feel free to proceed with your preferred method for configuring the static IP address.

Method 1: Assigning a Static IP Using nmcli (command-line)

#	Task
①	First, use the standard nmcli command to check f38s1's network settings configured by the VMnet8 DHCP service. You will confirm the information and hardcode the IP address, default gateway, and DNS information in the following steps.

```
[jdoe@f38s1 ~]$ nmcli device
DEVICE  TYPE      STATE                   CONNECTION
ens160  ethernet  connected               ens160
lo      loopback  connected (externally)  lo
[jdoe@localhost ~]$ nmcli device show ens160
GENERAL.DEVICE:                         ens160
GENERAL.TYPE:                           ethernet
GENERAL.HWADDR:                         00:0C:29:05:BC:8C
GENERAL.MTU:                            1500
GENERAL.STATE:                          100 (connected)
GENERAL.CONNECTION:                     ens160
GENERAL.CON-PATH:                       /org/freedesktop/
NetworkManager/ActiveConnection/2
WIRED-PROPERTIES.CARRIER:               on
IP4.ADDRESS[1]:                         192.168.127.130/24
IP4.GATEWAY:                            192.168.127.2
IP4.ROUTE[1]:                           dst = 192.168.127.0/24,
                                        nh = 0.0.0.0, mt = 100
IP4.ROUTE[2]:                           dst = 0.0.0.0/0,
                                        nh = 192.168.127.2, mt = 100
IP4.DNS[1]:                             192.168.127.2
IP4.DOMAIN[1]:                          localdomain
IP6.ADDRESS[1]:                         fe80::20c:29ff:fe05:bc8c/64
IP6.GATEWAY:                            --
IP6.ROUTE[1]:                           dst = fe80::/64, nh = ::,
                                        mt = 1024
```

(*continued*)

#	Task
②	Run the following sequence of `nmcli` commands to assign a static IP address, set the default gateway, set the DNS server(s), set the domain name, and change IP assignment to manual (static). Then shut down and bring back up the network interface to apply the changes.

```
[jdoe@f38s1 ~]$ sudo nmcli connection modify ens160 ipv4.addresses
192.168.127.130/24
[sudo] password for jdoe: ***************
[jdoe@f38s1 ~]$ sudo nmcli connection modify ens160 ipv4.gateway
192.168.127.2
[jdoe@f38s1 ~]$ sudo nmcli connection modify ens160 ipv4.dns
192.168.127.2,8.8.8.8
[jdoe@f38s1 ~]$ sudo nmcli connection modify ens160 ipv4.dns-search
pynetauto.com
[jdoe@f38s1 ~]$ sudo nmcli connection modify ens160 ipv4.method
manual
[jdoe@f38s1 ~]$ sudo nmcli connection down ens160; sudo nmcli
connection up ens160
```

Note: If you are running these commands as a root user, you can remove the word `sudo` from each command.

(*continued*)

#	Task
③	Verify the changes using the nmcli device show command.

```
[jdoe@f38s1 ~]$ nmcli device show ens160
GENERAL.DEVICE:                     ens160
GENERAL.TYPE:                       ethernet
GENERAL.HWADDR:                     00:0C:29:05:BC:8C
GENERAL.MTU:                        1500
GENERAL.STATE:                      100 (connected)
GENERAL.CONNECTION:                 ens160
GENERAL.CON-PATH:                   /org/freedesktop/Network
                                    Manager/ActiveConnection/3
WIRED-PROPERTIES.CARRIER:           on
IP4.ADDRESS[1]:                     192.168.127.130/24
IP4.GATEWAY:                        192.168.127.2
IP4.ROUTE[1]:                       dst = 192.168.127.0/24, nh =
                                    0.0.0.0, mt = 100
IP4.ROUTE[2]:                       dst = 0.0.0.0/0, nh =
                                    192.168.127.2, mt = 100
IP4.DNS[1]:                         192.168.127.2
IP4.DNS[2]:                         8.8.8.8
IP4.SEARCHES[1]:                    pynetauto.com
IP6.ADDRESS[1]:                     fe80::20c:29ff:fe05:bc8c/64
IP6.GATEWAY:                        --
IP6.ROUTE[1]:                       dst = fe80::/64, nh = ::,
                                    mt = 1024
```

Method 2: Assigning a Static IP Using nmtui (GUI)

Having learned the process of assigning a static IP address to your Fedora Server through the command-line method, you'll now delve into an alternative: the graphical user interface (GUI) approach using the nmtui tool. This technique is equally capable as the command-line method; however, it's important to note that for the GUI method, an Internet connection is required to install the necessary software package used for configuring the server network settings. Therefore, you still have to know how to configure IP settings from the command line, given that not all servers will have Internet access to reach package repositories.

#	Task

①	If you installed your Fedora Server using the minimal packages option, the nmtui tool needs to be installed first before it can be used. First verify whether the NetworkManager-tui package is already installed on your system.
	`[jdoe@f38s1 ~]$ rpm -q NetworkManager-tui`
	`package NetworkManager-tui is not installed`

②	Swiftly install the NetworkManager-tui package using the following command.
	`[jdoe@f38s1 ~]$ sudo dnf install NetworkManager-tui -y`
	`[sudo] password for jdoe: ***************`
	`[...omitted for brevity]`
	`Installed:`
	`NetworkManager-tui-1:1.42.8-1.fc38.x86_64        newt-0.52.23-`
	`2.fc38.x86_64        slang-2.3.3-3.fc38.x86_64`
	`Complete!`

③	You can now execute the nmtui command from either the VMware Workstation Console or a PuTTY SSH session. Simply type sudo nmtui and press the Enter key on your keyboard. `[jdoe@f38s1 ~]$ sudo nmtui`

(continued)

#	Task
④	When Fedora's NetworkManager TUI appears, choose Edit a Connection, as shown in Figure 6-15.

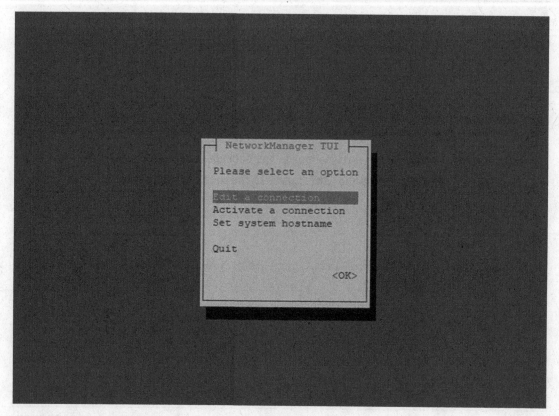

Figure 6-15. *Fedora configuration, start NetworkManager TUI*

(*continued*)

#	Task
⑤	Choose ens160 and use the Tab key or arrow keys to select the <Edit...> option, as illustrated in Figure 6-16.

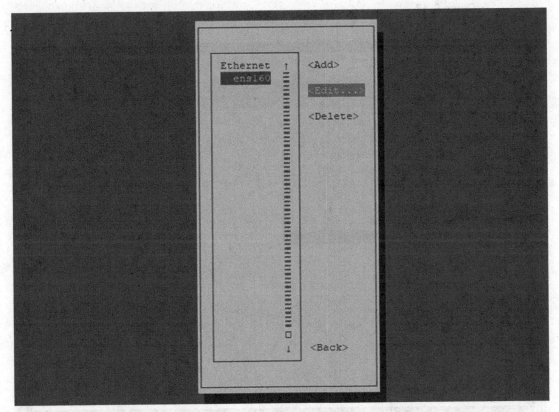

Figure 6-16. *Fedora configuration, selecting a network adapter*

(*continued*)

#	Task
⑥	Click the Automatic option located on the right side of the IPv4 Configuration section and change it to Manual. Then, click the Show option on the right side, as depicted in Figure 6-17.

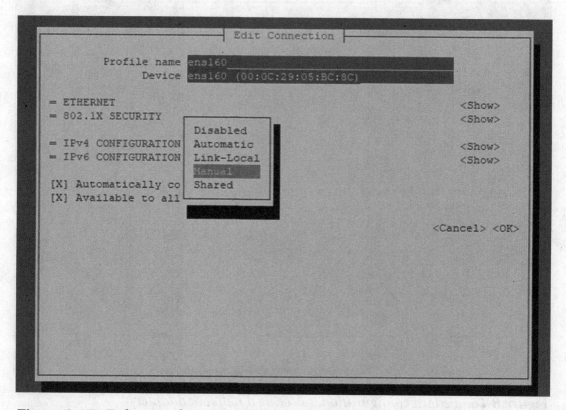

Figure 6-17. *Fedora configuration, selecting a manual configuration*

(*continued*)

#	Task
⑦	Referring to the details provided in Method 1, input your server's IP address, the default gateway's IP address, the DNS, and the domain information. Note that your IP addressing scheme and domain names might differ from mine presented in this example. Make the necessary adjustments to ensure accuracy according to your settings. After entering the details, scroll down and choose <OK>, following the example shown in Figure 6-18.

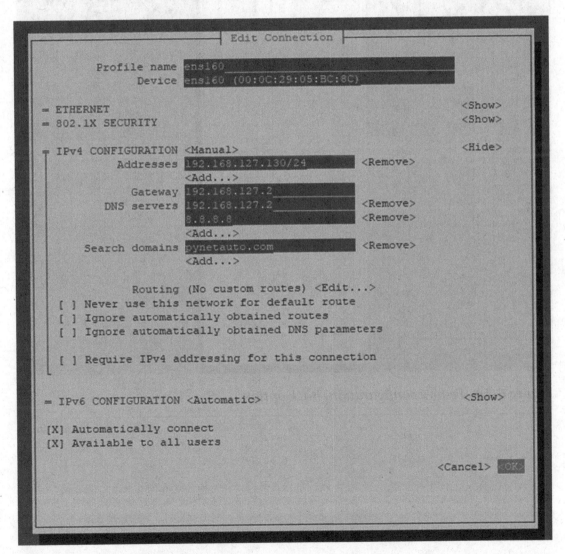

Figure 6-18. *Fedora configuration, saving manual changes*

(continued)

#	Task
⑧	Press the Tab key to navigate downwards and choose <Back> to return to the initial TUI interface, as depicted in Figure 6-19.

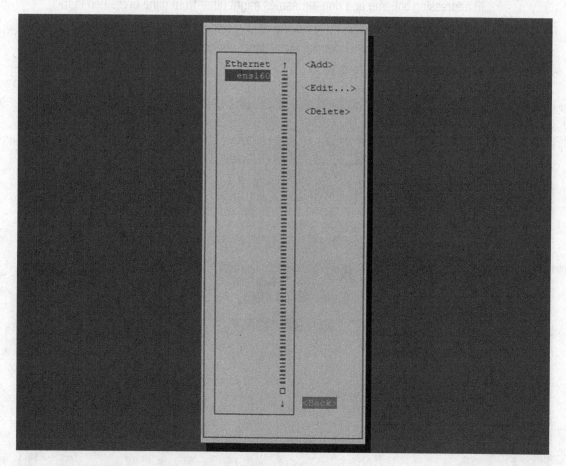

Figure 6-19. *Fedora configuration, Back option*

(*continued*)

#	Task
⑨	Choose Qui' and then select <OK> to save your changes and exit the application, as shown in Figure 6-20.

Figure 6-20.   *Fedora configuration, saving, and exiting TUI*

You have now acquired the knowledge to install the nmtui package and configure a static IP address on your Fedora Server. At this point, take some time to contemplate how you intend to utilize this server in your future labs and consider some of the tools that will help your lab experience. Unlike Windows, Linux gives the true power to the administrators and can also give you a lot more freedom and flexibility. Think of this server as a blank canvas, ready for your creative projects. Once you are content with the current setup of your Fedora Server, **I recommend creating a snapshot of its current state, as shown in Figure 6-21.**

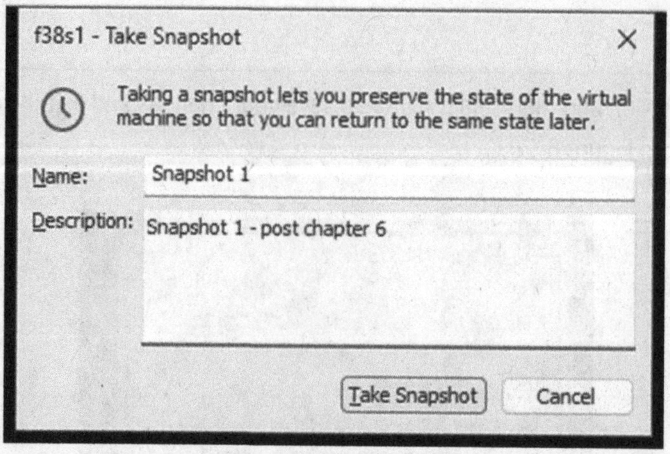

Figure 6-21. *Take a snapshot of f38s1*

Moving forward, in anticipation of the upcoming GNS3 integration, you will gain the knowledge of creating a virtual machine using an OVA file. This serves as an alternative method for establishing your VMs. An OVA (Open Virtualization Archive) file is a virtual appliance format utilized by VMware Workstation and Oracle VM VirtualBox. Essentially, an OVA file is a packaged unit containing various files that collectively define a virtual machine. This compilation includes an OVA descriptor file, optional manifest (.MF), and certificate files, as well as other related components. In simpler terms, an OVA file acts as a preconfigured VM template, thoughtfully prepared by another VM administrator to enable instant deployment of a designated server. Your next step involves downloading a GNS3 VM OVA file from the GNS3 GitHub repository and subsequently creating a GNS3 VM by importing this file. This action serves as a preparatory measure for the forthcoming GNS3 installation and integration, set to occur in Chapter 10. Therefore, **it's crucial not to overlook the GNS3 VM creation process detailed here.**

Creating a GNS3 VM by Importing a .ova File

The GNS3 VM .ova file, carefully maintained by community developers on www.gns3.org, serves the purpose of establishing a virtual machine that hosts network, security, and system images functioning within the GNS3 application. This specific server, an Ubuntu Linux-based application server, is intentionally designed to shoulder the processing load of the physical host running GNS3. Its purpose is to ensure the seamless operation of emulated GNS3 devices without causing any disruptions to the underlying physical host. An interesting surprise awaits: the capabilities of the GNS3 VM extend beyond merely simulating routers, switches, and firewalls. It can also serve as a platform for hosting containerized Linux servers and more. GNS3 is open-source and accessible to everyone. Throughout this book, I use VMware Workstation 17 Pro on Windows 11, requiring software tailored for Windows compatibility. At the time of writing this chapter, the most recent GNS3 version was v2.2.42, which you use in this book. The two GNS3 files required for this book are the installer (GNS3-2.2.42-all-in-one.exe) and the .ova file containing the GNS3.VM.VMware.Workstation.2.2.42.zip file. By the time this book is released, there will be newer versions of GNS3 files, so download the latest release for your installation and tasks, as newer versions tend to offer enhanced performance and address many existing bugs.

Anyway, for this section, you will only require the second file, which contains the .ova file. To download the latest GNS3 VM .ova file, visit https://github.com/GNS3/gns3-gui/releases. The procedure for downloading the GNS3 VM file and creating a GNS3 VM is outlined as follows:

#	Task
①	Begin by navigating to GNS3's official GitHub page, which is provided here for your convenience. From this location, download the GNS3 VM file. It is recommended to download the most recent version of this file. Specifically, the latest version available at the time of authoring this book was GNS3.VM.VMware.Workstation.2.2.42.zip. You must download this file and unzip it. You can access the GNS3/gns3-gui GitHub repository at the following URL: https://github.com/GNS3/gns3-gui/releases
②	Navigate to your Downloads folder and extract the GNS3.VM.VMware.Workstation.2.2.42.zip file in the same location.

(continued)

#	Task
③	Now go back to your VMware Workstation 17 Pro and select File ➤ Open…, as shown in Figure 6-22.

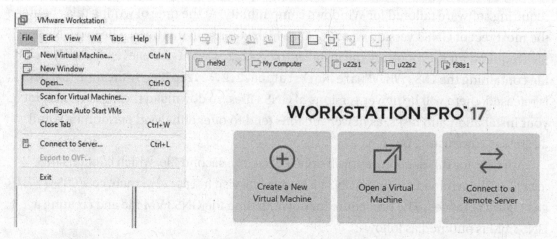

Figure 6-22. *VMware Workstation; select the Open… option under the File menu*

#	Task
④	Locate the extracted GNS3 VM .ova file, select the file, and then click Open. See Figure 6-23. The path to the .ova file should look similar to this, but replace it with your username. C:\Users\<Your_User_Name>\Downloads\GNS3.VM.VMware.Workstation.2.2.42

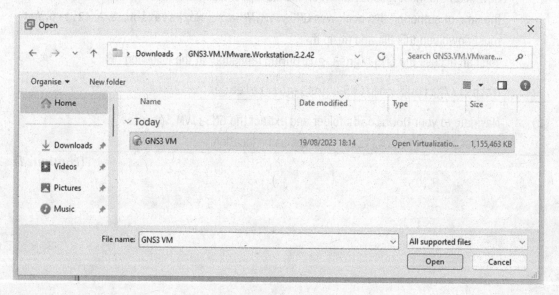

Figure 6-23. *VMware Workstation, GNS3 VM .ova file open*

(*continued*)

#	Task
⑤	In the subsequent window, click the Import button to initiate the GNS3 VM import process. You can keep the storage path at its default location. Refer to Figure 6-24 for guidance.

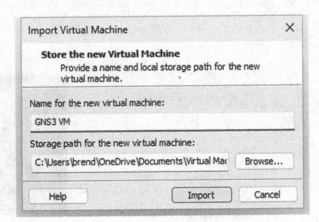

Figure 6-24. *VMware Workstation, GNS3 VM import*

This process will take a few seconds, so wait until the import process completes.

⑥	The GNS3 VM has now been successfully created in your VMware Workstation 17 Pro and is ready for use. At this point, there is no need to take any further actions with this VM. However, it's important to note that for this VM to become functional, you need to proceed with the installation and integration of the GNS3 software. You will be performing this task in a later chapter. Refer to Figure 6-25 for context.

(*continued*)

#	Task

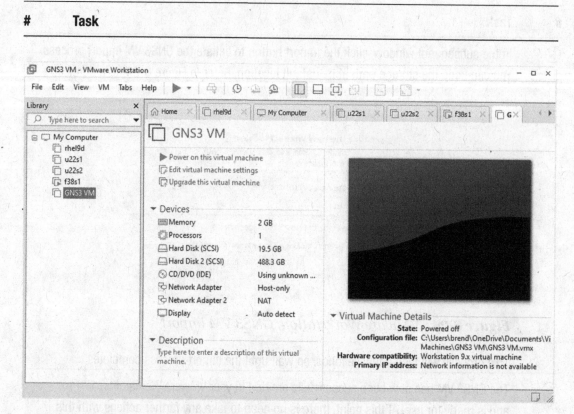

Figure 6-25.   VMware Workstation, GNS3 VM installed

You've finished all the necessary tasks for this chapter. Nevertheless, if you happened to skip taking a snapshot of your Fedora f38s1 server, I highly recommend you do that now. This precaution will help avoid the need to rebuild the server entirely in the event of any unexpected issues.

Summary

In this chapter, you downloaded, installed, and created a Fedora virtual machine. You learned how to enable root user SSH login, as well as how to recover a forgotten password for the root user. You mastered the process of assigning a static IP address to your Fedora Server's network interface using both the command-line (nmcli) and GUI (nmtui) methods. Additionally, you learned how to create a virtual machine from an .ova file, which sets the stage for GNS3 and IOS/CML OS integration in an upcoming chapter.

As a result, you now have two of the most popular Linux VMs and have handcrafted these Linux servers to suit your needs. Chapter 7 delves into Linux basics, and Chapter 8 covers IP Service application installations and even more customizations on Linux servers.

Storytime 3: The Origin of Hypervisors

Figure 6-26. *Cisco Catalyst 6500 WS-C6513-E Switch*

In the previous chapters, you delved into two distinct virtualization programs, categorized as Type-1 and Type-2 hypervisors. The surge in cloud computing, serverless architectures, and various "as-a-Service" concepts stems from rapid advancements in hardware, software, virtualization, and containerization technologies. Virtualization enables the creation of multiple virtual hardware instances on a single host. These instances, or virtual machines (VMs), operate autonomously with their own OSs and apps, simulating complete computers. VMs optimize resource utilization and segregate workloads, although they also demand significant resources due to emulating complete hardware. On the other hand, a containerization is a lightweight form of virtualization that packages apps and dependencies. Containers share the host OS kernel while maintaining separate user spaces, offering efficiency, portability, and consistency. This approach sidesteps full OS emulation, bundling apps, libraries, and configurations for consistent operation across environments.

The term "hypervisor" derives from "hyper" and "visor." "Hyper" harkens back to the Greek word for "above," while "visor" comes from Old Anglo-French, implying "to hide." It's akin to "supervisor" and denotes the "supervisor of supervisors," with "hyper" holding stronger linguistic weight than "super." Imagine a hypothetical DC Comics superhero named "Hyperman." If introduced, Hyperman would surpass even Superman's power.

To grasp virtualization, envision a hypervisor as an engine lubricant. Just as an engine comprises various moving parts, hypervisors facilitate seamless VM operation on host servers by reducing friction and wear among smaller components. Hypervisors obscure real hardware from VMs, enabling them to function like physical servers while residing as files managed by hypervisors. This is akin to fabricating a false environment, with VMs operating on software infrastructure.

Some legacy environments still use Cisco 6500/4500 Series enterprise switches and Cisco 9000 Series switches with supervisor modules, functioning as routers, switches, or both (see Figure 6-26). They accommodate multiple OSI layers and reflect Cisco's early hardware-based virtualization endeavors. Contemporary offerings like Nexus 3K/5K/6K/7K/9K switches and Enterprise 9K switches feature Python APIs and Python 2.7.2 or newer versions. The built-in Python version has certain functionality constraints. Further insights are available on Cisco's official website: www.cisco.com.

Linux Fundamentals I – Linux File and Directory Mastery

In this chapter, you dive deep into the heart of Linux, exploring the essential concepts and commands that will empower you to navigate and manipulate the file system with confidence. You'll begin by sharpening your skills with fundamental commands for working with directories and files, allowing you to create, move, copy, and delete them effortlessly. Along the way, you'll also unravel the mysteries of hidden files and directories, uncovering their significance in the Linux ecosystem. As you progress, you'll discover the power of the ls command, a versatile tool that provides a wealth of information about files and directories. You'll delve into the art of script creation and execution, equipping you with the knowledge to write your Python applications and make them executable. To further enhance your Linux prowess, you'll explore the intricacies of configuring your system's network settings, from IP addresses to hostnames, ensuring system stability and efficient communication. By the end of this chapter, you'll have honed your Linux skills to a fine point, enabling you to navigate, manage, and customize your Linux environment. So, let's embark on this journey to unlock the full potential of Linux, where the command line is your canvas, and the file system your playground.

© Brendan Choi 2024
B. Choi, *Introduction to Python Network Automation Volume I - Laying the Groundwork*,
https://doi.org/10.1007/979-8-8688-0146-4_7

Building a Strong Linux Base for Network Automation

In this pivotal chapter, you delve deep into the world of Linux, equipping you with the essential skills needed to navigate through the rest of this book. While I understand that not all readers are aiming to become aspiring Linux administrators, it's crucial to establish a solid foundation in basic Linux tasks and simple administration as you continue your Python Network Automation journey. This knowledge is indispensable, especially when working in production environments, as Linux administrators are often cautious about granting access to those outside the Linux specialization, including Microsoft Windows, network, security and DevOps administrators.

Your journey commences with an exploration of the origins of Linux in early Linux development. From there, the chapter will unravel the complexities of Linux directory and file structures, providing you with a sturdy foothold in this operating system's fundamentals. You'll then shift your focus to two essential Linux text editors: the classic and robust "vi" and the more user-friendly "nano." Mastery of these text editors is key to confidently navigating the Linux environment.

This chapter signifies a transformative step in your career, as you make the transition from the familiar Windows Desktop to the uncharted territory of Linux command lines. However, if your previous experience has revolved around enterprise networking devices such as routers, switches, and firewalls, your transition will likely be smoother, given that many of these devices still provide finer-grained configuration control through the command-line interface. Throughout this chapter, carefully crafted hands-on exercises guide you in gradually mastering the essentials of file and directory management. These exercises are designed to empower you, allowing you to fully harness the potential of the Linux terminal and use Linux text editors as versatile tools for manipulating directories and files without the aid of a GUI (Graphical User Interface).

By the end of this chapter, you will have acquired the proficiency to navigate the Linux terminal and handle files and directories with confidence. This newfound skillset is your first ticket to success in your Python Network Automation journey. So, let's embark on this Linux adventure together and unlock the power of the command line.

Warning

Stop! Are your Linux servers primed and ready?

This chapter assumes that you have diligently worked through and accomplished all the necessary tasks outlined in Chapters 1–6. This book was designed for sequential learning for most readers, which aids both future and current engineers in becoming well-rounded professionals, as discussed at the beginning of Chapter 1. Your tasks involve using both the Ubuntu 22 and Fedora 38 virtual servers, which you've previously installed and configured in the preceding chapters. If you haven't yet completed the installation and customization of your virtual machines (VMs), **I strongly urge you to backtrack to the earlier chapters and complete the creation of your VMs**.

Detailed guidelines for setting up Linux servers can be accessed from my GitHub repository:

URL: `https://github.com/jdoe/apress_jdoe_ed2.0/tree/main/pre_installation_guides`

In this chapter, you will acquire an understanding of Linux basics by utilizing the Fedora and Ubuntu server virtual machines. Figure 7-1 depicts the necessary logical lab topology for this chapter. Both Linux servers need to be operational and connected to the VMnet8 (NAT) network on the 192.168.127.0/24 subnet. Concurrently, your Windows host should be linked to the Internet through your home router network. Typically, home networks operate within the Local Area Network (LAN) with either the 192.168.0.0/24 or 192.168.1.0/24 local subnets. However, if you've adopted custom settings, you need to modify the IP addressing scheme to align with your network configuration. The third octet of your VMnet8 network subnet may differ from the one displayed in Figure 7-1. Should this be the case, you'll operate within the confines of your designated subnet, or you can adjust the VMnet8 subnet through VMware Workstation's Virtual Network Editor. This action ensures that your working natted subnet also operates within the 192.168.127.0/24 subnet.

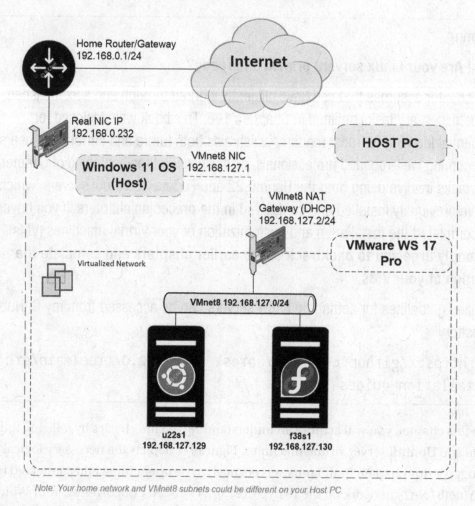

Figure 7-1. *Chapter 7 logical network topology*

Why Learn Linux?

This chapter is dedicated to learning Linux basics. You learn about the history of Linux, different types of Linux distributions, basic file and directory management, and how to use the vi/nano text editors for fundamental Linux administration. Whether you're already entrenched in the IT industry or aspiring to be, the question of "Why should I learn Linux?" might have crossed your mind, particularly if you're a content Windows user. The answer is simple: Learning Linux enhances your skillset as an IT professional, regardless of your specialization—be it network, security, systems, cloud, or software engineering. Surprisingly, despite Linux's over three-decade existence and the existence of UNIX for over half a century, the IT industry still faces a shortage of professionals fluent in Linux administration. This translates to more job opportunities for those with a strong grasp of Linux administration built on their chosen IT field.

Admittedly, from the perspective of a Microsoft Windows user, transitioning to and mastering the Linux operating system within a short time frame can be a challenging endeavor. The notion of parting with Windows and its GUI can be scary. Yet, if you're already well-versed in Linux, consider yourself ahead of the curve. Over two decades ago, I received advice from a mentor to explore Linux and potentially pursue a career as a Linux administrator. At that time, my focus was on Cisco networks, unified communications, and Windows, leaving Linux studies on the backburner. It wasn't until my venture into Python coding in 2015 that I regretted not following my mentor's counsel earlier. This personal journey highlights the significance of Linux for IT engineers. Many professionals, particularly network, security, and Microsoft engineers, unknowingly sideline Linux, echoing the mistake I once made. I share this story to encourage Windows users to remain open to Linux's potential. Don't let this opportunity pass you by.

Especially at the enterprise, cloud, and data center levels, a substantial portion of application servers run on Linux-based operating systems. Whether it's Amazon Web Services (AWS), Facebook, or Google in the cloud, these servers require a secure, reliable operating system to function consistently. In the past 18 years, the use of Linux servers has surged in parallel with the rise of containerization, cloud computing, big data, artificial intelligence (AI), and machine learning (ML). Linux's prevalence in enterprise IT and data center environments continues to grow as more systems migrate from Windows. Numerous factors contribute to this trend, including Linux's cost-effectiveness, superior reliability, scalability, security, and unmatched flexibility compared to Windows servers. Behind the scenes, Linux has become the new norm shaping our digital lives.

Expand Your Knowledge:

Learn about Windows Subsystem for Linux (WSL)

Visit the Microsoft Windows documentation site to read more about WSL.

URL: `https://learn.microsoft.com/en-us/windows/wsl/about`

Even for most devoted Windows users, the landscape has evolved. Microsoft's release of Windows versions featuring built-in Linux kernel support and Windows Subsystem for Linux (WSL) opens avenues for learning Linux within the Windows 10/11 Desktop environment. You can easily access various flavors of Linux from the Microsoft Store, bridging the gap between the two worlds.

Presented in the following "Expand Your Knowledge" are intriguing figures obtained from a quick Google search, aimed at providing you with some insights into the current utilization of Linux within the industry as of 2023.

Expand Your Knowledge:

Linux Continues to Impact Our Lives

According to 2023 research, the dominance of Linux is showcased, as it runs nearly 97 percent of the world's top web servers. This staggering dominance finds approval from revered platforms such as Twitter, Yahoo, Amazon, and eBay, firmly establishing Linux as the operating system of choice for e-commerce businesses. In a future market projection, the global Linux industry is poised to burgeon from $3.89 billion in 2023 to a whopping $15.64 billion by the year 2027, and $ 22.15 billion by 2029. Encompassing a staggering user base, approximately 32.8 million individuals worldwide embrace it. Notably, even the space exploration industry has witnessed 65 SpaceX flights relying on the power of Linux.

In the enterprise server market, Red Hat Enterprise Linux (RHEL) controls a 33.9 percent share of the global Linux server market. Curiously, despite many professional developers preferring Windows Desktop over Linux Desktop, about 47 percent of professional developers are using *nix-like operating systems. However, when the spotlight shifts to servers in the data centers, Linux emerges victorious, commanding an imposing 96.3 percent usage share for web servers. Ubuntu, a more desktop user-friendly Linux, commands a substantial 32.8 percent of the market. Usage-wise, Linux empowers a staggering 85 percent of smartphones and runs 90 percent of the premier web servers.

Unfolding the demographic needle point unveils that, as of July 2023, 80 percent of Linux administrators are male. Females contribute to 9.9 percent of the Linux kernel Git population, with around 330 female developers actively participating in Linux's evolution. The sheer breadth of Linux's impact is underscored by the presence of over two million Ubuntu websites solely within the United States. In the broader context of the global desktop OS market, Windows towers as the dominant force, trailed by macOS and Linux. Despite ranking as the third most prevalent OS, Linux's technological influence in behind-the-scenes data centers (cloud computing) remains undeniable, spanning from smartphones to space stations.

Further reading:

https://www.zdnet.com/article/linux-has-over-3-of-the-desktop-market-its-more-complicated-than-that/

https://www.cbtnuggets.com/blog/certifications/open-source/why-linux-runs-90-percent-of-the-public-cloud-workload

---

If you have been in the enterprise networking industry for some time, you will be most familiar with Cisco technologies. Just looking at Cisco as an example, about 20 years ago, most of Cisco's network, security, and voice services application servers were based on Windows 2000 and 2003. An excellent example of this is Cisco's IP PABX servers, known as Cisco CallManager (version 3 and 4.1), which were originally built on Windows 2000 servers. Other examples include the old UCCX, UCCE, and CiscoWorks servers; they all used Windows servers as their base platforms. However, in 2010, Cisco decided to ditch Windows servers and went with the appliance model; it migrated many of its application servers to a Red Hat–based Linux OS. Cisco's decision to drop Windows servers in favor of Linux was in line with the evolving IT trend back in 2010. In addition, an adaptation of the Linux OS can be found in Juniper's and Palo Alto's core operating systems, such as Junos and Palo Alto's PAN-OS products; they both use Linux as their base operating systems.

As mentioned, some key benefits of Linux over Windows include stability, high security, and lower ownership cost. Linux is an effective enterprise operating system that all IT engineers must learn and apply to their work. Not all of us indeed want to make a living as Linux system administrators, but you must know enough to keep your skin in the game for the next decade. In this book, you want to learn enough Linux fundamentals to be comfortable performing the basic lab tasks. If you're going to study Linux professionally to become a Linux system administrator, you can study Red Hat 9 certification systematically such as RH124 (Red Hat System Administration I) and RH134 (Red Hat System Administration II) first, and then you can have a go at RH294 (Red Hat

System Administration III). In this book, you learn selective Linux content from RH124 and RH134, as well as some content from my blog to get started with Linux, geared toward Python networking automation tasks.

To get to know a technology, it is always good to start with a little history, or where it all began. Let's get started with some Linux history, learn the different types of Linux distributions available, study Linux files and directory structures, and master both the vi and nano text editors to do things without the aid of a GUI. But just in case you may need a GUI for some reason, you already have the optional GUI-based Linux desktop on the Ubuntu servers. You are expected to perform essential learnings on both Ubuntu and Fedora Linux Servers. Let's step on the gas.

The Beginning of Linux

Before embarking on your exploration of the origins of Linux, it's important to acknowledge the robust connection it shares with UNIX. Many of Linux's foundational features were directly influenced by UNIX, leading to the Linux community often referring to both UNIX and Linux as *nix-like operating systems. In your journey to understand Linux, let's promptly explore key milestones in Linux's development, followed by an overview of the diverse Linux distributions in use today. The initial development highlights, spanning from 1969 to 2023, are outlined in Table 7-1 for your convenience. For further insights into the founding of Linux and to access other timelines, you can visit the following Wikipedia page: https://en.wikipedia.org/wiki/Linux.

Table 7-1. *Linux Development Timeline*

Year	Linux Development Highlights
1969	UNIX was developed at AT&T Labs by Ken Thompson, Dennis Ritchie, Douglas Mcilroy, and Joe Ossanna.
1971	UNIX was first written in Assembly language.
1973	Dennis Ritchie writes UNIX in the C language.
1983	Richard Stallman introduces the GNU Project.
1984	Complete UNIX-compatible software system. Free software development commences.

(continued)

Table 7-1. (*continued*)

Year	Linux Development Highlights
1985	Richard Stallman established the Free Software Foundation.
1989	Introduction of the General Public License (GNU).
1990	Development of many programs for the operating system.
Aug 25, 1991	Linus Benedict Torvalds, a 21-year-old Finnish student, publicly announces the free version of the Linux kernel. The 1991 Linux kernel was released under the GNU GPL license.
1992	Linux kernel version 0.12 was released.
1994	Development of the first stable release, Linux kernel version 1.0.
1996	Start of the 2.0 kernel series, introducing advanced features.
1998	Netscape releases the source code of its Communicator web browser as open-source, catalyzing the open-source movement.
2001	Introduction of the Linux 2.4 kernel with improved scalability and support for larger systems.
2005	Release of Linux kernel version 2.6 with significant performance enhancements and improved hardware support.
2011	Launch of the Linux 3.0 kernel series with improved power management and hardware support.
2015	Integration of the Linux kernel into various industries, from mobile devices to supercomputers.
2018	Introduction of the Linux 4.0 kernel series, offering advanced features and optimizations.
2020	Continued growth and adoption of Linux in cloud computing, IoT devices, and AI/ML applications.
2023	Linux maintains its status as a dominant force in various technological domains, powering critical infrastructure and services.

Source: https://en.wikipedia.org/wiki/Linux

As evident from Table 7-1, Linux finds its origins deeply intertwined with UNIX. This close lineage suggests that Linux syntax and operations share similarities with those of UNIX. Following Linus Torvalds' release of the free Linux kernel in 1991, a plethora of Linux distributions emerged, often distributed under the GNU license. These distributions encompass a range of purposes—some are commercially geared for business applications, while others are forged for communal or personal use. Notably, many Linux distributions possess the capability to support business-oriented applications. However, certain distributions go beyond this and excel as exceptional desktop versions. A prime example is the Ubuntu desktop, which not only serves as a robust platform for various business functions but also delivers an impressive desktop experience.

Table 7-2 lists the 12 most popular Linux distributions since 2017 and some characteristics of each Linux type. If you need a Linux OS in your enterprise infrastructure, the most recommended Linux system is Red Hat Enterprise Server. If you have to use it for work and study, Ubuntu, CentOS, and Debian are incredibly flexible and user-friendly Linux distributions. Out of these three very popular Linux distributions, Ubuntu has the most user-friendly features, has a great GUI if required, and is an excellent choice for beginners. Note that Ubuntu is a Debian derivative. CentOS uses the same Linux kernels and software as Red Hat and Fedora. The three Linux mentioned here—Red Hat, CentOS, and Fedora—are the same Linux distros with a minor aesthetical difference. Fedora is a development version of Red Hat. Red Hat is the enterprise-level commercialized Linux for large enterprises, and CentOS is the open-source version of Red Hat. Fedora offers the latest beta software but lacks the stability of CentOS and Red Hat Linux. Hence, when learning Linux, any version of the CentOS server or CentOS Stream should be your preferred Linux distribution for Red Hat–derived Linux versions. The main difference between the open-source versus commercial versions of Linux is whether you get full technical support from a vendor support team or get best-effort support from a Linux developer community. Now quickly review Table 7-2 and find the Linux distribution you want to use. Most of the Linux software is free for personal use with no commercial restrictions.

Table 7-2. *Top 12 Linux Server Distributions of 2023*

Rank	Linux Distro	OS Derivative	User Skill Level	Advantages
1	Ubuntu Server	Debian-based	Intermediate	Performance, stability, flexibility, data center support, security
2	Red Hat Enterprise Linux (RHEL)	Fedora-based	Advanced	Vendor support, performance, security, cloud and IoT support, data and virtualization support
3	SUSE Linux Enterprise Server	RPM-based	Intermediate	Open-source, stability, security, cloud service support
4	Rocky Linux	RHEL-based	Intermediate	Free community support; same as RHEL without the logo, fully compatible with RHEL
5	Almalinux OS	RHEL-based	Intermediate	Free, open-source, community-driven, designed as a CentOS Linux replacement
6	CentOS Stream	RHEL-based	Intermediate	A stable, open-source derivative of RHEL with a focus on collaboration with RHEL upstream
7	Debian	Debian-based	Intermediate to advanced	Free, open-source, stability, educational, suitable for commercial, government, and NGO use
8	Oracle Linux (Oracle Enterprise Linux)	RHEL-based	Advanced	Free, open-source, suited for off-cloud, SMB, and enterprise use, with cloud and data center support
9	Mageia	Mandriva-based	Intermediate	Free, stable, secure, community support, offers a range of software, includes support for MariaDB
10	ClearOS	RHEL/CentOS-based	Intermediate to Advanced	Open-source, SMB support, suitable for commercial use, provides network gateway and server support, web server support

(continued)

Table 7-2. (*continued*)

Rank	Linux Distro	OS Derivative	User Skill Level	Advantages
11	Arch Linux	Other	Advanced	Open-source, simplicity, optimized performance, stability, flexibility
12	Slackware Linux	Slackware-based	Advanced	Free, open-source, closest to UNIX system, simplicity, stability

Source: `https://www.tecmint.com/linux-server-distributions/`

Understanding the Linux Environment

Linux is an operating system installed on a physical or virtual machine for personal or commercial use. The significant difference between Linux Desktop and Linux Server is the graphical user interface. Linux servers are usually installed to provide a specific service to users or businesses and are usually managed by Linux administrators, who are well-versed in Linux commands. Linux usually gets installed with the minimum software for better performance, stability, and higher security.

This difference aside, the Linux desktop and server versions use the same base kernel for each release version of a Linux OS. As shown in the previous chapters, you can optionally install the GUI on Linux servers. Earlier in this book, you installed a desktop on an Ubuntu Linux server for learning and convenience. As you get familiar with Linux and its command line, you will slowly move away from the GUI and will be able to run all the basic Linux administration tasks using the command line only. As you will discover, in Linux, everything is made up of files and directories; it is a free, open-source, and very flexible operating system. Once again, if you are used to administering Cisco or Juniper devices through a command-line interface (CLI), then you will feel right at home. Even if you do not have a Cisco networking background or have zero Linux experience, you will be able to follow along; I try to cover the very basics of Linux (RH124 level) so you can run the labs to reach the end of your first Python Network Automation journey.

Understanding Linux Directories and File Formats

Earlier, you briefly looked at the Linux development timeline and learned about popular Linux distribution types. Next, let's take a quick look at the Linux directory structure. In Linux, everything is written in text and saved in various directories. Because the Windows operating system can also trace its roots to *nix, the Windows file and folder structure are similar. But Linux does not have a C: drive like Windows; instead, it has the root folder, or /. Figure 7-2 depicts a general Linux directory structure and what kinds of files usually reside in each directory. Of course, you can create your custom directories and files just like in Windows OS. Review Figure 7-2 and use it as a point of reference if you forget the purpose of each directory. You don't have to memorize it all at this stage, but take a glimpse at anything interesting that catches your eye. As you use Linux more and more, you will get more familiar with the directory structures and the type of files that belong to various directories.

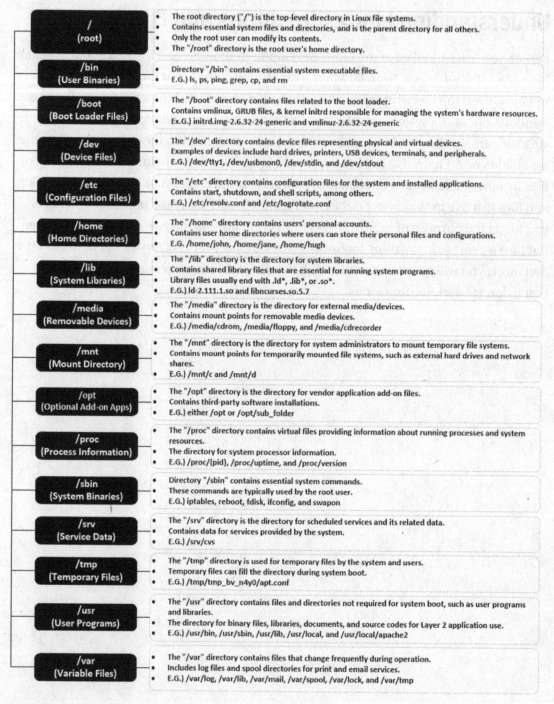

Figure 7-2. *Typical Linux directory and file structure*

Tip

Linux directory structures share similarities

A standard Linux directory structure is depicted in Figure 7-2. While various Linux distributions may exhibit slight variations in their directory and file arrangements, they largely maintain a consistent framework across the board.

Figure 7-3 displays the root directory of the Fedora 38 server. Upon closer examination and comparison of the listed directories, notice the striking resemblances to the layout depicted in Figure 7-2.

```
[root@f38s1 /]# ls -l
total 20
dr-xr-xr-x.   2 root root    6 Jan 19  2023 afs
lrwxrwxrwx.   1 root root    7 Jan 19  2023 bin -> usr/bin
dr-xr-xr-x.   5 root root 4096 Aug 15 22:39 boot
drwxr-xr-x.  20 root root 3940 Aug 19 12:53 dev
drwxr-xr-x. 106 root root 8192 Aug 19 13:37 etc
drwxr-xr-x.   3 root root   18 Aug 15 22:40 home
lrwxrwxrwx.   1 root root    7 Jan 19  2023 lib -> usr/lib
lrwxrwxrwx.   1 root root    9 Jan 19  2023 lib64 -> usr/lib64
drwxr-xr-x.   2 root root    6 Jan 19  2023 media
drwxr-xr-x.   3 root root   18 Aug 15 22:35 mnt
drwxr-xr-x.   2 root root    6 Jan 19  2023 opt
dr-xr-xr-x. 224 root root    0 Aug 19 12:53 proc
dr-xr-x---.   3 root root  163 Aug 19 13:32 root
drwxr-xr-x.  36 root root 1100 Aug 21 23:22 run
lrwxrwxrwx.   1 root root    8 Jan 19  2023 sbin -> usr/sbin
drwxr-xr-x.   2 root root    6 Jan 19  2023 srv
dr-xr-xr-x.  13 root root    0 Aug 19 12:53 sys
drwxrwxrwt.  14 root root  280 Aug 21 23:27 tmp
drwxr-xr-x.  12 root root  144 Aug 15 22:33 usr
drwxr-xr-x.  20 root root 4096 Aug 15 23:59 var
```

Figure 7-3. Fedora 38 Linux directory example

vi vs. nano

You've gained a brief understanding of the typical Linux directory and file structures. Now, let's delve into the realm of Linux files and directory management. Readers well-versed in Linux might wonder, "Why focus on teaching the use of the vi text editor here?" If you're an experienced Linux user, feel free to skip this chapter. However, do ensure you read Chapter 8 to install various IP services on the Fedora 38 server (f38s1) before progressing to Chapter 9. For those with little to no exposure to Linux, it's imperative to grasp vi (the visual editor) and nano before advancing to the next chapter. Familiarity with a Linux text editor is essential, as it enables you to accomplish tasks primarily through the terminal console or command lines.

On Linux servers, the essence largely revolves around text files, requiring proficiency with the terminal console for day-to-day management. Put simply, you must acquaint yourself with Linux's file structure and master file and directory management through the command line. When executing tasks on Linux servers, your intentions should be clear, and your desired outcomes well-defined. Proficiency in using Linux text editors is a cornerstone for delving into Python. Given that script-based coding demands extensive hours in your preferred text editor, this skill becomes pivotal.

Undoubtedly, various text editors exist for Linux, but vi stands as the standard on most modern Linux systems. To excel in Linux, mastery of vi is not just a choice, but a necessity. vi indeed lacks user-friendly controls against a black backdrop, potentially posing challenges for Linux newcomers. Let's demystify the vi editor once and for all, so you can bid farewell to the initial trepidation it might cause.

In this chapter, you're encouraged to explore file and directory management using vi, accompanied by the secondary text editor, nano. nano, catering to beginners with its pseudo-graphic layouts, is another Linux text editor worth acquainting yourself with. Unlike vi, it might not come pre-installed across all Linux distributions, but familiarity with both is beneficial. Remember, learning to use vi is not a mere option; it could be your sole recourse while overseeing enterprise servers and network devices in a client's production environment.

First and foremost, you'll learn to use the vi text editor, poised to become your primary Linux text-editing tool. Subsequently, you'll gain proficiency in the nano text editor, which offers an alternative to your textual endeavors. **This dual mastery will empower you in your Linux journey, enabling adept navigation, manipulation, and productivity within the Linux ecosystem.**

Introduction to vi

The origins of vi in Linux can be traced back to its UNIX predecessor. In Linux, vi closely resembles its UNIX counterpart, revealing the shared heritage of the Linux operating system and its applications. vi, which stands for "visual editor," uses two distinct modes to prevent unintentional edits by segregating commands and insert functionalities. vi operates in two modes:

- **Command mode:** Upon opening a file, vi starts in this mode. Each character typed in this mode serves as a command to modify the open text file.

- **Insert mode:** This mode is used for editing. When in insert mode, each character typed is added to the text in the file. Pressing the Esc key exits Insert mode and returns to Command mode.

Additionally, vi's Command mode offers numerous useful commands, although you'll only need a handful to get started. Basic yet highly useful vi commands are listed in Table 7-3. With practice, your fingers will remember these commands even before your mind does.

Table 7-3. *vi Text Editor Basic Commands*

vi command	Description
BASIC	
vi	Open the vi text editor
i	Enter Insert mode
Esc	Exit Insert mode
:x	Quit vi without saving changes
:q or :q!	Quit or quit forcefully
:w	Save changes
:wq or :wq!	Save changes and quit
MOVE	
j	Move the cursor down one line
k	Move cursor up one line
h	Move the cursor left one character
l (lowercase L)	Move the cursor right one character

(*continued*)

Table 7-3. (*continued*)

vi command	Description
0 **(zero)**	Move the cursor to the start of the current line
$	Move the cursor to the end of the current line
w	Move the cursor to the beginning of the next word
b	Move the cursor back to the beginning of the preceding word
:0	Move the cursor to the first line in the file
:n	Move the cursor to line n
:$	Move the cursor to the last line in the file
COPY/ PASTE	
dd	Cut (delete) line
p	Paste after the cursor
P	Paste before the cursor
UNDO	
u	Undo the last change
SEARCH TEXT	
/string	Search forward for the occurrence of string in text
?string	Search backward for the occurrence of string in text
n	Move to the next occurrence of the search string
N	Move to the previous occurrence of the search string

After having browsed through Table 7-3 approximately five times and having committed some of vi's key commands to memory, you are now ready to launch VMware Workstation and initiate an SSH connection to either the Fedora or Ubuntu Server in preparation for the first exercise in this chapter. In actual production environments, system administrators often establish remote connections to Linux servers and networking devices via SSH clients like PuTTY, Tera Term, or SecureCRT. The choice of which Linux server to use is inconsequential. Even though you're operating within a single computer environment and utilizing virtual machines, envision your server as a remote Linux server and your host's Windows OS as the remote client. Let's engage in practicing essential vi and Linux commands.

Basics of vi

For some people, mastering the use of vi might pose the initial hurdle in their Linux journey. However, for others, vi is simply another tool to add to their repertoire, one they can proudly incorporate into their skillset. With practice, familiarity with vi will grow, propelling you toward cultivating proficient Linux administration skills.

Tip

When you see <ENTER>, press your Enter key!

After entering each Linux command, it's essential to press the Enter key on your keyboard to execute the command. In certain sections of the exercises, where you're instructed to press the Enter key, you might encounter **<ENTER>** right after the last command, followed by a space. This signifies that you need to physically press the Enter key on your keyboard.

Here's an example: :wq <ENTER>

This signifies that once you've typed :wq, you must subsequently press the physical Enter key to execute the command.

For the following exercise, you will initiate an SSH connection to log in to the Fedora server, f38s1 (192.168.127.130) as the user jdoe.

Note 1: Your IP address scheme may be different from this book, so use your server IP address.

Note 2. If you have not updated the hostname in the previous chapter, your hostname will show as localhost.

#	Exercise

① Verify the current (present) working directory (pwd), create a new working directory (mkdir) named ex_vi. Then list (ls) the contents of the current working folder, and navigate (cd) to the ex_vi directory. Conclusively, confirm the present working directory (pwd) once more.

Objective: Acquire proficiency in checking, establishing, and navigating to a new directory.

```
[jdoe@f38s1 ~]$ pwd
/home/jdoe
[jdoe@f38s1 ~]$ ls
[jdoe@f38s1 ~]$ mkdir ex_vi
[jdoe@f38s1 ~]$ ls
ex_vi
[jdoe@f38s1 ~]$ cd ex_vi
[jdoe@f38s1 ex_vi]$ pwd
/home/jdoe/ex_vi
```

② As soon as the text file opens in vi, you will notice that this is a proper minimalistic text editor. The most exciting thing about vi is the information shown at the base of the application about the file name and line number. Try to type something on the keyboard; you cannot type anything in Command mode. Go to the next exercise to add data (text) to this file. You may create a new file by typing vi filename and then pressing the Enter key.

Objective: Learn how to create/open a file.

```
[jdoe@f38s1 ex_vi]$ vi file01.txt
```

When the new file opens, you will see blank lines, each line with a tilde (~) and a line at the bottom with the file name and status of the new file.

```
[...omitted for brevity]
~

~

"file01.txt" [New]                                    0,0-1              All
```

(*continued*)

#	Exercise
③	If you want to enter text into your text file, you must first enter Insert mode. Press the I key on your keyboard to enter --INSERT-- mode. If you see --INSERT-- in the lower-left corner, vi is now ready for your input.

Objective: Learn how to get into Insert mode in vi.

Press the I key on your keyboard.

[...omitted for brevity]

~

~

-- INSERT --   0,1   All

#	
④	Now type some text into this file and press the Esc key on your keyboard to exit Insert mode and move back into Command mode. As soon as you press the Esc key, look at the lower-left corner. The -- INSERT -- disappears from the screen, and you are in Ex mode. Now enter :wq or :wq! and press the Enter key to save the changes and exit vi.

Objective: Learn how to write, save, and exit a file in vi by pressing :wq <ENTER>.

Python lives in the jungle.

Also, python lives on my computer.

Have a Pythonic Day!

~

:wq <ENTER>

(continued)

#	Exercise
⑤	Like the previous example, after making changes to your file, you usually want to save the modified file while exiting vi. Another way to exit vi is by typing :x in Command mode.

Objective: Learn another way to save and exit a file in vi.

Python lives in the jungle.

Also, python lives on **your** computer.

Have a Pythonic Day!

~

:x <ENTER>

⑥	Once you have exited vi and are back in the Linux terminal console, issue ls (list) and then use the cat (concatenate) command to display the contents of file01.txt and verify the changes.

Objective: Learn to list (ls) files in the current directory and view the file contents in vi.

[jdoe@f38s1 ex_vi]$ **ls**

file01.txt

[jdoe@f38s1 ex_vi]$ **cat file01.txt**

Python lives in the jungle.

Also, python lives on your computer.

Have a Pythonic Day!

(*continued*)

#	Exercise
⑦	Now you are introduced to a few new Linux commands to perform the following tasks. You learn how to log in as a sudo user, check the current working directory, find your text file, copy the file to the root directory, and then return to normal user mode. You have just seen a glimpse of what will follow in this chapter.

Objective: Learn to log in as the root user, check that a file exists, search for the file, and copy a file to the root user folder.

```
[jdoe@f38s1 ex_vi]$ pwd

/home/jdoe/ex_vi

[jdoe@f38s1 ex_vi]$ su -

Password: ***************

[root@f38s1 ~]# pwd

/root

[root@f38s1 ~]# ls file01*

ls: cannot access 'file*': No such file or directory

[root@f38s1 ~]# find / -name file01*

/home/jdoe/ex_vi/file01.txt

[root@f38s1 ~]# cp /home/jdoe/ex_vi/file01.txt ~/

[root@f38s1 ~]# ls

anaconda-ks.cfg  file01.txt

[root@f38s1 ~]# find / -name file01.txt

/root/file01.txt

/home/jdoe/ex_vi/file01.txt
```

Reopening a File in vi

Here you will practice reopening and closing a file in vi.

#	Task
①	If you are continuing from the previous exercise, you should still be in root user mode. Go back to user mode using su - username. Check the current working directory and then move to the original ex_vi directory.

Replace the username with your own. Now you should be back to the user's home directory and in the ex_vi directory.

Objective: Learn to log back in as a standard user.

[root@f38s1 ~]# **su - jdoe**

[jdoe@f38s1 ~]$ **pwd**

/home/jdoe

[jdoe@f38s1 ~]$ **ls**

ex_vi

[jdoe@f38s1 ~]$ **cd ex_vi**

[jdoe@f38s1 ex_vi]$ **pwd**

/home/jdoe/ex_vi

(continued)

#	Task

② To reopen an existing file, simply type vi followed by the file name. If you opened a file by mistake and did not want to make any changes, simply type :q and press the Enter key.

Objective: Learn to reopen existing files and exit (quit) without modifying the file from vi.

[jdoe@f38s1 ex_vi]$ **ls**

file01.txt

[jdoe@f38s1 ex_vi]$ **vi file01.txt**

Python lives in the jungle.

Also, python lives on your computer.

Have a Pythonic Day!

~

[...omitted for brevity]

~

:q <ENTER>

(continued)

#	Task

③ If you opened the file, entered into Insert mode, and started editing the file but decide to quit without saving your changes, you can use :q!. In this example, "Goodbye." was added to the fourth line, but you want to discard it and exit without saving the change.

Objective: Learn to quit after modifying the file.

[jdoe@f38s1 ex_vi]$ **vi file01.txt**

Python lives in the jungle.

Also, python lives on your computer.

Have a Pythonic Day!

Goodbye.|

~

:q! <ENTER>

Note, if you modified the file and only use :q and the Enter key, vi will ask you to add !
after :q.

Python lives in the jungle.

Also, python lives on your computer.

Have a Pythonic Day!

Goodbye.

~

E37: No write since last change (add ! to override)   4,8
All

(*continued*)

#	Task
④	To view a file's contents without opening it in vi, you can use the cat, more, or less commands. Try all three commands. After running the more and less commands, you can exit the application by using the Ctrl+Z keys.

Objective: Learn to view file contents using the cat, more, and less commands.

```
[jdoe@f38s1 ex_vi]$ cat file01.txt
Python lives in the jungle.

Also, python lives on your computer.

Have a Pythonic Day!
[jdoe@f38s1 ex_vi]$ more file01.txt
[...omitted for brevity]
[5]+  Stopped                    more file01.txt <Ctrl + Z>
[jdoe@f38s1 ex_vi]$ less file01.txt
[...omitted for brevity]
[6]+  Stopped                    less file01.txt <Ctrl + Z>
```

Copying and Pasting a Line in vi

You can use dd to copy a line in vi and use the p key to paste a line below the cursor position. Or use the P key to paste a line above the cursor position. You can easily remember this operation. Try to use the p key to paste below the cursor position and use the P key to paste above the cursor position.

#	Task
①	Open `file01.txt` in vi again. Move the cursor to the third line, as you are going to cut the third line.

Objective: Move the cursor in vi Command mode.

```
Python lives in the jungle.

Also, python lives on your computer.

|Have a Pythonic Day!            # cursor line, place the cursor at 'H'

~

"file01.txt" 3L, 86B                      3,1            All
```

| ② | Press the D key twice in a row (dd). This operation will cut the line where the cursor was positioned. |

Objective: Cut strings on the active line using dd.

```
Python lives in the jungle.

|Also, python lives on your computer.        # cursor moves
one line up after the cutting action.

~

~

"file01.txt" 3L, 86B                      3,1            All
```

| ③ | Now press the P key to paste "Have a pythonic day!" before "Also, python lives on my computer." You have successfully swapped the second and third lines. |

Objective: Paste the copied line to the line above the cursor position.

```
Python lives in the jungle.

|Have a Pythonic Day!            # press <Shift + p> for upper
case P, paste action.

Also, python lives on your computer.

~

"file01.txt" 3L, 84C                      2,1            All
```

(continued)

#	Task
④	Now you want to add the same sentence in the fourth line. Move the cursor to the third line position.

Objective: Move the cursor down.

```
Python lives in the jungle.

Have a Pythonic Day!                                    # cursor line

|Also, python lives on your computer.

~

"file01.txt" 3L, 84C              3,1            All
```

⑤	This time press the p key to paste "Have a Pythonic day!" below the third line.

Objective: Paste the copied line to the line below the cursor position.

```
Python lives in the jungle.

Have a Pythonic Day!

|Also, python lives on your computer.               # cursor line

Have a Pythonic Day!

~

4,1              All
```

(continued)

#	Task
⑥	Now press the Esc key once and then use `:wq` to save the changes and exit vi.

Objective: Save changes and exit vi.

```
Python lives in the jungle.

Have a Pythonic Day!

Also, python lives on your computer.

Have a Pythonic Day!

~

[...omitted for brevity]

~

:wq <ENTER>
```

| ⑦ | Check the result by using the `cat file01.txt` command. |

```
[jdoe@f38s1 ex_vi]$ cat file01.txt

Python lives in the jungle.

Have a Pythonic Day!

Also, python lives on your computer.

Have a Pythonic Day!
```

Undo Last in vi

If you make a mistake, you can undo the last action using :u in Command mode.

#	Task
①	:u (undo) is one of the most essential commands, as it allows you to undo your last action. In vi, this acts as a toggle, undoing and redoing your most recent action. First, reopen file01.txt and type something in line 5 while you are in --INSERT-- mode. I am typing "You can do it!" on the fifth line.

Objective: Learn to undo the last action in vi.

```
Python lives in the jungle.

Have a Pythonic Day!

Also, python lives on your computer.

Have a Pythonic Day!

You can do it!|                              # cursor line

~

-- INSERT --                                      All
```

②	Press the Esc key to exit Insert mode and move back to Command mode. Type :u and press the Enter key on your keyboard to undo your last action.

```
Python lives in the jungle.

Have a Pythonic Day!

Also, python lives on my computer.

Have a Pythonic Day!|                          # cursor moved line

~

[...omitted for brevity]

~

1 line less; before #1   18 seconds ago          4,20        All
```

As soon as you type :u and press the Enter key, the fifth line you just added will be removed (undone), and the cursor position will move to the back of the fourth line.

(continued)

#	Task
③	Use the `:qa` command to quit the session.

Tip

Exploring gvim on Windows

Some text editor users hold a strong attraction for the vi editor, to the extent that they opt to install a Windows adaptation of vi named *gvim*. They then use gvim as their favored text editor within the Windows environment. Although it might require a period of adjustment, many newcomers find that vi gradually becomes more appealing. If you're interested in exploring gvim, you can download it at: `https://www.vim.org/download.php`.

Searching for Text in vi

The vi editor provides a powerful string search functionality within its Command mode. To locate a specific string, simply use the `/string` command. This handy feature is also accessible when working with Cisco IOS `show` commands. As an illustration, suppose you're executing the `show run` command on your Cisco router. In such a scenario, using `/line vty` will swiftly move you down to the end of the line you're interested in.

#	Task

①	Open the file01.txt file in vi. You can use a string to search through the text. Move your cursor position to the top, then type /python in Command mode. The search words will be highlighted. Remember that the p in python is in lowercase letters, so this search is case-sensitive. Notice that only the word python on the third line is highlighted.
	
	Objective: Learn to search a string and navigate through a text file in vi.
	
	`Python lives in the jungle.`
	
	`Have a Pythonic Day!`
	
	`Also, python lives on my computer.`
	
	`Have a Pythonic Day!`
	
	`~`
	
	/python | *# cursor line*
	
	Press the Enter key once to move to the first occurrence of the string Python. The cursor moves to the first letter of the searched word.

②	Now replace /python with /Python with the capital P. Note that the word Python is highlighted on three different lines. If you have multiple selected words like this, you can use the Enter key to move down to the next selection if your cursor is positioned at the first character of the top line.
	
	`Python lives in the jungle.`
	
	`Have a Pythonic Day!`
	
	`Also, python lives on my computer.`
	
	`Have a Pythonic Day!`
	
	`~`
	
	/Python | *# cursor line*

(continued)

#	Task
③	Press the Enter key and then the N key to move to the next occurrence of the string Python. By pressing the N key multiple times, you will see that it loops through the selections.

```
Python lives in the jungle.

Have a Pythonic Day!

Also, python lives on my computer.

Have a |Pythonic Day!                              # cursor line

~
```

/Python	4,8	All

#	Task
④	To loop through in reverse (up), try the Shift+N key combinations to move backward. Notice that the / sign changes to ? at the bottom-left corner.

```
Python lives in the jungle.

Have a |Pythonic day!                              # cursor line

Also, python lives on my computer.

Have a Pythonic day!

~
```

?Python	2,8	All

Display the Line Number in vi

When working in the vi text editor, managing a few lines of text or code is straightforward. However, as the volume of text or code increases, it's easy to become disoriented within the lines. To maintain awareness of your current position, vi offers a numbering feature. To activate line numbering, simply type :set number in Command mode.

#	Task
①	Reopen `file01.txt` in vi, type `:set number`, and press the Enter key.

Objective: Enable and disable the line number.

```
1 Python lives in the jungle.

2 Have a Pythonic day!

3 Also, python lives on my computer.

4 Have a Pythonic day!

~
```

:set number <ENTER>

4,1   All

②	If you want to turn off the numbering, type `:set nonumber` in Command mode.

```
Python lives in the jungle.

Have a Pythonic day!

Also, python lives on my computer.

Have a Pythonic day!

~
```

:set nononumber <ENTER>

4,1   All

While vi boasts numerous commands, the exercise you've just completed covers the fundamental ones necessary to begin your journey in the Linux OS. Next, you'll delve into the nano text editor. Particularly for Windows PC users, nano may serve as a more user-friendly text editor option while operating within a Linux OS environment.

Expand Your Knowledge:

Learn More about vi Features

If you want to learn more about vi, visit these URLs for more details:

URL: https://www.tecmint.com/vi-editor-usage/

URL: https://www.washington.edu/computing/unix/vi.html

Introduction to nano

Unlike vi, nano has almost no learning curve on Linux; it is an easy-to-use text editor with a versatile and straightforward user interface. Nano is typically installed by default on newer Linux distributions, but this might not be the case for the vast majority. For instance, on the latest Fedora 38 server, as of the time of writing this book, nano was not installed by default. Once installed, the latest version available should be version 7.2 or newer; however, as you read this book, you will have access to a newer version.

If you are using Ubuntu Server 22 or newer for the Linux chapter exercises, the pre-installed version will be at least 6.2 or newer. If it is not pre-installed, a single yum command will suffice to install the program on your Linux machine. Before proceeding to install the nano text editor on the Fedora server, f38s1, let's explore some key commands used in the nano text editor. These commands are readily available from the nano interface, so you don't have to memorize them in your head. Take a moment to review the available commands in Table 7-4 and read their descriptions at least once before progressing to the next section.

Table 7-4. *nano Text Editor Primary Keys*

Command	Description
nano[filename]	Open the editor command.
Ctrl+X	Exit edit mode key combo.
Y	Press Ctrl+X and choose Y to save the file.
N	Press Ctrl+X and choose N to ignore edit.
Cancel	Press Ctrl+X and select Cancel to return to the nano editor.
Ctrl+K	Copy (Cut).
Ctrl+U	Paste.

Installing nano

Let's quickly determine whether your Linux OS already includes a pre-installed version of nano. In the forthcoming example, the username jdoe is used for logging into Linux. If you set a different username during the Linux installation process, your username will differ accordingly.

#	Task
①	From your Linux terminal console, run nano -V or nano --version. The following example shows the output of the nano -V command on the Fedora server.

```
[jdoe@f38s1 ex_vi]$ cd ..
[jdoe@f38s1 ~]$ nano -V
-bash: nano: command not found
[jdoe@f38s1 ~]$ sudo dnf install nano -y          # use -y handle for yes
[sudo] password for jdoe: **************
Fedora 38 - x86_64 - Updates                      4.0 kB/s | 4.4 kB   00:01
[...omitted for brevity]
Installed:
nano-7.2-2.fc38.x86_64
Complete!
[jdoe@f38s1 ~]$ nano -V
GNU nano, version 7.2
(C) 2023 the Free Software Foundation and various contributors
Compiled options: --enable-utf8
```

(continued)

#	Task

② Another way to check if nano is installed on your Linux system is to create and open a new file using the nano [filename] command.

Objective: Check if nano is available on your Linux system by looking at the /usr/bin directory.

If the nano text editor is not installed on your Linux system, Linux will return a No such file or directory bash error.

```
[jdoe@f38s1 ~]$ nano test01.txt
-bash: /usr/bin/nano: No such file or directory
```

Also, when you studied the Linux directory structure earlier, you saw that the executable program files typically reside in /usr/bin/; quickly check if the nano executable file exists in this directory to reconfirm.

```
[jdoe@f38s1 ~]$ ls /usr/bin/nano
ls: cannot access '/usr/bin/nano': No such file or directory
```

If nano is installed, you can confirm that the nano file resides in the /usr/bin directory.

```
[jdoe@f38s1 ~]$ ls -lh /usr/bin/nano
-rwxr-xr-x. 1 root root 279K Jan 19  2023 /usr/bin/nano
```

③ If you encountered a similar error as before, it's time to install nano on your Linux OS. You can effortlessly install nano with a single command and the -y option for automatic confirmation. If you're logged in as a standard user, as demonstrated in the following example, execute the sudo yum install -y nano command and enter your sudo password. If you're logged in as a root user, you can omit sudo before the yum command. To uninstall nano, simply replace install with remove.

Objective: Install and uninstall nano on your Linux server.

```
# To install nano on Fedora/CentOS/Red Hat Linux
[jdoe@f38s1 ~]$ sudo dnf install nano
[sudo] password for jdoe: **********
# To uninstall nano
[jdoe@f38s1 ~]$ sudo dnf remove -y nano
```

(*continued*)

#	Task

	`# To install nano on Ubuntu/Debian/Mint Linux`
	
	`jdoe@u22s1:~$ sudo apt install -y nano`
	
	`[sudo] password for jdoe: **********`
	
	`# To uninstall nano`
	
	`jdoe@u22s1:~$ sudo apt remove -y nano`

④	If you are using Ubuntu Server 22 and do not have the nano editor, install it using the `apt-get install` nano command. The subtle syntax differences between CentOS and Ubuntu typically arise from the use of different package management tools. Red Hat-based distributions like CentOS, Red Hat, and Fedora use the yum (Yellowdog Updater Modified) command, while the newer package manager called dnf (using RPM Package Manager) is gradually replacing it. Debian-based distributions such as Ubuntu, Debian, and Mint Linux use apt (Advanced Package Tool) as their package manager.
	
	Now, quickly run the `ls /usr/bin/nano` command to confirm successful installation.
	
	Objective: Check for nano installation success.
	
	`# On Fedora/CentOS/Red Hat server`
	
	`[jdoe@f38s1 ~]$ ls /usr/bin/nano`
	
	`/usr/bin/nano`
	
	`# On Ubuntu/Debian/Mint Linux/PoP OS server`
	
	`jdoe@u22s1:~$ ls /usr/bin/nano`
	
	`/usr/bin/nano`
	
	This will verify whether nano has been installed successfully on your system.

Tip

Differences in package managers: Red Hat, Debian, and Arch Linux variants

In Red Hat-based Linux systems, RPM serves as a straightforward package manager primarily for installing and verifying packages, but it doesn't handle dependencies automatically. Yum, an older tool, builds upon RPM, providing dependency management, automatic updates, and removals. Its successor, DNF, is the modern default in later CentOS and Fedora. DNF inherits Yum's features while offering better performance and improved dependency handling, making it the preferred choice for its efficiency.

In Debian-based systems like Ubuntu, you'll find `apt-get` and `apt`, both serving as package managers. `apt-get`, being older, uses specific commands, lacking download progress indicators. On the other hand, `apt` is a newer, user-friendly alternative that simplifies commands and combines multiple tasks into one, enhancing the user experience with progress bars during downloads.

- `apt`: Advanced Package Tool
- `apt-get`: Advanced Package Tool with Get
- DNF: Dandified Yum (Dandified Package Manager)
- `emerge`: A Meta-Package Manager (Gentoo Linux package manager)
- `Pacman`: Package Manager for Arch Linux
- RPM: Red Hat Package Manager
- Yum: Yellowdog Updater Modified
- `Zypper`: Zypper is Not Yum (ZYpp package manager and solver for openSUSE)

In Arch Linux and its derivatives, `Pacman` stands out, offering simplicity and robust dependency resolution. For openSUSE, there's `zypper`, while older Red Hat systems use yum, and Gentoo uses `emerge`. These package managers share common functionalities such as package installation, updates, and removals but vary based on the Linux distribution. Newer package managers like `dnf` and `apt` tend to be more user-friendly and feature-rich. Additionally, Slackware Linux uses 'pkgtool' as its package manager.

Create/Open a File with nano

You have confirmed the successful installation of nano and are now prepared to edit files with this new text editor. As previously mentioned, you can use your Fedora or Ubuntu virtual server for all exercises. You can proceed by logging back in as a standard user and creating a new directory, called ex_nano, to initiate the nano exercises.

#	Task
①	First, make a new directory called ex_nano by typing `mkdir ex_nano`. You will use this directory to store exercise files created during your exercises. Change the working directory to ex_nano by typing `cd ex_nano`.

Objective: Create a new directory to practice using the nano text editor.

```
[jdoe@f38s1 ~]$ mkdir ex_nano && cd ex_nano          # notice the && usage
                                                      for simplification

[jdoe@f38s1 ex_nano]$ ls
[jdoe@f38s1 ex_nano]$ pwd

/home/jdoe/ex_nano
```

②	If you execute the command nano file02.txt as shown next, if a file with the same name does not exist, a new file will open. If a file with the same name exists, then it will reopen the existing file. Nano has a pseudo-graphical user interface, and as soon as you open a file, you feel at home with the help menu displaying at the base; you want to jump right in and use it. If you are used to Notepad on Windows, you will have no problem using this user-friendly tool.

Objective: Create a new file using the nano command.

```
[jdoe@f38s1 ex_nano]$ nano file02.txt          # press <ENTER> key

GNU nano 7.2                                    file02.txt

[...omitted for brevity]

[ New File ]

^G Help   ^O Write Out   ^W Where Is   ^K Cut   ^T Execute   ^C Location
M-U Undo

^X Exit   ^R Read File   ^\ Replace   ^U Paste   ^J Justify   ^/ Go To
Line    M-E Redo
```

(continued)

#	Task

③ ⸱ After opening a new file and immediately deciding to exit nano without editing the file, the file will be discarded. To exit nano, use ^X (the Ctrl+X keys). If you want to create a new file first, use touch file02.txt and then open it with the nano file02.txt command. In nano, if you see the ^ symbol, that means the Ctrl key.

Objective: Use the touch command to create a new file.

[jdoe@f38s1 ex_nano]$ **nano file02.txt**

[jdoe@f38s1 ex_nano]$ **ls**

[jdoe@f38s1 ex_nano]$ **touch file02.txt**

[jdoe@f38s1 ex_nano]$ **ls**

file02.txt

④ Now run the nano tta01.txt command to create a new file and enter a few text lines. I am entering the list of things to automate here but you can make up your own and follow the exercise. As you have discovered, the nano editor does not require you to press the I key to move you into -- INSERT -- mode as you do in the vi editor. After you have finished, to exit nano, press Ctrl+X (^X).

Objective: Write to a new file and exit.

[jdoe@f38s1 ex_nano]$ **nano tta01.txt**

GNU nano 2.9.8   tta01.txt
Modified

Things to automate:

Cisco router and switch upgrades

Palo Alto VM deployment (IaC)

Cisco PSIRT API integration with ServiceNow CI

(continued)

#	Task

Save modified buffer? **Y** *# Press the 'Y' key*

Y Yes

N No   ^C Cancel

File Name to Write: tta01.txt *# press <ENTER>*

^G Help   M-D DOS Format   M-A Append   M-B Backup
File

^C Cancel   M-M Mac Format   M-P Prepend   ^T Browse

---

⑤ Say you forgot to add an item to the list. Open the file again and add an item to the next line. This time, use Ctrl+S to save the file first, followed by Ctrl+X to quit nano. This time nano won't prompt you to confirm the changes.

Objective: Modify the file, then save and exit.

[jdoe@f38s1 ex_nano]$ **nano tta01.txt**

GNU nano 2.9.8   tta01.txt   Modified

Things to automate:

Cisco router and switch upgrades

Palo Alto VM deployment (IaC)

Cisco PSIRT API integration with ServiceNow CI

Vulnerabilities and CVE SQL DB integration   *# press 'Ctrl+S'*
and then 'Ctrl+X'.

(continued)

#	Task
⑥	Use the `cat`, `more`, or `less` command, followed by the file name you've saved, like this: `cat tta01.txt`. When you use the `more` or `less` commands, you can exit by pressing the Q key. These commands are system utilities (applications) in Linux. Novice Linux users often perceive `cat`, `more`, and `less` as simple text commands, but in reality, they are full-fledged Linux applications, typically implemented in the C programming language. These utilities are intentionally designed to be efficient and lightweight, making C an ideal choice for their development.

Objective: View the contents of the file using `cat`, `more`, or `less`.

```
[jdoe@f38s1 ex_nano]$ ls -lh

total 4.0K

-rw-r--r--. 1 jdoe jdoe   0 Sep  3 09:46 file02.txt

-rw-r--r--. 1 jdoe jdoe 139 Sep  3 09:47 tta01.txt

[jdoe@f38s1 ex_nano]$ cat tta01.txt            # try more or less
commands

Things to automate:

Cisco router and switch upgrades

Palo Alto VM deployment (IaC)

Cisco PSIRT API integration with ServiceNow CI

Vulnerabilities and CVE SQL DB integration
```

You've just acquired the essential skills in nano for creating, opening, saving, and closing a file. Linux boasts a variety of excellent text editors, including Emacs, Gedit, Leafpad, and Komodo. However, due to the scope of this chapter and book, I won't delve into these alternatives. Nevertheless, I encourage you to explore these Linux-based text editing tools in your spare time through a simple Google search. Also, with the introduction of ChatGPT-3.5 by OpenAII in March 2023, you can now learn the essential Linux commands and their applications to your heart's content from any computer on the Internet.

Using the Auto-Complete Feature to Reopen a File with nano

You can use the auto-complete feature to reopen a file with nano. To do this, follow these steps: open nano by entering the command, type nano f, and then press the Tab key to auto-completing the file name. As there is only one file beginning with the name file02.txt, tabbing will promptly complete the file name, sparing you from entering the entire name manually.

#	Task

① To reopen an existing text file in Nano, simply use the nano [filename] command, following the same format as in the previous exercise. To accomplish this quickly, type nano t, then utilize the Tab key to auto-complete the file name. Finally, press the Enter key to open the desired file.

Objective: Use the auto-complete feature to open an existing file.

```
[jdoe@f38s1 ex_nano]$ nano t|                    # press <Tab> key to
auto complete the filename

[jdoe@f38s1 ex_nano]$ nano tta01.txt             # auto-completed
filename, press <ENTER> key

GNU nano 2.9.8                        tta01.txt

Things to automate:

Cisco router and switch upgrades

Palo Alto VM deployment (IaC)

Cisco PSIRT API integration with ServiceNow CI

Vulnerabilities and CVE SQL DB integration

[ Read 5 lines ]

^G Help          ^O Write Out    ^W Where Is      ^K Cut           ^T
Execute          ^C Location    M-U Undo

^X Exit          ^R Read File    ^\ Replace   ^U Paste             ^J
Justify          ^/ Go To Line  M-E Redo

Use Ctrl+X to exit without changing the information.
```

Cut (Delete) and Paste with nano

#	Task
①	While working in nano, to cut a line, first navigate to the line you want to cut (or copy), and then use the Ctrl+K key combination to cut it. Then paste it using the Ctrl+U key combination. If you do not paste the cut information, it will be discarded from the computer's memory and will function similarly to a delete operation. To begin the exercise, reopen `file02.txt` and position the cursor on line 5.

Objective: Cut (delete) a line in nano.

```
[jdoe@f38s1 ex_nano]$ nano tta01.txt
```

Things to automate:

Cisco router and switch upgrades

Palo Alto VM deployment (IaC)

Cisco PSIRT API integration with ServiceNow CI

Vulnerabilities and CVE SQL DB integration   # cursor line

 # To delete line 5, press Ctrl+K. Line 5 appears to have been deleted, but nano cuts and puts line 5 in your server's random-access memory (RAM).

Things to automate:

Cisco router and switch upgrades

Palo Alto VM deployment (IaC)

Cisco PSIRT API integration with ServiceNow CI

| # cursor line

 # You can use the Ctrl+U keys to paste back the information.

Things to automate:

Cisco router and switch upgrades

Palo Alto VM deployment (IaC)

Cisco PSIRT API integration with ServiceNow CI

Vulnerabilities and CVE SQL DB integration

| # cursor line

(continued)

#	Task
②	If you want to copy and paste specific strings, first move your cursor to the first position of a string where you want to begin your copy.

Objective: Learn how to copy and paste a specific string.

 # In this example, move the cursor to the letter V of Vulnerabilities. You want to cut the words "Vulnerabilities and" from line 5.

Things to automate:

Cisco router and switch upgrades

Palo Alto VM deployment (IaC)

Cisco PSIRT API integration with ServiceNow CI

Vulnerabilities and CVE SQL DB integration   *# cursor line*

 # Then press Ctrl+6 and use the right arrow [→] to highlight a word or strings.

Things to automate:

Cisco router and switch upgrades

Palo Alto VM deployment (IaC)

Cisco PSIRT API integration with ServiceNow CI

Vulnerabilities and CVE SQL DB integration   *# cursor line*

 # Then press Ctrl+K to cut the string and remove the leading space on line 5, so it looks like this.

Things to automate:

Cisco router and switch upgrades

Palo Alto VM deployment (IaC)

Cisco PSIRT API integration with ServiceNow CI

CVE SQL DB integration   *# cursor line*

(*continued*)

#	Task

③   Now move the cursor to line 4 using the arrow keys and cut line 4. You want to move line 4 to line 3.

Objective: Use the cut-and-paste function in nano.

 # Place your cursor at the first position of line 4.

Things to automate:

Cisco router and switch upgrades

Palo Alto VM deployment (IaC)

Cisco PSIRT API integration with ServiceNow CI   *# cursor line*

CVE SQL DB integration

 # Press Ctrl+K to copy the fourth line. The cursor will be placed on the letter C.

Things to automate:

Cisco router and switch upgrades

Palo Alto VM deployment (IaC)

CVE SQL DB integration   *# cursor line*

 # Now move the cursor to the beginning of the second line.

Things to automate:

Cisco router and switch upgrades   *# cursor line*

Palo Alto VM deployment (IaC)

CVE SQL DB integration

 # Press Ctrl+U to paste (insert) the copied line.

Things to automate:

Cisco router and switch upgrades

Cisco PSIRT API integration with ServiceNow CI   *# cursor line*

Palo Alto VM deployment (IaC)

CVE SQL DB integration

Now you have successfully cut and pasted the fourth line and swapped line 4 with line 3.

(*continued*)

#	Task

④ If you want to cut multiple lines, place the cursor in the first position of the line you want to copy using the Ctrl+K keys, then press the Ctrl+K keys consecutively.

Objective: Cut and paste multiple lines in nano.

 # Place the cursor at the beginning of the fourth line. You will copy the fourth and fifth lines by pressing the Ctrl+K keys twice.

Things to automate:

Cisco router and switch upgrades

Cisco PSIRT API integration with ServiceNow CI

Palo Alto VM deployment (IaC)   *# cursor line*

CVE SQL DB integration

 # Use Ctrl+K twice to cut lines 4 and 5.

Things to automate:

Cisco PSIRT API integration with ServiceNow CI

Cisco router and switch upgrades

| *# cursor line*

 # Now move the cursor to the first position of the second line, in this case in front of the letter C in Cisco.

Things to automate:

Cisco PSIRT API integration with ServiceNow CI   *# cursor line*

Cisco router and switch upgrades

(continued)

#	Task

 # Now use the Ctrl+U to paste the fourth and fifth line, so the two lines beginning with the word Cisco are pushed down as shown:

Things to automate:

Palo Alto VM deployment (IaC)

CVE SQL DB integration

Cisco PSIRT API integration with ServiceNow CI   # cursor line

Cisco router and switch upgrades

Use Ctrl+S and Ctrl+X to save the change and exit. Now you know how to cut and paste multiple lines using nano's Ctrl+K and Ctrl+U keys.

String Search and Replacing String(s)

#	Task

① In nano, you can use Ctrl+W to search for a string, and the search is case-insensitive. Objective: Search for a specific word or string in nano.

In the following example, you will search for the word "integration."

 # Open the tta01.txt in nano again. Press Ctrl+W, and then type the word integration and press Enter.

Things to automate:

Palo Alto VM deployment (IaC)

CVE SQL DB integration

Cisco PSIRT API integration with ServiceNow CI

Cisco router and switch upgrades

Search: **integration**| # cursor line

^G Help   M-C Case Sens   M-B Backwards   ^P Older   ^T Go To Line

^C Cancel   M-R Reg.exp.   ^R Replace   ^N Newer

(continued)

#	Task

 # As soon as you press the Enter key, the cursor moves to the first match of the word integration.

Things to automate:

Palo Alto VM deployment (IaC)

CVE SQL DB |integration   *# cursor line*

Cisco PSIRT API integration with ServiceNow CI

Cisco router and switch upgrades

 # If you press Ctrl+W one more time and press the Enter key one more time, it will move to the next keyword match if it exists. If there is only a single match, it will remain on the first matched keyword. In this case, you have a second keyword match, so it will jump to the fourth line and highlight the word integration.

Things to automate:

Palo Alto VM deployment (IaC)

CVE SQL DB integration

Cisco PSIRT API |integration with ServiceNow CI   *# cursor line*

Cisco router and switch upgrades

(continued)

#	Task

(2) To search and replace a word or string, use Ctrl+W to locate the word, then use Ctrl+\.
Objective: Search for a specific word and replace it.

 # To perform this exercise, close the tta01.txt file and then reopen it in nano. You are going to search for the word Cisco and replace it with Juniper. Press the Ctrl+\ keys on your keyboard, then type the word Cisco.

[jdoe@f38s1 ex_nano]$ **nano tta01.txt**

Things to automate:

Palo Alto VM deployment (IaC)

CVE SQL DB integration

Cisco PSIRT API integration with ServiceNow CI

Cisco router and switch upgrades

Search (to replace): **Cisco**<ENTER>   # *cursor line*

^G Help   M-C Case Sens   M-B Backwards   ^P Older   ^T Go To Line

^C Cancel   M-R Reg.exp.   ^R Replace   ^N Newer

 # As soon as you press the Enter key, you will be prompted to enter the relacing word. Enter Juniper and press the Enter key once again.

Replace with: **Juniper**<ENTER>   # *cursor line*

^G Help   ^P Older

^C Cancel   ^N Newer

 # At the next prompt, you will be asked whether you want to replace a single instance or all the instances. Because you want to replace both instances of the word Cisco, respond with A.

Replace this instance?**A**   # *cursor line*

Y Yes   A All

N No   ^C Cancel

(*continued*)

#	Task

 # All the matched words Cisco have been replaced with the word Juniper as highlighted.

Things to automate:

Palo Alto VM deployment (IaC)

CVE SQL DB integration

Juniper PSIRT API integration with ServiceNow CI

Juniper router and switch upgrades

[Replaced 2 occurrences]

```
^G Help          ^O Write Out    ^W Where Is      ^K Cut          ^T
Execute      ^C Location     M-U Undo

^X Exit          ^R Read File    ^\ Replace       ^U Paste        ^J
Justify      ^/ Go To Line   M-E Redo
```

③ You can use ^O (Ctrl+O) and then the Enter key to save the changes without closing the nano editor. This command works like a Save button.

Objective: Save the file using the Ctrl+O option.

 # Press the Ctrl+O keys on your keyboard and press the Enter key.

Things to automate:

Palo Alto VM deployment (IaC)

CVE SQL DB integration

Juniper PSIRT API integration with ServiceNow CI

Juniper router and switch upgrades

File Name to Write: tta01.txt <ENTER>   *# cursor line*

```
^G Help     M-D DOS Format     M-A Append      M-B Backup File

^C Cancel   M-M Mac Format     M-P Prepend     ^T Browse
```

(continued)

403

#	Task

 # You will remain in nano but the change has been saved.

Things to automate:

Palo Alto VM deployment (IaC)

CVE SQL DB integration

Juniper PSIRT API integration with ServiceNow CI   *# cursor line*

Juniper router and switch upgrades

Use the Ctrl+X keys to exit the file tta01.txt.

[jdoe@f38s1 ex_nano]$

Customize nano for Python Coding

While writing Python code in nano, you may notice the absence of certain features, such as a four-space tab for reducing coding fatigue (instead of having to press the spacebar four times) and options for displaying line numbers to quickly identify your current working position. To customize these settings, you'll need to make changes in the /etc/nanorc file.

#	Task

① To modify the tab character in nano from eight spaces to four spaces, you can follow these steps. Objective: Enable four-space tabbing in nano for Python coding.

 # Begin by opening the nanorc configuration file. To do this, execute the following command:

[jdoe@f38s1 ex_nano]$ **sudo nano /etc/nanorc**

[sudo] password for jdoe: ******************

(*continued*)

#	Task

 # Search the nanorc file using the ^W (Ctrl+W) command with key set tabsize. Remove the hash signs for set tabsize **and** set tabstospaces **to activate the lines and replace numbers 8 to 4. Then save the file and exit.**

GNU nano 2.9.8   /etc/nanorc

[...omitted for brevity]

Use this tab size instead of the default; it must be greater than 0.

set tabsize 4   *# Remove # to activate & update 8 to 4*

Convert each typed tab to the fitting number of spaces.

set tabstospaces   *# Remove # to activate this line*

[...omitted for brevity]

 # Now it is time to check the changes. Reopen tta01.txt **in nano and use the Tab key to add four spaces to lines 2-5 to confirm.**

Things to automate:

Palo Alto VM deployment (IaC)   *# Tabbing adds 4 spaces*

CVE SQL DB integration

Juniper PSIRT API integration with ServiceNow CI
Juniper router and switch upgrades

Now, when you work in a .py file, every time you use the Tab key, you will be adding four spaces instead of the default eight spaces. If you want to reverse the previous change, you can re-open the /etc/nanorc file and add # to the two lines you changed.

(*continued*)

#	Task

② Use sudo nano /etc/nanorc to reopen the nanorc file one more time. Search for set linenumbers and remove the # sign at the beginning of this line. Then save the changes.

Objective: Enable line numbering in nano.

```
[jdoe@f38s1 ex_nano]$ sudo nano /etc/nanorc
```

```
[sudo] password for jdoe: **********
```

 # Remove the # in front of set linenumbers**. This will enable line numbering in nano.**

```
GNU nano 2.9.8              /etc/nanorc         Modified
```

[...omitted for brevity]

```
## Display line numbers to the left of the text.
```

```
set linenumbers                    # Remove # to activate this line
```

[...omitted for brevity]

 # To confirm the change, reopen the tta01.txt **file. You will see the line numbers next to each line.**

```
GNU nano 7.2                                    tta01.txt
```

```
1 Things to automate:
```

```
2      Palo Alto VM deployment (IaC)
```

```
3      CVE SQL DB integration
```

```
4      Juniper PSIRT API integration with ServiceNow CI
```

```
5      Juniper router and switch upgrades
```

```
6
```

(*continued*)

#	Task

```
[ line  1/6 (16%), col  1/20 (  5%), char   0/161 ( 0%) ]

^G Help          ^O Write Out    ^W Where Is      ^K Cut           ^T
Execute          ^C Location    M-U Undo

^X Exit          ^R Read File    ^\ Replace       ^U Paste         ^J
Justify          ^/ Go To Line  M-E Redo
```

If you want to reverse the change, you can open the /etc/nanorc file and add the # back
to the same line, such as # set linenumbers. Then save the nanorc file.

Initially, for Windows users, the vi and nano text editors might pose a challenge,
primarily because Windows users are unfamiliar with these programs. However,
as you invest more time using these applications, your comfort level will naturally
increase. Therefore, it's essential to take things at your own pace and persist with
these applications. If you can master the proper use of the vi text editor, you've already
conquered a significant aspect of Linux administration. Here's a little dad joke, but it
holds true: "Learning the first half of Linux administration is learning how to use vi."
Of course, the nano text editor offers a plethora of additional features, it is not pre-
installed on all Linux distributions by default. If you're interested in exploring more nano
commands, you can refer to this link: https://cheatography.com/pepe/cheat-sheets/
nano/. If the link address changes, a copy has been placed at https://github.com/
pynetauto/apress_pynetauto_ed2.0/tree/main/Other_files.

It's worth noting that many readers may find the Linux chapters less appealing,
especially as they involve transitioning away from the GUI and immersing themselves
in the terminal console for extended periods. However, this process is exceptionally
valuable in becoming proficient in Linux and, subsequently, when working on Python
code in a Linux environment.

Linux Basic Administration

As you're becoming more familiar with the vi and nano text editors, let's delve into
some fundamental Linux administration tasks to kickstart your journey. Having cleared
the initial hurdle, you can expect things to become progressively smoother and less
daunting. So, let's get started and embrace the learning process with enthusiasm!

To begin this exercise, power on both primary servers: f38s1 and u22s1. The cloned server u22s2 will not be required here and for the rest of the book and you will work with only two servers to better focus on the required tasks.

Changing and Hard-Coding IP Addresses for System Stability

Now that you have powered on f38s1 and u22s1, note that for the f38s1 server, you hard coded the server's IP to its originally DHCP-assigned IP address of 192.168.127.130/24 and the Ubuntu Server is still using its assigned IP address of 192.168.127.129/24. To update the servers to your preferred IP addresses, update f38s1's IP address to 192.168.127.10 and then update u22s1's IP address to a fixed IP address of 192.168.127.20. Follow the next steps to achieve your goals.

#	Task
①	Open your terminal session application such as PuTTY and SSH into f38s1. Check the current network interface configuration by running the nmcli device commands shown here.

```
[jdoe@f38s1 ~]$ nmcli device                                    # Check
connected network interfaces

DEVICE   TYPE      STATE                   CONNECTION

ens160   ethernet  connected               ens160

lo       loopback  connected (externally)  lo

[jdoe@f38s1 ~]$ nmcli device show ens160                        # Display
ens160 interface configurations

GENERAL.DEVICE:              ens160

GENERAL.TYPE:                ethernet

GENERAL.HWADDR:              00:0C:29:05:BC:8C

GENERAL.MTU:                 1500
```

(continued)

#	Task

GENERAL.STATE:	100 (connected)
GENERAL.CONNECTION:	ens160
GENERAL.CON-PATH:	/org/freedesktop/NetworkManager/ ActiveConnection/2
WIRED-PROPERTIES.CARRIER:	on
IP4.ADDRESS[1]:	192.168.127.130/24 *# Current IP address, update this IP Address to .10*
IP4.GATEWAY:	192.168.127.2
IP4.ROUTE[1]:	dst = 0.0.0.0/0, nh = 192.168.127.2, mt = 100
IP4.ROUTE[2]:	dst = 192.168.127.0/24, nh = 0.0.0.0, mt = 100
IP4.DNS[1]:	192.168.127.2
IP4.DNS[2]:	8.8.8.8
IP4.SEARCHES[1]:	pynetauto.com
IP6.ADDRESS[1]:	fe80::20c:29ff:fe05:bc8c/64
IP6.GATEWAY:	--
IP6.ROUTE[1]:	dst = fe80::/64, nh = ::, mt = 1024

(continued)

#	Task

② Next, update the current IP address, 192.168.127.130, to the new IP address of 192.168.127.10. The default gateway and DNS information is unchanged and you are only updating the IP address for this server here.

```
[jdoe@f38s1 ~]$ sudo nmcli connection modify ens160 ipv4.addresses
192.168.127.10/24 # Update to new IP Address

[sudo] password for jdoe: ***************

[jdoe@f38s1 ~]$ sudo nmcli connection ens160 down; sudo nmcli
connection up ens160  # Reset the interface

Error: argument 'ens160' not understood. Try passing --help instead.
# SSH disconnects
```

③ If you were connected via SSH, you have to restart your PuTTY session using the new IP address, 192.168.127.10, and log back in. When prompted with a new host key prompt, accept the ssh-ed25519 key fingerprint to access the server and log in. Run the nmcli device show ens160 command one more time for verification.

```
[jdoe@f38s1 ~]$ nmcli device show ens160

GENERAL.DEVICE:                       ens160

[...omitted for brevity]

IP4.ADDRESS[1]:                       192.168.127.10/24
# Newly updated IP address

IP4.GATEWAY:                          192.168.127.2

[...omitted for brevity]
```

You have now successfully changed the IP address of your Fedora server.

(continued)

#	Task

④ Open another PuTTY window and connect to u22s1 via SSH protocol using the current IP address, 192.168.127.129. Your IP address may be different if your DHCP server gave out a different IP address.

Now confirm the network configuration file in the /etc/netplan directory and the make a backup of the original file, so that you have a working copy of the file that works with DHCP.

jdoe@u22s1:~$ **ls /etc/netplan/**

00-installer-config.yaml

jdoe@u22s1:~$ **sudo cat /etc/netplan/00-installer-config.yaml**
Don't forget the 'sudo' command

This is the network config written by 'subiquity'

network:

ethernets:

ens33:

dhcp4: true

version: 2

jdoe@u22s1:~$ **sudo cp /etc/netplan/00-installer-config.yaml /etc/**
netplan/00-installer-config.yaml.org

[sudo] password for jdoe: ***************

jdoe@u22s1:~$ **ls /etc/netplan/**

00-installer-config.yaml   00-installer-config.yaml.org

(continued)

411

#	Task
⑤	Now that you have made the backup copy of the network configuration file, you can modify the file and hardcode or manually configure the IP address to your preferred IP, 192.168.127.20. Because this server is on the same subnet as f38s1, you can borrow the default gateway and DNS server IP addresses to make your life better.

```
jdoe@u22s1:~$ sudo vi /etc/netplan/00-installer-config.yaml

[sudo] password for jdoe: ****************

jdoe@u22s1:~$ sudo cat /etc/netplan/00-installer-config.yaml

network:

ethernets:

ens33:                                            # interface name

dhcp4: false                                       # disable DHCP

addresses: [192.168.127.20/24]             # IP address/subnet mask

routes:

- to: default

via: 192.168.127.2                      # default gateway

metric: 100

nameservers:

addresses: [192.168.127.2,8.8.8.8]              # name server to bind

search: [pynetauto.com]                      # my DNS search base
place holder

dhcp6: false

version: 2

jdoe@u22s1:~$ sudo netplan apply <ENTER>           # SSH Disconnects
```

(continued)

#	Task
⑥	Open another PuTTY session and connect to the new IP address, 192.168.127.20, via SSH. When prompted to accept the host key, accept the `ssh-ed25519` key fingerprint and SSH into the server.

```
jdoe@u22s1:~$ ip address show ens33

2: ens33: <BROADCAST,MULTICAST,UP,LOWER_UP> mtu 1500 qdisc fq_codel
state UP group default qlen 1000

link/ether 00:0c:29:cf:71:3d brd ff:ff:ff:ff:ff:ff

altname enp2s1

inet 192.168.127.20/24 brd 192.168.127.255 scope global ens33
# updated IP address

valid_lft forever preferred_lft forever

inet6 fe80::20c:29ff:fecf:713d/64 scope link

valid_lft forever preferred_lft forever
```

| ⑦ | Now try to ping (send ICMP packet test) Google's well-known DNS IP address to test the connectivity. You will get a command not found error, as you have installed the server version of Ubuntu and have to manually install the IP tools (`iputils-ping`) before you can use the `ping` command. Install the utility to test the connectivity in the next step. |

```
jdoe@u22s1:~$ ping 8.8.8.8

-bash: ping: command not found

jdoe@u22s1:~$ sudo apt install iputils-ping            # install ip
utility tool

[sudo] password for jdoe: ***************

[...omitted for brevity]

Which services should be restarted? 4                 # Press 4 to
ignore service restart

[...omitted for brevity]
```

(continued)

#	Task

⑧ Now ping the same IP address again. The Google DNS should reply with the ICMP replies. To stop the ping, use the Ctrl+C keys. Note that the ping statistics are provided with the details.

```
jdoe@u22s1:~$ ping 8.8.8.8

PING 8.8.8.8 (8.8.8.8) 56(84) bytes of data.

64 bytes from 8.8.8.8: icmp_seq=1 ttl=128 time=12.6 ms

64 bytes from 8.8.8.8: icmp_seq=2 ttl=128 time=17.0 ms

64 bytes from 8.8.8.8: icmp_seq=3 ttl=128 time=15.5 ms

^C

--- 8.8.8.8 ping statistics ---

3 packets transmitted, 3 received, 0% packet loss, time 2004ms

rtt min/avg/max/mdev = 12.582/15.028/17.016/1.838 ms          # notice
the statistics
```

⑨ This time, ping www.google.com, using its fully qualified domain name, but this time, stop the ping with the Ctrl+Z keys. Note that it simply stops the ping, but does not give any statistics.

```
jdoe@u22s1:~$ ping www.google.com

PING www.google.com (142.250.204.4) 56(84) bytes of data.

64 bytes from syd09s25-in-f4.1e100.net (142.250.204.4): icmp_seq=1
ttl=128 time=13.0 ms

64 bytes from syd09s25-in-f4.1e100.net (142.250.204.4): icmp_seq=2
ttl=128 time=15.6 ms

64 bytes from syd09s25-in-f4.1e100.net (142.250.204.4): icmp_seq=3
ttl=128 time=13.6 ms

^Z

[2]+  Stopped                      ping www.google.com
# notice that no statistics given
```

You have learned how to update an IP address on a Fedora (CentOS/Red Hat) Server and how to configure the IP address, default gateway, and DNS IPS on the Ubuntu Linux Server from the command line.

Changing the Hostname to a Fully Qualified Domain Name (FQDN)

In Chapters 5 and 6, you installed the Ubuntu 22 and Fedora 38 servers, and you configured their hostnames. However, these hostnames were simple and not fully qualified domain names (FQDN), which are typically used in real production environments. In Linux, DNS services are often provided by applications like BIND (Berkeley Internet Name Domain). Although you will update the hostnames to use placeholder (dummy) FQDNs in the following exercise, due to the scope of this book, I do not cover the installation and configuration of BIND. Instead, you will use the hosts file for simplicity.

#	Task
①	First, you'll learn how to check the hostname. There are a few ways to check the hostname currently assigned to your server, and here are some of the Linux commands. The hostnamectl command provides the most useful information if you are checking more than the hostname itself. Also, the file that contains the name is in the /etc/hostname file. All these commands are Linux commands, so they are case-sensitive.

Objective: Learn how to change the hostname on Linux using the command line.

```
[jdoe@f38s1 ~]$ hostname
f38s1
[jdoe@f38s1 ~]$ echo "$HOSTNAME"                              # prints
the HOSTNAME from the env variable
f38s1
```

(continued)

415

#	Task
	`[jdoe@f38s1 ~]$ printf "%s\n" $HOSTNAME`
	`f38s1`
	`[jdoe@f38s1 ~]$ sudo hostnamectl set-hostname f38s1.pynetauto.com`
	`[sudo] password for jdoe: **************`
	`[jdoe@f38s1 ~]$ hostname`
	`f38s1.pynetauto.com` `#` *updated to a dummy FQDN*
②	Update the Ubuntu server's hostname to a placeholder FQDN name.
	`jdoe@u22s1:~$ hostname`
	`u22s1`
	`jdoe@u22s1:~$ sudo hostnamectl set-hostname u22s1.pynetauto.com`
	`[sudo] password for jdoe: **************`
	`jdoe@u22s1:~$ hostname`
	`u22s1.pynetauto.com`

Bypass DNS Server Lookup Using /etc/hosts

In enterprise production environments, organizations typically use fully-fledged DNS servers running on either Windows or Linux OS servers. These same DNS services are also offered in the public cloud through services like AWS Route 53, Microsoft Azure DNS, and Google Cloud DNS. Here, you have the option to set up one of your Linux servers as a DNS server by installing BIND (Berkeley Internet Name Domain) along with bind utilities (`bind-utils`). You can achieve this by executing the `sudo dnf -y install bind bind-utils` command and then proceed to configure the `/etc/named.conf` file.

However, because this falls outside the scope of this book, you will not be installing the BIND applications here. Instead, you will use a simpler solution that still enables communication with devices using their hostnames. In this case, you will use the `/etc/hosts` file on each server. When the hostnames and their corresponding IP addresses are mapped in the /etc/hosts file, the server will prioritize the IP addresses listed in this file for each hostname, bypassing the need for DNS lookups. This method is often used in PoC (proof-of-concept) lab settings to fully leverage hostnames. You may also work with this file in some parts of the book to simplify ICMP communication tests.

Now, let's explore how the /etc/hosts files are configured to bypass DNS server lookups.

#	Task
①	Working from the f38s1 server, let's run a quick ping command using the hostname of the Ubuntu server, u22s1.

[jdoe@f38s1 ~]$ **ping u22s1**

ping: u22s1: Name or service not known

[jdoe@f38s1 ~]$ **ping u22s1.pynetauto.com**

ping: u22s1.pynetauto.com: Name or service not known

We've used both the hostname and FQDN names for an ICMP (ping) test, but both returned errors (failed).

②	To solve this problem quickly, you can modify and save the /etc/hosts file as shown here.

[jdoe@f38s1 ~]$ **cat /etc/hosts**

Loopback entries; do not change.

For historical reasons, localhost precedes localhost.localdomain:

127.0.0.1   localhost localhost.localdomain localhost4 localhost4.localdomain4   *# update to hostname & FQDN*

::1   localhost localhost.localdomain localhost6 localhost6.localdomain6

See hosts(5) for proper format and other examples:

192.168.1.10 foo.mydomain.org foo

192.168.1.13 bar.mydomain.org bar

(continued)

#	Task

[jdoe@f38s1 ~]$ **sudo nano /etc/hosts**

[sudo] password for jdoe: **************

[jdoe@f38s1 ~]$ **cat /etc/hosts**

Loopback entries; do not change.

For historical reasons, localhost precedes localhost.localdomain:

127.0.0.1   localhost localhost.localdomain **f38s1 f38s1.pynetauto.com**
updated to hostname & FQDN

::1   localhost localhost.localdomain localhost6 localhost6.
localdomain6

See hosts(5) for proper format and other examples:

192.168.1.10 foo.mydomain.org foo

192.168.1.13 bar.mydomain.org bar

192.168.127.20 u22s1 u22s1.pynetauto.com   # *Add remote*
hostname & FQDN

**# Perform the ICMP test using the ping command and the hostnames and
FQDNs.**

[jdoe@f38s1 ~]$ **ping u22s1**

PING u22s1 (192.168.127.20) 56(84) bytes of data.

64 bytes from u22s1 (192.168.127.20): icmp_seq=1 ttl=64 time=1.62 ms

[...omitted for brevity]

[jdoe@f38s1 ~]$ **ping u22s1.pynetauto.com**

PING u22s1 (192.168.127.20) 56(84) bytes of data.

64 bytes from u22s1 (192.168.127.20): icmp_seq=1 ttl=64 time=1.56 ms

[...omitted for brevity]

[jdoe@f38s1 ~]$ **ping f38s1**

(*continued*)

#	Task
	PING localhost (127.0.0.1) 56(84) bytes of data.
	64 bytes from localhost (127.0.0.1): icmp_seq=1 ttl=64 time=0.102 ms
	[...omitted for brevity]
	[jdoe@f38s1 ~]$ **ping f38s1.pynetauto.com**
	PING localhost (127.0.0.1) 56(84) bytes of data.
	64 bytes from localhost (127.0.0.1): icmp_seq=1 ttl=64 time=0.093 ms
	[...omitted for brevity]
	You have now reconfigured the /etc/hosts file on the Fedora server and can ping devices using their hostnames and FQDN.
③	On your Ubuntu server, u22s1, perform the same ICMP testing.
	jdoe@u22s1:~$ **ping f38s1**
	ping: f38s1: Temporary failure in name resolution
	jdoe@u22s1:~$ **ping f38s1.pynetauto.com**
	ping: f38s1.pynetauto.com: Name or service not known
④	Now perform the same task and tests shown in Step ②.

You can now perform connectivity tests using the servers' hostnames and FQDNs without relying on a DNS server. In the future, you will be able to do the same for your routers and switches as necessary.

Basic Linux File and Directory Commands

This section introduces essential commands for managing files and directories in the Linux operating system. Acquiring a deep understanding of Linux commands often requires significant time and practice. This book, however, is not designed for comprehensive Linux administration. Instead, this chapter aims to establish a foundation in Linux administration basics, allowing you to confidently perform fundamental tasks on Linux systems. Only the most fundamental and vocational commands are covered here.

Before proceeding with the exercises, take a moment to study each command listed in Table 7-5. While you don't need to memorize all the commands immediately, try to become familiar with their syntax.

Table 7-5. *Basic Linux File and Directory Commands*

Command	Description and Example
pwd	Present working directory $ **pwd**
ls	List segment: Lists files and directories in the present working directory $ **ls**
ls [directory]	$ **ls /home/jdoe/Documents**
ls -a	List all files, including hidden directories and files $ **ls -a .bashrc**
dir	Directory $ **dir**
mkdir	Make a directory $ **mkdir myapps**
cd	Change the directory $ **cd myapps** $ **cd /usr/local**
cd ..	Change the current directory to the parent directory /myapps$ **cd ..**
cd ~	Move to the user's home directory from anywhere $ **cd /usr/sbin** :/usr/sbin$ **cd ~** $ **pwd** /home/jdoe
cd -	Switch back to the previous directory where you were working earlier $ **cd /usr/local** :/usr/local$ **cd -** /home/jdoe

(continued)

Table 7-5. (*continued*)

Command	Description and Example
rm OR rm -r	Remove file(s) /myapps$ **rm router_app.py**
rmdir	Remove a directory $ **rmdir myapps**
mv	Rename a file name $ **mv file01.py myfile01.py**
mv file directory	Move a file to another directory $ **mv file01.py ./Documents**
mv directory_A directory_B	Rename one directory to another directory $ **mv myapps myscripts**
touch filename	Create a file(s) $ **touch file04.txt** $ **touch file05.txt file06.txt**
cp	Copy a file to another directory or copy and paste with another file name $ **cp file01.py /home/jdoe/Documents**
cp -a directory_A directory_B	Copy one directory to another directory $ **cp -a Documents Mydocs**
find	Find a file $ **find /home/jdoe -name "file*"**
grep	Search for a string from a file $ **grep jdoe /etc/passwd** $ **grep 'Python' /home/jdoe/file10.py**

Now that you've reviewed some fundamental Linux commands, let's dive right into the exercises. Practicing these commands on your keyboard will help you become more comfortable with all the commands described in Table 7-5.

Linux File and Directory Exercises – Set A

Now, let's delve into Linux's basic file and directory management through a series of exercises. Whenever you encounter commands highlighted in bold, make sure to type them into your Linux console terminal. The choice between the Fedora and Ubuntu servers doesn't matter for this exercise, but for the remainder of this chapter, you will log in to the Ubuntu server as the jdoe user to complete your tasks. So, roll up your sleeves, follow along, and remember that practice will significantly enhance your understanding.

Exercise 7-1. File and Directory Basics

#	Task
①	Use the pwd command to check the current working directory. As you learned in Table 7-5, pwd stands for present working directory. Think of this as your compass to navigate around the Linux system. jdoe@u22s1:~$ **pwd** /home/jdoe
②	The ls command is a UNIX/Linux-specific command used to display files and directories. You will delve into the detailed options of the ls command later in your learning journey. For now, let's check and create a directory using the ls and mkdir commands. After creating the dir1, cd (change directory) into dir1 and use the pwd command to check the current working directory. jdoe@u22s1:~$ **ls** Desktop Documents Downloads Music Pictures Public Templates Videos jdoe@u22s1:~$ **mkdir dir1** jdoe@u22s1:~$ **ls**

(*continued*)

#	Task

Desktop Documents Downloads Music Pictures Public Templates
Videos dir1   # a new directory

```
jdoe@u22s1:~$ cd dir1                      # change directory to dir1

jdoe@u22s1:~/dir1$ pwd

/home/jdoe/dir1
```

③ Continuing from the previous exercise, create a file named file1 using the touch file1
command and then use the ls command to see the newly created file under dir1. Notice
that I have not specified the file extension type purposefully to show you that Linux will allow
you to create a file without specifying the file extension type.

```
jdoe@u22s1:~/dir1$ touch file1

jdoe@u22s1:~/dir1$ ls

file01
```

Now, if you attempt to create a directory named file1 using the mkdir file1 command,
you'll encounter an issue. Linux prevents the creation of a directory with the same name as
an existing file, as demonstrated:

```
jdoe@u22s1:~/dir1$ mkdir file1

mkdir: cannot create directory 'file1': File exists
```

This behavior underscores an important point: In Linux, directories are treated as files, and
naming conflicts between files and directories are not allowed.

To avoid this issue, it's advisable to specify the type of file you're working with, as illustrated:

```
jdoe@u22s1:~/dir1$ touch file2.txt

jdoe@u22s1:~/dir1$ ls

file1  file2.txt

jdoe@u22s1:~/dir1$ mkdir file2
```

(continued)

423

#	Task
| | ```
jdoe@u22s1:~/dir1$ ls -l        # use "ls" with "-l" (long list) option
total 4
-rw-rw-r-- 1 jdoe jdoe    0 Sep  7 09:45 file1
drwxrwxr-x 2 jdoe jdoe 4096 Sep  7 09:54 file2         # directory
starts with 'd'
-rw-rw-r-- 1 jdoe jdoe    0 Sep  7 09:54 file2.txt              # a file
starts with '-'
``` |

By giving your files distinct extensions, like .txt in this example, you can avoid naming conflicts when creating directories and files. This practice helps maintain a clear distinction between different types of data in your directory. You will be learning this later but, in Linux, the permissions strings "drwxrwxr-x" and "-rw-rw-r--" represent the permission mode of files. This string is composed of various characters and symbols that denote different aspects of file permissions. If you don't understand these, do not worry too much, as you will become familiar as you use Linux more and more.

④ Having a directory named file2 is not very intuitive, so let's change the directory name to dir2 using the mv command. Then check the files using the ls command.

```
jdoe@u22s1:~/dir1$ mv file2 dir2         # change directory name
jdoe@u22s1:~/dir1$ ls
dir2  file1  file2.txt
```

Now move the text file, file2.txt, to the dir2 directory using the mv command. As you can see, the mv command can be used to move the file as well as update the name of the file.

```
jdoe@u22s1:~/dir1$ mv file2.txt dir2         # move file2.txt into dir2
directory
jdoe@u22s1:~/dir1$ ls
dir2  file1
```

(continued)
```

#	Task
	jdoe@u22s1:~/dir1$ **ls -d dir2** *# use 'ls -d' to check that dir2 exists*
	dir2
	jdoe@u22s1:~/dir1$ **ls -l dir2** *# use "ls -l" to check the content of dir2*
	total 0
	-rw-rw-r-- 1 jdoe jdoe 0 Sep 7 10:09 file2.txt

⑤ To display hidden files and folders together using the ls command, you can utilize the combination of -a, -al, or -alh options. The -a option stands for "all" and reveals hidden directories and files, making them visible in the listing.

```
jdoe@u22s1:~/dir1$ ls -a            # '-a' displays hidden files too
. .. dir2 file1
jdoe@u22s1:~/dir1$ ls -al           # '-l' displays long listing
information
total 12
drwxrwxr-x  3 jdoe jdoe 4096 Sep  7 10:19 .
drwxr-x--- 15 jdoe jdoe 4096 Sep  7 09:38 ..
drwxrwxr-x  2 jdoe jdoe 4096 Sep  7 10:10 dir2
-rw-rw-r--  1 jdoe jdoe    0 Sep  7 09:45 file1
jdoe@u22s1:~/dir1$ ls -alh          # '-h' option outputs human-
readable format
total 12K
drwxrwxr-x  3 jdoe jdoe 4.0K Sep  7 10:19 .    # "." represents the
current directory
drwxr-x--- 15 jdoe jdoe 4.0K Sep  7 09:38 ..        # ".." represents
the parent directory
drwxrwxr-x  2 jdoe jdoe 4.0K Sep  7 10:10 dir2
```

#	Task

	`-rw-rw-r-- 1 jdoe jdoe    0 Sep  7 09:45 file1`
	
	. (Dot): The single dot (.) represents the current directory. When you see . in a directory listing, it refers to the directory you are currently in.
	
	`jdoe@u22s1:~/dir1$ ls .`
	`dir2  file1`
	
	.. (Dot-Dot): The double dot (..) represents the parent directory. It allows you to refer to the directory immediately above the current directory.
	
	`jdoe@u22s1:~/dir1$ ls ..`
	`Desktop Documents Downloads Music Pictures Public Templates`
	`Videos  dir1`

⑥	In the example provided, note that the . symbol represents the current working directory. Additionally, you can use the . symbol in front of a file or directory name to create hidden files or directories. Let's perform the following tasks to see the effect:
	
	`jdoe@u22s1:~/dir1$ touch .file3` `# create a hidden file named`
	`.file3`
	
	`jdoe@u22s1:~/dir1$ ls` `# list the contents (no visible`
	`change)`
	
	`dir2  file1`
	
	`jdoe@u22s1:~/dir1$ mkdir .dir3` `# create a hidden directory named`
	`.dir3`
	
	`jdoe@u22s1:~/dir1$ ls` `# list the contents (still no`
	`visible change)`
	
	`dir2  file1`
	
	`jdoe@u22s1:~/dir1$ ls -a` `# list all contents, including`
	`hidden ones`
	
	`.  ..  .dir3  dir2  file1`

(*continued*)

#	Task

⑦ You've already used the `mkdir` command a few times; it's used to create new directories in Linux. A directory in Linux is similar to a folder in the Windows operating system; it can contain both child directories and files. To gain more practice, create another directory named `dir4`.

```
jdoe@u22s1:~/dir1$ ls

dir2  file1

jdoe@u22s1:~/dir1$ mkdir dir4          # create new directory, dir4

jdoe@u22s1:~/dir1$ ls -d d*            # list all directories starting
                                         with 'd'

dir2  dir4

jdoe@u22s1:~/dir1$ rmdir dir4          # remove an empty directory, dir4

jdoe@u22s1:~/dir1$ ls                  # check the directory

dir2  file1
```

⑧ Let's get some more practice with the `mv`, `ls`, and `ll` commands. The explanations are provided as embedded comments.

```
jdoe@u22s1:~/dir1$ ls

dir2  file1

jdoe@u22s1:~/dir1$ mv .file3 file3 && mv .dir3 dir3    # use && to run
two commands on a single line

jdoe@u22s1:~/dir1$ ls

dir2  dir3  file1  file3

jdoe@u22s1:~/dir1$ mv dir3 dir2                        # move directory
dir3 into directory, dir2

jdoe@u22s1:~/dir1$ ls

dir2  file1  file3

jdoe@u22s1:~/dir1$ mv file* dir2                       # move all files
starting with 'file' into dir2
```

(*continued*)

#	Task

```
jdoe@u22s1:~/dir1$ ls

dir2

jdoe@u22s1:~/dir1$ ls dir2

dir3  file1  file2.txt  file3

jdoe@u22s1:~/dir1$ ll dir2                          # "ll dir2" is
equivalent to running "ls -l dir2"

total 12

drwxrwxr-x 3 jdoe jdoe 4096 Sep  7 11:02 ./

drwxrwxr-x 3 jdoe jdoe 4096 Sep  7 11:02 ../

drwxrwxr-x 2 jdoe jdoe 4096 Sep  7 10:30 dir3/

-rw-rw-r-- 1 jdoe jdoe    0 Sep  7 09:45 file1

-rw-rw-r-- 1 jdoe jdoe    0 Sep  7 10:09 file2.txt

-rw-rw-r-- 1 jdoe jdoe    0 Sep  7 10:35 file3
```

The cp -a command allows you to copy an entire directory, including the files and child directories inside the original directory. In this exercise, you are copying dir2 to make another directory named dir4, containing the same files.

```
jdoe@u22s1:~/dir1$ cp -a dir2 dir4                  # use 'cp -a'
to copy the whole content of dir2

jdoe@u22s1:~/dir1$ ls -lh                           # notice the same
file sizes for dir2 and dir4

total 8.0K

drwxrwxr-x 3 jdoe jdoe 4.0K Sep  7 11:02 dir2

drwxrwxr-x 3 jdoe jdoe 4.0K Sep  7 11:02 dir4

jdoe@u22s1:~/dir1$ ls dir2

dir3  file1  file2.txt  file3
```

(continued)

#	Task
	jdoe@u22s1:~/dir1$ **ls dir4** *# dir4 contains* *the same files as dir2*
	dir3 file1 file2.txt file3

⑨ rmdir allows you to remove an empty directory; this command will delete the directory. dir4 is not empty, but try to delete it using the rmdir command anyway.

jdoe@u22s1:~/dir1$ **ls**

dir2   dir4

jdoe@u22s1:~/dir1$ **rmdir dir4**

rmdir: failed to remove 'dir4': Directory not empty   *# directory*
with files cannot be deleted.

jdoe@u22s1:~/dir1$ **rm -rf dir4/***   *# let's empty all files in dir4*

jdoe@u22s1:~/dir1$ **ls -l dir4**   *# check the files*

total 0

jdoe@u22s1:~/dir1$ **rmdir dir4**   *# re-run the rmdir command*

jdoe@u22s1:~/dir1$ **ls**

dir2

jdoe@u22s1:~/dir1$ **cp -r dir2 dir5**   *# copy dir2 and create a*
duplicate dir5 with '-r' (recursive) option

jdoe@u22s1:~/dir1$ **ls -lh**

(*continued*)

#	Task

total 8.0K

drwxrwxr-x 3 jdoe jdoe 4.0K Sep 7 11:02 dir2

drwxrwxr-x 3 jdoe jdoe 4.0K Sep 7 11:40 dir5   *# dir5 is not empty!*

jdoe@u22s1:~/dir1$ **rmdir dir5**   *# rmdir command fails again*

rmdir: failed to remove 'dir5': Directory not empty

jdoe@u22s1:~/dir1$ **rm -r dir5**   *# use the 'rm -r' command to recursively delete dir5 with the content*

jdoe@u22s1:~/dir1$ **ls**

dir2   *# dir5 has been deleted.*

⑩ As demonstrated in Step ⑨, when attempting to delete a directory containing other files or directories, you can use the rm -r command. However, it's crucial to exercise caution with this option, as it doesn't prompt user confirmation and deletes items immediately. To engage in interactive deletion, where you can confirm each item's removal, you should use the rm -ir command, as illustrated:

jdoe@u22s1:~/dir1$ **cp -a dir2 dir6**

jdoe@u22s1:~/dir1$ **ls -lh**

total 8.0K

drwxrwxr-x 3 jdoe jdoe 4.0K Sep 7 11:02 dir2

drwxrwxr-x 3 jdoe jdoe 4.0K Sep 7 11:02 dir6

jdoe@u22s1:~/dir1$ **rm -ir dir6**   *# use '-i' option for interactive deletion*

rm: descend into directory 'dir6'? **y**   *# answer 'y' for 'yes' to descend to directory*

(continued)

#	Task
	rm: remove directory 'dir6/dir3'? **y**
	rm: remove regular empty file 'dir6/file2.txt'? **y**
	rm: remove regular empty file 'dir6/file3'? **y**
	rm: remove regular empty file 'dir6/file1'? **y**
	rm: remove directory 'dir6'? **y** *# answer 'y' to delete dir6*
	jdoe@u22s1:~/dir1$ **ls**
	dir2 *# dir6 has been deleted.*

(11) You've already gained some experience with the mv command in previous exercises. The mv command is versatile, serving as a means to move and rename both files and directories. Furthermore, it allows you to relocate a file or directory to another location, offering a practical way to consolidate your knowledge, as demonstrated in the following exercise:

```
jdoe@u22s1:~/dir1$ ls -d dir*
dir2

jdoe@u22s1:~/dir1$ mv dir2 dir7        # renaming a directory

jdoe@u22s1:~/dir1$ ls -d dir*

dir7

jdoe@u22s1:~/dir1$ mkdir dir8

jdoe@u22s1:~/dir1$ ls -d dir*

dir7   dir8

jdoe@u22s1:~/dir1$ mv dir7 dir8         # moving a directory to
another directory

jdoe@u22s1:~/dir1$ ls -d dir*

dir8

jdoe@u22s1:~/dir1$ ls dir8              # dir7 is in dir8
dir7
```

431

Fantastic start! Your dedication and focus are key to your success. Keep up the excellent work as you progress through this chapter and navigate the content in this book.

Tip

Is there a better way to see directories and files in Linux at a glance?

Indeed, there is a useful Linux directory visualization tool known as "tree." After installing it, simply run the tree command in your current working directory to view directories and files in a tree-like structure. To install the software, use the sudo apt install tree command.

```
jdoe@u22s1:~/dir1$ sudo apt install tree -y
[sudo] password for jdoe: ***************
Reading package lists... Done
[...omitted for brevity]
jdoe@u22s1:~/dir1$ tree
.
└── dir8
└── dir7
├── dir3
├── file1
├── file2.txt
└── file3

3 directories, 3 files
```

Exercise 7-2. Freely Create Files/Directories and Freely Navigate Through the Directories

#	Task
①	Return to the user's home directory and run the `ls -d $PWD/*` command to display the paths of the working directories.

```
jdoe@u22s1:~/dir1$ cd ..

jdoe@u22s1:~$ ls -d $PWD/*

/home/jdoe/Desktop     /home/jdoe/Music      /home/jdoe/Templates

/home/jdoe/Documents   /home/jdoe/Pictures   /home/jdoe/Videos

/home/jdoe/Downloads   /home/jdoe/Public     /home/jdoe/dir1
```

②	Now, remove the existing directory, dir1, using the `rm -r dir1` command. Then you will create multiple directories using the `mkdir` command.

```
jdoe@u22s1:~$ rm -r dir1

jdoe@u22s1:~$ mkdir dir1 dir3 dir5              # create three
directories ending with odd numbers

jdoe@u22s1:~$ ls -d dir*

dir1  dir3  dir5

jdoe@u22s1:~$ mkdir dir1/dir2 dir3/dir4 dir5/dir6   # create three
nested sub-directories ending with even numbers

jdoe@u22s1:~$ ls -d dir*

dir1  dir3  dir5
```

(continued)

#	Task

jdoe@u22s1:~$ **tree dir***   # use the 'tree
dir*' command to check directory structure

```
dir1
└── dir2
dir3
└── dir4
dir5
└── dir6
1 directory, 0 files
```

Let's create a file named level1.txt in each of the directories ending with the odd numbers—that is dir1, dir3, and dir5. Here you will use the {} to abbreviate the command. The touch dir{1,3,5}/level1.txt and touch dir1/level1.txt dir3/level1.txt dir5/level1.txt commands will result in the same effect.

jdoe@u22s1:~$ **touch dir{1,3,5}/level1.txt**   # create 'level1.
txt' files in each of odd directories

jdoe@u22s1:~$ **tree dir***

```
dir1
├── dir2
└── level1.txt
dir3
├── dir4
└── level1.txt
dir5
├── dir6
└── level1.txt
1 directory, 1 file
```

(*continued*)

#	Task

\# Now, create a file called `level2.txt` in directories ending with the even numbers.
Use the `touch dir{1/dir2,3/dir4,5/dir6}/level2.txt` command, which is an
abbreviated command of `touch dir1/dir2/level2.txt dir3/dir4/level2.txt`
`dir5/dir6/level2.txt`.

`jdoe@u22s1:~$ touch dir{1/dir2,3/dir4,5/dir6}/level2.txt` *# create*
'level2.txt' files in each of even directories

`jdoe@u22s1:~$ tree dir*`

```
dir1
├── dir2
│   └── level2.txt
└── level1.txt
dir3
├── dir4
│   └── level2.txt
└── level1.txt
dir5
├── dir6
│   └── level2.txt
└── level1.txt
1 directory, 2 files
```

(continued)

#	Task
③	The cd commands, including cd, cd .., cd /, and cd ~, are essential for changing the user's working directory. Practicing these commands will significantly enhance your efficiency when working with files and directories. Let's explore some examples to illustrate their use.

```
# Move to dir2 directory and then use the "cd .." to move up
directories and return to home directory.

jdoe@u22s1:~$ cd dir1/dir2

jdoe@u22s1:~/dir1/dir2$ cd ..

jdoe@u22s1:~/dir1$ pwd

/home/jdoe/dir1

jdoe@u22s1:~/dir1$ cd ..

jdoe@u22s1:~$ pwd

/home/jdoe

# Move to dir1 directory and then use 'cd ~' command to return to
home directory.

jdoe@u22s1:~$ cd dir1

jdoe@u22s1:~/dir1$ pwd

/home/jdoe/dir1

jdoe@u22s1:~/dir1$ cd ~

jdoe@u22s1:~$ pwd

/home/jdoe

# Move to the dir4 directory and then use the 'cd' command to return
to the home directory.

jdoe@u22s1:~$ cd dir3/dir4

jdoe@u22s1:~/dir3/dir4$ pwd
```

(continued)

#	Task
	/home/jdoe/dir3/dir4

jdoe@u22s1:~/dir3/dir4$ **cd**<ENTER>

jdoe@u22s1:~$ **pwd**

/home/jdoe

Move to dir6 directory and then use the cd ../.. command to return to home directory. Notice that you can also use cd ../../ to jump up multiple levels.

jdoe@u22s1:~$ **cd dir5/dir6**

jdoe@u22s1:~/dir5/dir6$ **pwd**

/home/jdoe/dir5/dir6

jdoe@u22s1:~/dir5/dir6$ **cd ../..**

jdoe@u22s1:~$ **pwd**

/home/jdoe

Move to the root directory using the cd / command and then return to the home directory.

jdoe@u22s1:~$ **pwd**

/home/jdoe

jdoe@u22s1:~$ **cd /**

jdoe@u22s1:/$ **pwd**

/

jdoe@u22s1:/$ **cd ~**

jdoe@u22s1:~$ **pwd**

/home/jdoe

(*continued*)

437

#	Task
④	If you have the precise directory path, you can swiftly navigate between working directories by using the cd command followed by the specific directory path. The following exercise illustrates how to switch between specific directories and return to the home directory.

```
jdoe@u22s1:~/dir3/dir4$ cd /var     # Move to /var directory

jdoe@u22s1:/var$ pwd

/var

jdoe@u22s1:/$ cd /home/jdoe/dir3/dir4       # Move to /home/jdoe/dir3/
dir4 directory

jdoe@u22s1:~/dir3/dir4$ pwd

/home/jdoe/dir3/dir4

jdoe@u22s1:~/dir3/dir4$ cd ~/dir5        # Move to /home/jdoe/dir5
directory

jdoe@u22s1:~/dir5$ pwd

/home/jdoe/dir5

jdoe@u22s1:~/dir5$ cd ~                   # Return to home directory

jdoe@u22s1:~$ pwd

/home/jdoe
```

(*continued*)

#	Task
⑤	As you have seen in previous examples, the cd ~ or cd<ENTER> commands can be used to return to the user's home directory, basically from any directory. jdoe@u22s1:~$ **cd /tmp** jdoe@u22s1:/tmp$ **pwd** /tmp jdoe@u22s1:/tmp$ **cd ~** jdoe@u22s1:~$ **pwd** /home/jdoe jdoe@u22s1:~$ **cd dir5/dir6** jdoe@u22s1:~/dir5/dir6$ **pwd** /home/jdoe/dir5/dir6 jdoe@u22s1:~/dir5/dir6$ **cd ~** jdoe@u22s1:~$ **pwd** /home/jdoe
⑥	Unlike the ./ command, cd ~ enables you to navigate between directories without relying on the current working directory. Let's engage in more practice to enhance your directory navigation skills. jdoe@u22s1:~$ **pwd** /home/jdoe jdoe@u22s1:~/dir1$ **cd /var/log** jdoe@u22s1:/var/log$ **pwd** /var/log jdoe@u22s1:/var/log$ **cd ~** jdoe@u22s1:~$ **pwd** /home/jdoe

(continued)

#	Task
	jdoe@u22s1:~$ **cd ~/dir5/dir6**
	jdoe@u22s1:~/dir5/dir6$ **cd ~**
	jdoe@u22s1:~$ **pwd**
	/home/jdoe
	jdoe@u22s1:~$ **cd ~/dir3/dir4**
	jdoe@u22s1:~/dir3/dir4$ **pwd**
	/home/jdoe/dir3/dir4
	jdoe@u22s1:~/dir3/dir4$ **cd ~/dir1**
	jdoe@u22s1:~/dir1$ **pwd**
	/home/jdoe/dir1
⑦	The dir (directory) command is equivalent to the ls -C -b command, and it's designed to cater to both Linux and Windows users. However, there is a difference: when you use dir, the directory names are displayed in black, while using ls -C -b results in colored directory names, in my case blue.

```
jdoe@u22s1:~$ dir

Desktop    Downloads Pictures Templates dir1 dir5

Documents  Music     Public   Videos    dir3
# output is in black

jdoe@u22s1:~$ ls -C -b

Desktop    Downloads Pictures Templates dir1 dir5

Documents  Music     Public   Videos    dir3
# output is in blue
```

(continued)

#	Task
⑧	As demonstrated in Step ②, the touch command is used to create files. By simply entering touch file_name, you can create a file. Furthermore, you can use a single-line touch command to create multiple files. Additionally, a hidden feature of the touch command is its ability to update the timestamp of files. Let's check it out!

```
jdoe@u22s1:~$ pwd

/home/jdoe

jdoe@u22s1:~$ cd dir1

jdoe@u22s1:~/dir1$ touch f1.txt                    # create a single file

jdoe@u22s1:~/dir1$ ls -lh

total 4.0K

drwxrwxr-x 2 jdoe jdoe 4.0K Sep  8 10:00 dir2

-rw-rw-r-- 1 jdoe jdoe    0 Sep  8 11:27 f1.txt

-rw-rw-r-- 1 jdoe jdoe    0 Sep  8 09:54 level1.txt

jdoe@u22s1:~/dir1$ touch f2.txt f3.txt f4.txt f5.txt
# create multiple files

jdoe@u22s1:~/dir1$ ls -lh

total 4.0K

drwxrwxr-x 2 jdoe jdoe 4.0K Sep  8 10:00 dir2

-rw-rw-r-- 1 jdoe jdoe    0 Sep  8 11:27 f1.txt

-rw-rw-r-- 1 jdoe jdoe    0 Sep  8 11:28 f2.txt

-rw-rw-r-- 1 jdoe jdoe    0 Sep  8 11:28 f3.txt

-rw-rw-r-- 1 jdoe jdoe    0 Sep  8 11:28 f4.txt

-rw-rw-r-- 1 jdoe jdoe    0 Sep  8 11:28 f5.txt

-rw-rw-r-- 1 jdoe jdoe    0 Sep  8 09:54 level1.txt
# check the original time
```

(continued)

#	Task

	`jdoe@u22s1:~/dir1$ touch level1.txt` `# touch the file,`
	`level1.txt`
	
	`jdoe@u22s1:~/dir1$ ls -lh level1.txt`
	
	`-rw-rw-r-- 1 jdoe jdoe 0 Sep  8 11:29 level1.txt` `# file`
	`timestamp has been updated`

⑨	The cp (copy) command allows you to copy files or directories. Don't forget to use the −r (recursive) or −a (all) option when copying a directory. You will continue to work in the /home/jdoe/dir1 directory.
	
	`jdoe@u22s1:~/dir1$ pwd`
	
	`/home/jdoe/dir1`
	
	`jdoe@u22s1:~/dir1$ ls`
	
	`dir2  f1.txt  f2.txt  f3.txt  f4.txt  f5.txt  level1.txt`
	
	`jdoe@u22s1:~/dir1$ cp f2.txt f2c.txt`
	
	`jdoe@u22s1:~/dir1$ ls`
	
	`dir2  f1.txt  f2.txt  f2c.txt  f3.txt  f4.txt  f5.txt  level1.txt`
	
	`jdoe@u22s1:~/dir1$ ls -d dir*`
	
	`dir2`
	
	`jdoe@u22s1:~/dir1$ cp -r dir2 dir2c1`
	
	`jdoe@u22s1:~/dir1$ ls -d dir*`
	
	`dir2  dir2c1`
	
	`jdoe@u22s1:~/dir1$ cp -a dir2 dir2c2`
	
	`jdoe@u22s1:~/dir1$ ls -d dir*`
	
	`dir2  dir2c1  dir2c2`
	
	`jdoe@u22s1:~/dir1$ tree dir*`

(continued)

442

#	Task

```
dir2
└── level2.txt
dir2c1
└── level2.txt
dir2c2
└── level2.txt
0 directories, 1 file
```

⑩   The rm (remove) command is used to delete files or directories. In the following example, you use the -r option to delete directories.

```
jdoe@u22s1:~/dir1$ ls

dir2    dir2c2  f2.txt    f3.txt  f5.txt

dir2c1  f1.txt  f2c.txt  f4.txt  level1.txt

jdoe@u22s1:~/dir1$ rm *.txt         # use the wildcard * to delete
all files ending with file extension .txt

jdoe@u22s1:~/dir1$ ls

dir2  dir2c1  dir2c2

jdoe@u22s1:~/dir1$ rm -r dir2c*     # delete two copied directories
recursively, with -r option

jdoe@u22s1:~/dir1$ ls

dir2

jdoe@u22s1:~/dir1$ tree             # you are back to the original
state

.
└── dir2
└── level2.txt
1 directory, 1 file
```

Proceed to the next set of exercises to further enhance your familiarity with Linux command lines. Remember, practice makes perfect.

Exercise 7-3. Work with the Directories and Hidden Files

#	Task
①	The mv (move) command allows you to change the file name or move files and directories to another directory. Let's learn to use this through some examples.

```
jdoe@u22s1:~/dir1$ clear                # Use the 'clear' command or
'Ctrl+L' key to clear your screen

# Rename level2.txt in /home/jdoe/dir1/dir2 directory to L2.txt.

jdoe@u22s1:~/dir1$ pwd

/home/jdoe/dir1

jdoe@u22s1:~/dir1$ ls dir2

level2.txt

jdoe@u22s1:~/dir1$ ls ./dir2            # you can see that dir2 and
./dir2 is the same

level2.txt

jdoe@u22s1:~/dir1$ mv ./dir2/level2.txt ./dir2/L2.txt     # rename
level2.txt to L2.txt

jdoe@u22s1:~/dir1$ tree dir2

dir2
└── L2.txt

0 directories, 1 file

# Move L2.txt to the home directory, /home/jdoe.

jdoe@u22s1:~/dir1$ mv ./dir2/L2.txt ./

jdoe@u22s1:~/dir1$ ls

L2.txt  dir2
```

(continued)

#	Task

jdoe@u22s1:~/dir1$ **tree**

```
.
├── L2.txt
└── dir2
```

1 directory, 1 file

② First, let's quickly check the directories. You currently have dir1, dir3, and dir5 directories in the user's home directory, /home/jdoe, and the even-numbered directories in each—that is dir1/dir2, dir3/dir4, and dir5/dir6. In this exercise, you will try to nest dir3 into dir2 and then nest dir5 into dir4, so the directory path will be ~/dir1/dir2/dir3/dir4/dir5/dir6.

jdoe@u22s1:~/dir1$ **pwd**   *# take special note of the current working directory*

/home/jdoe/dir1

jdoe@u22s1:~/dir1$ **ls ../dir***

../dir1:

L2.txt dir2

../dir3:

dir4 level1.txt

../dir5:

dir6 level1.txt

jdoe@u22s1:~/dir1$ **ls**

L2.txt dir2

jdoe@u22s1:~/dir1$ **mv ../dir3 dir2**   *# move ~/dir3 to ~/dir1/dir2*

jdoe@u22s1:~/dir1$ **ls dir2**

dir3

(continued)

#	Task

jdoe@u22s1:~/dir1$ **mv ../dir5 dir2/dir3/dir4**   *# move ~/dir5 to*
~/dir1/dir2/dir3/dir4

jdoe@u22s1:~/dir1$ **tree ../dir1**   *# check the*
directory structure

```
../dir1
├── L2.txt
└── dir2
    └── dir3
        ├── dir4
        │   ├── dir5
        │   │   ├── dir6
        │   │   │   └── level2.txt
        │   │   └── level1.txt
        │   └── level2.txt
        └── level1.txt
```

5 directories, 5 files

③ Now, using the . (dot) method, move the dir files to the user's home directory, at the same level as the parent directory, dir1.

jdoe@u22s1:~/dir1$ **cd ..**

jdoe@u22s1:~$ **pwd**   *# take special note of*
the current working directory

/home/jdoe

jdoe@u22s1:~$ **mv ./dir1/dir2/dir3/dir4/dir5/dir6 .**   *# move dir6, the*
. represents current directory

jdoe@u22s1:~$ **mv ./dir1/dir2/dir3/dir4/dir5 .**

jdoe@u22s1:~$ **mv ./dir1/dir2/dir3/dir4 .**

(continued)

#	Task

jdoe@u22s1:~$ **mv ./dir1/dir2/dir3 .**

jdoe@u22s1:~$ **mv ./dir1/dir2 .**

jdoe@u22s1:~$ **ls**   *# you should find all six directories under your home directory*

Desktop   Downloads Pictures Templates dir1 dir3 dir5

Documents Music   Public   Videos   dir2 dir4 dir6

④ Now use the rm -ir command to clean the directories and files you have created. Because the -I option will ask you to confirm the deletions, you will have to answer 'y' to all prompts and confirmation. You must use the rm -r command with care, as it will remove the file instantaneously.

jdoe@u22s1:~$ **ls**

Desktop   Downloads Pictures Templates dir1 dir3 dir5

Documents Music   Public   Videos   dir2 dir4 dir6

jdoe@u22s1:~$ **rm -ir dir***
 # remove files interactively

rm: descend into directory 'dir1'? **y**

rm: remove regular empty file 'dir1/L2.txt'? **y**
 # answer 'y' to all prompts

[...omitted for brevity]

rm: remove regular empty file 'dir6/level2.txt'? **y**

rm: remove directory 'dir6'? **y**

jdoe@u22s1:~$ **ls**

Desktop Documents Downloads Music Pictures Public Templates
Videos

(continued)

447

#	Task
⑤	Create the my_secret file with your name and a secret password. Create a hidden directory called hide_me using the . (dot) method and move the secret file into the .hide_me directory. Optionally, to see the hidden files, use the ls -a command.

```
jdoe@u22s1:~$ vi my_secret
```

```
jdoe@u22s1:~$ cat my_secret
```

```
jdoe
```

```
fairdinkum!@#
```

```
jdoe@u22s1:~$ mkdir .hide_me                              # create a
hidden directory
```

```
jdoe@u22s1:~$ ls
```

```
Desktop  Documents  Downloads  Music  Pictures  Public  Templates
Videos  my_secret
```

```
jdoe@u22s1:~$ mv my_secret .hide_me/                      # move the
secret file to the hidden directory
```

```
jdoe@u22s1:~$ ls
```

```
Desktop  Documents  Downloads  Music  Pictures  Public  Templates
Videos
```

```
jdoe@u22s1:~$ tree .hide_me/                              # check the
hidden secret file in a hidden directory
```

```
.hide_me/
└── my_secret
```

```
0 directories, 1 file
```

Tip

There are two ways to view command options, --help and man

In Linux, the `linux_command --help` and `man linux_command` commands both offer valuable information for your Linux commands, yet they serve distinct purposes and provide varying levels of detail. Let's use the `ls` command as an example:

`jdoe@u22s1:~$ `**`ls --help`**` # gives you a quick reference to the most commonly used options`

The `--help` option gives you a quick reference to the most frequently utilized options, making it convenient for a rapid overview of the command's basic functionality.

`jdoe@u22s1:~$ `**`man ls`**` # provides a comprehensive and detailed manual page with information on all aspects of the command.`

The `man` command, followed by the command name, opens a comprehensive and detailed manual page that covers all aspects of the `ls` command. It offers in-depth explanations of the command's syntax, available options, and detailed guidance on its usage.

It's worth noting that when using these commands, `man` precedes the command name, while `--help` comes after the command. Additionally, if you have installed a server version of a Linux distribution, you might need to execute the `unminimize` command to enable all the necessary manual (man) packages. Running `unminimize` is optional and may take some time, as it installs various packages.

`jdoe@u22s1:~$ `**`unminimize`**` # optional on server OS`

Additionally, you can quickly search for Linux command cheat sheets on Google and your search result will return numerous search results. Here's one such website for your reference: `https://cheatography.com/davechild/cheat-sheets/linux-command-line/`

Linux File and Directory Exercises – Set B

You have just completed essential Linux file and directory exercises in Exercise 7-1, 7-2, and 7-3. Next, let's learn some more useful commands that are used daily. The user-friendly GUI is often a missing feature on enterprise Linux systems, and much of the administrator's tasks are carried out via a command-line or console interface.

Proficiency in Linux administration involves a wide range of skills and knowledge to effectively manage and maintain Linux-based systems. Proficiency also does not necessarily depend on the number of commands you know but rather on how effectively you can use them to perform daily tasks and troubleshoot issues. However, having a good grasp of a core set of essential Linux commands is important for a smooth Linux OS administration.

Now, let's put your knowledge from the previous exercises into practice and expand your familiarity with Linux commands. Table 7-6 presents greetings, expressions of love, friendship phrases, and farewells in ten different languages. You'll be using these expressions as you work through this set of exercises.

Table 7-6. *Table of Greetings, Love, Friend, and Farewells in 11 Languages*

Language	Greeting	Love	Friend	Farewell
English	Hi	Love	Friend	Bye
Arabic	Marhaban (مَرْحَبا)	Hubb (حب)	Sadiq (صديق)	Wada'an (وداعا)
French	Bonjour	Amour	Ami	Au revoir
Hebrew	Shalom (שלום)	Ahaba (אהבה)	Chaver (חבר)	Bahy (ביי)
Hindi	Namaste (नमस्ते)	Mohabbat (मोहब्बत)	Dost (दोस्त)	Alveedaa (अलवादिा)
Italian	Ciao	Amore	Amico	Arrivederci
Japanese	Konichiwa (こんにちは)	Ai (愛)	Tomodachi (友達)	Sah-yoh-na-rah (さようなら)
Korean	Anyoung (안녕)	Sarang (사랑)	Chingu (친구)	Anyoung (안녕)
Mandarin Chinese	Nihao (你好)	Ai (爱)	朋友 (Péngyǒu)	Zaijian (再见)
Spanish	Hola	Amor	Amigo	Adiós
Turkish	Merhaba	Ask	Arkadaş	Hoşça kal

Exercise 7-4. Echo, Cat, More, and Less Command Exercise

You can work on either the Fedora (f38s1) or Ubuntu (u22s1) Server by connecting via SSH using a terminal console program such as PuTTY, SecureCRT, or TerraTerm. It's worth noting that while this chapter uses Ubuntu, you can still perform the same tasks if you're using Fedora or any other Linux distribution.

#	Task
①	Create a new file named greet1 and use the echo command to write the following question into greet1: 'Can you say Hello in other languages?'

```
jdoe@u22s1:~$ pwd

/home/jdoe

jdoe@u22s1:~$ touch greet1                    # Create a new file named
'greet1'

jdoe@u22s1:~$ ls greet*

greet1

jdoe@u22s1:~$ echo "Can you say Hello in other languages?" > greet1
# use echo > to insert strings to a file

jdoe@u22s1:~$ more greet1                      # Display the content of
'greet1'

Can you say Hello in different languages?
```

(continued)

#	Task

② Create another file called greet2 and this time, you'll write the word Hello in various languages using the echo command. This exercise will teach you how to greet people in ten other languages.

```
jdoe@u22s1:~$ touch greet2                    # Create a new file named
'greet2'
```

```
jdoe@u22s1:~$ echo "Hi Bonjour Nihao Konichiwa Shalom Merhaba Hola
Namaste Ciao Anyoung Marhaban" > greet2 # Write greetings in other
languages
```

```
jdoe@u22s1:~$ cat greet2                       # Display the content of
'greet2'
```

```
Hi Bonjour Nihao Konichiwa Shalom Merhaba Hola Namaste Ciao Anyoung
Marhaban
```

In greet2, you've now learned how to say 'Hi' ('Hello') in ten languages other than English.

③ In the previous exercise, you used the cat command to display the contents of greet2. Another useful application of the cat command is to merge the contents of multiple files into a single file. In this exercise, you will merge greet1 and greet2 to create a new file named greet3.

```
jdoe@u22s1:~# cat greet1 greet2 > greet3      # Merge 'greet1' and
'greet2' into 'greet3'
```

```
jdoe @u22s1:~# ls -d greet*                    # List files starting with
'greet'
```

```
greet1  greet2  greet3
```

```
jdoe @u22s1:~# more greet3                      # Display the content of
'greet3'
Can you say Hello in other languages?
```

Hi Bonjour Nihao Konichiwa Shalom Merhaba Ola Namaste Ciao Anyoung Marhaban

Now, greet3 contains the merged contents from greet1 and greet2.

(continued)

#	Task

④ To add content to an existing file, you can utilize the `cat >>` command.

`jdoe@u22s1:~# `**`cat >> greet3`**

How do you say "Love" in other languages?

Love Amour Ai Ai Ahaba Ask Amor Amore Mohabbat Sarang Hubb

#To exit, press Ctrl+D keys.

After executing this command, you can view the updated greet3 file using the more command:

`jdoe @u22s1:~# `**`more greet3`**

Can you say Hello in other languages?

Hi Bonjour Nihao Konichiwa Shalom Merhaba Ola Namaste Anyoung

How do you say "Love" in other languages?

Love Amour Ai Ai Ahaba Ask Amor Amore Mohabbat Sarang Hubb

With this exercise, you've not only learned how to append content into an existing file but also discovered how to express the word Love in 11 different languages.

⑤ You can also create a new file using the `cat >` command. You are not creating a new file using the `cat >` command, instead, you are overwriting the contents of an existing file if there is an existing file with the same name or creating a new file if it doesn't exist. To create a new file using the `cat` command, you typically use `cat` with the input from the keyboard and then terminate the input with Ctrl+D.

`jdoe@u22s1:~$ `**`cat > greet4`**

How to say "Friend" in various languages?

Friend Ami Pengyou Tomodachi Chaver Arkadas Amigo Amico Dost Chingu Sadiq

#To exit, press Ctrl+D keys.

`jdoe@u22s1:~$ `**`more greet4`**

(continued)

453

#	Task
	How to say "Friend" in various languages?
	Friend Ami Pengyou Tomodachi Chaver Arkadas Amigo Amico Dost Chingu Sadiq
	With this exercise, you've written the word `Friend` in various languages, but you can use the same method to create your sentences and have some fun.

⑥ You can also use the `more` command to view the contents of your file. If the file is long, you can navigate through it using the spacebar to scroll down a page or the Enter key to scroll down line by line. To exit in the middle of reading, you can use the Ctrl+C or Ctrl+Z key combination.

Here's an example of creating greet5 by combining the contents of greet1, greet2, and greet4 using the cat command, then viewing the contents using the more command.

```
jdoe@u22s1:~$ cat greet1 greet2 greet4 > greet5
```

```
jdoe@u22s1:~$ more greet5
```

Can you say Hello in different languages?

Hi Bonjour Nihao Konichiwa Shalom Merhaba Hola Namaste Ciao Anyoung Marhaban

How to say "Friend" in various languages?

Friend Ami Pengyou Tomodachi Chaver Arkadas Amigo Amico Dost Chingu Sadiq

With more commands, you can easily navigate and read through long files.

(continued)

#	Task
⑦	You can also use the `less` command to view the contents of your file. Unlike the `cat` command, `less` does not immediately print the entire contents on the terminal, which is helpful for longer files. To navigate through the content, use the spacebar to scroll down a page and the Enter key to scroll down by line. To exit from `less`, you can use Ctrl+Z, or you can press Ctrl+C and then type `:q` and press Enter. Here's an example of using the `less` command to view greet5: jdoe@u22s1:~# **less greet5** Can you say Hello in different languages? Hi Bonjour Nihao Konichiwa Shalom Merhaba Hola Namaste Ciao Anyoung Marhaban How to say "Friend" in various languages? Friend Ami Pengyou Tomodachi Chaver Arkadas Amigo Amico Dost Chingu Sadiq greet5 (END) *< Ctrl+Z or Ctrl+C and then :q >* The `less` command allows for easy navigation and reading of files, especially when dealing with longer content.

Tip

In need of no-cost, beginner-friendly Linux learning resources?

Sometimes, the best resources come at no cost. Thanks to Paul Cobbaut's generosity in sharing his book, *Linux Fundamentals,* on the Linuxfun website, you can dive into the world of Linux with ease. I strongly recommend downloading this free PDF file and harnessing its valuable insights.

URL: `https://linux-training.be/linuxfun.pdf`

Exercise 7-5. ls Command with Options

You might be wondering how delving into these exercises relates to your immediate goal of achieving Python Network Automation. However, it's crucial to view these drills as the foundational building blocks for your journey. Just like constructing a sturdy house, you must lay one brick at a time. This process of building a strong foundation is vital. Make the most of the exercises in this chapter and consider exploring additional Linux command study materials, both online and offline.

Here are some fundamental Linux commands you focus on in this section:

> ls: Lists files and directories.

> ls -l: Displays detailed information about files and directories.

> ls -a: Lists all files in the current working directory, including hidden ones.

> ls -al: Shows detailed information about files and directories in the current working directory, including hidden files.

> ls -lh: Displays file sizes in a human-readable format (e.g., 1K, 2M) alongside other file and directory information.

Mastering these basic ls commands is essential for your Linux and Python journey.

#	Task
①	Use the ls command with the search keyword and the all-inclusive or greedy *. The following example lists all files or folders starting with the word greet in the current working directory.

```
jdoe@u22s1:~$ pwd

/home/jdoe

jdoe@u22s1:~$ ls g*                    # use the greedy * to display all
files starting with the letter 'g'

greet1  greet2  greet3  greet4  greet5

jdoe@u22s1:~$ ls greet*                # you can go a little bit specific
to perform a more refined search and display

greet1  greet2  greet3  greet4  greet5
```

(continued)

#	Task

② Create a new directory called `greetings` and use the `ls` command with the `-d` and `-l` (long listing) options to distinguish between files and directories. Pay attention to the letter d at the beginning of the `greetings` directory listing; it signifies that this is indeed a directory.

```
jdoe@u22s1:~$ mkdir greetings
jdoe@u22s1:~$ ls -d -l greet*
-rw-rw-r-- 1 jdoe jdoe   42 Sep  9 02:30 greet1
-rw-rw-r-- 1 jdoe jdoe   77 Sep  9 02:54 greet2
-rw-rw-r-- 1 jdoe jdoe  220 Sep  9 03:08 greet3
-rw-rw-r-- 1 jdoe jdoe  116 Sep  9 03:34 greet4
-rw-rw-r-- 1 jdoe jdoe  235 Sep  9 03:36 greet5
drwxrwxr-x 2 jdoe jdoe 4096 Sep  9 06:09 greetings
```

③ The `-a` command in `ls` lists all files, including hidden ones. Hidden files are denoted by a leading dot (`.`) in their names.

Here's an example of using `ls -a`:

```
jdoe@u22s1:~$ ls -a
.              .cache    .profile                   Documents  Templates  greet4
..             .config   .ssh                       Downloads  Videos     greet5
.bash_history  .hide_me  .sudo_as_admin_successful  Music                 greet1
greetings
.bash_logout   .lesshst  .viminfo                              Pictures   greet2
.bashrc        .local    Desktop                               Public     greet3
```

In the output, you can see hidden files with names starting with a dot (`.`), along with regular files and directories.

(continued)

#	Task
④	You can combine various ls options to list the files and directories as you like. Other options include –R, -o, -g, -i, -s, -t, -S, and -r. Use ls man and man --help to review various options. If you have the time to explore these options, go to the Internet and spend an hour or two to find each one of them and mix and match.

The following is the combined use of the –l (list) and –h (human-readable) commands:

```
jdoe@u22s1:~$ ls -lh greet*
-rw-rw-r-- 1 jdoe jdoe    42 Sep  9 02:30 greet1
-rw-rw-r-- 1 jdoe jdoe    77 Sep  9 02:54 greet2
-rw-rw-r-- 1 jdoe jdoe   220 Sep  9 03:08 greet3
-rw-rw-r-- 1 jdoe jdoe   116 Sep  9 03:34 greet4
-rw-rw-r-- 1 jdoe jdoe   235 Sep  9 03:36 greet5
greetings:
total 0
```

Tip

A quick study tip: How to increase the output in IT learning

Learning in IT is dynamic and multifaceted. Beyond textbooks, it involves reading, online research, videos, classroom training, and hands-on experience. The goal is to absorb and transform information into practical knowledge.

Effective learning hinges on active engagement. Ask questions, apply what you learn, teach others, and collaborate. Problem-solving and testing reinforce knowledge. Reflect and revisit concepts for retention.

Consistency is key. Stay engaged, pursue new knowledge, and strive for improvement. Dedicate yourself to lifelong learning, actively participating, practicing, teaching, and collaborating. This approach ensures knowledge retention and empowers career growth in the ever-changing IT landscape.

Exercise 7-6. Create, Delete, and Script Files and Directories

In this exercise, you gain more hands-on experience by practicing the deletion of files and directories.

#	Task

① If you want to delete all files starting with the same name in a directory, you can use `rm filename*`. If you want to delete all files in a directory, you can use `rm *`, but always use the rm command with care. Continuing from the previous exercise, let's move all files starting with the word greet into the greetings directory.

```
jdoe@u22s1:~$ pwd

/home/jdoe

jdoe@u22s1:~$ ls

Desktop     Downloads  Pictures  Templates  greet1  greet3  greet5

Documents   Music      Public    Videos     greet2  greet4  greetings

greetings:

total 0

jdoe@u22s1:~$ mv greet* greetings/        # encounters an error but
files are still moved to the greetings directory

mv: cannot move 'greetings' to a subdirectory of itself, 'greetings/
greetings'

jdoe@u22s1:~$ ls

Desktop  Documents  Downloads  Music  Pictures  Public  Templates
Videos  greetings

jdoe@u22s1:~$ cd greetings/

jdoe@u22s1:~/greetings$ ls

greet1  greet2  greet3  greet4  greet5
```

(continued)

#	Task

```
jdoe@u22s1:~/greetings$ rm *                    # delete all files in  the
directory, use with care

jdoe@u22s1:~/greetings$ ls -lh

total 0
```

② Now you'll re-create three files beginning with greet and three files beginning with bye. Then delete the files containing a specific string; your targets are the files ending with the number 3. The * is used as a wildcard that replaces all leading characters, so it only matches the files ending with the number 3.

```
jdoe@u22s1:~/greetings$ pwd

/home/jdoe/greetings

jdoe@u22s1:~/greetings$ touch greet1 greet2 greet3 bye1 bye2 bye3

jdoe@u22s1:~/greetings$ ls

bye1  bye2  bye3  greet1  greet2  greet3

jdoe@u22s1:~/greetings$ find . -name "*3"

./bye3

./greet3

jdoe@u22s1:~/greetings$ rm *3

jdoe@u22s1:~/greetings$ ls

bye1  bye2  greet1  greet2

# Next, let's delete all the files containing greet using "rm greet*".

jdoe@u22s1:~/greetings$ rm greet*

jdoe@u22s1:~/greetings$ ls

bye1  bye2
```

(continued)

#	Task

*# Then let's delete all files in the directory using the "rm *". You should have an empty directory.*

jdoe@u22s1:~/greetings$ **rm** *****

jdoe@u22s1:~/greetings$ **ls -lh**

total 0

③ If you want to delete a directory in the same manner, you must use the rm -r command. The r in this command signifies *recursive*. Without the -r option, Linux prohibits the deletion of directories, so exercise caution when using it. While working within the greetings directory, you'll create 20 directories using the bash shell's loop feature, denoted by {1..10}. The command mkdir sayhi{1..10} will generate ten directories starting with sayhi and mkdir saybye{1..10} will create another ten directories beginning with saybye. Because the operation is identical, you can execute a single command mkdir sayhi{1..10} saybye{1..10} to create all 20 directories, achieving the same result efficiently. This method can also be used to create multiple files; simply replace the mkdir command with touch. To remove directories containing specific strings, use the ' ' wildcard character. For instance, to delete directories containing the word hi, enclose the word with * wildcards, one at the beginning and one at the end. By the end of this exercise, you should have an empty directory.

jdoe@u22s1:~/greetings$ **mkdir sayhi{1..10} saybye{1..10}**

jdoe@u22s1:~/greetings$ **ls**

saybye1   saybye2   saybye4   saybye6   saybye8   sayhi1   sayhi2   sayhi4
sayhi6   sayhi8

saybye10   saybye3   saybye5   saybye7   saybye9   sayhi10   sayhi3   sayhi5
sayhi7   sayhi9

jdoe@u22s1:~/greetings$ **rm *hi***

rm: cannot remove 'sayhi1': Is a directory

[...omitted for brevity]

(continued)

461

#	Task

rm: cannot remove 'sayhi9': Is a directory

jdoe@u22s1:~/greetings$ **rm -r *hi***

jdoe@u22s1:~/greetings$ **ls**

saybye1   saybye10   saybye2   saybye3   saybye4   saybye5   saybye6
saybye7   saybye8   saybye9

jdoe@u22s1:~/greetings$ **rm -r *bye***

jdoe@u22s1:~/greetings$ **ls -lh**

total 0

---

④ Now you're stepping up a gear here. You'll use a simple shell loop script on a single command line to create 100 files named g1 to g100. Then, you list the files to confirm their creation. Next, you search for all files ending with the number 4 and remove (delete) them using the rm command. Finally, you remove all files starting with the letter g and display the resulting empty directory.

jdoe@u22s1:~/greetings$ **pwd**

/home/jdoe/greetings

jdoe@u22s1:~/greetings$ **for i in {1..100}; do touch "g$i"; done**   # use a simple shell loop to create 100 files

jdoe@u22s1:~/greetings$ **ls**

g1   g14 g2   g25 g30 g36 g41 g47 g52 g58 g63 g69 g74 g8
g85 g90 g96

[...omitted for brevity]

g13   g19 g24 g3 g35 g40 g46 g51 g57 g62 g68 g73 g79 g84
g9   g95

jdoe@u22s1:~/greetings$ **find . -name "*4"** # search for all files ending with the digit 4

./g94

./g84

(*continued*)

#	Task

[...omitted for brevity]

./g44

./g74

```
jdoe@u22s1:~/greetings$ rm *4          # remove (delete) all files
ending with the digit4
```

```
jdoe@u22s1:~/greetings$ ls
```

```
g1    g13  g19  g23  g29  g33  g39  g45  g5   g55  g6   g65  g7   g75
g8   g85  g9   g95
```

[...omitted for brevity]

```
g12   g18  g22  g28  g32  g38  g43  g49  g53  g59  g63  g69  g73  g79
g83  g89  g93  g99
```

```
jdoe@u22s1:~/greetings$ rm g*          # remove all files starting with
the letter 'g'
```

```
jdoe@u22s1:~/greetings$ ls -lh
```

```
total 0
```

⑤ Create 100 directories (d1, d2, d3, ... d100) in the greetings directory and populate each of these directories with a corresponding file (f1.txt, f2.txt, ... f100.txt) using nested for loops in the bash shell. The resulting directory structure is displayed using the tree command, which shows the hierarchical organization of directories and files, indicating 100 directories and 100 files. Finally, you use the rm -r d* command to remove all the directories starting with the letter d, effectively deleting the entire structure.

```
jdoe@u22s1:~/greetings$ for i in {1..100}; do mkdir "d$i"; done
# create 100 directories for a practice
```

```
jdoe@u22s1:~/greetings$ ls
```

```
d1    d14  d2   d25  d30  d36  d41  d47  d52  d58  d63  d69  d74  d8
d85  d90  d96
```

[...omitted for brevity]

(continued)

#	Task

d13   d19   d24   d3   d35   d40   d46   d51   d57   d62   d68   d73   d79   d84
d9   d95

jdoe@u22s1:~/greetings$ **for i in {1..100}; do touch "di/fi.txt"; done**
create 100 .txt files in each directory

jdoe@u22s1:~/greetings$ **tree**

.

```
├── d1
│   └── f1.txt
[...omitted for brevity]
└── d99
└── f99.txt
```

100 directories, 100 files

jdoe@u22s1:~/greetings$ **rm -r d***   # use a single rm command to
delete all directories and text files

jdoe@u22s1:~/greetings$ **ls -lh**

total 0

⑥ Use the bash script to exemplify a series of tasks aimed at automating the creation of directories and files in a Linux environment. This example writes these tasks into a shell script to achieve the creation of the directories and files. This scripted approach streamlines the otherwise tedious process of manual directory and file creation, exemplifying the efficiency and power of automation in a Linux environment.

jdoe@u22s1:~/greetings$ **vi create_100_d_f.sh**

jdoe@u22s1:~/greetings$ **cat create_100_d_f.sh**

#!/bin/bash

 # Create 100 directories

for i in {1..100}; do

(*continued*)

#	Task

mkdir "d$i"

done

 # Create a file in each directory with a corresponding name

for i in {1..100}; do

touch "di/fi.txt"

done

jdoe@u22s1:~/greetings$ **ls -lh**

total 4.0K

-rw-rw-r-- 1 jdoe jdoe 193 Sep 9 07:35 create_100_d_f.sh

jdoe@u22s1:~/greetings$ **chmod +x create_100_d_f.sh**   # make the script executable

jdoe@u22s1:~/greetings$ **ls -lh**

total 4.0K

-rwxrwxr-x 1 jdoe jdoe 193 Sep 9 07:35 create_100_d_f.sh

jdoe@u22s1:~/greetings$ **./create_100_d_f.sh**   # execute the shell script to create files

jdoe@u22s1:~/greetings$ **ls**

create_100_d_f.sh d13 d19 d24 d3   d35 d40 d46 d51 d57 d62 d68 d73 d79 d84 d9   d95

[...omitted for brevity]

d12   d18 d23 d29 d34 d4   d45 d50 d56 d61 d67 d72 d78 d83 d89 d94

(continued)

#	Task

⑦ While this isn't a Python-focused section, it's an excellent opportunity to demonstrate the same task using Python scripting. To achieve the same goal using Python, create a Python script with a .py extension. In this case, create a Python file named `create_100_d_f.py`. To distinguish the files created by Python, modify the directory names to begin with the letter p and the file names to begin with the letter x.

```
jdoe@u22s1:~/greetings$ vi create_100_d_f.py

jdoe@u22s1:~/greetings$ cat create_100_d_f.py

import os

for i in range(1, 101):          # Create 100 directories

d_name = f'p{i}'

os.makedirs(d_name, exist_ok=True)

for i in range(1, 101):          # Create a file in each directory

d_name = f'p{i}'

f_name = f'x{i}.txt'

f_path = os.path.join(d_name, f_name)

with open(f_path, 'w'):

pass

jdoe@u22s1:~/greetings$ python3 create_100_d_f.py

jdoe@u22s1:~/greetings$ ls

create_100_d_f.py  d17  d27  d37  d47  d57  d67  d77  d87  d97  p16
p26  p36  p46  p56  p66  p76  p86  p96

create_100_d_f.sh  d18  d28  d38  d48  d58  d68  d78  d88  d98  p17
p27  p37  p47  p57  p67  p77  p87  p97

[...omitted for brevity]
```

(continued)

#	Task

d16   d26   d36   d46   d56   d66   d76   d86   d96   p15   p25

p35   p45   p55   p65   p75   p85   p95

```
jdoe@u22s1:~/greetings$ tree
.
├── create_100_d_f.py
├── create_100_d_f.sh
├── d1
│   └── f1.txt
[...omitted for brevity]
└── p99
└── x99.txt
```

In the dynamite example, you created 100 files and 100 directories using Bash command lines. Then, you developed and used a shell program to generate 100 directories and 100 files within each directory. For a bit of fun, you replicated the same functionality using a Python program, resulting in an additional 100 directories and 100 files. When working with Linux, it's valuable to learn how to write Bash shell scripts, as they can complement your Python scripting skills. This section is included to showcase the true power and convenience of Bash shell scripting in Linux, as well as to demonstrate how you can achieve the same objectives using Python scripts.

Exercise 7-7. Create a Python Application, Make Your File Executable, Add a Shebang, and Run the Application

This exercise uses a combination of Linux commands you've acquired thus far to interact with Python files. Once you've created the Python .py file, you can modify the file's permissions using the chmod command. This Linux command proves useful when adjusting the properties of a Python script file to render it executable. Currently, there are no Python files in the user's home directory. Let's promptly generate a basic Python script and observe how this process unfolds in the context of that script:

#	Task

① To create a Python script in Linux, append a .py file extension to the file name. To create your
    Python script, you can use the familiar echo and cat commands or utilize the vi or nano text
    editors that you've become acquainted with in this chapter. The presence of \n after the word
    Automation signifies a newline character insertion or alteration within the script. Proceed to
    generate this file and execute the application using the command python3 print5times.
    py to confirm the smooth execution of your script.

```
jdoe@u22s1:~/greetings$ cd ..

jdoe@u22s1:~$ pwd

/home/jdoe

jdoe@u22s1:~$ mkdir myscript && cd myscript

jdoe@u22s1:~/myscript$ echo "x = 'Python Network Automation\n'" >
print5times.py

jdoe@u22s1:~/myscript$ more print5times.py

x = 'Python Network Automation\n'

jdoe@u22s1:~/myscript$ cat >> print5times.py

print(x*5)                                      # type in the code "print(x*5)"

<Ctrl+D> to exit

jdoe@u22s1:~/myscript$ more print5times.py

x = 'Python Network Automation\n'

print(x*5)

jdoe@u22s1:~/myscript$ python3 print5times.py

Python Network Automation

Python Network Automation

Python Network Automation

Python Network Automation

Python Network Automation
```

(continued)

#	Task
②	Now, you've successfully created a functional Python script (or application) and examined its file mode. This file can indeed be referred to as an application because it prints x five times each time it's executed. To check the file's access permissions, execute the `ls -l print5times.py` command and observe the output starting with `-rw-r--r--`. As you can discern, it lacks the x or executable-level access. To enable this file to run as an executable application without specifying Python 3 each time, you must modify its properties to include the x permission.

```
jdoe@u22s1:~/myscript$ ls -l print5times.py
```

```
-rw-rw-r-- 1 jdoe jdoe 45 Sep  9 08:23 print5times.py
```

```
jdoe@u22s1:~/myscript$ ./print5times.py
```

```
-bash: ./print5times.py: Permission denied
```

Use `chmod +x print5times.py` to make the script executable. The file color should change to green automatically, indicating that this is now an executable file.

```
jdoe@u22s1:~/myscript$ chmod +x print5times.py
```

```
jdoe@u22s1:~/myscript$ ls -l print5times.py
```

```
-rwxrwxr-x 1 jdoe jdoe 45 Sep  9 08:23 print5times.py
```

Try to run the application without the python3 command. But when you run the script, you will encounter an unexpected token error, as you did not add the infamous shebang (#!/usr/bin/python3) line on the top. A shebang line defines where the interpreter is located.
```
jdoe@u22s1:~/myscript$ ./print5times.py
```

```
./print5times.py: line 1: x: command not found
```

```
./print5times.py: line 2: syntax error near unexpected token `x*5'
```

```
./print5times.py: line 2: `print(x*5)'
```

(continued)

#	Task

③ Let's enhance this script by adding #!/usr/bin/python3 (shebang) at the beginning. To do this, you'll use the sed command with the -i and -e options. sed, short for Stream Editor, is a powerful Linux/UNIX tool designed for text manipulation. You don't need to be fully proficient in using it at this point, but having a basic understanding of how it operates will prove invaluable in the future.

```
jdoe@u22s1:~/myscript$ cat print5times.py

x = 'Python Network Automation\n'

print(x*5)

jdoe@u22s1:~/myscript$ sed -i -e '1i#!/usr/bin/python3\' print5times.
py # use sed to add shebang line on top

jdoe@u22s1:~/myscript$ cat print5times.py

#!/usr/bin/python3                              # This line has been
added by the above sed command

x = 'Python Network Automation\n'

print(x*5)
```

Now you checked that the shebang line is on the first line. Run the Python script from the working directory. It should print x five times, as shown here:

```
jdoe@u22s1:~/myscript$ ./print5times.py

Python Network Automation

[...omitted for brevity]
```

(*continued*)

#	Task
④	What if you wanted to run the application without using `./` each time? You can use the Linux command PATH="$(pwd):$PATH" but keep in mind that once your Linux terminal session ends, the added PATH will reset and disappear.

```
jdoe@u22s1:~/myscript$ ls -lh print5times.py

-rwxrwxr-x 1 jdoe jdoe 64 Sep  9 08:39 print5times.py

jdoe@u22s1:~/myscript$ PATH="$(pwd):$PATH"   # add a path to this
session only

jdoe@u22s1:~/myscript$ print5times.py

Python Network Automation

[...omitted for brevity]

jdoe@u22s1:~/myscript$ logout                    # You will be logged
out

# You have to log back in to begin this task.

jdoe@u22s1:~$ cd myscript/

jdoe@u22s1:~/myscript$ print5times.py

print5times.py: command not found
```

(continued)

#	Task

⑤ To permanently include the ~/myscript directory or your current working directory in the PATH variable, utilize the following command. This way, even after exiting the session and returning, you will still be able to run the script without using ./. After adding the path, remember to restart the bash by executing either source ~/.bashrc or exec bash to ensure the changes take effect.

```
jdoe@u22s1:~/myscript# echo "export PATH=\$PATH:$(pwd)" >> ~/.bashrc
# add a permanent path to .bashrc

jdoe@u22s1:~/myscript# exec bash #(source ~/.bashrc)  restarts bash

jdoe@u22s1:~/myscript# print5times.py

Python Network Automation

[...omitted for brevity]

jdoe@u22s1:~/myscript$ logout                 # You will be logged out

# You have to log back in to begin this task.

jdoe@u22s1:~$ cd myscript/

jdoe@u22s1:~/myscript$ print5times.py       # Even after a new login,
you can still run the Python application using the file name only

Python Network Automation

[...omitted for brevity]
```

Expand Your Knowledge:

Further Advancing Your Linux Knowledge and Get Certified?

If you're interested in delving deeper into Linux, consider pursuing certifications like the Linux Professional Institute 101 (LPI 101) and Red Hat's RHCSA/RHCE. Numerous free and paid training programs are accessible both online and offline for those who have the time and resources. If you want to explore the LPI and RHCE certification tracks further, consult the following links.

Linux Professional Institute URL: `https://www.lpi.org/`

Red Hat Certified System Administrator (RHCSA) URL: `https://www.redhat.com/en/services/certification/rhcsa`

Red Hat Certified Engineer URL: `https://www.redhat.com/en/services/certification/rhce`

Summary

In this chapter, you embarked on a true journey into the heart of Linux, building a rock-solid foundation in essential files and directory management skills. While not every reader may aspire to become a dedicated Linux administrator, possessing a competent grasp of Linux is undeniably invaluable, particularly when navigating the intricate landscapes of complex production environments. Unfortunately, many Python Network Automation resources tend to overlook the significance of sound Linux administration skills. However, this chapter underscores the intrinsic connection between Linux, Python, and network automation, marking the first confident stride toward achieving success in your network automation endeavors. You've diligently laid the groundwork for your Linux journey, and rest assured, the real adventure has just begun. As you wrap up the file and directory exercises in this chapter, it's crucial to recognize that you've merely scratched the surface of Linux's capabilities. Yet, the knowledge you've acquired here is more than sufficient to tackle tasks in the forthcoming Python Network Automation labs. Remember, regular practice in Linux files and directory navigation is the key to mastery, so make it a habit in your daily work. It's in this environment that the true magic of Python Network Automation unfolds.

The next chapter covers vital Linux commands for finding crucial system information. As you say goodbye to Chapter 7, take pride in your progress in mastering Linux's core skills; this foundation will serve you well in the upcoming chapters. Get ready to explore more Linux insights and enhance your understanding as you dive deeper into the world of Python Network Automation.

CHAPTER 8

Linux Fundamentals II – TCP/IP Services

This chapter takes you deeper into the practical aspects of Linux OS administration, building on the foundational knowledge acquired in previous chapters. Whether you're a Linux novice looking to expand your expertise or an experienced user aiming to deepen your understanding, this chapter offers invaluable insights. Your journey begins by uncovering essential details about your Linux system, including crucial information about its kernel and distribution version, forming the bedrock of your Linux experience. Moving forward, you explore versatile commands like netstat, nc, and telnet. These are powerful tools that help validate and troubleshoot TCP/IP and UDP ports, diagnose network issues, and effectively manage your Linux network infrastructure. In addition to this, you delve into the installation and configuration of essential file transfer and time services, including TFTP, FTP, SFTP, and NTP services, all on a single Linux server. Mastering the setup of these services is a pivotal step on your path to becoming a proficient Linux administrator.

© Brendan Choi 2024
B. Choi, *Introduction to Python Network Automation Volume I - Laying the Groundwork*,
https://doi.org/10.1007/979-8-8688-0146-4_8

Warning

This book is a stepping stone—further your Linux education with additional reading!

In the realm of Linux literature, numerous books are available, some exclusively dedicated to specific Linux distributions or focused on particular services, often spanning hundreds of pages. In contrast, the goal in this book is to streamline your learning experience, providing a strong foundation for Python Network Automation. With just four chapters dedicated to Linux topics, I've carefully selected the most essential subjects to prepare you for your journey into network automation using Linux servers. If you're new to Linux and desire a deeper understanding of the Linux operating system, I recommend exploring specialized Linux books tailored to your specific needs. A brief search on Amazon.com reveals a wealth of well-written Linux books to choose from.

Information on Linux: Kernel and Distribution Version

Many new Linux users often begin their journey with a fundamental question: **How can I determine the precise version of my Linux distribution and the currently running kernel?** The Linux kernel serves as the cornerstone of a Linux operating system, acting as the crucial intermediary between the computer's hardware and its running processes. So, how can you check the versions of both the Linux kernel and the distribution running on your system? The exercises in this chapter are primarily centered on two popular distributions: Fedora (which is based on Red Hat) and Ubuntu (a Debian-based OS). Keep in mind that there may be some variations in command syntax due to the different distributions, causing certain commands to function on one distribution but not the other. If such discrepancies arise, I provide reminders. Nevertheless, it's important to note that, for the most part, Linux commands remain consistent across various distributions. Adjusting to these minor differences is an integral part of the learning process when using the operating system. Initially, the distinctions between Fedora and Ubuntu may seem vast, but in reality, these distributions share many similarities. Additionally, it's worth mentioning that this chapter delves into a broader array of Linux networking tools and their respective use cases. This expanded coverage is particularly relevant because a significant portion of readers have a keen interest in networking and troubleshooting network-related issues on their Linux systems.

In this chapter, you perform most tasks using your Fedora 38 (f38s1, IP: 192.168.127.10) server. Additionally, you may utilize the Ubuntu Server (u22s1, IP: 192.168.127.20) and your Windows host for specific testing purposes as you enable various IP services.

#	Fedora 38	Ubuntu 22
①	How can you check the Linux kernel version? Use the uname command with various options. uname commands provide information about your system; the commands used on Fedora and Ubuntu are identical for the uname command.	

```
[jdoe@f38s1 ~]$ uname --a
Linux f38s1.pynetauto.com 6.2.9-
300.fc38.x86_64 #1 SMP PREEMPT_
DYNAMIC Thu Mar 30 22:32:5
[jdoe@f38s1 ~]$ uname -s # OS name
Linux
[jdoe@f38s1 ~]$ uname -n # network
or hostname
f38s1.pynetauto.com
[jdoe@f38s1 ~]$ uname -r # kernel
version
6.2.9-300.fc38.x86_64
[jdoe@f38s1 ~]$ uname -v #
additional kernel detail
#1 SMP PREEMPT_DYNAMIC Thu Mar 30
22:32:58 UTC 2023
[jdoe@f38s1 ~]$ uname -m # processor
type
x86_64
[jdoe@f38s1 ~]$ uname -p
unknown
[jdoe@f38s1 ~]$ uname -i
unknown
[jdoe@f38s1 ~]$ uname -o # OS name
GNU/Linux
```

```
jdoe@u22s1:~$ uname --all
Linux u22s1.pynetauto.com
5.15.0-83-generic #92-Ubuntu SMP
Mon Aug 14 09:30:42 UTC 2023 x8
jdoe@u22s1:~$ uname -s
Linux
jdoe@u22s1:~$ uname -n
u22s1.pynetauto.com
jdoe@u22s1:~$ uname -r
5.15.0-83-generic
jdoe@u22s1:~$ uname -v
#92-Ubuntu SMP Mon Aug 14
09:30:42 UTC 2023
jdoe@u22s1:~$ uname -m
x86_64
jdoe@u22s1:~$ uname -p # processor
type/architecture
x86_64
jdoe@u22s1:~$ uname -I # hardware
platform/archi.
x86_64
jdoe@u22s1:~$ uname -o
GNU/Linux
```

(continued)

#	Fedora 38	Ubuntu 22

② The options for the uname command can be used in any combination. To view all available command options and obtain assistance, utilize the uname --help command.

| | ```
[jdoe@f38s1 ~]$ uname -nr
f38s1.pynetauto.com 6.2.9-300.fc38.
x86_64
[jdoe@f38s1 ~]$ uname -nv
f38s1.pynetauto.com #1 SMP PREEMPT_
DYNAMIC Thu Mar 30 22:32:58 UTC
2023
[jdoe@f38s1 ~]$ uname -vr
6.2.9-300.fc38.x86_64 #1 SMP
PREEMPT_DYNAMIC Thu Mar 30 22:32:58
UTC 2023
[jdoe@f38s1 ~]$ uname -nmv
f38s1.pynetauto.com #1 SMP PREEMPT_
DYNAMIC Thu Mar 30 22:32:58 UTC
2023 x86_64
``` | ```
jdoe@u22s1:~$ uname -nr
u22s1.pynetauto.com
5.15.0-83-generic
jdoe@u22s1:~$ uname -nv
u22s1.pynetauto.com #92-Ubuntu
SMP Mon Aug 14 09:30:42 UTC 2023
jdoe@u22s1:~$ uname -vr
5.15.0-83-generic #92-Ubuntu SMP
Mon Aug 14 09:30:42 UTC 2023
jdoe@u22s1:~$ uname -nmv
u22s1.pynetauto.com #92-Ubuntu
SMP Mon Aug 14 09:30:42 UTC 2023
x86_64
``` |

③ On the Fedora, CentOS, and Red Hat operating systems, you can also use the grep command to inspect the Grub Environment Block. Utilize the grep saved_entry /boot/grub2/grubenv command. Note that this command is not functional on Debian-based Linux distributions, as you can see on the right.

| | ```
[jdoe@f38s1 ~]$ sudo grep saved_
entry /boot/grub2/grubenv
[sudo] password for jdoe:
**************
saved_entry=cd2656d3f38240e59171e3c
eff1aba99-6.2.9-300.fc38.x86_64
``` | ```
jdoe@u22s1:~$ sudo grep saved_
entry /boot/grub2/grubenv
[sudo] password for jdoe:
**************
grep: /boot/grub2/grubenv: No
such file or directory
``` |

(continued)

#	Fedora 38	Ubuntu 22

④ Use hostnamectl to inspect the hostname, operating system, kernel version, architecture, and additional information.

```
[jdoe@f38s1 ~]$ hostnamectl
    Static hostname: f38s1.
    pynetauto.com
        Icon name: computer-vm
          Chassis: vm ⊟
       Machine ID: cd2656d3f38240e
       59171e3ceff1aba99
          Boot ID: 1368b688822c4eb4
          88633abdcedf4a5a
   Virtualization: vmware
 Operating System: Fedora Linux
 38 (Server Edition)
      CPE OS Name: cpe:/o:fedora
      project:fedora:38
   OS Support End: Tue 2024-05-14
OS Support Remaining: 7month 4w 1d
           Kernel: Linux 6.2.9-
           300.fc38.x86_64
     Architecture: x86-64
  Hardware Vendor: VMware, Inc.
   Hardware Model: VMware Virtual
 Platform
 Firmware Version: 6.00
    Firmware Date: Thu 2020-11-12
```

```
jdoe@u22s1:~$ hostnamectl
    Static hostname: u22s1.
    pynetauto.com
        Icon name: computer-vm
          Chassis: vm
       Machine ID: aa52429b78514
       6cdbb5ad36ce024b15b
          Boot ID: 6b3245a926bc44
          5283b79022319291f9
   Virtualization: vmware
 Operating System: Ubuntu 22.04.3
 LTS
           Kernel: Linux 5.15.0-83-
           generic
     Architecture: x86-64
  Hardware Vendor: VMware, Inc.
   Hardware Model: VMware Virtual
 Platform
```

(continued)

#	Fedora 38	Ubuntu 22

⑤ You can also verify your operating system using the lsb_release -d command. Unlike Ubuntu, Fedora does not come with LSB (Linux Standard Base) pre-installed. You can install it by executing the yum install -y redhat-lsb command or simply by running lsb_release -d and responding with Y when prompted to install it. You can also utilize the -sc and -a options to access additional information about your Linux operating system.

```
[jdoe@f38s1 ~]$ lsb_release -d
-bash: lsb_release: command not
found
[jdoe@f38s1 ~]$ sudo dnf install
redhat-lsb -y
[...omitted for brevity]
[jdoe@f38s1 ~]$ lsb_release -d
Description:    Fedora release 38
(Thirty Eight)
[jdoe@f38s1 ~]$ lsb_release -sc
ThirtyEight
[jdoe@f38s1 ~]$ lsb_release -a
LSB Version:      :core-4.1-
amd64:core-4.1-noarch:cxx-4.1-
amd64:cxx-4.1-noarch:desktop-4.1-
amd64:desktop-4.1-noarch:languages-
4.1-amd64:languages-4.1-
noarch:printing-4.1-amd64:printing-
4.1-noarch
Distributor ID: Fedora
Description:    Fedora release 38
(Thirty Eight)
Release:        38
Codename:       ThirtyEight
```

```
jdoe@u22s1:~$ lsb_release -d
Description:    Ubuntu 22.04.3
LTS
jdoe@u22s1:~$ lsb_release -sc
jammy
jdoe@u22s1:~$ lsb_release -a
No LSB modules are available.
Distributor ID: Ubuntu
Description:    Ubuntu 22.04.3
LTS
Release:        22.04
Codename:       jammy
```

(*continued*)

#	Fedora 38	Ubuntu 22

⑥ You can also use the cat command with a wildcard (*) to access additional system information from the /etc/ directory. Notably, this method is effective on both Linux distributions. To check the release version information of your Linux distribution, simply run the cat /etc/*release command. This cat command is valuable to remember, as it provides a wealth of information about your Linux operating system.

```
[jdoe@f38s1 ~]$ cat /etc/*release        jdoe@u22s1:~$ cat /etc/*release
c/*release                                DISTRIB_ID=Ubuntu
Fedora release 38 (Thirty Eight)          DISTRIB_RELEASE=22.04
NAME="Fedora Linux"                       DISTRIB_CODENAME=jammy
VERSION="38 (Server Edition)"             DISTRIB_DESCRIPTION="Ubuntu
ID=fedora                                 22.04.3 LTS"
VERSION_ID=38                             PRETTY_NAME="Ubuntu 22.04.3 LTS"
VERSION_CODENAME=""                       NAME="Ubuntu"
PLATFORM_ID="platform:f38"                VERSION_ID="22.04"
PRETTY_NAME="Fedora Linux 38              VERSION="22.04.3 LTS (Jammy
(Server Edition)"                         Jellyfish)"
ANSI_COLOR="0;38;2;60;110;180"            VERSION_CODENAME=jammy
LOGO=fedora-logo-icon                     ID=ubuntu
CPE_NAME="cpe:/                           ID_LIKE=debian
o:fedoraproject:fedora:38"                HOME_URL="https://www.ubuntu.
HOME_URL="https://fedoraproject.          com/"
org/"                                     SUPPORT_URL="https://help.ubuntu.
DOCUMENTATION_URL="https://docs.          com/"
fedoraproject.org/en-US/fedora/f38/       BUG_REPORT_URL="https://bugs.
system-administrators-guide/"             launchpad.net/ubuntu/"
SUPPORT_URL="https://ask.                 PRIVACY_POLICY_URL="https://
fedoraproject.org/"                       www.ubuntu.com/legal/terms-and-
[...omitted for brevity]                  policies/privacy-policy"
Fedora release 38 (Thirty Eight)          UBUNTU_CODENAME=jammy
```

(continued)

#	Fedora 38	Ubuntu 22

⑦ The `lscpu` command provides detailed information about the CPU, including its architecture, number of cores, threads, and other processor-related details.

```
[jdoe@f38s1 ~]$ lscpu
Architecture:                 x86_64
  CPU op-mode(s):  32-bit, 64-bit
  Address sizes:          45 bits
  physical, 48 bits virtual
  Byte Order:        Little Endian
CPU(s):                            1
  On-line CPU(s) list:   0
Vendor ID:
GenuineIntel
  Model name:             Intel(R)
Core(TM) i7-6700HQ CPU @ 2.60GHz
    CPU family:             6
    Model:                 94
    Thread(s) per core:  1
    Core(s) per socket:  1
    Socket(s):            1
    Stepping:             3
[...omitted for brevity]
```

```
jdoe@u22s1:~$ lscpu
Architecture:                 x86_64
  CPU op-mode(s):  32-bit, 64-bit
  Address sizes:          45 bits
physical, 48 bits virtual
  Byte Order:        Little Endian
CPU(s):                            2
  On-line CPU(s) list:   0,1
Vendor ID:              GenuineIntel
  Model name:              Intel(R)
Core(TM) i7-6700HQ CPU @ 2.60GHz
    CPU family:             6
    Model:                 94
    Thread(s) per core:  1
    Core(s) per socket:  1
    Socket(s):            2
    Stepping:             3
[...omitted for brevity]
```

⑧ Inxi is a versatile command-line system information tool for Linux, offering comprehensive hardware and software details. This makes it valuable for system diagnostics and information gathering. To use it, you must install it first, and the `inxi -F` command provides extensive system information.

```
# For Fedora server
[jdoe@f38s1 ~]$ sudo dnf install inxi -y
[...omitted for brevity]
[jdoe@f38s1 ~]$ inxi -F
System:
  Host: f38s1.pynetauto.com Kernel: 6.2.9-300.fc38.x86_64 arch: x86_64
  bits: 64 Console: pty pts/0
  Distro: Fedora release 38 (Thirty Eight)
```

(*continued*)

#	Fedora 38	Ubuntu 22

Machine:
  Type: Vmware System: VMware product: VMware Virtual Platform v: N/A
  serial: <superuser required>
  Mobo: Intel model: 440BX Desktop Reference Platform serial: <superuser
  required> BIOS: Phoenix
    v: 6.00 date: 11/12/2020
CPU:
  Info: single core model: Intel Core i7-6700HQ bits: 64 cache: L2: 256
  KiB
  Speed (MHz): 2592 min/max: N/A core: 1: 2592
Graphics:
  Device-1: VMware SVGA II Adapter driver: vmwgfx v: 2.20.0.0
  Display: unspecified server: N/A driver: gpu: vmwgfx tty: 110x67
  API: N/A Message: No display API data available in console. Headless
machine?
Audio:
  Device-1: Ensoniq ES1371/ES1373 / Creative Labs CT2518 driver: snd_
  ens1371
  API: ALSA v: k6.2.9-300.fc38.x86_64 status: kernel-api
Network:
  Device-1: Intel 82371AB/EB/MB PIIX4 ACPI type: network bridge driver:
  N/A
  Device-2: VMware VMXNET3 Ethernet driver: vmxnet3
  IF: ens160 state: up speed: 10000 Mbps duplex: full mac:
  00:0c:29:05:bc:8c
Drives:
  Local Storage: total: 60 GiB used: 3.05 GiB (5.1%)
  ID-1: /dev/nvme0n1 vendor: VMware model: Virtual NVMe Disk VMware NVME
  size: 60 GiB
Partition:
  ID-1: / size: 14.94 GiB used: 2.83 GiB (19.0%) fs: xfs dev: /dev/dm-0
  ID-2: /boot size: 960 MiB used: 224.8 MiB (23.4%) fs: xfs dev: /dev/
  nvme0n1p2

(*continued*)

#	Fedora 38	Ubuntu 22

Swap:

  ID-1: swap-1 type: zram size: 3.81 GiB used: O KiB (0.0%) dev: /dev/
  zramO
Sensors:

  Src: lm-sensors+/sys Message: No sensor data found using /sys/class/
  hwmon or lm-sensors.
Info:

  Processes: 163 Uptime: 1h 46m Memory: total: 4 GiB available: 3.81
  GiB used: 614.6 MiB (15.7%)
  Init: systemd target: multi-user (3) Shell: Bash inxi: 3.3.29
For Ubuntu server
jdoe@u22s1:~$ **sudo apt install inxi -y**
[...omitted for brevity]
jdoe@u22s1:~$ **inxi -F**
System:

  Host: u22s1.pynetauto.com Kernel: 5.15.0-83-generic x86_64 bits: 64
  Console: pty pts/O
    Distro: Ubuntu 22.04.3 LTS (Jammy Jellyfish)
[...omitted for brevity]

(*continued*)

#	Fedora 38	Ubuntu 22

⑨ Neofetch is a fun and informative command-line system information tool in Linux. It must be installed before, by using the neofetch command. When it runs, neofetch displays a graphical representation of system information (see Figures 8-1 and 8-2), including details about the operating system, kernel, CPU, GPU, memory, and more. It's often used to display system information in a visually appealing way and can be customized to match user preferences.

```
# For the Fedora server
[jdoe@f38s1 ~]$ neofetch
-bash: neofetch: command not found
[jdoe@f38s1 ~]$ sudo dnf install neofetch -y
[...omitted for brevity]
[jdoe@f38s1 ~]$ neofetch
```

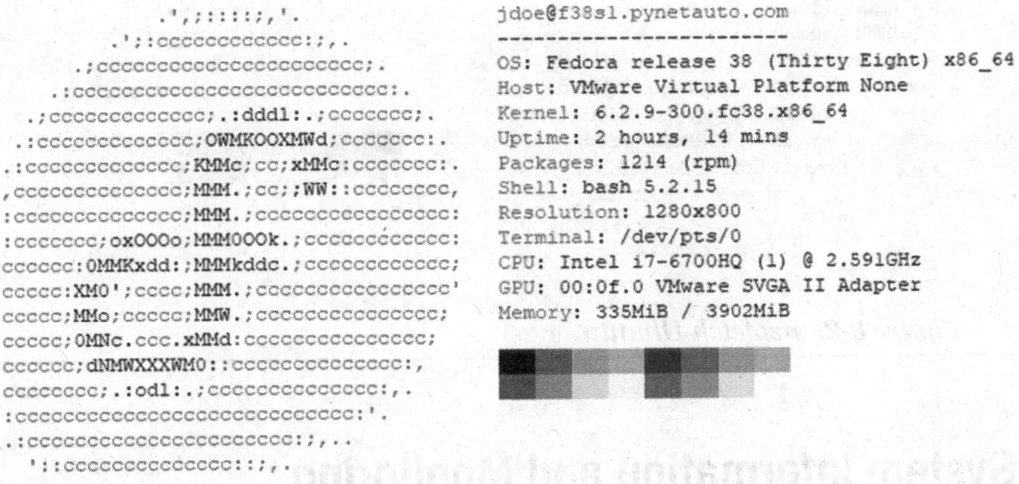

```
          .',;:::::;,'.                    jdoe@f38s1.pynetauto.com
       .';:cccccccccccc:;,.                -------------------------
    .;cccccccccccccccccccccc;.             OS: Fedora release 38 (Thirty Eight) x86_64
  .:cccccccccccccccccccccccccc:.           Host: VMware Virtual Platform None
.;cccccccccccc;.:dddl:.;ccccccc;.          Kernel: 6.2.9-300.fc38.x86_64
.:ccccccccccccc;OWMKOOXMWd;ccccccc:.       Uptime: 2 hours, 14 mins
.:ccccccccccccc;KMMc;cc;xMMc;ccccccc:.     Packages: 1214 (rpm)
,cccccccccccccc;MMM.;cc;;WW::cccccccc,     Shell: bash 5.2.15
:ccccccccccccc;MMM.;cccccccccccccccc:      Resolution: 1280x800
:ccccccc;ox0OOo;MMM0O0k.;ccccccccccc:      Terminal: /dev/pts/0
cccccc:0MMKxdd:;MMMkddc.;cccccccccccc;     CPU: Intel i7-6700HQ (1) @ 2.591GHz
ccccc:XMO';cccc;MMM.;cccccccccccccccc'     GPU: 00:0f.0 VMware SVGA II Adapter
ccccc;MMo;ccccc;MMW.;ccccccccccccccc;      Memory: 335MiB / 3902MiB
ccccc;0MNc.ccc.xMMd:cccccccccccccccc;
cccccc;dNMWXXXWM0::cccccccccccccccc:,
cccccccc;.:odl:.;ccccccccccccccc:,.
:cccccccccccccccccccccccccccccc:'.
.:ccccccccccccccccccccccc::;,...
  ':ccccccccccccccc::;,..
```

Figure 8-1. *neofetch Fedora*

(*continued*)

#	Fedora 38	Ubuntu 22

```
# For the Ubuntu server
jdoe@u22s1:~$ neofetch
Command 'neofetch' not found, but can be installed with:
sudo apt install neofetch
jdoe@u22s1:~$ sudo apt install neofetch -y
[...omitted for brevity]
jdoe@u22s1:~$ neofetch
```

```
              .-/+oossssoo+/-.               jdoe@u22s1.pynetauto.com
          ':+ssssssssssssssssss+:'           ------------------------
        -+ssssssssssssssssssyyssss+-         OS: Ubuntu 22.04.3 LTS x86_64
      .osssssssssssssssssssdMMMNysssso.      Host: VMware Virtual Platform None
     /ssssssssssshdmmNNmmyNMMMMhssssss/      Kernel: 5.15.0-83-generic
    +ssssssssshmydMMMMMMMNddddyssssssss+     Uptime: 2 hours, 12 mins
   /sssssssshNMMMyhhyyyyhmNMMMNhssssssss/    Packages: 1745 (dpkg), 4 (snap)
  .ssssssssdMMMNhsssssssssshNMMMdssssssss.   Shell: bash 5.1.16
  +sssshhhyNMMNysssssssssssssyNMMMysssssss+  Resolution: 800x600
  ossyNMMMNyMMhsssssssssssssshmmmhssssssso   Terminal: /dev/pts/0
  ossyNMMMNyMMhsssssssssssssshmmmhssssssso   CPU: Intel i7-6700HQ (2) @ 2.591GHz
  +sssshhhyNMMNysssssssssssssyNMMMysssssss+  GPU: 00:0f.0 VMware SVGA II Adapter
  .ssssssssdMMMNhsssssssssshNMMMdssssssss.   Memory: 696MiB / 3876MiB
   /sssssssshNMMMyhhyyyyhdNMMMNhssssssss/
    +sssssssssdmydMMMMMMMMddddyssssssss+
     /ssssssssssshdmNNNNmyNMMMMhssssss/
      .ossssssssssssssssssdMMMNysssso.
        -+sssssssssssssssssyyyssss+-
          ':+ssssssssssssssssss+:'
              .-/+oossssoo+/-.
```

Figure 8-2. *neofetch Ubuntu*

System Information and Monitoring

In the realm of system information and monitoring, there are several essential commands at your disposal. First, the hostname command provides the system's unique identifier, known as the hostname. If you need information about system uptime, user count, and load averages, you can turn to the uptime command. For a comprehensive view of disk space usage, including partition details in a human-readable format, the df -h command is your go-to choice. When it comes to memory usage, the free -m command displays statistics, including total, used, and free memory in megabytes. If you're interested in listing block devices such as disks and partitions, complete with their sizes and mount points, the lsblk command proves invaluable. Finally, for a detailed list of running processes, including user, process ID (PID), CPU use, and memory use, the ps aux command has you covered. These commands are essential tools for system administrators and users seeking to monitor and manage system resources effectively. Now, let's check out these commands on your Linux machine.

#	Task
①	hostname: Displays the system's unique identifier (hostname).

```
[jdoe@f38s1 ~]$ hostname
f38s1.pynetauto.com
```

| ② | uptime: Provides information about system uptime, user count, and load averages. |

```
[jdoe@f38s1 ~]$ uptime
14:13:39 up 3 min,  1 user,  load average: 0.46, 0.64, 0.30
```

| ③ | df -h: Shows disk space usage with partition details in a human-readable format. |

```
[jdoe@f38s1 ~]$ df -h
Filesystem              Size  Used Avail Use% Mounted on
devtmpfs                4.0M     0  4.0M   0% /dev
tmpfs                   2.0G     0  2.0G   0% /dev/shm
tmpfs                   781M  1.4M  780M   1% /run
/dev/mapper/fedora-root  15G  2.9G   13G  20% /
tmpfs                   2.0G     0  2.0G   0% /tmp
/dev/nvme0n1p2          960M  225M  736M  24% /boot
tmpfs                   391M  4.0K  391M   1% /run/user/1000
```

(continued)

#	Task

④ `free -m`: Displays memory usage, including total, used, and free memory in megabytes.

```
[jdoe@f38s1 ~]$ free -m
total      used    free     shared  buff/cache  available
Mem:       3902    269      3438    1           193         3417
Swap:      3901    0        3901
```

⑤ `lsblk`: Lists block devices such as disks and partitions, showing sizes and mount points. In Ubuntu, the disk name will be `sda`, and partition names will be something like `sda1`, `sda2`, `sda3`, In the case of a Red Hat Linux distribution like Fedora or CentOS Stream, the name of the disk takes the form of `nvme0n1`.

```
[jdoe@f38s1 ~]$ lsblk
NAME              MAJ:MIN RM  SIZE RO TYPE MOUNTPOINTS
sr0                11:0    1   2.3G  0 rom
zram0             252:0    0   3.8G  0 disk [SWAP]
nvme0n1           259:0    0   60G   0 disk
├─nvme0n1p1       259:1    0    1M   0 part
├─nvme0n1p2       259:2    0    1G   0 part /boot
└─nvme0n1p3       259:3    0   59G   0 part
  └─fedora-root   253:0    0   15G   0 lvm  /
```

⑥ `ps aux`: Lists running processes with user, PID, CPU, and memory usage details.

```
[jdoe@f38s1 ~]$ ps aux
USER        PID %CPU %MEM    VSZ    RSS TTY       STAT START   TIME
COMMAND
root          1  0.9  0.6 153112  26576 ?         Ss   14:10   0:03 /
usr/lib/systemd/systemd rhgb --switched-ro
root          2  0.0  0.0      0      0 ?         S    14:10   0:00
[kthreadd]
[...omitted for brevity]
```

(continued)

#	Task
⑦	systemctl list-units: Checks the running or inactive services on your Linux server. You can run the following systemctl list-units commands with the suggested options.

```
[jdoe@f38s1 ~]$ systemctl list-units --type=service --state=running
UNIT                        LOAD    ACTIVE SUB     DESCRIPTION
abrt-journal-core.service loaded active running ABRT coredumpctl
message creator
abrt-oops.service         loaded active running ABRT kernel log
watcher
[...omitted for brevity]
```

```
[jdoe@f38s1 ~]$ systemctl list-units --type=service --state=inactive
UNIT                        LOAD    ACTIVE   SUB  DESCRIPTION       >
abrt-vmcore.service        loaded  inactive dead ABRT kernel
panic detection
auth-rpcgss-module.service loaded  inactive dead Kernel Module
supporting RPCSEC_GSS
[...omitted for brevity]
```

#	Task
⑧	dmesg: Displays kernel ring buffer messages, providing insight into hardware-related issues. By running dmesg and piping it through less for easier navigation, you can access a log of kernel messages, including information about hardware components, errors, and system events, thus helping to diagnose and troubleshoot hardware problems.

```
[jdoe@f38s1 ~]$ dmesg | less
[    0.000000] Linux version 6.2.9-300.fc38.x86_64 (mockbuild@38f30b3c
0c69453fae61718fc43f33bc) (gcc (GCC) 13.0.1 20230318 (Red Hat 13.0.1-
0), GNU ld version 2.39-9.fc38) #1 SMP PREEMPT_DYNAMIC Thu Mar 30
22:32:58 UTC 2023
[...omitted for brevity]
[use Ctrl+Z to quit]
```

(continued)

#	Task

⑨ top/htop: The top and htop commands in Linux both monitor system processes, but they differ in user interface and functionality. top offers a basic, text-based interface with limited customization and updates its display every few seconds, typically around five seconds. On the other hand, htop provides an interactive, color-coded interface with real-time updates, detailed process information, and extensive customization options, refreshing its display at a faster rate, usually every second. htop offers a more user-friendly and flexible experience, making it a preferred choice for monitoring and managing processes on Linux systems.

```
[jdoe@f38s1 ~]$ sudo dnf install htop
[...omitted for brevity]
[jdoe@f38s1 ~]$ top
[...omitted for brevity] # use Ctrl+Z to quit
[jdoe@f38s1 ~]$ htop
[...omitted for brevity] # use Ctrl+Z to quit
```

Network administration, configuration, and troubleshooting differ among Linux OS, Windows OS, and vendor-specific devices like Cisco Routers, Palo Alto Firewalls, and Fortigate Firewalls. Linux and Windows operating systems serve different purposes in networking. Linux focuses on flexibility and customizability, often using command-line tools like ifconfig and iptables for configuration and troubleshooting. Windows offers a more user-friendly GUI, with tools like ipconfig and Network and Sharing Center. In contrast, vendor-specific devices, like Cisco routers and switches, are designed for dedicated networking tasks. They use proprietary operating systems and command-line interfaces (CLI) for configuration and troubleshooting. For example, Cisco devices use commands like show ip interface brief for network status. Palo Alto and Fortigate Firewalls have their own GUIs and CLIs for network and security configurations. Administrators use features like security policies and NAT rules to manage traffic and secure networks. While Linux servers aren't dedicated networking devices, administrators use similar networking concepts and troubleshooting techniques. Getting familiar with Linux networking commands is also beneficial for network professionals. Each platform serves unique purposes, and expertise in all three is valuable in modern-day network administration.

Linux Network Tools I: Introduction

This section focuses on the network troubleshooting exercises, where you delve into the essential realm of Linux commands and tools aimed at diagnosing and resolving network-related issues. This series of tasks is designed to empower you with the knowledge and skills necessary to navigate the intricacies of network troubleshooting. The ping command checks network connectivity by sending ICMP echo requests; traceroute is a tool that reveals the path that packets take to reach their destination, aiding in the diagnosis of network problems; netstat provides insights into network statistics and active connections; ss is a versatile alternative for socket statistics and network connection details; ifconfig and ip address show are essential commands for displaying network interface configurations and information; dig is a command-line utility used to query and retrieve information from DNS (Domain Name System) servers; and journalctl retrieves logs from the systemd journal, facilitating the viewing of system logs and troubleshooting system services. By the end of these exercises, you'll be well-equipped to tackle a variety of network challenges and optimize network performance.

First, let's quickly run each of these network commands on the f38s1 server and study their basic output. In the subsequent exercises, you delve deeper into some of these network commands.

#	Task
①	ping: This is a network utility that checks network connectivity to a host by sending ICMP (Internet Control Message Protocol) echo requests. In this task, you use Google's DNS server, 8.8.8.8, as the target. On a stable network, you should ideally receive a response from the target with 0% packet loss and 100% successful responses. You will deep dive into ping commands in the next section.

```
[jdoe@f38s1 ~]$ ping -c 4 8.8.8.8
PING 8.8.8.8 (8.8.8.8) 56(84) bytes of data.
64 bytes from 8.8.8.8: icmp_seq=1 ttl=128 time=14.3 ms
[...omitted for brevity]
--- 8.8.8.8 ping statistics ---
4 packets transmitted, 4 received, 0% packet loss, time 3004ms
rtt min/avg/max/mdev = 13.111/13.636/14.325/0.503 ms
```

(*continued*)

#	Task

(2)   `traceroute` (For Linux): Displays the route that packets take to reach a destination. This is used to diagnose network issues. This command also utilizes ICMP packets to trace the route to a destination host. On Windows systems, the equivalent command is `tracert`.

2-1. To test ICMP communication on your local network from your Windows Host PC, run `tracert 8.8.8.8`. You should receive a normal response if ICMP communication is allowed within your local network.

```
C:\Users\brend>tracert 8.8.8.8

Tracing route to dns.google [8.8.8.8]
over a maximum of 30 hops:
1     1 ms    <1 ms    <1 ms   mymodem.modem [192.168.0.1]
2    10 ms    10 ms    10 ms   gateway.nb11.sydney.asp.telstra.net
[58.162.26.75]
[...omitted for brevity]
8    10 ms    11 ms    11 ms   216.239.57.119
9    11 ms    11 ms    11 ms   dns.google [8.8.8.8]
```

2.2. Now, try running the `traceroute -I 8.8.8.8` command on your Fedora Server. Make sure to include the `-I` option to ensure you receive the final response from `dns.google`.

```
[jdoe@f38s1 ~]$ traceroute -I 8.8.8.8
traceroute to 8.8.8.8 (8.8.8.8), 30 hops max, 60 byte packets
1  _gateway (192.168.127.2)  1.222 ms *  0.457 ms
2  * * *
3  * * *
[...omitted for brevity]
9  * * *
10  dns.google (8.8.8.8)  17.041 ms  16.880 ms  16.292 ms
```

You are currently utilizing NAT (Network Address Translation) in the VMware settings. When you execute a `traceroute` command from a virtual machine (VM) running behind NAT on a Windows host PC, the VM sends ICMP echo requests to the destination with varying Time to Live (TTL) values, representing the number of hops. However, due to the NAT configuration in VMware Workstation, the Windows 11 host receives the responding ICMP packets but is not configured to relay traceroute details to the VM console. This behavior is not uncommon and should not be interpreted as an issue with your network configuration.

(continued)

#	Task

③ netstat: Displays network statistics and active network connections. You can delve into the wealth of information it offers through various options. These commands provide valuable insights into network connections, routing, interface statistics, and more. You can explore the specific details by executing these commands on your Linux system and reviewing the output.

```
[jdoe@f38s1 ~]$ netstat -tuln # TCP, UDP, listening, IP/port
[...omitted for brevity]
[jdoe@f38s1 ~]$ netstat -tulp # TCP, UDP, listening, PID/program
[...omitted for brevity]
[jdoe@f38s1 ~]$ netstat -tua # TCP, UDP, all sockets
[...omitted for brevity]
[jdoe@f38s1 ~]$ netstat -tuna # TCP, UDP, IP/port, all sockets
[...omitted for brevity]
```

While I won't delve into the output of these commands in detail here, I cover this topic more comprehensively later. To become familiar with these commands, take a few moments to execute them and examine the resulting output. Run man netstat and netstat --help to review and get familiar with this network utility.

④ ss (Socket Statistics): This Linux network tool replaces the older netstat tool. Just like its predecessor, the ss serves the purpose of displaying network-related information, but it also provides more advanced network diagnostics and analysis with a richer feature set and performance.

Like the more familiar netstat tool, in the context of network socket inspection using the ss command on a Linux system, you can use several command options to retrieve specific socket-related information. For instance, you can use the ss -a command to list all sockets, regardless of their current status. If you are interested in exclusively viewing listening sockets that are actively waiting for incoming connections, ss -l is the appropriate command. Furthermore, ss -t allows you to focus solely on TCP sockets, while ss -u is used to display UDP sockets. To obtain a summary of socket statistics, such as the number of sockets in different states, ss -s provides a concise overview. Additionally, ss -x helps identify UNIX domain sockets, ss -4 filters for IPv4 sockets, and ss -6 isolates IPv6 sockets. Lastly, ss -o is used to reveal various timers associated with TCP sockets, aiding in network performance analysis and troubleshooting. These ss commands serve as valuable tools for network administrators and engineers to gain insights into network connections and socket-related details.

(continued)

#	Task

4-1. Execute ss commands with single options.

```
[jdoe@f38s1 ~]$ ss -a # list all sockets
[jdoe@f38s1 ~]$ ss -l # list listening sockets
[jdoe@f38s1 ~]$ ss -t # display TCP sockets
[jdoe@f38s1 ~]$ ss -u # display UDP sockets
[jdoe@f38s1 ~]$ ss -s # display summary statistics
[jdoe@f38s1 ~]$ ss -x # show Unix domain sockets
[jdoe@f38s1 ~]$ ss -4 # display Ipv4 sockets
[jdoe@f38s1 ~]$ ss -6 # display Ipv6 sockets
[jdoe@f38s1 ~]$ ss -o # show timers for TCP sockets
```

By executing ss commands with various combinations of options, you will get extensive insight into network socket details, connections, routing, and more. The flexibility and comprehensiveness of the ss command makes it a preferred choice for network administrators and engineers, enabling them to effectively manage and troubleshoot network-related issues. The ss tool inherits and builds on many of the options and functionalities originally found in the netstat tool.

4-2. Here are some examples. Execute and explore these ss commands with various options.

```
[jdoe@f38s1 ~]$ ss -t -i # show detailed socket information
[jdoe@f38s1 ~]$ ss -t -p # show PID and process information
[jdoe@f38s1 ~]$ ss -tuln # list all TCP, UDP, and listening sockets and
numerical addresses
[jdoe@f38s1 ~]$ ss -tua # list all TCP and UDP sockets
[jdoe@f38s1 ~]$ ss -t -l -n -p '( sport = :22 )' # show details of the
socket with source port 22 (SSH)
[jdoe@f38s1 ~]$ ss -t -a -n | grep ESTAB # list all established TCP
connections, expand your knowledge by studying other states
```

(continued)

#	Task

⑤   ifconfig/ip addr show: The ifconfig and ip addr show commands provide network interface details on Linux. ifconfig displays interface info, including flags, MTU, IP, netmask, and broadcast. ip addr show provides similar data with additional details like state, MAC address, and scope. Both commands are vital for configuring, monitoring, and troubleshooting network connections on Linux systems, helping to ensure proper connectivity and diagnose network problems.

```
[jdoe@f38s1 ~]$ ifconfig
ens160: flags=4163<UP,BROADCAST,RUNNING,MULTICAST>  mtu 1500
inet 192.168.127.10  netmask 255.255.255.0  broadcast 192.168.127.255
[...omitted for brevity]
lo: flags=73<UP,LOOPBACK,RUNNING>  mtu 65536
inet 127.0.0.1  netmask 255.0.0.0
[...omitted for brevity]

[jdoe@f38s1 ~]$ ip address show
1: lo: <LOOPBACK,UP,LOWER_UP> mtu 65536 qdisc noqueue state UNKNOWN
group default qlen 1000
link/loopback 00:00:00:00:00:00 brd 00:00:00:00:00:00
inet 127.0.0.1/8 scope host lo
[...omitted for brevity]
2: ens160: <BROADCAST,MULTICAST,UP,LOWER_UP> mtu 1500 qdisc fq_codel
state UP group default qlen 1000
link/ether 00:0c:29:05:bc:8c brd ff:ff:ff:ff:ff:ff
altname enp3s0
inet 192.168.127.10/24 brd 192.168.127.255 scope global noprefixroute
ens160
[...omitted for brevity]
```

(continued)

#	Task

⑥ dig (Domain Information Groper): A tool for querying DNS servers. It retrieves information about domain names, such as IP addresses, DNS records, and name server details. It is a valuable tool for troubleshooting and analyzing domain-related data.

```
[jdoe@f38s1 ~]$ dig # Default DNS query
[jdoe@f38s1 ~]$ dig www.google.com # Query for 'www.google.com'.
[jdoe@f38s1 ~]$ dig MX www.google.com # Query MX records for 'www.
google.com'.
[jdoe@f38s1 ~]$ dig -x 8.8.8.8  # Reverse lookup for '8.8.8.8'.
[jdoe@f38s1 ~]$ dig @8.8.4.4 www.google.com # Specify DNS server
(8.8.4.4), query 'www.google.com'.
[jdoe@f38s1 ~]$ dig +dnssec www.google.com # Request DNSSEC data for
'www.google.com'.
[jdoe@f38s1 ~]$ dig +short www.google.com # Display IP only for 'www.
google.com'.
```

⑦ journalctl: A Linux command that retrieves logs from the systemd journal, providing a valuable tool for viewing system logs and troubleshooting system services. The example output displays kernel-related logs, showing details like the Linux version, kernel command line, and specific events. It's a crucial resource for monitoring system health and diagnosing issues, making it an essential utility for system administrators.

```
[jdoe@f38s1 ~]$ journalctl
Aug 15 23:59:45 localhost kernel: Linux version 6.2.9-300.fc38.x86_64
(mockbuild@38f30b3c0c69453fae61718fc43f>
Aug 15 23:59:45 localhost kernel: Command line: BOOT_IMAGE=(hd0,gpt2)/
vmlinuz-6.2.9-300.fc38.x86_64 root=/dev>
[...omitted for brevity]
```

Linux Network Tools II: Packet INternet Groper (Ping)

If you are reading this book, you are likely already familiar with the general purpose of the ping command. The term "ping" in the context of computer networking comes from the sonar analogy used in submarines. Ping is an abbreviation that stands for "Packet INternet Groper." However, have you ever delved into the meanings of the responses or attempted to simulate them to understand why certain ICMP messages are returned? In the context of network troubleshooting, the ping command serves as a versatile tool for assessing network connectivity between your computer and a destination node. When using this command on Linux servers, you will encounter five distinct responses, each with its own significance. To gain a deeper understanding and simulate various ping response scenarios, let's explore different network troubleshooting scenarios. This hands-on exercise is designed to clarify and solidify your knowledge.

Now, let's quickly simulate the five most common ping response scenarios using f38s1 (192.168.127.10), u22s1 (192.168.127.20), and your Windows host PC. Ensure that both VMs are powered on and connected to the Internet.

#	Task

① **Successful ping response**: On your Fedora 38s1 server, execute the ping -c 4 www. google.com command. The output should include details such as the IP address of the target host, the size of the ICMP packets sent and received, and the response time (measured in milliseconds). The response time represents the time it took for the packet to travel to the target host and back.

Use ping 0 to test ping to localhost
```
[jdoe@f38s1 ~]$ ping 0 # this command pings localhost, use Ctrl+Z or
Ctrl+C to stop
PING 0 (127.0.0.1) 56(84) bytes of data.
64 bytes from 127.0.0.1: icmp_seq=1 ttl=64 time=0.085 ms
[...omitted for brevity]
```

Use the '-c' option to control the packet numbers.
```
[jdoe@f38s1 ~]$ ping -c 4 www.google.com
PING www.google.com (172.217.24.36) 56(84) bytes of data.
64 bytes from hkg07s23-in-f4.1e100.net (172.217.24.36): icmp_seq=1
ttl=128 time=13.7 ms
[...omitted for brevity]
```

Use '-v' to enable the verbose option for more information.
```
[jdoe@f38s1 ~]$ ping -v -c 4 8.8.8.8
ping: sock4.fd: 3 (socktype: SOCK_DGRAM), sock6.fd: 4 (socktype: SOCK_
DGRAM), hints.ai_family: AF_UNSPEC
ai->ai_family: AF_INET, ai->ai_canonname: '8.8.8.8'
PING 8.8.8.8 (8.8.8.8) 56(84) bytes of data.
64 bytes from 8.8.8.8: icmp_seq=1 ttl=128 time=14.4 ms
[...omitted for brevity]
```

Use the '-q' option only to view the ping statistics.
```
[jdoe@f38s1 ~]$ ping -q -c 4 8.8.8.8
PING 8.8.8.8 (8.8.8.8) 56(84) bytes of data.

--- 8.8.8.8 ping statistics ---
4 packets transmitted, 4 received, 0% packet loss, time 3013ms
rtt min/avg/max/mdev = 14.477/16.703/18.138/1.353 ms
```

(continued)

#	Task

② **Request timed out:** When you encounter Request timed out in the Windows command prompt, it indicates that the ping command sent ICMP echo requests to the target host but did not receive any response within the specified timeout period. This can happen for various reasons, including network congestion, firewall settings, or the target host being offline.

2-1. To replicate this scenario, execute the following iptables command on the u22s1 server to block (drop) incoming ping (ICMP) messages. This command can be used on both Fedora and Ubuntu Servers to drop ICMP packets, essentially making the server unresponsive to ping probes. If prompted, enter your sudo password.

```
jdoe@u22s1:~$ sudo iptables -A INPUT -p icmp --icmp-type
echo-request -j DROP
```

2-2. To verify the outcome of this command, open the command prompt on your Windows host and execute the ping command directed at the u22s1 server. If the packets are dropped, you will receive Request timed out responses.

```
C:\Users\brend>ping 192.168.127.20

Pinging 192.168.127.20 with 32 bytes of data:
Request timed out.
[...omitted for brevity]
Ping statistics for 192.168.127.20:
Packets: Sent = 4, Received = 0, Lost = 4 (100% loss),
```

2-3. To confirm the same result from another Linux server, in this case, the f38s1 server, execute the ping command directed at the u22s1 server and wait for the ping operation to finish. Unlike Windows, the Linux server will not display the Request timed out message; rather, u22s1 will silently drop the ping packets originating from the f38s1 server.

```
[jdoe@f38s1 ~]$ ping -c 4 192.168.127.20
PING 192.168.127.20 (192.168.127.20) 56(84) bytes of data.

--- 192.168.127.20 ping statistics ---
4 packets transmitted, 0 received, 100% packet loss, time 3077ms
```

(*continued*)

#	Task

2-4. To test the `ping` command from the u22s1 server, send `ping` requests to the f38s1 server, as shown here. Normal `ping` behavior will occur and remain unaffected.

```
jdoe@u22s1:~$ ping -c 4 192.168.127.10
PING 192.168.127.10 (192.168.127.10) 56(84) bytes of data.
64 bytes from 192.168.127.10: icmp_seq=1 ttl=64 time=1.59 ms
[...omitted for brevity]
--- 192.168.127.10 ping statistics ---
4 packets transmitted, 4 received, 0% packet loss, time 3004ms
rtt min/avg/max/mdev = 0.771/1.451/1.784/0.399 ms
```

2-5. To remove the packet loss rule on f38s1 and restore normal `ping` behavior, run the following reverse command. If you are prompted to enter your `sudo` password, do so.

```
[jdoe@f38s1 ~]$ sudo iptables -D INPUT -p icmp --icmp-type echo-request -j DROP
```

System and network engineers often disable ICMP packets in their networks to safeguard their operating environments, and firewalls operate on the same theoretical basis. Now you've gained basic insights into how probing ICMP packets are dropped on Linux and other network devices.

(continued)

#	Task

③ **Destination host unreachable**: When the ping command is unable to reach the target host due to the destination host being considered unreachable, you will receive a Destination Host Unreachable ICMP response. This situation can occur due to network routing issues, misconfigured network settings, or the nonexistence of the target host.

To demonstrate this scenario, you can execute the ping command on your f38s1 server targeting a nonexistent server IP, such as 192.168.127.55.

```
[jdoe@f38s1 ~]$ ping -c 4 192.168.127.55
PING 192.168.127.55 (192.168.127.55) 56(84) bytes of data.
From 192.168.127.10 icmp_seq=1 Destination Host Unreachable
[...omitted for brevity]
--- 192.168.127.55 ping statistics ---
4 packets transmitted, 0 received, +4 errors, 100% packet loss, time
3068ms
pipe 4
```

On your host PC, execute a ping command and observe the distinctions between Linux and Windows.

```
C:\Users\brend>ping 192.168.127.55

Pinging 192.168.127.55 with 32 bytes of data:
Reply from 192.168.127.1: Destination host unreachable.
Request timed out.
[...omitted for brevity]
Ping statistics for 192.168.127.55:
Packets: Sent = 4, Received = 1, Lost = 3 (75% loss),
```

If you see the Destination Host Unreachable message with uppercase H and U, it originates from a Linux-based server. Conversely, if the output contains Destination host unreachable with lowercase h and u, it is a Windows output. Additionally, Windows reports 75% packet loss, whereas Linux reports 100% packet loss from the ping test.

(*continued*)

#	Task

④ **TTL exceeded**: `Time to live exceeded` means that the ICMP packet reached a router (in this example, `www.google.com` or 172.217.24.36), but the router's Time to Live (TTL) value was decremented to zero. Routers decrement the TTL for each hop they traverse, and if the TTL reaches zero, the packet is discarded. This response can help you identify network routing issues.

In most Linux distributions, the default TTL (Time to Live) value for the `ping` command is 64, while in Windows, the default TTL value for the `ping` command is typically 128. This value signifies the maximum number of network hops a packet can make before being discarded. It's important to note that TTL is not a measure of time in seconds or milliseconds. Instead, as a packet is forwarded through routers or network hops, the TTL value decreases by one. If it reaches zero, the packet is discarded, and an ICMP `Time to Live Exceeded` message is sent back to the source. With a TTL value of 64, a packet can traverse up to 64 network hops. However, the actual time it takes for the packet to reach its destination depends on network routing and router processing speed. TTL can serve as a mechanism to prevent endless packet circulation due to routing issues.

To simulate this scenario and analyze the output, execute the following `ping` command from the `f38s1` server to ping `www.google.com` with a reduced TTL value of 1 (using the `-t 1` option).

```
[jdoe@f38s1 ~]$ ping -c 4 -t 1 www.google.com
PING www.google.com (172.217.24.36) 56(84) bytes of data.
From _gateway (192.168.127.2) icmp_seq=1 Time to live exceeded
[...omitted for brevity]
--- www.google.com ping statistics ---
4 packets transmitted, 0 received, +4 errors, 100% packet loss, time
3006ms
```

It's important to use the `-t 1` option for this test, because setting the TTL value to 2 or greater would allow the packets to reach their destination, and the `Time to live exceeded` message would not be generated.

(*continued*)

#	Task
⑤	**Unknown host:** When you attempt to ping a host that doesn't exist or has an invalid hostname, you'll receive an unknown host error. This error indicates that the hostname you specified couldn't be resolved to an IP address.

To emulate the Unknown Host scenario, you can use the ping command with a hostname that doesn't exist or has an invalid hostname. Here's how you can do it on your Fedora and Ubuntu Servers:

The server name ubuntu22server1 does not exist on the Fedora Server (f38s1):

```
[jdoe@f38s1 ~]$ ping -c 4 ubuntu22server1
ping: ubuntu22server1: Name or service not known
```

In the same manner, the server name edora38server1 does not exist on the Ubuntu Server (u22s1):

```
jdoe@u22s1:~$ ping -c 4 fedora38server1
ping: fedora38server1: Temporary failure in name resolution
```

The hostnames provided could not be resolved to an IP address because they do not exist. This emulates the Unknown Host scenario in both Ubuntu and Fedora.

Additionally, if you want to perform a successful ping to a valid host, you should ensure that the hostname is properly defined in the /etc/hosts file, or if you are using a DNS, add the entry to your DNS. If you missed this step, refer back to the previous chapter for instructions on modifying the local host file.

```
[jdoe@f38s1 ~]$ ping -c 4 u22s1
PING u22s1 (192.168.127.20) 56(84) bytes of data.
64 bytes from u22s1 (192.168.127.20): icmp_seq=1 ttl=64 time=1.54 ms
[...omitted for brevity]
--- u22s1 ping statistics ---
4 packets transmitted, 4 received, 0% packet loss, time 3005ms
rtt min/avg/max/mdev = 1.543/1.715/1.863/0.115 ms
```

While using the ping commands, you've simulated these five common responses. Additionally, beyond these common responses, two other scenarios to explore are *packet loss,* where some packets are lost during transmission, often due to network congestion, excessive hops, or target host/network issues, and *ping flood,* which represents an aggressive ping test used for network stress-testing and provides statistics about packet transmission and round-trip times.

Expand Your Knowledge:

Update Kernel Parameters to Control the Behavior

In most Linux distributions, you can use the sysctl command to control various kernel parameters, including those related to network settings. The following commands can be used to drop incoming ICMP echo requests (ping requests) and then reverse that configuration.

Drop incoming pings: This command sets the kernel parameter net.ipv4. icmp_echo_ignore_all to 1. When this parameter is set to 1, it means the system will ignore (drop) all incoming ICMP echo requests, effectively blocking incoming pings. This can be useful for enhancing security or reducing network noise.

```
$ sudo sysctl -w net.ipv4.icmp_echo_ignore_all=1
```

Reverse the configuration (allow incoming pings):

This command reverses the previous configuration by setting the net.ipv4. icmp_echo_ignore_all parameter back to 0. When set to 0, the system will no longer ignore incoming ICMP echo requests, allowing incoming pings to be processed and responded to as usual.

```
$ sudo sysctl -w net.ipv4.icmp_echo_ignore_all=0
```

These commands provide a way to temporarily control the behavior of the Linux kernel regarding ICMP echo requests. By changing the value of net.ipv4. icmp_echo_ignore_all, you can either allow or block incoming pings on the system. It's important to use this functionality thoughtfully, considering security and network monitoring needs.

Linux Network Tools III: Trace Route (traceroute)

The traceroute tool is a valuable networking tool used to trace the route that packets take from your computer to a destination host. It helps you understand the path that data packets follow through the network, revealing the intermediate routers or hops along the way. Traceroute is particularly useful for diagnosing network routing issues, identifying slow or problematic network segments, and understanding the network path between your computer and a remote host. In contrast, the ping command, while related, serves a different purpose.

The following tasks were performed on a separate PC running Ubuntu 22 LTS. If you have a spare laptop/PC, install your favorite Linux distribution and run the commands. You can still run these commands on your VMs, but it will not give you the same result due to the Microsoft firewall.

#	Task
①	**Basic traceroute to a host**: Traces the route to the specified host, showing each hop's IP address and response time.

```
brendan@Precision-T1650:~$ traceroute dns.google
traceroute to dns.google (8.8.8.8), 64 hops max
1    192.168.0.1  0.764ms   1.030ms   1.144ms
[...omitted for brevity]
7    *  *  *
8    142.251.64.179  12.325ms   10.178ms   10.544ms
9    8.8.8.8  9.933ms   14.212ms   9.745ms
```

#	Task
②	**Traceroute with maximum hops**: Specifies the maximum number of hops the traceroute should attempt.

```
brendan@Precision-T1650:~$ traceroute -m 30 google.com
traceroute to google.com (142.250.76.110), 30 hops max
1    192.168.0.1  1.534ms   0.729ms   0.717ms
[...omitted for brevity]
7    *  *  *
8    142.251.64.178  10.923ms   10.763ms   11.600ms
9    142.250.76.110  10.879ms   11.070ms   9.884ms
```

(continued)

#	Task

③ **Use ICMP echo requests**: Forces the use of ICMP echo requests (like `ping`) instead of UDP packets.

```
brendan@Precision-T1650:~$ traceroute -I google.com
traceroute to google.com (142.250.76.110), 64 hops max
1    192.168.0.1  0.826ms  0.716ms  0.687ms
[...omitted for brevity]
7    108.170.247.65  11.161ms  11.026ms  16.436ms
8    142.250.212.137  12.082ms  12.597ms  12.904ms
9    142.250.76.110  14.085ms  11.236ms  11.548ms
```

④ **Specify source IP address**: Specifies a source IP address for the `traceroute`.

```
brendan@Precision-T1650:~$ traceroute -s 192.168.127.20 dns.google
[...omitted for brevity]
```

If you want to test similar commands from your Windows Host PC, you can use the `tracert` command with the options specified in the `tracert` usage. Simply type `tracert` into your Windows Command Prompt and press the Enter key to reveal the usage and options.

Information on Linux: Use the netstat Command to Validate TCP/UDP Ports

To prepare you for the IP services installation—enabling your Linux servers to be useful for this lab and applying what you have learned—you must first learn how to use various Linux IP Services on the network. Because all devices connect to each network segment, it's crucial to identify open and closed ports. In essence, understanding which IP services are running and available to users contributes to server network security and network access control. Let's explore how you can check network ports and protocols running on your Linux systems.

Log in to f38s1 via SSH and perform the following tasks to gain more hands-on practice.

#	Task

① First, to obtain a list of all network interfaces on your Linux server, use the `netstat -i` command.

```
[jdoe@f38s1 ~]$ netstat -i
Kernel Interface table
Iface   MTU   RX-OK  RX-ERR RX-DRP RX-OVR  TX-OK TX-ERR TX-DRP TX-OVR
Flg
ens160  1500  12052      0      0 0        9980      0      0      0 BMRU
lo      65536    55      0      0 0          55      0      0      0 LRU
```

② To practice `netstat` commands, install the Nginx web server on the Fedora Server and start the web service. After starting Nginx, run the `netstat -tulpn | grep :80` command to confirm that your Fedora Server is listening on port 80 on the local interface.

Install, check installation, and start the nginx web services on the `f38s1` server. When prompted, input your sudo password.

```
[jdoe@f38s1 ~]$ sudo dnf install -y nginx # If prompted, enter your
sudo password
[...omitted for brevity]
```

```
[jdoe@f38s1 ~]$ whatis nginx
nginx (3pm)      - Perl interface to the nginx HTTP server API
nginx (8)        - "HTTP and reverse proxy server, mail proxy server"
```

```
[jdoe@f38s1 ~]$ whereis nginx
nginx: /usr/sbin/nginx /usr/lib64/nginx /etc/nginx /usr/share/nginx /
usr/share/man/man3/nginx.3pm.gz /usr/share/man/man8/nginx.8.gz
```

On Fedora, Nginx gets installed but requires manual starting and enabling. Because you only need Nginx for this chapter, you will start the service but not enable it. When a service is enabled on a Linux server, it automatically starts during the boot-up process.

```
[jdoe@f38s1 ~]$ systemctl start nginx
==== AUTHENTICATING FOR org.freedesktop.systemd1.manage-units ====
Authentication is required to start 'nginx.service'.
Authenticating as: John Doe (jdoe)
Password: ***************
```

(continued)

#	Task

==== AUTHENTICATION COMPLETE ====

[jdoe@f38s1 ~]$ **systemctl status nginx**

● nginx.service - The nginx HTTP and reverse proxy server
Loaded: loaded (/usr/lib/systemd/system/nginx.service; disabled;
preset: disabled)
Drop-In: /usr/lib/systemd/system/service.d
└─10-timeout-abort.conf
Active: active (running) since Mon 2023-09-25 16:48:11 AEST; 3s ago
Process: 2522 ExecStartPre=/usr/bin/rm -f /run/nginx.pid (code=exited,
status=0/SUCCESS)
[...*omitted for brevity*]

Run the following netstat command to check if the server is listening on port 80 for an HTTP connection.

[jdoe@f38s1 ~]$ **netstat -tulpn | grep :80**
(Not all processes could be identified, non-owned process info
will not be shown, you would have to be root to see it all.)
tcp   0   0 0.0.0.0:80   0.0.0.0:*   LISTEN   -
tcp6   0   0 :::80   :::*   LISTEN   -

(continued)

#	Task

③ To permanently allow HTTP connections on port 80 to reach the web services, add the HTTP service to the Fedora firewall's services list. Some refer to this process as punching the hole for a service. Then, verify that the firewall service is running correctly to allow HTTP connections on port 80. To apply the changes, you must reload the firewall service using the `firewall-cmd --reload` command. Here are the full steps:

```
[jdoe@f38s1 ~]$ sudo firewall-cmd --permanent --add-service=http # If
prompted, enter your sudo password
success
[jdoe@f38s1 ~]$ sudo firewall-cmd --permanent --list-all
FedoraServer
target: default
icmp-block-inversion: no
[...omitted for brevity]
[jdoe@f38s1 ~]$ sudo firewall-cmd --reload
success
```

You haven't provisioned a DNS server in your network, so you need to use the server's IP address. While you already know that the server's IP is 192.168.127.10, for the sake of learning a new command, you can verify this information by running the following command. Alternatively, you can use the `ip addr` command to browse through the information.

```
[jdoe@f38s1 ~]$ ip addr show ens160 | grep inet | awk '{ print $2; }'
| sed 's/\/.*$//'
192.168.127.10
fe80::20c:29ff:fe05:bc8c
[jdoe@f38s1 ~]$ ip address show ens160
2: ens160: <BROADCAST,MULTICAST,UP,LOWER_UP> mtu 1500 qdisc fq_codel
state UP group default qlen 1000
link/ether 00:0c:29:05:bc:8c brd ff:ff:ff:ff:ff:ff
altname enp3s0
```

(continued)

509

#	Task

```
inet 192.168.127.10/24 brd 192.168.127.255 scope global noprefixroute
ens160
valid_lft forever preferred_lft forever
inet6 fe80::20c:29ff:fe05:bc8c/64 scope link noprefixroute
valid_lft forever preferred_lft forever
```

At this point, if you open your favorite web browser on your Windows host PC, you will be able to access the Fedora Nginx test page using http://192.168.127.10, as shown in Figure 8-3.

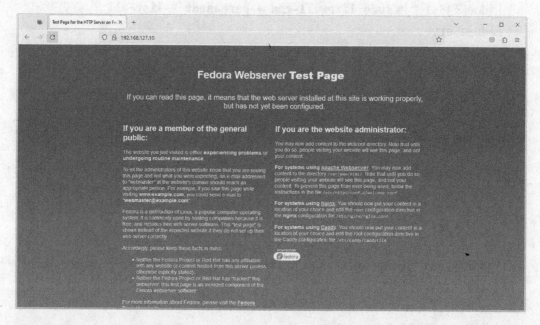

Figure 8-3. *Open the Nginx test page on your Windows host's web browser*

(continued)

#	Task

④ To list all the TCP or UDP ports on your Linux server, you can use the netstat -a command; the -a option stands for all. You can specify the -t option for TCP ports only or the -u option for UDP ports in use.

For TCP:

```
[jdoe@f38s1 ~]$ netstat -at
Active Internet connections (servers and established)
Proto Recv-Q Send-Q Local Address          Foreign Address         State
tcp         0      0 0.0.0.0:http           0.0.0.0:*               LISTEN
tcp         0      0 0.0.0.0:ssh            0.0.0.0:*               LISTEN
[...omitted for brevity]
```

For UDP:

```
[jdoe@f38s1 ~]$ netstat -au
Active Internet connections (servers and established)
Proto Recv-Q Send-Q Local Address          Foreign Address         State
udp         0      0 0.0.0.0:mdns           0.0.0.0:*
udp         0      0 0.0.0.0:hostmon        0.0.0.0:*
[...omitted for brevity]
```

⑤ If you want to list only the listening ports, you can use netstat -l. The list was too long, so the following output only shows the top of the listening port information. Run this command on your Fedora VM and study the returned result.

```
[jdoe@f38s1 ~]$ netstat -l
Active Internet connections (only servers)
Proto Recv-Q Send-Q Local Address          Foreign Address         State
tcp         0      0 0.0.0.0:http           0.0.0.0:*               LISTEN
tcp         0      0 0.0.0.0:ssh            0.0.0.0:*               LISTEN
tcp         0      0 _localdnsstub:domain   0.0.0.0:*               LISTEN
tcp         0      0 0.0.0.0:hostmon        0.0.0.0:*               LISTEN
[...omitted for brevity]
```

(continued)

#	Task
⑥	Similar to the netstat -a command, netstat -l can also be combined with the -t or -u option to filter TCP or UDP information, respectively. netstat -lt will list only TCP listening ports, while netstat -lu will list only UDP listening ports.

```
[jdoe@f38s1 ~]$ netstat -lt
Active Internet connections (only servers)
Proto Recv-Q Send-Q Local Address            Foreign Address        State
tcp        0      0 0.0.0.0:http             0.0.0.0:*              LISTEN
tcp        0      0 0.0.0.0:ssh              0.0.0.0:*              LISTEN
[...omitted for brevity]
[jdoe@f38s1 ~]$ netstat -lu
Active Internet connections (only servers)
Proto Recv-Q Send-Q Local Address            Foreign Address        State
udp        0      0 0.0.0.0:mdns             0.0.0.0:*
udp        0      0 0.0.0.0:hostmon          0.0.0.0:*
[...omitted for brevity]
```

#	Task
⑦	If you want to check which process uses a specific port, you can do so by typing netstat -an combined with a pipe (|) and grep followed by :port_number. The port number, enclosed in single quotation marks, indicates that the data type is a string. For example, if you want to check who is using SSH (port 22), you issue the netstat -an	grep ':22' command.

```
[jdoe@f38s1 ~]$ netstat -an | grep ':22'
tcp        0      0 0.0.0.0:22               0.0.0.0:*              LISTEN
tcp        0     64 192.168.127.10:22        192.168.127.1:60179    STABLISHED
tcp6       0      0 :::22                    :::*                   LISTEN
[jdoe@f38s1 ~]$ netstat -an | grep ':80'
tcp        0      0 0.0.0.0:80               0.0.0.0:*              LISTEN
tcp6       0      0 :::80                    :::*                   LISTEN
```

(continued)

#	Task

⑧ To check which IP network services are running on your server, you can use the netstat -ap command. Here's an example of the netstat -ap | grep ssh command:

```
[jdoe@f38s1 ~]$ netstat -ap | grep ssh
(Not all processes could be identified, non-owned process info will
not be shown, you would have to be root to see it all.)
tcp         0        0 0.0.0.0:ssh              0.0.0.0:*             LISTEN     -
tcp         0      176 f38s1.pynetauto.com:ssh 192.168.127.1:fido
ESTABLISHED -
tcp6        0        0 [::]:ssh                 [::]:*               LISTEN     -
```

⑨ To display the process ID (PID) and program names in your output, you can use the netstat -pt command. This command will provide information about the protocol, IP service, and IP addresses in use. Here's an example of the netstat -pt output for an active SSH connection:

```
[jdoe@f38s1 ~]$ netstat -pt
(Not all processes could be identified, non-owned process info
will not be shown, you would have to be root to see it all.)
Active Internet connections (w/o servers)
Proto Recv-Q Send-Q Local Address            Foreign Address
State        PID/Program name
tcp         0      832 f38s1.pynetauto.com:ssh 192.168.127.1:fido
ESTABLISHED -
```

(continued)

#	Task

⑩ The final set of commands involves statistical commands using `netstat` options. Because the output can be quite lengthy, it's best to run these commands directly from your Fedora VM via a SSH connection. Look for the keyword `statistics` to identify these commands on the man page. Feel free to run and study the following commands on your Fedora Linux server at your own pace:

```
[jdoe@f38s1 ~]$ netstat -s # provides a comprehensive summary of
various network statistics, including TCP, UDP, ICMP, and IP
statistics.
Ip:
Forwarding: 2
13704 total packets received
1 with invalid addresses
[...omitted for brevity]
```

```
[jdoe@f38s1 ~]$ netstat -st # displays TCP-related statistics. It's
useful for monitoring TCP connections, errors, and other TCP-specific
metrics.
[...omitted for brevity]
Tcp:
39 active connection openings
5 passive connection openings
[...omitted for brevity]
```

```
[jdoe@f38s1 ~]$ netstat -su # focuses on UDP-related statistics. It
shows information about UDP datagrams, errors, and other UDP-specific
details.
[...omitted for brevity]
Udp:
683 packets received
0 packets to unknown port received
0 packet receive errors
[...omitted for brevity]
```

You have learned how to use netstat commands, enabling you to efficiently access and locate TCP and UDP-related information, thereby making it a valuable tool for diagnosing network issues and monitoring network activity. The next section shifts focus to practical applications and explores how to transform your Fedora Server into a versatile file-sharing and time server.

Installing TFTP, FTP, SFTP, and NTP Servers

For some, this section may be the most intriguing part of this chapter, while others might not find as much enjoyment in the process of installing and building components themselves. Nevertheless, **it is essential to work through this section from start to finish to gain mastery in installing various IP services on Linux in a comprehensive manner**. This knowledge will not only serve as a foundation but will also be vital for effectively utilizing these services in the labs presented in Part 2.

Tip

Not a CCNA student? No problem!

Here's a brief vocabulary lesson for those who might not be familiar with CCNA terminology:

- FTP: File Transfer Protocol
- SFTP: Secure File Transfer Protocol
- TFTP: Trivial File Transfer Protocol
- NTP: Network Time Protocol

In the business world, both PC end users and IT engineers regularly use various network services within company networks, as well as increasingly on private and public cloud networks. Among the numerous IP services available, FTP, SFTP, TFTP, and NTP are some of the most popular ones supported by today's network and system engineers. Each of these services can be installed on multiple distributed servers or even on dedicated networking platforms, depending on the supported installation and configuration options. Alternatively, you can configure these services in the public cloud, although cost considerations must be taken into account. In a lab environment, there's typically no need to distribute network services across multiple virtual servers to accommodate various services. While it's feasible to install all services on a single Linux server for testing purposes, in a real production environment, these services are often distributed across multiple servers and across multiple locations for system and location redundancy. For the convenience of this lab, you will install multiple IP services on a single Fedora Server, f38s1.

Expand Your Knowledge:

FTP, SFTP, TFTP, and NTP Services on the Public Cloud?

Here's a summary of the FTP, SFTP, TFTP, and NTP services offered by major public cloud service providers. While some perceive public cloud services as cost-effective, it's important to exercise caution, as improper use can lead to significant expenses. Migrating to the public cloud presents advantages and disadvantages. Public cloud costs are itemized, and increased usage results in higher expenses, making ongoing costs not as budget-friendly as you might assume. While some promote the public cloud as abundant and free, it's crucial to recognize that it's a marketing strategy. From an enterprise network and security perspective, it's wise to only migrate services to the public cloud that align with your security standards and budgetary constraints. Like most things in life, the cloud isn't free, and what you receive often correlates with what you pay for.

FTP (File Transfer Protocol):

AWS: AWS Transfer Family (SFTP, FTPS, FTP)

Azure: Azure Blob Storage (FTP access with Azure Blob FUSE)

GCP: Google Cloud Storage (FTP/SFTP access via third-party clients)

SFTP (Secure File Transfer Protocol):

AWS: AWS Transfer Family (SFTP)

Azure: Azure Logic Apps (with SFTP connector)

GCP: Google Cloud Storage (secured via SSH keys, accessed with SFTP clients)

TFTP (Trivial File Transfer Protocol):

None of the major cloud providers offer direct TFTP services, as it's less common and not secure in cloud environments, as well as primarily used for network booting.

NTP (Network Time Protocol):

AWS: Amazon Time Sync Service

Azure: Azure Time Series Insights

GCP: Built-in NTP service for accurate time synchronization.

In a production environment, FTP, SFTP, and TFTP are file services that typically require a substantial amount of storage space. Due to their storage demands, these services are commonly installed on enterprise-grade Linux or Windows servers rather than on networking devices like routers, switches, or firewalls. NTP, on the other hand, is a time service and can often run directly from Cisco routers. NTP ensures that both servers and network devices maintain accurate time synchronization. In the lab setup, you can consolidate all four of these IP services onto a single server for convenience. If you come from a predominantly networking background, you may have limited experience in building and supporting enterprise IP services on Linux servers. Expanding your skillset to include both network and systems administration can be highly beneficial. Let's proceed with the installation of FTP, SFTP, TFTP, and NTP servers on the Fedora Server for lab purposes. Remember that you've reserved the Ubuntu Server for later labs, where it will serve as a Python, Docker, and IPAM (IP Address Management) server.

FTP Server Installation

File Transfer Protocol (FTP) is a robust network service designed for secure file exchange between servers and clients. Unlike the slower TFTP, FTP allows simultaneous file uploads and downloads, making it highly efficient. FTP typically uses TCP port 21 as its default communication port, but it's worth noting that it is less secure than its encrypted counterpart, SFTP. Linux offers several open-source FTP server options, including PureFTPd, ProFTPD, and vsftpd. In this example, you will install and utilize Very Secure FTP daemon (vsftpd) due to its reputation for security, stability, and speed. Let's begin by verifying whether the FTP service is currently running on your Fedora Server, followed by the installation process.

#	Task
①	You have probably not yet installed the vsftpd on f38s1, but as a validation, run the vsftpd -version command to check if vsftpd is installed on your Fedora Server.

```
[jdoe@f38s1 ~]$ vsftpd -version
-bash: vsftpd: command not found
```

| ② | As expected, the application is not present on the server, so you have to install it using the sudo dnf install vsftpd command. |

```
[jdoe@f38s1 ~]$ sudo dnf install vsftpd # If prompted, enter your
sudo password
Last metadata expiration check: 1:25:28 ago on Mon 25 Sep 2023
21:33:00.
[...omitted for brevity]
[jdoe@f38s1 ~]$ vsftpd -version
vsftpd: version 3.0.5
```

| ③ | Just like in the case of Nginx, the vsftpd service doesn't start automatically. To ensure the service starts during system boot, execute systemctl enable vsftpd, initiate the services with the systemctl start vsftpd command, and then verify the service status using systemctl status vsftpd. |

```
[jdoe@f38s1 ~]$ sudo systemctl enable vsftpd # If prompted, enter
your sudo password
Created symlink /etc/systemd/system/multi-user.target.wants/vsftpd.
service → /usr/lib/systemd/system/vsftpd.service.

[jdoe@f38s1 ~]$ sudo systemctl start vsftpd # You have provided the
sudo password in the previous step.
[jdoe@f38s1 ~]$ sudo systemctl status vsftpd
● vsftpd.service - Vsftpd ftp daemon
Loaded: loaded (/usr/lib/systemd/system/vsftpd.service; enabled;
preset: disabled)
```

(continued)

#	Task

Drop-In: /usr/lib/systemd/system/service.d
└─10-timeout-abort.conf
Active: active (running) since Mon 2023-09-25 23:03:07 AEST; 3s ago
Process: 2998 ExecStart=/usr/sbin/vsftpd /etc/vsftpd/vsftpd.conf
(code=exited, status=0/SUCCESS)
[...omitted for brevity]
Use 'Ctrl+C' to exit from the vsftpd status file.

④ To use FTP for your labs, a few lines of the vsftpd.conf file need to be updated. Open the vsftpd.conf file in the vi or nano text editor, check the existing configuration, and modify the configurations.

[jdoe@f38s1 ~]$ **sudo nano /etc/vsftpd/vsftpd.conf**
The following configuration should be ready out of the box, but
configure the settings as follows if they are different:
anonymous_enable=**NO** # Check the value
local_enable=**YES** # Check the value
write_enable=**YES** # Check the value

To control access to the FTP server using user_list, add the following lines after the last line:

userlist_enable=YES # line 127, the last line
userlist_file=/etc/vsftpd/user_list # add this line
userlist_deny=NO # add

To grant your user writable access to their home directory, use this:

allow_writeable_chroot=YES # add

Also, vsftpd can use any port range for passive FTP connections. It is best practice to specify the port range for this, so you have full control of the port numbers in use. Append the following configuration to the end of the vsftpd.conf file and save the file:

pasv_enable=YES # add
pasv_min_port=40000 # add
pasv_max_port=41000 # add

(continued)

#	Task

To change where the files are uploaded and downloaded, update the local_root
configuration. In this example, $USER will take your user's ID and open FTP sessions from
the /home/jdoe/ftp directory.

user_sub_token=$USER # add

local_root=/home/$USER/ftp # add

After appending all the lines to the end of the /etc/vsftpd/vsftpd.conf file, it should
look similar to lines 127 to 135 in Figure 8-4.

```
122 # Make sure, that one of the listen options is commented !!
123 listen_ipv6=YES
124
125 pam_service_name=vsftpd
126 userlist_enable=YES
127 # ADDED BY JDOE
128 userlist_file=/etc/vsftpd/user_list
129 userlist_deny=NO
130 allow_writeable_chroot=YES
131 pasv_enable=YES
132 pasv_min_port=40000
133 pasv_max_port=41000
134 user_sub_token=$USER
135 local_root=/home/$USER/ftp
```

Figure 8-4. Configuring FTP server on f38s1

⑤	One more step before moving to task 5—save the file and note the last line: local_root = /home/$USER/ftp. Ensure that you create a local folder named ftp for FTP access. You will use a standard user to log in to the FTP server. In my example, the directory is called /home/jdoe/ftp.

```
[jdoe@f38s1 ~]$ pwd
/home/jdoe
[jdoe@f38s1 ~]$ mkdir ftp
```

(continued)

#	Task
⑥	Use either the vi or nano editor to modify the FTP server configuration file, granting access to all users. Next, append your user ID to the user_list file located at /etc/vsftpd/. Remember to save the file once you have added your username.

```
[jdoe@f38s1 ~]$ sudo nano /etc/vsftpd/user_list
# vsftpd userlist
[...omitted for brevity]
games
nobody
jdoe # append your username
```

#	Task
⑦	Next, configure the firewall to allow FTP and passive ports using firewall-cmd commands. To grant access to FTP ports 20 and 21 and enable passive TCP port ranges from 40000 to 41000, execute the following commands:

```
[jdoe@f38s1 ~]$ sudo firewall-cmd --add-service=ftp --permanent
# OR
[jdoe@f38s1 ~]$ sudo firewall-cmd --permanent --add-port=20-21/tcp #
If prompted, enter your sudo password
success
[jdoe@f38s1 ~]$ sudo firewall-cmd --permanent --add-port=40000-41000/
tcp
success
[jdoe@f38s1 ~]$ sudo setsebool -P ftpd_full_access on
[jdoe@f38s1 ~]$ sudo firewall-cmd --reload
success
```

Note that FTP uses TCP ports 20 and 21. Port 21 handles control and negotiation, while port 20 manages the actual data transfer. These ports ensure reliable communication between FTP clients and servers.

(continued)

#	Task
⑧	Ensure that you issue the `systemctl enable vsftpd` command to enable `vsftpd` to start automatically at system startup. Here are some essential FTP troubleshooting commands for maintaining the service:

```
[jdoe@f38s1 ~]$ sudo systemctl enable vsftpd.service
[jdoe@f38s1 ~]$ sudo systemctl start vsftpd.service
[jdoe@f38s1 ~]$ sudo systemctl restart vsftpd.service
[jdoe@f38s1 ~]$ sudo systemctl stop vsftpd.service
[jdoe@f38s1 ~]$ sudo systemctl status vsftpd.service
```

In addition to these commands, you can use `netstat` to check the status of FTP services. These `netstat` commands help verify the smooth operation of FTP services.

```
[jdoe@f38s1 ~]$ sudo netstat -ap | grep ftp
[jdoe@f38s1 ~]$ sudo netstat -tupan | grep 21
[jdoe@f38s1 ~]$ sudo netstat -na | grep tcp6
[jdoe@f38s1 ~]$ sudo netstat -tuln | grep 21
tcp6        0       0 :::21                      :::*              LISTEN
```

Do not be alarmed about `tcp6`, as this indicates that the FTP server is listening on IPv6 addresses for incoming connections on port 21. This is perfectly normal and indicates that your system is capable of handling both IPv4 and IPv6 connections for FTP.

(continued)

#	Task
⑨	Log in to your Ubuntu Server, u22s1, at IP address 192.168.127.20, and test the FTP server's functionality from another Linux server using three methods: nc (Netcat), telnet, and ftp. If your FTP server is working, you should see a similar result as shown here:

```
jdoe@u22s1:~$ nc -vz 192.168.127.10 21
Connection to 192.168.127.10 21 port [tcp/ftp] succeeded!
```

```
jdoe@u22s1:~$ telnet 192.168.127.10 21
Trying 192.168.127.10...
Connected to 192.168.127.10.
Escape character is '^]'.
220 (vsFTPd 3.0.5)
quit # or press 'Ctrl+]'
221 Goodbye.
Connection closed by foreign host.
```

```
jdoe@u22s1:~$ ftp 192.168.127.10
Connected to 192.168.127.10.
220 (vsFTPd 3.0.5)
Name (192.168.127.10:jdoe): jdoe
331 Please specify the password.
Password: ****************
230 Login successful.
Remote system type is UNIX.
Using binary mode to transfer files.
ftp> quit # or press 'Ctrl + Z'
221 Goodbye.
```

If you want to learn more about FTP server installation and testing with Cisco devices, visit my blog: https://italchemy.wordpress.com/2021/12/06/installing-ftp-server-on-centos-red-hat-fedora-ec2-linux-the-complete-guide/

(continued)

#	Task
⑩	Optionally, you can download the WinSCP or FileZilla FTP client on your Windows host PC and establish a connection to your FTP server via port 21. This example illustrates the use of WinSCP in Figures 8-5 and 8-6.

You can download WinSCP or FileZilla clients at no cost by visiting the following URLs:

WinSCP: `https://winscp.net/eng/download.php`

FileZilla: `https://filezilla-project.org/download.php?platform=win64`

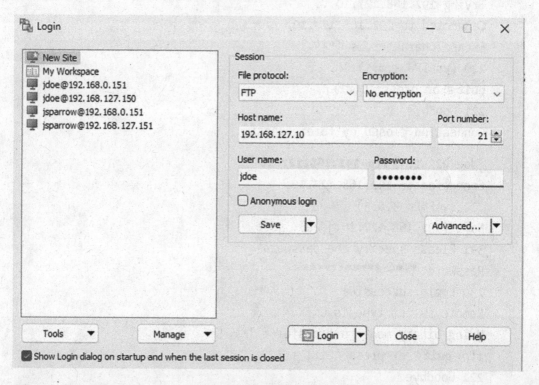

Figure 8-5. *WinSCP, connecting to the Fedora FTP server*

(continued)

#	Task
	Drag a test file from your Windows host PC and drop it into your new FTP server, as shown in Figure 8-6.

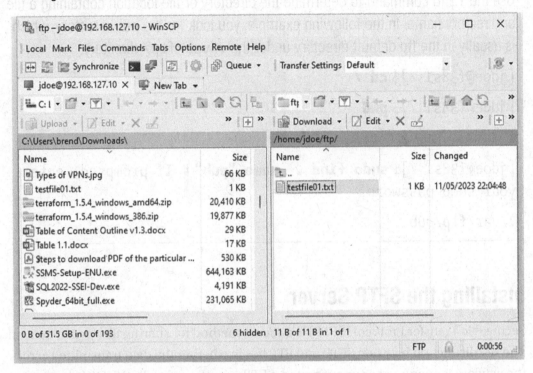

Figure 8-6. *WinSCP, connected to the Fedora FTP server*

Congratulations, you have successfully set up and tested the FTP server login. You can now utilize this server for seamless file-sharing applications in your lab, whether it's for uploading the IOS or configuration files among network devices or safeguarding essential router and switch configurations.

Tip

Searching for a file?

Use the `find` command to determine the directory or file location containing a file or directory name. In the following example, you look for the pub directory, which is usually in the ftp default directory under the `./var/ftp/` directory.

```
[jdoe@f38s1 /]$ cd /
[jdoe@f38s1 /]$ pwd
/
[jdoe@f38s1 /]$ sudo find . -name "pub" # If prompted, enter
your sudo password
./var/ftp/pub
```

Installing the SFTP Server

Secure File Transfer Protocol (SFTP) is a secure method for sharing files over a network. The key distinction between SFTP and FTP lies in whether the data transmitted across the network is encrypted or unencrypted. SFTP operates using TCP/UDP port 22 as its default port, and in the majority of file transfer scenarios involving the SFTP protocol, TCP port 22 is used. While UDP port 22 was initially introduced during the TCP/IP development process at the developer's request, it was not fully implemented. Consequently, it is accurate to assert that SFTP primarily utilizes TCP port 22.

The `vsftpd` server was initially configured as an FTP server, but it also supports SFTP. As you already have `vsftpd` version 3.0.5 installed, you can configure it to function as an SFTP server alongside the FTP server. Follow along to configure your new SFTP server.

#	Task
①	First, log in to the Fedora VM as the root user using the SSH client, PuTTY. You don't need to install any new software for SFTP, but to get started, you need to create a dedicated SFTP user account. Use adduser and passwd to establish a new user account specifically for SFTP file transfers; in this case, the username created is sftpuser.

```
[jdoe@f38s1 ~]$ sudo adduser sftpuser # If prompted, enter your sudo
password
[jdoe@f38s1 ~]$ sudo passwd sftpuser
Changing password for user sftpuser.
New password: ****************
Retype new password: ****************
passwd: all authentication tokens updated successfully.
```

A quick tip: If you want to remove and then re-create a user, you can use the userdel command. To delete the user's home directory and mail pool, include the -r option.

```
[jdoe@f38s1 ~]$ sudo userdel -r sftpuser
```

| ② | Create a directory called sftp within the /var/ directory, and within this sftp directory, create another subdirectory named sftpdata, where you store and share your files. The directory name sftpdata is provided here as an example. Typically, a file-sharing directory is established under the /var directory, and in this instance, follow the same convention. |

Here are the commands to create these directories:

```
[jdoe@f38s1 ~]$ sudo mkdir -p /var/sftp/sftpdata # '-p' option creates
the necessary parent directories
```

| ③ | Change the ownership of the sftp directory to grant sftpuser the ability to modify its contents within /var/sftp. Assign ownership of the /var/sftp/ directory to the root user. Change the permissions to 755, allowing sftpuser to modify directories and files. Additionally, designate sftpuser as the owner of the /var/sftp/sftpdata directory. |

```
[jdoe@f38s1 ~]$ sudo chown root:root /var/sftp # If prompted, enter
your sudo password
[jdoe@f38s1 ~]$ sudo chmod 755 /var/sftp
[jdoe@f38s1 ~]$ sudo chown sftpuser:sftpuser /var/sftp/sftpdata
```

(continued)

#	Task

④ To restrict SSH access to the /var/sftp/sftpdata directory, you need to make modifications to the sshd_config file located in the /etc/ssh/ directory. Open the sshd_config file and add or modify the following configuration settings. Copy the provided contents and append them to the end of the configuration file, then save your changes.

[jdoe@f38s1 ~]$ **sudo nano /etc/ssh/sshd_config**

Append lines 133 to 140 to the end of your file, as shown in Figure 8-7.

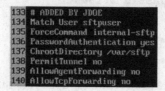

Figure 8-7. *Modify the /etc/ssh/sshd_config file to restrict SSH access*

⑤ Restart the sshd service to apply the previously made changes.

[jdoe@f38s1 ~]$ **sudo systemctl restart sshd**

⑥ If you attempt to SSH into the Fedora Server using the sftpuser account, the connection will be refused and terminated. Despite SSH and SFTP utilizing the same connection port, the sftpuser account is exclusively designated for SFTP connections and cannot be used for SSH connections. You can conduct this test either from the same server or from another Linux server. Feel free to try it.

[jdoe@f38s1 ~]$ **ssh sftpuser@192.168.127.10**
The authenticity of host '192.168.127.10 (192.168.127.10)' can't be
established.
ED25519 key fingerprint is SHA256:gSB2Nu/vnEdfkwhOaV9P+WVXwSB49TLTO1+
pWgzEz2k.
This key is not known by any other names
Are you sure you want to continue connecting (yes/no/[fingerprint])? **yes**
Warning: Permanently added '192.168.127.10' (ED25519) to the list of
known hosts.
sftpuser@192.168.127.10's password: ****************
This service allows sftp connections only.
Connection to 192.168.127.10 closed.

(continued)

#	Task
⑦	This time, attempt to connect to the SFTP server from the u22s1 server, using the sftp command. Enter your password to log in, and then use Ctrl+Z to disconnect from the SFTP server.

```
jdoe@u22s1:~$ sftp sftpuser@192.168.127.10
The authenticity of host '192.168.127.10 (192.168.127.10)' can't be
established.
ED25519 key fingerprint is SHA256:gSB2Nu/vnEdfkwhOaV9P+WVXwSB49TLTO1+pWgzE
z2k.
This key is not known by any other names
Are you sure you want to continue connecting (yes/no/[fingerprint])? yes
Warning: Permanently added '192.168.127.10' (ED25519) to the list of
known hosts.
sftpuser@192.168.127.10's password: ****************
Connected to 192.168.127.10.
sftp># Press Ctrl+Z to disconnect from the sftp server.
```

#	Task
⑧	Now, return to the f38s1 server and use the following netstat commands to confirm the proper operation of port 22 and sshd. Note that your output may differ from what is shown here.

```
[root@centos8s1 ~]# sudo netstat -na | grep tcp6
[...omitted for brevity]
[root@centos8s1 ~]# sudo netstat -ap | grep sshd
[...omitted for brevity]
[root@centos8s1 ~]# sudo netstat -tupan | grep 22
tcp    0  0 0.0.0.0:22        0.0.0.0:*          LISTEN        1728/sshd: /usr/sbi
tcp    0  0 192.168.127.10:22     192.168.127.10:33410    ESTABLISHED
1762/sshd: sftpuser
tcp    0  0 192.168.127.10:22     192.168.127.1:51651     ESTABLISHED
1147/sshd: jdoe [pr
tcp    0  0 192.168.127.10:33410  192.168.127.10:22       ESTABLISHED
1761/ssh
tcp    0  0 192.168.127.10:22     192.168.127.20:50532    ESTABLISHED
1782/sshd: sftpuser
tcp6   0  0 :::22             :::*               LISTEN        1728/sshd: /usr/sbi
```

(continued)

#	Task
⑨	Finally, confirm that your SFTP server is operating correctly. You can use Windows applications such as FileZilla (or WinSCP). Enter the user ID `sftpuser` and your password, and then connect to port 22. To establish the connection to your SFTP server, refer to Figure 8-8 and utilize the Quickconnect button. Once connected, perform a test by dragging and dropping a test file, as demonstrated in Figure 8-9, to assess the end-to-end functionality.

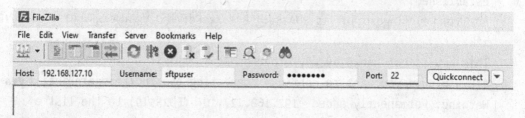

Figure 8-8. *FileZilla client, SFTP connection example*

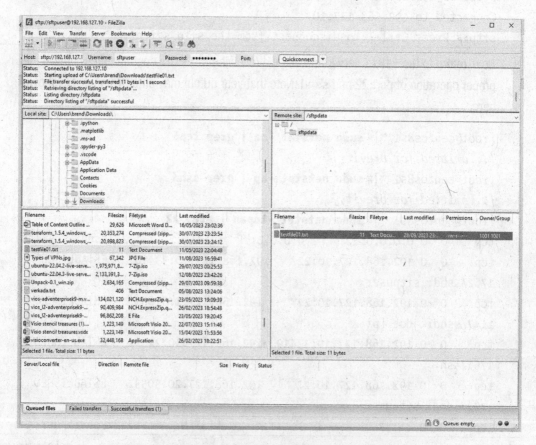

Figure 8-9. *FileZilla SFTP file transfer example*

Now, your Fedora Server is hosting SFTP services for secure file sharing across your lab network. Whenever possible, SFTP should be the preferred choice over FTP or TFTP for secure file transfers between two devices. However, some older devices may only support FTP or TFTP, so it is highly recommended that you become familiar with configuring each of these file-sharing methods. While it is possible to use Windows-based FTP, SFTP, or TFTP servers, taking a step forward toward network automation requires you to install, configure, and set up these servers on your new Linux servers. Next, you learn how to install and configure a TFTP server.

Tip

Printing all the usernames configured on your Linux server

This command displays a list of usernames from the /etc/passwd file, including system and user accounts:

[jdoe@f38s1 ~]$ **awk -F ':' '{print $ 1}'** /etc/passwd

[…omitted for brevity]

jdoe

avahi

rtkit

pipewire

colord

geoclue

nginx

sftpuser

awk, a versatile Linux text-processing tool, extracts, manipulates, and reports data, supporting custom actions. Its name comes from its authors' initials: Alfred **A**ho, Peter **W**einberger, and Brian **K**ernighan.

Installing the TFTP Server

Trivial File Transfer Protocol (TFTP) operates over UDP port 69 as its default communication channel. Due to its lightweight nature, TFTP is often used over FTP or SFTP for file transfers. It's commonly used for sharing Cisco IOS or NX-OS images and configuration files within internal networks. However, TFTP uses plain text communication and lacks the reliability and security of FTP or SFTP.

In a real production environment, FTP, SFTP, and TFTP services typically run on separate servers. In your lab environment, you're consolidating all three services into one for convenience and demonstration purposes. Installing TFTP on Fedora resembles the vsftpd installation process. Let's proceed with setting up the TFTP server for your lab use. **Building every component of your lab environment is a valuable learning experience and priceless.**

#	Task
①	First, log in to f38s1 using the jdoe account and SSH into the server using PuTTY. Once you have successfully logged in, verify the firewall status by executing the sudo systemctl status firewalld command.

```
[jdoe@f38s1 ~]$ sudo systemctl status firewalld # If prompted, enter
your sudo password
● firewalld.service - firewalld - dynamic firewall daemon
Loaded: loaded (/usr/lib/systemd/system/firewalld.service; enabled;
preset: enabled)
Drop-In: /usr/lib/systemd/system/service.d
└─10-timeout-abort.conf
Active: active (running) since Thu 2023-09-28 19:25:39 AEST; 12h
ago
Docs: man:firewalld(1)
Main PID: 735 (firewalld)
[...omitted for brevity]
```

(continued)

#	Task

② Check the current zone configuration, and then modify the server's firewall settings with the following commands to enable TFTP traffic to communicate with your server:

```
[jdoe@f38s1 ~]$ sudo firewall-cmd --zone=public --list-all # check
the zone configuration
public
target: default
[...omitted for brevity]
sources:
services: dhcpv6-client mdns ssh
ports:
[...omitted for brevity]
[jdoe@f38s1 ~]$ sudo firewall-cmd --permanent --zone=public --add-
service=tftp
success
[jdoe@f38s1 ~]$ sudo firewall-cmd --reload # Run firewall reload
command
success
[jdoe@f38s1 ~]$ sudo firewall-cmd --zone=public --list-all
public
target: default
[...omitted for brevity]
sources:
services: dhcpv6-client mdns ssh tftp
ports:
[...omitted for brevity]
```

(continued)

#	Task

③	Use the `sudo dnf install` command to install the `tftp-server`, the `xinetd` service daemon, and the `tftp` client package. Execute the following set of commands to complete the installation on your Fedora Server:
	
	`[jdoe@f38s1 ~]$ `**`sudo dnf install tftp-server tftp -y`**` # If prompted, enter your sudo password`
	`Last metadata expiration check: 0:12:16 ago on Fri 29 Sep 2023 08:31:00.`
	`[...omitted for brevity]`

④	This installation creates the `tftp.service` and `tftp.socket` files under the `/usr/lib/systemd/system/` directory. You have to copy these two files and rename them under the `/etc/systemd/system` directory. In other words, make copies of both files from the `lib` directory into the `system` directory.
	
	First, copy the `tftp-socket` file and rename it `tftp-server.socket`.
	
	`[jdoe@f38s1 ~]$ `**`sudo cp /usr/lib/systemd/system/tftp.socket /etc/systemd/system/tftp-server.socket`**
	
	Next, copy the `tftp.service` file and rename it `tftp-server.service`. You have to modify the TFTP service settings, as shown here:
	
	`[jdoe@f38s1 ~]$ `**`sudo cp /usr/lib/systemd/system/tftp.service /etc/systemd/system/tftp-server.service`**
	`[jdoe@f38s1 ~]$ `**`sudo nano /etc/systemd/system/tftp-server.service`**
	`[jdoe@f38s1 ~]$ `**`sudo cat /etc/systemd/system/tftp-server.service`**
	`[Unit]`
	`Description=Tftp Server`
	`#Requires=tftp.socket # Add '#' to disable this original line and add the next line`
	`Requires=tftp-server.socket`` # tells systemd that TFTP service depends on the 'teft-server.socket'`
	`Documentation=man:in.tftpd`

(continued)

#	Task

[Service]
#ExecStart=/usr/sbin/in.tftpd -s /var/lib/tftpboot # add '#' to disable this original line and add the next line
ExecStart=/usr/sbin/in.tftpd -c -p -s /var/lib/tftpboot # The '-c' option allows new file creation, the '-p' option is for additional file permission control and the '-s' option helps with compatibility and security.
StandardInput=socket
[Install]
#Also=tftp.socket # add '#' to disable this original line and add the next line
WantedBy=multi-user.target #tells systemd to enable multi-user mode and TFTP service to be started
Also=tftp-server.socket #tells systemd to start TFTP server service when 'tftp=server.socket' to be started

Note that under [Service], it specifies that the default upload or download location for file transfers is /var/lib/tftpboot. Once you are satisfied with your changes, save the file to proceed to the next task.

(continued)

#	Task
⑤	Let's reload the systemd daemon and then enable and check the TFTP server. All seems to be working, so now let's change the permission of the TFTP share directory to allow uploading and downloading.

```
[jdoe@f38s1 ~]$ sudo systemctl daemon-reload # If prompted, enter
your sudo password
[jdoe@f38s1 ~]$ sudo systemctl enable --now tftp-server
Created symlink /etc/systemd/system/multi-user.target.wants/tftp-
server.service → /etc/systemd/system/tftp-server.service.
Created symlink /etc/systemd/system/sockets.target.wants/tftp-
server.socket → /etc/systemd/system/tftp-server.socket.
[jdoe@f38s1 ~]$ sudo systemctl status  tftp-server
• tftp-server.service - Tftp Server
Loaded: loaded (/etc/systemd/system/tftp-server.service; enabled;
preset: disabled)
Drop-In: /usr/lib/systemd/system/service.d
└─10-timeout-abort.conf
Active: active (running) since Fri 2023-09-29 09:16:27 AEST; 11s
ago
TriggeredBy: • tftp-server.socket
Docs: man:in.tftpd
Main PID: 2290 (in.tftpd)
Tasks: 1 (limit: 4632)
Memory: 180.0K
CPU: 4ms
CGroup: /system.slice/tftp-server.service
└─2290 /usr/sbin/in.tftpd -c -p -s /var/lib/tftpboot
```

Sep 29 09:16:27 f38s1.pynetauto.com systemd[1]: Started tftp-server.service - Tftp Server.

(continued)

#	Task
⑥	Use the following change mode command with caution, as TFTP is insecure. Only modify the permission within secure and known networks. Change the permissions of the tftpdir directory so the tftp system account has permissions to this directory. To allow some freedom, you'll modify the directory with chmod 777.

[jdoe@f38s1 ~]$ **sudo chmod 777 /var/lib/tftpboot**

Then create a test file named server_file01.txt, so that you can test downloading from the client machine.

[jdoe@f38s1 ~]$ **cat > /var/lib/tftpboot/f38s1_file06.txt** # create a
server-side for client download
This is a server file 06 from f38s1.
^C # use CTRL+C or CTRL+Z to exit
[jdoe@f38s1 ~]$ **ls -lh /var/lib/tftpboot/**
total 4.0K
-rw-r--r--. 1 jdoe jdoe 37 Sep 30 10:06 f38s1_file06.txt

⑦	Go to u22s1 and install the tftp client. This will allow you to connect to your tftp server.

jdoe@u22s1:~$ **sudo apt install tftp -y**
[...omitted for brevity]

⑧	On the u22s1 VM, create a new working folder named ch08 and change the directory to it. To download a file from the TFTP server at 192.168.127.10, establish a connection with the TFTP server and then execute the get (download) command. This command takes the form of get remote_file_name local_file_name. If you do not specify the local_file_name, the file will retain the remote_file_name.

jdoe@u22s1:~$ **mkdir ch08 && cd ch08**
jdoe@u22s1:~/ch08$ **tftp 192.168.127.10** # Connect to TFTP server
tftp> **get f38s1_file06.txt server_file06.txt** # download a remote
file and rename to server_file06.txt
Received 38 bytes in 0.1 seconds

(continued)

#	Task
| | ```
tftp> quit # quit or CTRL+Z to exit
jdoe@u22s1:~/ch08$ ls
server_file06.txt
jdoe@u22s1:~/ch08$ cat server_file06.txt
This is a server file 06 from f38s1.
``` |
| ⑨ | Continuing from u22s1, if you want to upload a local file to the TFTP server (192.168.127.10), start by creating a local file named u22s1_file08.txt. Next, reestablish a connection with the TFTP server and then execute the put (upload) command. This command follows the format put local_file_name remote_file_name. If you do not specify the remote_file_name, the file will retain the local_file_name.

```
jdoe@u22s1:~/ch08$ cat > u22s1_file09.txt
This is a client file 9 from u22s1.
^C # use CTRL+C or CTRL+Z to exit
jdoe@u22s1:~/ch08$ ls
server_file06.txt  u22s1_file09.txt
jdoe@u22s1:~$ tftp 192.168.127.10
tftp> put u22s1_file09.txt # upload a client file to the server,
retain the same file name
Sent 37 bytes in 0.0 seconds
tftp> quit # quit or CTRL+Z to exit
``` |
| ⑩ | To verify the file upload on f38s1, execute the ls and cat commands.

```
[jdoe@f38s1 ~]$ ls -lh /var/lib/tftpboot/
total 8.0K
-rw-r--r--. 1 jdoe    jdoe   37 Sep 30 10:06 f38s1_file06.txt
-rw-r--r--. 1 nobody nobody 36 Sep 30 10:28 u22s1_file09.txt
[jdoe@f38s1 ~]$ cat /var/lib/tftpboot/u22s1_file09.txt
This is a client file 9 from u22s1.
``` |
```

You have successfully installed TFTP on the Fedora Server and verified TFTP operations between the server (f38s1) and a client (u22s1). To this point, FTP, SFTP, and TFTP have all been configured, and their functionalities have been confirmed. Next, you will promptly install time services (NTP server) software on Fedora. These servers will prove invaluable when testing various scenarios in your lab or work environment. The advantage of this setup is that you have configured these IP services, providing you with a deep understanding of their operations.

Tip

Verifying TFTP functionality with net-tool on Fedora VM

You can verify whether TFTP is functioning correctly by using the net-tools command. If the netstat command is not recognized on your FedoraVM, you can install it using dnf install net-tools -y and then execute the following set of commands to inspect the TFTP-related port operations:

netstat -na | grep udp6

netstat -lu

netstat -ap | grep tftp

netstat -tupan

netstat -tupan | grep 69

Installing the NTP Server

Network Time Protocol (NTP) is used to synchronize the time on enterprise devices such as servers, firewalls, routers, and switches. The NTP services use UDP port 123 and an IP network service that must be present in the corporate network to keep accurate time. The devices running in the same network segment or timezone need to have a consistent time, and the NTP server can provide this service to other devices. If hundreds or thousands of networked devices on a network all run on their hardware clock time, there will be no consistent timestamps for log and system files. NTP servers serve as a time aid to help the network equipment agree on a single referenced time.

Expand Your Knowledge:

Hardware Clock vs. System Time

In the world of computing, two distinct times coexist within your system: the hardware clock and the system time.

The **hardware clock**, also known as the BIOS clock or real-time clock (RTC), resides within your computer's BIOS or motherboard, especially in physical servers. Its primary function is to persistently track time, unaffected by system reboots or power cycling. While it serves this critical role, it is typically considered less precise than the system time, which is governed by your operating system.

In contrast, the **system time** is under the diligent management of your operating system while your computer is operational. It encompasses both the current time and date, playing a pivotal role in assisting the OS and applications in event tracking, task scheduling, and the provision of accurate timestamps for files and logs. For superior precision and synchronization, the system time often relies on external NTP servers to ensure its accuracy, making it a crucial component for various operations. Moreover, it also can adjust automatically for daylight saving time shifts under the configured timezone.

This harmonious interplay between the hardware clock and system time is fundamental to the seamless operation of your computer, ensuring accurate timekeeping and event tracking.

Let's proceed with the NTP server configuration on the Fedora Server and conduct a quick test run for confirmation. On Fedora, the chrony daemon provides both NTP server and NTP client services. While it's also possible to install and use ntpq as an alternative to chrony, you'll observe that chrony is already operational on your Fedora Server. Hence, you will utilize this NTP application in the following example.

#	Task
①	First, use the SSH client to log into the Fedora VM, f38s1. After the login, check the server's clock (BIOS time) and the system time (time and timezone). If any of this information is incorrect, follow these directions to set your clock and timezone correctly:

```
[jdoe@f38s1 ~]$ sudo clock # view Hardware Clock (a.k.a. BIOS
Clock) # If prompted, enter your sudo password
2023-09-30 12:40:43.990554+10:00
[jdoe@f38s1 ~]$ date # view date and time settings on your OS
Sat 30 Sep 2023 12:41:07 AEST
[jdoe@f38s1 ~]$ timedatectl # view date, time, and timezone
settings on the OS
Local time: Sat 2023-09-30 12:42:12 AEST
Universal time: Sat 2023-09-30 02:42:12 UTC
RTC time: Sat 2023-09-30 02:42:12
Time zone: Australia/Sydney (AEST, +1000)
System clock synchronized: yes
NTP service: active
RTC in local TZ: no
[jdoe@f38s1 ~]$ # timedatectl list-timezones # display and locate
your timezone
[...omitted for brevity]
[jdoe@f38s1 ~]$ timedatectl set-timezone Australia/Sydney # set the
timezone to Australia/Sydney
[jdoe@f38s1 ~]$ date # check time, date and timezone
Sat 30 Sep 2023 12:43:52 AEST
```

Note, if you want to synchronize the hardware clock to the system time, you can do so using sudo timedatectl set-local-rtc 1, but this may create various problems with timezone changes and daylight-saving time adjustments. So, the best approach is to leave this as the default, unsynchronized.

(continued)

541

#	Task
②	Next run the following `systemctl` command and check if the chronyd is installed and active.

```
[jdoe@f38s1 ~]$ sudo systemctl list-units --type=service # If
prompted, enter your sudo password
[...omitted for brevity]
auditd.service                      loaded active running Security
Auditing Service
avahi-daemon.service                loaded active running Avahi
mDNS/DNS-SD Stack
chronyd.service                     loaded active running NTP
client/server
crond.service                       loaded active running Command
Scheduler
dbus-broker.service                 loaded active running D-Bus
System Message Bus
dracut-shutdown.service             loaded active exited  Restore /
run/initramfs on shutdown
firewalld.service                   loaded active running
firewalld - dynamic firewall daemon
[...omitted for brevity]
```

If chronyd is not yet installed, install the NTP server and client using the dnf install command.

```
[jdoe@f38s1 ~]$ sudo dnf install chrony
```

(continued)

#	Task
③	To make chronyd run at startup, enable the chrony services by typing systemctl enable chronyd. [jdoe@f38s1 ~]$ **sudo systemctl enable chronyd** # If prompted, enter your sudo password [jdoe@f38s1 ~]$ **sudo systemctl status chronyd** • chronyd.service - NTP client/server Loaded: loaded (/usr/lib/systemd/system/chronyd.service; enabled; preset: enabled) Drop-In: /usr/lib/systemd/system/service.d └─10-timeout-abort.conf Active: active (running) since Thu 2023-09-28 19:25:35 AEST; 1 day 17h ago Docs: man:chronyd(8) man:chrony.conf(5) Main PID: 718 (chronyd) Tasks: 1 (limit: 4632) *[...omitted for brevity]*
④	Now configure chronyd to synchronize with NTP servers in your region. First, go to https://www.ntppool.org/en/ and locate your nearest NTP servers to use. In my case, the closest servers available to me are the 0 to 3 servers in the au.pool.ntp.org list. Yours will be different, so visit ntppool.org to locate your NTP servers. [jdoe@f38s1 ~]$ **sudo nano /etc/chrony.conf** [jdoe@f38s1 ~]$ **sudo cat /etc/chrony.conf** # Use public servers from the pool.ntp.org project. # Please consider joining the pool (https://www.pool.ntp.org/join.html). #pool 2.fedora.pool.ntp.org iburst # add the '#' to disable the default ntp pool server 0.au.pool.ntp.org iburst # Add the new pools located on ntppool.org page

(continued)

#	Task
	server 1.au.pool.ntp.org iburst

```
server 1.au.pool.ntp.org iburst
server 2.au.pool.ntp.org iburst
server 3.au.pool.ntp.org iburst
[...omitted for brevity]
[jdoe@f38s1 ~]$ sudo systemctl restart chronyd # restart the
chrond.service
[jdoe@f38s1 ~]$ sudo systemctl status chronyd # check the chrond.
service
[...omitted for brevity]
[jdoe@f38s1 ~]$ chronyc tracking # track time synchronization
Reference ID    : 6EE87216 (mansfield.id.au)
Stratum         : 3 # The "Stratum" line will indicate the stratum
level of external NTP server.
Ref time (UTC)  : Sat Sep 30 03:53:52 2023
System time     : 0.000000280 seconds slow of NTP time
Last offset     : +0.000321391 seconds
RMS offset      : 0.000321391 seconds
Frequency       : 0.148 ppm fast
Residual freq   : +95.791 ppm
Skew            : 0.124 ppm
Root delay      : 0.024532856 seconds
Root dispersion : 0.005232252 seconds
Update interval : 1.5 seconds
Leap status     : Normal
```

In this output, the Stratum 3 is the external NTP server's value, which makes your server's (f38s1) stratum, meaning that f38s1's NTP Stratum value is 4 (one level up to the referenced clock).

(continued)

#	Task
⑤	Reopen the chrony.conf file located at /etc/chrony/chrony.conf. This time, you'll configure it to allow communication between your NTP server and the lab network. Because the server operates at Stratum 4, it can be utilized within your lab environment. Most of the network devices and servers will readily synchronize their time with a Linux-based NTP server that has a stratum level equal to or lower than 5. It's worth noting that when using Windows as the NTP server, some network devices may decline to synchronize time with Windows-based NTP services. Therefore, it is essential to consult the vendor's documentation when planning and designing an enterprise NTP architecture.

```
[jdoe@f38s1 ~]$ sudo nano /etc/chrony.conf
[...omitted for brevity]
# Allow NTP client access from local network.
#allow 192.168.0.0/16
allow 192.168.127.0/24 # add this line and save the file
[...omitted for brevity]
```

| ⑥ | Open the firewall port to permit incoming NTP requests on the network, and then reload the firewall settings. |

```
[jdoe@f38s1 ~]$ sudo firewall-cmd --permanent --add-service=ntp #
If prompted, enter your sudo password
success
[jdoe@f38s1 ~]$ sudo firewall-cmd --reload
success
```

| ⑦ | To apply the change, restart the chronyd daemon and verify the service status for further validation. |

```
[jdoe@f38s1 ~]$ sudo systemctl restart chronyd
[jdoe@f38s1 ~]$ sudo systemctl status chronyd
```

(continued)

#	Task
⑧	Navigate to your Ubuntu 22 LTS (u22s1) server, configure the timezone, install `ntpdate`, and utilize the `ntpdate 192.168.127.10` command to synchronize the time with this server. If your NTP server's IP address differs, make sure to update the IP address accordingly.

8-1. Check the timezone using the `date` and `timedatectl` commands. Then update the timezone using the `timedatectl` commands.

```
jdoe@u22s1:~$ date
Sat Sep 30 04:28:13 UTC 2023
jdoe@u22s1:~$ timedatectl
Local time: Sat 2023-09-30 04:26:19 UTC
Universal time: Sat 2023-09-30 04:26:19 UTC
RTC time: Sat 2023-09-30 04:26:19
Time zone: Etc/UTC (UTC, +0000)
System clock synchronized: yes
NTP service: active
RTC in local TZ: no
jdoe@u22s1:~$ timedatectl list-timezones # lists all timezones
[...omitted for brevity]
jdoe@u22s1:~$ sudo timedatectl set-timezone Australia/Sydney #
Update to your timezone
jdoe@u22s1:~$ timedatectl
Local time: Sat 2023-09-30 14:31:30 AEST
Universal time: Sat 2023-09-30 04:31:30 UTC
RTC time: Sat 2023-09-30 04:31:30
Time zone: Australia/Sydney (AEST, +1000)
System clock synchronized: yes
NTP service: active
RTC in local TZ: no
jdoe@u22s1:~$ date
Sat Sep 30 14:31:53 AEST 2023
jdoe@u22s1:~$ sudo cat /etc/timezone
Australia/Sydney
```

(continued)

#	Task
	For those who are curious, you can also check the hardware clock using the following sudo command. This command works on both Ubuntu and Fedora Servers: jdoe@u22s1:~$ **sudo hwclock --show** 2023-09-30 14:32:04.985838+10:00
⑨	9-1. To synchronize the time with the NTP server on the Ubuntu client, you first need to install ntpdate. root@ubuntu20s1:~# **sudo apt install ntpdate** # If prompted, enter your sudo password *[...omitted for brevity]* 9-2. After installing ntpdate, proceed to synchronize the time of u22s1 with the NTP server on f38s1. When the NTP service is functioning correctly, the client machine will synchronize its clock and begin relying on the NTP server for time requests. jdoe@u22s1:~$ **ntpdate -d 192.168.127.10** 30 Sep 14:32:58 ntpdate[5591]: ntpdate 4.2.8p15@1.3728-o Wed Feb 16 17:13:02 UTC 2022 (1) Looking for host 192.168.127.10 and service ntp host found : 192.168.127.10 transmit(192.168.127.10) *[...omitted for brevity]* 30 Sep 14:33:04 ntpdate[5591]: adjust time server 192.168.127.10 offset -0.002302 sec 9-3. Now, utilize the ntpdate command with the -q and -d options to validate the service information. Pay close attention to the available information. This step provides valuable insight into the workings of NTP server-to-client communications. jdoe@u22s1:~$ **sudo ntpdate -q 192.168.127.10** server 192.168.127.10, stratum 4, offset -0.002534, delay 0.02727 30 Sep 14:35:33 ntpdate[5597]: adjust time server 192.168.127.10 offset -0.002534 sec jdoe@u22s1:~$ **sudo ntpdate -q -d 192.168.127.10**

(continued)

#	Task
	30 Sep 14:37:22 ntpdate[5633]: ntpdate 4.2.8p15@1.3728-o Wed Feb 16 17:13:02 UTC 2022 (1) Looking for host 192.168.127.10 and service ntp host found : 192.168.127.10 transmit(192.168.127.10) receive(192.168.127.10) server 192.168.127.10, port 123 stratum 4, precision -24, leap 00, trust 000 refid [162.159.200.1], root delay 0.017075, root dispersion 0.002869 reference time: e8c22382.e3f1341f Sat, Sep 30 2023 14:33:06.890 originate timestamp: e8c22482.2ad3be72 Sat, Sep 30 2023 14:37:22.167 transmit timestamp: e8c22482.2b2a3bb1 Sat, Sep 30 2023 14:37:22.168 delay 0.02702, dispersion 0.00000, offset -0.002316 30 Sep 14:37:22 ntpdate[5633]: adjust time server 192.168.127.10 offset -0.002316 sec
⑩	If you are using SuperPutty or SecureCRT, you can simultaneously execute the date command while connected to both f38s1 and u22s1 servers from the command line. Issue the date command concurrently. The output on f38s1 and u22s1 will display at the same time, as u22s1 is obtaining its time from the local NTP server, f38s1. Time on the NTP server: [jdoe@f38s1 ~]$ **date** Sat 30 Sep 2023 14:34:10 AEST Time on the client machine. jdoe@u22s1:~$ **date** Sat Sep 30 14:34:10 AEST 2023 Optionally, you can use the ntpdate 192.168.127.10 or ntpdate -u 192.168.127.10 command to update and resynchronize the time from the client machine.

You've learned how to install and configure NTP services using chronyd and have tested its functionalities both as a server and a client. You'll put this NTP server to use in one of the labs later, so it's crucial to develop a solid understanding of NTP, including its inner workings.

NTP plays a critical role in ensuring that all systems within an enterprise network operate with synchronized time, maintaining alignment with a single point of truth. Consistency in time across systems is essential in numerous scenarios, serving as a cornerstone for troubleshooting and safeguarding against data loss and corruption. Therefore, it's imperative to grasp the concept of NTP thoroughly.

With the successful installation of the NTP server, you've now completed the installation and verification of NTP, FTP, SFTP, and TFTP services. These servers will not only add depth to your lab scenarios but also provide you with the tools to explore, challenge, and rebuild your labs, much like your favorite childhood toys.

Tip

Securing your progress: Snapshotting the Fedora Server after IP service setup

You have successfully installed and configured four different IP services on the f38s1 server. Now is the perfect time to take a snapshot of your Fedora Server to preserve its current working state, as illustrated in Figure 8-10. This snapshot will serve as a valuable resource in the future; if any services encounter issues or break, you can quickly restore to this snapshot, saving time and effort in troubleshooting.

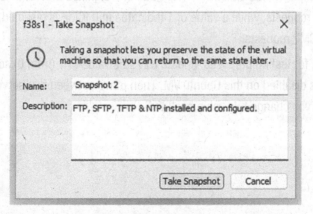

Figure 8-10. *CentOS, taking a snapshot*

Here are commands to check the health status of the FTP, SFTP, TFTP, and chronyd NTP services:

[jdoe@f38s1 ~]$ **sudo systemctl status vsftpd** # Check the status of the FTP and SFTP services

[jdoe@f38s1 ~]$ **sudo systemctl status tftp-server** # Check the status of the TFTP service

[jdoe@f38s1 ~]$ **sudo systemctl status chronyd** # Check the status of the chronyd NTP service

These commands will help ensure that your installed services are running smoothly and provide valuable information for monitoring their health.

Linux TCP/IP Troubleshooting Exercise

This marks the final exercise of this chapter. Here, you will acquire some fundamental Linux networking troubleshooting tips to diagnose TCP- and IP-related issues. When you encounter server networking problems, you'll be equipped to troubleshoot them independently instead of relying on a Linux administrator.

#	Task
①	The initial exercise involves verifying whether your server permits ping (ICMP) requests. You can do this by checking the value of /proc/sys/net/ipv4/icmp_echo_ignore_all. The output will be either 0 or 1. A value of 0 signifies that ICMP is enabled and will respond to requests, while a value of 1 indicates that ICMP is disabled, causing the server to ignore ICMP requests.
	On Ubuntu, for testing purposes, update u22s1's value to 1 (from 0) so the ICMP response is disabled on this Ubuntu VM. Then ping between two servers. After testing, make sure you change this value back to 0.

(continued)

#	Task

jdoe@u22s1:~$ **sudo cat /proc/sys/net/ipv4/icmp_echo_ignore_all** #
If prompted, enter your sudo password

0

jdoe@u22s1:~$ **echo 1 | sudo tee /proc/sys/net/ipv4/icmp_echo_**
ignore_all # use echo to update the value to 1

1

jdoe@u22s1:~$ ping 192.168.127.10 -c 4
PING 192.168.127.10 (192.168.127.10) 56(84) bytes of data.
64 bytes from 192.168.127.10: icmp_seq=1 ttl=64 time=1.79 ms
64 bytes from 192.168.127.10: icmp_seq=2 ttl=64 time=1.71 ms
64 bytes from 192.168.127.10: icmp_seq=3 ttl=64 time=1.89 ms
64 bytes from 192.168.127.10: icmp_seq=4 ttl=64 time=1.42 ms
--- 192.168.127.10 ping statistics ---
4 packets transmitted, 4 received, 0% packet loss, time 3038ms
rtt min/avg/max/mdev = 1.423/1.701/1.885/0.172 ms

On the Fedora Server, confirm that the icmp_echo_ignore_all value is 0. Send ICMP
packets to the Ubuntu client. The expected result is 100% packet loss, as u22s1 will
ignore all ICMP packets.

[jdoe@f38s1 ~]$ **sudo cat /proc/sys/net/ipv4/icmp_echo_ignore_all** #
If prompted, enter your sudo password

0

[jdoe@f38s1 ~]$ ping 192.168.127.20 -c 4
PING 192.168.127.20 (192.168.127.20) 56(84) bytes of data.
--- 192.168.127.20 ping statistics ---
4 packets transmitted, 0 received, 100% packet loss, time 3128ms
On u22s1, restore the value to 0 to allow the ICMP traffic.
jdoe@u22s1:~$ **echo 0 | sudo tee /proc/sys/net/ipv4/icmp_echo_**
ignore_all

0

(continued)

#	Task

②	To test the open ports of a server from a remote machine, you can borrow the `telnet` command, specifying the IP address of the remote server and the TCP port number. Telnet is useful for evaluating basic network socket connectivity, but it is limited to testing TCP ports; it does not function with UDP ports. For instance, if you want to assess the FTP (21) and SFTP (22) TCP connections from the Ubuntu Server to the Fedora FTP/SFTP Server, you can execute the following `telnet` tests to confirm end-to-end connectivity. Once you're connected, to exit, simply type QUIT and press Enter.
	
	2-1. On u22s1, perform the FTP connection test:
	
	`jdoe@u22s1:~$ `**`telnet 192.168.127.10 21`**
	`Trying 192.168.127.10...`
	`Connected to 192.168.127.10.`
	`Escape character is '^]'.`
	`220 (vsFTPd 3.0.5)`
	`QUIT`
	`221 Goodbye.`
	
	Connection closed by foreign host.
	
	2-2. Here is the SSH/SFTP connection test:
	
	`jdoe@u22s1:~$ `**`telnet 192.168.127.10 22`**
	`Trying 192.168.127.10...`
	`Connected to 192.168.127.10.`
	`Escape character is '^]'.`
	`SSH-2.0-OpenSSH_9.0`
	`QUIT`
	
	Invalid SSH identification string.
	
	Connection closed by foreign host.

(continued)

#	Task
③	An even better tool for testing open ports is the nc (netcat) command, which enables you to test open TCP and UDP ports. Here's a quick series of open port tests for TCP 21 (FTP), TCP 22 (SSH), UDP 69 (TFTP), and UDP 123 (NTP).

```
jdoe@u22s1:~$ nc -vz 192.168.127.10 21
Connection to 192.168.127.10 21 port [tcp/ftp] succeeded!
jdoe@u22s1:~$ nc -vz 192.168.127.10 22
Connection to 192.168.127.10 22 port [tcp/ssh] succeeded!
jdoe@u22s1:~$ nc -u -z -v 192.168.127.10 69 # '-u' option means
UDP
Connection to 192.168.127.10 69 port [udp/tftp] succeeded!
jdoe@u22s1:~$ nc -u -z -v 192.168.127.10 123 # '-u' option means
UDP
Connection to 192.168.127.10 123 port [udp/ntp] succeeded!
```

The -v option enables verbose mode, providing more detailed output, and the -z option tells nc to scan for open ports without sending any data.

#	Task
④	To determine whether a program or process is actively listening on a port, ready to accept incoming packets, you can utilize the netstat command. Here are various netstat arguments (options) that you can mix and match to suit your needs when running this command on your Ubuntu Server:

t – Show TCP ports.

u – Show UDP ports.

a – Display all connections and listening ports.

l – Show only listening processes.

n – Display numerical IP addresses and port numbers without resolving hostnames.

p – Include the process names associated with the ports.

(continued)

#	Task
	You can experiment with these options to tailor your netstat command. For example, you can run the netstat -tulnp and netstat -tuna commands and carefully observe the differences in their output: jdoe@u22s1:~$ **netstat -tulnp** **[...output omitted for brevity...]** jdoe@u22s1:~$ netstat -tuna **[...output omitted for brevity...]** These commands will provide you with valuable insights into the listening ports and associated processes on your server.
⑤	You can also utilize the ss command with various arguments to inspect listening ports or check port readiness. To determine if a program or process is actively listening on a port, prepared to receive packets, you can use ss. These ss commands function effectively on Ubuntu and Fedora Servers: t – Display TCP sockets. u – Display UDP sockets. l – Display listening sockets. n – Display numerical addresses without resolving names. p – Show the processes associated with the sockets. For example, you can run the ss -nutlp command to examine the status of TCP and UDP sockets along with their associated processes: jdoe@u22s1:~$ **ss -nutlp** **[...output omitted for brevity...]** These commands will provide you with valuable information about the listening ports and the processes using them on your server

(continued)

#	Task
⑥	Utilize lsof to generate a list of open ports on a Linux OS. To display the process names, associated PID numbers and open ports, enter sudo lsof -i. This command is compatible with most Linux operating systems. Refer to Figure 8-11 for examples.

[jdoe@f38s1 ~]$ **sudo lsof -i**

```
COMMAND     PID          USER   FD   TYPE DEVICE SIZE/OFF NODE NAME
systemd       1          root   66u  IPv6  22700     0t0  TCP  *:websm (LISTEN)
systemd       1          root   99u  IPv6  89610     0t0  UDP  *:tftp
systemd-r   653 systemd-resolve  10u  IPv4  22667     0t0  UDP  *:hostmon
systemd-r   653 systemd-resolve  11u  IPv4  22668     0t0  TCP  *:hostmon (LISTEN)
systemd-r   653 systemd-resolve  12u  IPv6  22670     0t0  UDP  *:hostmon
systemd-r   653 systemd-resolve  13u  IPv6  22671     0t0  TCP  *:hostmon (LISTEN)
systemd-r   653 systemd-resolve  16u  IPv4  22674     0t0  UDP  _localdnsstub:domain
systemd-r   653 systemd-resolve  17u  IPv4  22675     0t0  TCP  _localdnsstub:domain (LISTEN)
systemd-r   653 systemd-resolve  18u  IPv4  22676     0t0  UDP  _localdnsproxy:domain
systemd-r   653 systemd-resolve  19u  IPv4  22677     0t0  TCP  _localdnsproxy:domain (LISTEN)
avahi-dae   695         avahi   12u  IPv4  23271     0t0  UDP  *:mdns
avahi-dae   695         avahi   13u  IPv6  23272     0t0  UDP  *:mdns
avahi-dae   695         avahi   14u  IPv4  23273     0t0  UDP  *:44235
avahi-dae   695         avahi   15u  IPv6  23274     0t0  UDP  *:34846
vsftpd     1333          root    3u  IPv6  29559     0t0  TCP  *:ftp (LISTEN)
sshd       1728          root    3u  IPv4  75371     0t0  TCP  *:ssh (LISTEN)
sshd       1728          root    4u  IPv6  75380     0t0  TCP  *:ssh (LISTEN)
sshd       2530          root    4u  IPv4  95922     0t0  TCP  f38s1.pynetauto.com:ssh->192.168.127.1:59660 (ESTABLISHED)
sshd       2534          jdoe    4u  IPv4  95922     0t0  TCP  f38s1.pynetauto.com:ssh->192.168.127.1:59660 (ESTABLISHED)
chronyd    3069        chrony    5u  IPv4 113820     0t0  UDP  localhost:323
chronyd    3069        chrony    6u  IPv6 113821     0t0  UDP  localhost:323
chronyd    3069        chrony    7u  IPv4 113822     0t0  UDP  *:ntp
sshd       3230          root    4u  IPv4 118983     0t0  TCP  f38s1.pynetauto.com:ssh->192.168.127.1:61366 (ESTABLISHED)
sshd       3234          jdoe    4u  IPv4 118983     0t0  TCP  f38s1.pynetauto.com:ssh->192.168.127.1:61366 (ESTABLISHED)
```

Figure 8-11. *Fedora, lsof -i output example*

OR

jdoe@u22s1:~$ **sudo lsof -i**
[...output omitted for brevity...]

(continued)

#	Task
⑦	Use the `iptables` command to retrieve additional TCP/IP communication details. Execute `iptables -xvn -L` to showcase information about packets, interfaces, source and destination IP addresses, as well as the ports in use.

```
[jdoe@f38s1 ~]$ sudo iptables -xvn -L
Chain INPUT (policy ACCEPT 0 packets, 0 bytes)
pkts      bytes target     prot opt in      out      source
destination
Chain FORWARD (policy ACCEPT 0 packets, 0 bytes)
pkts      bytes target     prot opt in      out      source
destination
Chain OUTPUT (policy ACCEPT 0 packets, 0 bytes)
pkts      bytes target     prot opt in      out      source
destination
jdoe@u22s1:~$ sudo iptables -xvn -L
[...output omitted for brevity...]
```

#	Task
⑧	If you are connecting to your FTP server from a Windows client, you may wonder how to establish an FTP connection to your server from your Windows PC. You can achieve this using Windows PowerShell. `Test-NetConnection` is a built-in PowerShell command that is handy for testing basic connectivity, including FTP port 21.

To begin, launch PowerShell from your Windows 10 host PC or laptop and promptly assess the FTP connection to the FedoraFTP server to ensure it functions correctly. Refer to Figure 8-12 for a guide.

```
PS C:\Users\brend> test-NetConnection -ComputerName
192.168.127.10 -Port 21
```

(*continued*)

#	Task

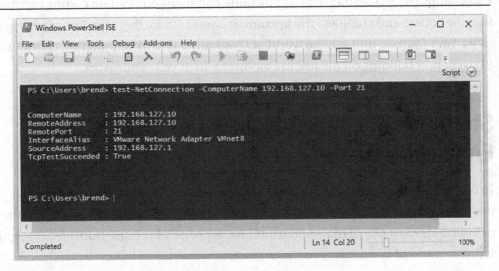

Figure 8-12. *Windows 10 host PC, PowerShell test-NetConnection example*

Source: My blog at https://italchemy.wordpress.com/2023/08/03/testing-connections-on-open-port-on-windows-powershell-ise/

Summary

In this chapter, you embarked on a journey of Linux TCP/IP administration, expanding your skillset with practical knowledge. You learned how to view system information and validate TCP/UDP ports on Linux systems, laying the groundwork for effective network management. I then guided you through the installation of essential IP services on a Fedora Server, creating an all-in-one lab server capable of hosting TFTP, FTP, SFTP, and NTP services. This server, a pivotal resource, will play a central role in Python network automation labs featured in the second half of this book. Additionally, you acquired the fundamental skills necessary for TCP/IP troubleshooting, equipping you to confidently address connectivity issues on the go. I trust that this chapter has been both engaging and enlightening.

As you advance to Chapter 9, you'll dive into another intriguing subject—Regular Expressions (regex)—which can significantly enhance your Python coding capabilities. Stay the course and complete the upcoming chapter to further your knowledge and skills. Your journey through the world of Linux and network automation continues, with each chapter building on the last to empower you in your endeavors.

Storytime 4: Linux Odyssey: Unleashing the IT Engineer's Dream

In the world of IT, becoming a proficient Linux administrator is akin to chasing a dream—an aspiration I, too, once held. Do you recall your maiden voyage into the world of Linux? Here's a tale of trials and triumphs, especially for those transitioning from the familiar world of Windows:

- Ubuntu Desktop, touted as beginner-friendly, beckoned. You embarked on the Linux voyage, only to find yourself returning to the familiar embrace of Windows 11 within days. It was as if your Linux escapade had never occurred.

- The allure of dual booting was irresistible. Windows and Linux coexisted on your laptop, side by side. Yet, weeks later, as you gazed at a conspicuously unused partition within Windows' precincts, you realized you had forgotten about your Linux companion. What a waste of storage space!

- Time passed, and increasingly, you found yourself gravitating toward Windows. Despite having the multi-booting option, you became ensnared by the charms of the Windows OS.

- The Ubuntu and Gnome Desktop experience was acceptable, but you couldn't help but long for the comforting familiarity of the Windows graphical user interface (GUI). You were hooked, and the allure of the Windows GUI was unshakable.

- Everyone emphasized the importance of learning Linux commands, yet no one offered guidance on how to tackle this daunting task. Countless websites and videos preached the necessity of memorization. You fervently tried to etch every command into your brain, but the following day, you could not recall a single command from your previous study session.

- There was always a Linux guru lurking at your workplace, nudging you to rekindle your relationship with Linux, even if it had been neglected for years. "Never give up," they said.

Perhaps Linux initially didn't ignite your passion, serving as a formidable barrier in your Python network automation journey. Yet, you must persist. A glance at industry statistics reveals a dearth of true Linux administrators. In my last job, out of 80 IT engineers, only three were Linux experts. Presently, in my team of 20, only one is well-versed in Linux. Every engineer who can write code knows that developing and running services solely on Windows servers is implausible. As a novice network automation engineer, it's imperative to embrace Linux and Python in tandem, for the two are inseparable. To excel in Python or any coding endeavor, a solid foundation in Linux is a prerequisite.

Learning Linux administration might seem daunting, but take it one step at a time. Progress may be gradual, but it's inevitable. The knowledge you gain will not only carry you through this book but also reorient your career. Since delving into Python, my Linux skills have flourished, prompting me to reconsider my career trajectory. I wholeheartedly recommend giving Linux another chance. Press on and persist in your pursuit of Linux mastery!

CHAPTER 9

Regular Expressions for Network Automation

In this chapter, you venture into the powerful world of Regular Expressions, a universal key to working with text and data in various programming languages, including Python. Regular Expressions, often abbreviated as *regex*, are a fundamental tool for processing complex strings of text. Regardless of the programming language you use, a deep understanding of Regular Expressions can significantly enhance your data processing capabilities. The chapter begins by exploring the basics of Regular Expressions and learning about character classes, repetition, anchors, and metacharacters. Understanding these fundamentals will set the stage for more advanced applications. Python provides native support for regular expressions through the re module. This chapter delves into the various string methods the re module offers, such as re.match(), re.search(), re.findall(), and re.finditer(), allowing you to perform powerful string-matching operations. Additionally, you explore the usage of named groups, lookahead, lookbehind, and non-capturing groups, which can make your Regular Expressions more readable and efficient.

By the end of this chapter, you'll gain a strong foundation in Regular Expressions, a skill that's indispensable for real-world automation challenges and data manipulation. Regular Expressions are like a secret weapon that can help you extract, transform, and manipulate data with precision, making you a more effective and capable programmer.

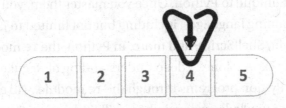

© Brendan Choi 2024
B. Choi, *Introduction to Python Network Automation Volume I - Laying the Groundwork*,
https://doi.org/10.1007/979-8-8688-0146-4_9

Unlocking the Power of Regular Expressions: A Universal Key to Programming Languages

This essential chapter delves into the fundamental concepts of regular expressions for Python Network Automation. While Python offers native methods to manipulate and dissect text strings for data processing, these often demand an extensive amount of code to locate specific substrings. For some readers, Regular Expressions might appear unfamiliar or uneasy. Regular Expressions might not be the most glamorous subject, but they are an indispensable tool in a programmer's toolkit. However, conquering this hurdle is essential for every engineer looking to advance in their programming journey and beyond. In the world of computing, data processing reigns supreme, whether dealing with structured or unstructured information. As IT professionals, we must always consider the significance of data and how we can harness it to achieve our business objectives. Utilizing Regular Expressions to process data elevates your data-processing skills to the next level compared to those who rely solely on native programming language methods. Learning Regular Expressions in Python is akin to mastering another application, as you gain proficiency in the inner workings of the re module and expand your understanding of regex concepts. I cannot emphasize more the critical skill of data wrangling through Regular Expressions to succeed in Python Network Automation. Unlike many Python Network Automation resources that underestimate the importance of mastering regex topics, this book acknowledges and recognizes its indispensable role in general programming and network automation. While this chapter may appear challenging at first, I encourage you to persist for the sake of your future benefit. By diligently working through the content presented here, you will acquire a skill that will prove invaluable in your programming journey. Your future self will undoubtedly express gratitude for mastering Regular Expressions. Gracefully embrace the challenge of text manipulation and automation.

Regular Expressions are universally applicable to all computer programming languages and are not unique to Python. Once you master them, you can apply them to a wide range of programming languages, including but not limited to Java, C++, JavaScript, Ruby, Perl, R, PHP, Swift, ShellScript, and more. In Python, the re module serves as the gateway to Regular Expressions. A deep understanding of Regular Expressions, when applied to your Python programs through the re module, will elevate your skills as a Python coder. The knowledge you gain here will find practical application in the development of network automation applications in your labs and future projects.

Mastering Regular Expressions is a topic that no Python coder should overlook. Although this chapter is relatively complex and challenging at first attempt, the skills you acquire will last a lifetime. If you find that any part of the book is unclear, revisit the chapter repeatedly until you have a complete understanding of the concepts and applications of Regular Expressions.

After grasping the basic syntax and concepts of Python, your goal will be to write working Python applications fluently. As I emphasize throughout this book, Python coding isn't solely about syntax and concepts. Like all aspects of computing, writing code hinges on effective data handling. This data could originate from users, application variables, file reading, web scraping, or logs exchanged between two computers. In nearly all programming languages, writing code invariably involves data manipulation. After spending some time writing Python code, you will soon realize that a comprehensive understanding of Regular Expressions is indispensable for developing any efficient network automation application. If you are serious about network automation using Python or any other programming language, you must master the art of Regular Expressions and the re module. You will explore the basics of regex and apply Regular Expressions to actual Cisco router and switch text files, allowing you to relate the knowledge to real-world production scenarios.

To complete this regex-dedicated chapter, you need access to your Windows 11 host PC and the Ubuntu Server VM (u22s1) running on VMware Workstation 17 Pro, as illustrated in Figure 9-1.

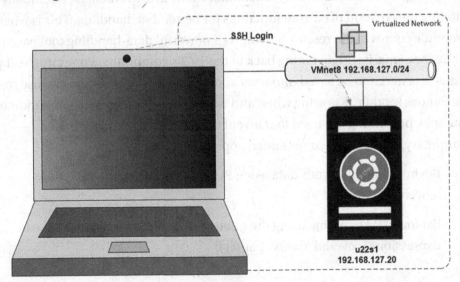

Figure 9-1. *Devices required in this chapter*

Mastering Regular Expressions: A Universal Key to Data Processing in Python and Beyond

A Regular Expression (regex) is a standard method used in computing to process complex strings of text. Its use is not limited to Python; it is used universally in data processing tasks. Initially, learning Regular Expressions might appear unrelated to mastering Python or network automation, but as you progress to an intermediate level, the true power of Regular Expressions becomes obvious. In Python, Regular Expressions are supported through a built-in module called the re module. While some readers may argue that learning Regular Expressions isn't an essential part of mastering Python, the reality is that as you tackle real-world automation challenges, you will frequently need to extract specific strings (data) from source files or large text strings. In coding, every comma, period, and whitespace is critical when handling data to create variables and run applications to prevent data-related errors.

When someone asks me what programming languages like C, C++, JavaScript, Perl, Ruby, R, and Python have in common, my immediate response is data processing. Virtually every program written in a computer programming language must handle and process data to fulfill its purpose. In other words, you require tools to enhance your data-handling and processing capabilities. As you learned in Chapter 2, there are built-in methods to slice, concatenate, and index data in strings. However, when dealing with extensive datasets, you'll encounter many inconveniences, potentially necessitating the creation of custom functions for better data handling. This is where the re module comes to the rescue. Serving as a powerful data-handling tool based on Regular Expressions, its origin dating back to the 1970s computing. For example, if your significant data needs to be saved into rows and columns as in SQL, you can use regex with the Pandas module. Knowing when and where to use different Python modules can save you time, preventing the need to reinvent the wheel (custom functions).

In summary, here's the recommended approach:

1. Begin by handling your data using Python's native methods (covered in Chapter 2).

2. Explore data handling using the built-in re module for Regular Expressions (covered in this chapter).

3. Dive even deeper into advanced data-handling methods using widely-used Python libraries such as NumPy and Pandas. NumPy provides objects for multidimensional arrays, while Pandas offers an in-memory 2D table object called a dataframe (expand your knowledge after reading this book).

Every Python coder should master Regular Expressions and leverage them to handle data efficiently and extract specific pieces of text.

Furthermore, my decision to include a dedicated chapter on Regular Expressions is based on my own experience and challenges while studying network automation using Python. Regular Expressions are indispensable when working on Python code for various network automation projects, especially beyond an intermediate level. As you advance in Python coding, you will inevitably encounter data-handling challenges, and a solid grasp of Regular Expressions is essential to make progress.

By completing the exercises in this chapter, you will be well-equipped with one of the most valuable Python coding tools available. While the examples presented here may not cover every possible scenario, they provide a foundation to enhance your data-handling skills through Python's re module. Because each string-matching requirement is unique, I encourage you to explore additional regex tutorials beyond this book and invest time in researching use cases that align with your specific data-handling needs. Numerous free online training materials are available to help you practice regex for various data-processing scenarios.

To re or Not to re

Let's begin with a simple example. Imagine you've applied for a job as a Python developer with a networking background. After successfully passing the initial technical interview, the hiring manager assigns you a take-home task. Your task is to analyze and transform a given text string. Specifically, you need to extract switch names and their MAC addresses and present the information in a specific format.

You've been provided with the following string. Your objective is to print the switch name, followed by the MAC address represented in 12 hexadecimal characters. It's essential to preserve the first six digits of the Organizationally Unique Identifier (OUI) to identify the manufacturer's ID, while the last six digits should be masked with asterisks (*) to conceal the actual MAC address.

Here's a given string:

```
sw_mac = '"pynetauto-sw01 84:3d:c6:05:09:11
pynetauto-sw17 80:7f:f8:80:71:1b
pynetauto-sw05 f0:62:81:5a:53:cd"'
```

Also, any letters, including the hexadecimal a–f, must be capitalized, so the result must match the expected output shown here:

```
PYNETAUTO-SW01 843DC6******
PYNETAUTO-SW17 807FF8******
PYNETAUTO-SW05 F06281******
```

If you haven't studied Regular Expressions, you can follow these steps to write your program:

1. Remove colons and convert the string to capital letters.

2. Split the strings in whitespace and add them to a list.

3. Eliminate whitespace using the `strip()` method, creating an updated list.

4. Utilize the `len()` method to distinguish names and MAC addresses based on the list's item lengths. If an item has 14 characters, it's a switch name; add it to the `sw` list. If it has 12 characters, it's a MAC address; add it to the MAC list. When appending MAC addresses, replace the second half with ******.

5. Use Python dictionary's zip method to combine the two lists into a single dictionary.

6. Use a `for` loop to print the key-value pairs from the dictionary.

In programming languages, it's often said, "There's more than one way to achieve a goal." However, one of the methods (through code) that accomplishes the desired result without using the `re` module will resemble Listing 9-1.

Tip

Where can you locate and download Chapter 9's source code and files?

All the code presented in this chapter as listings is available for download from pynetauto on GitHub. For the actual listings used in chapter, look in the ch09 folder and navigate your way to apress_pynetauto_ed2.0/source_codes/ch09_ Listings_1-83.txt.

URL: https://github.com/pynetauto/apress_pynetauto_ed2.0/tree/ main/source_codes/ch09

Listing 9-1. Native Python Methods

```
sw_mac = '''pynetauto-sw01 84:3d:c6:05:09:11
    pynetauto-sw17 80:7f:f8:80:71:1b
    pynetauto-sw05 f0:62:81:5a:53:cd'''

sw_mac = sw_mac.replace(":", "").upper() # 1
sw_mac
'\nPYNETAUTO-SW01 843DC6050911 \nPYNETAUTO-SW17 807FF880711B
\nPYNETAUTO-SW05 F062815A53CD\n'
list1 = sw_mac.split(" ") # 2
list1
['\nPYNETAUTO-SW01', '843DC6050911', '\nPYNETAUTO-SW17', '807FF880711B',
'\nPYNETAUTO-SW05', 'F062815A53CD\n']
list2 = [] # 3
for i in list1:  # 4
    list2.append(i.strip())  # 5

list2
['PYNETAUTO-SW01', '843DC6050911', 'PYNETAUTO-SW17', '807FF880711B',
'PYNETAUTO-SW05', 'F062815A53CD']

sw_list =  [] # 6
mac_list = [] # 7
for i in list2: # 8
    if len(i) == 14: # 9
        sw_list.append(i) # 10
```

```
    if len(i) == 12:  # 11
        i = i[:6] + "******" # 12
        mac_list.append(i) # 13
sw_list
['PYNETAUTO-SW01', 'PYNETAUTO-SW17', 'PYNETAUTO-SW05']
mac_list
['843DC6******', '807FF8******', 'F06281******']
sw_mac_dict = dict(zip(sw_list, mac_list)) # 14
for k,v in sw_mac_dict.items(): # 15
    print(k, v) # 16 lines
```

Output:
```
PYNETAUTO-SW01 843DC6******
PYNETAUTO-SW17 807FF8******
PYNETAUTO-SW05 F06281******
```

You don't need to worry about or understand how to read the previous code. What's important is your ability to count the number of code lines required to achieve the expected result. Excluding the newline and data lines, precisely 16 code lines were needed to produce the result using only Python methods, without relying on any modules. Yes, it works, but it takes many lines of code to reach the goal.

Once you've learned how to use a Regular Expression, you can use Python's re module to perform the same task, making data manipulation a breeze. The number of code lines decreases, making it easier to both write and read. Count the number of code lines in Listing 9-2; precisely four code lines were necessary to display the expected result, not including the newline and data lines. So, when you compare the number of code lines between the two listings, you can observe significant savings in the number of code lines used. This was a simple example, but consider more complex tasks involving extensive data. Writing lengthy custom code to achieve the end goal can consume a lot of time and effort. By using the Regular Expression module in Python code, your application code will become more concise, easier to write, and easier to read.

Listing 9-2. re Example

```
sw_mac = '''pynetauto-sw01 84:3d:c6:05:09:11
pynetauto-sw17 80:7f:f8:80:71:1b
pynetauto-sw05 f0:62:81:5a:53:cd'''

import re # 1
sw_mac = sw_mac.replace(":", "").upper() # 2
pattern = re.compile("([0-9A-F]{6})" "([0-9A-F]{6})") # 3
print(pattern.sub("\g<1>******", sw_mac)) # 4 lines
```

Output:
```
PYNETAUTO-SW01 843DC6******
PYNETAUTO-SW17 807FF8******
PYNETAUTO-SW05 F06281******
```

At this stage, there's no need to write the code yourself. You can simply download and run the code by visiting my pynetauto GitHub site, where you can find Listings 9-1 and 9-2.

Studying Regular Expressions Using Python

There are multiple ways to study Regular Expressions with Python, and I discuss a few of them here. Choose a study method that suits you best and commit to it until you finish the exercises in this chapter.

Method 1: Using Notepad++

In Chapter 2, you installed Notepad++, which serves as an excellent tool for delving into Regular Expressions. With Notepad++, there are two methods for studying Regular Expressions, and your choice between them depends on the size of the data or text you are working with. For smaller string data, as illustrated in Figure 9-2, you can incorporate the actual data as a Python variable, import the re module, and craft the necessary Regular Expressions to match specific strings. By executing the script using either Ctrl+F6 or the F6 keys within Notepad++, you can achieve the desired matches.

In Figure 9-2, the entire show version output is stored as the sh_ver variable, represented as a string. I utilized the Regular Expression re.findall(r'C\d{4}[^\s]+', sh_ver) to match the Catalyst/Router model, such as C8300-1N1S-6T. At this stage, it is not essential to fully comprehend the intricacies of Regular Expressions; the primary goal is to become acquainted with the process for now.

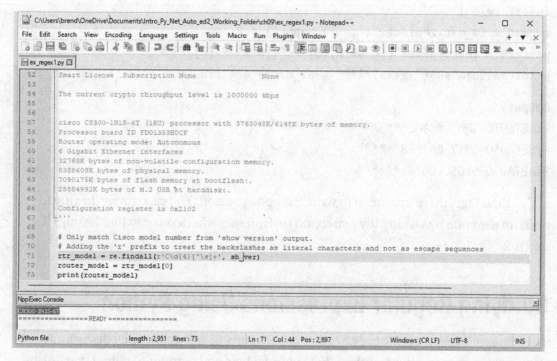

Figure 9-2. *Studying Regular Expressions using Notepad++ with a single script*

If the text data is lengthy or there are multiple files to process, you can use the file-reading method to read the files into your Python script and execute the Python code you've written. Figures 9-3 and 9-4 illustrate this example. You do not have to perform any task for this section.

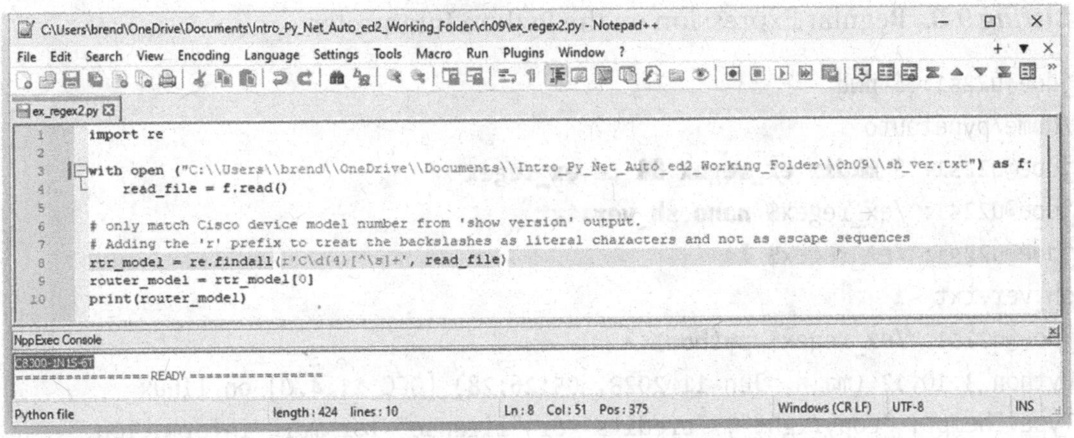

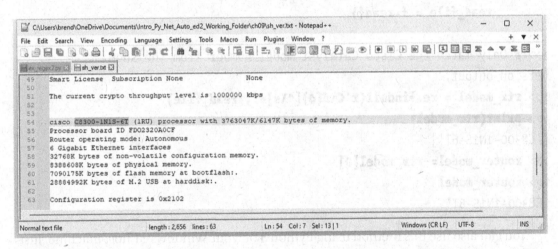

Figure 9-3. *Regular Expression using Notepad++, read file method re script*

Figure 9-4. *Regular Expression using Notepad++, read file method data file*

Method 2: Using the Linux Shell

Similar to the Notepad++ method, you can run one of your Linux VM servers and SSH into the server to practice Regular Expressions in Python. If you want to test a simple Regular Expression, you can initiate an interactive session with the Python Interpreter (as demonstrated in Listing 9-3). After entering the expression and pressing the Enter key, it promptly provides the result, or no result if your expression doesn't match any strings.

Listing 9-3. Regular Expression on the Python Interpreter

```
jdoe@u22s1:~$ pwd
/home/pynetauto
jdoe@u22s1:~$ mkdir ex_regex && cd ex_regex
jdoe@u22s1:~/ex_regex$ nano sh_ver.txt
jdoe@u22s1:~/ex_regex$ ls
sh_ver.txt
jdoe@u22s1:~/ex_regex$ python3
Python 3.10.12 (main, Jun 11 2023, 05:26:28) [GCC 11.4.0] on linux
Type "help", "copyright", "credits" or "license" for more information.
>>> import re
>>> with open("/home/jdoe/ex_regex/sh_ver.txt") as f:
...     read_file = f.read()
...
>>> # Only match the Cisco Catalyst model number from the show
version output.
>>> rtr_model = re.findall(r'C\d{4}[^\s]+', read_file)
>>> print(rtr_model)
['C8300-1N1S-6T']
>>> router_model= rtr_model[0]
>>> router_model
'C8300-1N1S-6T'
```

You can also use this method using Python 3 on your Windows 11 host machine. Just like in Notepad++, you can write the Python code first and execute it from the terminal console to run the re match script, as depicted in Listing 9-4. This method may initially seem challenging, but after practicing a few examples, you'll become familiar with it, and using Regular Expressions with Python will become more straightforward.

Listing 9-4. Regular Expression Writing Python Code on Linux

```
jdoe@u22s1:~/ex_regex$ pwd
/home/jdoe/ex_regex
jdoe@u22s1:~/ex_regex$ ls
sh_ver.txt
jdoe@u22s1:~/ex_regex$ nano ex9.4_sh_ver.py
```

```
jdoe@u22s1:~/ex_regex$ cat ex9.4_sh_ver.py
import re
with open("/home/jdoe/ex_regex/sh_ver.txt") as f:
    read_file = f.read()
# Only match the Cisco Catalyst model number from the show version output.
rtr_model = re.findall(r'C\d{4}[^\s]+', read_file)
print(rtr_model)
router_model = rtr_model[0]
print(router_model)
jdoe@u22s1:~/ex_regex$ python3 ex9.4_sh_ver.py
['C8300-1N1S-6T']
C8300-1N1S-6T
```

Regular expression breakdown: r'C\d{4}[^\s]+'

r	Adds the r prefix to treat the backslashes as literal characters and not as escape sequences.
C	Matches the character C literally.
\d{4}	\d is shorthand for matching any digit (0-9), and {4} specifies that it should match exactly four consecutive digits.
[^\s]+	[^\s] matches any character that is not whitespace. The ^ inside the square brackets negates the character class, so it matches anything except whitespace. The + sign indicates that the preceding character class ([^\s]) should be matched one or more times.

Method 3: Using the Internet to Study Regular Expressions

One of the most effective ways to study Regular Expressions is by using a web browser to access Regular Expression content and resources on the Internet. Numerous websites offer free Regular Expression exercises. Some of these sites may favor one programming language over another, but try to find programming language-neutral platforms and engage in more practice. As you gain confidence in Regular Expressions, you can begin using one of the first two Python re methods mentioned earlier. Practicing with the re module in Python is crucial, as it's the way you'll be utilizing Regular Expressions in Python. A particularly valuable platform for Regular Expression practice is regex101 (https://regex101.com/), as illustrated in Figure 9-5.

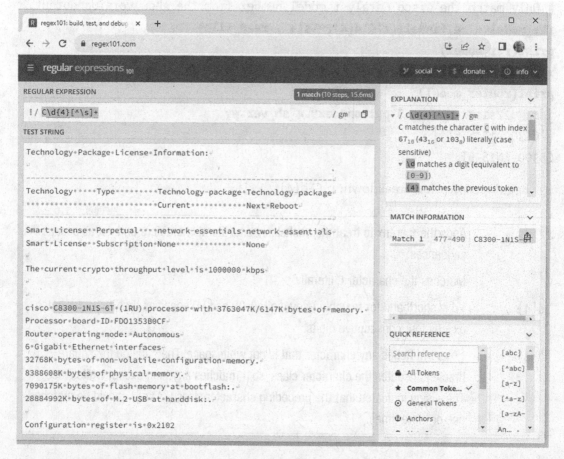

Figure 9-5. *Regular Expressions practice website*

If you're frequently on the move but still want to practice Regular Expressions, you can do so conveniently on your Android or Apple iOS devices. There are dedicated mobile applications—like RegexH for Android devices and RegEx Lab for iOS devices—designed to assist users in practicing and experimenting with Regular Expressions right on their respective mobile platforms. These apps provide a user-friendly way for individuals to enhance their knowledge of Regular Expressions, conduct tests, and refine their skills while on the move. Whether you are using an Android device with

RegexH or an iOS device with RegEx Lab, you have the opportunity to delve into Regular Expressions, perform tests, and enhance your proficiency through the interactive features offered by these applications.

To get started, simply download apps like RegexH (for Android phones) or RegEx Lab (for iOS devices), or similar alternatives, onto your mobile device. These applications offer a convenient means for quick, on-the-go Regular Expression practice, allowing you to engage with Regular Expressions anytime and anywhere, as illustrated in Figure 9-6.

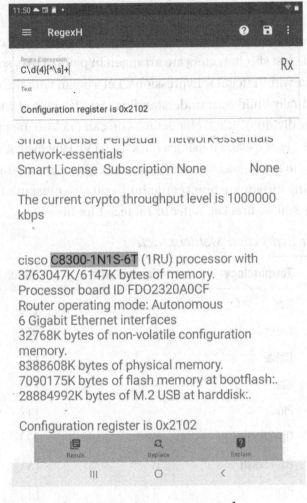

Figure 9-6. *Android Regular Expression app example*

Regex Operation: The Basics

Regular Expressions utilize metacharacters to match static or dynamic data strings. The word "meta" comes from Latin (Greek) and means beyond, after, or behind. When used in a programming language, metacharacters take on special meanings different from their literal representations, essentially serving as characters with hidden meanings. The metacharacters used in Python encompass the following set:

. ^ $ * + ? \ | ( ) [ ] { }

Each of these metacharacters, when used in Regular Expressions, carries a specific, special meaning. The last six characters are arranged in pairs of two, so the brackets must be used in pairs within Regular Expressions. Let's begin with the simplest Regular Expression and gradually build your understanding. Additionally, if you want to express these characters as individual, literal characters, you can enclose the metacharacter in square brackets ([ ]) or escape it using a backslash (\). However, it's important to pay special attention to the metacharacter ^ (called a carat). This character cannot be directly matched using the square bracket method, you also must use the escaping backslash within the square bracket. Refer to Table 9-1 for details.

Table 9-1. *Regular Expression Metacharacters*

Metacharacter	Terminology	Escape with \	Match Literally Using [ ]
.	Dot	\.	[.]
^	Caret	\^	[\^]
$	Dollar	\$	[$]
*	Star	*	[*]
+	Plus	\+	[+]
?	Question mark	\?	[?]
\	Backslash	\\	[\\]
|	Pipe	|	[|]
( )	Round brackets	\(\)	[(] [)]
[ ]	Square brackets	\[\]	[[][]]
{ }	Curly brackets	\{ \}	[{] [}]

To work with the literal matching method for ^ and \, you can append a backslash like this \^ and \\ within the square brackets. Open your Python Interpreter to learn more, as demonstrated in Listing 9-5.

Listing 9-5. Matching Metacharacters ^ and \ Using Square Brackets ([ ])

```
>>> import re
>>> expr = " . ^ $ * + ? \ | ( ) [ ] { }"
>>> re.search(r'[\^]', expr)
<re.Match object; span=(3, 4), match='^'>
>>> re.search(r'[\\]', expr)
<re.Match object; span=(13, 14), match='\\'>
```

Tip

Interactive learning through the Python Interpreter

As in all previous chapters, for a complete comprehension of Regular Expression concepts, you are encouraged to open your Python Interpreter and enter the content marked in bold in each listing. This involves everything following the three greater-than signs (>>>).

When ^ or \ are used within a square bracket set, it is necessary to include an escape backslash preceding these metacharacters. This requirement serves specific purposes. Within square brackets, ^ is utilized to negate the character immediately following it. To gain a better understanding, enter the code provided in Listing 9-6 into your Python Interpreter and study it carefully. [^a] signifies the matching of all characters except a. In Listing 9-6, observe that all characters are matched, except for the letter a.

Listing 9-6. Meaning of [^a]

```
>>> import re
>>> re.findall('[^a]', 'abracadabra')
['b', 'r', 'c', 'd', 'b', 'r']
```

The backslash placed within the brackets, [ ], presents a slight issue, as the Regular Expression interprets the backslash as a negating character for the closing square bracket,] itself. Therefore, to negate the backslash, you need to include an additional backslash. Take a look at Listing 9-7, where a backslash was used to match both the backslash and a closing square bracket,].

Listing 9-7. Meaning of [\]]

```
>>> import re
>>> re.search(r"[\\]", r"match \ or ]")
<re.Match object; span=(6, 7), match='\\'>
>>> re.search(r"[\]]", r'match \ or ]')
<re.Match object; span=(11, 12), match=']'>
```

Character Class ([])

Let's begin by learning about the first metacharacter, which is the **character class metacharacter**. Usually, a Regular Expression constructed using character classes is defined between an opening square bracket ([) and a closing square bracket (]). Character classes allow for the inclusion of all characters enclosed within the square brackets, [ ].

For instance, a Regular Expression like [aei] will match any one of the vowel letters a, e, or i. Let's consider real words associated with alarms: ding, buzz, beep, clang.

Regular Expression	Words (String)	Matched	Explanation
[aei]	ding	ding	Matches the character *i* literally (case sensitive).
	buzz	buzz	No match; *buzz* does not contain *a*, *e*, or *i*
	beep	beep	Matches the character *e* twice.
	clang	clang	Matches the character *a* literally.

When a hyphen (-) is used within square brackets alongside letters or numbers, it functions as shorthand for denoting a range. For example, [a-z] encompasses all lowercase letters, while [A-Z] includes all uppercase letters from A to Z. As you may have already inferred, to include all letters in both lowercase and uppercase, the Regular Expression becomes [a-zA-Z]. You can also use the Regular Expression [[:alpha:]] in place of [a-zA-Z], although [a-zA-Z] is more commonly used.

A common Regular Expression used to match a single digit between 0 to 9 is [0-9], which signifies the range from 0 to 9, essentially [0 1 2 3 4 5 6 7 8 9]. Also, to capture MAC addresses that use hexadecimal numbers, you can use [0-9a-fA-F], which includes all whole numbers and both lowercase and uppercase letters from a to f or A to F. In regex, capitalization holds significance and you will see it later, but to ignore capitalization, you can append re.IGNORECASE as part of your search expression.

Almost any valid characters can be used within square brackets [ ], with the sole exception of the caret (^) symbol (^ metacharacter). When ^ is used inside square brackets, it negates the expression, effectively meaning NOT. For instance, if you want to create an expression that excludes all whole numbers, you can use [^0-9]. Similarly, to avoid matching uppercase letters, you can use [^A-Z].

For commonly used Regular Expressions such as [0-9] and [a-zA-Z], there are specific shorthand expressions available to save you time and enhance the readability of Regular Expressions. These are tabulated here for your reference:

Regular Expression	Interchangeable Expression	Explanation	Example
\d	[0-9]	Matches whole numbers from 0 to 9.	import re re.findall(r'\d', 'Match 123 and 456') Output: ['1', '2', '3', '4', '5', '6']
\D	[^0-9]	Matches all characters except whole numbers.	import re re.findall(r'\D', 'Match 123 and 456') Output: ['M', 'a', 't', 'c', 'h', ' ', ' ', 'a', 'n', 'd', ' ']

(continued)

Regular Expression	Interchangeable Expression	Explanation	Example
\s	[\t\n\r\f\v]	Matches all types of whitespace. Whitespace is included.	import re re.findall(r'\s', 'Match\twhite spaces\nand\rnewline\fand\ vvertical tab') Output: ['\t', ' ', '\n', '\r', '\x0c', '\x0b', ' ']
\S	[^ \t\n\r\f\v]	Matches all characters except whitespace characters.	import re re.findall(r'\S', 'Match\twhite spaces\nand\rnewline\fand\ vvertical tab') Output: ['M', 'a', 't', 'c', 'h', 'w', 'h', 'i', 't', 'e', 's', 'p', 'a', 'c', 'e', 's', 'a', 'n', 'd', 'n', 'e', 'w', 'l', 'i', 'n', 'e', 'a', 'n', 'd', 'v', 'e', 'r', 't', 'i', 'c', 'a', 'l', 't', 'a', 'b']
\w	[a-zA-Z0-9]	Matches all alphanumeric letters.	import re re.findall(r'\w', 'Match 123 and $pecial characters') Output: ['M', 'a', 't', 'c', 'h', '1', '2', '3', 'a', 'n', 'd', 'p', 'e', 'c', 'i', 'a', 'l', 'c', 'h', 'a', 'r', 'a', 'c', 't', 'e', 'r', 's']
\W	[^a-zA-Z0-9]	Does not match alphanumeric letters. Matches all symbols such as % # @.	import re re.findall(r'\W', 'Match 123 and $pecial characters') Output: [' ', ' ', ' ', '$', ' ']

In the world of programming, the backslash (\) is commonly used to negate the meaning of the expression that follows it. For instance, d is a letter in the alphabet, but when combined with the backslash to become \d, it takes on a different meaning. Additionally, the backslash expressions with capital letters always have the opposite meaning of their lowercase counterparts.

Dot (.): Single Character Match

The Regular Expression . (dot) matches any single character except for line terminators like \n. Interestingly, Regular Expressions provide a method to include \n, as you will see in a later example. By using the re.DOTALL option, the . (dot) can also match the newline character, \n.

Study the following Regular Expression example.

Regular Expression	Explanation
d.g	Matches d, then matches any single character, and then matches the letter g. (For example, dog, dig, and dug will be matched.)

Any character specified must match. For example, the letter d must be matched in the first position, and the letter g must match in the third position. The middle character can match any character except the newline character \n.

Regular Expression	Words (String)	Matched	Explanation
d.g	dog	dog	Matches all characters d, o, and g.
	d%g	d%g	Matches all characters d, % sign, and g.
	d\ng	None	Not matched, \n is ignored and not matched. d and g are matched, but \n is ignored, so d\ng is not matched.

What if the dot character is in between the square brackets, [ ]?

Regular Expression	Explanation
d[.]g	The dot character between the brackets takes its literal meaning as a single dot (.). So, it will only match d.g but not dog or d%g.

Asterisk (*): Repetition

Let's zoom through this one and look at the following Regular Expression.

Regular Expression	Explanation
zo*m	Match if the character in front of the star occurs zero, one, or many times. The preceding expression is matched. In this case, the letter *o*.

The metacharacter * signifies repetition and can match the preceding expression zero, one, or an almost infinite number of times. * is particularly useful when attempting to match unpredictable occurrences, where a character may or may not appear, allowing for flexible matching. One of the most commonly used Regular Expressions is .*; this combination of a dot followed by a star will match any character for any length.

All of the following examples are matched by the * metacharacter.

Regular Expression	Words (String)	Matched	Explanation
zo*m	zm	zm	Matches *o* zero times. Even without *o*, zm is matched.
	zom	zom	Matches *o* once.
	zoom	zoom	Matches *oo* in the middle.

Plus (+): Repetition

A plus sign (+) is another metacharacter associated with the repetition. It is similar to the star (*), but slightly different because zero times is not considered a match. With the use of the + metacharacter, at least one character must be matched. Let's use the same character again for an explanation.

Regular Expression	Explanation
zo+m	Matches the letter *o* if appears one or more times.

The + metacharacter matches some words.

Regular Expression	Words (String)	Matched	Explanation
zo+m	zm	None	No o in the middle, so no match.
	zom	zom	Matches *z*, *o*, and *m*.
	zoom	zoom	Matches *z*, *oo*, and *m*.

{m, n}: Repetition

Using the metacharacter {m, n }, you can match the number of repetitions. The letter m is the start of the match count, and n is the end of the match count. For example, o{1, 3} takes the meaning of matching the character *o* one to three times. Another example is o{3, }, which means that the repetition of the prepending character *o* must match at least three times or more. Another example is o{, 3}, which will match the same character *o* up to three times. So, the Regular Expression of {0, } is equivalent to +, and {1, } is equivalent to *. Let's study {m, n} by looking at some examples first.

{m}

The reference letter or m is the exact number of repetitions required to match the prepending character. Look at a simple example and explanation.

Regular Expression	Explanation
Zo{1}e	Matches the first letter *Z*, then matches the letter *o* m number of times (m=1), in this case once only, and then matches the letter *e*. So, the expected match letter is Zoe. Note, the Regular Expressions are case-sensitive.

Let's look at more examples to help your understanding. If you can type these on your computer keyboard while following the book, you will learn more.

Regular Expression {m}	Words (String)	Matched	Explanation
o{2}	oo	oo	Matches characters *oo*.
	zoo	zoo	Matches characters *oo*.
	boom	boom	Matches characters *oo*.
zo{2}m	zm	None	Missing *oo*, so not matched.
	zom	None	Missing *oo*, so not matched.
	zoom	zoom	Matches characters *z*, *oo*, and *m*.

{m, n}

The first reference number, or m, is the minimum repetition number, and the second reference number, or n, is the maximum repetition number. First, a simple explanation of how {m, n} works.

Regular Expression	Explanation	Example(s)

o{2, 5}	Matches characters *oo*, *ooo*, *oooo*, or *ooooo*. Matches from two to five occurrences of the letter *o*.	`import re`
		`x = 'zoooooom'`
		`re.findall(r'o{2,5}', x)`
		Output:
		`['ooooo']`
		`import re`
		`t = "Look at the balloons: o, oo, ooo,`
		`oooo, ooooo"`
		`re.findall(r'o{2,5}', t)`
		Output:
		`['oo', 'oo', 'oo', 'ooo', 'oooo', 'ooooo']`

Now let's look at some simple examples.

Regular Expression {m, n}	Words (String)	Matched	Explanation
zo{1,3}m	zm	None	Not matched, *o* matches 0 times.
	zoom	zoom	Matches *z*, *oo*, and *m*.
	zooom	None	Not matched, one too many o.

? (Question Mark: Repetition)

The metacharacter ? has the same meaning as {0, 1} and can be used interchangeably. Again using a simple example, here is more explanation of how ? works in a Regular Expression.

Regular Expression	Explanation
Zoe?	Matches *Zo* or *Zoe*. The character before the question mark, which is *e*, becomes optional. So, even if the string is Zo, the Regular Expression will still match the word. This can be written as Zoe{0, 1}.

Use the same example as before to better understand the ?.

Regular Expression ?	Words (string)	Matched	Explanation
zo?m	zm	zm	Matches z and m. Letter *o* is optional, so it does not have to match.
	zom	zom	Matches *z*, *o*, and *m*.
	zoom	None	Not matched, as only expecting one *o*.

As shown earlier, the *, +, and ? metacharacters can be replaced by {m, n} methods, but using *, +, and ? makes Regular Expressions easier to read and comprehend, so whenever possible, try to use *, +, and ? instead of the {m, n} format.

Python's re Module

As mentioned earlier, Python offers built-in support for Regular Expressions through a standard module known as re (short for Regular Expression). This module comes pre-installed as part of the standard Python library when you install Python on your operating system. As you embark on your journey with the Python re module, it's important to be aware of the different styles you can use when writing Python code with this module. You have the flexibility to keep your script structure simple, standard, or structured.

In the simple style, you can express the Regular Expression in a single line of code, as demonstrated in the example in Table 9-2. When using the standard style, there's no need to use a re.compile statement, but you can improve the code's readability by separating the string and Regular Expression statements. For those seeking a higher level of consistency in their code, the compiler style can be adopted, using the re.compile statement. Any of these coding styles will yield the desired results, but it's worth noting that using the re.compile statement provides a clear advantage. It imparts more control and structure to your code, resulting in a more consistent and stylized code appearance.

Table 9-2. *Different Ways to Use the re Module in Python*

Style	Example

Simple	`>>> import re`
	`>>> m = re.findall(r'\dx\d{4}', "Configuration register is`
	`0x2102")` # re.findall returns a list of strings
	`>>> print(m[0])` # output the first element of a list
	`0x2102`

Standard	`>>> import re`
	`>>> expr = "Configuration register is 0x2102"` # expr stands
	for expression
	`>>> m = re.findall(r'\dx\d{4}', expr)` # m stands for match
	`>>> print(m[0])`
	`0x2102`

Compiler	`>>> import re`
	`>>> expr = "Configuration register is 0x2102"` # expr stands
	for expression
	`>>> p = re.compile(r'\dx\d{4}')` # p stands for pattern
	`>>> m = p.findall(expr)` # m stands for match
	`>>> print(m[0])`
	`0x2102`

Note: "Configuration register is 0x2102" in Cisco devices signifies they will boot using the startup configuration stored in NVRAM at 9600 bps console speed. On the other hand, "Configuration register 0x2142" signifies the device to boot without using the startup configuration, facilitating password recovery.

Let's quickly compare the three styles by examining examples of each using the Cisco IOS register string, `"Configuration register is 0x2102"`. The Regular Expression \dx\d{4} is used to match patterns in text. It matches a digit (\d), then matches the literal x, then matches exactly four more digits based on \d{4}. All three examples will yield the same result—0x2102—but will be written in three different styles. Try each example on your Python Interpreter.

In Python, the r prefix before a string literal denotes a "raw" string literal. Raw string literals treat backslashes (\) as literal characters rather than interpreting them as escape characters. Using the raw string literal (r'...') ensures that backslashes are not interpreted by Python, but are passed directly to the regex engine, allowing it to interpret \d as intended, representing a digit. In short, when working with Regular Expressions in Python, using raw string literals (r'...') is a good practice to ensure proper interpretation of special characters by the regex engine.

In the third compiler style, you designate a separate variable p for the compiler statement, which contains the desired Regular Expression for matching. Subsequently, the variable m is utilized to execute the match function, using expr and p as variables. If you anticipate using the compiled Regular Expression more than twice, adopting this method becomes advantageous over the simpler approaches. It's important to note that Python permits the use of shortcuts, which may reduce the code's length but at the expense of structure and style. Conversely, using more lines of code offers greater control and structure, albeit at the cost of writing additional lines to achieve the same result. In my honest opinion, there are no definitive right or wrong answers in this context; the choice primarily hinges on your style and preferences.

Python re String Methods

Four fundamental types of Regular Expression search methods need to be studied next. First you'll briefly explore these methods and then reinforce your understanding through practical exercises in the Python Interpreter. Refer to Table 9-3.

Table 9-3. *re String Methods*

Method	Explanation
re.match()	**Searches the Regular Expression pattern on the first line** and returns the match object. (Limited to the first line.) Returns None if no match is found.
re.search()	Searches the Regular Expression pattern and **returns the first occurrence**. Unlike re.match(), this method checks all lines. Returns None if no match is found.
re.findall()	Searches the Regular Expression pattern and **matches all occurrences**. Unlike re.match() or re.search(), this method **returns all non-overlapping pattern matches in a string as a list of strings.**
re.finditer()	**Searches the Regular Expression pattern and returns an iterator that yields** MatchObject **instances for all non-overlapping matches** of the string's re pattern.

re.match()

Listings 9-8, 9-9, and 9-10 produce identical match results while using three distinct coding styles with the re.match() method. Analyze their approaches. In programming, multiple paths can lead to the same goal.

Listing 9-8. re.match() Method 1

```
>>> import re
>>> re.match(r'\d\w\d{4}', '0x2142 Configuration register is 0x2102')
<re.Match object; span=(0, 6), match='0x2142'>
```

Listing 9-9. re.match() Method 2

```
>>> import re
>>> expr = '0x2142 Configuration register is 0x2102'
>>> re.match(r'\d\w\d{4}', expr)
<re.Match object; span=(0, 6), match='0x2142'>
```

Listing 9-10. re.match() Method 3

```
>>> import re
>>> expr = '0x2142 Configuration register is 0x2102'
>>> p = re.compile(r'\d\w\d{4}')
>>> m = p.match(expr)
>>> print(m)
<re.Match object; span=(0, 6), match='0x2142'>
```

Let's do another re matching exercise. In Listing 9-11, the match object is returned with the span indicating the start and end positions of the matching string. Conversely, in Listing 9-12, when no matching object is found, the returned value is None. In Python, None serves a similar role as null in other programming languages, signifying that no match was found.

Listing 9-11. re.match() Exercise 1

```
>>> import re
>>> p = re.compile('[a-z]+')
>>> expr = "five regular expressions"
>>> m = p.match(expr)
>>> print(m)
<re.Match object; span=(0, 4), match='five'>
```

Listing 9-12. re.match() Exercise 2

```
>>> import re
>>> p = re.compile('[a-z]+')
>>> expr = "5 regular expressions"
>>> m = p.match(expr)
>>> print(m)
None
```

The previous listings are crucial in shaping the structure of your Python Regular Expression script flow. Observing the returned values, one recommendation is to construct your Python re scripts in the following format, ensuring that the script proceeds only if a match is found, and otherwise printing "Match not found":

Recommended Regular Expression Script Format for Chapter 9

```
import re # import 're' module
p = re.compile("Enter_re_here") # compile a pattern, 'p' stands for pattern
expr = 'string_to_search_here' # data or expression, 'expr' stands for
expression
m = p.match(expr) # matching patterns using pattern, 'm' stands for match
if m: # execute only if a match is found
  print('Match found: ', m.group())
else:
  print('Match not found')
```

---

re.search()

As shown earlier, you can use the re.search() method to perform a matching operation, and in Listing 9-13, the returned result is the same as re.match() when the Regular Expression matches the target string and returns the first matched object. The Regular Expression [a-z]+ matches one or more lowercase letters in the range from a to z. However, in this case, it will only match the string 'five' because you are using the re.search() method.

Listing 9-13. re.search() Exercise 1

```
>>> import re # import the 're' module
>>> p = re.compile('[a-z]+') # write your regex expression using
re.compile method
>>> expr = "five regular expressions" # add the string you want to perform
a search
>>> m = p.search(expr) # use re.search() to match the first item
>>> print(m)
<re.Match object; span=(0, 4), match='five'>
>>> print(m[0])
five
```

Let's apply this code to a real example, as shown here:

```
>>> import re
>>> p = re.compile(r"(\S+) (\d) (\S+) (\S+) (\w)")
>>> arp = "33.33.33.1 0 b3:a9:5a:ff:c8:35 VLAN#33 L"
>>> m = p.search(arp)
>>> m.group()
'33.33.33.1 0 b3:a9:5a:ff:c8:35 VLAN#33 L'
>>> m.group(1)
'33.33.33.1'
>>> m.group(2)
'0'
>>> m.group(3)
'b3:a9:5a:ff:c8:35'
```

```
>>> m.group(4)
'VLAN#33'
>>> m.group(5)
'L'
```

On the other hand, in Listing 9-14, unlike the re.match() method in Listing 9-12, the re.search() method's Regular Expression skips the digit 5, moves to the next match, and returns the matched string 'regular'. Therefore, **the** match() **method is typically used when searching from the beginning of the string, while the** search() **method can be used to find the first instance by searching the entire string.**

Listing 9-14. re.search() Exercise 2

```
>>> import re
>>> p = re.compile('[a-z]+') # pattern
>>> expr = "5 regular expressions" # expression
>>> m = p.search(expr) # match
>>> print(m)
<re.Match object; span=(2, 9), match='regular'>
```

re.findall()

This time, let's practice using the findall() method with the same Regular Expression pattern. Enter each line into your Python Interpreter console to gain more hands-on experience. Unlike the previous two methods, the findall() method returns the matched objects as a list. In Listing 9-15, each word has been returned as individual strings as a list.

Listing 9-15. re.findall() Exercise 1

```
>>> import re
>>> p = re.compile('[a-z]+')
>>> expr = "five regular expressions"
>>> m = p.findall(expr)
>>> print(m)
['five', 'regular', 'expression']
```

In Listing 9-16, findall() matches all strings satisfying the Regular Expression condition, but ignores the digit 5. This method will try to match and return all matched objects in a list format.

Listing 9-16. re.findall() Exercise 2

```
>>> import re
>>> p = re.compile('[a-z]+')
>>> expr = "5 regular expressions"
>>> m = p.findall(expr)
>>> print(m)
['regular', 'expression']
```

re.finditer( )

The next exercise focuses on the finditer() method. As before, type the code and practice through the exercises (refer to Listings 9-17 and 9-18). The finditer() method returns results similar to the findall() method but provides an iterator for all non-overlapping matches of the string's Regular Expression pattern. While it can be a powerful tool for text processing, the use cases for the finditer() method are rather limited.

Listing 9-17. re.finditer() Exercise 1

```
>>> import re
>>> p = re.compile('[a-z]+')
>>> expr = "five regular expressions"
>>> m = p.finditer(expr)
>>> print(m)
<callable_iterator object at 0x000001E581F1B5E0>
>>> for r in m:
...     print(r) # don't forget to add four whitespaces before the print
        statement
...
<re.Match object; span=(0, 4), match='five'>
<re.Match object; span=(5, 12), match='regular'>
<re.Match object; span=(13, 23), match='expression'>
```

Listing 9-18. re.finditer() Exercise 2

```
>>> import re
>>> p = re.compile('[a-z]+')
>>> expr = "5 regular expression"
>>> m = p.finditer(expr)
>>> print(m)
<callable_iterator object at 0x000001E581F1B5E0>
>>> for r in m: print(r) #A loop statement on a single line can be concise
but may be confusing.
...
<re.Match object; span=(2, 9), match='regular'>
<re.Match object; span=(10, 20), match='expression'>
```

Match Object Method

Earlier, you observed the returned objects resulting from Regular Expression matches using the match and search methods. However, there were still some questions regarding the matched strings and how they precisely function. To gain a better understanding of the attributes of these returned objects, following the execution of the match and search methods, you can rely on match object methods to find answers to your questions. First, let's quickly study the re match object methods in Table 9-4.

Table 9-4. *re Match Object Methods*

Match Method	Explanation
group()	Returns the matched string.
start()	Returns the starting position of the matched string.
end()	Returns the ending position of the matched string.
span()	Returns the starting and ending positions of matched string in tuple format.

Now that you have some understanding of the available match object methods, let's look at learning these methods through exercises to verify the returned objects. In the first exercise involving the match method, you will individually access the match object attributes using the group, start, end, and span match methods. You will continue to use the recommended re format to keep the learning more structured. To get the most out of this exercise, enter the lines of Python code provided in Listing 9-19 into the interpreter and interactively check the results.

Listing 9-19. re.match()

```
>>> import re
>>> p = re.compile('[a-z]+') # pattern
>>> expr = "automation" # expression
>>> m = p.match(expr) # match
>>> print(m)
<re.Match object; span=(0, 10), match='automation'>
>>> m.group()
'automation'
>>> m.start() # the first matched position is 0, indexing begins with
0 in Python
0
>>> m.end() # the object (word) has 10 characters (index 0-9), so the end
position is 10 (or n-1)
10
>>> m.span() # span will display both the start and end positions of the
matched object
(0, 10)
```

In the search match method demonstrated in Listing 9-20, if you want to determine the precise location of the match object in memory, you can use group, start, end, and span without the round brackets at the end. Nevertheless, the primary focus should be on the results of the group(), start(), end(), and span() methods to access the match object attributes.

Listing 9-20. re.search()

```
>>> import re
>>> p = re.compile('[a-z]+') # compile for alphabets 'a-z'
>>> expr = "5 regular expressions"
>>> m = p.search(expr)
>>> print(m)
<re.Match object; span=(2, 9), match='regular'>
```

```
>>> m.group # use the method without the brackets to display attributes
<built-in method group of re.Match object at 0x7faa9fc0f0c0>
>>> m.group() # group matches the first object, 'regular'
'regular'
>>> m.start() # the starting 'r' in 'regular' has an index of 2
2
>>> m.end() # the ending 'r' in 'regular' has an index of 9
9
>>> m.span # use the method without the brackets to display attributes
<built-in method span of re.Match object at 0x7faa9fc0f0c0>
>>> m.span() # to see the attributes in a friendly format, add the round
brackets
(2, 9)
```

Compile Options

When compiling Regular Expressions, you have the option to include specific modifiers in your expressions. First, let's have a quick overview of these options. When utilizing these Regular Expression options, you can either use the full descriptive option names like re.DOTALL, re.IGNORECASE, re.MULTILINE, and re.VERBOSE, or opt for their abbreviated versions, such as re.S, re.I, re.M, and re.X. Refer to Table 9-5 for more details.

Table 9-5. *re Compile Options*

Options	Abbreviation	Explanation
DOTALL	S	Matches any character including a newline, \n.
IGNORECASE	I	Makes the regex case-insensitive or ignore case. All major regex engines match in case-sensitive mode; I mode disables case sensitivity.
MULTILINE	M	^ and $ will match the start and end of a line, instead of the whole string. It enables the Regular Expression engine to handle an input string that consists of multiple lines.
VERBOSE	X	Allows the use of verbose mode. Whitespace is ignored. Spaces, tabs, and carriage returns are not matched as spaces, tabs, and carriage returns.

If you have reviewed this table and are ready to engage in practical learning, remember the phrase, "no pain, no gain." Proceed by typing the following exercises into the Python Interpreter so you can gain valuable insights from the provided examples.

re.DOTALL (re.S)

The DOTALL option is used to include a newline character in the match string. Let's now examine how the DOTALL option operates in a practical scenario. You can refer to Listings 9-21 and 9-22 for further demonstration of this in action.

Listing 9-21. Without re.DOTALL()

```
>>> import re
>>> expr = 'a\nb' # expression
>>> p = re.compile('a.b') # pattern
>>> m = p.match(expr) # match
>>> print(m)
None # No match found due to the use of the newline character, '\n'
```

In Listing 9-21, the \n character literally signifies a newline, and because of this, the Regular Expression 'a.b' alone cannot match 'a\nb'.

Listing 9-22. re.DOTALL()

```
>>> import re
>>> expr = 'a\nb' # define a string with a newline character.
>>> p = re.compile('a.b', re.DOTALL) # compile the regular expression with
the DOTALL option.
>>> m = p.match(expr) # attempt to match the expression.
>>> m
<re.Match object; span=(0, 3), match='a\nb'> # Match object successfully
captures 'a\nb'.
>>> print(m[0]) # print the matched substring, which includes the newline
character.
a
b
```

In Listing 9-22, when you activate the DOTALL option using re.DOTALL, it becomes clear that even the \n character is considered a part of the matched string. Typically, you wouldn't use the DOTALL option to match newline characters directly. Instead, it's primarily used to match strings that span multiple lines while disregarding the newline characters within them. I'm optimistic that this is beginning to make sense, and your expertise in Regular Expressions is taking shape.

re.IGNORECASE (re.I)

When the IGNORECASE option is activated, it renders the Regular Expression case insensitive. This means that both uppercase and lowercase letters are matched, regardless of the letter casing. To gain a practical understanding of how re.IGNORECASE (or re.I) functions, let's engage in some exercises. Refer to Listing 9-23 for a demonstration.

Listing 9-23. re.IGNORECASE()

```
>>> import re
>>> expr1 = 'automation'
>>> expr2 = 'Automation'
>>> expr3 = 'AUTOMATION'
>>> p = re.compile('[a-z]+', re.IGNORECASE)
>>> m1 = p.match(expr1)
>>> print(m1)
<re.Match object; span=(0, 10), match='automation'>
>>> m2 = p.match(expr2)
>>> print(m2)
<re.Match object; span=(0, 10), match='Automation'>
>>> m3 = p.match(expr3)
>>> print(m3)
<re.Match object; span=(0, 10), match='AUTOMATION'>
```

Let's apply this code to a simple network example. Extract the interface information only using re.IGNORECASE.

```
import re

log_data = """
ERROR: Interface Gi1/0/0 DOWN
Error encountered on interface gi1/0/1
WARNING: INTERFACE GI2/0/1 DOWN
"""

pattern = r'interface gi\d+/\d/\d?'
matches = re.findall(pattern, log_data, re.IGNORECASE)
print("Matches for interface names:", matches)

Output:
Matches for interface names: ['Interface Gi1/0/0', 'interface gi1/0/1',
'INTERFACE GI2/0/1']
```

A single exercise is enough to comprehend the use of re.IGNORECASE or re.I. In Listing 9-23, the identical pattern has been used three times to match patterns within three distinct expressions (strings). You used three different casing styles (all lowercase, first-letter capitalization, and all uppercase expressions) as the target strings. Thanks to the re.I option being activated in the Regular Expression pattern, it successfully matches all three strings, regardless of their letter casing. I believe that you're grasping this concept and that your competence in working with Regular Expressions is improving.

re.MULTILINE (re.M)

Next, let's take a closer look at how the re.MULTILINE (or re.M) option is used in conjunction with the ^ and $ Regular Expression metacharacters. As previously explained, the ^ metacharacter serves to signify the start of a string, while $ is utilized to denote the end of a string. In simple terms, a Regular Expression like ^Network implies that the first string must commence with the word "network", whereas automation$ means the last string must conclude with the word "automation". Once again, you can gain a practical understanding of the MULTILINE option by putting it into action. Follow along with Listings 9-24 and 9-25 to grasp the re.M string matching.

Listing 9-24. Without re.MULTILINE()

```
>>> import re
>>> expr = '''Regular Engineers
... Regular Network Engineers
... Regular but not so regular Engineers'''
>>> p = re.compile('^R\w+\S') # match 'R' at the line start and end at the
first non-whitespace character
>>> m = p.findall(expr)
>>> print(m)
['Regular'] # only matches the first substring on the first line
```

Listing 9-25. ^ and re.MULTILINE()

```
>>> import re
>>> expr = '''Regular Engineers
... Regular Network Engineers
... Regular but not so Regular Engineers'''
>>> p = re.compile('^R\w+\S', re.MULTILINE) # match 'R' at the line start
and end at the first non-whitespace character on multiple lines
>>> m = p.findall(expr)
>>> print(m)
['Regular', 'Regular', 'Regular'] # matches all three substrings on three
different lines
```

In both of the provided listings, the data (expression) comprises three lines that all commence with the word "Regular." Each line begins with this same word, and the Regular Expression ^R\w+\S is designed to match the first word only, which starts with a capital R and is followed by alphanumeric characters up to the first non-whitespace character (\S). In Listing 9-24, where the re.MULTILINE option is not enabled, the search operation exclusively matches the first occurrence of the word "Regular." Conversely, in Listing 9-25, with the re.MULTILINE option activated, the search can match the word "Regular" at the start of each new line within the multiple lines of the input. I have faith that this information is resonating with you and that your proficiency in Regular Expressions is on the rise.

Tip

Accessing the listings from GitHub

Try to type as much as you can and maintain accuracy in your work. If you need to double-check for typos, you can access the exercises used in this chapter by downloading them from my GitHub. If necessary, you may also choose to copy and paste the required information.

URL: `https://github.com/pynetauto/apress_pynetauto_ed2.0/tree/main/source_codes/ch09`

re.VERBOSE (re.X)

Most of the Regular Expression examples introduced in this chapter have been relatively basic in comparison to the Regular Expressions used in real, production-ready scripts. Now, consider the following two examples presented in Listings 9-26 and 9-27; despite their differences in appearance, they are, in fact, identical scripts that return the same results. The Regular Expression is designed to collectively attempt to match all digits, including the comma, and then return them as a list of digits.

Listing 9-26. Without re.VERBOSE

```
>>> import re
>>> expr = 'I was born in 2,009 and I am 15 years old. I started my primary
school in 2,015'
>>> p = re.compile(r'[1-9](?:\d{0,2})(?:,\d{3})*(?:\.\
d*[1-9])?|0?\.\d*[1-9]|0')
>>> m = p.findall(expr)
>>> print(m)
['2,009', '15', '2,015']
```

Listing 9-27. With re.VERBOSE

```
>>> import re
>>> expr = 'I was born in 2,009 and I am 15 years old. I started my primary
        school in 2,015'
>>> # Define a regular expression pattern with comments
```

```
>>> p = re.compile(r"""
... [1-9] # Match a single digit between 1 and 9
... (?:\d{0,2}) # Match a digit between 0-9, 0 to 2 times
... (?:,\d{3})* # Match a comma, followed by 3 digits, zero or more times
... (?:\.\d*[1-9])? # Match a dot, followed by digits (optional), ending
    with a non-zero digit (optional)
... | # OR
... 0?\.\d*[1-9] # Match 0 once or not at all, then a dot, followed by
    digits (optional), ending with a non-zero digit
... | # OR
... 0 # Match a single 0
... """, re.VERBOSE)
>>> m = p.findall(expr)
>>> print(m)
['2,009', '15', '2,015']
```

For novice Python coders with limited exposure to Regular Expressions, the compiled Regular Expression in the first example (r'[1-9](?:\d{0,2}) (?:,\d{3})*(?:\.\d*[1-9])?|0?\.\d*[1-9]|0') may appear to be nothing more than gibberish. This complex Regular Expression is designed to match date-related digits, including both standalone digits and those with commas used for thousands. The first example is what you have become familiar with so far. However, the second example leverages the re.VERBOSE option to enhance readability by adding comments and explanations that clarify how the Regular Expression functions. While both examples produce the same outcome, the latter significantly improves readability, even for the person who originally authored the Regular Expression. With the re.VERBOSE (or re.X) option, you can demystify the Regular Expression and include optional comments to enhance its comprehensibility and readability. I hope that this information is sinking in, and that your expertise in mastering Regular Expressions is progressing steadily.

\: The Confusing Backslash Character

In Python, the backslash \ gives special meaning to a metacharacter. It acts as an escape character both in Python strings and in the regex engine, which eventually processes your patterns. The use of the backslash in the Python regex engine can sometimes lead to confusion regarding the number of escape characters needed to precisely match the desired string from the data. To eliminate this confusion, when you compile a Regular Expression in Python, **you can append r (raw string notation) immediately before the Regular Expression. This helps ensure that backslashes are treated literally and don't require additional escaping.**

Let's examine this concept through two examples presented in Listings 9-28 and 9-29. In the first example, raw string notation is not used, while the second example uses it. In the provided code, various Regular Expressions are used to test against the input string 'Our team \scored three goals\', which includes escape characters (backslashes). The purpose is to identify matches for the substring "\scored".

Listing 9-28. Backslashes Without Raw String Notation

```
>>> import re
>>> expr = 'Our team \scored three goals\\'
>>> p1 = re.compile('\scored')
>>> p2 = re.compile('\\scored')
>>> p3 = re.compile('\\\scored')
>>> p4 = re.compile('\\\\scored')
>>> p5 = re.compile('\\\\\scored')
>>> print(p1.findall(expr))
[] # no match, returns an empty list
>>> print(p2.findall(expr))
[]
>>> print(p3.findall(expr))
['\\scored']
>>> print(p4.findall(expr))
['\\scored']
>>> print(p5.findall(expr))
[]
```

A crucial point to remember is that while working with Regular Expressions in Python, it's essential to manage backslashes attentively, considering their role as escape characters in both Python strings and regex patterns. In numerous instances, opting for raw string notation (by adding an r before the regex pattern) can streamline the handling of backslashes and enhance the readability of your patterns.

In Listing 9-29, both the compiled Regular Expression with three backslashes and the one with four backslashes match and return the same result. This situation can be perplexing, leaving you uncertain about whether you should use three or four backslashes to successfully match the word with the literal backslash character, "\ scored".

Listing 9-29. Backslash with Raw String Notation

```
>>> import re
>>> expr = 'Our team \scored three goals\\'
>>> p1 = re.compile(r'\scored')
>>> p2 = re.compile(r'\\scored')
>>> p3 = re.compile(r'\\\scored')
>>> p4 = re.compile(r'\\\\scored')
>>> print(p1.findall(expr))
[] # no match, returns an empty list
>>> print(p2.findall(expr))
['\\scored']
>>> print(p3.findall(expr))
[]
>>> print(p4.findall(expr))
[]
```

Listing 9-30 uses raw string notation, r, and it becomes clear that the result shows you need to use two backslashes to match the intended string "\scored". Using one, three, or four backslashes in conjunction with raw string notation will not return a successful match for the target string.

Listing 9-30. Backslash with Raw String Notation

```
>>> import re
>>> expr = 'Our team \scored three goals\\'
>>> p2 = re.compile(r'\\scored')
>>> m = p2.findall(expr)
>>> print(m)
```

```
['\\scored']
>>> n = m[0] # assign the first element of the list m to the variable n.
>>> n
'\\scored'
>>> for x in n:
...     print(x, end='')
...
\scored
```

In Listing 9-30, the raw string match method is used effectively. It matches both backslashes (\\) in the input string and returns the matched string, "\scored", as a list. To store a specific item from this list into a variable, you can use the indexing method, as demonstrated by n = m[0]. This process differs from **casting**, where one data type is converted into another. For instance, consider s = "123", which can be transformed into n = int(x). This conversion turns the string '123' into the numeric value 123.

Regular Expressions: A Brief Review and More

This section conducts a quick review of what you've learned so far and then looks into a few additional metacharacters and Regular Expression methods, such as grouping, lookahead, and lookbehind search. If you've completed the exercises in each listing and have reached the second half of this chapter, you're making excellent progress, and you're already halfway there. It took me a full three months to write this single chapter, so if you can digest the information in a week or two, you're doing better than I did. Let your fingers do the walking as you read through this chapter.

Exploring More Metacharacters

While I've already covered the most commonly used metacharacters, there are a few more that you need to understand to deepen your understanding. These additional metacharacters exhibit slightly different behaviors compared to those discussed earlier in this chapter. You've already studied metacharacters like +, *, [ ], and { }, which perform a single search as they change positions in a matching string. Now, let's expand your metacharacter repertoire by introducing some new ones. After that, you'll study examples of grouping, lookahead, and lookbehind.

The OR Operator (|)

In a Regular Expression, the | (pipe) metacharacter carries the same meaning as OR. The Regular Expression a|b is functionally similar to [ab], but their operation differs. Both | and [ ] function as OR operators, attempting to match specific characters in the string. However, the matched results and their interpretations vary slightly. To gain a precise understanding of the distinction between | and [ ], study the examples demonstrated in Listings 9-31 and 9-32.

Listing 9-31. a[bc]

```
>>> import re
>>> re.findall('a[bc]', 'a, ab, ac, abc, acb, ad')
['ab', 'ac', 'ab', 'ac']
```

In Listing 9-31, the Regular Expression [ ] was used to match either 'b' or 'c'. The returned values from this Regular Expression also include the leading 'a'.

Listing 9-32. a(b|c)

```
>>> re.findall('a(b|c)', 'a, ab, ac, abc, acb, ad')
['b', 'c', 'b', 'c']
```

However, Listing 9-32 replaced [ ] with |, and the returned values only consisting of the matched 'b' or 'c', without the leading 'a'. So, the key difference between [ ] and | lies in how they handle the leading character(s) in the match, with one returning the leading character(s) and the other not.

Now, when you examine Listings 9-33 and 9-34, this distinction is further emphasized using a Regular Expression's range option, making it more evident that one displays the leading character while the other does not.

Listing 9-33. 3[a-f]

```
>>> re.findall('3[a-f]', '3, 3a, 3c, 3f, 3g')
['3a', '3c', '3f']
```

Listing 9-34. 3(a|b|c|d|e|f)

```
>>> re.findall('3(a|b|c|d|e|f)', '3, 3a, 3c, 3f, 3g')
['a', 'c', 'f']
```

Listings 9-35 and 9-36 provide straightforward examples of the | (OR) operator using the words "apple" and "raspberry."

Listing 9-35. apple|raspberry

```
>>> re.match('apple|raspberry', 'raspberry pie')
<re.Match object; span=(0, 8), match='raspberry'>
```

In Listing 9-35, the Regular Expression 'apple|raspberry' is used with re.match to find a match for the word "raspberry" in the text "raspberry pie," and it successfully finds a match.

Listing 9-36. apple|rasberry

```
>>> print(re.findall('apple|raspberry', 'raspberry and apple pie'))
['raspberry, 'apple']
```

In Listing 9-36, the same Regular Expression 'apple|raspberry' is applied with re.findall to search for occurrences of 'raspberry' and 'apple' in the text 'raspberry and apple pie.' It identifies both words and returns them as a list.

^ and $ (Anchors)

In Regular Expressions, the ^ (caret) character is known as the "caret anchor" because it is used to find a match starting at the first character of a string. Similarly, the $ character is called the "dollar anchor" and is used to find a match at the end of a string. When combined with the re.MULTILINE or re.M option, these anchors enable the Regular Expression to operate at each newline in your data or strings. To gain a better understanding, let's perform some exercises using your Python Interpreter. Check out Listings 9-37 and 9-38.

Listing 9-37. ^Start

```
>>> re.findall('^Start', 'Start to finish')
['Start']
```

In Listing 9-37, the ^ character instructs the Regular Expression '^Start' to find and match the word 'Start' at the beginning of the string.

Listing 9-38. finish$

```
>>> re.findall('finish$', 'Start to finish')
['finish']
```

In Listing 9-38, the $ character instructs the Regular Expression to search for and match the word 'finish' at the end of the string.

Listing 9-39. ^S.+sh$

```
>>> re.findall('^S.+sh$', 'Start to finish')
['Start to finish']
```

Listing 9-40 explores a combined example of ^ and $. The Regular Expression '^S.+sh$' is designed to match an exact string that starts with 'S' and ends with 'sh', which is precisely what it does in the given example, matching the entire string 'Start to finish'.

Listing 9-40. ^S.+sh$' and re.M

```
>>> re.findall('^S.+sh$', 'Start to finish\nSpecial fish\nSuper fresh',
re.MULTILINE)
['Start to finish', 'Special fish', 'Super fresh']
```

In Listing 9-40, by using the re.MULTILINE module, you successfully matched three lines of strings that all start with 'S' and end with 'sh'.

Now, let's explore a simplified practical example through another exercise. You can access the Listing 9-40. sh ip int brief.txt file for this exercise on my GitHub website. Check out Listing 9-41 for more details.

Listing 9-41. ^Gig.+up$ and re.M

```
>>> import re
>>> expr = '''
... sydcbdpit-st01#sh ip int brief # '... ' is not part of the expression.
... Interface              IP-Address      OK? Method Status      Protocol
... Vlan1                  unassigned      YES NVRAM  up               up
... Vlan50                 10.50.50.11     YES NVRAM  up               up
... FastEthernet0          unassigned      YES NVRAM  down           down
... GigabitEthernet1/0/1   unassigned      YES unset  down           down
```

```
...  GigabitEthernet1/0/2     unassigned        YES unset  up                       up
...  GigabitEthernet1/0/3     unassigned        YES unset  up                       up
... '''
>>> p1 = re.compile('^Gig.+down$', re.MULTILINE) # Look for a line starting
with Gig and ending with the word 'down'.
>>> m1 = p1.findall(expr) # match 1
>>> print(m1)
['GigabitEthernet1/0/1    unassigned        YES unset  down                  down']
>>> p2 = re.compile('^Gig.+up$', re.MULTILINE) # change to 'up' to find
online Gig interfaces
>>> m2 = p2.findall(expr) # match 2
>>> for up_gint in m2: # use the for loop to print each item on each line
...        print(up_gint)
...
GigabitEthernet1/0/2    unassigned       YES unset  up                       up
GigabitEthernet1/0/3    unassigned       YES unset  up                       up
```

You can readily apply this concept to a real-world scenario, such as when you need to extract interface information from the show commands of your network devices. Listing 9-41 illustrated this by using the lines of a Cisco switch's show ip interface brief commands. With the Regular Expression '^Gig.+up$' or '^Gig.+down$', you efficiently identify Gigabit Ethernet interfaces with either up or down status. While this example is oversimplified for demonstration purposes, in a real-world environment where you manage hundreds or even thousands of switchport interfaces, the power of Regular Expressions becomes indispensable for processing the collected data. Reflect on situations where you can harness the capabilities of these Regular Expressions with Python and explore them further based on your practical knowledge and experience.

\A and \Z

\A matches the start of the string, locating a match exclusively at the string's very beginning. It is commonly used to specify that a pattern should commence from the start of the string. Conversely, \Z matches the end of the string, identifying a match solely at the string's conclusion. It is used to indicate that a pattern should conclude at the string's end. In single-line string matching, ^ and \A behave identically. However, their behaviors differ when attempting to match multi-line strings, as demonstrated in Listings 9-42 and 9-43.

Listing 9-42. ^S.+sh

```
# Matches lines starting with 'S' and ending with 'sh' in a single-
line string.
>>> re.findall('^S.+sh', 'Start to finish')
['Start to finish']
```

Listing 9-43. \AS.+sh

```
# Matches lines starting with 'S' and ending with 'sh' but only if it's at
the start of the entire single-line string.
>>> re.findall('\AS.+sh', 'Start to finish')
['Start to finish']
```

Similarly, the behavior also applies to $ and \Z, when attempting to match multi-line strings, as demonstrated in Listing 9-44. With the re.M or re.MULTILINE option enabled, ^ can match both at the start of strings and after each line break, while \A only matches at the start of the string, as exemplified in Listing 9-45.

Listing 9-44. ^S.+sh with re.MULTILINE

```
# Matches lines starting with 'S' and ending with 'sh', where 'S' can
appear anywhere before 'sh', across multiple lines.
>>> import re
>>> re.findall('^S.+sh', 'Start to finish\nSuper special fish\nSuper fresh
fish\nSuper smelly fish', re.M)
['Start to finish', 'Super special fish', 'Super fresh fish', 'Super
smelly fish']
```

Listing 9-45. \AS.+sh with re.MULTILINE

```
# Matches lines starting with 'S' and ending with 'sh', but only at the
start of each line in the multi-line string.
>>> re.findall('\AS.+sh', 'Start to finish\nSuper special fish\nSuper fresh
fish\nSuper smelly fish', re.M)
['Start to finish']
```

Additionally, $ can match both at the end of the string and before each line break, as demonstrated in Listing 9-46. In contrast, \Z exclusively matches at the end of the string, as shown in Listing 9-47.

Listing 9-46. S.+sh$ with re.MULTILINE

```
# Matches lines ending with 'sh', where 'S' can appear anywhere before
'sh', across multiple lines.
>> re.findall('S.+sh$', 'Start to finish\nSuper special fish\nSuper fresh
fish\nSuper smelly fish', re.M)
['Start to finish', 'Super special fish', 'Super fresh fish', 'Super
smelly fish']
```

Listing 9-47. S.+sh\Z with re.MULTILINE

```
# Matches lines ending with 'sh', where 'S' can appear anywhere before
'sh', but only if they are the whole string, not just a part, across
multiple lines.
>>> re.findall('S.+sh\Z', 'Start to finish\nSuper special fish\nSuper fresh
fish\nSuper smelly fish', re.M)
['Super smelly fish']
```

The following exercises illustrate how the combined use of ^ or \A and $ or \Z influences the results of matched returns. I've introduced intentional newlines by separating each line with \n to replicate the newline effect. To enhance your comprehension, create your examples and experiment with these metacharacters. Gain more insights by running the code in your Python Interpreter all at once, following the examples in Listings 9-48, 9-49, 9-50, and 9-51.

Listing 9-48. ^S.+sh$ with re.M

```
# Matches lines starting with 'S' and ending with 'sh', across
multiple lines.
>>> re.findall('^S.+sh$', 'Start to finish\nSuper special fish\nSuper fresh
fish\nSuper smelly fish', re.M)
['Start to finish', 'Super special fish', 'Super fresh fish', 'Super
smelly fish']
```

Listing 9-49. \AS.+sh$ with re.M

```
# Matches lines starting with 'S' and ending with 'sh', but only at the
start of the entire string.
>>> re.findall('\AS.+sh$', 'Start to finish\nSuper special fish\nSuper
fresh fish\nSuper smelly fish', re.M)
['Start to finish']
```

Listing 9-50. ^S.+sh\Z with re.M

```
# Matches lines starting with 'S' and ending with 'sh', but only if they
are the whole string, not just a part.
>>> re.findall('^S.+sh\Z', 'Start to finish\nSuper special fish\nSuper
fresh fish\nSuper smelly fish', re.M)
['Super smelly fish']
```

Listing 9-51. \AS.+sh\Z with re.M

```
# Tries to match lines starting with 'S' and ending with 'sh', but it can't
find a complete match, resulting in an empty list.
>>> re.findall('\AS.+sh\Z', 'Start to finish\nSuper special fish\nSuper
fresh fish\nSuper smelly fish', re.M)
[]
```

\b and \B (Word Boundaries in Regular Expressions)

In Regular Expressions, \b represents a word boundary. Within a sentence, these boundaries correspond to the spaces between words, where one side is a word character (e.g., \w), and the other side is not (e.g., space or the beginning of the string).

Word Boundary	Description
\b	Matches positions where one side is a word character (like \w), and the other side is not. It's similar to the anchors ^ and $, and often represents the beginning or end of a word.
\B	The negation of \b, \B, matches positions where \b does not match. It's useful for finding patterns surrounded by word characters.

To avoid confusion, always use the raw string notation (r) when using \b in Regular Expressions, as \b is a backspace character in literal notation.

Listing 9-52 attempts to match the word "computers". The pattern includes leading \b and trailing \b to specify word boundaries. This ensures the match occurs when the word is surrounded by spaces, returning the expected result.

Listing 9-52. \b(word)\b Matched

```
>>> import re
>>> expr = "Small computers include smartphones."
>>> p = re.compile(r'\bcomputers\b')
>>> m = p.search(expr)
>>> print(m)
<re.Match object; span=(6, 15), match='computers'>
```

In Listing 9-53, the word 'microcomputers' contains the term 'computers' but begins with 'micro', which means that the word boundary \b cannot match the word 'computers' when it follows 'micro'. As a result, the expected outcome is None.

Listing 9-53. \b(word)\b Not Matched

```
>>> import re
>>> expr = "Microcomputers include smartphones."
>>> p = re.compile(r'\bcomputers\b')
>>> m = p.search(expr)
>>> print(m)
None
```

In Listing 9-54, the first \b in the Regular Expression is omitted, and now it successfully matches the target word, 'computers', returning the expected result.

Listing 9-54. (word)\b Matched

```
>>> import re
>>> expr = "Microcomputers include smartphones."
>>> p = re.compile(r'computers\b')
>>> m = p.search(expr)
>>> print(m)
<re.Match object; span=(5, 14), match='computers'>
```

613

\B has the opposite meaning to \b and is used to achieve the reverse effect. In Listing 9-55, the goal is to match the word 'computer' without the plural s at the end. To do this, you utilize a leading \B and ending \B to precisely target and match the word.

Listing 9-55. \B(word)\B Matched

```
>>> import re
>>> expr = "Microcomputers include smartphones."
>>> p = re.compile(r'\Bcomputer\B')
>>> m = p.search(expr)
>>> print(m)
<re.Match object; span=(5, 13), match='computer'>
```

Grouping

Imagine you have a string representing the up and down status of a flapping link on a router. You want to find and match continuous "up" status. After identifying these sequences, you can use the group() option to retrieve and print the output, as demonstrated in Listing 9-56. To create a group in a Regular Expression, you enclose the pattern within parentheses ( ). While this example might seem impractical, it serves to introduce the concept of Regular Expression grouping. In the next example, you'll explore a more practical application.

Listing 9-56. Grouping Exercise 1

```
>>> import re
>>> expr = "downupupupdowndownupdowndown"
>>> p = re.compile("(up)+")
>>> m = p.search(expr)
>>> print(m)
<re.Match object; span=(4, 10), match='upupup'>
>>> print(m.group(0))
upupup
```

Let's explore an example where you need to extract the country name along with the fully qualified telephone number of a technical assistance center, specifically for the United States. The objective is to compile a regular expression that can accurately match the entire string, starting with the country name and then continuing with the technical assistant center's telephone number. For a practical demonstration, refer to Listing 9-57.

Listing 9-57. Grouping Exercise 2

```
>>> import re
>>> expr = "United States 1 408 526 1234"
>>> p = re.compile(r"\w+\s\w+\s\d\s\d{3}\s\d{3}\s\d+")
>>> m = p.search(expr)
>>> print(m)
<re.Match object; span=(0, 28), match='United States 1 408 526 1234'>
```

In Listing 9-57, a combination of shorthand characters—such as \w for alphanumeric characters, \s for whitespace, and \d for digits, along with repetition {n}—is used to match various characters within the string. However, the data captured in this example is not fully leveraged. To extract specific information from the matched strings, you can use grouping.

Suppose the goal is to extract only the country name, as illustrated in Listing 9-58.

Listing 9-58. Grouping Exercise 3

```
>>> import re
>>> expr = "United States 1 408 526 1234"
>>> p = re.compile(r"(\w+\s\w+)\s\d?\s\d{3}\s\d{3}\s\d+")
>>> m = p.search(expr)
>>> print(m)
<re.Match object; span=(0, 28), match='United States 1 408 526 1234'>
>>> country = m.group(1)
>>> country
'United States'
```

Listing 9-58 uses the group(1) method to isolate specific information from the entire matched string. This extracted data can now be utilized as a variable or incorporated into the script. To gain a better understanding of how regular expression groupings are numbered, take a moment to review the index of the group() method. Refer to Table 9-6 for further clarification.

Table 9-6. *Group Method Index Meanings*

Group Index	Explanation
group(0)	Whole matched string
group(1)	Matched first group
group(2)	Matched second group
group(3)	Matched third group
group(n)	Matched n[th] group

To better comprehend grouping method indexing, look at practical examples, as demonstrated in Listings 9-59 and 9-60.

Listing 9-59. Grouping Method Indexing Exercise 1

```
>>> import re
>>> expr = "United States 1 408 526 1234"
>>> p = re.compile(r"(\w+\s\w+)\s(\d?\s\d{3}\s\d{3}\s\d+)")
>>> m = p.search(expr)
>>> print(m)
<re.Match object; span=(0, 28), match='United States 1 408 526 1234'>
>>> phone_number = m.group(2)
>>> phone_number
'1 408 526 1234'
```

Listing 9-60. Grouping Method Indexing Exercise 2

```
>>> import re
>>> expr = "United States 1 408 526 1234"
>>> p = re.compile(r"(\w+\s\w+)\s((\d?)\s(\d{3})\s(\d{3}\s\d+))")
>>> m = p.search(expr)
>>> m.group(0)
'United States 1 408 526 1234'
>>> m.group(1)
'United States'
>>> m.group(2)
'1 408 526 1234'
```

```
>>> m.group(3)
'1'
>>> m.group(4)
'408'
>>> m.group(5)
'526 1234'
```

In Listing 9-59, group(1) captures the country name, while group(2) retrieves the telephone number. Listing 9-60 further breaks down the groups, allowing you to access specific components of the matched string, as illustrated in Figure 9-7.

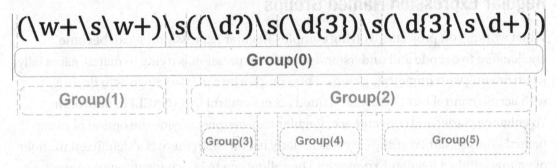

Figure 9-7. Group index in Regular Expression example

In Listing 9-61, the groups have been further divided into smaller segments, allowing you to isolate the country code 1, area code 408, and local number 526 1234 individually. This showcases the flexibility and power of Regular Expression groupings.

Imagine the multitude of possibilities and applications in real networking automation scenarios. With the capability to precisely capture and analyze data from production routers and switches, you can gain invaluable insights and exercise control over your devices based on the collected and processed information. The potential for automation and network management is boundless.

Listing 9-61. Referencing Grouped String

```
>>> import re
>>> expr = "Did you know that that 'that', that that person used in that
    sentence, is wrong."
>>> p = re.compile(r'(\bthat)\s+\1')  # Matches "that" followed by spaces
    and the same "that" again.
>>> m = p.search(expr)
```

```
>>> print(m)
<re.Match object; span=(13, 22), match='that that'>
>>> m = p.search(expr).group()
>>> print(m)
that that
```

Group indexing offers the advantage of shorthand references like +\1. In the Regular Expression (\bthat)\s+\1, the + matches the same strings as the previous group, and \1 re-references group 1. For a second group, \2 is used for reference.

Regular Expression Named Groups

When working on projects involving complex Regular Expressions, it can become challenging to decode and understand what the expression is trying to match, especially when dealing with numerous groups. This complexity can be analogous to dealing with access control lists (ACL) and named access control lists (NACL) in networking. To enhance clarity and convenience, Regular Expressions provide the option of using named groups. Named groups are particularly useful when there is a significant number of groups within a Regular Expression. They allow you to attach meaningful names to groups, making data manipulation more straightforward. This proves handy when conducting advanced search and replace operations, ensuring your code remains both readable and maintainable.

Consider an example where you need to extract information from a line borrowed from a router's show version command. This line includes the router's name and uptime information, specifying the number of years, weeks, days, hours, and minutes the device has been operational.

```
expr = "SYD-GW1 uptime is 1 year, 9 weeks, 2 days, 5 hours, 26 minutes"
```

To match and extract these components individually using Regular Expression groups, the expression may seem intimidating at first, but there's no need to be alarmed. You'll soon break down and unravel each group.

```
(\w+[-]\w+)\s.+((\d+\sy\w+),\s(\d+\sw\w+),\s(\d+\sd\w+),\s(\d+\sh\w+),
\s(\d+\sm\w+))
```

In real-world scenarios, when confronted with numerous complex groupings and attempting to comprehend someone else's code featuring multiple Regular Expression groups, it can be quite challenging, especially if your knowledge of Regular Expressions is limited. For a visual representation of the complexity involved, refer to Figure 9-8.

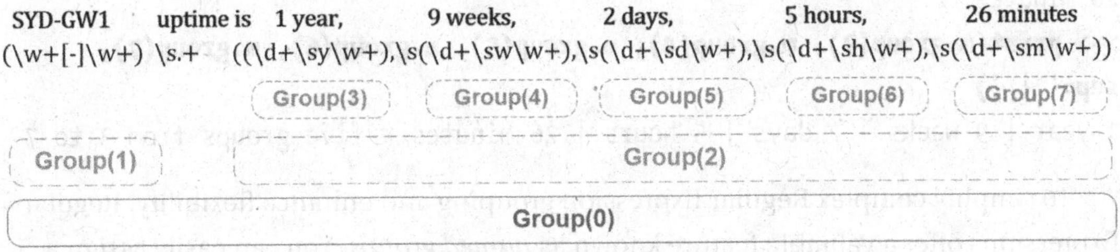

Figure 9-8. *Regular Expression multiple numbered groups example*

Now, let's dive into a practical exercise to understand how this Regular Expression functions in Python. Following the recommended flow for working with Regular Expressions, you'll compile your Regular Expression and apply it to the provided string. As expected, you can extract the router name SYD-GW1 as group 1, print the entire uptime by accessing group 2, and then look at the smaller groups nested within group 2, including groups 3 (years), 4 (weeks), 5 (days), 6 (hours), and 7 (minutes).

If you're not feeling confused at this point, you're certainly making excellent progress. Proceed with confidence as you explore Listing 9-62.

Listing 9-62. Multiple Numbered Groups Exercise

```
>>> import re
>>> expr = "SYD-GW1 uptime is 1 year, 9 weeks, 2 days, 5 hours, 26 minutes"
>>> p = re.compile(r'(\w+[-]\w+)\s.+((\d+\sy\w+),\s(\d+\sw\w+),
    \s(\d+\sd\w+),\s(\d+\sh\w+),\s(\d+\sm\w+))')
>>> m = p.search(expr)
>>> print(m.group(0))
SYD-GW1 uptime is 1 year, 9 weeks, 2 days, 5 hours, 26 minutes
>>> print(m.group(1))
SYD-GW1
>>> print(m.group(2))
1 year, 9 weeks, 2 days, 5 hours, 26 minutes
>>> print(m.group(2), sep=' | ')
1 year, 9 weeks, 2 days, 5 hours, 26 minutes # single group, group 2 only
```

```
>>> print(m.group(3))
1 year
[...omitted for brevity]
>>> print(m.group(7))
26 minutes
>>> print(m.group(3), m.group(4), m.group(5), m.group(6), m.group(7),
sep=' | ')
1 year | 9 weeks | 2 days | 5 hours | 26 minutes # five groups from 3 to 7
```

To simplify complex Regular Expression grouping and enhance flexibility, Regular Expressions offer a valuable feature known as *named groups*. You can easily assign a name to a group by using the syntax ?P<group_name> at the beginning of the group, allowing you to reference the group by the specified name. In the context of the previous example, providing group names transforms the expression, as demonstrated in Listing 9-63. Assigning names to groups adds clarity and meaning to the data they match, eliminating the need for extensive decoding of the Regular Expression.

Listing 9-63. Named Group Exercise

```
>>> import re
>>> expr = "SYD-GW1 uptime is 1 year, 9 weeks, 2 days, 5 hours, 26 minutes"
>>> p_named = re.compile(r'(?P<hostname>\w+[-]\w+)\s.+(?P<uptime>
    (?P<years>\d+\sy\w+),\s(?P<weeks>\d+\sw\w+),\s(?P<days>\d+\sd\w+),
    \s(?P<hours>\d+\sh\w+),\s(?P<minutes>\d+\sm\w+))')
>>> m = p_named.search(expr)
>>> print(m.group("hostname"))
SYD-GW1
>>> print(m.group("uptime"))
1 year, 9 weeks, 2 days, 5 hours, 26 minutes
>>> print(m.group("years"), m.group("weeks"), m.group("days"),
m.group("hours"), m.group("minutes"), sep=" | ")
1 year | 9 weeks | 2 days | 5 hours | 26 minutes
```

When you examine the named groups demonstrated here with the string data in mind, the groupings will be represented as depicted in Figure 9-9.

SYD-GW1	uptime is	1 year,	9 weeks,	2 days,	5 hours,	26 minutes
(\w+[-]\w+)	\s.+	(((\d+\sy\w+),\s(\d+\sw\w+),\s(\d+\sd\w+),\s(\d+\sh\w+),\s(\d+\sm\w+))				
		years	weeks	days	hours	minutes
hostname		uptime				
Group(0)						

Figure 9-9. *Regular Expression named groups example*

Notice how the named groups directly correlate with the information you intend to match, resulting in minimal confusion amid multiple groupings. Instead of investing time in deciphering cryptic Regular Expressions created by others, you can allocate your valuable work hours to tackle mission-critical tasks or improve customer support experiences.

Lookahead and Lookbehind Assertions

Before you jump into this section, it's important to be honest. If you're new to Regular Expressions, the concepts of **lookahead** and **lookbehind** may not immediately capture your interest or stick to you. To facilitate your learning experience and kindle your enthusiasm for this topic, I've put together some practical, yet easy-to-follow exercises. Nevertheless, it might require a few iterations to fully comprehend this concept. Once you've mastered the concepts of lookahead and lookbehind in Regular Expressions, they will elevate your regex skills to such a level that you'll find yourself wanting to use them extensively.

Lookahead, Lookbehind, and Non-Capturing group

Lookaheads and lookbehinds, collectively known as *lookarounds*, often perplex novice regex learners. They might initially appear confusing, given that they all begin with a ?. The distinction between them becomes apparent with the use of the second and third metacharacters. Once you've become proficient in their applications, they evolve into valuable tools for streamlining your Regular Expressions. Don't feel pressured to grasp this section after a first read; take your time to learn about lookarounds. Consider this section as a future reference point. There are four types of lookarounds and a non-capturing group, all commencing with the ? symbol.

As a quick reminder, before you move further, Table 9-7 provides a concise overview of lookarounds along with basic examples.

Table 9-7. *The re Lookahead, Lookbehind, and Non-Capturing Groups*

Lookaround	Name	String	Example	Explanation
?=	Lookahead	abc	a(?=b)	Positive lookahead matches "a" only if it is followed by "b".
?!	Negative lookahead	abc	a(?!b)	Negative lookahead matches "a" only if it is *not* followed by "b".
?<=	Lookbehind	abc	(?<=a)b	Positive lookbehind matches "b" only if it is preceded by "a".
?<!	Negative lookbehind	abc	(?<!a)b	Negative lookbehind matches "b" only if it is *not* preceded by "a".
?:	Non-capturing group	abc	a(?:b)	Non-capturing group (?:b) matches "ab" but doesn't capture it as a separate group in the regex match result.

Now proceed by entering the text marked in bold into your Python Interpreter and observe how the returned objects vary. In the subsequent exercises, you utilize a shortened print function in combination with a Regular Expression and the target string 'abc'. A detailed explanation accompanies each exercise. Stay motivated; type the code in the Python Interpreter for practical application. Active engagement enhances memory retention.

#	Exercise	Explanation

①	>>> **print(re.search('a(?=b)', 'abc'))**
	 <re.Match object; span=(0, 1), match='a'>
	 >>> **print(re.search('a(?=b)', 'xbc'))**
	 None
		Matches a, as the next letter is b. No match, as the first letter is not a before letter b.

②	>>> **print(re.search('a(?!b)', 'abc'))**
	 None
	 >>> **print(re.search('a(?!b)', 'acd'))**
	 <re.Match object; span=(0, 1), match='a'>
		No match, as the next letter is b. Matches a, as the next letter is not b (it is c).

(continued)

#	Exercise	Explanation

③	`>>> print(re.search('(?<=a)b', 'abc'))`
	`<re.Match object; span=(1, 2), match='b'>`
	`>>> print(re.search('(?<=a)b', 'xbc'))`
	`None`
		Matches b, as the previous letter is a.
		
		No match, as the previous letter is not a.

④	`>>> print(re.search('(?<!a)b', 'abc'))`
	`None`
	`>>> print(re.search('(?<!a)b', 'xbc'))`
	`<re.Match object; span=(1, 2), match='b'>`
		No match, as the previous letter is a.
		Matches b, as the previous letter is not a.

⑤	`>>> print(re.search('a(?:b)', 'abc'))`
	`<re.Match object; span=(0, 2),`
	`match='ab'>`
	`>>> print(re.search('a(?=b)', 'abc'))`
	`<re.Match object; span=(0, 1), match='a'>`
		Matches a and b, because b is followed by a. Both ab are matched.
		Matches a, as the next letter is b.
		(This is the same as exercise 1.)

⑥	`>>> import re`
	`>>> expr = "+1 408 526 1234"`
	`>>> p = re.compile(r"((?:(\+1)[ -])?\`
	`(?(\d{3})\)?[ -]?\d{3}[ -]?\d{4})")`
	`>>> m = p.search(expr)`
	`>>> print(m)`
	`<re.Match object; span=(0, 15), match='+1 408 526 1234'>`
	`>>> print(m.group(2))`
	`+1`
		`?:`: represents a non-capturing group. Without `?:`, +1 and the trailing space are captured as a group. However, when you use `?:`, the Regular Expression still matches the group inside the parentheses but doesn't capture it for backreferencing, which is why it's called a non-capturing group.

Expand Your Knowledge:

Visit RexEgg to Explore More Regex Concepts!

Explore RexEgg for in-depth insights and additional Regular Expression examples. It's a valuable, free resource to enhance your understanding of regex. You could spend days on this website, given the wealth of regex knowledge it offers!

URL: `https://www.rexegg.com/`

Practice More Lookarounds

To grasp this concept, practice is essential. Let's use the simple string 'abba' to structure your learning with the full compile method. Although 'abba' sounds like the iconic 70's Swedish pop group, this exercise is purely about the literal string 'abba' for learning purposes.

expr = 'abba'

To fully comprehend this topic, practice is essential. Open your Python Interpreter and enter the text marked in bold next to the three greater-than signs. Reading alone won't help you retain the information; complete all exercises from 1 to 10.

#	Exercise	Regex	Explanation

①	```>>> import re```
	```>>> expr = 'abba'```
	```>>> p = re.compile('a(?=b)')```
	```>>> m = p.search(expr)```
	```>>> print(m)```
	```<re.Match object;```
	```span=(0, 1), match='a'>```
		a(?=b)	Positive lookahead for 'a' followed by 'b'; matches 'a' only if followed by 'b'.

②	```>>> p = re.compile('b(?=b)')```
	```>>> m = p.search(expr)```
	```>>> print(m)```
	```<re.Match object;```
	```span=(1, 2), match='b'>```
		b(?=b)	Positive lookahead for 'b' followed by 'b'; matches 'b' only if followed by another 'b'.

③	```>>> p = re.compile('a(?!b)')```
	```>>> m = p.search(expr)```
	```>>> print(m)```
	```<re.Match object;```
	```span=(3, 4), match='a'>```
		a(?!b)	Negative lookahead for 'a' not followed by 'b'; matches 'a' only if not followed by 'b'.

(continued)

#	Exercise	Regex	Explanation

④	`>>> p = re.compile('b(?!b)')`
	`>>> m = p.search(expr)`
	`>>> print(m)`
	`<re.Match object;`
	`span=(2, 3), match='b'>`
		b(?!b)	Negative lookahead for 'b' not followed by 'b'; matches 'b' only if not followed by another 'b'.

⑤	`>>> p = re.compile`
	`('(?<=a)b')`
	`>>> print(m)`
	`<re.Match object;`
	`span=(1, 2), match='b'>`
		(?<=a)b	Positive lookbehind for 'a' before 'b'; matches 'b' preceded by 'a' in the string.

⑥	`>>> p = re.compile`
	`('(?<=b)b')`
	`>>> m = p.search(expr)`
	`>>> print(m)`
	`<re.Match object;`
	`span=(2, 3), match='b'>`
		(?<=b)b	Positive lookbehind for 'b' before 'b'; matches 'b' preceded by 'b' in the string.

⑦	`>>> p = re.compile`
	`('(?<!a)b')`
	`>>> m = p.search(expr)`
	`>>> print(m)`
	`<re.Match object;`
	`span=(2, 3), match='b'>`
		(?<!a)b	Negative lookbehind for 'a' before 'b'; matches 'b' not preceded by 'a' in the string.

⑧	`>>> p = re.compile`
	`('(?<!b)b')`
	`>>> m = p.search(expr)`
	`>>> print(m)`
	`<re.Match object;`
	`span=(1, 2), match='b'>`
		(?<!b)b	Negative lookbehind for 'b' before 'b'; matches 'b' not preceded by 'b' in the string.

(continued)

#	Exercise	Regex	Explanation

⑨	`>>> p1 = re.compile('a(?:b)')`
	`>>> m1 = p1.search(expr)`
	`>>> print(m1)`
	`<re.Match object;`
	`span=(0, 2), match='ab'>`
		a(?:b)	Non-capturing group for 'ab'; matches 'ab' but doesn't capture it in parentheses.

⑩	`>>> p2 = re.compile('a(?=b)')`
	`>>> m2 = p2.search(expr)`
	`>>> print(m2)`
	`<re.Match object;`
	`span=(0, 1), match='a'>`
		a(?=b)	Positive lookahead for 'a' followed by 'b'; asserts 'a' is followed by 'b' without including 'b' in the match.

Note that all these exercises use expr = 'abba' for better comprehension.

Lookaround Application Examples

For current and aspiring engineers learning the Python programming language, there's a vast amount to explore. The true value and power of Regular Expressions may not become apparent until you start working on real projects. You've been introduced to basic Regular Expressions through exercises, gradually building your regex skills. However, unless you work with regex daily, reaching an advanced level takes time. You can learn the fundamentals from this chapter and complement your knowledge with additional resources online and reading other books to advance your skills.

Let's practice with the Cisco TAC's URL http://www.cisco.com/techsupport. See Listing 9-64 for an example.

Listing 9-64. Only Use Lookahead Method to Print http

```
>>> import re
>>> m = (re.search(r"\w{4,5}(?=:)", "http://www.cisco.com/techsupport"))
>>> print(m.group())
http
```

In Listing 9-64, the Regular Expression \w{4,5}(?=:) matches the preceding alphanumeric characters occurring four to five times, which are followed by a colon (:).

Listing 9-65. Only Use Lookahead and Lookbehind Method to Print www.cisco.com

```
>>> import re
>>> m = (re.search(r"(?<=\/)\w.+[.]\w+[.]\w+(?=/)", "http://www.cisco.com/
techsupport"))
>>> print(m.group())
www.cisco.com
```

To match www.cisco.com exclusively, you used a lookbehind method (?<=), starting with a forward slash (/), and matched the www format. You then used a lookahead (?=) ending with /. Lookarounds allow for quick and precise string matching.

The following expression can match any file names with any file extension types, such as vlan.dat, sw1.bak, config.txt, or even a Cisco switch IOS-XE file such as cat9k_iosxe.16.12.01.SPA.bin. In the example that follows, you will compare the negative lookahead method with the ^ negation method.

.*[.].*$

In the expr (expression or string), note that \n has been used between file names to create a newline effect in a single string. This is also for the sake of simplicity and space-saving. Explanations follow each exercise.

Listing 9-66 uses the Regular Expression .*[.].*$ to match all files in expr.

Listing 9-66. Match All File Types Using Regular Expression - .*[.].*$

```
>>> import re
>>> expr = "vlan.dat\nsw1.bak\nconfig.txt\njdoe.dat\nsw1_old.bak\
    ncat9k_iosxe.16.12.01.SPA.bin"
>>> m = re.findall(".*[.].*$", expr, re.M)
>>> m
['vlan.dat', 'sw1.bak', 'config.txt', 'jdoe.dat', 'sw1_old.bak',
'cat9k_iosxe.16.12.01.SPA.bin']
```

In Listing 9-67, the ^ (caret) method is used to exclude any files ending with the .dat extension, returning all matched file names in a list. Note that this example uses the re. findall and re.M (MULTILINE) methods you learned about earlier in this chapter.

Listing 9-67. Filter Files with File Extensions Not Starting with the Letter d (Not Using the Lookaround Method)

```
>>> import re
>>> expr = "vlan.dat\nsw1.bak\nconfig.txt\njdoe.dat\nsw1_old.bak\
    ncat9k_iosxe.16.12.01.SPA.bin"
>>> m = re.findall(r".*[.][^d].*$", expr, re.M)
>>> m
['sw1.bak', 'config.txt', 'sw1_old.bak', 'cat9k_iosxe.16.12.01.SPA.bin']
```

Listing 9-68 provides a negative lookahead example that returns the same results as Listing 9-67. There's often more than one way to extract the same data.

Listing 9-68. Filter Files with File Extensions Not Starting with the Letter d (Using the Lookaround Method)

```
>>> import re
>>> expr = "vlan.dat\nsw1.bak\nconfig.txt\njdoe.dat\nsw1_old.bak\
    ncat9k_iosxe.16.12.01.SPA.bin"
>>> m = re.findall(r".*[.](?!dat$).*$", expr, re.M)
>>> m
['sw1.bak', 'config.txt', 'sw1_old.bak', 'cat9k_iosxe.16.12.01.SPA.bin ']
```

In Listings 9-69 and 9-70, you have negated any file names ending with .dat or .bak using both negation methods. Still, the latter method has an advantage if the file extension extensions begin with the same letter or if the length of the extension starts to vary.

Listing 9-69. Filter Any Files Ending with .dat and .bak Without Using the Lookaround Method

```
>>> import re
>>> expr = "vlan.dat\nsw1.bak\nconfig.txt\njdoe.dat\nsw1_old.bak\
    ncat9k_iosxe.16.12.01.SPA.bin"
>>> m = re.findall(r".*[.][^d|^b].*$", expr, re.M)
>>> m
['config.txt', 'cat9k_iosxe.16.12.01.SPA.bin']
```

Listing 9-70. Filter Any Files Ending with dat and bak Using the Lookaround Method

```
>>> import re
>>> expr = "vlan.dat\nsw1.bak\nconfig.txt\njdoe.dat\nsw1_old.bak\
    ncat9k_iosxe.16.12.01.SPA.bin"
>>> m = re.findall(r".*[.](?!dat$|bak$).*$", expr, re.M)
>>> m
['config.txt', 'cat9k_iosxe.16.12.01.SPA.bin']
```

In Listings 9-71 and 9-72, the returned results are different, as the Regular Expressions used in Listing 9-71 filtered or negated all files, but in Listing 9-72, only the files ending with .dat or .bak have been filtered.

Listing 9-71. Filter Any Files Ending with dat or bak Using the ^ Negation Method

```
>>> import re
>>> expr = "file1.bak\nfile2.dat\nfile3.bakup\nfile4.data"
>>> m = re.findall(r".*[.][^d|^b].*$", expr, re.M)
>>> m
[] # no match, returns an empty list
```

If you try to write a working Regular Expression without the negative lookahead method in Listing 9-72, the Regular Expression will be lengthy and cryptic. In Listing 9-72, using the negative lookahead method, you can simply append the exact extension name with the | (OR) sign in the Regular Expression.

Listing 9-72. Filter Any Files Ending with dat or bak Using Negative Lookahead Method

```
>>> import re
>>> expr = "file1.bak\nfile2.dat\nfile3.bakup\nfile4.data"
>>> m = re.findall(r".*[.](?!dat$|bak$).*$", expr, re.M)
>>> m
['file3.bakup', 'file4.data'] # returns all file types excluding the .dat
or .bak files
```

sub Method: Substituting Strings

Using the sub method in Regular Expressions, you can replace or exchange matched strings. Let's start with an exercise to see it in action and review the results.

Substitute Strings Using sub

Let's begin with an exercise before we go into the details. Refer to Listing 9-73.

Listing 9-73. Use sub to Substitute Multiple Matching Words

```
>>> import re
>>> p = re.compile('HP|Juniper|Arista')
>>> p.sub('Cisco', 'Juniper router, HP switch, Arista AP and Palo Alto
firewall')
'Cisco router, Cisco switch, Cisco AP and Palo Alto firewall'
```

Listing 9-73 demonstrates using the sub method to replace the vendors Juniper, HP, or Arista, and Cisco. However, in Listing 9-74, we are controlling the number of replacements using the count=1 parameter, which only replaces the first matched item.

Listing 9-74. Use sub to Substitute a Matching Word Only Once

```
>>> p.sub('Cisco', 'Juniper router, HP switch, Arista AP and Palo Alto
    firewall', count=1)
'Cisco router, HP switch, Arista AP and Palo Alto firewall'
```

Suppose you need to find out the number of replacements in a longer string. In such cases, you can utilize the subn method to accomplish this task. Listing 9-75 explores how this works.

Listing 9-75. Use subn to Count the Number of Replacements

```
>>> import re
>>> expr = '''Juniper router, HP switch, Palo Alto firewall, Juniper
router, HP switch, Palo Alto firewall, Juniper router, HP switch, Palo Alto
firewall, Juniper router, HP switch, Palo Alto firewall, Juniper router, HP
switch, Palo Alto firewall, Juniper router, HP switch, Palo Alto firewall,
and Arista router'''
>>> p = re.compile('HP|Juniper|Arista')
>>> p.subn('Cisco', expr)
('Cisco router, Cisco switch, Palo Alto firewall, Cisco router, Cisco
switch, Palo Alto firewall, Cisco router, Cisco switch, Palo Alto firewall,
Cisco router, Cisco switch, Palo Alto firewall, Cisco router, Cisco switch,
Palo Alto firewall, Cisco router, Cisco switch, Palo Alto firewall, and
Cisco router', 13)
```

You can use the subn method to substitute strings and count the number of replacements. In Listing 9-75, 13 instances of strings like HP, Juniper, and Arista have been replaced with the word Cisco.

Using sub and \g to Swap Positions

When you use the sub method in a Regular Expression, you can combine it with relative group referencing (\g). Let's say you have a string like 'Model Number: C8300-1N1S-6T', and you want to swap the positions of 'C8300-1N1S-6T' and 'Model Number' so that it looks like this:

From	To
Model Number : C8300-1N1S-6T →	C8300-1N1S-6T: Model Number

Type the code from each exercise into your Python Interpreter to gain a better understanding. In Listing 9-76, you've compiled the match Regular Expression into three groups and, using the sub method, reversed the group sequence after matching each group. The groups stay in the same positions, but groups 1 and 3 have switched places.

Listing 9-76. Use sub and Grouping to Swap Positions

```
>>> import re
>>> expr = "Model Number : C8300-1N1S-6T"
>>> p = re.compile(r"(\w+\s\w+)(\s[:]\s)(\w+[-]\w+[-]\w+)") # (grp1)
    (grp2)(grp3)
>>> m = p.sub("\g<3>\g<2>\g<1>", expr)
>>> print(m)
C8300-1N1S-6T : Model Number
```

In Listing 9-77, you can apply named grouping and provide meaningful names to each group to achieve your goal. This is a named group example that accomplishes the same result as before. Note that the group was not given a name like (?P<comma>\s[:]\s) to demonstrate that you can mix and match named groups with numbered groups.

Listing 9-77. Mix and Match Numbered and Named Groups

```
>>> import re
>>> expr = "Model Number : C8300-1N1S-6T"
>>> p = re.compile(r"(?P<Desc>\w+\s\w+)(\s[:]\s)(?P<Model>(\w+[-]\w+[-]\w+))")
>>> m = p.sub("\g<Model>\g<2>\g<Desc>", expr)
>>> print(m)
C8300-1N1S-6T : Model Number
```

In Listing 9-78, you used only two named groups and omitted the "comma" group. However, when you applied the sub method to perform the matching, you included the colon (:) in your replacement expression to achieve the desired result.

Listing 9-78. Use sub and the Named Group Method to Swap Positions

```
>>> import re
>>> expr = "Model Number : C8300-1N1S-6T"
>>> p = re.compile(r"(?P<Desc>\w+\s\w+)\s[:]\s(?P<Model>(\w+[-]\
    w+[-]\w+))")
>>> m = p.sub("\g<Model> : \g<Desc>", expr)
>>> print(m)
C8300-1N1S-6T : Model Number
```

Insert a Function in the sub Method

In network design and operations, you frequently work with binary, decimal, and hexadecimal values. Hexadecimal values are commonly used in MAC addresses and IPv6 addresses. Understanding how to convert between hexadecimal, binary, and decimal is crucial for IPv6 addressing.

In the upcoming exercises, you will practice using functions with the sub method. In Listing 9-79, you have to use the standard Python methods to convert a randomly chosen decimal IP address into binary numbers. The same conversion can be achieved using the sub command, as demonstrated in Listing 9-80.

Listing 9-79. Decimal to Binary Using the join Method

```
>>> ip = '172.168.123.245'
>>> print ('.'.join([bin(int(x)+256)[3:] for x in ip.split('.')]))
10101100.10101000.01111011.11110101
```

Listing 9-80. Decimal to Binary Using the sub Method

```
>>> ip = '172.168.123.245'
>>> def dec2bin(match):
...     value = int(match.group())
...     return bin(value)
...
>>> p = re.compile(r'\d+')
>>> p.sub(dec2bin, ip)
'0b10101100.0b10101000.0b1111011.0b11110101' # '0b' indicates a
binary number.
```

When the sub method is used, the compiled return result starts with 0b, which indicates that this is a binary number.

Listing 9-81. Binary to Decimal Using the join Method

```
>>> ip = "00001010.11010110.10001011.10111101"
>>> ip1 = ip.replace(".", "") # remove the . characters
>>> ip1
'00001010110101101000101110111101'
>>> def bin2dec():
...     return ".".join(map(str, int(ip1, 2).to_bytes(4, "big")))
...
>>> bin2dec()
'10.214.139.189'
```

In Listing 9-81, you created a function called dec2bin and used it in the sub method to get the decimal IP address into binary numbers. Listing 9-81 chooses a random binary IP address and showcases the conversion from binary to decimal numbers using Python's join method. After this conversion, the listing confirms that the IP address you are looking for is 10.214.139.189.

Listing 9-82. Hexadecimal to Decimal Numbers

```
>>> mac = "84:3d:c6:f5:c9:ba"
>>> mac1 = mac.replace(":", "")
>>> mac1
'843dc6f5c9ba'
>>> i = int(mac1, 16)
>>> str(i)
'145400865868218'
```

Listing 9-82 captures the MAC address of a switch and wants to convert these hexadecimal numbers into decimal numbers. Using the basic Python methods, you can easily convert hexadecimal numbers into decimals. This is a good example of how efficient Python can be in converting numbers from one form to another.

Listing 9-83. Decimal to Hexadecimal

```
>>> def hexrepl(match):
...       value = int(match.group())
...       return hex(value)
...
>>> p = re.compile(r"\d+")
>>> p.sub(hexrepl, 'MAC address: 145400865868218')
'MAC address: 0x843dc6f5c9ba' # '0x' indicates a hexadecimal number.
```

In Listing 9-83, you've written Python code using the sub method to reverse the decimal MAC address back into a hexadecimal number for demonstration purposes. The 0x at the beginning of the number indicates that it's a hexadecimal value.

That concludes the last listing or exercise in this comprehensive chapter. I've done my best to distill the essence of Regular Expressions into a single chapter, even though the topic could fill an entire book with multiple chapters. I hope you've enjoyed mastering Regular Expression concepts using Python and its re module. Congratulations if you've completed this chapter in its entirety. As mentioned, it might not be enough to fully comprehend the content of this chapter in a single reading or practice session. If you're still unsure about some parts, I encourage you to go over this chapter at least one to two more times. Once you have, think about real-world applications where you can tap into the potential of these Regular Expressions in Python and explore them more deeply based on your work experience. Real-world problem-solving using book knowledge is how IT professionals maintain their expertise.

Tip

Handy cheat sheets for taming Regular Expressions

For those new to Regular Expressions, this chapter might have been challenging. However, mastering Regular Expressions is essential in general programming; this is not an optional learning.

For additional help on this topic, check out these Regular Expressions Cheat Sheets:

1. https://cheatography.com/davechild/cheat-sheets/
   regular-expressions/

2. `https://web.mit.edu/hackl/www/lab/turkshop/slides/` `regex-cheatsheet.pdf`

3. `https://italchemy.wordpress.com/2020/07/09/` `regular-expression-cheatsheet/` (My Regular Expression Cheat Sheet)

The last URL leads to my personal Regular Expression Cheat Sheet. However, I believe that the most valuable cheat sheet is one crafted by you, reflecting your unique experiences. Hence, while the referenced cheat sheets serve as excellent reference points, endeavor to create your personalized Regular Expression cheat sheet for future reference.

Optionally, if you want to get some more practice to solidify what you have learned in this book, you can find more exercises from my blog: `https://` `wordpress.com/post/italchemy.wordpress.com/5830`.

Summary

This chapter delved into the world of Regular Expressions for network automation. It served as a foundational guide to mastering the versatile tool that is Regular Expressions. In this chapter, readers discovered the power of Regular Expressions as a universal key to programming languages, unlocking a skillset that is crucial for handling data in computing. Three different methods were explored to understand Regular Expressions, including using Notepad++, the Linux shell, and online resources. This chapter covered the basics of regex operations, including character classes, the dot (single character match), repetition using the * (star), +, and {m,n}, as well as other advanced metacharacters.

The re module in Python took center stage, offering methods like re.match(), re.search(), re.findall(), and re.finditer, along with match object methods and compile options. Essential regex concepts like DOTALL, ignore case, multiline, and the verbose options were mastered. The sometimes confusing backslash character was clarified. As you proceeded, a review of regex basics was followed by the exploration of more metacharacters like the OR operator, anchors (^ and $), and word boundaries (\b and \B). The chapter introduced grouping and the use of named groups to enhance regex readability.

The chapter concluded with in-depth insights into lookahead and lookbehind assertions and their applications. The sub method for substituting strings was explored, allowing you to manipulate text effectively. By mastering Regular Expressions, you equip yourself with invaluable skills for handling data efficiently, making you a more proficient programmer.

CHAPTER 10

GNS3 Basics

This chapter takes a deep dive into the world of GNS3, an essential tool for networking and automation students and enthusiasts. It starts with an overview of GNS3, including the software and installation procedures. Once you have GNS3 up and running, you'll explore various aspects of its functionality, from the user interface to the nuances of setting up a Cisco IOS router. The chapter includes a step-by-step guide on installing the Microsoft Loopback Adapter, a crucial component for seamless communication between GNS3 devices and the host PC. But that's not all; you'll also venture into the realm of network automation by configuring a GNS3 IOS router using a Python script from a Windows host PC. This chapter is packed with hands-on labs and practical insights, setting the stage for the networking automation adventures to come. So, whether you're a novice looking to gain networking skills or an experienced engineer seeking to expand your knowledge, this chapter is your gateway to mastering GNS3 and network automation.

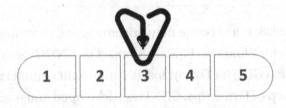

Exploring GNS3 and VMware Networking Labs

To gain a deep understanding of your networking lab, you need to build it yourself. Crafting your virtual lab is a potent method to master specific IT skills. In this chapter, you embark on a journey to create a fundamental networking lab using GNS3 and VMware Workstation Pro. You are guided through every installation and configuration step, ensuring your setup is primed for network automation testing. This chapter also unveils various GNS3 features on the Windows platform. The beauty is that you can eliminate the need for physical

639

© Brendan Choi 2024
B. Choi, *Introduction to Python Network Automation Volume I - Laying the Groundwork*,
https://doi.org/10.1007/979-8-8688-0146-4_10

networking hardware. As you construct a simple lab topology, you will use an older Cisco IOS router image and subject the lab to various set-up validations, thus enhancing your familiarity with the lab environment. Building these basic IOS labs in GNS3 will equip you with essential skills that can be applied to diverse network automation labs. You can even extend the use of these labs to your professional work, whether for proof-of-concept testing or to pursue various vendor networking certifications. As you reach the midway point of this book, you stand at a crossroads—the last leg of groundwork before you delve into the exciting Python Network Automation labs that lie ahead.

GNS3 at a Glance

Warning

The pre-task must be finished before proceeding

At the end of Chapter 6, you downloaded the GNS3 VM.ova file specific to your GNS3 version and subsequently imported it as a virtual server to host your networking devices. If you have not yet accomplished this task, return to the section titled "Downloading and Installing the GNS3 VM from a .ova File" and complete it before proceeding with this chapter.

GNS3, introduced in 2008, is a versatile network emulator that supports multiple vendors. It is available for Windows, Linux, and macOS. GNS3 is also known as the graphical user interface (GUI) for Dynamips. It's important to understand that the GUI-based GNS3 runs on top of Dynamips. GNS3 was developed and is supported by the community, and you can download it for free after registering on the GNS3.org website (https://www.gns3.com/software) or download it from the Developer's GitHub without account registration (https://github.com/GNS3/gns3-gui/releases).

For this chapter, you need the latest version of GNS3 to set it up as a virtual server on VMware Workstation. Running GNS3 on VMware Workstation Pro as a virtual machine is recommended, and it's considered a best practice for your Python Network Automation learning lab setup. As a new GNS3 is released often, your latest version will always be newer than the version used in this book. At the time of writing this chapter, the latest supported version was GNS3 version 2.2.43, and the newer version 3.0.0 alpha 4 was already available to the community for early testing use. When GNS3 runs as a local server on the host operating system, it can significantly degrade Windows performance. Therefore, it is advisable to run GNS3 as a separate virtual machine (VM) on VMware Workstation. This configuration prevents CPU and memory contention issues between the host PC and the GNS3 server.

Another reason for using GNS3 is to create an integrated lab with Linux virtual machines (VMs). You can use these Linux servers as Python servers to control virtual routers and switches in various proof-of-concept (PoC) labs, facilitating the study and testing of networking concepts.

When installing GNS3 on a Windows machine, you only need a single installation .exe file, but some additional software will be automatically installed during the installation process. Ensure that your computer is directly connected to the Internet during the installation. The installation procedures detailed in this book include tips I've accumulated over the years, and I recommend following each step closely to replicate all the tasks in this chapter.

To test routers, switches, or firewalls, you need to locate the necessary software separately and integrate it into GNS3 for various labs. It's worth noting that GNS3 doesn't support all IOS types and versions. It primarily supports older IOS 12.x versions for testing purposes. While Cisco's 7200 router IOS version 15.x can be still supported, it has two notable issues: it consumes significant CPU and memory resources, and it lacks support for the layer 2 switching function.

Tip

Cisco CML vs. Cisco VIRL?

In this chapter and throughout this book, the term *Cisco CML* is consistently used. It essentially represents the newer version of the previous Cisco VIRL. Cisco CML is a software platform designed for emulating Cisco networking devices in virtual environments. While VIRL stands for Virtual Internet Routing Lab, CML stands for Cisco Modelling Lab. In 2020, CML replaced VIRL. For the sake of clarity in this book, I exclusively use the term *CML* to refer to Cisco's network device emulation software.

Cisco's IOU was initially available to internal Cisco TAC engineers, and a spinoff from IOU resulted in the new VIRL L2 and L3 software for networking studies. Cisco has since renamed VIRL to CML Personal Edition (PE). The new CML-PE L2 and L3 images are identical to the previous VIRL images, so in this book, you can use either image from Cisco.

GNS3 offers more valuable features for integrating other software and serves as an excellent study tool for networking students and IT professionals. CML-PE, VIRL, and IOU images support the use of Qemu as a key feature in the new GNS3. There's also support for appliance integration via Docker images. In GNS3, Docker and virtualization programs can run concurrently on the GNS3 VM server. A significant advantage of configuring such a lab setup has been the support for the layer 2 switching function through L2 IOSv images because the introduction of IOU and VIRL. GNS3 continues to support both CML-PE's L2 and L3 images., which are IOS-XE based.

If you want to study Cisco routing and switching, I highly recommend using either Cisco CML-PE or EVE-NG lab solutions. If you're new to GNS3, you'll find the installation procedures in this chapter straightforward. For longtime GNS3 users, this chapter offers various installation and configuration tips to improve your existing GNS3 integration skills.

GNS3 was briefly discussed in Chapter 1 when comparing various emulation and simulation software for cost-effective and time-saving networking studies. You also examined the advantages and disadvantages of each software. By the end of Chapter 6, you learned how to create a virtual machine, specifically a GNS3 VM from a .ova file, which is a pre-installed virtual machine for quicker deployment. You've already downloaded and created a virtual machine named GNS3 VM as part of this process. You've been gradually acquiring essential IT skills in Python, virtualization, Linux administration, and Regular Expressions in preparation for the Python Network Automation labs.

Starting in this chapter, you build an environment where you can learn, test, validate, and master various network automation scenarios using Python. The GNS3 installation in this chapter is a continuation of where you left off in Chapter 6. You proceed with the installation of GNS3 to integrate Cisco IOS in this chapter, and later, you'll integrate the CML-PE L2 and L3 IOSv images, so the virtual networking devices can communicate with the Windows host PC and Linux VMs on the same network.

Installing GNS3 the First Time

Creating the GNS3 VM virtual machine on VMware Workstation 17 Pro in Chapter 6 was a preparatory step for integrating GNS3 with VMware Workstation and Cisco CML software. GNS3 software is used to configure and control Cisco's IOS and

CML images, but these images will run from the GNS3 VM, which, in turn, runs on VMware Workstation. This setup, with a VM running within another VM, is known as a nested virtualization environment.

Before downloading the GNS3 installation (.exe) file for Windows 11, it's important to verify the version of your GNS3 VM to ensure compatibility with the software you download. As mentioned, download the latest installable file to proceed with this chapter. This book is using GNS3 version 2.2.42, which was the latest available at the time of writing the first chapter. Because newer GNS3 software versions are already available, either version 2.2.42 or the latest version of GNS3, possibly version 3 or higher, should work perfectly fine.

Downloading the GNS3 Installation File

If you haven't already downloaded the GNS3 installation file, visit the GNS3 download URL at `https://github.com/GNS3/gns3-gui/releases` and download the suitable GNS3 .exe file for your GNS3 VM version (refer to Figure 10-1). The version used in this book is 2.2.42 (`GNS3-2.2.42-all-in-one.exe`). You can reasonably assume that the GNS3 VM version used in this book is also 2.2.42, and this virtual machine is already pre-installed on your VMware Workstation. To precisely follow the steps in this book, you can use the same software versions. However, if you are using VMware Workstation 16 Pro and the latest GNS3 files, the installation and setup processes will be nearly identical, so you should not encounter major challenges when configuring your GNS3 environment.

Assets 20		
GNS3-2.2.42-all-in-one.exe	99.5 MB	Aug 9
GNS3-2.2.42-all-in-one.exe.sha256	93 Bytes	Aug 9
GNS3-2.2.42.dmg	115 MB	Aug 9
GNS3-2.2.42.dmg.sha256	82 Bytes	Aug 9
GNS3-2.2.42.source.zip	18.7 MB	Aug 9
GNS3-2.2.42.source.zip.sha256	89 Bytes	Aug 9
GNS3.VM.ARM64.2.2.42.zip	1.02 GB	Aug 9
GNS3.VM.ARM64.2.2.42.zip.sha256	91 Bytes	Aug 9
GNS3.VM.Hyper-V.2.2.42.zip	1.05 GB	Aug 9
GNS3.VM.Hyper-V.2.2.42.zip.sha256	93 Bytes	Aug 9
GNS3.VM.KVM.2.2.42.zip	1020 MB	Aug 9
GNS3.VM.KVM.2.2.42.zip.sha256	89 Bytes	Aug 9
GNS3.VM.VirtualBox.2.2.42.zip	1.01 GB	Aug 9
GNS3.VM.VirtualBox.2.2.42.zip.sha256	96 Bytes	Aug 9
GNS3.VM.VMware.ESXI.2.2.42.zip	1.08 GB	Aug 9
GNS3.VM.VMware.ESXI.2.2.42.zip.sha256	97 Bytes	Aug 9
GNS3.VM.VMware.Workstation.2.2.42.zip	1.08 GB	Aug 9
GNS3.VM.VMware.Workstation.2.2.42.zip.sha256	104 Bytes	Aug 9
Source code (zip)		Aug 9
Source code (tar.gz)		Aug 9

Figure 10-1. *GNS3 installation file download for Windows*

In this example, the software is downloaded from the developer's GitHub website by clicking the Assets option. Alternatively, you can also download the same software from the GNS3.org website after logging in with your user account. It is always less cumbersome to access these files through GitHub.

GNS3 Installation and Setup

As part of the installation process, GNS3 will install essential software components such as Microsoft Visual C++ 2017 Redistributable (x64), Wireshark, WinPcap, and Npcap. If your PC already has these essential software components installed, the GNS3 installation wizard will automatically detect them. However, if these components are not installed, GNS3 will automatically take care of their installation. In most installation scenarios, the GNS3 installation will proceed without any hiccups. But if you encounter any difficulties during the installation, you have the option to pre-install the correct versions

644

of Wireshark, WinPcap, and Npcap before initiating the GNS3 installation. During the installation process, you may also be presented with an offer to sign up and install SolarWinds software. In my opinion, this software can be considered as bloatware and may impact your computer's performance. Therefore, if you are concerned about your computer's performance, I recommend declining SolarWinds' free offer.

GNS3 Installation

The basic installation procedures have been comprehensively documented in a dedicated installation, integration, and troubleshooting guide. This approach ensures the incorporation of high-quality supplementary content and saves pages for more important content in this book. Installing GNS3 on your Windows host PC is a straightforward process, mainly involving a few clicks of the Next button until the installation is complete. For detailed, step-by-step guidance on the initial GNS3 installation process, consult Chapter 10's pre-task installation guide, titled Ch10_VMware_GNS3_install_integrate_ and_tshoot_VTx_v1.1.pdf, accessible at https://github.com/pynetauto/apress_ pynetauto_ed2.0/tree/main/pre_installation_guides. If you encounter challenges while setting up GNS3 and the GNS3 VM on your Windows laptop/PC, it's imperative to reference this documentation before proceeding to the next section.

Warning

Prerequisite: GNS3 installation required to proceed

As mentioned, this book uses GNS3 version 2.2.42, which was the latest version at the time of writing Chapter 6. GNS3 receives regular updates, and version 2.2.43 and a Beta version 3 was released toward the end of 2023. GNS3 VM is essentially an Ubuntu 20.04 LTS server that hosts virtualized devices in a nested setup. In the newer GNS3 3.x Beta version, the base host image changed to Ubuntu 22.04 LTS, and there were plans to phase out the GNS3 VM hosting on VMware Workstation. If you're comfortable installing and following the version 3 method, you can do so at your own risk. However, if you want to follow this book, I recommend that all readers use the same software versions while honing their new skills.

To follow along with each task on your laptop, you must download and complete the installation, integration, and troubleshooting of GNS3 and GNS3 VM on the Workstation Pro.

GNS3 Setup Procedures

You have completed all the standard GNS3 installation procedures and confirmed that both your GNS3 application and GNS3 VM are running, as depicted in Figures 10-2 and 10-3. If you encounter any issues during the GNS3-to-GNS3 VM integration process, it's essential to diagnose and resolve these integration problems before moving on to construct your network lab. **At this stage in the book, it is assumed that all readers have successfully set up GNS3 and GNS3 VM on their laptops/PCs**, as illustrated here.

#	Task
①	After launching the GNS3 app, it should automatically initiate the startup of the GNS3 VM on the VMware Workstation. It might take 1-2 minutes for the GNS3 VM to power up and for the system resources to stabilize. See Figure 10-2.

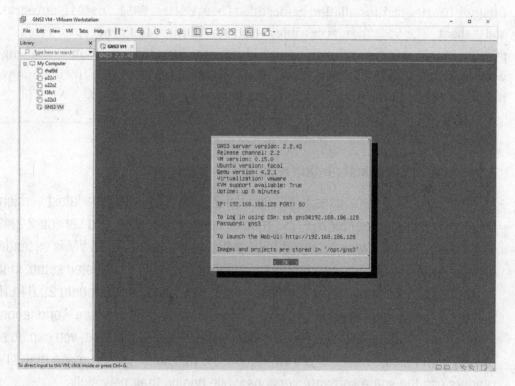

Figure 10-2. GNS3 VM powered-on by the GNS3 App

(continued)

#	Task
②	After the GNS3 VM is powered on, you should observe the red circle in the Server Summary Window change to green (see Figure 10-3). If it remains red, you may be encountering issues; in other words, your GNS3 VM might not have started correctly. In such a scenario, it's a must to troubleshoot and resolve the issue before proceeding to the next section to learn more about GNS3.

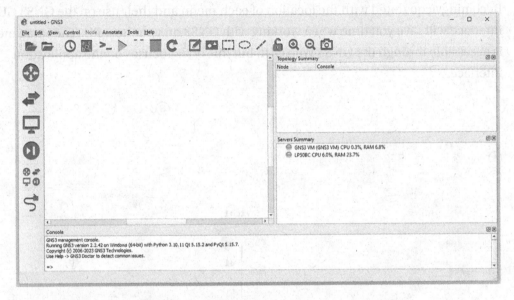

Figure 10-3. *GNS3 is operational and ready for some work*

You have GNS3 at your fingertips now, so it's time to dive into its menus and familiarize yourself with the interface, enabling you to efficiently use this application to achieve your learning objectives.

Getting Familiar with GNS3

Now that GNS3 has been successfully installed and launched, you are all set to utilize the application. Before diving into GNS3 and creating test network topologies, it's a good idea to take a moment to explore the user interface. Understanding the functionalities and options of each menu will be of great help. All the icon menus, as well as additional menu options, can be accessed from the main drop-down menu. The following sections provide a brief introduction to the GNS3 menu and offer useful tips to help you smoothly navigate the menus and run networking labs using GNS3.

GNS3 Menus and GUI

Figure 10-4 displays GNS3's main window, and Table 10-1 describes each option. Becoming acquainted with the location of each menu and their use on the GNS3 GUI interface will save you time when working with GNS3 on your host PC. The same menu is accessible through the GNS3 Web GUI, but this book focuses on the application interface.

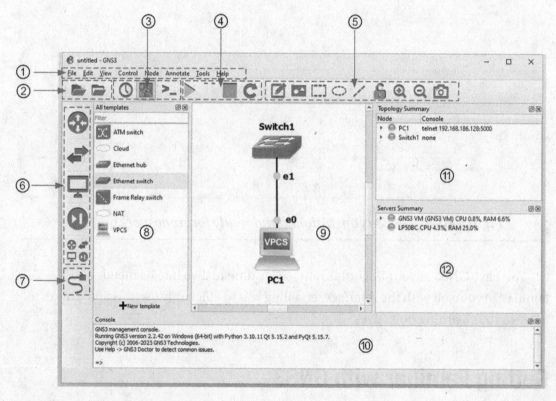

Figure 10-4. *GNS3 GUI*

Here are brief explanations of each GNS3 GUI menu component to assist you in understanding them better. The circled numbers in Figure 10-4 correspond to the circled numbers in Table 10-1.

Table 10-1. *GNS3 GUI Components*

#	Menu	Explanation
①	Menu option	Access options from the drop-down menu.
②	File option	Open or save GNS3 projects.
③	Device and Topology option	Manage snapshots, show/hide connectors, and console into devices.
④	Simulation option	Power on/off, pause, and restart devices.
⑤	Drawing tools	Decorate the GNS3 Topology canvas with drawing tools.
⑥	Device Type icons	Show devices based on different device types.
⑦	Add a Link tool	Connect various devices.
⑧	Device List	List installed devices and use the search menu to filter displayed devices.
⑨	Topology canvas	Select and drop devices onto the canvas to create a working topology.
⑩	Log window	Display GNS3 operational status and send commands using this window.
⑪	Topology/Node Summary	View the current GNS3 device summary.
⑫	Server Summary	Check the GNS3 VM and local server status, including CPU and memory utilization for each server.

Now is a good time to discover some general user tips for smoothly running your GNS3 network labs. First, let's consider why it's essential to handle your lab environment with care and diligence.

Gracefully Shutting Down GNS3 and GNS3 VM

Before you start arranging icons on GNS3's Topology canvas, it's important to keep in mind that due to GNS3's sensitivity to Windows installations and the software's emulation of physical hardware, GNS3 running on a Windows OS may not always be 100 percent reliable. To minimize potential issues and save troubleshooting time, it's crucial to approach the starting and closing of GNS3 on your Windows OS with care.

When you start GNS3, allow it sufficient time to launch all its background services, especially if you're using the GNS3 VM to host virtual network devices. Most importantly, when shutting down GNS3, it's imperative to follow a specific set of procedures to prevent configuration loss and avoid the risk of project file corruption resulting from abrupt application closures. While GNS3 is an excellent free tool for studying essential networking concepts, it may not offer the same level of reliability as enterprise-grade solutions. In the end, the stability of your labs depends on your system's performance and how you treat the application.

After completing each lab, whether for Cisco or other vendor devices, on GNS3, it's critical to save the running configurations. For Cisco IOS devices, you can achieve this by running copy running-config startup-config or write memory to save the running configurations to the startup configuration. Subsequently, ensure that all devices are appropriately powered off by using the Big Red Stop button or individually selecting and shutting down each device (see Figure 10-5). Once all configurations are saved and the devices are powered down, you can gracefully shut down GNS3 by clicking the X in the top-right corner (see Figure 10-6).

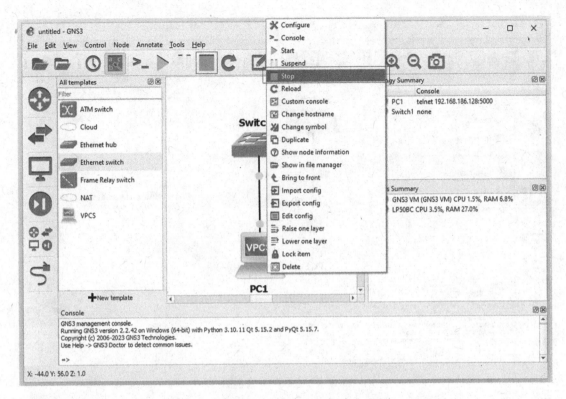

Figure 10-5. *GNS3, stopping a device using the right-click option*

After GNS3 shuts down, the GNS3 VM running on VMware Workstation 17 Pro will also automatically power down. It's important not to manually shut down the VM from the workstation. Instead, it is recommended that you use the X button in the top-right corner to close the GNS3 application (see Figure 10-6). As you become more familiar with GNS3 and its intricacies, this shutdown process will become a standard procedure. If you're not careful, improper shutdown procedures can often lead to malfunctions in your working lab configurations and projects. Developing sound GNS3 user habits can spare you from wasting time while mastering a range of concepts and skills.

651

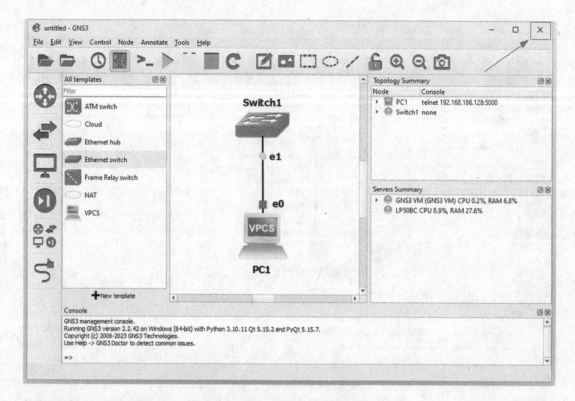

Figure 10-6. *GNS3, graceful shutdown using the X key*

Let's explore another crucial tip to ensure smooth lab operation without unnecessary interruptions. Few things are more frustrating than spending time troubleshooting minor and major issues during crucial lab work. What may appear to be a minor problem can turn into hours or even days of troubleshooting. Therefore, it's advisable to address these behaviors or settings proactively before encountering such challenges. I'm familiar with this from my own experiences both at work and when creating technical documentation.

Starting GNS3 as an Administrator

Here's a quick tip while launching GNS3 for the first time on your Windows operating system. If you created the Desktop shortcut during the installation, GNS3 will create a startup icon on your Windows desktop by default. Using this icon is the fastest way to start the program. However, be aware that not starting GNS3 as an administrator may restrict your ability to make configuration changes to network adapter settings and other preferences. Therefore, it's considered best practice to always launch GNS3 as an administrator. One tip for ensuring you always start GNS3 as an administrator is to adjust the settings under the GNS3 icon.

#	Task
①	Start by navigating to your host PC's desktop, finding the GNS3 icon (see Figure 10-7), and right-clicking it to access the Properties menu.

Figure 10-7. *GNS3, changing the program icon startup settings*

(continued)

#	Task
②	Next, navigate to the Compatibility tab. In the Settings section, choose the Run This Program as an Administrator option. Then, click the Apply and OK buttons to save the settings. Refer to Figure 10-8 for visual guidance.

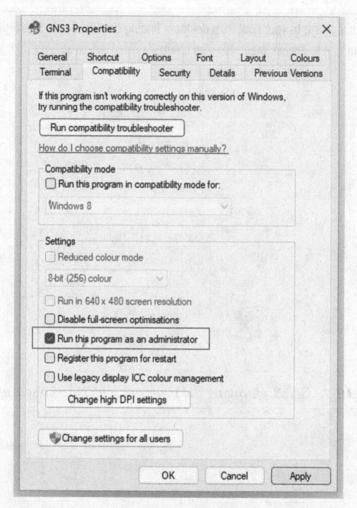

Figure 10-8. *GNS3, changing the program icon startup settings*

You are now ready to learn some valuable GNS3 techniques to improve your skills. Throughout the remainder of this chapter, you are introduced to some useful GNS3 tricks. These include connecting GNS3 devices to your host, establishing an Internet connection within GNS3, integrating the Microsoft loopback into your lab topology, and cloning a GNS3 project to create your base lab template.

Using GNS3 the First Time: Cisco IOS and Windows Lab

In the past, the primary method of studying Cisco technologies and certifications involved physical hardware-based labs with routers, switches, PIX/ASA Firewalls, and physical severs. However, the landscape changed significantly when Christophe Fillot developed Dynamips in August 2005. Dynamips allowed the emulation of older Cisco router platforms and revolutionized how networking students approached Cisco technology studies. Before Dynamips, there was Cisco's Packet Tracer, but it functioned more as a simulator rather than an emulator. GNS3, as mentioned, is the graphical user interface (GUI) version of Dynamips, and it still relies on Dynamips as its underlying application.

For some time, it was something of an open secret that Cisco used UNIX-based Cisco IOU (IOS on UNIX) for internal staff training. However, IOU was not made commercially available. During a transitional period, Cisco IOU was leaked to Cisco partners, and networking students began to use it. Cisco eventually moved IOU running on UNIX to Cisco CML (Cisco Modelling Lab) running on Linux and more recently rebranded the CML as VIRL (Virtual Internet Routing Lab). They developed it into a subscription-based product that is now available to networking students.

Before GNS3 developers incorporated VIRL and IOU images, traditional networking students used somewhat dated Cisco IOS images on GNS3 for Cisco certification preparation. Even today, GNS3 continues to support older Cisco IOS images. This is particularly useful to CCNA students, as it offers a way to emulate over 90 percent of CCNA routing topics without requiring physical equipment. While there have been advancements in networking technologies and the education market, many core routing and switching concepts remain integral to CCNA studies. Therefore, for foundational networking concepts, the older Cisco IOS 12.4.x version is more than sufficient for your initial learning needs.

There are two main limitations when using older IOS-based GNS3 labs for networking studies. First, it can typically support only older IOS 12.4 versions on extremely old router platforms, except for the Cisco 7200 series. Second, for switching and layer 2 support, it relies on the NM-16ESW module installed on router platforms. This does not offer the same feature sets as a working L2 switch. By utilizing newer VIRL L2 and L3 images, you can create more robust Cisco routing and switching labs on GNS3, enriched with additional IOS-XE features.

As part of the GNS3 introduction, integrating older Cisco IOS into a lab serves as a solid starting point. In VIRL integration, the primary difference is replacing the IOS image with more recent VIRL images. This chapter gradually introduces you to a series of techniques for using Cisco IOS on GNS3. Importantly, the skills acquired in this chapter are extendable to the VIRL labs in Part 2 Chapters, enhancing your ability to build versatile GNS3 labs with greater efficiency and flexibility. Even if you are a seasoned CCNA/CCNP student familiar with the older IOS integration on GNS3, do not skip this chapter, as it introduces new skills that will prove valuable throughout the learning journey and your career as well.

To begin, let's delve into a brief discussion of the Cisco software license model, including Cisco IOS, IOU, and VIRL images.

Cisco IOS Software License and Downloading an Older Cisco IOS

First, to set up your GNS3 lab with Cisco IOS, you need to locate and download Cisco Internet Operating System (IOS) images that are compatible with the Cisco router models supported by GNS3. It is assumed that you have either completed Cisco's CCNA R&S certification or are currently working toward it. Additionally, I assume that you are interested in gaining insights into how Cisco operates and aspire to work in the enterprise networking industry as network, security, or data center engineers. Alternatively, some of you may come from different IT backgrounds and possess a strong desire to expand your expertise in the field of networking. This, in itself, is a relatively uncommon Endeavor in today's IT landscape. In the ICT world, it's more common to see network and security engineers venturing into the realm of public cloud technologies to broaden their understanding of cloud services. Nonetheless, Cisco's revenue generation relies on the sale of its hardware, software, and service support contracts. To comprehend how Cisco uses software to maximize its revenue, you must have a deep understanding of Cisco's software ownership and licensing agreements, which are closely intertwined with its business model. Cisco still is a prominent vendor in the enterprise and SMB ICT markets, selling networking equipment and services. The company's profitability is driven by the sale of technical support contract packages for its hardware and software. These packages include the right to use Cisco's software. In essence, when customers purchase equipment through Cisco's partners via regular channels, they gain the privilege to use platform-specific software on their networking devices and access 24/7 support from the industry's best Cisco TAC throughout the service contract's duration.

Second, it's important to note that if you purchase a device running Cisco IOS version 16, you are typically limited to minor patch upgrades within the same software version. Exceptions include security vulnerabilities or field notices that require upgrading to the latest major software version. As devices age, the minimum hardware requirements for newer software versions tend to increase. Therefore, there's a limit to how much you can upgrade an aging device's software, eventually requiring an upgrade to newer hardware models. Cisco discontinues support for end-of-life (EoL) devices, and because most of Cisco's software is considered proprietary and part of Cisco's intellectual property, the distribution of their software for commercial use without a support contract is prohibited. This policy applies to both new and older software. After procuring Cisco equipment through a channel partner, the technical support service contract facilitates software downloads and access to technical support from Cisco TAC. Those working for Cisco partners can generally download the latest IOS software with ease, though getting an older IOS software might be more challenging. An effective way to get an older IOS for study purposes is to purchase used lab routers from online auction sites like eBay, Craigslist, or Gumtree, or perhaps from someone who no longer requires their old CCNA/CCNP lab equipment. These routers typically come with a functional IOS in their flash memory, which can be copied to your PC via TFTP file transfer and subsequently used as a GNS3 IOS base image. Even if you have the right to download IOS from Cisco's official site, finding older GNS3-compatible IOS versions can be tricky because most older devices have already reached EoL and the download is no longer available. For full-time students aspiring to work in the networking industry as network or security engineers, Google searches may lead to websites where older IOS versions can be located. This chapter relies on the older IOS version sourced from my old Cisco CCNA lab equipment, but ultimately, it is your responsibility to source a working copy of the required older IOS version to follow along.

Third, when visiting GNS3's official site, you'll notice that GNS3 provides support for older Cisco routers, including the C1700, C2600, C2691, C3600, C3700, and C7200 series routers, along with older-style Cisco PIX firewalls. For this chapter's quick demonstrations, an older Cisco 3745 router's IOS version 12.4.15 T15 is used, which is still compatible with GNS3 version 2.2.42. While the Cisco 7200 router's IOS version 15.x is supported, it requires 512MB RAM, which consumes more system memory compared to older 3700 series routers. Those with PCs featuring strong CPUs and ample memory can opt for the Cisco 7200 IOS version 15.x in place of the 3745 IOS. In this chapter, the specific IOS version used is `c3745-adventerprisek9-mz.124-25d.bin`, which should still work on GNS3 2.2.42. Recently, my schedule doesn't permit much experimentation with these older IOS versions, but **I still consider these older Cisco IOSs the best resource for those embarking on their CCNA studies.**

Here are some older IOS versions suitable for CCNA study purposes:

- `c3725-adventerprisek9-mz.124-15.T14.bin` (old)
- `c3745-adventerprisek9-mz.124-25d.bin` (old, used in this chapter)
- `c7200-adventerprisek9-mz.124-24.T5.bin` (old)
- `c7200-adventerprisek9-mz.152-4.M7.bin` (newer)

Warning

Each reader is responsible for acquiring the software referenced in this book.

Readers are responsible for acquiring and downloading all the necessary software referenced in this book. The author (or the publisher) of this book does not provide the software but directs you to the sources where you can find and download the appropriate software. It's essential to note that this book includes disclaimers to clarify that the author or publisher does not endorse, guarantee, or take legal responsibility for the software or its suitability for specific purposes. Ultimately, each reader is accountable for sourcing and using the software to meet their unique learning needs and system requirements.

Decompressing Cisco IOS for GNS3 Use

To follow along with this book, you should have successfully located and downloaded the `c3745-adventerprisek9-mz.124-25d.bin` file into your Downloads folder. The file ending with the .bin file is compressed, so for systems to use it, it needs to be decompressed first. On Cisco routers, the same decompression process takes place when the system boots up—the file gets decompressed and saved in the Random Access Memory for the IOS system to run. By decompressing this .bin file into the .image file, GNS3 is presented with the file already in usable format and hence, GNS3 does not have to decompress the .bin file every time a new Cisco router is powered on in GNS3. Next, let's decompress the

.bin file into an .image file to make it usable in GNS3. Various methods can be used to decompress a Cisco IOS .bin file, depending on your operating system. However, I'll guide you through the two most common methods for decompressing the older IOS file on a Windows system. The first method involves using Unpack-0.1_win.zip, and the second method integrates GNS3 with Dynamips to achieve the decompression. You can use one of the methods to decompress the old IOS image for a quick IOS lab build.

Decompressing Cisco IOS Method: Using the Unpack.exe

In this method, you need to download Unpack.exe for Windows and use it to decompress a Cisco IOS file for GNS3. Follow these instructions to complete the decompression process, ensuring that you save the resulting file with the .image file extension and place it in your PC's Downloads folder.

#	Task
①	To begin, download the Cisco Image Unpack-0.1_win.zip file for Windows to your Downloads folder. I provide the download link for this software in Chapter 1's software requirement table; however, note that the Source Forge URL for this file keeps changing. So, my recommendation is to perform a Google search using the file name to locate the correct file and download it to a folder. After downloading, extract the file in your Downloads folder.
②	If you still have your IOS file in the Downloads folder, copy it to the Unpack folder, as shown in Figure 10-9.

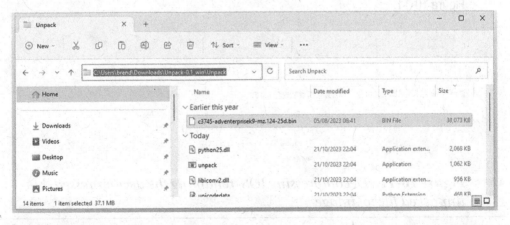

Figure 10-9. Decompressing IOS, moving the IOS file to the Unpack folder

(*continued*)

#	Task

③ Referring to Figure 10-10, open the Windows command-line prompt and change your directory using the cd command to the Unpack folder. Run the unpack.exe command to extract the image file in the same folder. Once the file is decompressed, the decompressed file will be called c3745-adventerprisek9-mz.124-25d.bin.unpacked. Replace the file path with your Unpack folder path.

C:\Users\brend>**cd C:\Users\your_name\Downloads\Unpack-0.1_win\Unpack**

C:\Users\your_name\Downloads\Unpack-0.1_win\Unpack**unpack.exe --format IOS c3745-adventerprisek9-mz.124-25d.bin**

Figure 10-10. *Unpacking and converting Cisco IOS .bin file to an image file*

④ Next, locate the unpacked file and rename the file called c3745-adventerprisek9-mz.124-25d.bin.unpacked to c3745-adventerprisek9-mz.124-25d.image. In other words, you're replacing the word .bin.unpacked with .image. Note that the decompressed image file is significantly larger than the original .bin file, as illustrated in Figure 10-11.

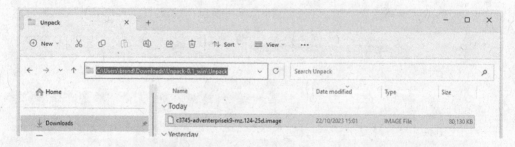

Figure 10-11. *Decompressing IOS, renaming the decompressed .bin. unpacked file to .image*

(continued)

#	Task
⑤	After updating the file name with the correct file extension, make sure to copy and paste the file into the Downloads folder. This step is crucial because GNS3 will first look for a compatible .image file in your Windows Downloads folder (and the /GNS3/images folder). Refer to Figure 10-12 for visual guidance.

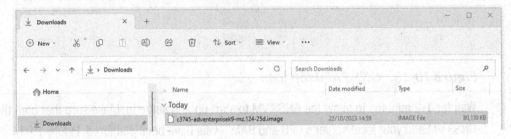

Figure 10-12. *Decompressing IOS, moving the .image file to the Downloads folder*

If you want to learn how to decompress the IOS file using the second method—the Dynamips method—you can continue reading the next optional section. However, if you're eager to start building your network lab right away, feel free to skip to the next section.

Decompressing Cisco IOS Method 2: Using Dynamips Server (Optional)

Just like in method 1, you can use the GNS3 Dynamips Server method to decompress your IOS .bin file into the .image format. Upon completing these steps, confirm that a copy of the .image file is stored in your host PC's Downloads folder. Some readers may find this approach more user-friendly than the first method. Let's quickly check the tasks at hand.

#	Task
①	First, if you haven't already started GNS3, begin by double-clicking the GNS3 start icon (shown in Figure 10-13) on your desktop.

Figure 10-13. *GNS3 desktop icon*

②	Wait for 1-2 minutes to allow the GNS3 VM to start up and settle in. Make sure that both the GNS3 VM and your local server's CPU and RAM levels have been stabilized. Figure 10-14 shows the Servers Summary window in GNS3.

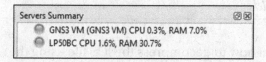

Figure 10-14. *GNS3, Servers Summary window*

③	GNS3 will prompt you with the Project window. Because you are only interested in decompressing the IOS, click the Cancel button. You can refer to Figure 10-15 for visual guidance.

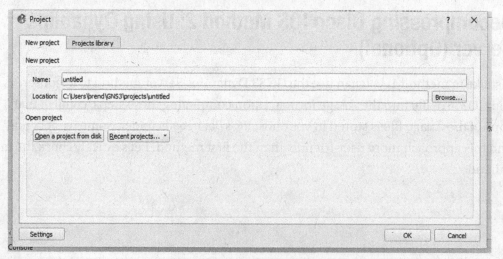

Figure 10-15. *GNS3, Project window, press the Cancel button*

(continued)

#	Task

④　Next, to open the Preferences menu in GNS3, select Edit, then click the Preferences… option, as depicted in Figure 10-16.

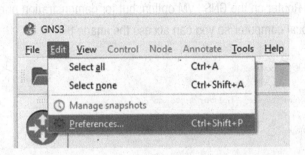

Figure 10-16. *GNS3, opening the Preferences from the Edit menu*

⑤　Once the Preferences window opens, navigate to the Dynamips option and select IOS Routers, as illustrated in Figure 10-17.

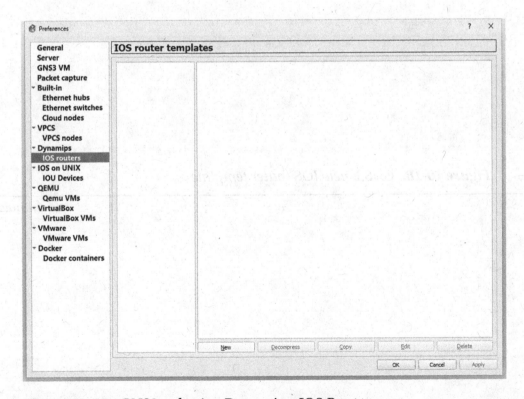

Figure 10-17. *GNS3, selecting Dynamips, IOS Routers*

(*continued*)

#	Task

⑥   Click the New button to open the New IOS router template window shown in Figure 10-18. In the Server screen, choose Run this IOS Router on My Local Computer. You can also opt for the Run this IOS Router on the GNS3 VM option, but for demonstration purposes, it's better to run it from the local computer so you can access the image file.

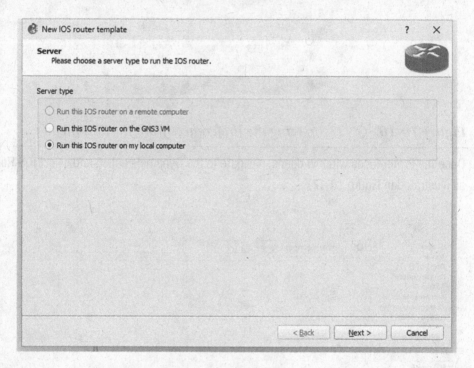

Figure 10-18. *GNS3, new IOS router template*

(continued)

#	Task
⑦	To locate the .bin file, in the IOS Image window, click the Browse button on the right. You can find a visual reference in Figure 10-19.

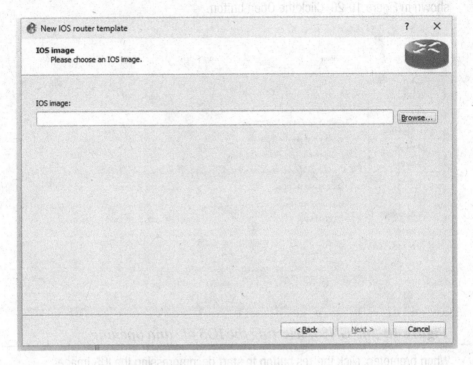

Figure 10-19. *GNS3, browsing to the IOS image*

(continued)

#	Task
⑧	Locate and select your IOS image from the folder and click the Open button. You saved the `c3745-adventerprisek9-mz.124-25d.bin` file in the `Downloads` folder previously, as shown in Figure 10-20. Click the Open button.

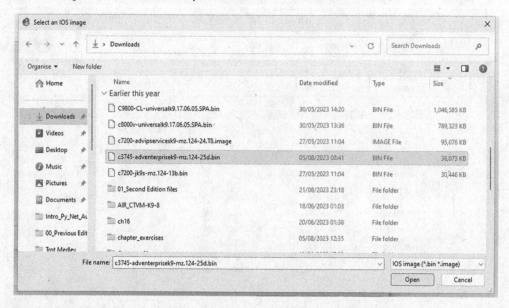

***Figure 10-20.** GNS3, selecting the IOS file and opening*

⑨	When prompted, click the Yes button to start decompressing the IOS image. See Figure 10-21.

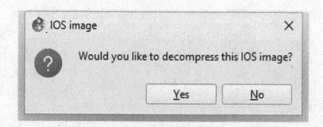

***Figure 10-21.** GNS3, decompressing IOS image*

(continued)

#	Task

(10) When you come back to the IOS image window, GNS3 will tell you where the .image file will be stored. For this demonstration, it is extracted to the user's GNS3\images\IOS\ folder, as displayed in Figure 10-22. When the GNS3 template looks for .images files, this is one of the file locations it will look in, along with your Downloads folder.

C:\Users\your_name\GNS3\images\IOSc3745-adventerprisek9-mz.124-25d.image

*Note: Replace your_name with your name and remember the full file path.

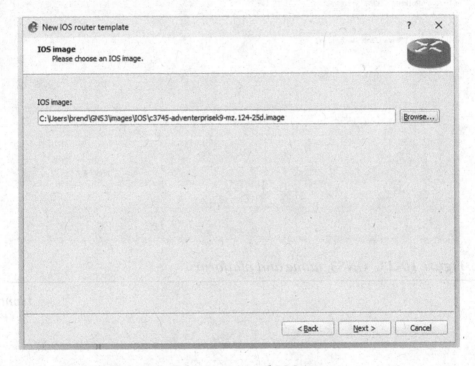

Figure 10-22. *GNS3, saving decompressed IOS image*

(*continued*)

#	Task
⑪	For the name and platform, leave all the settings as the defaults and click the Next button. See Figure 10-23.

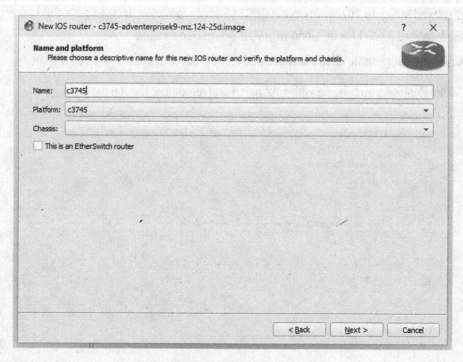

Figure 10-23. GNS3, name and platform

(*continued*)

#	Task
⑫	The recommended RAM size for 3745 is 256MB. Click the OK button to continue. See Figure 10-24.

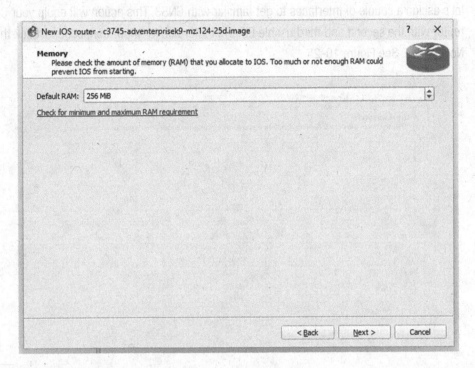

Figure 10-24. *GNS3, router memory allocation*

(*continued*)

#	Task
⑬	In the Network Adapters window, add NM-1FE-TX for slots 1 and 2 for training purposes. Because this will be removed after the file decompression, this won't affect your lab later, but let's assign a couple of interfaces to get familiar with GNS3. This action will equip your Cisco router with the second and third usable Ethernet interface for multi-connections. Click the Next button. See Figure 10-25.

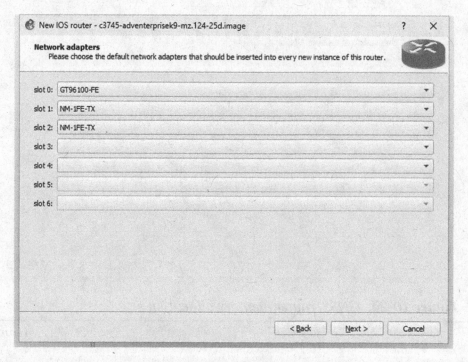

Figure 10-25. *GNS3, extra FastEthernet interface assignment*

(*continued*)

#	Task
⑭	Similarly, in the WIC modules window, add WIC-1T in WIC 0 and 1. This will give two Serial WAN interfaces for multiple serial connections. You can optionally choose the 2T option to get even more connectivity options. Click the Next button again, as depicted in Figure 10-26.

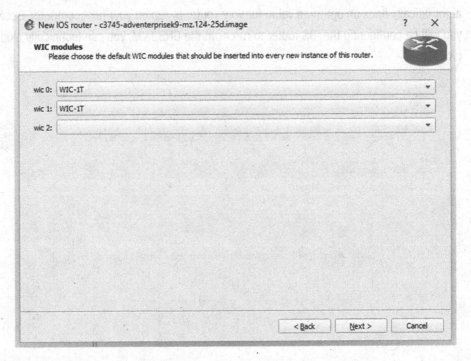

Figure 10-26. *GNS3, WIC interface assignment*

(*continued*)

#	Task
⑮	In the Idle-PC window, click the Idle-PC Finder button, as demonstrated in Figure 10-27. You will not be using the local server in this chapter, but this is demonstrated here to teach you what the feature does, so follow along. Click OK and then click the Finish button.

*Note: If you choose to run the IOS router on the local machine and Dynamips, Idle-PC Finder automatically finds an optimum value for your router to run on your host computer. Because you will be configuring the IOS router to run from the GNS3 VM, you can technically skip this process. |

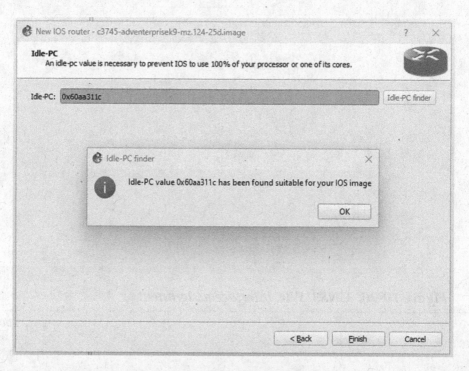

Figure 10-27. *GNS3, IOS idle-PC finder example only*

(*continued*)

#	Task
⑯	Now go to the following folder path, C:\Users\your_name\GNS3\images\IOS. Locate a copy of the decompressed IOS image file with the file extension .image. Copy the file to the Downloads folder, as shown in Figure 10-28.

*Note: Replace your_name with your username. |

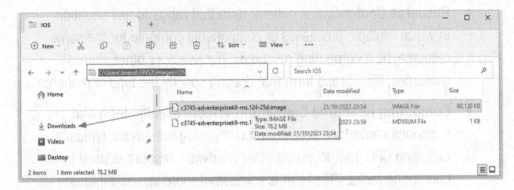

Figure 10-28. *Host PC, copying the extracted .image file to the Downloads folder*

Now you are ready to install the legacy Cisco IOS router on GNS3 VM and have some networking fun. To get comfortable with GNS3, let's follow through with some more tasks.

Installing Cisco IOS on the GNS3 VM

Great, now that you've successfully decompressed your IOS image using one of the previous methods, you're all set to create a GNS3 project using the .image file. For this guide, you use the GNS3 VM as the GNS3 server to avoid CPU and memory performance issues associated with running devices on the local Dynamips server. In virtualization technology, the terminology for this behavior is known as "computer resource contention."

Expand Your Knowledge:

Resource Contention, Understanding the Finer Details

The choice of terminology depends on the specific context and personal writing style, but let's delve into the nuances of "resource contention: and its variations in the world of computing.

- **Resource Contention**: A general term that refers to any situation in which multiple processes or components compete for the same resource, be it computing resources, hardware, or other shared resources. It's a broad term that doesn't specify the type of resource.

- **Computing Resource Contention**: A more specific term that describes contention concerning computing resources, typically including CPU, memory, and other hardware resources used in computing tasks. This term is somewhat more specific than the general resource contention term.

- **Computer Resource Contention**: An even more specific term that directly refers to resource contention within a computer system. It may encompass not only computing resources but also other resources within a computer, such as storage, network interfaces, and peripherals.

The choice among these terms depends on the level of specificity you need for your context. If you aim to be more general, resource contention suffices. If you want to emphasize computing resources, computing resource contention should serve the purpose. If your focus is specifically on resources within a computer system, computer resource contention is the most appropriate choice.

If your GNS3 is not already running, start the application and let it initialize the GNS3 VM on Workstation. Wait for about one to two minutes for the GNS3 VM to boot up correctly. Also, ensure that your computer's CPU and memory usage have settled down. Assuming that both GNS3 and the GNS3 VM on Workstation are running on your computer, you can proceed with the following set of tasks to create your first GNS3 project and install the .image file on the GNS3 VM server.

#	Task
①	At the GNS3 launch, when the GNS3 project window appears, create a new GNS3 project and give it a meaningful name. Alternatively, you can use the New Project icon to open the Project menu and begin this task. You can choose your preferred project name that suits this purpose. In this example, the project was named ch10_ios_lab, but you can use your own naming convention. Refer to Figure 10-29 for visual guidance.

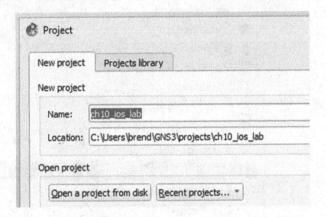

Figure 10-29. *GNS3, creating a new project*

(*continued*)

#	Task
②	Next, from the GNS3's main menu, select File and then + New Template. Or, click the large Router icon under Devices on the left and click + New Template. The first selection method is shown in Figure 10-30.

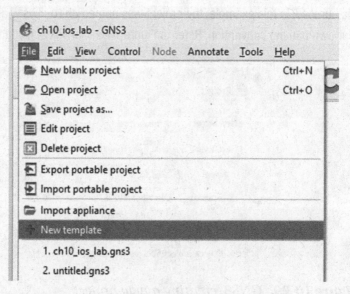

Figure 10-30. *GNS3, opening the New template menu*

(*continued*)

#	Task
③	When the New Template window appears, select the Install an Appliance from the GNS3 Server (Recommended) option. Click the Next button, as shown in Figure 10-31.

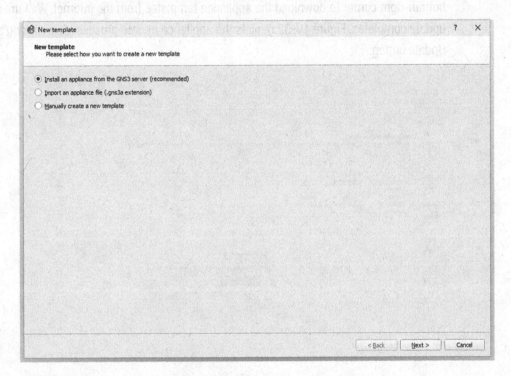

Figure 10-31. *GNS3, new template option*

(*continued*)

#	Task
④	When the New Template window appears, you will notice that the working appliance templates are blank, so you need to use the Update from Online Registry button at the bottom-right corner to download the appliance templates from the Internet. Wait until the update completes. Figure 10-32 depicts the appliance update process after clicking the Update button.

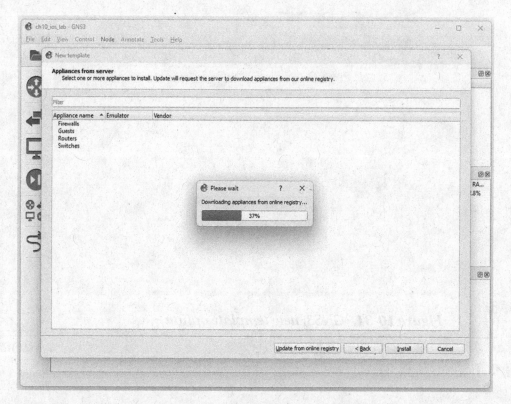

Figure 10-32. *GNS3, update appliance template from online registry*

(*continued*)

#	Task
⑤	After the update from the online registry process is completed, you will receive the Appliances Are Up to Date message, as shown in Figure 10-33, and you will also notice that the devices under the Appliance name now have the selection arrows next to the names. Click the OK button to continue.

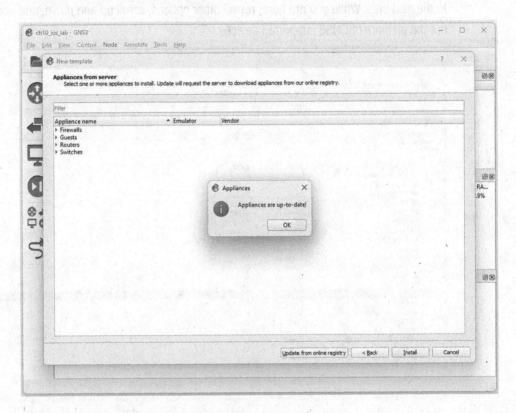

Figure 10-33. *GNS3, appliances are up to date!*

(continued)

#	Task
⑥	On the same window, click the Routers option to reveal various router platforms. Locate your IOS router model. Figure 10-34 shows the Cisco 3745 with Dynamips selected as the Emulator and Cisco as the Vendor. The newer IOS-XE routers use Qemu as the emulator, but the older IOS uses Dynamips as its preferred emulator. Click the Install button to move to the next step. While you are here, reveal other options, scroll up and down, and check out the plethora of GNS3 supported devices.

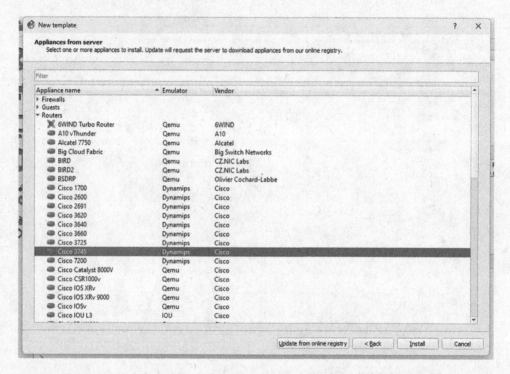

Figure 10-34. *GNS3, selecting the Cisco 3745 appliance template*

(*continued*)

#	Task
⑦	When the New template window appears, leave the default selection, which is the Install the Appliance on the GNS3 VM (Recommended) option, and click the Next button, as shown in Figure 10-35.

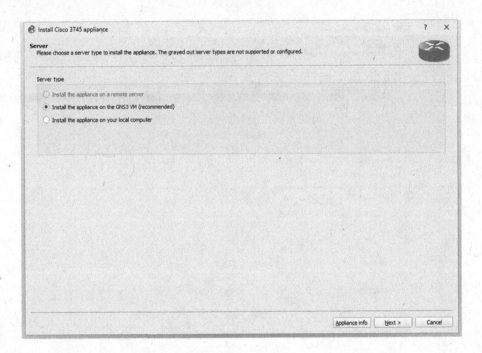

Figure 10-35. GNS3, server type selection

(*continued*)

681

#	Task
⑧	If you have successfully followed the previous steps, the Required Files window will locate your IOS .image file automatically, and you will see the window shown in Figure 10-36. Select the image file by highlighting it and then click the Next button to install.

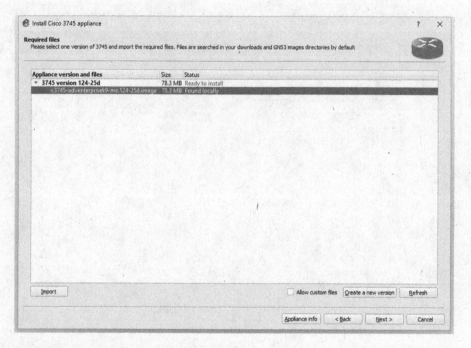

Figure 10-36. *GNS3, highlight the required file*

⑨	Because you intend to install the legacy Cisco IOS on GNS3, without thinking twice, click the Yes button shown in Figure 10-37.

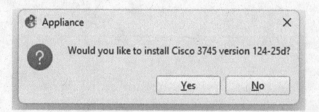

Figure 10-37. *GNS3, appliance installation confirmation message*

(continued)

#	Task
⑩	You are almost there; click the Finish button to finish the installation. See Figure 10-38.

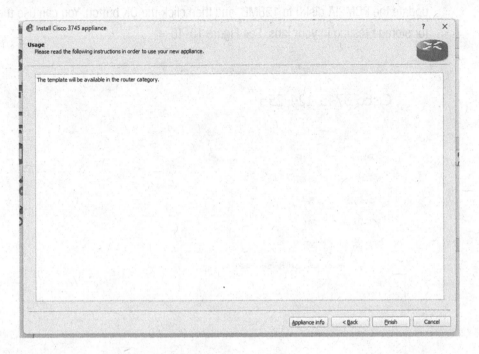

Figure 10-38. *GNS3, usage prompt*

⑪	Now let's check the correct RAM size for 3745 and customize the settings to suit your lab. Go to the GNS3 main window and click the router icon. You will see the installed Cisco 3745 IOS router. Under the router icon, right-click the icon and select Configure Template, as shown in Figure 10-39.

Figure 10-39. *GNS3, configuring the template*

(*continued*)

#	Task
⑫	Navigate to the Memories and Disks tab, verify that the default RAM size is 256MB, update the PCMCIA disk0 to 128MB, and then click the OK button. You can use the disk0 for storage testing in your labs. See Figure 10-40.

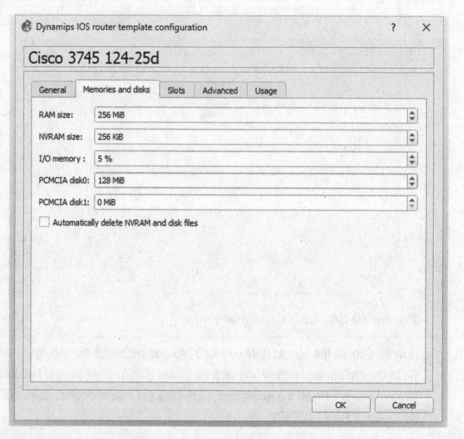

Figure 10-40. GNS3, checking memory and adding disk0 to the IOS router

#	Task
⑬	On the Slots tab, keep an NM-1FE-TX on slot 1 and update slots 2 and 3 to NM-1FE-TX, as shown in Figure 10-41. You can use NM-4T for four more routed FastEthernet interfaces or NM-16ESW, which adds 16 L2 interfaces. If you want to use this router as an L2 switch, then NM-16ESW can be added, but this has little relevance in the current technologies. You can leave the three WIC-1T cards populated in WIC 0 to 2. Because you are only going to connect through FastEthernet, you can optionally leave the WIC slots empty. Click the OK button to complete the customization.

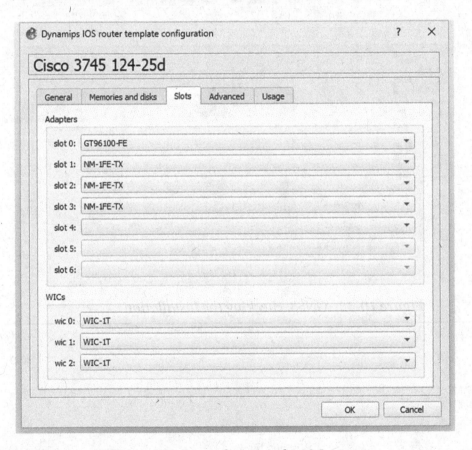

Figure 10-41. *GNS3, adding interfaces on the IOS router*

(*continued*)

#	Task
⑭	Now click the router icon and then drag and drop it into the Topology canvas on the right, as shown in Figure 10-42. If no error is encountered, then your device should boot up normally, and you are now ready to rock and roll. You have successfully installed a legacy IOS image on the GNS3 for your study.

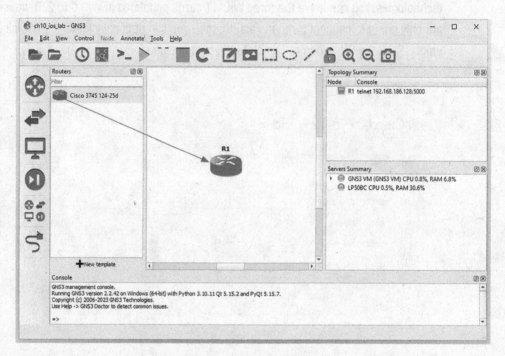

Figure 10-42. *GNS3, checking the installation*

(*continued*)

#	Task
⑮	Now close GNS3 by clicking the top-right X button (see Figure 10-43) and the GNS3 VM running on Workstation. Your GNS3 project will be saved and the GNS3 VM will be shut down automatically if you do not have other VMs running. If you have another virtual machine running on VMware Workstation, the other VMs on Workstation will continue to run.

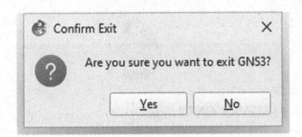

Figure 10-43. *GNS3, closing GNS3 (and GNS3 VM)*

If you've made it this far without encountering major challenges, you're all set for some exciting and interesting labs. Keep up the good work!

Creating an IOS Lab Topology on GNS3 and Connecting to the Internet

Warning

A physical Internet connection may be required for this section.

For consistent and reliable lab results, the tasks described in this section require a physical Internet connection, and it is strongly recommended that your computer is connected via an Ethernet cable, not through a wireless connection. Labs conducted over wireless adapters may yield different results than those outlined in this book. The labs are primarily performed with an Ethernet cable connected to a home router's Ethernet port. While most labs can work well over a wireless connection after this chapter, if you encounter any issues, it's advisable to connect your PC to a physical Ethernet port on your router or switch to ensure proper functionality.

You were instructed to close both GNS3 and GNS3 VM in the previous task. This was intentional so that you could correctly reopen the previous lab. Now, let's proceed with the steps to reopen the project and continue building your IOS lab.

#	Task
①	First, relaunch GNS3 using the GNS3 icon on your Windows desktop (see Figure 10-44).

Figure 10-44. *GNS3, GNS3 desktop icon*

②	When the GNS3 project window appears, wait for one to two minutes for the GNS3 VM to boot up. Click the Recent Projects button under Open Project to select the ch10_ios_lab.gns3 project (see Figure 10-45). Then, click the OK button to reopen the project.

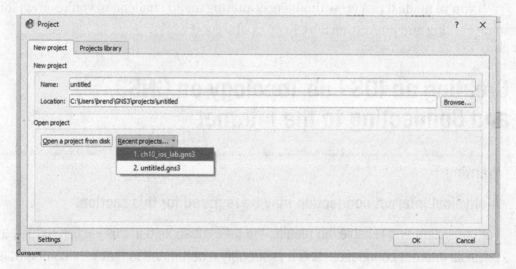

Figure 10-45. *GNS3, opening a recent project*

(*continued*)

#	Task
③	As soon as the ch10_ios_lab.gns3 project opens, click the All Devices icon on the left (see Figure 10-46), then drag and drop one NAT (NAT1), second router (R2), one GNS3 built-in unmanaged Switch (Switch1), and two VPCS (PC1 and PC2) on to the Topology canvas. When you drag and drop these devices, you will be prompted to select a server to run them. Pay close attention to which server you select here.

Figure 10-46. *GSN3, All Devices icon*

④ For NAT1, my local host LP50BC is selected, as displayed in Figure 10-47. Your computer name will be different, so you should select your local hostname.

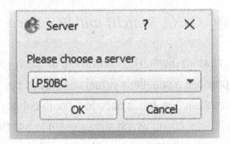

Figure 10-47. *GSN3, NAT1 server selection*

This NAT device will run on the local server's NATted network, and the DHCP service will allocate an IP address from the VMnet8 network subnet 192.168.127.0/24, as shown in Figure 10-48.

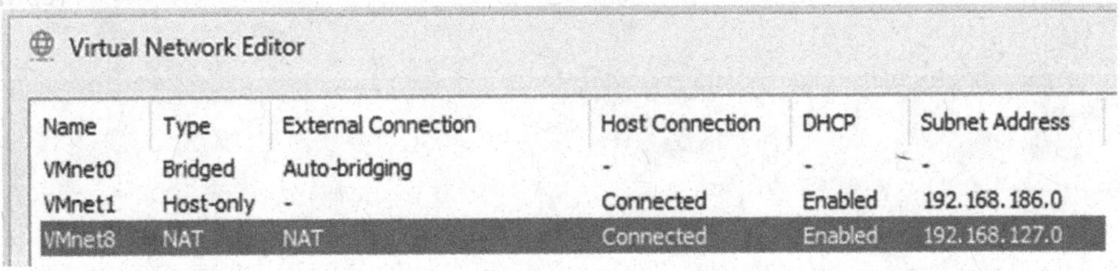

Name	Type	External Connection	Host Connection	DHCP	Subnet Address
VMnet0	Bridged	Auto-bridging	-	-	-
VMnet1	Host-only	-	Connected	Enabled	192.168.186.0
VMnet8	NAT	NAT	Connected	Enabled	192.168.127.0

Virtual Network Editor

Figure 10-48. *VMware Workstation Virtual network editor, VMnet8 NAT subnet*

(*continued*)

#	Task
	You could connect to the Internet via GNS3 VM's NATted network (192.168.186.0/24), but connecting to the outside network via GNS3 VM sometimes could be unreliable. Using the local server NAT address via VMnet8 provides a more reliable connection to the Internet and your Linux servers with Python sharing the same VMnet8's subnet to reach your network devices.
⑤	For routers, GNS3 Switch1 and VPCSs, select GNS3 VM (GNS3 VM) as the server (see Figure 10-49). These devices will run on the GNS3 VM server.

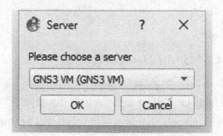

Figure 10-49. *GSN3, Switch1 and PC1 server selection*

A GNS3 built-in switch (Switch1) is used here to teach you the preferred way to connect devices, as it provides a seamless virtual connection between devices. It is not a managed switch like Cisco switches, but is used to smooth out any connection issues. VPCS is GNS3's handy built-in PC-like client, which allows users to use them as end devices for simple communication testing. VPCS saves a lot of computing power compared to running another virtual machine as end clients. Using a VPC is like configuring a dummy loopback interface on a Cisco router or switch for end-device reachability testing. You can ping and traceroute from VPCS, just like a real end device.

(continued)

#	Task
⑥	Click the Add a Link icon on the bottom left and connect all devices, as shown in Figure 10-50. Enable the Show Interface Label and rearrange the device names. Your GNS3 window for ch10_ios_lab should look similar to this figure. Hint: Refer to the Topology and Servers summaries to connect your devices.

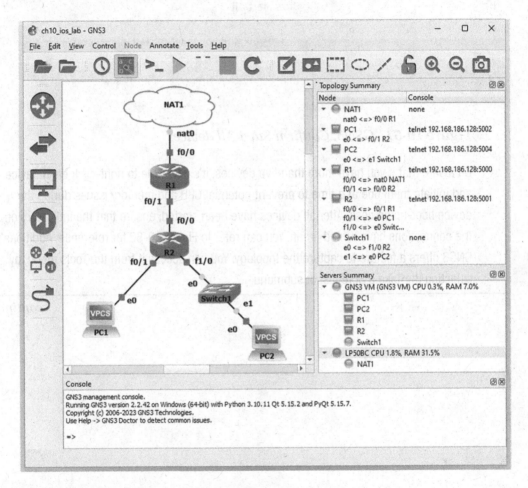

Figure 10-50. *GSN3, connecting devices*

(continued)

#	Task
⑦	You can use the Add a Note decoration tool to include IP addresses for each interface you plan to configure. Once you're satisfied with your topology, click the large green play icon to initiate all devices. A confirmation prompt will appear, as shown in Figure 10-51.

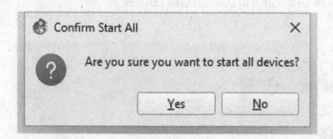

Figure 10-51. *GSN3, Confirm Start All devices*

Be aware that if you have more than five devices, it's advisable to right-click each device and initiate them one at a time to prevent potential CPU and memory issues during the device boot-up process. After all devices have been started, ensure that the indicators on the connections have turned green. You can refer to Figure 10-52 for reference. Additionally, GNS3 offers a feature to capture the topology. You can access it from the Tools menu, by selecting the Take a Screenshot submenu.

(continued)

#	Task

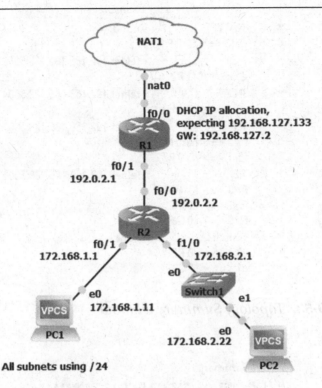

Figure 10-52. *GSN3, Topology screenshot*

⑧ Make sure that all indicators under the Topology Summary (see Figure 10-53) and Server
   Summary (see Figure 10-54) are displaying green lights. Additionally, verify that there are no
   unaddressed errors in the Console window (see Figure 10-55).

(continued)

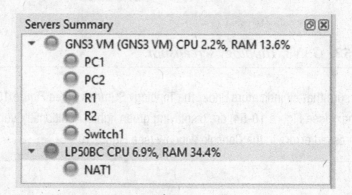

Topology Summary window

Node	Console
▼ ● NAT1	none
nat0 <=> f0/0 R1	
▼ ● PC1	telnet 192.168.186.128:5002
e0 <=> f0/1 R2	
▼ ● PC2	telnet 192.168.186.128:5004
e0 <=> e1 Switch1	
▼ ● R1	telnet 192.168.186.128:5000
f0/0 <=> nat0 NAT1	
f0/1 <=> f0/0 R2	
▼ ● R2	telnet 192.168.186.128:5001
f0/0 <=> f0/1 R1	
f0/1 <=> e0 PC1	
f1/0 <=> e0 Switc...	
▼ ● Switch1	none
e0 <=> f1/0 R2	
e1 <=> e0 PC2	

Figure 10-53. *Topology Summary window*

Servers Summary

- ▼ ● GNS3 VM (GNS3 VM) CPU 2.2%, RAM 13.6%
  - ● PC1
  - ● PC2
  - ● R1
  - ● R2
  - ● Switch1
- ▼ ● LP50BC CPU 6.9%, RAM 34.4%
  - ● NAT1

Figure 10-54. *Servers Summary window*

Console

GNS3 management console.
Running GNS3 version 2.2.42 on Windows (64-bit) with Python 3.10.11 Qt 5.15.2 and PyQt 5.15.7.
Copyright (c) 2006-2023 GNS3 Technologies.
Use Help -> GNS3 Doctor to detect common issues.

=>

Figure 10-55. *GSN3, Console window*

#	Task
⑨	To start a console of R1, simply double-click the R1 icon on the Topology or right-click and select the Console menu. At the console prompt, configure R1 for your first lab. If you want to study how DHCP works, enable debug dhcp on R1 before starting the configuration. The debugging example can be found in the next Expand Your Knowledge section, entitled "Debug and Study DHCP Communication."

configure terminal

hostname R1 # Assigns R1 as the hostname for the router.

ip name-server 8.8.8.8 # Configures the name server with the DNS address 8.8.8.8.

interface FastEthernet0/0

duplex full

ip address dhcp # Configures the IP address for interface Fa0/0 using DHCP.

no shut # Activates the interface (brings it up).

interface FastEthernet0/1

ip address 192.0.2.1 255.255.255.0 # Assigns the IP address 192.0.2.1 with a subnet mask of 255.255.255.0 to Fa0/1.

no shut # Activates the interface (brings it up).

exit

router ospf 1 # Configures OSPF (Open Shortest Path First) routing protocol with pro. ID 1.

network 192.0.2.0 0.0.0.255 area 0 # Specifies a network (192.0.2.0/24) to be advertised via OSPF in Area 0.

network 192.168.127.0 0.0.0.255 area 0 # Specifies another network (192.168.183.0/24) for OSPF advertisement in Area 0.

end

copy running-config startup-config # Saves the router's running configuration to the startup configuration. Prompts for Destination filename confirmation.

(continued)

#	Task

Check the interface status and IP address allocation. Make sure a correct IP address has been assigned from your VMnet8 subnet range. Your IP addressing scheme and address may be different from those shown here:

R1#**show ip int brief**

```
Interface          IP-Address      OK? Method Status        Protocol

FastEthernet0/0    192.168.127.133 YES DHCP    up            up # An IP
                                                             is assigned
                                                             & up/up

Serial0/0          unassigned      YES unset  administratively down down

FastEthernet0/1    192.0.2.1       YES manual up                    up

[...omitted for brevity]
```

Don't forget to perform the communication check on the Internet.

R1#**ping 8.8.8.8**

```
Type escape sequence to abort.

Sending 5, 100-byte ICMP Echos to 8.8.8.8, timeout is 2 seconds:

.!!!! # check if ICMP communication works to the Google DNS, notice
that the first packet is dropped.

Success rate is 80 percent (4/5), round-trip min/avg/max = 28/36/48 ms
```

When R1 (a router) sends a packet to the next hop or a directly connected destination without an ARP table entry, it first sends an ARP request. However, during this process, the router may drop one to two initial packets. The first ARP packet is often dropped because it's sent to discover the MAC (Media Access Control) address of the destination, and there may be a brief period during which the router attempts to send the original packet without knowing the destination's MAC address. This can result in packet loss. Subsequent packets are not dropped because the router caches the MAC address after receiving an ARP response, allowing it to forward packets without delay.

(continued)

#	Task
⑩	Now let's configure R2. The configuration is similar to R1, but it has three interfaces on three different subnets.

```
configure terminal
hostname R2 # Assigns R2 as hostname
ip dhcp excluded-address 172.168.2.1 172.168.2.21 # Excludes
reserved IP addresses, PC2 should get the next IP address, which is
172.168.2.22 via DHCP.
ip dhcp pool VPCS_2 # PC2's DHCP pool configuration
network 172.168.2.0 255.255.255.0
default-router 172.168.2.1
interface FastEthernet0/0 # Connection to uplink R1's f0/1
ip address 192.0.2.2 255.255.255.0
no shut # Bring up the interface.
interface FastEthernet0/1 # Configure an IP address on f0/1, direct
connection to PC1.
ip address 172.168.1.1 255.255.255.0
no shut # Bring up the interface.
interface FastEthernet1/0 # Configure an IP address on f1/0.
ip address 172.168.2.1 255.255.255.0    # Connects to PC2
no shut # Bring up the interface.
exit
router ospf 1 # Configure OSPF 1 for internal network advertisement.
network 172.168.0.0 0.0.0.255 area 0
network 172.168.1.0 0.0.0.255 area 0
network 172.168.2.0 0.0.0.255 area 0
network 192.0.2.0 0.0.0.255 area 0
exit
ip route 0.0.0.0 0.0.0.0 192.0.2.1 # Configure a static route for
Gateway of last resort; static route to R1
exit
write memory # Save R2's running configuration to startup
configuration
```

(*continued*)

#	Task
⑪	Now open the PC1 (VPCS) console and practice configuring PC1's IP address manually. Type the commands exactly as shown here:

PC1> **ip 172.168.1.11/24 172.168.1.1** # Assign IP address and Gateway
Checking for duplicate address...
PC1 : 172.168.1.11 255.255.255.0 gateway 172.168.1.1
PC1> **ip dns 8.8.8.8** # Configure DNS IP address

PC1> **show ip** # Show ip address details
NAME   : PC1[1]
IP/MASK   : 172.168.1.11/24
GATEWAY   : 172.168.1.1
DNS   : 8.8.8.8
MAC   : 00:50:79:66:68:00
LPORT   : 20019
RHOST:PORT   : 127.0.0.1:20020
MTU   : 1500

Now validate your configuration by sending some ICMP messages from PC1 to R2, R1, and the Internet. If you get the ICMP responses from all three destinations, then your configuration is good and your network is working as designed.

PC1> **ping 192.0.2.2 -c 2** # to R2's f0/0
84 bytes from 192.0.2.2 icmp_seq=1 ttl=255 time=16.044 ms
84 bytes from 192.0.2.2 icmp_seq=2 ttl=255 time=16.198 ms

PC1> **ping 192.168.127.133 -c 2** # to R1's f0/0
84 bytes from 192.168.127.133 icmp_seq=1 ttl=254 time=47.766 ms
84 bytes from 192.168.127.133 icmp_seq=2 ttl=254 time=47.830 ms

PC1> **ping 8.8.8.8 -c 2** # to Google's public DNS server, 8.8.8.8
84 bytes from 8.8.8.8 icmp_seq=1 ttl=126 time=94.321 ms
84 bytes from 8.8.8.8 icmp_seq=2 ttl=126 time=80.163 ms

(continued)

#	Task
⑫	This time, open the console of PC2 (VPCS) and configure the IP address using the `ip dhcp` method. Unlike the previous configuration, PC2 will get its IP from R2's DHCP service, so R2 is the DHCP server and PC2 is the DHCP client here. If you have configured everything precisely as shown, then PC2 should be assigned with an IP address of 172.168.2.22.

```
PC2> ip dhcp
DDORA IP 172.168.2.22/24 GW 172.168.2.1 # "DDORA" stands for D:
Discover, O: Offer, R: Request, A: Acknowledge. Do not get confused
with the kid's character, 'DORA the Explorer'.
PC2> show ip
NAME         : PC2[1]
IP/MASK      : 172.168.2.22/24
GATEWAY      : 172.168.2.1
DNS          :
DHCP SERVER  : 172.168.2.1
DHCP LEASE   : 86373, 86400/43200/75600
MAC          : 00:50:79:66:68:01
LPORT        : 20021
RHOST:PORT   : 127.0.0.1:20022
MTU          : 1500
```

Although PC2 (VPCS) has printed DDORA while negotiating the IP address from the DHCP server, the standard version of the acronym is "DORA," representing the four main stages in the DHCP process. These are four stages in the DHCP processes:

D: Discover: The client broadcasts a DHCP Discover message to find available DHCP servers.
O: Offer: DHCP servers respond with DHCP Offer messages, suggesting available IP addresses.
R: Request: The client selects one IP address and sends a DHCP Request message to request it.
A: Acknowledge: The DHCP server confirms the allocation of the IP address with a DHCP Acknowledgment message.

(continued)

#	Task
	Now validate your configuration by sending some ICMP messages to R2, PC1, R1, and the Internet.

PC2> **ping 192.0.2.2 -c 2** # to R2's f0/0
84 bytes from 192.0.2.2 icmp_seq=1 ttl=255 time=16.112 ms
84 bytes from 192.0.2.2 icmp_seq=2 ttl=255 time=15.769 ms

PC2> **ping 172.168.1.11 -c 2** # to PC1
84 bytes from 172.168.1.11 icmp_seq=1 ttl=63 time=
31.787 ms
84 bytes from 172.168.1.11 icmp_seq=2 ttl=63 time=32.212 ms

PC2> **ping 192.168.127.133 -c 2** # to R1's f0/0
84 bytes from 192.168.127.133 icmp_seq=1 ttl=254 time=48.480 ms
84 bytes from 192.168.127.133 icmp_seq=2 ttl=254 time=47.722 ms

PC2> **ping 8.8.8.8 -c 2** # to Google's public DNS server, 8.8.8.8
84 bytes from 8.8.8.8 icmp_seq=1 ttl=126 time=94.982 ms # On
wireless you may get timeouts
84 bytes from 8.8.8.8 icmp_seq=2 ttl=126 time=79.944 ms

During this lab, you have accomplished the following:

- Built a GNS3 Topology.
- Configured two routers.
- Set up and used two VPCS PCs.
- Learned router basics.
- Explored DHCP.
- Tested ICMP connectivity.
- Set up OSPF routing.
- Configured a default gateway.
- Saved router configurations.

Wow, there were many different networking concepts to grasp from this first lab. You were introduced to basic OSPF routing, ICMP, and DHCP communications while working with two Cisco IOS routers, an unmanaged GNS3 switch, and two VPCS PCs. Although this book doesn't solely focus on routing and switching, having a fundamental understanding of networking concepts is crucial for maximizing the benefits of the book's content. Congratulations on completing your first GNS3 network lab. After each lab, remember to save the configuration, gracefully shut down your devices, and follow the standard procedure to close your project.

Expand Youcackets on a Cisco Router

In Step ⑨, if you wanted to find out more about how an IP address is allocated to an IP interface, you could enable the debug command debug dhcp and it would look something like this. This teaches you exactly how an IP address negotiation takes place between the DHCP server and a client. Here, the DHCP server is the VMnet8 interface and the client is R1.

R1#**debug dhcp** # Disable DHCP debugging.

DHCP client activity debugging is on

R1#**configure terminal**

R1(config)#**debug dhcp**

R1(config-if)#**ip address dhcp**

R1(config-if)#

*Mar 1 00:44:03.123: DHCP: DHCP client process started: 10

*Mar 1 00:44:03.135: RAC: Starting DHCP discover on FastEthernet0/0

*Mar 1 00:44:03.135: DHCP: Try 1 to acquire address for FastEthernet0/0

*Mar 1 00:44:03.143: DHCP: allocate request

*Mar 1 00:44:03.143: DHCP: new entry. add to queue, interface FastEthernet0/0

*Mar 1 00:44:03.147: DHCP: SDiscover attempt # 1 for entry:

*Mar 1 00:44:03.147: DHCP: SDiscover: sending 291 byte length DHCP packet

*Mar 1 00:44:03.147: DHCP: SDiscover 291 bytes

*Mar 1 00:44:03.147: B'cast on FastEthernet0/0 interface from 0.0.0.0

*Mar 1 00:44:04.223: DHCP: Received a BOOTREP pkt

*Mar 1 00:44:04.223: DHCP: offer received from 192.168.127.254

*Mar 1 00:44:04.227: DHCP: SRequest attempt # 1 for entry:

*Mar 1 00:44:04.227: DHCP: SRequest- Server ID option: 192.168.127.254

*Mar 1 00:44:04.227: DHCP: SRequest- Requested IP addr option: 192.168.127.133

*Mar 1 00:44:04.227: DHCP: SRequest placed lease len option: 1800

*Mar 1 00:44:04.227: DHCP: SRequest: 309 bytes

*Mar 1 00:44:04.227: DHCP: SRequest: 309 bytes

*Mar 1 00:44:04.231: B'cast on FastEthernet0/0 interface from 0.0.0.0

*Mar 1 00:44:04.275: DHCP: Received a BOOTREP pkt

*Mar 1 00:44:08.291: DHCP Client Pooling: ***Allocated IP address: 192.168.127.133

*Mar 1 00:44:08.403: Allocated IP address = 192.168.127.133 255.255.255.0

*Mar 1 00:44:08.403: %DHCP-6-ADDRESS_ASSIGN: Interface FastEthernet0/0 assigned DHCP address 192.168.127.133, mask 255.255.255.0, hostname R1

R1#**show dhcp server** # Check DHCP server information

DHCP server: ANY (255.255.255.255)

Leases: 2

Offers: 1   Requests: 3   Acks : 2   Naks: 0

Declines: 0   Releases: 0   Query: 0   Bad: 0

DNS0:   192.168.127.2,   DNS1: 0.0.0.0

NBNS0: 192.168.127.2,   NBNS1: 0.0.0.0

Subnet: 255.255.255.0   DNS Domain: localdomain

R1#**show dhcp lease** # Check DHCP lease information

Temp IP addr: 192.168.127.133 for peer on Interface: FastEthernet0/0

Temp sub net mask: 255.255.255.0

```
DHCP Lease server: 192.168.127.254, state: 3 Bound

DHCP transaction id: CC1

Lease: 1800 secs,  Renewal: 900 secs,  Rebind: 1575 secs
```

Temp default-gateway addr: 192.168.127.2

```
Next timer fires after: 00:07:19

Retry count: 0   Client-ID: cisco-c401.2915.0000-Fa0/0

Client-ID hex dump: 636973636F2D633430312E323931352E

303030302D4661302F30

Hostname: R1
```

R1#**undebug all** # Disable all debugging.

All possible debugging has been turned off

Next, let's explore the process of installing the Microsoft Loopback Adapter. This adapter facilitates communication between Windows hosts and networking/system devices running within GNS3 topologies.

Installing the Microsoft Loopback Adapter

To communicate, control, and manage Cisco devices in your GNS3 setup from your Windows 11 host PC, you can install the Microsoft Loopback Adapter. This adapter serves as a virtual network interface for testing purposes, making it easy to connect to GNS3 devices from your host operating system. Follow these steps to install the Microsoft Loopback Adapter on your Windows PC. If you are still using Windows 10 as your host operating system, the steps are quite similar to was outlined in the first edition of this book. Keep in mind that if you're using a company-provided standard operating environment (SOE) laptop or PC, the process may vary, and the menus and options might look different on such devices. However, if you are using your personal computer, you can follow these steps.

#	Task
①	Press the Windows and R keys simultaneously on your keyboard. This will open the Run dialog.
②	In the Run dialog, type devmgmt.msc and click the OK button, as shown in Figure 10-56.

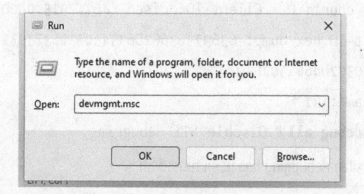

Figure 10-56. *Open Device Manager using the Run dialog*

(*continued*)

#	Task
③	The Device Manager window will open, allowing you to view and manage the devices on your computer. In the Device Manager window, first click Network Adapters to highlight it, then click Action, which is located in the top menu. Finally, click Add Legacy Hardware, as shown in Figure 10-57.

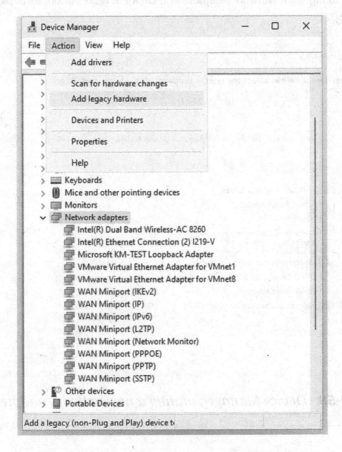

Figure 10-57. *Device Manager, network adapters, adding legacy hardware*

(*continued*)

#	Task
④	When the Add Hardware pop-up window appears, click the Next button.
⑤	In the next window, select Install the Hardware That I Manually Select from a List (Advanced). Then click the Next button.
⑥	Scroll down to highlight Network Adapters and click the Next button, as depicted in Figure 10-58.

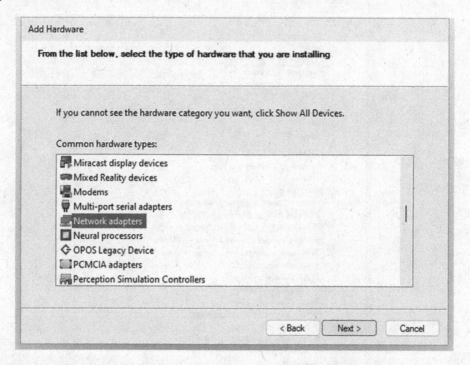

Figure 10-58. *Device Manager, adding a new network adapter*

(*continued*)

#	Task
⑦	When the hardware device driver window appears, select Microsoft under Manufacturer, and then select Microsoft KM-TEST Loopback Adapter under Model on the right. Click the Next button again. Refer to Figure 10-59.

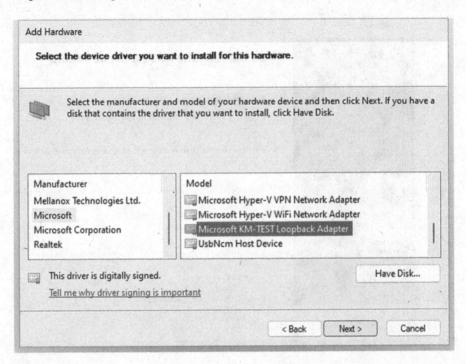

Figure 10-59. *Device Manager, adding the Microsoft loopback adapter*

#	Task
⑧	On the next screen, click the Next button to install the hardware driver.

(*continued*)

#	Task
⑨	When the driver installation is completed and the Completing the Add Hardware Wizard message appears, click the Finish button (see Figure 10-60). Also, close the Device Manager so all windows are closed.

Figure 10-60. *Device Manager, finishing the Microsoft loopback adapter installation*

⑩	One more time, press the Windows and R keys simultaneously on your keyboard. This will open the Run dialog.

(continued)

#	Task
⑪	Next, type ncpa.cpl in the Run dialog, as shown in Figure 10-61. This will open the Network Connections window with network adapters.

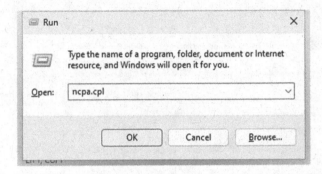

Figure 10-61. *Windows 11, a shortcut to running network connections*

#	Task
⑫	Highlight the newly added Microsoft KM-TEST Loopback Adapter icon, then select the Rename this Connection option on the top, as shown in Figure 10-62.

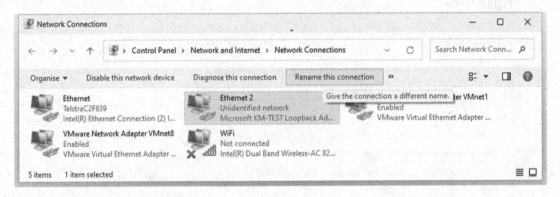

Figure 10-62. *Windows 11, renaming the Microsoft loopback adapter*

(*continued*)

#	Task

Now change the name of the Ethernet 2 to Loopback, as shown in Figure 10-63. This will help you identify this adapter more easily from others.

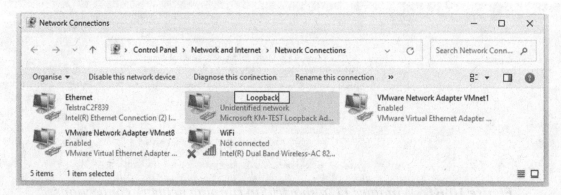

Figure 10-63. *Windows 11, renaming the Microsoft loopback adapter*

⑬   This time, right-click the loopback adapter, then select the Properties option, as shown in Figure 10-64.

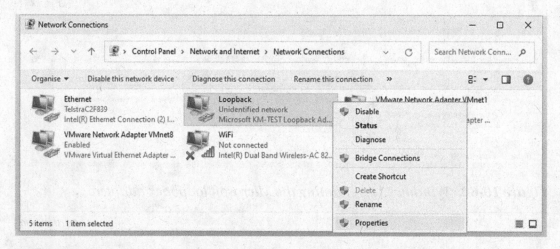

Figure 10-64. *Windows 11, select the Microsoft loopback adapter properties option*

(*continued*)

#	Task
⑭	Highlight Internet Protocol Version 4 (TCP/IP4) and then click the Properties button, as displayed in Figure 10-65.

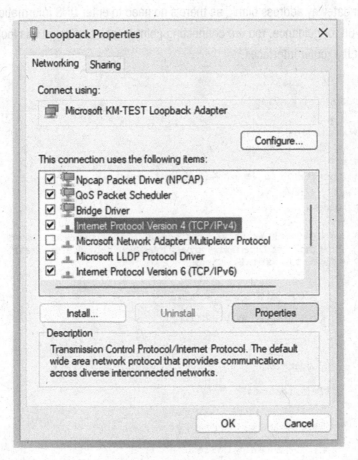

Figure 10-65. *Windows 11, selecting IPv4 properties*

(*continued*)

#	Task
⑮	For testing purposes, assign an IP address to the loopback adapter. In this example, I used the IP address 7.7.7.1 with a subnet mask of 255.255.255.0 for the 7.7.7.0/24 subnet. Leave the default gateway address blank, as there's no need to enter DNS information. Refer to Figure 10-66 for guidance. You are connecting point-to-point between this loopback interface and one of the router interfaces.

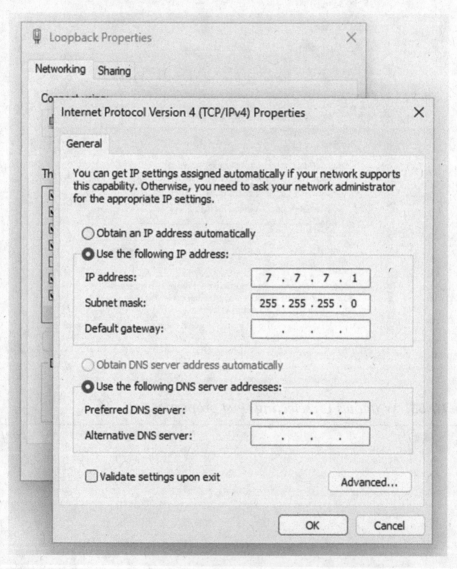

Figure 10-66. *Windows 11, configure a static IP address on the MS loopback adapter*

#	Task
⑯	Click OK to confirm the settings, and then close all windows and running applications, including GNS3. To ensure that GNS3 recognizes the newly installed Microsoft Loopback interface, restart your Windows host once more. Proceed with the system restart.

After the PC restart, you can create a new GNS3 project utilizing the Microsoft Loopback Adapter. You'll set up a router and establish a connection between your Windows host machine and a virtual Cisco IOS Router for testing. This same connection method can be applied to connect to Cisco's VIRL L2 and L3 devices, as well as GNS3 virtual device platforms. This will allow you to use Windows SSH Client tools such as PuTTY or Secure CRT to connect to the virtual network devices running on the GNS3 VM, adding more convenience to your lab.

Accessing GNS3 Network Devices Using MS Loopback

After creating a basic GNS3 project, you will be testing the communication between R1 and the Windows 11 host. Because a single image conveys more than a thousand words, Figure 10-67 displays the basic logical topology to help your understanding.

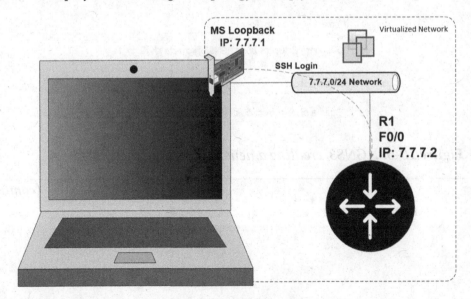

Figure 10-67. Host PC to GNS3 router communication

713

To configure your second lab using a simple Microsoft Loopback and a single virtual IOS router, follow these instructions:

#	Task
①	Launch GNS3 using the GNS3 icon on the desktop (see Figure 10-68). Wait until the GNS3 VM starts and the CPU settles down.

Figure 10-68. *GNS3 desktop icon*

#	Task
②	Now, go ahead and create a new project named `ch10_lo_to_r1`. See Figure 10-69. You do not have to follow this naming convention, so use your imagination and give it a meaningful name.

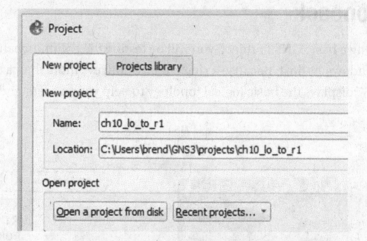

Figure 10-69. *GNS3, creating a new project, loopback_to_r1*

(continued)

#	Task
③	Now put together a simple lab topology. Open the All Devices menu and drop one IOS router and one cloud (not the NAT cloud) onto the Topology canvas. R1 will run on the GNS3 VM, and Cloud-1 will be running on the host PC. Look at the server's summary for your reference. Do not connect or start the router yet, as shown in Figure 10-70.

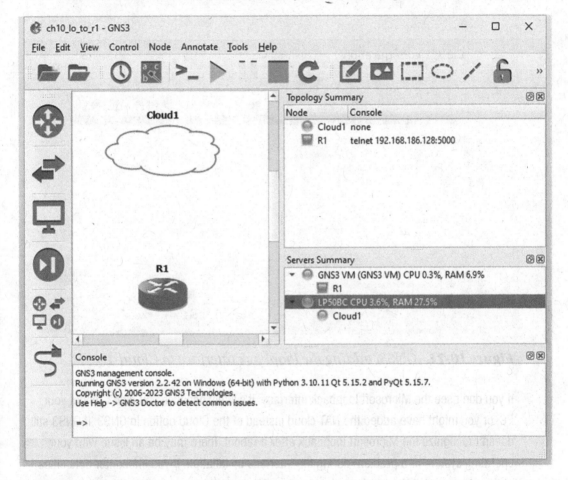

Figure 10-70. *GNS3, creating a topology*

(*continued*)

#	Task
④	In this step, refer to Figure 10-71 and right-click Cloud-1. Next, select Configure and check the Show Special Ethernet Interfaces box located at the bottom-left corner of the window. Remove the default Ethernet entry and add the Loopback interface from the drop-down menu. Finally, click the Apply button and then select the OK button to complete the task.

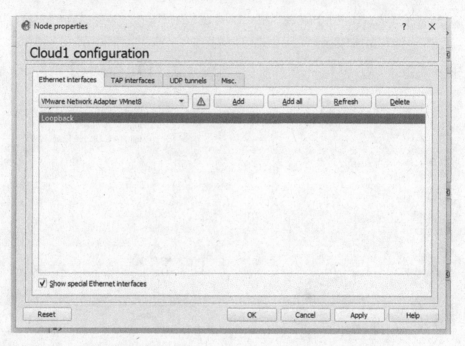

Figure 10-71. *GNS3, adding the loopback interface to Cloud-1*

If you don't see the Microsoft loopback interface, it's likely because you didn't reboot your PC, or you might have added the NAT cloud instead of the Cloud option in GNS3. If GNS3 still doesn't recognize the Microsoft loopback after a reboot, there may be an issue with your operating system or a problem during the interface installation. If you encounter difficulties at this stage, revisit the previous steps and rectify the problem.

(*continued*)

#	Task
⑤	Right-click Cloud-1 and change the hostname to Host-PC. Then connect the Loopback interface to R1's f0/0 interface, as shown in Figure 10-72. After connecting the two interfaces, power on R1 and wait a minute or two for R1 to start.

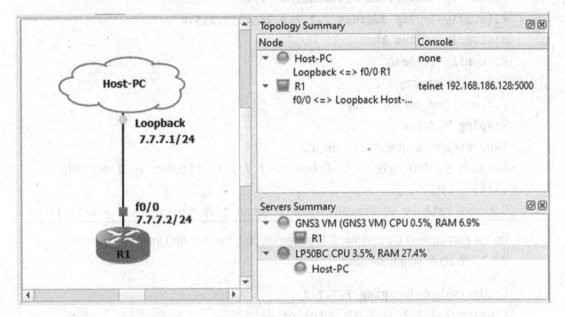

Figure 10-72. *GNS3, connecting the Microsoft loopback to R1's f0/0*

Note: If your GNS3 throws an error and refuses to connect, you may need to change the User Account Control Setting on your Windows host PC.

(continued)

#	Task
⑥	Double-click the R1 icon to open R1's console and configure R1's f0/0 interface, as shown here:

```
R1#config t
R1(config)#interface FastEthernet 0/0
R1(config-if)#ip address 7.7.7.2 255.255.255.0
R1(config-if)#no shut
R1(config-if)#end
R1# write memory
[...omitted for brevity]
R1#ping 7.7.7.1
Type escape sequence to abort.
Sending 5, 100-byte ICMP Echos to 7.7.7.1, timeout is 2 seconds:
.!!!!
Success rate is 80 percent (4/5), round-trip min/avg/max = 8/11/12 ms
```

#	Task
⑦	On the host laptop/PC's command-line prompt, ping the R1's f0/0 interface IP address 7.7.7.2 to verify communication.

```
C:\Users\brendan>ping 7.7.7.2
Pinging 7.7.7.2 with 32 bytes of data:
Reply from 7.7.7.2: bytes=32 time=22ms TTL=255
Reply from 7.7.7.2: bytes=32 time=6ms TTL=255
Reply from 7.7.7.2: bytes=32 time=8ms TTL=255
Reply from 7.7.7.2: bytes=32 time=11ms TTL=255
Ping statistics for 7.7.7.2:
Packets: Sent = 4, Received = 4, Lost = 0 (0% loss),
Approximate round trip times in milli-seconds:
Minimum = 6ms, Maximum = 22ms, Average = 11ms
```

(continued)

#	Task
⑧	For testing purposes, configure the username and Telnet on R1. Telnet is configured here:

R1#**configure terminal**
R1(config)# **username jdoe privilege 15 password Lion2Roar!**
R1(config)#**line vty 0 15**
R1(config-line)#**login local**
R1(config-line)#**transport input telnet**
R1(config-line)#**do wri**
Building configuration...
[OK]

(continued)

#	Task
⑨	Using PuTTY, enter R1's IP address 7.7.7.2 and change the port to Telnet port 23, as shown in Figure 10-73. Click the Open button to log in.

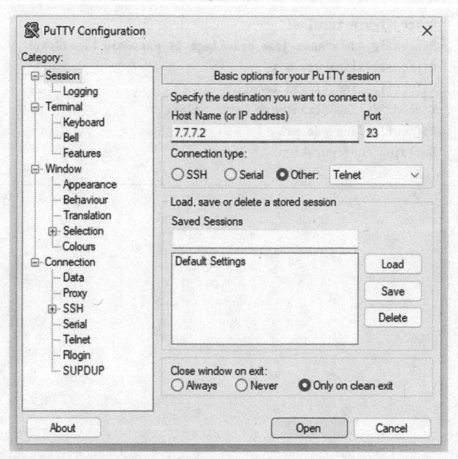

Figure 10-73. *PuTTY, Telnet to R1*

(*continued*)

#	Task
(10)	When prompted for the username and password, enter the credentials and log in to R1 (see Figure 10-74).

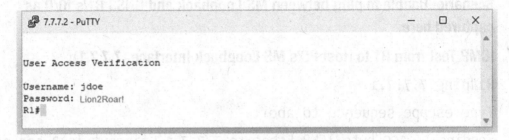

Figure 10-74. PuTTY, a successful Telnet login to R1

You have now completed your second GNS3 practice lab. In this lab, you gained knowledge about adding a Microsoft Loopback interface to your host PC, connecting it to R1 through the GNS3 Cloud, and configuring the f0/0 interface along with user account and telnet settings on R1. You also used PuTTY to establish a Telnet connection to R1 via port 23. If you've reached this point in the lab, congratulations! You can now proceed to the next step, which involves creating a simple Python Telnet script to configure R1's interfaces.

If you encounter issues, particularly the GNS3 MS Loopback communication problem, there's no need to worry. I've meticulously documented each troubleshooting step to assist readers facing similar challenges. While every computer running various builds of Windows 11 may exhibit unique settings and specific issues, the methods documented here represent general Windows troubleshooting steps. If the problem persists, review this section carefully. If you're still facing ICMP-related problems, it's essential to troubleshoot and resolve the issue before progressing to the next section of your learning journey.

Tip

Troubleshooting ping issues through the Windows 11 Firewall with GNS3 and MS Loopback

Scenario: Unable to ping between MS Loopback and GNS3 R1's f0/0 as captured here.

ICMP Test from R1 to Host PC's MS Loopback Interface (7.7.7.1):

R1#ping 7.7.7.1

Type escape sequence to abort.

Sending 5, 100-byte ICMP Echos to 7.7.7.1, timeout is 2 seconds:

.....

Success rate is 0 percent (0/5)

ICMP Test from Host PC to R1's FastEthernet 0/0 (7.7.7.2):

C:\Users\brend>ping 7.7.7.2

Pinging 7.7.7.2 with 32 bytes of data:

Reply from 7.7.7.1: Destination host unreachable.

Request timed out.

Request timed out.

Request timed out.

Ping statistics for 7.7.7.2:

Packets: Sent = 4, Received = 1, Lost = 3 (75% loss)

Note

If you encounter this issue, try the following troubleshooting methods to resolve it. **Perform one troubleshooting method at a time. After each method is performed and if the Windows Firewall settings have changed, restart your system and then perform these ICMP tests to check if the issue has been resolved.**

① **Method 1: Change the User Account control setting.**

From the Control Panel, open User Account Control Setting and change the setting to Never Notify. This will allow you to connect the MS Loopback interface with GNS3 devices. After making this change, you must restart the PC one more time.

1. Press Win+R on your keyboard to open the Run dialog.
2. Enter this command: `control.exe /name Microsoft.UserAccounts`.
3. Select Change User Account Control settings.
4. When the User Account Control Settings window opens, use the slider to set it to Never Notify (see Figure 10-75).
5. Click the OK button to save the settings.
6. Restart your system.

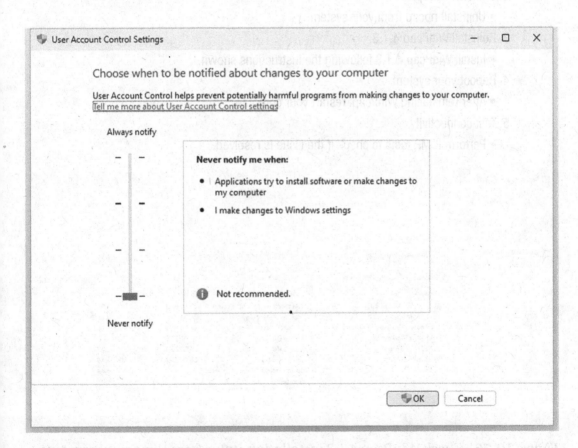

Figure 10-75. *User account control setting, changing to Never Notify*

(continued)

② **Method 2: Check Npcap (Nmap), uninstall Npcap and reinstall WinPcap 4.1.3**

If Npcap was installed instead of WinPcap 4.1.3, it's recommended to uninstall Npcap and then install WinPcap 4.1.3, as shown in Figure 10-76. This process can help resolve issues related to MS Loopback interface reachability. After reinstalling WinPcap, remember to reboot your system. Attempting to resolve the problem by configuring Npcap with options like WinPcap API Compatible or Legacy Loopback Support is generally not recommended, as they may not allow you to connect the cloud to MS Loopback and ping it.

Here is a step-by-step instructions:

1. Check npcap (Nmap).
   - Verify if npcap (Nmap) is installed.
   - If npcap is installed instead of WinPcap 4.1.3, proceed to the next steps.
2. Uninstall npcap.
   - Uninstall npcap from your system.
3. Reinstall WinPcap 4.1.3.
   - Install WinPcap 4.1.3 following the instructions shown.
4. Reboot your system.
   - After reinstalling WinPcap, restart your computer.
5. Test connectivity.
   - Perform ICMP tests to check if the issue is resolved.

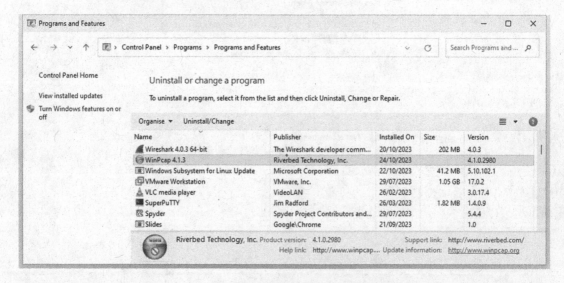

Figure 10-76. *Check WinPcap 4.1.3 installation status from Windows Programs and Features*

(*continued*)

③ **Method 3: Allow Ping from Windows Security Settings**

The most frequently used method to enable ping in the Windows 11 Firewall is by adjusting the settings for applications permitted to pass through the Windows Firewall:

1. Type **Windows Security** in the Windows 11 search bar and press Enter.
2. The Windows Security app will open. Choose Firewall & Network Protection from the left panel.
3. Click the Allow an App Through Firewall hyperlink.
4. The window for allowed apps will be displayed on your screen.
5. Click the Change Settings button.
6. Check the boxes next to File and Printer Sharing to enable pings through the firewall (see Figure 10-77).
7. Click the OK button to save the changes.

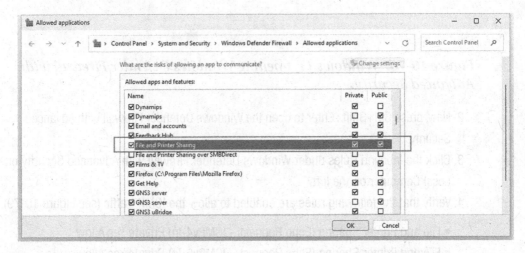

Figure 10-77. *Windows Defender Firewall allowed applications*

(continued)

④   **Method 4: Check File and Printer Sharing Echo Requests in Windows Defender Firewall with Advanced Security**

You can also enable ping through the Windows 11 Firewall using the Command Prompt. Here's how:

1. Press the Windows+R keys to open the Run dialog box and type wf.msc in the field (see Figure 10-78).

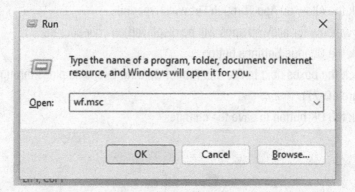

Figure 10-78. *Windows 11, opening Windows Defender Firewall with Advanced Security*

2. Now, press Ctrl+Shift+Enter to open the Windows Defender Firewall with Advanced Security.
3. Click the Inbound Rules under Windows Defender Firewall with Advanced Security on Local Computer on the left.
4. Verify that the following rules are enabled to allow the ICMP traffic (see Figure 10-79).

- File and Printer Sharing (Echo Request – ICMPv4-In) Private Yes Allow
- File and Printer Sharing (Echo Request – ICMPv6-In) Private Yes Allow

(continued)

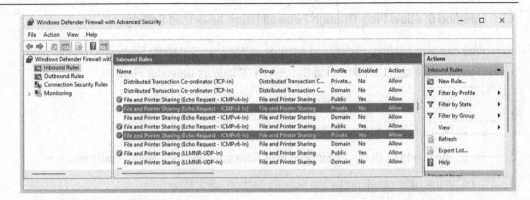

Figure 10-79. *Inbound rules under Windows Defender Firewall with Advanced Security*

⑤   **Method 5: Enable ICMP Echo Request Using Command Prompt**

You can also enable ping through the Windows 11 Firewall using the Command Prompt. Here's how:

1. Press the Windows+R keys to open the Run dialog box and type cmd in the field.
2. Now, press Ctrl+Shift+Enter to open the Command Prompt with administrative privileges.
3. In the Command Prompt, type the following command and press Enter:`netsh advfirewall firewall add rule name="ICMPv4 Allow Ping Requests" protocol=icmpv4:8,any dir=in action=allow`
4. Next, type the following command and press Enter to allow another type of ICMP request: `netsh advfirewall firewall add rule name="ICMPv6 Allow Ping Requests" protocol=icmpv6:8,any dir=in action=allow`

Once these commands are executed successfully, you have enabled ping through the Windows 11 Firewall.

(*continued*)

⑥   **Method 6: Allow Ping Through Firewall Using Advanced Settings**

You can also configure advanced settings in Windows Defender Firewall to enable ping. Follow these steps to allow ping through the Windows Defender Firewall.

1. Press the Windows+R keys to open the Run dialog box.

2. Type `wf.msc` and press Enter.

3. The Windows Defender Firewall with Advanced Security window will open.

4. In the right panel, under the Actions section, click New Rule.

5. The New Inbound Rule Wizard will appear.

6. Select the Custom button and click Next.

7. Choose All Programs and click Next.

8. Click Protocol Type to open the drop-down list.

9. Select either ICMPv4 or ICMPv6, depending on your preference.

10. Click Customize.

11. In the Customize ICMP Settings wizard, select Specific ICMP Types.

12. Check the Echo Request option and click OK.

13. The wizard will close, and you'll return to the Inbound Rule Wizard. Click Next.

14. With Any IP Address selected for both options, click Next.

15. Choose Allow the Connection and click Next.

16. Under the Profile section, select Domain, Private, and Public, and then click Next.

17. Provide a name for this new rule and click Finish.

(continued)

⑦ **Method 7: Allow Ping Using a Local Group Policy**

You can configure the local group policy editor to allow ping through the firewall. Follow these steps:

1. Open the Run dialog by pressing the Windows+R keys.

2. Type gpedit.msc and press Enter to launch the Local Group Policy Editor.

3. In the left panel, select Computer Configuration.

4. Double-click Windows Settings to expand it.

5. Choose Security Settings and expand Windows Firewall with Advanced Security.

6. Select Inbound Rules, then right-click it.

7. Click New Rule...

8. In the new rule wizard, choose the Custom option and click Next.

9. Select All Programs and click Next.

10. Open the Protocol Type drop-down menu and select either ICMPv4 or ICMPv6, depending on your preference.

11. Click the Customize button on the same screen.

12. Choose the Specific ICMP Types option and check the box for Echo Request. Click Next.

13. Select Any IP Address for both options and click Next again.

14. Choose the Allow the Connection radio button and click Next.

15. Check the boxes for all the options: Domain, Private, and Public.

16. Finally, provide a name for the new rule and click Finish to complete the process of allowing ping through the firewall.

(continued)

⑧   **Method 8: Allowing ICMP Echo Request Using PowerShell**

Likewise, similar to Step ⑤, you can allow ICMP Echo Request using PowerShell. Run the following PowerShell commands in Administrator mode (the detailed steps are not described here).

1. `netsh advfirewall firewall add rule name="ICMP Allow incoming V4 echo request" protocol=icmpv4:8,any dir=in action=allow`
2. `netsh advfirewall firewall add rule name="ICMP Allow incoming V6 echo request" protocol=icmpv6:128,any dir=in action=allow`

As a result of the troubleshooting steps previously outlined, you should now be able to establish communication between R1 and the MS Loopback interface on your host PC. This means you have successfully connected to the IOS device running on GNS3 from your Windows PC. You are now ready to configure the GNS3 router from the convenience of your Windows PC, using a Python script.

Configuring the GNS3 IOS Router Using a Python Script from the Windows Host PC

In your third GNS3 practice lab, you will create a Python script to achieve the following objectives:

- Locate Python resources and reuse code for your learning.

- Telnet into a single Cisco IOS device.

- Configure a loopback interface and FastEthernet 0/1.

Even if you haven't written a Python script before, follow along and complete each task in this Python Network primer lab. I sourced the Python Telnet example script from the Python.org documentation and modified it slightly to be used in this third GNS3 practice lab. By copying this example, you will create your first Cisco router interaction script, which works via Telnet. This script utilizes Python's built-in libraries and the getpass module to get user input and passwords. A Python library is a collection of useful modules. These Python modules can be thought of as small programs that are pre-written and tested for other users, saving you from reinventing the wheel each time.

Built-in or standard libraries are installed by default when Python is installed on your machine, while external or nonstandard libraries are modules that are installed on your operating system as needed. When you reach the next level, you could also choose to write and compile your own Python module, which serves a specific purpose for your work.

Don't attempt to grasp every detail in the sample code. Explanations are provided later. Concentrate on the assigned task and meticulously check for typing errors. When writing code, even the smallest details—such as commas, periods, and spacing—are crucial, especially in Python scripting. Developing a healthy typing habit is essential for any programmer, as it helps avoid typos and errors, ultimately saving time and headaches.

#	Task
①	On your Windows host PC, start by navigating to your Python installation folder. In my case, the installation location is C:\Python312, so I will use this folder for my work. Your Python installation location might be different from mine. Next, create a new folder to store your scripts. In this example, I've named my folder ch10, as shown in Figure 10-80.

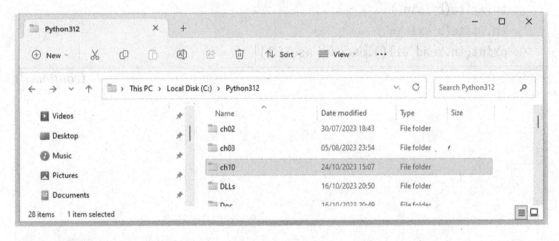

Figure 10-80. *Host PC, creating a new folder*

(*continued*)

#	Task
②	Both the getpass and telnet libraries used in this script are built-in, standard Python libraries, so there's no need to install them separately. You can find a Telnet example by visiting the following URL and scrolling to the end:

```
https://docs.python.org/3/library/telnetlib.html
import getpass
import telnetlib
HOST = "localhost"
user = input("Enter your remote account: ")
password = getpass.getpass()
tn = telnetlib.Telnet(HOST)
tn.read_until(b"login: ")
tn.write(user.encode('ascii') + b"\n")
if password:
tn.read_until(b"Password: ")
tn.write(password.encode('ascii') + b"\n")
tn.write(b"ls\n")
tn.write(b"exit\n")
print(tn.read_all().decode('ascii'))
```

(continued)

#	Task
③	Copy and paste this Python Telnet example to a Notepad++ file. Save the file as ch10_telnet1.py in the C:\python312\ch10 folder on your Windows PC (see Figure 10-81). Modify the code as follows, with the modified portions in bold. Save the script as a .py file once you've made the changes. While this script will be thoroughly explained later, for now, follow the lab instructions precisely. When you're starting your Python coding journey, you often learn the most by imitating or adapting other people's work, much like how infants learn to talk by hearing and imitating parents' voices and those around them.

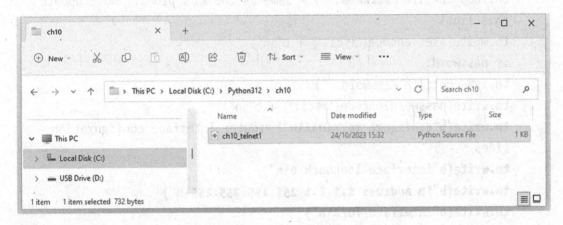

Figure 10-81. *Save the Python code as ch10_telnet1.py*

(continued)

#	Task

```
# Filename: ch10_telnet1.py
import getpass
import telnetlib
HOST = "7.7.7.2" # R1's f0/0 interface IP address
user = input("Enter your telnet username: ")
password = getpass.getpass()
tn = telnetlib.Telnet(HOST)
tn.read_until(b"Username: ") # Same as the R1's prompt, must update
this line!
tn.write(user.encode('ascii') + b"\n")
if password:
tn.read_until(b"Password: ")
tn.write(password.encode('ascii') + b"\n")
tn.write(b"configure terminal\n") #router interface configuration
lines
tn.write(b"interface loopback 0\n")
tn.write(b"ip address 1.1.1.1 255.255.255.255\n")
tn.write(b"interface f0/1\n")
tn.write(b"ip address 20.20.20.1 255.255.255.0\n")
tn.write(b"no shut\n")
tn.write(b"end\n")
tn.write(b"show ip interface brief\n")
tn.write(b"write memory\n")
tn.write(b"exit\n")
print(tn.read_all().decode('ascii'))
```

(continued)

#	Task

④ As displayed in Figure 10-82, open R1's console using PuTTY to Telnet to R1 (7.7.7.2). You can also use the GNS3 R1 console for this task. After you are connected, you can check the current interface status by running the show ip interface brief command, or sh ip int bri for short. This command will display the information about the configured interfaces, allowing you to verify the current interface status.

R1#**show ip interface brief**

```
 7.7.7.2 - PuTTY                                                      ─    □    ✕
R1#show ip interface brief
Interface                  IP-Address      OK? Method Status                 Protoc
ol
FastEthernet0/0            7.7.7.2         YES NVRAM  up                         up

Serial0/0                  unassigned      YES NVRAM  administratively down down

FastEthernet0/1            unassigned      YES NVRAM  administratively down down

Serial0/1                  unassigned      YES NVRAM  administratively down down

Serial0/2                  unassigned      YES NVRAM  administratively down down

FastEthernet1/0            unassigned      YES NVRAM  administratively down down

FastEthernet2/0            unassigned      YES NVRAM  administratively down down

FastEthernet3/0            unassigned      YES NVRAM  administratively down down

R1#
```

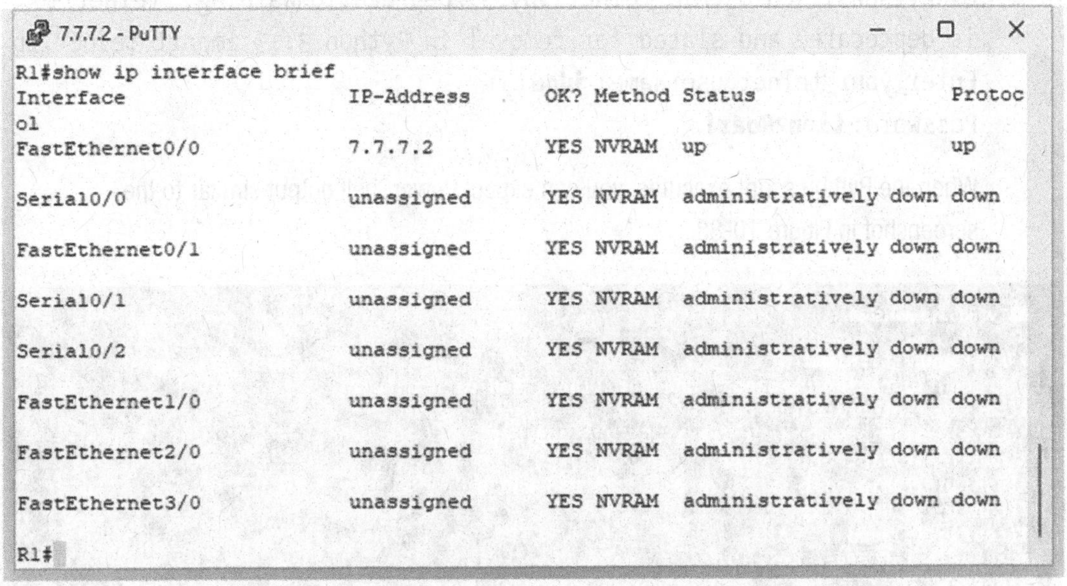

Figure 10-82. PuTTY, R1 show ip interface brief output

⑤ On R1's telnet connection, enable debugging for Telnet and enable the terminal monitor to observe the router activities. The terminal monitor command is only required for remote login sessions such as Telnet and SSH, so if you're connected via GNS3 Console, you do not have to issue this command. When you run the script and authenticate, keep R1's console window open and observe the logs.

R1#**debug telnet**
R1# **terminal monitor** # for Telnet and SSH connections

(continued)

#	Task
⑥	Now open Windows PowerShell, navigate to the C:\Python312\ch10\ folder, and run python ch10_telnet1.py. When prompted for a username and password, authenticate using the credentials you created in the previous section. As you type the password, you will not see any characters, as the getpass module hides this information automatically.

```
PS C:\Users\brend> cd C:\Python312\ch10\
PS C:\Python312\ch10> python ch10_telnet1.py
C:\Python312\ch10\ch10_telnet1.py:3: DeprecationWarning: 'telnetlib'
is deprecated and slated for removal in Python 3.13 import telnetlib
Enter your telnet username: jdoe
Password: Lion2Roar!
```

When the Python script executes, you can expect PowerShell output similar to the screenshot in Figure 10-83.

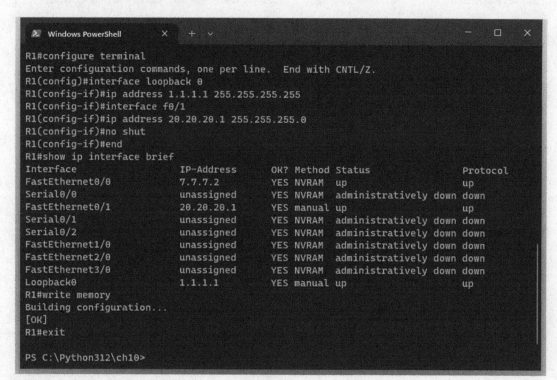

Figure 10-83. *Windows PowerShell, R1 configuration output*

(*continued*)

#	Task
⑦	Return to your remote Telnet session with R1 on PuTTY and monitor the Telnet logs. After successfully configuring the router interfaces, it's essential to disable debugging by running the undebug all command. Following that, execute show ip int bri to verify the configuration of Loopback0 and FastEthernet0/1. Both interfaces should now have assigned IP addresses in up/up operational state. After running the Python script, you will observe output similar to what's depicted in Figure 10-84.

```
R1#un all
R1#show ip int bri
```

```
7.7.7.2 - PuTTY                                                          —    □    ×
R1#
*Mar  1 00:19:35.363: Telnet163: 1 1 251 1
*Mar  1 00:19:35.363: TCP163: Telnet sent WILL ECHO (1)
*Mar  1 00:19:35.363: Telnet163: 2 2 251 3
*Mar  1 00:19:35.363: TCP163: Telnet sent WILL SUPPRESS-GA (3)
*Mar  1 00:19:35.363: Telnet163: 80000 80000 253 24
*Mar  1 00:19:35.363: TCP163: Telnet sent DO TTY-TYPE (24)
*Mar  1 00:19:35.363: Telnet163: 10000000 10000000 253 31
*Mar  1 00:19:35.367: TCP163: Telnet sent DO WINDOW-SIZE (31)
*Mar  1 00:19:35.371: TCP163: Telnet received DONT ECHO (1)
*Mar  1 00:19:35.371: TCP163: Telnet sent WONT ECHO (1)
*Mar  1 00:19:35.383: TCP163: Telnet received DONT SUPPRESS-GA (3)
*Mar  1 00:19:35.383: TCP163: Telnet sent WONT SUPPRESS-GA (3)
*Mar  1 00:19:35.383: TCP163: Telnet received WONT TTY-TYPE (24)
*Mar  1 00:19:35.383: TCP163: Telnet sent DONT TTY-TYPE (24)
*Mar  1 00:19:35.383: TCP163: Telnet received WONT WINDOW-SIZE (31)
*Mar  1 00:19:35.383: TCP163: Telnet sent DONT WINDOW-SIZE (31)
*Mar  1 00:19:35.403: TCP163: Telnet received DONT ECHO (1)
*Mar  1 00:19:35.415: TCP163: Telnet received DONT SUPPRESS-GA (3)
*Mar  1 00:19:35.427: TCP163: Telnet received WONT TTY-TYPE (24)
*Mar  1 00:19:35.435: TCP163: Telnet received WONT WINDOW-SIZE (31)
*Mar  1 00:19:36.991: %SYS-5-CONFIG_I: Configured from console by jdoe on vty1 (7.7.7.1)
R1#un all
All possible debugging has been turned off
R1#show ip int bri
Interface              IP-Address      OK? Method Status                Protocol
FastEthernet0/0        7.7.7.2         YES NVRAM  up                    up
Serial0/0              unassigned      YES NVRAM  administratively down down
FastEthernet0/1        20.20.20.1      YES manual up                    up
Serial0/1              unassigned      YES NVRAM  administratively down down
Serial0/2              unassigned      YES NVRAM  administratively down down
FastEthernet1/0        unassigned      YES NVRAM  administratively down down
FastEthernet2/0        unassigned      YES NVRAM  administratively down down
FastEthernet3/0        unassigned      YES NVRAM  administratively down down
Loopback0              1.1.1.1         YES manual up                    up
R1#
```

Figure 10-84. *PuTTY, ch10_telnet1.py run logs on R1 and show ip int bri output*

Well done on completing your third GNS3 practice lab, where you configured R1's f0/1 and a loopback using a Python Telnet script! I hope you're enjoying each lab and retaining a wealth of practical knowledge. While studying concepts from various resources is valuable, reinforcing that knowledge through hands-on experience is equally crucial in making it your own. You're on the right track in your Python Network Automation journey, and next, I introduce the out-of-the-box GNS3 appliance server into your topology to explore its capabilities.

Cisco IOS and GNS3 Appliance Lab

GNS3 provides a plethora of useful Appliance templates that prove invaluable when delving into networking, security, and systems concepts. You can improve your experience by adding preconfigured templates, installing them on the GNS3 VM as appliances, and seamlessly integrating them into your lab. This versatility extends to even installing Palo Alto and Fortinet firewalls, complete with a full GUI interface, for practical lab utilization. GNS3 offers a plethora of pre-installed appliance Dockerized and QEMU images, designed to facilitate easy access to tens of pre-installed systems, network, and security platforms. In particular, the Network Automation Docker image is essentially an Ubuntu 20.04.2 LTS server Dockerized image that enables you to set up and run efficient network labs with minimum fuss. It's important to note that any changes made while Docker is active will revert to the original settings once it's powered off. Docker operates as a lightweight appliance and isn't a fully-fledged virtual machine, unlike your Fedora or Ubuntu VMs. Instead, it relies on the hosting server's kernels for its functionality and operations.

To illustrate this, this lab showcases the importation of a plain Linux Docker image and subsequently engages in an interactive Telnet session using this Linux Docker image.

This lab's key objectives include:

- Learn how to use a GNS3 appliance device in your topology.

- Practice IP address configuration on a Linux server's interface.

- Learn how to Telnet to a Cisco router from a Linux appliance server.

This fourth practice lab seamlessly extends from the previous two labs. You'll continue to work on the ch10_lo_to_r1 project. This lab introduces a Linux Docker appliance into your topology using the GNS3 template. Let's explore how GNS3 appliances can expedite your setup process.

#	Task
①	In the GNS3 main window, navigate to File > + New Template (see Figure 10-85). Alternatively, you can also open All Devices and select + New Template from there.

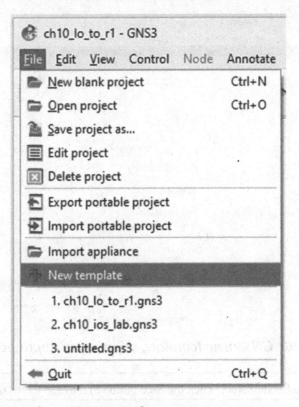

Figure 10-85. *GNS3, select +New Template*

②	In the New Template wizard window, leave the selection Install an Appliance from the GNS3 Server (Recommended) checked and click the Next button.

(continued)

#	Task
③	On the Appliances from the server screen, type Network Automation or use the drop-down menu under Guests and select Network Automation Docker. Then click the Install button, as shown in Figure 10-86. This will add a Dockerized Linux server to the GNS3's End Devices.

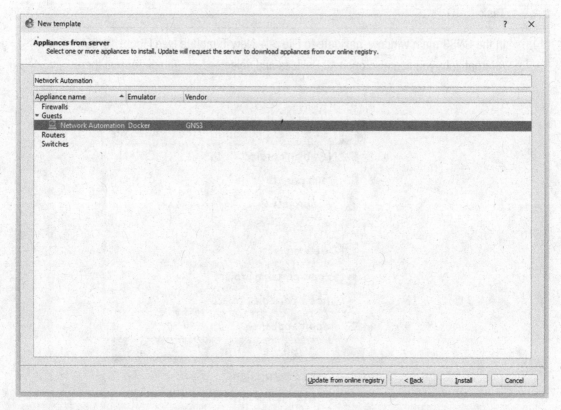

Figure 10-86. GNS3 *new template, selecting an appliance Linux server*

④	On the Server screen, click the Next button to move to the next screen.
⑤	On the Usage screen, to finish and close the New template window, click the Finish button.

(continued)

#	Task
⑥	Click the OK button to add the Network Automation Server template. See Figure 10-87.

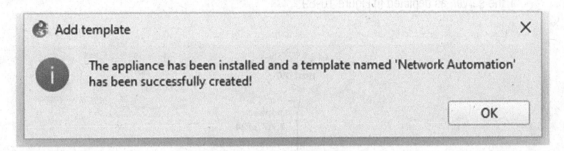

Figure 10-87. *GNS3 new template, Add Template window*

#	Task
⑦	Now go back to GNS3's main user interface and select the End Devices icon on the left. The End Devices icon is the one that looks like a computer screen. You will see your newly added appliance device, the Network Automation server. **Make sure your computer is connected to the Internet**. Select the Network Automation end device icon, then drag and drop it onto the Topology canvas. This action will initiate the Docker pull action and start downloading the Docker image from the Internet (DockerHub), as depicted in Figure 10-88.

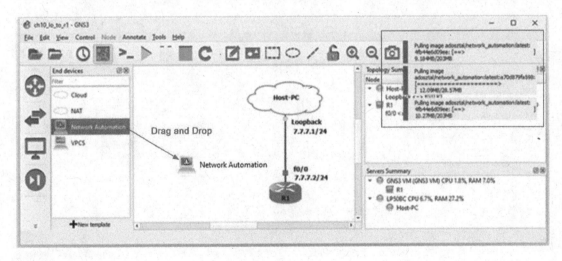

Figure 10-88. *GNS3, pulling the Network Automation appliance from the DockerHub*

(continued)

#	Task
⑧	Now connect eth0 of the NetworkAutomation-1 server to R1's f0/1 interface and power on the server, as depicted in Figure 10-89.

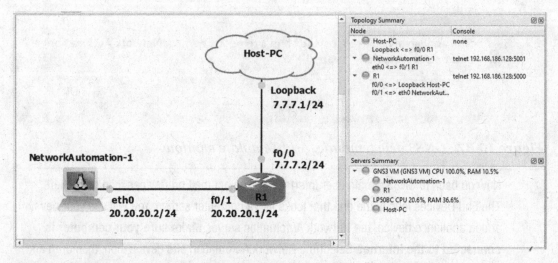

Figure 10-89. *GNS3, connecting NetworkAutomation-1 to R1*

(*continued*)

#	Task
⑨	As you can see in Figure 10-90, you can check the OS version of the appliance server by running the standard Linux command, `cat /etc/*release`. This server is a containerized (Docker) Ubuntu 20.04.2 LTS Server image for easy access. It only took a few minutes to gain access to a pre-built Ubuntu 20 Server at your fingertips.

```
root@NetworkAutomation-1:~# cat /etc/*release
```

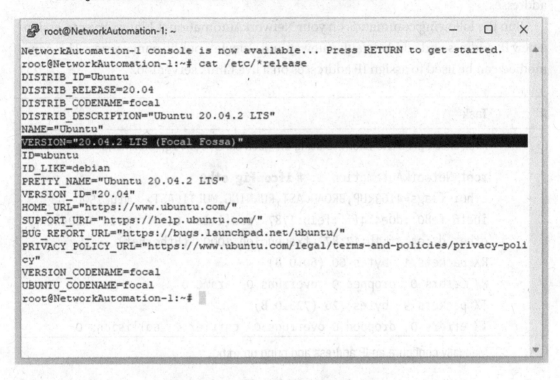

Figure 10-90. NetworkAutomation-1 Ubuntu Server version

Congratulations! You now have an additional server for practicing your Python scripts. You'll learn more about creating a Docker image in a Part 2 chapter. It's important to note that a Docker image functions as an ad hoc server, and when the Docker machine is powered off, everything resets to the default state, causing you to lose your previous work. To save your work, you may need to save it to a mapped drive or capture another Docker image while it's running. This topic is beyond the scope of the current discussion, but it's worth delving into Docker and Kubernetes concepts, as they are highly relevant in the field of systems and cloud services automation.

Manually Assigning an IP Address to GNS3 Linux Appliance Server

In the following steps, you'll practice assigning an IP address, default gateway, and DNS server to the Linux appliance server you've recently installed. It's essential to confirm proper communication by sending a ping to the default gateway. In the next section, you'll establish an Internet connection, eliminating the need to ping external Internet addresses.

Run the following commands on your NetworkAutomation-1 Linux server to assign a new IP address and add a default gateway and Google's public name server. This same method can be used to assign IP addresses on a live Linux server too.

#	Task

①	First, check the eth0 interface using the good old `ifconfig/` command.
	
	 `root@NetworkAutomation-1:~#` **`ifconfig eth0`**
	 `eth0: flags=4163<UP,BROADCAST,RUNNING,MULTICAST>  mtu 1500`
	 `    inet6 fe80::d0e4:4fff:fe1b:1787  prefixlen 64  scopeid 0x20<link>`
	 `    ether d2:e4:4f:1b:17:87  txqueuelen 1000  (Ethernet)`
	 `    RX packets 1  bytes 60 (60.0 B)`
	 `    RX errors 0  dropped 9  overruns 0  frame 0`
	 `    TX packets 9  bytes 726 (726.0 B)`
	 `    TX errors 0  dropped 0 overruns 0  carrier 0  collisions 0`

②	Manually configure an IP address and bring up eth0. `root@NetworkAutomation-1:~#` **`ifconfig eth0 20.20.20.2 netmask`** **`255.255.255.0 up`**
③	Configure R1's f0/1 interface as the default gateway for this appliance server. `root@NetworkAutomation-1:~#` `route add default gw 20.20.20.1`
④	Use the Linux echo command to add the DNS server information to the /etc/resolve.conf file. `root@NetworkAutomation-1:~#` **`echo "nameserver 8.8.8.8" > /etc/`** **`resolve.conf`**

(*continued*)

#	Task
⑤	Check the eth0 interface configuration before the ping test. root@NetworkAutomation-1:~# **ifconfig eth0** eth0: flags=4163<UP,BROADCAST,RUNNING,MULTICAST> mtu 1500 inet 20.20.20.2 netmask 255.255.255.0 broadcast 20.20.20.255 inet6 fe80::d0e4:4fff:fe1b:1787 prefixlen 64 scopeid 0x20<link> ether d2:e4:4f:1b:17:87 txqueuelen 1000 (Ethernet) RX packets 10 bytes 904 (904.0 B) RX errors 0 dropped 17 overruns 0 frame 0 TX packets 11 bytes 866 (866.0 B) TX errors 0 dropped 0 overruns 0 carrier 0 collisions 0
⑥	Test the reachability to R's f0/1 interface with the IP address of 20.20.20.1. root@NetworkAutomation-1:~# **ping 20.20.20.1 -c 3** PING 20.20.20.1 (20.20.20.1) 56(84) bytes of data. 64 bytes from 20.20.20.1: icmp_seq=1 ttl=255 time=11.7 ms 64 bytes from 20.20.20.1: icmp_seq=2 ttl=255 time=15.7 ms 64 bytes from 20.20.20.1: icmp_seq=3 ttl=255 time=16.2 ms --- 20.20.20.1 ping statistics --- 3 packets transmitted, 3 received, 0% packet loss, time 2023ms rtt min/avg/max/mdev = 11.740/14.556/16.200/2.000 ms

Tip

Another way to configure network interfaces for the appliance machine

You can also configure the network interface of an appliance machine by right-clicking the NetworkAutomation-1 icon and selecting the Edit Config option. From here, you can manually configure the settings or remove the # symbols to get a valid IP address from a DHCP server. Because you haven't set up a DHCP service on the 20.20.20.0/24 network, you can configure the IP address manually. Refer to Figure 10-91 for a visual representation.

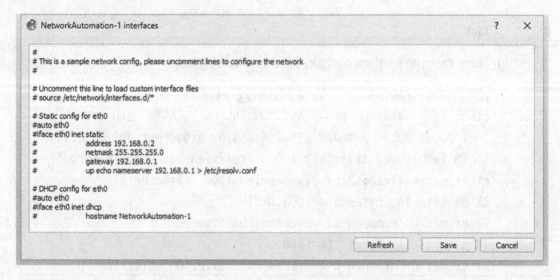

Figure 10-91. *NetworkAutomation-1, editing the config file*

You have successfully configured a GNS3 Appliance server's eth0 interface and connected it to your R1, the legacy Cisco IOS router. Using GNS3 appliances, you can add numerous firewalls, end devices, routers, and switches to your topology for study and testing purposes. If you have some spare time after reading this chapter, take a break from the book and explore the various devices at your disposal. While there's no substitute for working with physical equipment, this approach is far more user-friendly and cost-effective than the days when network engineers had to work hard with physical equipment in their labs to test a single concept.

Using the GNS3 Appliance Linux's Python to Manage R1

The goal of this lab is to provide you with hands-on experience in interacting with your network device, R1, using Python running on a Linux platform, which serves as the Python Network Automation environment. While you could configure R1 from the console, this lab aims to compose a Python script and let Python handle all the tasks for you. This experience provides a glimpse into the daily life of a network automation engineer. Pay close attention to every comma, period, and space, and avoid any typographical errors. Python coding isn't as glamorous as some Python enthusiasts may portray; every keystroke matters, and you must type out each character diligently. Remain discerning and don't buy the snake oil!

In this concluding GNS3 practice lab, you will use Python 3 running on the GNS3 Appliance Linux server (Ubuntu 20) to interact with R1 through an active Telnet session. You are honing your skills in communicating with your router through the assistance of Python, your trusty companion. Continue to work in the previous lab settings as you begin on this last practice run within GNS3. This preparation will serve as a final step before delving into more exciting labs in the second half of the book.

#	Task
①	First, check which Python versions are pre-installed on this server using the `which python` and `python version` commands. If you have downloaded the same Dockerized Linux server as this book, you will notice that Python 2.7 is no longer in use on Ubuntu 20, and Python 3.8.5 is installed on this system.

```
root@NetworkAutomation-1:~# which python # no more Python 2.7 on
Ubuntu 20 LTS
root@NetworkAutomation-1:~# python -version # no Python version 2
here
bash: python: command not found
root@NetworkAutomation-1:~# which python3 # /usr/bin/python3
contains Python program
/usr/bin/python3
root@NetworkAutomation-1:~# python3 -V # Python version is 3.8.5
Python 3.8.5
```

#	Task
②	Now, initiate the Python 3 interactive session by entering `python3` in the terminal. Once you see the three right-pointing arrows, it indicates that Python is ready to receive your next input. Let's put Python to work.

```
root@NetworkAutomation-1:~# python3
Python 3.8.5 (default, Jan 27 2021, 15:41:15)
[GCC 9.3.0] on linux
Type "help", "copyright", "credits" or "license" for more
information.
>>>
```

(continued)

#	Task

③	Now in the Python interpreter window of the GNS3 Appliance Linux server, type the following Python commands word by word. Do not worry too much about these commands' deep meanings; for now, try to get familiar with the process within the environment.
	
	Here, you add a loopback 5 to R1 via a Telnet session and then print out the session logs. After initiating the Telnet session, you send multiple tn.write commands for loopback 5 configurations. Then you must exit the session by sending the tn.write(b"exit\n") command to close the Telnet session. Then, you can print them out of your Telnet session.
	
	``python
	>>> import getpass # Import getpass module
	>>> import telnetlib # Import telnetlib module
	>>> tn = telnetlib.Telnet("20.20.20.1") # Create a telnet session
	to 20.20.20.1
	>>> tn.write("pynetauto".encode('ascii') + b"\n") # Send username
	'jdoe' to R1
	>>> tn.write("Lion2Roar!".encode('ascii') + b"\n") # Send password
	'Lion2Roar!' to R1
	>>> tn.write(b"configure terminal\n") # Enter config mode
	>>> tn.write(b"interface loopback 5\n")
	>>> tn.write(b"ip address 5.5.5.5 255.255.255.255\n")
	>>> tn.write(b"end\n")
	>>> tn.write(b"exit\n")
	>>> print(tn.read_all().decode('ascii')) # Print all session logs
	in tn
	``
	
	<div align="right">(*continued*)</div>

#	Task

| • | On a successful interactive session, the output will look similar to Figure 10-92. |

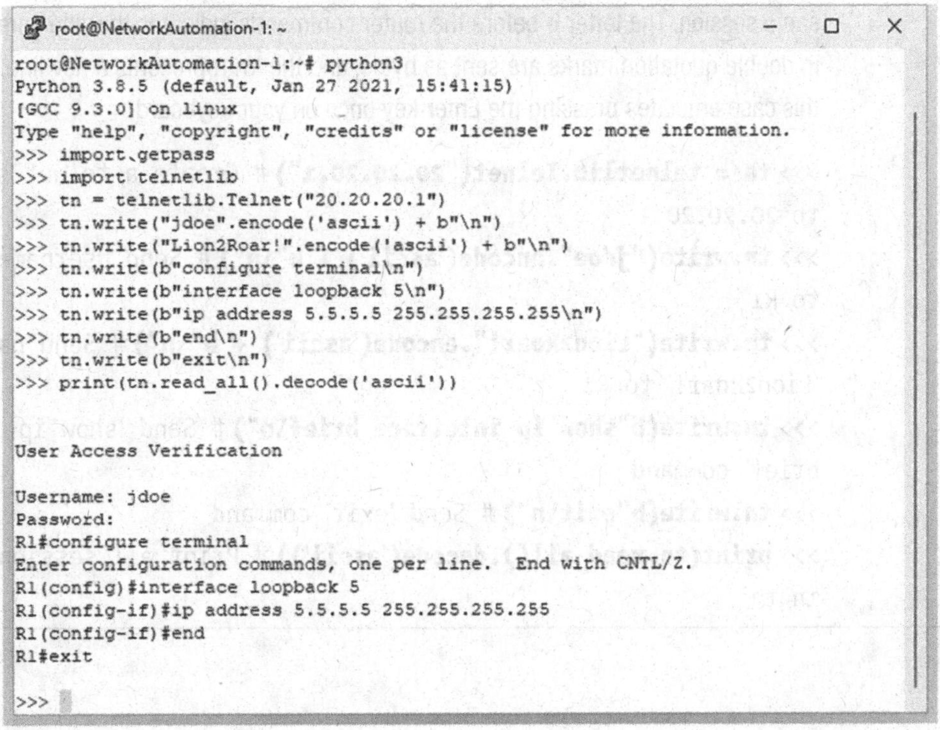

```
root@NetworkAutomation-1: ~                                          –    □    ×
root@NetworkAutomation-1:~# python3
Python 3.8.5 (default, Jan 27 2021, 15:41:15)
[GCC 9.3.0] on linux
Type "help", "copyright", "credits" or "license" for more information.
>>> import getpass
>>> import telnetlib
>>> tn = telnetlib.Telnet("20.20.20.1")
>>> tn.write("jdoe".encode('ascii') + b"\n")
>>> tn.write("Lion2Roar!".encode('ascii') + b"\n")
>>> tn.write(b"configure terminal\n")
>>> tn.write(b"interface loopback 5\n")
>>> tn.write(b"ip address 5.5.5.5 255.255.255.255\n")
>>> tn.write(b"end\n")
>>> tn.write(b"exit\n")
>>> print(tn.read_all().decode('ascii'))


User Access Verification

Username: jdoe
Password:
R1#configure terminal
Enter configuration commands, one per line.  End with CNTL/Z.
R1(config)#interface loopback 5
R1(config-if)#ip address 5.5.5.5 255.255.255.255
R1(config-if)#end
R1#exit

>>>
```

Figure 10-92. *NetworkAutomation-1, interacting with R1 using Python telnetlib 1*

(continued)

#	Task
④	Now continue with the show ip interface brief command and print out the logs. Notice that you do not have to import the modules again, as you have remained in the same session. The letter b before the router commands indicates that the commands in double quotation marks are sent as bytes, and the \n represents a newline, which in this case emulates pressing the Enter key once on your keyboard.

```
>>> tn = telnetlib.Telnet("20.20.20.1") # Create a telnet session
to 20.20.20.1
>>> tn.write("jdoe".encode('ascii') + b"\n") # Send username 'jdoe'
to R1
>>> tn.write("Lion2Roar!".encode('ascii') + b"\n") # Send password
'Lion2Roar!' to R1
>>> tn.write(b"show ip interface brief\n") # Send 'show ip int
brief' command
>>> tn.write(b"exit\n") # Send 'exit' command
>>> print(tn.read_all().decode('ascii')) # Print all session logs
in tn
```

(continued)

#	Task
	Upon completing the lab task, you will see the result of the show ip interface brief command output on your screen, as shown in Figure 10-93.

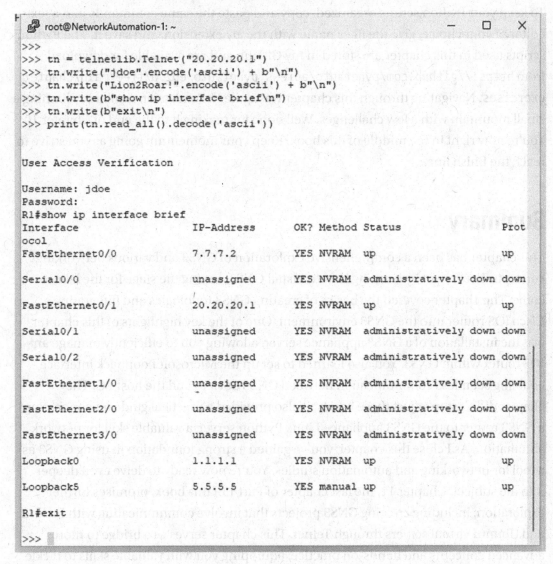

```
root@NetworkAutomation-1: ~                                    —    □    ×

>>>
>>> tn = telnetlib.Telnet("20.20.20.1")
>>> tn.write("jdoe".encode('ascii') + b"\n")
>>> tn.write("Lion2Roar!".encode('ascii') + b"\n")
>>> tn.write(b"show ip interface brief\n")
>>> tn.write(b"exit\n")
>>> print(tn.read_all().decode('ascii'))


User Access Verification

Username: jdoe
Password:
R1#show ip interface brief
Interface                 IP-Address      OK? Method Status                     Prot
ocol
FastEthernet0/0           7.7.7.2         YES NVRAM  up                             up

Serial0/0                 unassigned      YES NVRAM  administratively down down

FastEthernet0/1           20.20.20.1      YES NVRAM  up                             up

Serial0/1                 unassigned      YES NVRAM  administratively down down

Serial0/2                 unassigned      YES NVRAM  administratively down down

FastEthernet1/0           unassigned      YES NVRAM  administratively down down

FastEthernet2/0           unassigned      YES NVRAM  administratively down down

FastEthernet3/0           unassigned      YES NVRAM  administratively down down

Loopback0                 1.1.1.1         YES NVRAM  up                             up

Loopback5                 5.5.5.5         YES manual up                             up

R1#exit

>>>
```

Figure 10-93. *NetworkAutomation-1, interacting with R1 using Python telnetlib 2*

You have completed an interactive Telnet session with R1 using Python 3 running on the GNS3 NetworkAutomation appliance server (Ubuntu). This practice allows you to develop, validate, and verify Python code for interacting with network devices. When you create code for such purposes, you can test individual parts of your Python code. To keep your Python scripts organized, copy and paste the same commands into a text editor of your choice, give the file a name with the .py extension, and save it. The Python scripts used in this chapter are stored in my GitHub and are available for download from `https://github.com/pynetauto/apress_pynetauto_ed2.0/tree/main/chapter_exercises`. Navigating through this chapter was quite the endeavor, similar to climbing a small mountain with a few challenges. Well done for making it to the end of Chapter 10. You're now right in the middle of this book. Keep your momentum going as you strive to reach the finish line.

Summary

This chapter has been a comprehensive exploration of GNS3 and various networking concepts. You began by learning how to install GNS3, setting the stage for the labs to come. The chapter covered the basics of creating GNS3 topologies and integrating a Cisco IOS router into the GNS3 environment. One of the key highlights of this chapter was the installation of a GNS3 appliance server, allowing you to efficiently manage an IOS router within GNS3. You also learned to set up the Microsoft Loopback interface, enabling seamless communication between GNS3 devices and the host PC. The chapter didn't stop at just these basics; it also provided a practical guide on connecting a GNS3 router to the GNS3 appliance Linux Python server, a valuable skill for network automation. As I close this chapter, you've gained a strong foundation in using GNS3 as a tool for networking and automation studies. You're now ready to delve even deeper into the subject. Chapter 11, the last chapter of Part 1 of this book, promises further exploration, including creating GNS3 projects that involve communicating with Fedora and Ubuntu virtual servers through Telnet. This chapter serves as a bridge to more advanced concepts and hands-on practice, equipping you with valuable skills to tackle the challenges that lie ahead.

CHAPTER 11

Cisco IOS, Linux, TFTP, and Telnet Labs

This chapter serves as the epilogue to Part 1, setting the stage for what follows. This chapter dives into the intricacies of Cisco IOS router administration, leveraging the power of Telnet and Linux VMs for an in-depth exploration. You commence your journey by creating a new GNS3 project that integrates with Linux VMs, Cisco IOS Tcl scripting, Python telnetlib scripts, and TFTP capabilities, setting the stage for efficient Cisco device control through a blend of Tcl and Python scripts. This is an attempt to push you away from the command lines and push you into writing code to replace your tasks. Along the way, I revisit the Python PEP 8 style guide, emphasizing the significance of adhering to coding standards, as exemplified by a simple Python list. This exploration culminates in mastering the art of script-based file transfers to Cisco IOS routers, making the often-complex task of managing IOS configurations and uploading images a streamlined process. As you navigate this landscape, you'll harness the telnetlib library for Python, using it to manage device control and file transfers. Additionally, you venture into the GNS3 project replication by copying (cloning) a GNS3 project, ensuring that your configurations and progress remain intact for the next chapter. In summary, this chapter provides a comprehensive foundation for controlling a single Cisco device using Python scripts, encompassing tasks such as saving running configurations and uploading IOS images. Note that the remaining practical Python Network Automation Labs are exclusively reserved for Part 2 of this book.

© Brendan Choi 2024
B. Choi, *Introduction to Python Network Automation Volume I - Laying the Groundwork*,
https://doi.org/10.1007/979-8-8688-0146-4_11

Cisco IOS, Linux VM, TFTP Server, and Telnet Practice Labs

In the opening lab, you will connect your Linux virtual machines, which you built in earlier chapters, to GNS3 devices. In most production environments, it is the norm to run Python on Linux platforms to leverage the numerous advantages offered by Linux in an enterprise setting. Therefore, merely understanding how to write Python code is insufficient for creating a useful application that can automate and streamline a network engineer's tasks. You need to have a deeper understanding of the entire IT ecosystem and understand how different systems and technologies coexist harmoniously within it. You must be willing to step outside your comfort zone and invest personal effort in comprehending and appreciating other technologies within the IT ecosystem.

In this example involving Cisco IOS and Linux VMs, you will configure a new topology in preparation for the next chapter. Figure 11-1 illustrates the topology you are going to set up. Note that the Fedora 38 and Ubuntu 22 LTS Linux servers are already connected to VMnet8 on VMware Workstation, as depicted in the topology. In GNS3, I use representational icons to indicate that they belong to the 192.168.127.0/24 subnet. If you are using a different IP subnet for VMnet8, your IP addresses will differ, and you will have to factor in this difference while running your labs.

Chapter 11 Network Topology Explained

The topology in Figure 11-1 relies on NAT-1, running on the host PC, to connect to VMnet8 of VMware Workstation. It also serves as a DHCP server (192.168.127.254) and gateway (192.168.127.2) to provide Internet connectivity via my home network router (192.168.0.1). Note that your home network's IP address may differ, so you will need to account for this during your lab setup. In Chapter 10, you learned how to access GNS3 devices from your Windows 11 hosting PC, which is a valuable feature of GNS3. You will continue to utilize this feature to facilitate the management of your labs. The host PC, with an IP address of 7.7.7.1, serves as the cloud with the Microsoft loopback interface connecting to R1's F0/1 (7.7.7.2) on the 7.7.7.0/24 network. Are you prepared to apply the GNS3 and other skills you've gained in the first half of this book effectively? It's time to dive in!

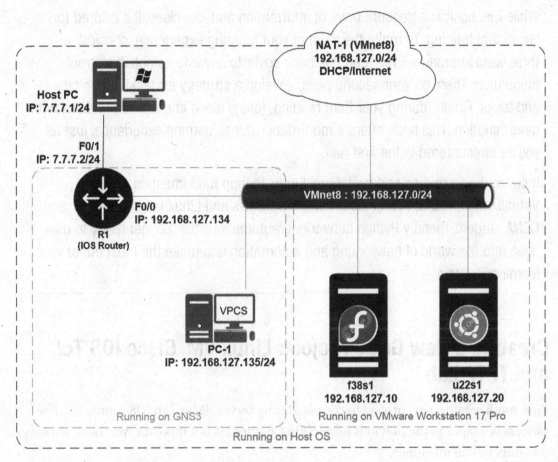

Figure 11-1. *lxvm2ios project, lab topology*

Tip

Optimize your learning with hands-on practice

Prepare for an exciting journey into the world of networking and automation! You'll find all the source code you need on my GitHub at this URL: GitHub Source Code for Chapter 11. `https://github.com/pynetauto/apress_pynetauto_ed2.0/` `tree/main/source_codes/Part1/ch11`

While this book is a treasure trove of information and exercises, it's tailored for vocational training. To make the most of your learning experience, consider a three-step approach. First, read this book cover to cover to establish a strong foundation. Then, on your second pass, develop a strategy for tackling the labs and tasks. Finally, during your third reading, follow along and tackle the tasks with determination. This book offers a multi-dimensional learning experience, just as you've encountered in the first half.

It covers basic routing and switching, Linux, Python fundamentals, VMware Virtualization, GNS3, virtual lab creation, Windows and Linux lab integration, and CCNA student-friendly Python networking automation labs. So, get ready to dive deep into the world of networking and automation and make the most out of your learning journey!

Creating a New GNS3 Project: Linux VM, Cisco IOS Tcl, and TFTP Lab

First you'll create a new project to connect Linux server VMs to an IOS router, R1. The process is similar to the previous projects in Chapter 10, but this time, you need to power on Linux virtual machines.

#	Task
①	To begin the lab, open a new project window by selecting File ➤ New Blank Project from the GNS3 main menu.
②	Give your new project a new name. The new project name used for this lab is lxvm2ios (Linux VM to IOS). You do not have to conform to this naming convention. Feel free to give your project a unique and meaningful name. Refer to Figure 11-2 for reference.

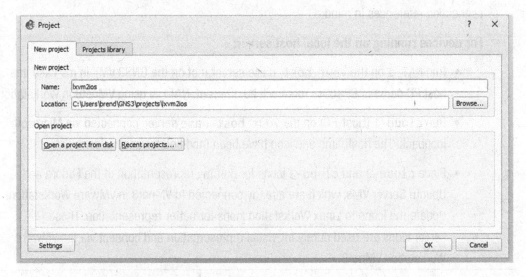

Figure 11-2. *GNS3, creating a new GNS3 project, lxvm2ios*

(continued)

#	Task

③ Configure the GNS3 topology as depicted in Figure 11-3. While setting up the new topology, use GNS3's Topology and Servers summary window for additional information. It provides an overview of how each device is interconnected. Once all the devices are connected, start R1 only for now. You will start PC-1 (VPC) in a later step.

When creating and configuring the topology on the GNS3 topology canvas, keep the following connection references in mind.

For devices running on the local host server:

- Run NAT-1 on the your_host_name server (not on the GNS3 VM). In my case, the host PC name is LP50BC. Yours will be different. NAT1 is using VMnet8 in Workstation.

- Run cloud-1 (Host-PC) on the your_host_name server, connected via Microsoft loopback. The hostname and icon have been modified for aesthetics.

- Place cloud-2 and cloud-3 icons for dummy representation of the Fedora and Ubuntu Server VMs, which are already connected to VMnet8 in VMware Workstation. Update the icons to Linux Workstation icons for better representation. These server icons are used purely for visual representation and connect via the VMware Workstation VMnet8.

(continued)

#	Task

For devices running on the GNS3 VM server:

- Run Ethernetswitch-1 (Switch1) on the GNS3 VM server, which will primarily serve as a dummy switch to facilitate connections between multiple devices.

- R1 is a Cisco 3745 IOS router. Run this device on the GNS3 VM server too.

- Run PC-1 (VPCS) on the GNS3 VM server, providing a convenient means to test communication between the devices. It's like configuring dummy loopback interfaces on the router.

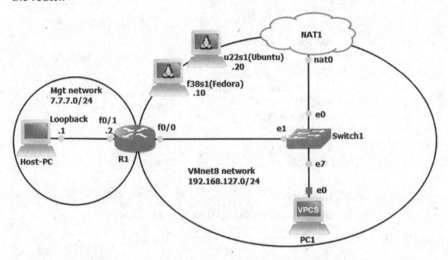

Figure 11-3. *lxvm2ios project, GNS3 topology connection*

④ When you drag and drop devices such as NAT1, PC1 (VPCS), Switch1, Host-PC (cloud-1), f38s1 (cloud-2), and u22s1 (cloud-3) onto the canvas, GNS3 will prompt you to select the appropriate server, as illustrated in Figure 11-4. In GNS3 networking labs, it's crucial to choose the right servers for running your devices, so exercise special care. Also, note that your PC's name is different, so your host server name will differ from what's shown in Figure 11-4.

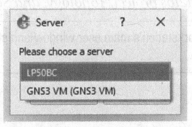

Figure 11-4. *lxvm2ios project, selecting the correct GNS3 server*

(continued)

#	Task
⑤	Use the Topology and Servers Summary windows shown in Figure 11-5 as a reference point while configuring and running your GNS3 topology.

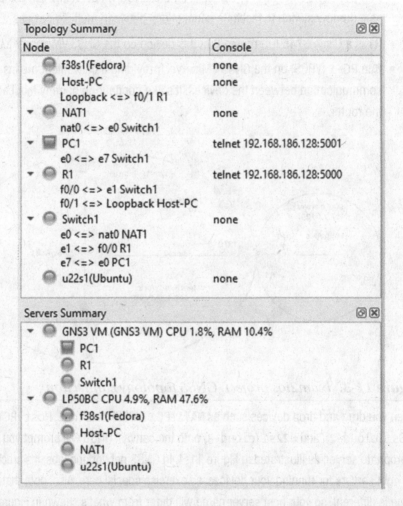

Figure 11-5. lxvm2ios project, Topology, and Servers Summary windows

#	Task
⑥	Next, go to VMware Workstation's main user window and start your Fedora and Ubuntu Server VMs.

(*continued*)

#	Task

⑦   On the VMware Workstation main console, log in to your u22s1 Ubuntu Server's Desktop, as shown in Figure 11-6. **You have already configured and know the IP address of this server from the Linux chapters, but imagine that you've forgotten the previously set IP address.** How good is your memory? Yes, humans tend to forget things, and it is sometimes a blessing that we don't have to remember everything.

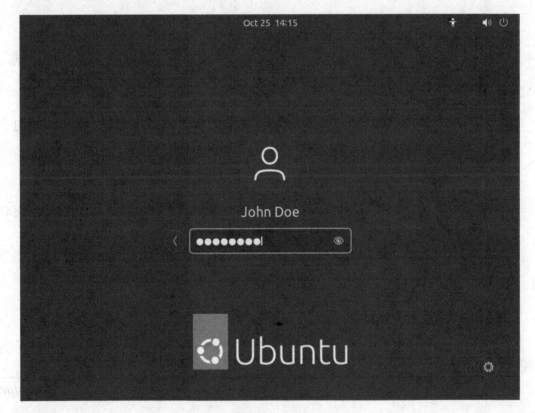

Figure 11-6. *u22s1 server desktop login*

(*continued*)

#	Task

	Log in to the Ubuntu Server's Desktop and use the terminal to determine the IP address of the server. Use the `ip link` command to identify network adapters, as well as the `ifconfig`, `ifconfig ens33`, `ifconfig enp2s1`, or `ip address show` commands to retrieve adapter details, including the IP address. Note that your IP address scheme may vary depending on your virtual machine's subnet.
	
	`jdoe@u22s1:~$` **`ip link`** `# Use this command to check installed network adapter names`
	`1: lo: <LOOPBACK,UP,LOWER_UP> mtu 65536 qdisc noqueue state UNKNOWN mode DEFAULT group default qlen 1000`
	`    link/loopback 00:00:00:00:00:00 brd 00:00:00:00:00:00`
	`2: ens33: <BROADCAST,MULTICAST,UP,LOWER_UP> mtu 1500 qdisc fq_codel state UP mode DEFAULT group default qlen 1000`
	`    link/ether 00:0c:29:cf:71:3d brd ff:ff:ff:ff:ff:ff`
	`    altname enp2s1`
	`jdoe@u22s1:~$` **`ifconfig ens33`** `# include adapter name to print targeted information`
	`ens33: flags=4163<UP,BROADCAST,RUNNING,MULTICAST>  mtu 1500`
	`    inet 192.168.127.20  netmask 255.255.255.0  broadcast`
	`    192.168.127.255`
	`[…omitted for brevity]`
	
	We've just verified that the IP address 192.168.127.20 was previously assigned to the ens33 interface.

(*continued*)

#	Task
⑧	This time, let's also assume that you've forgotten the IP address of your Fedora server. To retrieve the IP address, proceed to the workstation's main console and log in to the Fedora server f38s1 using your user credentials. Execute the ip link command to inspect the installed network adapters. Then, use ip address show, ipconfig, ip add show ens160, ipconfig ens160, or ipconfig enp3s0 to reveal the network interface details, including the assigned IP address. Keep in mind that if you are using a different subnet for VMnet8, you may receive a different IP address.

```
[jdoe@f38s1 ~]$ ip link
1: lo: <LOOPBACK,UP,LOWER_UP> mtu 65536 qdisc noqueue state UNKNOWN
mode DEFAULT group default qlen 1000
    link/loopback 00:00:00:00:00:00 brd 00:00:00:00:00:00
2: ens160: <BROADCAST,MULTICAST,UP,LOWER_UP> mtu 1500 qdisc fq_codel
state UP mode DEFAULT group default qlen 1000
    link/ether 00:0c:29:05:bc:8c brd ff:ff:ff:ff:ff:ff
    altname enp3s0
[jdoe@f38s1 ~]$ ip add show ens160
2: ens160: <BROADCAST,MULTICAST,UP,LOWER_UP> mtu 1500 qdisc fq_codel
state UP group default qlen 1000
    link/ether 00:0c:29:05:bc:8c brd ff:ff:ff:ff:ff:ff
    altname enp3s0
    inet 192.168.127.10/24 brd 192.168.127.255 scope global
    noprefixroute ens160
[…omitted for brevity]
```

In my example, the ens160 interface was previously assigned the IP address 192.168.127.10. Now that you have confirmed the IP addresses of both servers, you can easily SSH into them from an SSH client and manage the servers.

(continued)

#	Task
⑨	Now, in GNS3, ensure that R1 is powered on correctly. Open the console of R1 by double-clicking the R1 icon, and then configure the router's initial configurations. Configure the hostname, IP domain lookup, enable password, local admin account with privilege 15, and remote access interfaces with telnet access. Then continue to configure the FastEthernet 0/0 interface to obtain an IP address from VMnet8's DHCP server. Additionally, set up interface FastEthernet 0/1 with the IP address 7.7.7.2 and subnet mask 255.255.255.0. This interface connects to the Microsoft loopback of the Windows host PC and serves as the management plane for your lab.

```
R1#conf t
R1(config)#hostname R1
R1(config)#ip domain lookup
R1(config)#enable password Druken1Tiger!
R1(config)#username jdoe privilege 15 password Lion2Roar!
R1(config)#line vty 0 15
R1(config-line)#login local
R1(config-line)#transport input all # allows both Telnet and SSH
connections
R1(config-line)#no exec-timeout
R1(config-line)#int f0/0
R1(config-if)#ip address dhcp
R1(config-if)#no shut
*Mar  1 00:40:28.559: %LINK-3-UPDOWN: Interface FastEthernet0/0,
changed state to up
*Mar  1 00:40:29.559: %LINEPROTO-5-UPDOWN: Line protocol on Interface
FastEthernet0/0, changed state to up
*Mar  1 00:40:36.699: %DHCP-6-ADDRESS_ASSIGN: Interface
FastEthernet0/0 assigned DHCP address 192.168.127.134, mask
255.255.255.0, hostname R1
R1(config-if)#do show ip int bri
```

(*continued*)

#	Task

```
Interface          IP-Address       OK? Method Status                 Protocol
FastEthernet0/0    192.168.127.134  YES DHCP   up                     up
Serial0/0          unassigned       YES unset  administratively down  down
FastEthernet0/1    unassigned       YES unset  administratively down  down
[...omitted for brevity]
R1(config-if)# int f0/1
R1(config-if)#ip add 7.7.7.2 255.255.255.0
R1(config-if)#no shut
R1(config-if)#
*Mar  1 00:41:59.803: %LINK-3-UPDOWN: Interface FastEthernet0/1, changed
state to up
*Mar  1 00:42:00.803: %LINEPROTO-5-UPDOWN: Line protocol on Interface
FastEthernet0/1, changed state to up
R1(config-if)#end
R1# wri
```

192.168.127.134/24 was assigned to R1's f0/0 by VMnet8 DHCP server and we
assigned a static IP address of 7.7.7.2/24 to R1's f0/1 interface.

(*continued*)

#	Task
⑩	To check network reachability for all IP addresses, initiate ICMP (ping) messages from R1 to the following destinations: 7.7.7.1 (Host-PC's MS Loopback interface), 192.168.127.2 (NAT-1 gateway), 192.168.127.10 (f38s1), 192.168.127.20 (u22s1), and 8.8.8.8 (Google's famous public DNS IP). If you receive ICMP responses from all these destinations, you're on the right track.

While you can manually ping each IP address one at a time, imagine having hundreds of IPs to test. **To make this lab more engaging and to remind you how traditional network engineers used to tackle this problem in the past, use Tcl on R1 to assess network connectivity. This will give you a chance to practice the older methods of network testing before appreciating the advantages of modern methods, such as Python scripting**.

There are three ways to ping an IP address using Tcl. You can use the interactive Tcl shell for pinging IP addresses, but in this case, you'll create a Tcl shell script and save it to your flash: storage to run it as an application. Alternatively, you could place the same script on a TFTP server and execute it from the router. Can you recall the 128MB PCMCIA disk 0 assignment on the Cisco 3745 router template's Memories and Disks? Before proceeding to Tcl scripting, you need to format the 128MB disk 0 running on R1. Follow these steps to format the flash drive:

10-1. Check the health of R1's flash storage, and you'll receive a warning that disk 0 must be formatted correctly for the router to utilize this storage.

R1#**show flash:**

No files on device

134051840 bytes available (0 bytes used)

*Mar 1 01:15:35.887: %PCMCIAFS-5-DIBERR: PCMCIA disk 0 is formatted from a different router or PC. A format in this router is required before an image can be booted from this device

(*continued*)

#	Task

10-2. Run the show file system command to check the details of your 128MB flash card as highlighted.

R1#**show file system**

File Systems:

Size(b)	Free(b)	Type	Flags	Prefixes
-	-	opaque	rw	archive:
-	-	opaque	rw	system:
155640	155186	nvram	rw	nvram:
-	-	opaque	rw	null:
-	-	network	rw	tftp:
* 134051840	134051840	disk	rw	flash:
-	-	flash	rw	slot0:
-	-	opaque	wo	syslog:

[...omitted for brevity]

10-3. Run format flash: to format the disk 0.

R1#**format flash:**

Format operation may take a while. Continue? [confirm] # press
<Enter>
Format operation will destroy all data in "flash:". Continue?
[confirm] # press <Enter>
Format: Drive communication & 1st Sector Write OK...
[...omitted for brevity]

10-4. Check the flash again. You should now notice that the warning message is gone and 128MB of storage is ready for use.

R1#**show flash:**

No files on device
133918720 bytes available (0 bytes used)

(continued)

#	Task

⑪ Now, on to more interesting tasks. Let's write a Tcl script named ch11_ping_ips.tcl.
You can choose a different name for this file, but it must have the .tcl file extension for it to
function. Follow these steps to create your Tcl script:

11-1. In privileged mode on R1, run the tclsh command.

R1#**tclsh**

11-2. When you're in the Tcl shell, you can use the Tcl script in ch11_ping_ips.tcl.txt
in the ch11 directory on my GitHub. Alternatively, you can manually type in each line if you
enjoy typing and are a fast typist.

```
R1(tcl)#puts [open "flash:ch11_ping_ips.tcl" w+] {
+>(tcl)## Define the list of IP addresses to ping
+>(tcl)#set ip_addresses {
+>(tcl)#    7.7.7.1
+>(tcl)#    192.168.127.2
+>(tcl)#    192.168.127.10
+>(tcl)#    192.168.127.20
+>(tcl)#    8.8.8.8
+>(tcl)#}
+>(tcl)#
+>(tcl)## Loop through the IP addresses and ping each one
+>(tcl)#foreach ip $ip_addresses {
+>(tcl)#    set result [exec "ping $ip repeat 4"]
+>(tcl)#    puts "Pinging $ip..."
+>(tcl)#    puts "$result"
+>(tcl)#    puts "========== pynetauto_ed2 =========="
+>(tcl)#}
+>(tcl)#}
```

11-3. Save and close the script with the tclquit command.

R1(tcl)#**tclquit**

(continued)

#	Task

11-4. As an extra precaution, verify the file's existence by running show flash: and more ch11_ping_ips.tcl. This should provide you with output similar to the following:

```
R1#show flash:
-#- --length-- -----date/time------ path
1           347 Mar 1 2002 01:39:12 +00:00 ch11_ping_ips.tcl

133914624 bytes available (4096 bytes used)
R1#more ch11_ping_ips.tcl
# Define the list of IP addresses to ping
set ip_addresses {
    7.7.7.1
    192.168.127.2
    192.168.127.10
    192.168.127.20
    8.8.8.8
}

# Loop through the IP addresses and ping each one
foreach ip $ip_addresses {
    set result [exec "ping $ip repeat 4"]
    puts "Pinging $ip..."
    puts "$result"
    puts "=========== pynetauto_ed2 =========="
}
```

(continued)

#	Task

⑫   You can now enjoy the results of your hard work by executing the Tcl script from R1. As you learned in the previous chapter, the initial packet drop in ICMP communication to unknown destinations is a common occurrence. In the first run of your test, you will observe the first packet being dropped, which is an expected and normal ARP behavior. If you run the script a second time using `tclsh flash:ch11_ping_ips.tcl`, you should expect to get perfect responses, as depicted in Figure 11-7.

R1#**tclsh flash:ch11_ping_ips.tcl**

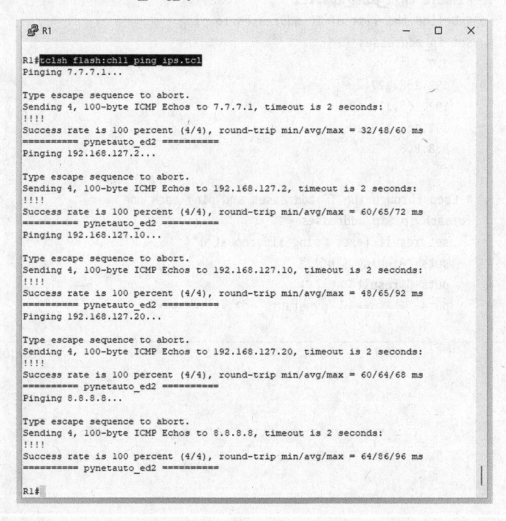

```
R1#tclsh flash:ch11_ping_ips.tcl
Pinging 7.7.7.1...

Type escape sequence to abort.
Sending 4, 100-byte ICMP Echos to 7.7.7.1, timeout is 2 seconds:
!!!!
Success rate is 100 percent (4/4), round-trip min/avg/max = 32/48/60 ms
========== pynetauto_ed2 ==========
Pinging 192.168.127.2...

Type escape sequence to abort.
Sending 4, 100-byte ICMP Echos to 192.168.127.2, timeout is 2 seconds:
!!!!
Success rate is 100 percent (4/4), round-trip min/avg/max = 60/65/72 ms
========== pynetauto_ed2 ==========
Pinging 192.168.127.10...

Type escape sequence to abort.
Sending 4, 100-byte ICMP Echos to 192.168.127.10, timeout is 2 seconds:
!!!!
Success rate is 100 percent (4/4), round-trip min/avg/max = 48/65/92 ms
========== pynetauto_ed2 ==========
Pinging 192.168.127.20...

Type escape sequence to abort.
Sending 4, 100-byte ICMP Echos to 192.168.127.20, timeout is 2 seconds:
!!!!
Success rate is 100 percent (4/4), round-trip min/avg/max = 60/64/68 ms
========== pynetauto_ed2 ==========
Pinging 8.8.8.8...

Type escape sequence to abort.
Sending 4, 100-byte ICMP Echos to 8.8.8.8, timeout is 2 seconds:
!!!!
Success rate is 100 percent (4/4), round-trip min/avg/max = 64/86/96 ms
========== pynetauto_ed2 ==========

R1#
```

Figure 11-7. *tcl ping application on flash output*

(continued)

#	Task

⑬   In Chapter 8, you installed and configured a TFTP server on f38s1 (Fedora) for testing in your
lab. You made this server into a Swiss Army Knife server. Let's SSH into the server and check
the running status of the TFTP services on f38s1:

13-1. Check the TFTP server's health by running the sudo systemctl status tftp-
server command. This command requires sudo privilege, so provide the password on the
first command.

[jdoe@f38s1 ~]$ **sudo systemctl status tftp-server**
[sudo] password for jdoe: **************

```
o tftp-server.service - Tftp Server
     Loaded: loaded (/etc/systemd/system/tftp-server.service; enabled; preset: disabled)
    Drop-In: /usr/lib/systemd/system/service.d
             └─10-timeout-abort.conf
     Active: inactive (dead) since Wed 2023-10-25 13:58:56 AEDT; 3h 2min ago
   Duration: 15min 1.349s
TriggeredBy: ● tftp-server.socket
       Docs: man:in.tftpd
    Process: 709 ExecStart=/usr/sbin/in.tftpd -c -p -s /var/lib/tftpboot (code=exited, status=0/SUCCESS)
   Main PID: 709 (code=exited, status=0/SUCCESS)
        CPU: 3ms

Oct 25 13:43:54 f38s1.pynetauto.com systemd[1]: Started tftp-server.service - Tftp Server.
Oct 25 13:58:56 f38s1.pynetauto.com systemd[1]: tftp-server.service: Deactivated successfully.
```

Figure 11-8. *f38s1, TFTP server is inactive (dead), not running*

13-2. Unfortunately, the service is in inactive (dead), status as shown in Figure 11-8. This
means your TFTP server is not working at this point. You can quickly troubleshoot this by
starting the service.

[jdoe@f38s1 ~]$ **sudo systemctl start tftp-server**
[jdoe@f38s1 ~]$ **sudo systemctl status tftp-server**

```
● tftp-server.service - Tftp Server
     Loaded: loaded (/etc/systemd/system/tftp-server.service; enabled; preset: disabled)
    Drop-In: /usr/lib/systemd/system/service.d
             └─10-timeout-abort.conf
     Active: active (running) since Wed 2023-10-25 17:03:05 AEDT; 2s ago
TriggeredBy: ● tftp-server.socket
       Docs: man:in.tftpd
   Main PID: 1501 (in.tftpd)
      Tasks: 1 (limit: 4632)
     Memory: 172.0K
        CPU: 5ms
     CGroup: /system.slice/tftp-server.service
             └─1501 /usr/sbin/in.tftpd -c -p -s /var/lib/tftpboot

Oct 25 17:03:05 f38s1.pynetauto.com systemd[1]: Started tftp-server.service - Tftp Server.
```

Figure 11-9. *f38s1, TFTP started and active (running)*

(continued)

#	Task
	After starting the server, the TFTP services change to active (running) status, as shown in Figure 11-9. If your TFTP service is not functioning correctly, troubleshoot the issue before proceeding to the next step. You can refer to the TFTP installation guide in Chapter 8 for troubleshooting help.
⑭	Now that the server is running, recall that the file-sharing path on the TFTP server was /var/lib/tftpboot/. Create a .tcl script with the same lines of code found in Step ⑪ and in the ch11_ping_ips.tcl file.

```
[jdoe@f38s1 ~]$ ls /var/lib/tftpboot/
f38s1_file06.txt u22s1_file09.txt
[jdoe@f38s1 ~]$ cd /var/lib/tftpboot/
[jdoe@f38s1 tftpboot]$ cat > ch11_ping_ips.tcl # use cat tool to
create your tcl script
# Define the list of IP addresses to ping
set ip_addresses {
    7.7.7.1
    192.168.127.2
    192.168.127.10
    192.168.127.20
    8.8.8.8
}

# Loop through the IP addresses and ping each one
foreach ip $ip_addresses {
    set result [exec "ping $ip repeat 4"]
    puts "Pinging $ip..."
    puts "$result"
    puts "========== pynetauto_ed2 =========="
} # press Ctrl+D to save the content and exit.

[jdoe@f38s1 tftpboot]$ ll /var/lib/tftpboot/
total 12
-rw-r--r--. 1 jdoe    jdoe     357 Oct 25 17:27 ch11_ping_ips.tcl
-rw-r--r--. 1 jdoe    jdoe      37 Sep 30 10:06 f38s1_file06.txt
-rw-r--r--. 1 nobody  nobody    36 Sep 30 10:28 u22s1_file09.txt
```

(continued)

#	Task
⑮	If everything is running smoothly, executing the following tclsh command to read the file contents from the TFTP server and run it on R1 will produce output similar to what's shown in Figure 11-10.

R1#**tclsh tftp://192.168.127.10/**ch11_ping_ips.tcl

Figure 11-10. tcl ping application on TFTP server output

(*continued*)

#	Task
	When router R1 runs the `tclsh tftp://192.168.127.10/ch11_ping_ips.tcl` command, it does not download the entire Tcl script file to its memory. Instead, it reads the contents of the Tcl script directly from the remote TFTP server (192.168.127.10) and executes it in memory without storing the script file locally on R1. This is a common way to run Tcl scripts from a remote source without consuming additional storage on the router. The router temporarily fetches and interprets the script in memory during execution.
⑯	Now start PC-1 (VPCS) on GNS3, open the PC-1 console, and follow the steps detailed here to assign an IP address to the PC-1 endpoint. Run the `ip dhcp` command to receive an IP address from the VMnet8 DHCP server, then use the `show ip` command to check the IP configuration on PC-1. You should see output similar to that shown in Figure 11-11.

PC1> **ip dhcp**
PC1> **show ip**

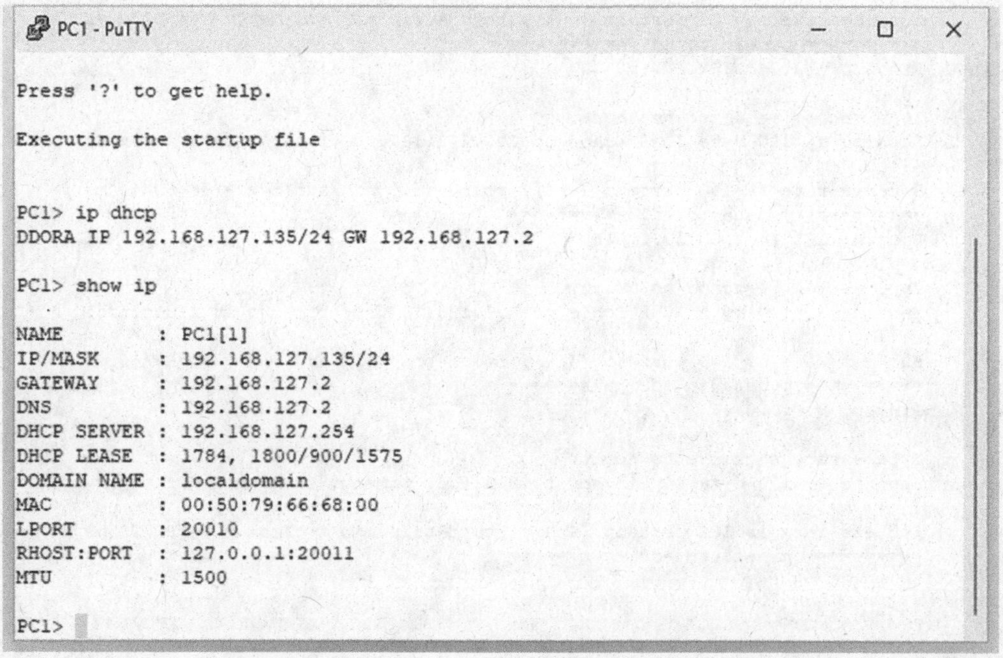

```
PC1 - PuTTY                                          —    □    ×

Press '?' to get help.

Executing the startup file


PC1> ip dhcp
DDORA IP 192.168.127.135/24 GW 192.168.127.2

PC1> show ip

NAME        : PC1[1]
IP/MASK     : 192.168.127.135/24
GATEWAY     : 192.168.127.2
DNS         : 192.168.127.2
DHCP SERVER : 192.168.127.254
DHCP LEASE  : 1784, 1800/900/1575
DOMAIN NAME : localdomain
MAC         : 00:50:79:66:68:00
LPORT       : 20010
RHOST:PORT  : 127.0.0.1:20011
MTU         : 1500

PC1>
```

Figure 11-11. PC1 (VPCS), DHCP IP assignment

(*continued*)

#	Task
	PC1's interface has been assigned the IP address 192.168.127.135 with a subnet mask of /24. As a reminder, DDORA is not the name of a children's cartoon character (Dora the Explorer)—instead, it stands for Discovery, Offer, Request, Acknowledge and represents the communication messages used in the process of assigning an IP address through DHCP services between a server and a client.
⑰	From your host PC's Windows Desktop, SSH into the f38s1(192.168.127.10) Linux server using PuTTY and perform a similar ping test using the Python telnetlib library. Here, you are trying to control the router to ping to destinations, controlling R1 from the Python Linux server. Follow these steps carefully to write the Python scripts:

17-1. Let's create a simplified version of the ping Python script that targets only a single IP address, for example, 7.7.7.1, which is the MS Loopback IP address. In this version, you will hardcode the host IP (R1), port, router username, and password directly into the script. I named this script ch11_ping_ip.py with a singular ip to describe its specific function. Note that embedding and hardcoding the username and password in your script is not recommended for production environments. However, to learn and test in this environment, you can be a bit more flexible. Now follow the steps and write your script. All scripts are available in the source_codes folder of my GitHub.

```
[jdoe@f38s1 ~]$ mkdir ch11 && cd ch11
[jdoe@f38s1 ch11]$ vi ch11_ping_ip.py
[jdoe@f38s1 ch11]$ cat ch11_ping_ip.py
import telnetlib

# Define the router's information
host = "192.168.127.134" # Replace with your router's IP address
port = 23 # Default Telnet port
username = "jdoe" # R1 username
password = "Lion2Roar!" # R1 user password

# Create a Telnet connection
tn = telnetlib.Telnet(host, port)
```

(continued)

775

#	Task

```
# Log in to the router
tn.read_until(b"Username: ")
tn.write(username.encode('utf-8') + b"\n")
if password:
    tn.read_until(b"Password: ")
    tn.write(password.encode('utf-8') + b"\n")

# Send the ping command
tn.write(b"ping 7.7.7.1\n") # Replace IP with your target IP
tn.write(b"\n") # Wait for the default prompts to display
# Read the ping results
output = tn.read_until(b"ms", timeout=10).decode('utf-8') # wait
until the string "ms" is received, i.e.) ... round-trip min/avg/max =
32/38/48 ms
print(output)
# Close the Telnet connection
tn.close()
```

17-2. After creating the Python script, run it using python3 ch11_ping_ip.py. The output in your PuTTY window should resemble Figure 11-12. Notice that the last two letters of the output are ms and that is used in the script to detect the end of the output.

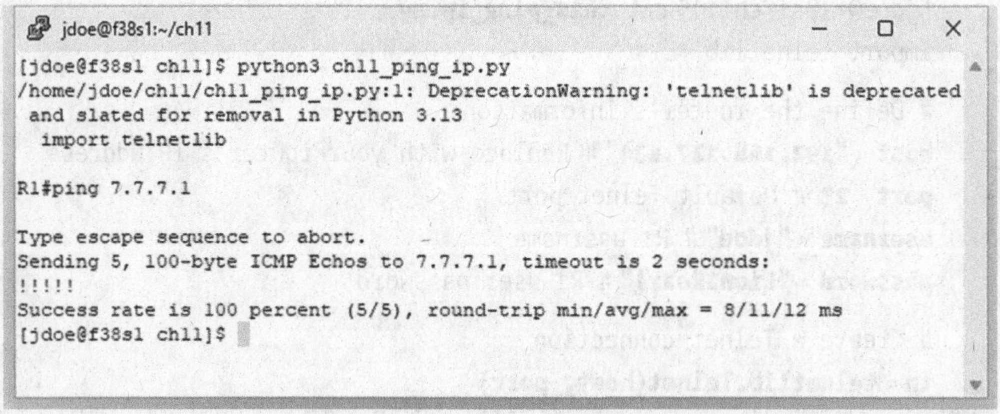

```
jdoe@f38s1:~/ch11                                              —    □    ✕

[jdoe@f38s1 ch11]$ python3 ch11_ping_ip.py
/home/jdoe/ch11/ch11_ping_ip.py:1: DeprecationWarning: 'telnetlib' is deprecated
 and slated for removal in Python 3.13
  import telnetlib

R1#ping 7.7.7.1

Type escape sequence to abort.
Sending 5, 100-byte ICMP Echos to 7.7.7.1, timeout is 2 seconds:
!!!!!
Success rate is 100 percent (5/5), round-trip min/avg/max = 8/11/12 ms
[jdoe@f38s1 ch11]$ ▊
```

Figure 11-12. *Run ch11_ping_ip.py on f38s1, ping output to a single destination*

(*continued*)

#	Task

17-3. A host with the IP address 7.7.7.7 does not exist in this network, and if you ping this IP address, it will time out in 10 seconds, as specified in the Python script. Therefore, it won't produce the line starting with the `Success rate`. Compare the two outputs carefully in Figures 11-13 and 11-14.

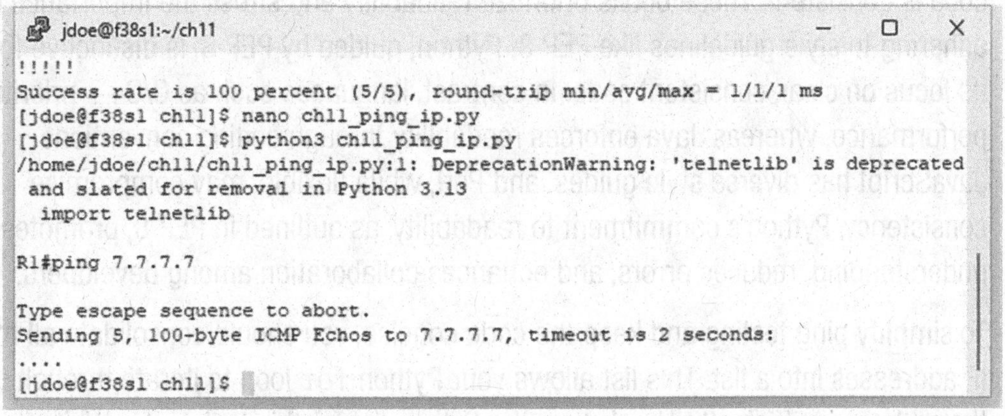

```
🖳 jdoe@f38s1:~/ch11                                               —    □    X
!!!!!
Success rate is 100 percent (5/5), round-trip min/avg/max = 1/1/1 ms
[jdoe@f38s1 ch11]$ nano ch11_ping_ip.py
[jdoe@f38s1 ch11]$ python3 ch11_ping_ip.py
/home/jdoe/ch11/ch11_ping_ip.py:1: DeprecationWarning: 'telnetlib' is deprecated
 and slated for removal in Python 3.13
  import telnetlib

R1#ping 7.7.7.7

Type escape sequence to abort.
Sending 5, 100-byte ICMP Echos to 7.7.7.7, timeout is 2 seconds:
....
[jdoe@f38s1 ch11]$
```

Figure 11-13. *Run ch11_ping_ip.py on f38s1, ping output to a non-existing destination*

You'll now enhance the single ICMP script to ping multiple targets. You'll remove the username and password from the file, utilizing the `getpass` module, as you did in the initial Telnet script. Additionally, you'll add PC-1's IP address, 192.168.127.135, to the existing target list used in the Tcl script. Before you proceed with the new script, it's essential to understand a PEP 8 topic based on your IP address list example. This is crucial for all Python programmers.

#	Task

Expand Your Knowledge:

Pythonic PEP 8: Enhancing Code Readability

In every Python book I've encountered, an emphasis on readability over writing code is consistent. These books prioritize readability and stress the importance of adhering to style guidelines like PEP 8. Python, guided by PEP 8, is distinctive for its focus on clear, consistent code. In contrast, languages such as C/C++ prioritize performance, whereas Java enforces readability through coding conventions. JavaScript has diverse style guides, and Perl, while flexible, may compromise consistency. Python's commitment to readability, as outlined in PEP 8, promotes understanding, reduces errors, and enhances collaboration among developers.

To simplify ping testing and keep the code concise, you should consolidate all the IP addresses into a list. This list allows your Python `for` loop to iterate through the addresses efficiently. Here's how the Python list for this task looks. While this format may be suitable for a computer, it significantly hampers readability for humans after the first few IP addresses.

```
#----------------------79-characters----------------------#
ip_addresses = ["7.7.7.1", "192.168.127.2", "192.168.127.10",
"192.168.127.20", "192.168.127.135", "8.8.8.8"]
#----------------------79-characters----------------------#
```

This is where Python's PEP 8 style guide proves valuable. I previously covered this concept in the Python chapter, and as explained, PEP 8 is the Python style guide, outlining coding conventions for consistency, readability, and maintainability in Python programming. It enables you to format the list in a more human-friendly manner, as demonstrated here. By following PEP 8 guidelines, you enhance code readability and maintainability.

(continued)

#	Task

```
#----------------------79-characters----------------------#
ip_addresses = [
    "7.7.7.1",
    "192.168.127.2",
    "192.168.127.10",
    "192.168.127.20",
    "192.168.127.135",
    "8.8.8.8"
]
#----------------------79-characters----------------------#
```

According to PEP 8, the recommended maximum line length for code is 79 characters. However, PEP 8 allows lines of code up to 99 characters in certain circumstances, but **it is generally better to keep lines shorter than 79 characters for improved readability and compatibility with standard terminal and console displays**. For docstrings and comments, the recommended maximum line length is 72 characters, and the limit for these lines is 89 characters. Visit the Official Python PEP 8 style guide website (`https://peps.python.org/pep-0008/`) for more details.

(continued)

#	Task
⑱	With the IP addresses formatted in a human-friendly PEP 8 style, you can merge them with the previous code to develop and create a new ICMP testing Python code. Let's move forward and write the new script.

18-1. On your f38s1 server, create a new Python script named ch11_ping_ips.py. Using the plural ips in the name conveys its purpose for pinging multiple IP addresses, ensuring a clear naming convention.

```python
import getpass # For username and password gathering
import telnetlib
# Define the router's information
host = "192.168.127.134" # Replace with your router's IP address
port = 23  # Default Telnet port
username = input("Enter your username: ")
password = getpass.getpass()
# List of IP addresses to ping
ip_addresses = [
    "7.7.7.1",
    "192.168.127.2",
    "192.168.127.10",
    "192.168.127.20",
    "192.168.127.135",
    "8.8.8.8"
]
# Create a Telnet connection
tn = telnetlib.Telnet(host, port)
# Log in to the router
tn.read_until(b"Username: ")
tn.write(username.encode('utf-8') + b"\n")
if password:
    tn.read_until(b"Password: ")
    tn.write(password.encode('utf-8') + b"\n")
```

(continued)

#	Task

```
# Loop through the list of IP addresses and ping each one
for ip in ip_addresses:
    tn.write(f"ping {ip}\n".encode('utf-8'))
    tn.write(b"\n")  # Wait for the default prompts to display
    output = tn.read_until(b"ms", timeout=10).decode('utf-8')
    print(f"Ping results for {ip}:\n{output}")
# Close the Telnet connection
tn.close()
```

18-2. On your Fedora server, after meticulously writing the provided code and saving it as a file named ch11_ping_ips.py, execute the script using the python3 ch11_ping_ips. py command. Upon successful execution, you should receive output on your PuTTY screen similar to Figure 11-14.

```
jdoe@f38s1:~/ch11                                          –    □    X
[jdoe@f38s1 ch11]$ python3 ch11_ping_ips.py
/home/jdoe/ch11/ch11_ping_ips.py:2: DeprecationWarning: 'telnetlib' is deprecate
  import telnetlib
Enter your username: jdoe
Password:
Ping results for 7.7.7.1:

R1#ping 7.7.7.1

Type escape sequence to abort.
Sending 5, 100-byte ICMP Echos to 7.7.7.1, timeout is 2 seconds:
!!!!!
Success rate is 100 percent (5/5), round-trip min/avg/max = 4/9/12 ms
Ping results for 192.168.127.2:

R1#ping 192.168.127.2

Type escape sequence to abort.
Sending 5, 100-byte ICMP Echos to 192.168.127.2, timeout is 2 seconds:
!!!!!
Success rate is 100 percent (5/5), round-trip min/avg/max = 20/64/236 ms
Ping results for 192.168.127.10:

R1#ping 192.168.127.10

Type escape sequence to abort.
Sending 5, 100-byte ICMP Echos to 192.168.127.10, timeout is 2 seconds:
!!!!!
Success rate is 100 percent (5/5), round-trip min/avg/max = 20/59/212 ms
```

Figure 11-14. *Run ch11_ping_ips.py on f38s1, ping output to multiple destinations*

Congratulations on completing the Cisco IOS ICMP testing lab with a unique twist. You've transitioned from manual ping commands on R1 to utilizing different scripts, often referred to as applications. First, you utilized the traditional Cisco IOS Tcl script stored on R1's flash to initiate pings. Later, you set up a TFTP server, stored the script on it, and conducted ICMP testing using the remote file server approach, although R1 still had to trigger the initial command to read the file for these tasks.

To move one step forward, you also developed Python scripts for both single- and multiple-destination ICMP testing. A significant distinction between Tcl and Python methods is that Tcl scripts executed directly on R1, while Python scripts ran from an SSH-connected Linux server. This approach empowered you with greater control and scalability, effectively transforming the Linux server into a proficient Python Network Automation Engineer. **What you've witnessed during this lab is a miniature version of how tasks can be replaced by lines of code, illustrating the gradual transition to artificial intelligence (AI), machine learning (ML), big data, ChatGPT, and various IT automation tools as preferred alternatives to traditional engineering tasks.** This trend, which began with Google's introduction of the concept of Site Reliability Engineering (SRE) in the early 2000s, has persisted for over two decades and continues to evolve. Consequently, the concern for job security among IT engineers has become increasingly prominent.

Mastering Script-Based File Transfers to Cisco IOS Routers

You will continue your Python journey with the file uploading and downloading lab using a Cisco router, TFTP server, and Python server. In this lab, you use the flash memory of GNS3's IOS router, R1, to upload and download files from a TFTP server (f38s1). You will write and run a Python script directly from the Ubuntu Server, u22s1, to achieve the following tasks:

- Check that the TFTP service is running correctly on f38s1.

- Make a backup of R1's running configuration to the TFTP server.

- Upload an IOS to the flash memory of R1 for a quick test.

In GNS3, while creating the Cisco 3745 IOS router template, you've already allocated 128MB to the router's PCMCIA disk0. You've also formatted the flash memory (flash:) and utilized the router's storage space in the previous lab. However, it's good practice to verify the overall health and status of the router's flash memory to ensure it's functioning correctly. To begin let's check the health of R1's flash: (disk 0). **The temptation here is to SSH into R1 and start blasting off show commands, but in a major part of this lab, you will log in to the Ubuntu Server, u22s1, and attempt to run commands and perform the tasks using Python scripts.** First, connect to u22s1 (192.168.127.20) server via an SSH connection.

#	Task
①	1-1. Create a working directory called ch11, as you did in the previous lab.

```
jdoe@u22s1:~$ mkdir ch11 && cd ch11
jdoe@u22s1:~/ch11$ pwd
/home/jdoe/ch11
```

1-2. You know which commands you want to run to check the health of flash: storage on R1. Here are the commands and a brief explanation of what they are used for.

- show file systems—Displays information about the different file systems.
- show flash:—Provides information about the flash memory, including available space and the contents of the flash:.
- show version—Checks the flash memory as part of the overall system information by using the show version command.

It's now time to write a simple Python script to log in to R1 via Telnet, run the three commands, and print the output to your u22s1's SSH session monitor. You are controlling R1 using u22s1 as your avatar or zombie. Once again, this code is available from my GitHub in the ch11 folder.

```
# ch11_r1_cf1.py
# This script runs show commands and prints output to your screen.
import telnetlib

# Define the router's information.
# Have you noticed anything different here? Converted 4 lines into a
single line. In Python, this is known as "multiple assignments" or
"tuple unpacking". Following PEP 8, characters count <79.
host, port, username, password = "192.168.127.134", 23, "jdoe",
"Lion2Roar!"
```

(continued)

#	Task

```python
# Create a Telnet connection
tn = telnetlib.Telnet(host, port)

# Log in to the router
tn.read_until(b"Username: ") #check your spelling and typing for
"Username: "
tn.write(username.encode('utf-8') + b"\n")
if password:
    tn.read_until(b"Password: ")
    tn.write(password.encode('utf-8') + b"\n")

# List of commands to run
commands = [
    "show file systems",
    "show flash:",
    'terminal length 0', # A prerequisite command to capture all
    output of the next command
    "show version"
]

# Execute the commands and capture the output
output = ""
for command in commands:
    tn.write(command.encode('utf-8') + b"\n")
    tn.write(b"\n") # Wait for command to complete
    output += tn.read_until(b"0x2102", timeout=3).decode('utf-8') #
    using "0x2102" to wait for the end output of 'show version' but
    this will still work with other commands. This is important for
    your code to work well.

print(output) # Print the combined output
```

(*continued*)

#	Task

tn.close()`# Close the Telnet connection`

When you run this Python code on your Linux server, you should see a response similar to Figure 11-15.

jdoe@u22s1:~/ch11$ **python3 ch11_r1_cf1.py**

[…output omitted for brevity]

```
  jdoe@u22s1: ~/ch11                                              —  ☐  ✕

jdoe@u22s1:~/ch11$ python3 ch11_r1_cf1.py

R1#show file systems
File Systems:

       Size(b)       Free(b)       Type  Flags   Prefixes
           -             -        opaque    rw    archive:
           -             -        opaque    rw    system:
       155640        153044        nvram    rw    nvram:
           -             -        opaque    rw    null:
           -             -       network    rw    tftp:
*   133918720     133914624         disk    rw    flash:#
           -             -         flash    rw    slot0:
           -             -        opaque    wo    syslog:
           -             -        opaque    rw    xmodem:
           -             -        opaque    rw    ymodem:
           -             -       network    rw    rcp:
           -             -       network    rw    pram:
           -             -       network    rw    ftp:
           -             -       network    rw    http:
           -             -       network    rw    scp:
           -             -       network    rw    https:
           -             -        opaque    ro    cns:
```

Figure 11-15. *u22s1, R1 flash health check 1*

1-3. Now copy the ch11_r1_cf1.py file. Name the new file ch11_r1_cf2_save.py and add the highlighted file, saving the Python code at the end of the script. Leave all the other code intact, as it is the same. You are only adding the highlighted code.

```
# ch11_r1_cf2_save.py
# This script runs show commands, prints output, and save the output
to a .txt file.
[…omitted for brevity]
    output += tn.read_until(b"0x2102", timeout=3).decode('utf-8')
```

(continued)

#	Task

with open("ch11_r1_cf2_saved.txt", "w") as file: # Save the combined output to a file

    file.write(output)

print(output)

tn.close()

When you run the modified Python code on your Linux server, you should see a response similar to Figure 11-16.

jdoe@u22s1:~/ch11$ **python3 ch11_r1_cf2_save.py**

[...output omitted for brevity]

jdoe@u22s1:~/ch11$ **ls -lh *saved.txt**

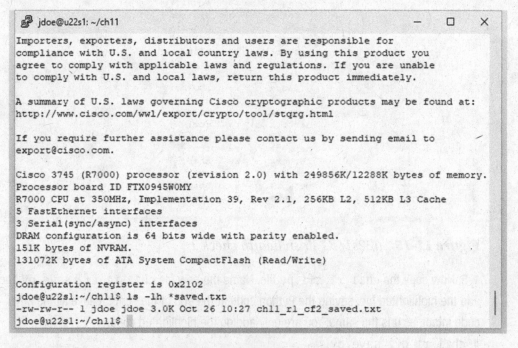

Figure 11-16. *u22s1, R1 flash health check 2*

(continued)

#	Task

1-4. As in the previous steps, make a copy of the last working script and create a new file called ch11_r1_cf3_ui_save.py. Refactor the Python code so you can ask the users to input the commands that they want to run on R1. This basically makes this script into a user interactive application where you can enter a single command or multiple Cisco IOS commands and run the commands from your Python Linux server.

jdoe@u22s1:~/ch11$ **cp ch11_r1_cf2_save.py ch11_r1_cf3_ui_save.py**

jdoe@u22s1:~/ch11$ **vi ch11_r1_cf3_ui_save.py**

1-4a. Add import telnetlib to the top of the code.

```
# ch11_r1_cf3_ui_save.py
# Runs interactively accepts show commands from user, prints output
and saves the output a file.
import getpass # Add this line to use getpass
import telnetlib
[...omitted for brevity]
```

1-4b. Delete the commands lines and replace them with the following code.

```
[...omitted for brevity]
# Get user input for commands to run
commands = []
while True:
  command = input("Enter a command to run (or press Enter to finish): ")
  if not command:
    break
  commands.append(command)
[...omitted for brevity]
```

1-4c. In the Saving Output to a File section, rename the file to reflect the change in code, as highlighted.

```
[...omitted for brevity]
with open("ch11_r1_cf3_ui_saved.txt", "w") as file:
    file.write(output)
[...omitted for brevity]
```

(continued)

#	Task

1-4d. When you run the updated Python script on u22s1, you will be prompted to enter any Cisco IOS commands. You should see a response similar to Figure 11-17.

jdoe@u22s1:~/ch11$ **python3 ch11_r1_cf3_ui_save.py**

jdoe@u22s1:~/ch11$ **ls -lh *saved.txt**

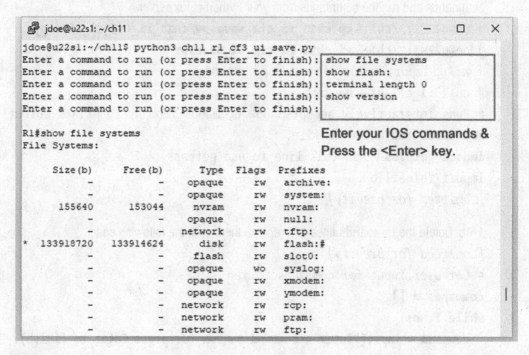

Figure 11-17. *u22s1, R1 flash health check 2*

(*continued*)

#	Task

② 2-1. Now create a new Python script to make a running configuration of R1 to your TFTP server (f38s1, 192.168.127.10). I named the file ch11_r1_bk_rcf.py. The bk_rcf part stands for backup_running-config.

jdoe@u22s1:~/ch11$ **vi ch11_r1_bk_rcf.py**

```
import getpass
import telnetlib

# Define the router's information
HOST = "192.168.127.134"
user = input("Enter your telnet username: ")
password = getpass.getpass()

# Create a Telnet connection
tn = telnetlib.Telnet(HOST)

# Log in to the router
tn.read_until(b"Username: ")
tn.write(user.encode('ascii') + b"\n")

if password:
  tn.read_until(b"Password: ")
  tn.write(password.encode('ascii') + b"\n")

# Initiate the backup process
tn.write(b"copy running-config tftp://192.168.127.10/running-
config\n") # copy command
tn.write(b"\n") # Confirm TFTP IP address, take a default IP
tn.write(b"\n") # Confirm file name, take a default name

# End the Telnet session
tn.write(b"exit\n")

# Print the result of the backup process
print(tn.read_all().decode('ascii'))
```

(*continued*)

#	Task

2-2. This script is not without its flaws, but it will work fine. Once you are happy with the quality of your first code, and you have checked the working status of your TFTP server on 192.168.127.10 (f38s1), run the script to save the running-config of your R1 to TFTP's root folder (see Figure 11-18). **You can always make your application work first and then make improvements. This is referred to as "refactoring the code" in programming.**

jdoe@u22s1:~/ch11$ **python3 ch11_r1_bk_rcf.py**

```
jdoe@u22s1: ~/ch11                                          —   □   ×

jdoe@u22s1:~/ch11$ vi ch11_r1_bk_config.py
jdoe@u22s1:~/ch11$ python3 ch11_r1_bk_rcf.py
Enter your telnet username: jdoe
Password:

R1#copy running-config tftp://192.168.127.10/running-config
Address or name of remote host [192.168.127.10]?
Destination filename [running-config]?
!!
1494 bytes copied in 0.788 secs (1896 bytes/sec)
R1#exit

jdoe@u22s1:~/ch11$
```

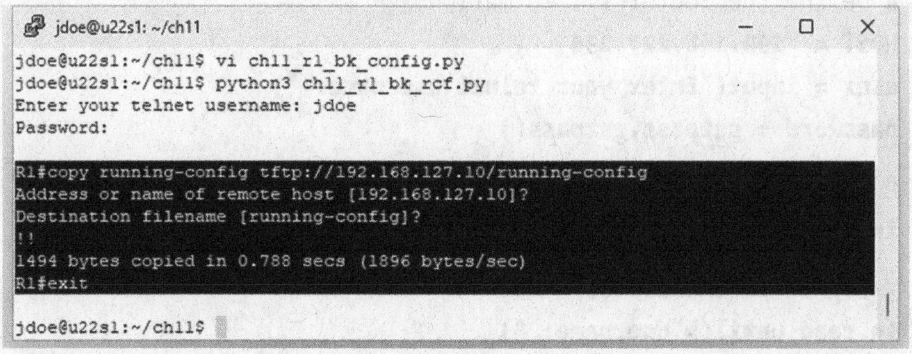

Figure 11-18. *u22s1, run the backup script to save a running-config of R1*

2-3. SSH into your TFTP server and check that the running configuration of R1 has been saved in the /var/lib/tftpboot directory. Figure 11-19 displays what the Linux ls command outputs before and after the backup script runs. If you can see that the running-config file has been copied as highlighted, then you have made a backup of R1's running configuration to a TFTP server. This seems to be a simple file with simple task automation, but you have just refrained from running this command from your router's console.

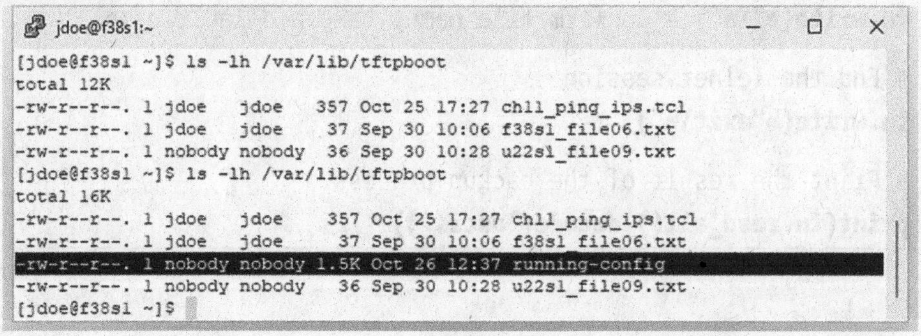

```
jdoe@f38s1:~                                                —   □   ×

[jdoe@f38s1 ~]$ ls -lh /var/lib/tftpboot
total 12K
-rw-r--r--. 1 jdoe    jdoe    357 Oct 25 17:27 ch11_ping_ips.tcl
-rw-r--r--. 1 jdoe    jdoe     37 Sep 30 10:06 f38s1_file06.txt
-rw-r--r--. 1 nobody nobody    36 Sep 30 10:28 u22s1_file09.txt
[jdoe@f38s1 ~]$ ls -lh /var/lib/tftpboot
total 16K
-rw-r--r--. 1 jdoe    jdoe    357 Oct 25 17:27 ch11_ping_ips.tcl
-rw-r--r--. 1 jdoe    jdoe     37 Sep 30 10:06 f38s1_file06.txt
-rw-r--r--. 1 nobody nobody  1.5K Oct 26 12:37 running-config
-rw-r--r--. 1 nobody nobody    36 Sep 30 10:28 u22s1_file09.txt
[jdoe@f38s1 ~]$
```

Figure 11-19. *f38s1, check running-config file on TFTP server*

(*continued*)

#	Task

③ 3-1. Now you need to upload an IOS image to GNS3's IOS router's flash. You have already formatted the flash drive in the previous lab—if you haven't yet, format the flash. Then open R1's console and follow these instructions:

R1#**show flash**

R1#**show file system**

R1#**format flash:**

3-2. You can use the FileZilla client for Windows or WinSCP to upload any IOS file or any file for file transfer testing. In this example, you will WinSCP, so if you do not have WinSCP on your Windows host PC, download it from the Internet and install it.

3-3. Using WinSCP, log in to your server. When prompted to accept the host ssh-ed key, click the Yes button.

File protocol: **SCP**

Host name: **192.168.127.10 (Your u38s1 IP address)**

Username: **jdoe (Your u38s1 username)**

Password : ********** **(Your u38s1 password)**

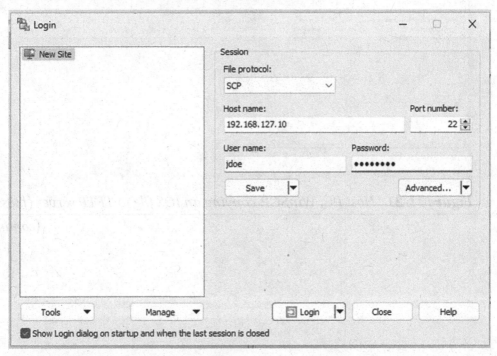

Figure 11-20. WinSCP, connection to TFTP server (CentOS8.1)

(continued)

#	Task

3-4. Once you're logged in, navigate to the /var/lib/tftpboot directory on your TFTP server (the right pane of Windows).

3-5. In this example, I am using the old IOS file, c3745-adventerprisek9-mz.124-25d.bin (37.1MB), which was used before and can be found in my Downloads folder. You can simply drop this file into the TFTP server's root directory, as shown in Figure 11-21. Alternatively, you can use another file, as I am only demonstrating the file-uploading process with a Python script.

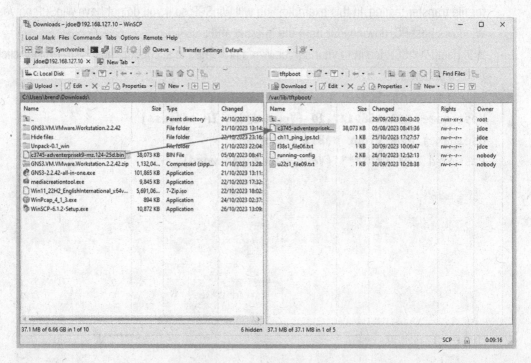

Figure 11-21. *Host PC, WinSCP, copying an IOS file to TFTP server (f38s1)*

(continued)

#	Task

3-6. Go back to your Python server, u22s1, and **copy the** ch11_r1_bk_rcf.py **file and name it** ch11_r1_up_ios.py. Then modify the Python code so it looks like the following code. The updated parts are highlighted. You can type in the script from scratch, but it is easier to reuse the previous script and make the required modifications. Also, the script is available for download from the official download site.

```
jdoe@u22s1:~/ch11$ cp ch11_r1_bk_rcf.py ch11_r1_up_ios.py
jdoe@u22s1:~/ch11$ vi ch11_r1_up_ios.py

import getpass
import telnetlib

HOST = "192.168.127.134"

user = input("Enter your telnet username: ")
password = getpass.getpass()

tn = telnetlib.Telnet(HOST)
tn.read_until(b"Username: ")
tn.write(user.encode('ascii') + b"\n")

if password:
    tn.read_until(b"Password: ")
    tn.write(password.encode('ascii') + b"\n")

tn.write(b" copy tftp://192.168.127.10/c3745-adventerprisek9-mz.124-
25d.bin flash:c3745-adventerprisek9-mz.124-25d.bin\n") # use the full
copy tftp command

tn.write(b"\n")
tn.write(b"exit\n")

print(tn.read_all().decode('ascii'))
```

(*continued*)

#	Task

3-7. Run the Python code. It may appear that the application is hanging, but it is transferring the file from the TFTP server to R1's flash memory. TFTP is a slow protocol, and it takes a considerable amount of time to transfer this 37.1MB file. If you use a smaller file, you can speed up this process. At the end of your file upload, you will need to use Ctrl+Z or Ctrl+C to manually exit the script. You are solely learning and testing this concept in this lab, so this approach is acceptable. However, in a production environment, we typically do not use the Python telnetlib. Additionally, note that telnetlib is deprecated and slated for removal in Python 3.13. If you want to use this library, your Python 3 version must be older than 3.13.

jdoe@u22s1:~/ch11$ **python3 ch11_r1_up_ios.py**

Enter your telnet username: **jdoe**

Password: ********

3-8. After running the previous script, return to R1's console. Use the show users command to inspect the vty session for Telnet and use the dir or show flash: command to verify that the file transfer is in progress. Figure 11-22 displays the completed file upload with the correct file size in bytes.

```
🖳 7.7.7.2 - PuTTY                                                    —    □    ✕
R1#
R1#show flash:
-#- --length-- -----date/time------ path
1            359 Mar 1 2002 01:55:56 +00:00 ch11_ping_ips.tcl

133914624 bytes available (4096 bytes used)

R1#show flash:
-#- --length-- -----date/time------ path
1            359 Mar 1 2002 01:55:56 +00:00 ch11_ping_ips.tcl
2         344064 Mar 1 2002 03:45:52 +00:00 c3745-adventerprisek9-mz.124-25d.bin

133570560 bytes available (348160 bytes used)

R1#show flash:
-#- --length-- -----date/time------ path
1            359 Mar 1 2002 01:55:56 +00:00 ch11_ping_ips.tcl
2       38986688 Mar 1 2002 03:59:40 +00:00 c3745-adventerprisek9-mz.124-25d.bin

94924800 bytes available (38993920 bytes used)

R1#show flash:
-#- --length-- -----date/time------ path
1            359 Mar 1 2002 01:55:56 +00:00 ch11_ping_ips.tcl
```

Figure 11-22. R1, show flash: output

If you are uploading recent IOS-XE files in a production environment, it will take hours to complete the upload via TFTP, as newer files are hundreds of megabytes in size. The TFTP protocol uses the UDP port for file transfer but it is a slow file transfer protocol in both lab and production settings. In production, SFTP or FTP is always the preferred choice when it comes to router and switch upgrades. You are only uploading a file to learn the concept of TFTP file transfer using a Python 3 script. Unfortunately, with GNS3 devices, you cannot update the IOS and boot into the new IOS image, as this is not a supported feature of GNS3. This is one of the downsides of using IOS on GNS3. However, by using the newer Cisco Catalyst c8000v or older Cisco CSR1000v or Cisco Nexus 9000v on hypervisors, you can still simulate the actual IOS upgrade processes, including booting into the newly upgraded IOS.

Copying (Cloning) a GNS3 Project

To prepare for the next chapter, you'll create a copy of the current project. There are approximately three ways to duplicate a GNS3 project on VMware Workstation 17 Pro running on Windows 11. The first method is to use the Save Project As... feature in the GNS3 menu. The second method involves exporting it as a portable project and then re-importing it on another host PC. The last method is to use the Export Config method to export your devices' configurations and manually clone your GNS3 project. These methods are listed in order of increasing difficulty.

Note that if you use the first method, your existing lab's configuration will be transferred to the newly saved project folder. But, you will lose the existing configurations of your devices' running configuration. The recommended way to clone a GNS3 project is by using the third method, which preserves your existing lab status and carries the same settings to the new project.

Lastly, but most importantly, if you want to create a full backup of your GNS3 project at any time, you can copy the entire project folder in C:\Users\[your_name]\GNS3\ project.

Because you will not be using the lxvm2ios project beyond this point in the book, let's explore how to clone the GNS3 project using a copying method. In a later chapter, you'll learn about another method for cloning.

#	Task
①	Ensure that all the work performed on your devices is properly saved in your GNS3 and that all the nodes are powered off. To save the existing lxvm2ios project with a new project name, first open GNS3's main user window. Go to the File menu and select Save Project As, as shown in Figure 11-23.

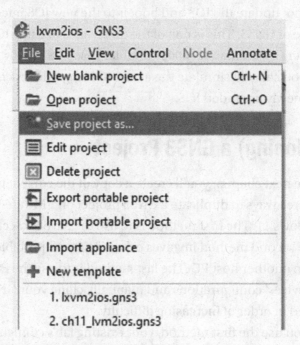

Figure 11-23. *GNS3, Save Project as... menu*

#	Task
②	The GNS3 projects are saved in the C:\Users\[your_name]\GNS3\project folder. Note that my GNS3 project folder location is C:\Users\brend\GNS3\projects. You will have to replace the path name with your username. Rename your new project for Chapter 12. As displayed in Figure 11-24, I named this project pynetauto-lab. This project will be used across subsequent labs.

Figure 11-24. *GNS3, cloning the existing lxvm2ios project to pynetauto-lab*

(*continued*)

#	Task
③	Immediately after you save the new project, navigate to the GNS3 projects folder (C:\ Users\[your_name]\GNS3\projects) and check the original and new project folders' file sizes. The original project's folder size was around 25.6KB for lxvm2ios, whereas the new project's folder size is 2.11MB for pynetauto-lab, as shown in Figure 11-25.

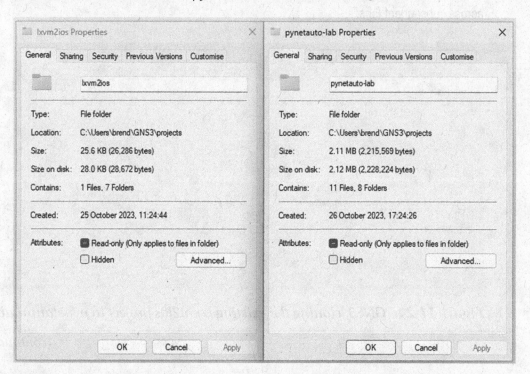

Figure 11-25. *GNS3 projects, compare original vs cloned folder size*

(*continued*)

#	Task
	When you open both project folders and cross-check them, you quickly realize that the original project folder is missing two large folders, namely the dynamips and vpcs folders, which constitute a significant portion of the lab, as depicted in Figure 11-26. These folders and files have been moved to the pynetauto-lab project's project-files folder.

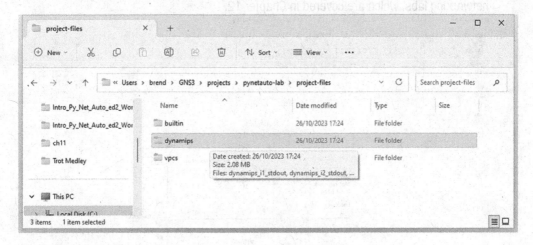

Figure 11-26. *pynetauto-lab, the largest folder in size*

(*continued*)

#	Task
④	Your new project should be opened in GNS3, ready for you to power it up. Power on R1 and PC1 and perform the configuration validations to confirm that all settings have also migrated to your devices. If you have saved the project correctly, it should run smoothly with no errors, as shown in Figure 11-27. Now you are ready for some Cisco CML-PE imaged-based networking labs, which are covered in Chapter 12.

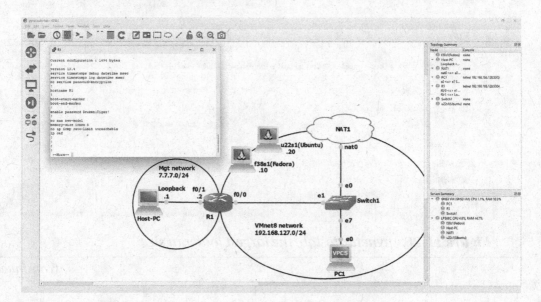

Figure 11-27. GNS3, running the pynetauto-lab project

If you've completed all the given tasks, congratulations and well done! This marks the end of Part 1 of this book. In the next chapters in Part 2 of this book, you will utilize the Cisco CML-based router and switch images for Python networking labs. Then, in later chapters, you'll use a Catalyst 8000v image on VMware Workstation to emulate the complete IOS-XE router upgrade process. You have used Python telnetlib and TFTP services to manage files on an old Cisco router, moving away from the IOS command-line console to control the router from a more powerful machine, Linux. This has also consolidated your knowledge and familiarized you with scripting approaches.

A significant portion of a network engineer's work involves security vulnerability patching and OS upgrades, tasks that include uploading IOS files to many routers, switches, and firewalls. Imagine yourself writing lines of code that can upload multiple IOS files to 100s of Cisco routers and switches overnight while you peacefully sleep.

In reality, this was one of the very first tools I worked on for regularly patching my clients' network devices. These lines of code, often referred to as scripts or applications, run on computer operating systems, with many of them operating on specialized Linux machines in production environments. **These applications have replaced and will continue to replace numerous tasks traditionally performed by IT engineers, including network engineers, marking a significant shift in the industry.**

In the future, the work of 100 engineers today could be effectively handled by a few exceptionally talented individuals. Now you understand how computing systems can indeed replace average IT engineers, echoing Steve Jobs' analogy regarding the impact of hiring exceptional talent. According to Jobs, in a 1998 interview, it typically takes 1-1.5 years to hire the best people, resulting in a one-to-two output ratio for good vs. average people. However, introducing the best people can increase the output ratio to 50 or even 100 to 1. **Extending and building upon Jobs' insights into exceptional talent, in the field of networking engineering, these exceptional talents are the engineers who build their careers on a strong foundation of networking engineering while expanding their horizons into software engineering. They are crossbred, multi-talented, and capable of working in both network engineering and software engineering domains like SD-WAN, public and private cloud, application development, cybersecurity, and various other related areas.**

Every day, put in the effort and focus on your studies to nurture your career. But don't hesitate to set yourself apart from the rest of your group.

Summary

In this chapter, you embarked on a comprehensive exploration of Cisco IOS management, harnessing the capabilities of Telnet and the Linux VM Labs to your advantage. The journey began with the creation of a new GNS3 project, seamlessly integrating Linux VM, Cisco IOS Tcl, and TFTP functionalities. This set the stage for efficient Cisco device control through the clever use of Tcl and Python scripts. Your mastery extended to script-based file transfers to Cisco IOS routers, simplifying the intricate tasks of IOS configuration management and image uploads. Central to these endeavors was the dependable Telnetlib library for Python, serving as a key tool for device control and file transfers. Moreover, you revisited the Python PEP 8 style guide, reinforcing the importance of adhering to coding standards. This was exemplified using a simple Python list, ensuring that your code remains both functional and aesthetically pleasing.

The upcoming chapters in Part 2 of this book will elevate the complexity as it introduces L2 switches and L3 routers. You can anticipate a wealth of exciting labs that will delve deeper into the realm of Python Network Automation, promising an enriching learning experience. Prepare to expand your knowledge and skills as you navigate the world of network automation and Cisco device management with confidence and finesse. As we conclude Part 1 of this book, this chapter acts as a bridge to Part 2, inviting you to delve deeper into 'Introduction to Python Network Automation II - Stepping up: Beyond the Essentials for Success.' I'm excited about our journey ahead and look forward to exploring the next phase together.

Index

© Brendan Choi 2024
B. Choi, *Introduction to Python Network Automation Volume I - Laying the Groundwork*,
https://doi.org/10.1007/979-8-8688-0146-4

Y

Z

Printed in the United States
by Baker & Taylor Publisher Services